COMMENTARIES
ON THE
CONSTITUTION
OF THE
UNITED STATES

by

Joseph Story

LEGAL LEGENDS SERIES

QUID PRO BOOKS

New Orleans, Louisiana

Commentaries on the Constitution of the United States

Published in 2013 by Quid Pro Books, as part of the *Legal Legends Series*.

ISBN 978-1-61027-195-0 (pbk.)
ISBN 978-1-61027-196-7 (hc.)

Quid Pro, LLC
5860 Citrus Blvd., Suite D-101
New Orleans, Louisiana 70123
www.quidprobooks.com

Publisher's Cataloging in Publication

Story, Joseph, 1779-1845.
 Commentaries on the Constitution of the United States / Joseph Story ; reprinted with an introduction by Kermit Roosevelt III.
  Reprint. Originally published : Boston : Hilliard, Gray, & Co., 1833.
   p. cm. — (Legal legends)
  Includes index.
   ISBN 978-1-61027-195-0 (pbk.)
1. Constitutional law — United States. 2. Constitutional history — United States. 3. United States — Constitution. I. Title. II. Series. III. Roosevelt III, Kermit.
KF4541.S7 2013
342.81'1—dc22
                                                        2013013983
                                                        CIP

TABLE OF CONTENTS

[The Table below, as in the original printing, references the pagination of the 1833 abridged edition, not the section numbers. Those page numbers are inserted into this modern edition by the use of {brackets}. They are retained for purposes of citation, continuity with the previous editions, functionality of the Contents and the Index, and standardized pagination within digital formats. A detailed Table of Sections is omitted.]

Foreword, 2013, by Kermit Roosevelt III. i

Preface. . . {page v} xix

The Constitution . . . {xvii} xxiii

Preliminary Chapter . . . {1} 1

BOOK I

HISTORY OF THE COLONIES.

Chapter I
Origin and Title to the Territory of the Colonies . . . {3-7} 5

Chapter II
Origin and Settlement of Virginia . . . {8-12} 9

Chapter III
Origin and Settlement of New-England, and
Plymouth Colony . . . {13-18} 11

Chapter IV
Massachusetts . . . {19-27} 14

Chapter V
New-Hampshire . . . {28-30} 19

Chapter VI
Maine . . . {31-33}. 21

Chapter VII
Connecticut . . . {34-36}. 23

Chapter VIII
Rhode Island . . . {37-40}. 25

Chapter IX
Maryland . . . {41-43} 27

Chapter X
New-York . . . {44-46} 29

Chapter XI
New-Jersey . . . {47-49} 31

Chapter XII
Pennsylvania . . . {50-53}. 33

Chapter XIII
    Delaware ... {54-55} 35
Chapter XIV
    North and South Carolina ... {56-60} 36
Chapter XV
    Georgia ... {61-61} 39
Chapter XVI
    General Review of the Colonies ... {62-66} 40
Chapter XVII
    General Review of the Colonies ... {67-83} 43

BOOK II

HISTORY OF THE REVOLUTION
AND OF THE CONFEDERATION.

Chapter I
    The History of the Revolution ... {84-90} 55
Chapter II
    Origin of the Confederation ... {91-93} 59
Chapter III
    Analysis of the Articles of the Confederation ... {94-104} 61

BOOK III

THE CONSTITUTION OF THE UNITED STATES.

Chapter I
    Origin and Adoption of the Constitution ... {105-109} 69
Chapter II
    Objections to the Constitution ... {110-115} 72
Chapter III
    Nature of the Constitution – Whether a Compact ... {116-122} 75
Chapter IV
    Who is the Final Judge or Interpreter in
    Constitutional Controversies ... {123-133} 79
Chapter V
    Rules of Interpretation of the Constitution ... {134-162} 85
Chapter VI
    The Preamble ... {163-194} 100
Chapter VII
    Distribution of Powers ... {195-198} 116
Chapter VIII
    The Legislature ... {199-209} 118
Chapter IX
    The House of Representatives ... {210-251} 124
Chapter X
    The Senate ... {252-290} 145

Chapter XI
Elections and Meetings of Congress ... {291-297} 165

Chapter XII
Privileges and Powers of Both
Houses of Congress ... {298-314} 169

Chapter XIII
Mode of Passing Laws – President's Negative ... {315-328} 178

Chapter XIV
Powers of Congress – Taxes ... {329-357} 185

Chapter XV
Power to Borrow Money and Regulate Commerce ... {358-382} 200

Chapter XVI
Power Over Naturalization and Bankruptcy ... {383-391} 213

Chapter XVII
Power to Coin Money and Fix the Standard
of Weights and Measures ... {392-395} 218

Chapter XVIII
Power to Establish Post-Offices and Post-Roads ... {396-401} 220

Chapter XIX
Power to Promote Science and Useful Arts ... {402-404} 223

Chapter XX
Power to Punish Piracies and Felonies on the High Seas ... {405-408} 225

Chapter XXI
Power to Declare War and Make Captures – Army – Navy ... {406-419} 228

Chapter XXII
Power Over the Militia ... {420-426} 234

Chapter XXIII
Power Over Seat of Government and
Other Ceded Places ... {427-430} 238

Chapter XXIV
Powers of Congress – Incidental ... {431-443} 240

Chapter XXV
Powers of Congress – National Bank ... {444-452} 247

Chapter XXVI
Powers of Congress – Internal Improvements ... {453-458} 252

Chapter XXVII
Powers of Congress – Purchases of Foreign
Territory – Embargoes ... {459-465} 255

Chapter XXVIII
Power of Congress to Punish Treason ... {466-469} 259

Chapter XXIX
Power of Congress as to Proof of State Records
and Proceedings ... {470-472} 261

Chapter XXX
Powers of Congress – Admission of New States, and
Acquisition of Territory ... {473- 475} 263

Chapter XXXI
Powers of Congress – Territorial Governments ... {476-480} 265

Chapter XXXII
    Prohibitions on the United States... {481-488} 270
Chapter XXXIII
    Prohibitions on the States... {489-497} 272
Chapter XXXIV
    Prohibitions on the States – Impairing Contracts... {498-511} 277
Chapter XXXV
    Prohibitions on the States – Tonnage Duties – Making War... {512-514} 284
Chapter XXXVI
    Executive Department – Organization of... {515-545} 286
Chapter XXXVII
    Executive – Powers and Duties... {546-580}..................................... 302
Chapter XXXVIII
    The Judiciary – Importance, Organization, and Powers of... {581-668}........... 320
Chapter XXXIX
    Definition and Evidence of Treason... {669-672} 363
Chapter XL
    Privileges of Citizens – Fugitives – Slaves... {673-676}........................ 365
Chapter XLI
    Guaranty of Republican Government – Mode of
    Making Amendments... {677-682} 367
Chapter XLII
    Public Debts – Supremacy of Constitution and Laws... {683-687}................. 370
Chapter XLIII
    Oaths of Office – Religious Test – Ratification of the
    Constitution... {688-692} 373
Chapter XLIV
    Amendments to the Constitution... {693-714} 376
Chapter XLV
    Concluding Remarks... {715-719} 387

Index... 391

FOREWORD

Introduction

Mehitabel Pedrick Story left one recorded quote for posterity. "Now, Joe, I've sat up and tended you many a night when you were a child, and don't you dare not to be a great man."[1] Her son Joseph, recipient of this admonition, took it to heart. By the time he died in 1845, he was one of the most influential legal thinkers of the young American Republic. He left an extraordinary legacy: among his writings were almost three hundred Supreme Court opinions, including some of the most fundamental foundations of our modern constitutional understandings, and eleven treatises, among them the tremendously influential Commentaries on the Conflict of Laws (1834) and the Constitution (1833). (There was also a book of poetry, but the critical consensus deems it awful.)

We offer this edition of Story's *Commentaries on the Constitution of the United States* in the hope and with the expectation that it will prove useful to modern readers, both those interested in Story's historical perspective and those engaged with modern constitutional doctrine. Story's Constitution is in some ways very different from ours. The specter of civil war is a looming presence in the Commentaries, but Story did not live to see that ghost made flesh, nor the Reconstruction that laid it finally to rest. The Constitution he described had only twelve amendments and was missing two of the provisions—the Equal Protection and Due Process Clauses of the Fourteenth Amendment—that generate many modern constitutional controversies. Still, many of the provisions are unchanged, and much of Story's analysis is still relevant.

Indeed, to judge by the Supreme Court, Story's views are actually increasing in importance. The Court cited Story's Commentaries only twice before the Civil War and only eleven times before World War Two. Between 1941 and 2012, however, there were 97 citations, including 20 after the year 2000. The list of cases in which the Court has cited or relied on Story reads like a greatest hits compilation. It features landmark cases dealing with issues as disparate as the right to privacy,[2] the federal-state balance,[3] religious freedom,[4] affirmative action,[5] the Second Amendment,[6] and the rights of Guantánamo detainees and other terrorism issues.[7]

---

[1] R. Kent Newmyer, *Supreme Court Justice Story: Statesman of the Old Republic* 19 (1985).

[2] Griswold v. Connecticut, 381 U.S. 479, 490 (1965).

[3] Alden v. Maine, 527 U.S. 706 (1999); Printz v. United States, 521 U.S. 898 (1997); New York v. United States, 505 U.S. 144 (1992); National League of Cities v. Usery, 426 U.S. 833, 863 (1976)

[4] Wallace v. Jafree, 472 U.S. 38 (1985); Lynch v. Donnelly, 465 U.S. 668, 678 (1984); Van Orden v. Perry, 544 U.S. 677 (2005).

[5] City of Richmond v. Croson, 488 U.S. 469, 521 (1989).

[6] McDonald v. City of Chicago, 130 S. Ct. 3020, 3038 (2010); District of Columbia v. Heller, 554 U.S. 570, 593, 608 (2008).

[7] Boumediene v. Bush, 553 U.S. 723, 741 (2008); Hamdi v. Rumsfeld, 524 U.S. 507 (2004).

How could someone writing in the nineteenth century have insights the Supreme Court would deem important to the controversies of the twenty-first? Each generation makes the Constitution its own; in some sense, each generation makes it anew. Each regards different provisions as settled and different ones as disputed; each seizes on different ones as the site of its struggle. Each makes different claims about how the words should be understood. But we all rely on the same document. Story allows us to see the field on which these battles are waged through the eyes of someone who was there when the lines were first laid down.

Story's Commentaries have been published in two forms, the original three-volume set and the one-volume abridgment offered here. Story created the abridged version to serve as a textbook for law school and college. The material he removed consists largely of esoterica: footnotes referencing sources no longer available to a general readership, cross-references, and some technical analyses of legal issues circa 1833. The abridgement is far superior in terms of readability. Even in Story's time, it seems to have been more widely read and influential. In addition, it represents Story's views, which the multivolume work—extended past the Civil War and updated by subsequent editors—no longer does. In this introduction, I will give a brief sketch of Story's life, including a general discussion of his constitutional views, and then offer some perspective on the Commentaries themselves.

Biographical Sketch

Joseph Story was a child of the Revolution. He was born in 1779, three years after independence was declared and two before the American victory at Yorktown would make it a reality. Marblehead, Massachusetts, his birthplace, was the second city of New England. To the cause of liberty, it supplied fishermen, who joined the Continental Army after a British blockade idled their boats, and Elbridge Gerry, a signer of the Declaration and later a delegate to the Philadelphia convention. To constitutional law, it gave Story.

What Marblehead gave to Story himself is somewhat less clear. Marblehead Academy prepared him for college, though not, as far as the available evidence discloses, especially well. The last lesson imparted was the stroke of a ruler on his hand: in the fall of his last year, Story was beaten in front of the entire school (the occasion seems to have been simple vengeance by the headmaster), whereupon his father withdrew him and sent him to Harvard. There Story learned he would have to take the regular entrance exam and also be examined on what the freshmen had studied that fall. He buckled down, prepped intensely for six weeks, and triumphed.

Harvard at the time had five professors and 173 students, all drawn from within 50 miles of the school. Still, Story found it, in his words, "Elysium."[8] He studied hard, splashing his face with water from the College Pump in Harvard Yard when his energies flagged. Again, his effort was rewarded; in 1798, Story graduated second in his class. He was elected class poet and wrote for graduation a poem called *Reason*.

---

[8] Newmyer, *Supreme Court Justice Story, supra* note 1, at 22.

But Reason was not Story's sole guide, nor his motivating force. "Ambition," he wrote soon after graduation, "is truly the food of my existence, and for that alone life is desirable."[9] The statement is not surprising. The Founding generation taught its heirs ambition by example—ambition, and optimism that their labors would not be in vain. Three million colonists had faced down the world's greatest military power and won a clean slate on which to write the principles of government. Now the New World had slipped the bonds of the Old; now it was truly new.

Story also learned ambition at home. He was the eldest son of a mother new to the family. Elisha Story, Joseph's father, had eight children with his first wife, the last of whom died at birth along with his mother in 1778. Elisha married Mehitable Pedrick the following year; she bore him eleven children, of whom Joseph was the first. Elisha participated in the Boston Tea Party wearing war paint; he joined the Sons of Liberty and fought at Lexington, Concord, and Bunker Hill. Despite these adventures, Elisha was a tolerant and loving man who seems to have formed the basis for Joseph's vision of God. Mehitable may have been the more dynamic force in the household, the one who carefully set her son on the path to greatness.

Story's early model in this quest was George Washington; he hoped to shape his world in the same way. The cyclic view of history suggested he might find the opportunity. Story believed in an ongoing struggle between light and dark, with opportunities for each generation to make its mark. But war was not his path to glory. Story started instead with law and politics. He went directly from his Harvard graduation to an apprenticeship in Samuel Sewall's Marblehead law office. Sewall advised Story that there were already too many lawyers but also supervised his legal education. The studies were tedious—Story lamented the "dry and technical principles ... and the repulsive and almost unintelligible forms of processes and pleadings"—but he engaged them with his customary ardor. "It is the part of cowardice to shrink," he wrote, "and of imbecility to hesitate. I have determined, and will execute."[10] For months, he read fourteen hours a day, the classic English commentaries of Blackstone and Coke, then the more foreign treatises of Grotius, Puffendorf, and Vattel. American law, he thought, was yet to be born. It demanded a transformation of old principles for the New World.

Story's legal career was one of engagement and steadily increasing success in what he deemed a grand calling. Law, he once wrote, "employ[ed] the noblest faculties of the human mind." His political progress was more checkered. The New England of his birth was a bastion of the conservative Federalists, who saw law primarily as a means to support the existing order. Story's views differed, and when drawn into the political fray, he did not shy away. He dared to align himself with the Jeffersonian Republicans, who in Massachusetts were still referred to as Antifederalists, the ancient foes of the Constitution. Story acquired enemies and once considered proposing a duel to repair his honor after a series of public insults. The duel never happened, but physical violence did: he was knocked down and kicked by one Federalist and chased through the streets by others.

---

[9] *Id.* at 34.

[10] *Id.* at 39-40.

Story's political fortunes rose with those of the Republican Party, though he never thought of himself as a party man. Parties demanded discipline and obedience from their members, but good government, Story believed, required independence. He was elected to the Massachusetts House of Representatives in 1805 and demonstrated that independence, unafraid to take the side of the Federalists when he believed them in the right. Elected to the U.S. House of Representatives in 1808, he gave the Massachusetts legislature a farewell speech that warned of the danger of parties. As a federal Representative, Story was equally independent. His great success came in championing a Federalist cause, the opposition to the Embargo Acts. This earned him the enmity of President Thomas Jefferson, and he served only one term.

Story returned to the Massachusetts legislature in 1811, and even served as Speaker, but his refusal to align consistently with a party made his long-term political future dim. Ever independent, he accepted this prospect. Story had come to believe that political parties—which the Framers of the Constitution had not foreseen—were dangerous to good government. Law, he hoped, could substitute for the politics that had fallen into corruption: law as a science, a system of neutral principles that could guide the ship of state.

At the least, law rescued Story from his flagging political career. In November 1811, he became the youngest man ever appointed to the Supreme Court, at 32 years and two months of age. Story was James Madison's fourth choice, and politically acceptable perhaps precisely because he had antagonized all sides equally. He came to the Court with no judicial experience, but he brought ten years of practice, including several Supreme Court arguments, substantial published scholarship, and the fierce dedication to study that had served him so well in the past.

The Court was an immediate refuge for Story. He found he had a natural affinity for Justice Bushrod Washington, the favorite nephew and heir of the childless George, and also formed a close relationship with Chief Justice John Marshall. Marshall had written a biography of George Washington; he had also, when Story arrived, written 147 of the Supreme Court's 171 existing opinions. Story's intellect and capacity for hard work promoted a more equal division of labor. In some areas, such as a choice of law (the topic of Story's first opinion), his scholarly acumen even outstripped Marshall's.

When Story came to the Court, the Constitution—the nation itself—still had the uncertainty of a great experiment. The Marshall Court's task was to prove the experiment a success, to transform the Constitution from speculative political philosophy to the bedrock principles of a real republic. Story took to the task eagerly. He shared Marshall's nationalist and pro-commercial philosophy. His opinions frequently promote federal authority in the hopes of securing legal uniformity.

Not all of these opinions have won the approval of history. One, *Martin v. Hunter's Lessee*,[11] affirmed the federal Supreme Court's power to reverse the judgments of state supreme courts and is now one of the most fundamental decisions about the structure of the federal judicial system. Another, *Swift v. Tyson*[12] extended the federal judicial power to issues we now consider properly within the

---

[11] 14 U.S. 304 (1816).
[12] 41 U.S. 1 (1842).

authority of the states and is famous primarily for its 1938 repudiation in *Erie Railroad v. Tompkins*.[13]

Whatever the future held, Story's early years on the Court found him an enthusiastic participant in the generally successful project of affirming federal supremacy. His first real opponents in his capacity as Supreme Court Justice were the New England Federalists. He had championed their cause against Jefferson's Embargo, but their opposition to the War of 1812 led to talk of regional secession. Story believed in Union above all, and when cases gave him the opportunity he made quite clear that a conspiracy to dismember the Union was treason.

Story believed fervently in the United States as a single nation. He tended to imagine that single nation in the image of the New England of his youth, which was his template and reference for the true America, but unity was the most important element. He championed the United States against all comers—first, the New England Federalists, then later the Southerners whose theories of states' rights created the legal arguments for secession. The belief in Union overcame his regional affection for New England during the War of 1812, and later it overcame his distaste for slavery. It is quite clear that Story was personally opposed to slavery. He spoke out against it in strong terms and in a written opinion condemned the slave trade as inconsistent with "any system of law that purports to rest on the authority of reason or revelation."[14] In the case of *The Amistad*,[15] he ruled that Africans who had overpowered their Spanish captors and taken control of a slave ship were neither pirates nor property but victims of kidnapping.

But Story was not an abolitionist. He wanted a gradual and peaceful end to slavery, not war. Abolitionists, like the pro-slavery forces, claimed the Constitution for their side, and Story wanted to withhold it from both as the property of the Union. His most infamous decision, *Prigg v. Pennsylvania*,[16] illustrates this desire.

Prigg arose out of the conflict between the laws of the states that recognized slavery and those that prohibited it. Part of the Constitution's compromise was to allow each state to decide for itself whether to permit or prohibit slavery within its borders. Interstate travel required further refinements. When slaveowners brought their slaves voluntarily into other states, the consequence was left up to the states they visited. Those states could, if they wished, provide that mere momentary presence within the state liberated the slaves, or they could (as most states did) follow the rule that visitors did not gain freedom, only residents did.

For fugitives, on the other hand, the Constitution provided a mandatory rule. Article IV, Section 2 of the Constitution, in the Fugitive Slave Clause, provided that slaves ("persons held to service," in the Constitution's delicate phrasing) who escaped into free states did not thereby acquire freedom. (Absent the clause, such a result would have been permissible if the free states' laws so provided, as, for instance, the law of England did.) They remained slaves and had to be returned upon the demand of the person to whom service was owed. But unlike the adjacent

13 304 U.S. 64 (1938).

14 United States v. La Jeune Eugenie, 26 Fed. Cas. 832, 845-46 (C.C.D. Mass. 1822) (No. 15551).

15 40 U.S. 518 (1841).

16 41 U.S. 539 (1842).

interstate extradition clause, which provided that interstate fugitives from justice must be returned if they were merely *charged* with a crime, the Fugitive Slave Clause applied only to people who were in fact slaves. It seemed possible, then, for free states to require slaveowners to prove their claims in local courts before alleged fugitives would be returned. Several states, Pennsylvania among them, adopted Personal Liberty Laws requiring just that. *Prigg* tested the constitutionality of Pennsylvania's law.

Margaret Morgan was a resident of Pennsylvania. She was born into slavery in Maryland but had apparently been informally freed and had married a free black. In 1832 the family moved across the border to Pennsylvania. They had children, at least some of whom were born in Pennsylvania. In 1837, slavecatcher Edward Prigg entered Pennsylvania on behalf of a Maryland resident asserting a claim to Margaret. There, rather than complying with the requirements of the Pennsylvania Personal Liberty Law, he abducted Margaret and her children and dragged them back across the border. Margaret was likely not a fugitive (the records do not decisively establish whether she had been freed or not) and her Pennsylvania-born children were clearly not; under Pennsylvania law, they were free from birth. Pennsylvania authorities, not unreasonably, deemed the abduction a kidnapping and invoked the interstate extradition clause to demand that Maryland surrender Prigg to face justice. Maryland refused.

Eventually Maryland agreed to return Prigg to Pennsylvania for trial on the condition that if convicted he not be imprisoned until the United States Supreme Court had ruled on the constitutional issues involved. Pennsylvania agreed. Prigg was tried and convicted but retained his liberty while the Supreme Court considered his case. (Margaret Morgan and her children, meanwhile, were adjudged slaves by a Maryland court and sold.)

The question for the Supreme Court was whether Pennsylvania's Personal Liberty Law should be held unconstitutional on the grounds that it conflicted with the Fugitive Slave Clause. Justice Story surely had no sympathy for the kidnapper Prigg and the defiant state of Maryland. But he had little more for the Pennsylvania authorities seeking to promote their state's anti-slavery views or the abolitionists who rallied to the cause. All were fomenters of chaos, he believed, twisting the Constitution for partisan aims. "It is astonishing," he wrote, "how easily men satisfy themselves that the Constitution is exactly what they wish it to be."[17] Story's opinion sought to take the matter out of the hands of the states and the individuals on both sides. State officials, he ruled, could not participate at all in rendition of fugitive slaves; the issue was entirely federal.

An inability to use state process might have caused difficulty for slavecatchers if some process was required and nothing else was available. On these grounds, some people—Story himself included—attempted to portray *Prigg* as a victory for freedom. But the argument is unconvincing. Federal process did exist—first the federal Fugitive Slave Act of 1793, in force at the time of *Prigg*, and later the substantially harsher Act of 1850. (The 1850 Act paid federal officials for each accusation of fugitive status they heard, but rather shockingly paid them twice as much if they decided the accused was a fugitive slave.) And in the absence of

---

[17] Newmyer, *Supreme Court Justice Story, supra* note 1, at 358.

federal process, Story suggested that self-help was authorized—which is to say, the unreviewable abduction of alleged fugitives, in defiance of free state kidnapping laws.

As between freedom and slavery, *Prigg* was a victory for the pro-slavery forces. But Story saw the case more as a contest between federal and state authority and was content if the federal side prevailed. Story's hope for the future lay in the strength of federal power, and that formed the heart of his view of the Constitution. (Unsurprisingly, Story did not consider this view a potentially partisan interpretation akin to those of the abolitionists and the slaveholders. He believed that *Prigg* was simply an execution of the judge's duty to faithfully implement the Constitution.)

As it turned out, of course, neither *Prigg* nor the Supreme Court's later and more desperate attempt in *Dred Scott*[18] to placate southern states could save the Union. Federal power would, but only in military form and at the cost of over half a million American lives. Story did not live to see the war, but he heard its rumors. From 1831 on, he felt that the Court was adrift, the Constitution disregarded. Party had come to the marble palace, and the Justices' frequent and bitter divisions revealed the politicization of the judicial process.

One might fairly ask whether the Court had become more ideological, as Story believed, or simply less ideologically cohesive. But in any case, the later years of Story's tenure were far less satisfying than the early ones. He retired at the end of October Term 1844, with what seems to have been some relief. He returned to Harvard, whose law school was in some sense his creation, anticipating years of productive scholarly work. It was not to be. In September 1845 he died. He left a tremendous legacy to the legal world, not only in his many important opinions but also in his scholarship, which included eleven treatises, mostly on commercial law. The Commentaries on the Constitution, however, stand out as his masterwork.

The Commentaries

In 1829, Story accepted the Dane Professorship at Harvard Law School and agreed to deliver lectures to students "from time to time in a familiar way."[19] One might as well say that he accepted the task of creating the law school; in 1828, Harvard Law's student body numbered precisely one. The apprentice system, which had educated Story, was still dominant. But it was becoming increasingly evident that office training did not provide the breadth of knowledge required by lawyers. At Harvard, students would learn from scholars—they would learn from Story and his Commentaries.

Story began work on the Commentaries soon after accepting Harvard's offer, and he certainly intended them at least in part for use by students. But his ambitions were broader. He was also a sitting Justice of the United States Supreme Court, engaged in a struggle over the meaning of the Constitution and the proper allocation of power between the states and the federal government, and he intended his Commentaries to advance the nationalist cause. They were in some sense

---

[18]   60 U.S. 393 (1857).

[19]   Newmyer, *supra* note 1, at 240.

a successor to the Federalist Papers, which had analyzed particular constitutional provisions with the aim of securing ratification. Story undertook the same task, his eye likewise on task of winning acceptance for his vision.

The Commentaries comprise three books. The first begins with a history of the colonies. It contains some interesting tidbits in its own right. How many people know, for instance, that John Locke wrote the constitution of the Carolinas—and produced a document contrary to all his philosophical writings? ("Probably," Story suggests, "there were many circumstances attending this transaction, which are now unknown," and which might furnish "if not a justification, at least some apology for this extraordinary instance of unwise and visionary legislation.")[20] But its main value is in disclosing the legal sources from which our constitutional structure came. The early colonies experimented with some forms of government radically different from those eventually adopted in the Constitution. Virginia's first charters, for instance, combined legislative and executive functions in a single council appointed by the king. Restiveness among the settlers led to the formation of a representative legislature.

The colony of New Plymouth, by contrast, vested legislative power in the whole body of male inhabitants. But increasing number and geographical dispersion eventually compelled a representative assembly. Massachusetts Bay, meanwhile, began its existence under the rule of a parent corporation based in England. When potential settlers proved unwilling to cross the ocean just to be governed from the land they had left, the company selected officers from among those who traveled to America, and the colony prospered. If there is a single lesson to be drawn from Book One, it is the importance of a local representative legislature. It is no accident that our Constitution creates the House of Representatives first, before the Supreme Court, the President, or even the Senate.

Book Two discusses the history surrounding the drafting of the Constitution. Here, too, Story's analysis helps deepen our understanding of why our Constitution takes the form it does. Constitution makers tend to fight the last war: the struggle that creates the opportunity for a new framing of government informs that framing. The Revolution taught that a distant general government was a threat to liberty and the states could intervene to protect their citizens. The Articles of Confederation embodied that lesson: they created a federal government so weak that it could never pose a threat of tyranny. But it was quickly clear that for just this reason they were a failure. Under the Articles, the national government had no executive branch and no judicial system, and while it could estimate the financial needs of the United States and apportion that amount among the states, it had no way to compel payment. The states were independent sovereigns in practice, and perhaps in theory too: since the Articles were ratified by the state legislatures, the states arguably retained the power to withdraw from the Confederation or modify its terms.

The Constitution, Story asserts, was designed to remedy these defects. The imminent failure of the Confederation was the "war" that loomed in the minds of the Constitution's drafters. And the Constitution does, clearly, attempt to respond to some of the inadequacies of the Articles. The national government it creates

---

[20] 1 Joseph Story, *Commentaries on the Constitution of the United States*, § 63.

has a powerful executive branch; it has its own judicial system and the power to tax. The Constitution was also submitted for ratification to the national People, a sovereign Story places above the states.

But the Constitution also preserves the lessons of the Revolution. It maintains state authority as a check on federal overreaching, and, notably in the Second Amendment, it reflects the view that this check may take the form of military opposition. As with the Articles, the national government is seen as the likely threat to liberty and states as its protectors. This tension—between the lessons of the Revolution and those imparted by the failures of the Articles—is one of the central fault lines of the original Constitution, along which the nation would eventually come apart.

The Founders' Constitution, which Story applied as a Justice and interpreted in his Commentaries, contained two fundamental compromises. The first was between the vision of the Revolution and the somewhat different perspective occasioned by the failure of the Articles of Confederation. The second was on slavery, which proved less a durable accommodation than a wound that never healed. The Constitution never used the word "slave," but several provisions—the Fugitive Slave Clause[21] and the prohibition on congressional interference with the international slave trade before 1818[22]—are clearly designed to protect the institution of slavery. More notoriously, the Three-Fifths Compromise[23] gave slave states extra representation in the federal government based on their slave populations.

The two compromises were connected. Only the federal government could ever abolish slavery against the will of slaveholding states, so abolitionists tended to lean towards nationalism, while the slaveholders relied on doctrines of state sovereignty. Book Two shows us where these competing visions of ultimate sovereignty came from, and Story's frantic arguments against state sovereignty show that he saw too well where they were headed.

Book Three is the largest and most substantial part of the Commentaries. It amounts to 85% of the text, and it consists of Story's statement of his approach to constitutional interpretation and his clause-by-clause exposition of the Constitution. Story's analysis relies substantially on the Federalist Papers and the opinions of the Marshall Court. There were contrary views, of course—the anti-Federalist writers had their own interpretations of the proposed Constitution (which may have been overstated for rhetorical effect) and the Marshall Court had its opponents, devotees of states' rights. Story sought to present the view of the Constitution "maintained by its founders and friends, and confirmed and illustrated by the actual practice of the government."[24] In that, he succeeded.

Story's Constitution is a nationalist document. He takes pains to emphasize the sovereignty of the national people as against the states. He devotes a whole chapter (the third) of Book Three to the question of whether the constitution is a compact among states. It is not, says Story. The states were never true sovereigns. They were subordinate to the Crown, and when they threw off that allegiance with

---

[21] U.S. Const. Art. IV, § 3, Cl. 2.

[22] U.S. Const. Art. I, § 9, Cl. 1.

[23] U.S. Const. Art. I., § 2, Cl. 3.

[24] 1 Story, *Commentaries*, Preface.

the Declaration of Independence they immediately became subject to the general authority of the national people. As for the Constitution, Story claims, the Preamble makes clear that it is the act of a national people establishing something, not of sovereign states compacting with each other. The Preamble invokes We the People "of the *United States*," Story notes, "not the distinct people of a *particular state* with the people of the other states."[25]

Story may have overplayed his hand with the textual argument. Drafting history reveals that the Preamble originally announced the deed of "We the people of the United States of New Hampshire, Massachusetts, Rhode Island and Providence Plantations, Connecticut, New York, New Jersey, Pennsylvania, Delaware, Maryland, Virginia, North Carolina, South Carolina, and Georgia," with the enumeration cut for reasons of style and to save embarrassment should some of the states refuse to ratify, as indeed Rhode Island and North Carolina initially did.[26] Even worse for Story, when the original Constitution uses the phrase "United States," it is a plural noun, which suggests a confederation with states as ultimate sovereigns, rather than a unitary nation.[27]

But Story's argument ultimately carried the day. John Marshall endorsed it in *McCulloch v. Maryland*.[28] And when Abraham Lincoln, in the Gettysburg Address, looked back for the beginning of the nation, he identified it with the Declaration and not the Constitution—1863 minus the famous fourscore and seven gives 1776, not 1789. Lincoln's words could not decide the issue, but Union arms could. The Civil War gave us a second Founding, which would confirm Story's vision—though averting that war was Story's whole purpose. The Reconstruction Amendments, the Thirteenth, Fourteenth, and Fifteenth, solidified the nationalist victory. They are designed to restrict state sovereignty and empower the national government. Indeed, they go beyond even Story's version of nationalism; they invert the Framing paradigm. Now, in the minds of the drafters, the states are the threats to liberty, and the federal government will be its protector. (Story's Commentaries of course do not include the Reconstruction Amendments, but he is still a help in understanding them. The drafters of the Amendments quite consciously used pre-existing concepts, which Story does discuss. The Fourteenth Amendment, for instance, takes privileges and immunities from Article IV, due process from the Fifth Amendment, and the idea of "appropriate" enforcement legislation from *McCulloch*. Story never saw this new cathedral of liberty, but he can tell us much about the blocks from which it was built.)

After the Civil War, the trend towards nationalism continued. The Seventeenth Amendment took selection of Senators out of the hands of state legislators and gave it to the people of the states. Whatever the intent, its effect was to make the Senate less likely to consider the value of state sovereignty. (If anyone cares about preserving meaningful state authority, it is state legislators, and depriving them of representation in the national government will surely lead to greater

---

[25] 3 Story, *Commentaries*, Ch. 3 § 153.

[26] *See* "Madison's Notes on the Debates in the Federal Convention" for August 6, 1787, available at http://avalon.law.yale.edu/18th_century/debates_806.asp.

[27] *See, e.g.*, U.S. Const. Art. I, § 9, Cl. 7 ("them"); *id.* Art. III, § 3, Cl. 1 ("them").

[28] 17 U.S. 316 (1819).

disregard of state interests.) Through the twentieth century, with brief and spasmodic interludes of resistance by the Supreme Court, the power of the federal government grew. In 1995, the Court revisited the issue of ultimate sovereignty in *United States Term Limits v. Thornton*,[29] and again the nationalist side prevailed.

But this evolutionary process does not mean that time has left Story behind. His analysis provides rich material for anyone seeking to understand the original constitution, and even for those seeking guidance in resolving contemporary constitutional quarrels. Under the surface of apparently novel issues lie the great constitutional debates that never go away. Arguments about secession in the 1830s, social security in the 1930s, civil rights legislation in the 1960s, or healthcare reform in the 2010s are all arguments about the distribution of power between the states and the federal government. That was Story's central concern, and in each of these eras, the Court has relied on him. Indeed, in several cases, including *Thornton*, both the majority and the dissenting opinions have invoked Story to bolster their arguments.

That is not to say that the Commentaries can give a precise resolution to such questions. It may be that there is, in fact, no objectively correct answer as a matter of original meaning or understanding. The question of whether Congress had the power to create a national bank, which the Supreme Court would eventually decide in *McCulloch v. Maryland*, first arose in 1791—only two years after the ratification of the Constitution. James Madison and Alexander Hamilton, who were not only important Framers but actually co-authors of the Federalist Papers, disagreed on the answer. The idea that sufficient diligence will unearth an answer to questions the Framers never contemplated is a bit hard to maintain when, so soon after ratification, the Framers were unable to agree on the correct answer to questions they *had* contemplated. But Story can show us the framework within which arguments should be constructed.

He can also teach us something else. There are serious questions as to whether the Constitution is adequate to the modern world, the world of the party system, of mass media and ever-increasing influence of money on politics. The party system, for example, poses a serious threat to the traditional understanding of separation of powers, under which the different branches of the government would check each other and compete for the public's loyalty. A Congress under the control of the party that holds the Presidency is unlikely to be much of a check on executive power. One under the control of the other party may see its task not as governing but as ensuring that the President fails, in order to enable its party to capture the Executive Branch in the next election. And in conjunction with the filibuster, the party system seems to have rendered Congress all but incapable of action on any contested issue.

Story's deepest insight is that the Constitution cannot be counted on to save us, that instead, it needs our protection. History shows that different schools of thought have contended over the Constitution, that our understandings of it have ebbed and flowed with the forces of social and political movements. The Constitution exists for the People, but it belongs it to those who claim it, who are willing to fight to make it their own.

---

[29]   514 U.S. 779 (1995).

In this sense, the Constitution has always been a battleground. Broad public awareness and understanding are crucial to prevent it from being captured by narrow partisans, of whatever stripe. Story wrote his Commentaries in an attempt to promote that understanding and thereby avert the disaster he feared. His attempt failed, and his Constitution failed too. The one we have now is better in some ways. But we can still profit from Story's learning—and from his warning as well. Some of Story's specific concerns, like the fear of secession, have been overtaken by history. Others, like his worries about the effect of the party system, are still with us. Most relevant of all is his conclusion. "Republics," he cautioned, "are created by the virtue, public spirit, and intelligence of the citizens. They fall, when the wise are banished from the public councils, because they dare to be honest, and the profligate are rewarded, because they flatter the people in order to betray them."[30]

KERMIT ROOSEVELT III

Professor of Law,
University of Pennsylvania Law School

Philadelphia, Pennsylvania
February, 2013

---

[30] 3 Story, *Commentaries*, Ch. 45, § 1016.

Commentaries on the

Constitution of the

United States

COMMENTARIES ON THE CONSTITUTION OF THE UNITED STATES

WITH A PRELIMINARY REVIEW OF THE CONSTITUTIONAL HISTORY OF THE COLONIES AND STATES, BEFORE THE ADOPTION OF THE CONSTITUTION.

BY JOSEPH STORY, LL. D.,

DANE PROFFESSOR OF LAW IN HARVARD UNIVERSITY.

ABRIDGED BY THE AUTHOR,

FOR THE USE OF COLLEGES AND HIGH SCHOOLS.

"Magistratibus igitur opus est; sine quorum prudentiâ ac diligentiâ esse civitas non potest; quorumque descriptione omnis Reipublicæ moderatio continetur."

CIECERO DE LEG. lib. 3. cap. 2.

"Government: a contrivance of human Wisdom to provide for human wants."

BURKE.

BOSTON: HILLIARD, GRAY, AND COMPANY.
CAMBRIDGE: BROWN, SHATTUCK, AND CO.

1833

CAMBRIDGE:
CHARLES FOLSOM,
Printer to the University.

TO THE HONORABLE JOHN MARSHALL, LL. D.,

CHIEF JUSTICE OF THE UNITED STATES OF AMERICA.

SIR,

I ask the favour of dedicating this work to you. I know not, to whom it could with so much propriety be dedicated, as to one, whose youth was engaged in the arduous enterprises of the Revolution; whose manhood assisted in framing and supporting the national Constitution; and whose maturer years have been devoted to the task of unfolding its powers, and illustrating its principles. When, indeed, I look back upon your judicial labours during a period of thirty-two years, it is difficult to suppress astonishment at their extent and variety, and at the exact learning, the profound reasoning, and the solid principles, which they every where display. Other Judges have attained an elevated reputation by similar labours in a single department of jurisprudence. But in one department, (it need scarcely be said that I allude to that of constitutional law,) the common consent of your countrymen has admitted you to stand without a rival. Posterity will assuredly confirm by its deliberate award, what the present age has approved, as an act of undisputed justice. Your expositions of constitutional law enjoy a rare and extraordinary authority. They constitute a monument of fame far beyond the ordinary memorials of political and military glory. They are destined to enlighten, instruct, and convince future generations; and can scarcely perish but with the memory of the constitution itself. They are the victories of a mind accustomed to grapple with difficulties, capable of unfolding the most comprehensive truths with masculine simplicity, and severe logic, and prompt to dissipate the illusions of ingenious doubt, and subtle argument, and impassioned eloquence. They remind us of some mighty river of our own country, which, gathering in its course the contributions of many tributary streams, pours at last its own current into the ocean, deep, clear, and irresistible.

But I confess, that I dwell with even more pleasure upon the entirety of a life adorned by consistent principles, and filled up in the discharge of virtuous duty; where there is nothing to regret, and nothing to conceal; no friendships broken; no confidence betrayed; no timid surrenders to popular clamour; no eager reaches for popular favour. Who does not listen with conscious pride to the truth, that the disciple, the friend, the biographer of Washington, still lives, the uncompromising advocate of his principles?

I am but too sensible, that to some minds the time may not seem yet to have arrived, when language, like this, however true, should meet the eyes of the public. May the period be yet far distant, when praise shall speak out with that fulness of utterance, which belongs to the sanctity of the grave.

But I know not, that in the course of providence the privilege will be allowed me hereafter, to declare, in any suitable form, my deep sense of the obligations, which the jurisprudence of my country owes to your labours, of which I have been for twenty-one years a witness, and in some humble measure a companion. And if any apology should be required for my present freedom, may I not say, that at your age all reserve may well be spared, since all your labours must soon belong exclusively to history?

Allow me to add, that I have a desire (will it be deemed presumptuous?) to record upon these pages the memory of a friendship, which has for so many years been to me a source of inexpressible satisfaction; and which, I indulge the hope, may continue to accompany and cheer me to the close of life.

I am with the highest respect,
affectionately your servant,

JOSEPH STORY.

Cambridge, January, 1833.

PREFACE.

TO THE ORIGINAL WORK.

————

I NOW offer to the public another portion of the labours devolved on me in the execution of the duties of the Dane Professorship of Law in Harvard University. The importance of the subject will hardly be doubted by any persons, who have been accustomed to deep reflection upon the nature and value of the Constitution of the United States. I can only regret, that it has not fallen into abler hands, with more leisure to prepare, and more various knowledge to bring to such a task.

Imperfect, however, as these Commentaries may seem to those, who are accustomed to demand a perfect finish in all elementary works, they have been attended with a degree of uninviting labour, and dry research, of which it is scarcely possible for the general reader to form any adequate estimate. Many of the materials lay loose and scattered; and were to be gathered up among pamphlets and discussions of a temporary character; among obscure private and public documents; and from collections, which required an exhausting diligence to master their contents, or to select from unimportant masses, a few facts, or a solitary argument. Indeed, it required no small labour, even after these sources were explored, to bring together the irregular fragments, and to form them into groups, in which they might illustrate and support each other.

From two great sources, however, I have drawn by far the greatest part of my most valuable materials. These are, The Federalist, an incomparable commentary of three of the greatest statesmen of their age; and the extraordinary Judgments of Mr. Chief Justice Marshall upon constitutional law. The former have discussed the structure and organization of the national government, in all its departments, with admirable fulness {vi} and force. The latter has expounded the application and limits of its powers and functions with unrivalled profoundness and felicity. The Federalist could do little more, than state the objects and general bearing of these powers and functions. The masterly reasoning of the Chief Justice has followed them out to their ultimate results and boundaries, with a precision and clearness, approaching, as near as may be, to mathematical demonstration. The Federalist, being written to meet the most prevalent popular objections at the time of the adoption of the Constitution, has not attempted to pursue any very exact order in its reasoning; but has taken up subjects in such a manner, as was best adapted at the time to overcome prejudices, and win favour. Topics, therefore, having a natural connexion, are sometimes separated; and illustrations appropriate to several important points, are sometimes presented in an incidental discussion. I have transferred into my own pages all, which seemed to be of permanent importance in that great work; and have thereby endeavoured to make its merits more generally known.

The reader must not expect to find in these pages any novel views, and novel constructions of the Constitution. I have not the ambition to be the author of any new plan of interpreting the theory of the Constitution, or of enlarging or narrowing its powers by ingenious subtleties and learned doubts. My object will be sufficiently attained, if I shall have succeeded in bringing before the reader the true view of its powers maintained by its founders and friends, and confirmed and illustrated by the actual practice of the government. The expositions to be found in the work are less to be regarded, as my own opinions, than as those of the great minds, which framed the Constitution, or which have been from time to time called upon to administer it. Upon subjects of government it has always appeared to me, that metaphysical refinements are out of place. A constitution of government is addressed to the common sense of the people; and never was designed for trials of logical skill, or visionary speculation.

The reader will sometimes find the same train of reasoning brought before him in different parts of these Commentaries. {vii} It was indispensable to do so, unless the discussion was left imperfect, or the reader was referred back to other pages, to gather up and combine disjointed portions of reasoning. In cases, which have undergone judicial investigation, or which concern the judicial department, I have felt myself restricted to more narrow discussions, than in the rest of the work; and have sometimes contented myself with a mere transcript from the judgments of the court. It may readily be understood, that this course has been adopted from a solicitude, not to go incidentally beyond the line pointed out by the authorities.

In dismissing the work, I cannot but solicit the indulgence of the public for its omissions and deficiencies. With more copious materials it might have been made more exact, as well as more satisfactory. With more leisure and more learning it might have been wrought up more in the spirit of political philosophy. Such as it is, it may not be wholly useless, as a means of stimulating abler minds to a more thorough review of the whole subject; and of impressing upon Americans a reverential attachment to the Constitution, as in the highest sense the palladium of American liberty.

January, 1833.

ADVERTISEMENT TO THE ABRIDGMENT.

THE present work is an abridgment, made by the author, of his original work, for the use of Colleges and High-schools. It presents in a compressed form the leading doctrines of that work, so far as they are necessary to a just understanding of the actual provisions of the constitution. Many illustrations and vindications of these provisions are necessarily omitted. But sufficient are retained to enable every student to comprehend and apply the great principles of constitutional law, which were maintained by the founders of the constitution, and which have been since promulgated by those, who have, from time to time, administered it, or expounded its powers. I indulge the hope, that even in this reduced form the reasoning {viii} in favour of every clause of the constitution will appear satisfactory and conclusive; and that the youth of my country will learn to venerate and admire it as the only solid foundation, on which to rest our national union, prosperity, and glory.

April, 1833.

CONSTITUTION
OF THE
UNITED STATES OF AMERICA
[in 1833]

WE, the people of the United States, in order to form a more perfect union, establish justice, ensure domestic tranquillity, provide for the common defence, promote the general welfare, and secure the blessings of liberty to ourselves and our posterity, do ordain and establish this Constitution for the United States of America.

ARTICLE I.

SECTION 1.

1. All legislative powers herein granted, shall be vested in a congress of the United States, which shall consist of a senate and house of representatives.

SECTION 2.

1. The house of representatives shall be composed of members chosen every second year by the people of the several states, and the electors in each state shall have the qualifications requisite for electors of the most numerous branch of the state legislature.

2. No person shall be a representative who shall not have attained to the age of twenty-five years, and been seven years a citizen of the United States, and who shall not, when elected, be an inhabitant of that state in which he shall be chosen. {xviii}

3. Representatives and direct taxes shall be apportioned among the several states which may be included within this Union, according to their respective numbers, which shall be determined by adding to the whole number of free persons, including those bound to service for a term of years, and excluding Indians not taxed, three-fifths of all other persons. The actual enumeration shall be made within three years after the first meeting of the congress of the United States, and within every subsequent term of ten years, in such manner as they shall by law direct. The number of representatives shall not exceed one for every thirty thousand, but each state shall have at least one representative; and until such enumeration shall be made, the state of New Hampshire shall be entitled to choose three, Massachusetts eight, Rhode Island and Providence Plantations one, Connecticut five, New York six, New Jersey four, Pennsylvania eight, Delaware one, Maryland six, Virginia ten, North Carolina five, South Carolina five, and Georgia three.

4. When vacancies happen in the representation from any state, the executive authority thereof shall issue writs of election to fill such vacancies.

5. The house of representatives shall choose their speaker and other officers; and shall have the sole power of impeachment.

SECTION 3.

1. The senate of the United States shall be composed of two senators from each state, chosen by the legislature thereof, for six years; and each senator shall have one vote.

2. Immediately after they shall be assembled in consequence of the first election, they shall be divided as equally as may be into three classes. The seats of the senators of the first class shall be vacated at the expiration of the second year, of the second class, at the expiration of the fourth year, and of the third class, at the expiration of the sixth year, so that one-third may be chosen every second year; and if vacancies happen by resignation, or otherwise, during the recess of the legislature {xix} of any state, the executive thereof may make temporary appointments until the next meeting of the legislature, which shall then fill such vacancies.

3. No person shall be a senator who shall not have attained to the age of thirty years, and been nine years a citizen of the United States, and who shall not, when elected, be an inhabitant of that state for which he shall be chosen.

4. The vice-president of the United States shall be president of the senate, but shall have no vote, unless they be equally divided.

5. The Senate shall choose their other officers, and also a president *pro tempore*, in the absence of the vice-president, or when he shall exercise the office of president of the United States.

6. The senate shall have the sole power to try all impeachments. When sitting for that purpose, they shall be on oath or affirmation. When the president of the United States is tried, the chief justice shall preside; and no person shall be convicted without the concurrence of two-thirds of the members present.

7. Judgment in cases of impeachment shall not extend further than to removal from office, and disqualification to hold and enjoy any office of honour, trust, or profit, under the United States; but the party convicted shall nevertheless be liable and subject to indictment, trial, judgment, and punishment, according to law.

SECTION 4.

1. The times, places, and manner of holding elections for senators and representatives, shall be prescribed in each state by the legislature thereof: but the congress may, at any time by law, make or alter such regulations, except as to the places of choosing senators.

2. The congress shall assemble at least once in every year and such meeting shall be on the first Monday in December, unless they shall by law appoint a different day. {xx}

SECTION 5.

1. Each house shall be the judge of the elections, returns, and qualifications of its own members, and a majority of each shall constitute a quorum to do business; but a smaller number may adjourn from day to day, and may be authorized to compel the attendance of absent members, in such manner, and under such penalties as each house may provide.

2. Each house may determine the rules of its proceedings, punish its members for disorderly behaviour, and, with the concurrence of two-thirds, expel a member.

3. Each house shall keep a journal of its proceedings, and from time to time publish the same, excepting such parts as may, in their judgment, require secrecy; and

the yeas and nays of the members of either house on any question, shall, at the desire of one-fifth of those present, be entered on the journal.

4. Neither house, during the session of congress, shall, without the consent of the other, adjourn for more than three days, nor to any other place than that in which the two houses shall be sitting.

SECTION 6.

1. The senators and representatives shall receive a compensation for their services, to be ascertained by law, and paid out of the treasury of the United States. They shall, in all cases, except treason, felony, and breach of the peace, he privileged from arrest during their attendance at the session of their respective houses, and in going to, and returning from, the same; and for any speech or debate in either house, they shall not be questioned in any other place.

2. No senator or representative shall, during the time for which he was elected, be appointed to any civil office under the authority of the United States, which shall have been created, or the emoluments whereof shall have been increased during such time; and no person holding any office under the United States, shall be a member of either house during his continuance in office. {xxi}

SECTION 7.

1. All bills for raising revenue shall originate in the house of representatives; but the senate may propose or concur with amendments as on other bills.

2. Every bill which shall have passed the house of representatives and the senate, shall, before it become a law, be presented to the president of the United States; if he approve he shall sign it, but if not be shall return it, with his objections, to that house in which it shall have originated, who shall enter the objections at large on their journal, and proceed to reconsider it. If after such reconsideration two-thirds of that house shall agree to pass the bill, it shall be sent, together with the objections, to the other house, by which it shall likewise be reconsidered, and if approved by two-thirds of that house, it shall become a law. But in all such cases the votes of both houses shall be determined by yeas and nays, and the names of the persons voting for and against the bill shall be entered on the journal of each house respectively. If any bill shall not be returned by the. president within ten days, (Sundays excepted,) after it shall have been presented to him, the same shall be a law, in like manner as if he had signed it, unless the congress by their adjournment prevent its return, in which case it shall not be a law.

3. Every order, resolution, or vote, to which the concurrence of the senate and house of representatives may be necessary, (except on a question of adjournment,) shall be presented to the president of the United States; and before the same shall take effect, shall be approved by him, or being disapproved by him, shall be re-passed by two-thirds of the senate and house of representatives, according to the rules and limitations prescribed in the case of a bill.

SECTION 8.

The congress shall have power

1. To lay and collect taxes, duties, imposts, and excises, to pay the debts and provide for the common defence and general {xxii} welfare of the United States; but all duties, imposts, and excises, shall be uniform throughout the United States:

2. To borrow money on the credit of the United States:

3. To regulate commerce with foreign nations, and among the several states, and with the Indian tribes:

4. To establish an uniform rule of naturalization, and uniform laws on the subject of bankruptcies throughout the United States:

5. To coin money, regulate the value thereof, and of foreign coin, and fix the standard of weights and measures:

6. To provide for the punishment of counterfeiting the securities and current coin of the United States:

7. To establish post-offices and post-roads:

8. To promote the progress of science and useful arts, by securing, for limited times, to authors and inventors the exclusive right to their respective writings and discoveries:

9. To constitute tribunals inferior to the Supreme Court:

10. To define and punish piracies, and felonies, committed on the high seas, and offences against the law of nations:

11. To declare war, grant letters of marque and reprisal, and make rules concerning captures on land and water:

12. To raise and support armies, but no appropriation of money to that use shall be for a longer term than two years:

13. To provide and maintain a navy:

14. To make rules for the government and regulation of the land and naval forces:

15. To provide for calling forth the militia to execute the laws of the Union, suppress insurrections, and repel invasions:

16. To provide for organizing, arming, and disciplining the militia, and for governing such part of them as may be employed in the service of the United States, reserving to the states respectively, the appointment of the officers, and the authority of training the militia according to the discipline prescribed by congress:

17. To exercise exclusive legislation in all cases whatsoever, over such district, (not exceeding ten miles square,) as may, by cession of particular states, and the acceptance of congress, {xxiii} become the seat of the government of the United States, and to exercise like authority over all places purchased by the consent of the legislature of the state in which the same shall be, for the erection of forts, magazines, arsenals, dock-yards, and other needful buildings: — And

18. To make all laws which shall be necessary and proper for carrying into execution the foregoing powers, and all other powers vested by this Constitution in the government of the United States, or in any department or officer thereof.

SECTION 9.

1. The migration or importation of such persons, as any of the states now existing shall think proper to admit, shall not be prohibited by the congress prior to the year one thousand eight hundred and eight, but a tax or duty may be imposed on such importation, not exceeding ten dollars for each person.

2. The privilege of the writ of *habeas corpus* shall not be suspended, unless when in cases of rebellion or invasion the public safety may require it.

3. No bill of attainder or *ex post facto* law shall be passed.

4. No capitation, or other direct tax shall be laid, unless in proportion to the *census* or enumeration herein before directed to be taken.

5. No tax or duty shall be laid on articles exported from any state. No preference shall be given by any regulation of commerce or revenue to the ports of one state over those of another; nor shall vessels bound to, or from, one state, be obliged to enter, clear, or pay duties, in another.

6. No money shall be drawn from the treasury, but in consequence of appropriations made by law; and a regular statement and account of the receipts and expenditures of all public money shall be published from time to time.

7. No title of nobility shall be granted by the United States: And no person holding any office of profit or trust under them, shall, without the consent of the congress, accept of any present, emolument, office, or title of any kind whatever, from any king, prince, or foreign state. {xxiv}

SECTION 10.

1. No state shall enter into any treaty, alliance, or confederation; grant letters of marque and reprisal; coin money.; emit bills of credit; make any thing but gold and silver coin a tender in payment of debts; pass any bill of attainder, *ex post facto* law, or law impairing the obligation of contracts, or grant any title of nobility.

2. No state shall, without the consent of the congress, lay any imposts or duties on imports or exports, except what may be absolutely necessary for executing its inspection laws; and the net produce of all duties and imposts, laid by any state on imports or exports, shall be for the use of the treasury of the United States; and all such laws shall be subject to the revision and control of the congress. No state shall, without the consent of congress, lay any duty of tonnage, keep troops, or ships of war, in time of peace, enter into any agreement or compact with another state, or with a foreign power, or engage in war, unless actually invaded, or in such imminent danger as will not admit of delay.

ARTICLE II.

SECTION 1.

1. The executive power shall be vested in a president of the United States of America. He shall hold his office during the term of four years, and together with the vice-president, chosen for the same term, be elected as follows:

2. Each state shall appoint, in such manner as the legislature thereof may direct, a number of electors equal to the whole number of senators and representatives to which the state may be entitled in the congress: but no senator or representative, or person holding an office of trust or profit under the United States, shall be appointed an elector.

3. The electors shall meet in their respective states, and vote by ballot for two persons, of whom one at least shall not be an inhabitant of the same state with themselves. And they shall make a list of all the persons voted for, and of the number of votes for each; which list they shall sign and certify, {xxv} and transmit, sealed, to the seat of the government of the United States, directed to the president of the senate. The president of the senate shall, in the presence of the senate and house of representatives, open all the certificates, and the votes shall then be counted. The person having the greatest number of votes shall be the president, if such number be a majority of the whole number of electors appointed; and if there be

more than one who have such majority, and have an equal number of votes, then the house of representatives shall immediately choose by ballot one of them for president; and if no person have a majority, then, from the five highest on the list the said house shall in like manner choose the president. But in choosing the president the votes shall be taken by states, the representation from each state having one vote; a quorum for this purpose shall consist of a member or members from two-thirds of the states, and a majority of all the states shall be necessary to a choice. In every case, after the choice of the president, the person having the greatest number of votes of the electors shall be the vice-president. But if there should remain two or more who have equal votes, the senate shall choose from them by ballot the vice-president.

4. The congress may determine the time of choosing the electors, and the day on which they shall give their votes; which day shall be the same throughout the United States.

5. No person except a natural born citizen, or a citizen of the United States, at the time of the adoption of this Constitution, shall be eligible to the office of president; neither shall any person be eligible to that office who shall not have attained to the age of thirty-five years, and been fourteen years a resident within the United States.

6. In case of the removal of the president from office, or of his death, resignation, or inability to discharge the powers and duties of the said office, the same shall devolve on the vice-president, and the congress may by law provide for the case of removal, death, resignation, or inability, both of the president and vice-president, declaring what officer shall then act as president, {xxvi} and such officer shall act accordingly until the disability be removed, or a president shall be elected.

7. The president shall, at stated times, receive for his services, a compensation, which shall neither be increased nor diminished during the period for which he shall have been elected, and he shall not receive within that period any other emolument from the United States or any of them.

8. Before he enter on the execution of his office, he shall take the following oath or affirmation:

9. "I do solemnly swear, (or affirm,) that I will faithfully execute the office of president of the United States, and will, to the best of my ability, preserve, protect, and defend the Constitution of the United States."

SECTION 2.

1. The president shall be commander-in-chief of the army and navy of the United States, and of the militia of the several states, when called into the actual service of the United States; he may require the opinion, in writing, of the principal officer in each of the executive departments, upon any subject relating to the duties of their respective offices, and he shall have power to grant reprieves and pardons for offences against the United States, except in cases of impeachment.

2. He shall have power, by and with the advice and consent of the senate, to make treaties, provided two thirds of the senators present concur; and he shall nominate, and by and with the advice and consent of the senate, shall appoint ambassadors, other public ministers and consuls, judges of the supreme court, and all other officers of the United States, whose appointments are not herein otherwise

provided for, and which shall be established by law: but the congress may by law vest the appointment of such inferior officers, as they think proper, in the president alone, in the courts of law, or in the heads of departments.

3. The president shall have power to fill up all vacancies that may happen during the recess of the senate, by granting commissions, which shall expire at the end of their next session. {xxvii}

SECTION 3.

1. He shall from time to time give to the congress information of the state of the Union, and recommend to their consideration such measures as he shall judge necessary and expedient; he may, on extraordinary occasions, convene both houses, or either of them, and in case of disagreement between them with respect to the time of adjournment, he may adjourn them to such time as he shall think proper; he shall receive ambassadors and other public ministers; he shall take care that the laws be faithfully executed, and shall commission all the officers of the United States.

SECTION 4.

1. The president, vice-president, and all civil officers of the United States shall be removed from office on impeachment for, and conviction of, treason, bribery, or other high crimes and misdemeanors.

ARTICLE III.

SECTION 1.

1. The judicial power of the United States, shall be vested in one Supreme Court, and in such inferior courts as the congress may from time to time ordain and establish. The judges, both of the supreme and inferior courts, shall hold their offices during good behaviour, and shall, at stated times, receive for their services, a compensation, which shall not be diminished during their continuance in office.

SECTION 2.

1. The judicial power shall extend to all cases, in law and equity, arising under this Constitution, the laws of the United States, and treaties made, or which shall be made, under their authority; to all cases affecting ambassadors, other public ministers and consuls; to all cases of admiralty and maritime jurisdiction; to controversies to which the United States shall be a party; to controversies between two or more states, between {xxviii} a state and citizens of another state, between citizens of different states, between citizens of the same state claiming lands under grants of different states, and between a state, or the citizens thereof, and foreign states, citizens, or subjects.

2. In all cases affecting ambassadors, other public ministers and consuls, and those in which a state shall be a party, the supreme court shall have original jurisdiction. In all the other cases before mentioned, the supreme court shall have appellate jurisdiction, both as to law and fact, with such exceptions, and under such regulations as the congress shall make.

3. The trial of all crimes, except in cases of impeachment, shall be by jury; and such trial shall be held in the state where the said crimes shall have been commit-

ted; but when not committed within any state, the trial shall be at such place or places as the congress may by law have directed.

SECTION 3.

1. Treason against the United States, shall consist only in levying war against them, or in adhering to their enemies, giving them aid and comfort. No person shall be convicted of treason unless on the testimony of two witnesses to the same overt act, or on confession in open court.

2. The congress shall have power to declare the punishment of treason, but no attainder of treason shall work corruption of blood, or forfeiture, except during the life of the person attainted.

ARTICLE IV.

SECTION 1.

1. Full faith and credit shall be given in each state to the public acts, records, and judicial proceedings of every other state. And the congress may by general laws prescribe the manner in which such acts, records, and proceedings shall be proved, and the effect thereof.

SECTION 2.

1. The citizens of each state shall be entitled to all privileges and immunities of citizens in the several states. {xxix}

2. A person charged in any state with treason, felony, or other crime, who shall flee from justice, and be found in another state, shall, on demand of the executive authority of the state from which he fled, be delivered up, to be removed to the state having jurisdiction of the crime.

3. No person held to service or labour in one state, under the laws thereof, escaping into another, shall, in consequence of any law or regulation therein, be discharged from such service or labour, but shall be delivered up on claim of the party to whom such service or labour may be due.

SECTION 3.

1. New states may be admitted by the congress into this Union; but no new state shall be formed or erected within the jurisdiction of any other state; nor any state be formed by the junction of two or more states, or parts of states, without the consent of the legislatures of the states concerned, as well as of the congress.

2. The congress shall have power to dispose of and make all needful rules and regulations respecting the territory or other property belonging to the United States; and nothing in this Constitution shall be so construed as to prejudice any claims of the United States, or of any particular state.

SECTION 4.

1. The United States shall guarantee to every state in this Union a republican form of government, and shall protect each of them against invasion; and on application of the legislature, or of the executive, (when the legislature cannot be convened,) against domestic violence.

ARTICLE V.

1. The congress, whenever two-thirds of both houses shall deem it necessary, shall propose amendments to this Constitution, or, on the application of the legislatures of two-thirds of the several states, shall call a convention for proposing amendments, which, in either case, shall be valid to all intents and {xxx} purposes, as part of this Constitution, when ratified by the legislatures of three-fourths of the several states or by conventions in three-fourths thereof, as the one or the other mode of ratification may be proposed by the congress: Provided, that no amendment, which may be made prior to the year one thousand eight hundred and eight, shall in any manner affect the first and fourth clauses in the ninth section of the first article; and that no state, without its consent, shall be deprived of its equal suffrage in the senate.

ARTICLE VI.

1. All debts contracted and engagements entered into, before the adoption of this Constitution, shall be as valid against the United States under this Constitution, as under the confederation.

2. This Constitution, and the laws of the United States which shall be made in pursuance thereof; and all treaties made, or which shall be made, under the authority of the United States, shall be the supreme law of the land; and the judges in every state shall be bound thereby, any thing in the constitution or laws of any state to the contrary notwithstanding.

3. The senators and representatives before mentioned, and the members of the several state legislatures, and all executive and judicial officers, both of the United States and of the several states shall be bound, by oath or affirmation, to support this Constitution; but no religious test shall ever be required as a qualification to any office or public trust under the United States.

ARTICLE VII.

1. The ratification of the conventions of nine states, shall be sufficient for the establishment of this Constitution between the states so ratifying the same. {xxxi}

AMENDMENTS TO THE CONSTITUTION.

ARTICLE I.

Congress shall make no law respecting an establishment of religion, or prohibiting the free exercise thereof; or abridging the freedom of speech, or of the press; or the right of the people peaceably to assemble, and to petition the government for a redress of grievances.

ARTICLE II.

A well regulated militia being necessary to the security of a free state, the right of the people to keep and bear arms shall not be infringed.

ARTICLE III.

No soldier shall, in time of peace, be quartered in any house without the consent of the owner; nor in time of war, but in a manner to be prescribed by law.

ARTICLE IV.

The right of the people to be secure in their persons, houses, papers, and effects, against unreasonable searches and seizures, shall not be violated; and no warrants shall issue, but upon probable cause, supported by oath or affirmation, and particularly describing the place to be searched, and the persons or things to be seized.

ARTICLE V.

No person shall be held to answer for a capital or otherwise infamous crime, unless on a presentment or indictment of a grand jury, except in cases arising in the land or naval forces, or in the militia, when in actual service, in time of war or public danger; nor shall any person be subject for the same offence to be twice put in jeopardy of life or limb; nor shall {xxxii} be compelled, in any criminal case, to be a witness against himself, nor be deprived of life, liberty, or property, without due process of law; nor shall private property be taken for public use without just compensation.

ARTICLE VI.

In all criminal prosecutions, the accused shall enjoy the right to a speedy and public trial, by an impartial jury of the state and district wherein the crime shall have been committed, which district shall have been previously ascertained by law; and to be informed of the nature and cause of the accusation; to be confronted with the witnesses against him; to have compulsory process for obtaining witnesses in his favour; and to have the assistance of counsel for his defence.

ARTICLE VII.

In suits at common law, where the value in controversy shall exceed twenty dollars, the right of trial by jury shall be preserved; and no fact tried by a jury shall be otherwise reexamined in any court of the United States, than according to the rules of the common law.

ARTICLE VIII.

Excessive bail shall not be required, nor excessive fines imposed, nor cruel and unusual punishments inflicted.

ARTICLE IX.

The enumeration in the Constitution of certain rights, shall not be construed to deny or disparage others retained by the people.

ARTICLE X.

The powers not delegated to the United States by the Constitution, nor prohibited by it to the states, are reserved to the states respectively, or to the people. {xxxiii}

ARTICLE XI.

The judicial power of the United States shall not be construed to extend to any suit in law or equity, commenced or prosecuted against one of the United States by citizens of another state, or by citizens or subjects of any foreign state.

ARTICLE XII.

1. The electors shall meet in their respective states, and vote by ballot for president

and vice-president, one of whom, at least, shall not be an inhabitant of the same state with themselves; they shall name in their ballots the person voted for as president, and in distinct ballots the person voted for as vice-president; and they shall make distinct lists of all persons voted for as president, and of all persons voted for as vice president, and of the number of votes for each, which lists they shall sign and certify, and transmit sealed to the seat of the government of the United States, directed to the president of the senate; the president of the senate shall, in the presence of the senate and house of representatives, open all the certificates, and the votes shall then be counted: the person having the greatest number of votes for president, shall be the president, if such number be a majority of the whole number of electors appointed; and if no person have such majority, then from the persons having the highest numbers, not exceeding three, on the list of those voted for as president, the house of representatives shall choose immediately, by ballot, the president. But in choosing the president, the votes shall be taken by states, the representation from each state having one vote; a quorum for this purpose shall consist of a member or members from two thirds of the states, and a majority of all the states shall be necessary to a choice. And if the house of representatives shall not choose a president, whenever the right of choice shall devolve upon them, before the fourth day of March next following, then the vice-president shall act as president, as in the case of the death or other constitutional disability of the president. {xxxiv}

2. The person having the greatest number of votes as vice-president, shall be the vice-president, if such number be a majority of the whole number of electors appointed; and if no person have a majority, then from the two highest numbers on the list, the senate shall choose the vice-president: a quorum for the purpose shall consist of two-thirds of the whole number of senators, a majority of the whole number shall be necessary to a choice.

3. But no person constitutionally ineligible to the office of president, shall be eligible to that of vice-president of the United States.

COMMENTARIES.

PRELIMINARY CHAPTER.

PLAN OF THE WORK.

{1}

THE principal object of these Commentaries is to present a full analysis and exposition of the Constitution of Government of the United States of America. In order to do this with clearness and accuracy, it is necessary to understand, what was the political position of the several States, composing the Union, in relation to each other at the time of its adoption. This will naturally conduct us back to the American Revolution; and to the formation of the Confederation consequent thereon. But if we stop here, we shall still be surrounded with many difficulties in regard to our domestic institutions and policy, which have grown out of transactions of a much earlier date, connected on one side with the common dependence of all the Colonies upon the British Empire, and on the other with the particular charters of government and internal legislation, which belonged to each Colony, as a distinct sovereignty, and which have impressed upon each peculiar habits, opinions, attachments, and even prejudices. Traces of these peculiarities are every where discernible in the actual jurisprudence of each State; and are silently or openly referred to in several of the provisions {2} of the Constitution of the United States. In short, without a careful review of the origin and constitutional and juridical history of all the colonies, of the principles common to all, and of the diversities, which were no less remarkable in all, it would be impossible fully to understand the nature and objects of the Constitution; the reasons on which several of its most important provisions are founded; and the necessity of those concessions and compromises, which a desire to form a solid and perpetual Union has incorporated into its leading features.

The plan of the work will, therefore, naturally comprehend three great divisions. The first will embrace a sketch of the charters, constitutional history, and ante-revolutionary jurisprudence of the Colonies. The second will embrace a sketch of the constitutional history of the States during the Revolution, and the rise, progress, decline, and fall of the Confederation. The third will embrace the history of the rise and adoption of the Constitution; and a full exposition of all its provisions, with the reasons, on which they were respectively founded, the objections, by which they were respectively assailed, and such illustrations drawn from contemporaneous documents, and the subsequent operations of the government, as may best enable the reader to estimate for himself the true value of each. In this way (as it is hoped) his judgment as well as his affections will be enlisted on the side of the Constitution, as the truest security of the Union, and the only solid basis, on which to rest the private rights, the public liberties, and the substantial prosperity of the people composing the American Republic.

1

BOOK I.

HISTORY OF THE COLONIES.

CHAPTER I.

ORIGIN OF THE TITLE TO TERRITORY OF THE COLONIES.

§ 1. THE discovery of the Continent of America by Columbus in the fifteenth century awakened the attention of all the maritime States of Europe. Stimulated by the love of glory, and still more by the hope of gain and dominion, many of them early embarked in adventurous enterprises, the object of which was to found colonies, or to search for the precious metals, or to exchange the products and manufactures of the old world for whatever was most valuable and attractive in the new. England was not behind her continental neighbours in seeking her own aggrandizement, and nourishing her then infant commerce. The ambition of Henry the Seventh was roused by the communications of Columbus, and in 1495 he granted a commission to John Cabot, an enterprising Venetian, then settled in England, to proceed on a voyage of discovery, and to subdue and take possession of any lands unoccupied by any Christian Power, in the name and for the benefit of the British Crown. In the succeeding year Cabot sailed on his voyage, and having first discovered {4} the Islands of Newfoundland and St. Johns, he afterwards sailed along the coast of the continent from the 56th to the 38th degree of north latitude, and claimed for his sovereign the vast region, which stretches from the Gulf of Mexico to the most northern regions.

§ 2. Such is the origin of the British title to the territory composing these United States. That title was founded on the right of discovery, a right, which was held among the European nations a just and sufficient foundation, on which to rest their respective claims to the American continent. Whatever controversies existed among them, (and they were numerous,) respecting the extent of their own acquisitions abroad, they appealed to this as the ultimate fact, by which their various and conflicting claims were to be adjusted. It may not be easy upon general reasoning to establish the doctrine, that priority of discovery confers any exclusive right to territory. It was probably adopted by the European nations as a convenient and flexible rule, by which to regulate their respective claims. For it was obvious, that in the mutual contests for dominion in newly discovered lands, there would soon arise violent and sanguinary struggles for exclusive possession, unless some common principle should be recognised by all maritime nations for the benefit of all. None more readily suggested itself than the one now under consideration; and as it was a principle of peace and repose, of perfect equality of benefit in proportion to the actual or supposed expenditures and hazards attendant upon such enterprises, it received a universal acquiescence, if not a ready approbation. It became the basis of European polity, and regulated the exercise of the rights of sovereignty and settlement in all the cis-Atlantic Plantations. In respect to desert and {5} uninhabited lands, there does not seem any important objection, which

5

can be urged against it. But in respect to countries, then inhabited by the natives, it is not easy to perceive, how, in point of justice, or humanity, or general conformity to the law of nature, it can be successfully vindicated. As a conventional rule it might properly govern all the nations, which recognised its obligation; but it could have no authority over the aborigines of America, whether gathered into civilized communities, or scattered in hunting tribes over the wilderness. Their right, whatever it was, of occupation or use, stood upon original principles deducible from the law of nature, and could not be justly narrowed or extinguished without their own free consent.

§ 3. There is no doubt, that the Indian tribes, inhabiting this continent at the time of its discovery, maintained a claim to the exclusive possession and occupancy of the territory within their respective limits, as sovereigns and absolute proprietors of the soil. They acknowledged no obedience, or allegiance, or subordination to any foreign sovereign whatsoever; and as far as they have possessed the means, they have ever since asserted this plenary right of dominion, and yielded it up only when lost by the superior force of conquest, or transferred by a voluntary cession.

§ 4. The European nations found little difficulty in reconciling themselves to the adoption of any principle, which gave ample scope to their ambition, and employed little reasoning to support it. They were content to take counsel of their interests, their prejudices, and their passions, and felt no necessity of vindicating their conduct before cabinets, which were already eager to recognise its justice and its policy. The Indians were a savage race, sunk in the depths of ignorance and {6} heathenism. If they might not be extirpated for their want of religion and just morals, they might be reclaimed from their errors. They were bound to yield to the superior genius of Europe, and in exchanging their wild and debasing habits, for civilization and Christianity they were deemed to gain more than an equivalent for every sacrifice and suffering. The Papal authority, too, was brought in aid of these great designs; and for the purpose of overthrowing heathenism, and propagating the Catholic religion, Alexander the Sixth, by a Bull issued in 1493, granted to the crown of Castile the whole of the immense territory then discovered, or to be discovered, between the poles, so far as it was not then possessed by any Christian prince.

§ 5. The principle, then, that discovery gave title to the government, by whose subjects or by whose authority it was made, against all other European governments, being once established, it followed almost as a matter of course, that every government within the limits of its discoveries excluded all other persons from any right to acquire the soil, by any grant whatsoever, from the natives. No nation would suffer, either its own subjects, or those of any other nation, to set up or vindicate any such title. It was deemed a right, exclusively belonging to the government, in its sovereign capacity to extinguish the Indian tide, and to perfect its own dominion over the soil, and dispose of it according to its own good pleasure.

§ 6. It may be asked, what was the effect of this principle of discovery in respect to the rights of the natives themselves. In the view of the Europeans it created a peculiar relation between themselves and the aboriginal inhabitants. The latter were admitted to possess a present right of occupancy, or use in the soil, {7} which was subordinate to the ultimate dominion of the discoverer. They were admitted to be the rightful occupants of the soil, with a legal, as well as just claim to retain possession of it, and to use it according to their own discretion. In a certain sense, they were permitted to exercise rights of sovereignty over it. They might sell or transfer it to the sovereign, who discovered it; but they were denied the authority to dispose of it to any other persons; and until such a sale or transfer, they were generally permitted to occupy it as sovereigns *de facto*. But, notwithstanding this occupancy, the European discoverers claimed and exercised the right to grant the soil, while yet in possession of the natives, subject however to their right of occupancy; and the title so granted was universally admitted to convey a sufficient title in the soil to the grantees in perfect dominion, or, as it is sometimes expressed in treatises of public law, it was a transfer of *plenum et utile dominium*.

CHAPTER II.

ORIGIN AND SETTLEMENT OF VIRGINIA.

§ 7. HAVING thus traced out the origin of the title to the soil of America asserted by the European nations, we may now enter upon a consideration of the manner in which the settlements were made, and the political constitutions, by which the various Colonies were organized and governed.

§ 8. The first permanent settlement made in America, under the auspices of England, was under a charter granted to Sir Thomas Gates and his associates by James the First, in the fourth year after his accession to the throne of England (in 1606.) That charter granted to them the territories in America, then commonly called Virginia, lying on the sea-coast between the 34th and the 45th degrees of north latitude and the islands adjacent within 100 miles, which were not belonging to, or possessed by any Christian prince or people. The associates were divided into two companies, one of which was required to settle between the 34th and 41st degrees of north latitude, and the other between the 38th and 45th degrees of north latitude, but not within 100 miles of the prior colony. By degrees, the name of Virginia was confined to the first or south colony. The second assumed the name of the Plymouth Company, from the residence of the original grantees; and New-England was founded under their auspices. Each colony had exclusive propriety in all the territory within fifty miles from the first seat of their plantation.

§ 9. The charter of the first or Virginia colony was successively altered in 1609 and 1612, without any {9} important change in its substantial provisions, as to the civil or political rights of the colonists. It is surprising, indeed, that charters, securing such vast powers to the crown, and such entire dependence on the part of the emigrants, should have found any favour in the eyes either of the proprietors, or of the people. By placing the whole legislative and executive powers in a council nominated by the crown, and guided by its instructions, every person settling in America seems to have been bereaved of the noblest privileges of a free man. But without hesitation or reluctance, the proprietors of both colonies prepared to execute their respective plans; and under the authority of a charter, which would now be rejected with disdain, as a violent invasion of the sacred and inalienable rights of liberty, the first permanent settlements of the English in America were established. From this period the progress of the two provinces of Virginia and New-England form a regular and connected story. The former in the South, and the latter in the North, may be considered as the original and parent colonies, in imitation of which, and under whose shelter, all the others have been successively planted and reared.

§ 10. The settlements in Virginia were earliest in point of date, and were fast advancing under a policy, which subdivided the property among the settlers, in-

8

stead of retaining it in common, and thus gave vigour to private enterprise. As the colony increased, the spirit of its members assumed more and more the tone of independence; and they grew restless and impatient for the privileges enjoyed under the government of their native country. To quiet this uneasiness, Sir George Yeardley, then the governor of the colony, in 1619, called a general assembly, composed of representatives {10} from the various plantations in the colony, and permitted them to assume and exercise the high functions of legislation. Thus was formed and established the first representative legislature, that ever sat in America. The conduct of the colonists, as well as the company, soon afterwards gave offence to King James; and the disasters, which accomplished an almost total destruction of the colony by the successful inroads of the Indians, created much discontent and disappointment among the proprietors at home. The king found it no difficult matter to satisfy the nation, that an inquiry into their conduct was necessary. It was accordingly ordered; and the result of that inquiry, by commissioners appointed by himself, was a demand, on the part of the crown, of a surrender of the charters. The demand was resisted by the company; a *quo warranto* was instituted against them, and it terminated, as in that age it might well be supposed it would, in a judgment, pronounced in 1624 by judges holding their offices during his pleasure, that the franchises were forfeited and the corporation should be dissolved.

§ 11. With the fall of the charter the colony came under the immediate government and control of the crown itself; and the king issued a special commission appointing a governor and twelve counsellors, to whom the entire direction of its affairs was committed. In this commission no representative assembly was mentioned; and there is little reason to suppose that James, who, besides his arbitrary notions of government, imputed the recent disasters to the existence of such an assembly, ever intended to revive it. While he was yet meditating upon a plan or code of government, his death put an end to his projects, which were better {11} calculated to nourish his own pride and conceit, than to subserve the permanent interests of the province. Henceforth, however, Virginia continued to be a royal province until the period of the American Revolution.

§ 12. Charles the First adopted the notions and followed out, in its full extent, the colonial system of his father. He declared the colony to be a part of the empire annexed to the crown, and immediately subordinate to its jurisdiction. During the greater part of his reign, Virginia knew no other law, than the will of the sovereign, or his delegated agents; and statutes were passed and taxes imposed without the slightest effort to convene a colonial assembly. It was not until the murmurs and complaints, which such a course of conduct was calculated to produce, had betrayed the inhabitants into acts of open resistance to the governor, and into a firm demand of redress from the crown against his oppressions, that the king was brought to more considerate measures. He did not at once yield to their discontents; but pressed, as he was, by severe embarrassments at home, he was content to adopt a policy, which would conciliate the colony and remove some of its just complaints. He accordingly, soon afterwards, appointed Sir William Berkeley governor, with powers and instructions, which breathed a far more benign spirit. He was authorized to proclaim, that in all its concerns, civil as well as ecclesiastical, the colony should be governed according to the laws of England. He was directed to issue writs for electing representatives of the people, who with the governor and council should form a general assembly, clothed with supreme legislative authority; and to establish courts of justice, whose proceedings should be guided by the forms of the parent country. The rights of Englishmen were {12} thus, in a great measure, secured to the colonists; and under the government of this excellent magistrate, with some short intervals of interruption, the colony flourished with a vigorous growth for almost forty years. The revolution of 1688 found it, if not in the practical possession of liberty, at least with forms of government well calculated silently to cherish its spirit.

CHAPTER III.

ORIGIN AND SETTLEMENT OF NEW-ENGLAND.

§ 13. WE may now advert in a brief manner to the history of the Northern, or Plymouth Company. That company possessed fewer resources and less enterprise than the Southern; and though aided by men of high distinction, its first efforts for colonization were feeble and discouraging. Capt. John Smith, so well known in the History of Virginia by his successful adventures under their authority, lent a transient lustre to their attempts; and his warm descriptions of the beauty and fertility of the country procured for it from the excited imagination of the Prince, after King Charles the First, the flattering name of *New-England*, a name, which effaced from it that of Virginia, and which has since become dear beyond expression, to the inhabitants of its harsh but salubrious climate.

§ 14. While the company was yet languishing, an event occurred, which gave a new and unexpected aspect to its prospects. It is well known, that the religious dissensions consequent upon the reformation, while they led to a more bold and free spirit of discussion, failed at the same time of introducing a correspondent charity for differences of religious opinion. Each successive sect entertained not the slightest doubt of its own infallibility in doctrine and worship, and was eager to obtain proselytes, and denounce the errors of its opponents. If it had stopped here, we might have forgotten, in admiration of the sincere zeal for Christian truth, the desire of power, and the pride of mind, which lurked within the inner folds of their devotion. But unfortunately {14} the spirit of intolerance was abroad in all its stern and unrelenting severity. To tolerate errors was to sacrifice Christianity to mere temporal interests. Truth, and truth alone, was to be followed at the hazard of all consequences; and religion allowed no compromises between conscience and worldly comforts. Heresy was itself a sin of a deadly nature, and to extirpate it was a primary duty of all, who were believers in sincerity and truth. Persecution, therefore, even when it seemed most to violate the feelings of humanity and the rights of private judgment, never wanted apologists among those of the purest and most devout lives. It was too often received with acclamations by the crowd, and found an ample vindication from the learned and the dogmatists; from the policy of the civil magistrate, and the blind zeal of the ecclesiastic. Each sect, as it attained power, exhibited the same unrelenting firmness in putting down its adversaries. The papist and the prelate, the puritan and the presbyterian, felt no compunctions in the destruction of dissentients from their own faith. They uttered, indeed, loud complaints of the injustice of their enemies, when they were themselves oppressed; but it was not from any abhorrence of persecution itself, but of the infamous errors of the persecutors. There are not wanting on the records of the history of these times abundant proofs, how easily sects, which had borne every

11

human calamity with unshrinking fortitude for conscience' sake, could turn upon their inoffensive, but, in their judgment, erring neighbours, with a like infliction of suffering. Even adversity sometimes fails of producing its usual salutary effects of moderation and compassion, when a blind but honest zeal has usurped domin- ion over the mind. If such a picture of human infirmity may justly add to our {15} humility, it may also serve to admonish us of the Christian duty of forbearance. And he, who can look with an eye of exclusive censure on such scenes, must have forgotten, how many bright examples they have afforded of the liveliest virtue, the most persuasive fidelity, and the most exalted piety.

§ 15. Among others, who suffered persecutions from the haughty zeal of Elizabeth, was a small sect, called, from the name of their leader, Brownists, to whom we owe the foundation of the now wide spread sect of Congregationalists or Independents. After sufferings of an aggravated nature, they were compelled to take refuge in Holland under the care of their pastor, Mr. John Robinson, a man distinguished for his piety, his benevolence, and his intrepid spirit. After remain- ing there some years, they concluded to emigrate to America in the hope, that they might thus perpetuate their religious discipline, and preserve the purity of an apostolical church. In conjunction with other friends in England they embarked on the voyage with a design of settlement on Hudson's river in New-York. But against their intention they were compelled to land on the shores of Cape Cod in the depth of winter, and the place of their landing was called Plymouth, which has since become so celebrated as the first permanent settlement in New-England. Not having contemplated any plantation at this place, they had not taken the pre- caution to obtain any charter from the Plymouth Company.

§ 16. On the 11th of November, 1620, these humble but fearless adventur- ers, before their landing, drew up and signed an original compact, in which, after acknowledging themselves subjects of the crown of England, they proceed to de- clare: "Having undertaken, {16} for the glory of God and the advancement of the Christian faith and the honor of our king and country, a voyage to plant the first colony in the northern parts of Virginia, we do by these presents solemnly and mutually, in the presence of God and of one another, covenant and combine our- selves together into a civil body politic, for our better ordering and preservation and furtherance of the ends aforesaid. And by virtue hereof do enact, constitute, and frame such just and equal laws, ordinances, acts, constitutions, and officers from time to time, as shall be thought most meet and convenient for the general good of the colony; unto which we promise all due submission and obedience." This is the whole of the compact, and it was signed by forty-one persons. It is in its very essence a pure democracy; and in pursuance of it the colonists proceeded soon afterwards to organize the colonial government, under the name of the Col- ony of New Plymouth, to appoint a governor and other officers, and to enact laws. The governor was chosen annually by the freemen, and had at first one assistant to aid him in the discharge of his trust. Four others were soon afterwards added, and finally the number was increased to seven. The supreme legislative power resided in, and was exercised by the whole body of the male inhabitants, every freeman, who was a member of the church, being admitted to vote in all public affairs. The number of settlements having increased, and being at a considerable distance from each other, a house of representatives was established in 1639; the members of which, as well as all other officers, were annually chosen. They adopted the common law of England, as the general basis of their jurisprudence, varying it however from time to time by municipal regulations {17} better adapted to their situation, or conforming more exactly to their stern notions of the absolute authority and universal obligation of the Mosaic Institutions.

§ 17. The Plymouth Colonists acted, at first, altogether under the voluntary compact and association already mentioned. But they daily felt embarrassments from the want of some general authority, derived directly or indirectly from the crown, which should recognise their settlement and confirm their legislation. After several ineffectual attempts made for this purpose, they at length succeeded in obtaining, in January, 1629, a patent from the council established at Plymouth, in England, under the charter of King James of 1620.

§ 18. This patent or charter seems never to have been confirmed by the crown; and the colonists were never, by any act of the crown, created a body politic and corporate with any legislative powers. They, therefore, remained in legal contemplation a mere voluntary association, exercising the highest powers and prerogatives of sovereignty, and yielding obedience to the laws and magistrates chosen by themselves.

§ 19. The charter of 1629 furnished them, however, with the colour of delegated sovereignty, of which they did not fail to avail themselves. They assumed under it the exercise of the most plenary executive, legislative, and judicial powers with but a momentary scruple, as to their right to inflict capital punishments. They were not disturbed in the free exercise of these powers, either through the ignorance or the connivance of the crown, until after the restoration of Charles the Second. Their authority under their charter was then questioned; and several unsuccessful attempts were made to procure a confirmation from the crown. They {18} continued to cling to it, until, in the general shipwreck of charters in 1684, theirs was overturned. An arbitrary government was then established over them in common with the other New-England colonies; and they were finally incorporated into a province with Massachusetts under the charter granted to the latter by William and Mary in 1691.

CHAPTER IV.

MASSACHUSETTS.

§ 20. ABOUT the period when the Plymouth colonists completed their voyage, James the First, with a view to promote more effectually the interests of the second or northern company, granted to the Duke of Lenox and others of the company a new charter, by which its territories were extended in breadth from the 40th to the 48th degree of north latitude; and in length by all the breadth aforesaid throughout the main land from sea to sea, excluding however all possession of any other Christian prince, and all lands within the bounds of the southern colony. To the territory thus bounded he affixed the name of New-England, and to the corporation itself so created, the name of "The Council established at Plymouth in the county of Devon, for the planting, ruling, ordering, and governing of New-England in America."

§ 21. Some of the powers granted by this charter were alarming to many persons, and especially those, which granted a monopoly of trade. The efforts to settle a colony within the territory were again renewed, and again were unsuccessful. The spirit of religion, however, soon effected, what the spirit of commerce had failed to accomplish. The Puritans, persecuted at home, and groaning under the weight of spiritual bondage, cast a longing eye towards America, as an ultimate retreat for themselves and their children. They were encouraged by the information, that the colonists at Plymouth were allowed to worship their Creator according to the dictates of their consciences, without {20} molestation. They opened a negotiation, through the instrumentality of a Mr. White, a distinguished nonconforming minister, with the council established at Plymouth; and in March, 1627, procured from them a grant to Sir Henry Rosewell and others of all that part of New-England lying three miles south of Charles river and three miles north of Merrimack river, and extending from the Atlantic to the South Sea.

§ 22. Other persons were soon induced to unite with them, if a charter could be procured from the crown, which should secure to the adventurers the usual powers of government. Application was made for this purpose to King Charles, who, accordingly, in March 1628, granted to the grantees and their associates the most ample powers of government. The charter confirmed to them the territory already granted by the council established at Plymouth, to be holden of the crown, as of the royal manor of East Greenwich, "in free and common soccage, and not in *capite*, nor by knight's service," yielding to the crown one fifth part of all ore of gold and silver, &c, with the exception, however, of any part of the territory actually possessed or inhabited by any other Christian prince or state, or of any part of it within the bounds of the southern colony [of Virginia] granted by King James. It also created the associates a body politic by the name of "The Governor and Company of the Massachusetts Bay in New-England," with the usual powers of corporations. It provided, that the government should be administered by a governor, a deputy governor, and eighteen assistants, from time to time elected out of the freemen of the company, which officers should have the care of the general business and affairs of the lands and plantations, and the government of the people there; and it appointed the {21} first governor, deputy governor, and assistants by name. It further provided, that a court or quorum for the transaction of business should consist of the governor, or the deputy governor, and seven or more assistants, which should assemble as often as once a month for that purpose, and also, that four great general assemblies of the company should be held in every year. In these great and general assemblies, (which were composed of the governor, deputy, assistants, and freemen present,) freemen were to be admitted free of the company, officers were to be elected, and laws and ordinances for the good and welfare of the colony made; "so as such laws and ordinances be not contrary or repugnant to the laws and statutes of this our realm of England." At one of these great and general assemblies held in Easter Term, the governor, deputy, and assistants, and other officers were to be annually chosen by the company present. The company were further authorized to transport any subjects or strangers willing to become subjects of the crown to the colony, and to carry on trade to and from it, without custom or subsidy for seven years, and were to be free of all taxation of imports or exports to and from the English dominion for the space of twenty-one years, with the exception of a five per cent duty. The charter further provided, that all subjects of the crown, who should become inhabitants, and their children born there, or on the seas going or returning, should enjoy all liberties and immunities of free and natural subjects, as if they and every of them were born within the realm of England. Full legislative authority was also given, subject to the restriction of not being contrary to the laws of England, as also for the imposition of fines and mulcts "according to the course of other corporations in England." Many other provisions {22} were added, similar in substance to those found in the antecedent colonial charters of the crown.

§ 23. Such were the original limits of the colony of Massachusetts Bay, and such were the powers and privileges conferred on it. It is observable, that the whole structure of the charter presupposes the residence of the company in England, and the transaction of all its business there. The experience of the past had not sufficiently instructed the adventurers, that settlements in America could not be well governed by corporations resident abroad; or if any of them had arrived at such a conclusion, there were many reasons for presuming, that the crown would be jealous of granting powers of so large a nature, which were to be exercised at such a distance, as would render any control or responsibility over them wholly visionary.

§ 24. But a bolder step was soon afterwards taken by the company itself. It was ascertained, that little success would attend the plantation, so long as its affairs were under the control of a distant government, knowing little of its wants and insensible to its difficulties. Many persons, indeed, possessed of fortune and character, warmed with religious zeal, or suffering under religious intolerance, were ready to embark in the enterprise, if the corporation should be removed, so that the powers of government might be exercised by the actual settlers. The company had already become alarmed at the extent of their own expenditures, and there were but faint hopes of any speedy reimbursement. They entertained some doubts of the legality of the course of transferring the charter. But at length it was determined in August, 1629, "by the general consent of the company, that the government and patent should be settled in New-England." This resolution infused {23} new life into the association; and the next election of officers was made from among those proprietors, who had signified an intention to remove to America. The government and charter were accordingly removed; and henceforth the whole management of all the affairs of the colony was confided to persons and magistrates resident within its own bosom. The fate of the colony was thus decided; and it grew with a rapidity and strength, that soon gave it a great ascendancy among the New-England settlements, and awakened the jealousy, distrust, and vigilance of the parent country.

§ 25. The government of the colony immediately after the removal of the charter was changed in many important features; but its fundamental grants of territory, powers, and privileges were eagerly maintained in their original validity. It is true, as Dr. Robertson has observed, that as soon as the Massachusetts emigrants had landed on these shores, they considered themselves for many purposes as a voluntary association, possessing the natural rights of men to adopt that mode of government, which was most agreeable to themselves, and to enact such laws, as were conducive to their own welfare. They did not, indeed, surrender up their charter, or cease to recognise its obligatory force. But they extended their acts far beyond its expression of powers; and while they boldly claimed protection from it against the royal demands and prerogatives, they nevertheless did not feel, that it furnished any limit upon the freest exercise of legislative, executive, or judicial functions. They did not view it, as creating an English corporation under the narrow construction of the common law; but as affording the means of founding a broad political government, subject to the crown of England, but yet enjoying many exclusive privileges. {24}

§ 26. It may be well to state in this connexion, that the council established at Plymouth in a very short period after the grant of the Massachusetts charter (in 1635) finally surrendered their own patent back to the crown. They had made other grants of territory, which we shall hereafter have occasion to notice, which had greatly diminished the value, as well as importance of their charter. But the immediate cause of the surrender was the odious extent of the monopolies granted to them, which roused the attention of Parliament, and of the nation at large, and compelled them to resign, what they could scarcely maintain against the strong current of public opinion. The surrender, so far from working any evil, rather infused new life into the colonies, which sprung from it, by freeing them from all restraint and supervision by a superior power, to which they might perhaps have been held accountable. Immediately after this surrender legal proceedings were instituted against the proprietors of the Massachusetts charter. Those who appeared were deprived of their franchises. But fortunately the measure was not carried into complete execution against the absent proprietors acting under the charter in America.

§ 27. After the fall of the first colonial charter in 1684, Massachusetts remained for some years in a very disturbed state under the arbitrary power of the crown. At length a new charter was in 1691 granted to the colony by William and Mary; and it henceforth became known as a province, and continued to act under this last charter until after the Revolution. The charter comprehended within its territorial limits all the old colony of the Massachusetts Bay, the colony of New-Plymouth, the Province of Maine, the territory called Acadia, or Nova Scotia, and all the lands lying between Nova Scotia {25} and Maine; and incorporated the whole into one Province by the name of the Province of the Massachusetts Bay in New-England, to be holden as of the royal manor of East Greenwich, in the county of Kent. It confirmed all prior grants made of lands to all persons, corporations, colleges, towns, villages, and schools. It reserved to the crown the appointment of the Governor, and Lieut. Governor, and Secretary of the province, and all the officers of the Court of Admiralty. It provided for the appointment annually of twenty-eight Counsellors, who were to be chosen by the General Court, and nominated the first board. The Governor and Counsellors were to hold a council for the ordering and directing of the affairs of the Province. The Governor was invested with the right of nominating and with the advice of the council of appointing all military officers, and all sheriffs, provosts, marshals, and justices of the peace, and other officers of courts of justice. He had also the power of calling the General Court, and of adjourning, proroguing, and dissolving it. He had also a negative upon all laws passed by the General Court. The General Court was to assemble annually on the last Wednesday of May, and was to consist of the Governor and Council for the time being, and of such representatives being freeholders, as should be annually elected by the freeholders in each town, who possessed a freehold of forty shillings annual value, or other estate to the value of forty pounds. Each town was entitled to two representatives; but the General Court was from time to time to decide on the number, which each town should send. The General Court was invested with full authority to erect courts, to levy taxes, and make all wholesome laws and ordinances, "so as the same be not repugnant or contrary to the laws of {26} England;" and to settle annually all civil officers, whose appointment was not otherwise provided for. All laws, however, were to be sent to England for approbation or disallowance; and if disallowed, and so signified under the sign manual and signet, within three years, the same thenceforth to cease and become void; otherwise to continue in force according to the terms of their original enactment. The General Court was also invested with authority to grant any lands in the colonies of Massachusetts, New Plymouth, and Province of Maine, with certain exceptions. The Governor and Council were invested with full jurisdiction as to the probate of wills and granting administrations. The Governor was also made commander-in-chief of the militia, with the usual martial powers; but was not to exercise martial law without the advice of the Council. In case of his death, removal, or absence, his authority was to devolve on the Lieut. Governor, or, if his office was vacant, then on the Council. With a view also to advance the growth of the Province by encouraging new settlements, it was expressly provided, that there should be "a liberty of conscience allowed in the worship of God to all Christians, except Papists;" and that all subjects inhabiting in the Province and their children born there, or on the seas going or returning, should have all the liberties and immunities of free and natural subjects, as if they were born within the realm of England. And in all cases an appeal was allowed from the judgments of any courts of the Province to the King in the Privy Council in England, where the matter in difference exceeded three hundred pounds sterling. And finally there was a reservation of the whole admiralty jurisdiction to the crown; and of a right to all subjects to fish on the coasts. Considering the {27} spirit of the times, it must be acknowledged, that, on the whole, this charter contains a liberal grant of authority to the Province; and a reasonable reservation of the royal prerogative. It was hailed with sincere satisfaction by the colony after the dangers, which had for so long a time menaced its liberties and its peace.

CHAPTER V.

NEW-HAMPSHIRE.

§ 28. HAVING gone into a full consideration of the origin and political organization of the primitive colonies in the South and North, it remains only to take rapid view of those, which were subsequently established in both regions. An historical order will probably be found as convenient for this purpose, as any, which could be devised.

§ 29. In November, 1629, Capt. John Mason obtained a grant from the council of Plymouth of all that part of the main land in New-England "lying upon the seacoast, beginning from the middle part of Merrimack river, and from thence to proceed northwards along the sea-coast to Piscataqua river, and so forwards up within the said river and to the furthest head thereof; and from thence northwestwards until three score miles be finished from the first entrance of Piscataqua river; and also from Merrimack through the said river and to the furthest head thereof, and so forwards up into the lands westwards, until three score miles be finished; and from thence to cross over land to the three score miles and accounted from Piscataqua river, together with all islands and islets within five leagues distance of the premises." This territory was afterwards called New-Hampshire. The land so granted was expressly subjected to the conditions and limitations In the original patent; and there was a covenant on the part of Mason that he would establish such government therein, and continue the same, "as shall be agreeable, as near as may be, to the laws and customs of the realm of England." {29} A further grant was made to Mason by the council of Plymouth about the time of the surrender of their charter, (22 April, 1635,) "beginning from the middle part of Naumkeag river [Salem], and from thence to proceed eastwards along the sea-coast to Cape Ann and round about the same to Piscataqua harbor; and then covering much of the land in the prior grant, and giving to the whole the name of New-Hampshire." This grant included a power of judicature in all cases, civil and criminal, "to be exercised and executed according to the laws of England as near as may be," reserving an appeal to the council. No patent of confirmation of this grant appears to have been made by the crown after the surrender of the Plymouth patent.

§ 30. Various detached settlements were made within this territory; and so ill defined were the boundaries, that a controversy soon arose between Massachusetts and Mason in respect to the right of sovereignty over it. In the exposition of its own charter Massachusetts contended, that its limits included the whole territory of New-Hampshire; and being at that time comparatively strong and active, she succeeded in establishing her jurisdiction over it, and maintained it with unabated vigilance for forty years. The controversy was finally brought before the king in council; and in 1679 it was solemnly adjudged against the claim of Massachusetts. And it being admitted, that Mason, under his grant, had no right to exercise any powers of government, a commission was, in the same year, issued by the crown for the government of New-Hampshire. By the form of government, described in this commission, the whole executive power was vested in a president and council, appointed by the crown, to whom also {30} was confided the judiciary power with an appeal to England. In the administration of justice it was directed, that "the form of proceedings in such cases, and the judgment thereon to be given, be as consonant and agreeable to the laws and statutes of this our realm of England, as the present state and condition of our subjects inhabiting within the limits aforesaid, and the circumstances of the place will admit." The legislative power was entrusted to the president, council, and burgesses, or representatives chosen by the towns; and they were authorized to levy taxes and to make laws for the interest of the province; which laws being approved by the president and council were to stand and be in force, until the pleasure of the king should be known, whether the same laws and ordinances should receive any change or confirmation, or be totally disallowed and discharged. And the president and council were required to transmit and send over the same by the first ship, that should depart thence for England after their making. Liberty of conscience was allowed to all protestants, those of the Church of England to be particularly encouraged. And a pledge was given in the commission to continue the privilege of an assembly in the same manner and form, unless by inconvenience arising therefrom the crown should see cause to alter the same.

CHAPTER VI.

MAINE.

§ 31. IN August, 1622, the council of Plymouth (which seems to have been extremely profuse and inconsiderate in its grants) granted to Sir Ferdinando Gorges and Capt. John Mason all the lands lying between the rivers Merrimack and Sagadahock, extending back to the great lakes and rivers of Canada; which was called Laconia. In April, 1639, Sir Ferdinando obtained from the crown a confirmatory grant of all the land from Piscataqua to Sagadahock and the Kennebeck river, and from the coast into the northern interior one hundred and twenty miles; and it was styled "The Province of Maine." Of this province he was made Lord Palatine, with all the powers, jurisdiction, and royalties belonging to the bishop of the county Palatine of Durham; and the lands were to be holden, as of the manor of East Greenwich. The charter contains a reservation of faith and allegiance to the crown, as having the supreme dominion; and the will and pleasure of the crown is signified, that the religion of the Church of England be professed, and its ecclesiastical government established in the province. It also authorizes the Palatine, with the assent of the greater part of the freeholders of the province, to make laws not repugnant or contrary, but as near as conveniently may be to the laws of England, for the public good of the province; and to erect courts of judicature for the determination of all civil and criminal causes, with an appeal to the Palatine. But all the powers of government, so granted, were to {32} be subordinate to the "power and *regement*," of the lords commissioners for foreign plantations for the time being. The Palatine also had authority to make ordinances for the government of the province, under certain restrictions; and a grant of full admiralty powers, subject to that of the Lord High Admiral of England. And the inhabitants, being subjects of the crown, were to enjoy all the rights and privileges of natural born subjects in England.

§ 32. Under these ample provisions Gorges soon established a civil government in the province, and made ordinances. The government, such as it was, was solely confided to the executive, without any powers of legislation. The province languished in imbecility under his care; and began to acquire vigour only when he ceased to act as proprietary and lawgiver. Massachusetts soon afterwards set up an exclusive right and jurisdiction over the territory, as within its chartered limits; and was able to enforce obedience and submission to its power. It continued under the jurisdiction of Massachusetts until 1665, when the commissioners of the crown separated it for a short period; but the authority of Massachusetts was soon afterwards re-established. The controversy between Massachusetts and the Palatine, as to jurisdiction over the province, was brought before the privy council at the same time with that of Mason respecting New-Hampshire, and the claim of

Massachusetts was adjudged void. Before a final adjudication was had, Massachusetts had the prudence and sagacity, in 1677, to purchase the title of Gorges for a trifling sum; and thus to the great disappointment of the crown, (then in treaty for the same object,) succeeded to it, and held it, and governed {33} it as a provincial dependency, until the fall of its own charter; and it afterwards, as we have seen, was incorporated with Massachusetts in the provincial charter of 1691.

CHAPTER VII.

CONNECTICUT.

§ 33. CONNECTICUT was originally settled under the protection of Massachusetts; but the inhabitants in a few years afterwards (1638) felt at liberty (after the example of Massachusetts) to frame a constitution of government and laws for themselves. In 1630 the Earl of Warwick obtained from the council of Plymouth a patent of the land upon a straight line near the seashore towards the southwest, west and by south, or west from Narraganset river forty leagues, as the coast lies towards Virginia, and all within that breadth to the South sea. In March, 1631, the Earl of Warwick conveyed the same to Lord Say and Seale and others. In April, 1635, the same council granted the same territory to the Marquis of Hamilton. Possession under the title of Lord Say and Seale and others was taken of the mouth of the Connecticut in 1635. The settlers there were not, however, disturbed; and finally, in 1644, they extinguished the title of the proprietaries, or Lords, and continued to act under the constitution of government, which they had framed in 1638.

§ 34. The colony of New-Haven had a separate origin, and was settled by emigrants immediately from England, without any title derived from the patentees. They began their settlement in 1638, purchasing their lands of the natives; and entered into a solemn compact of government.

§ 35. Soon after the restoration of Charles the Second to the throne, the colony of Connecticut, aware of the doubtful nature of its title to the exercise of sovereignty, {35} solicited and in April, 1662, obtained from that monarch a charter of government and territory. The charter included within its limits the whole colony of New-Haven; and as this was done without the consent of the latter, resistance was made to the incorporation, until 1665, when both were indissolubly united, and have ever since remained under one general government.

§ 36. The charter of Connecticut, which has been objected to by Chalmers, as establishing "a mere democracy, or rule of the people," contained, indeed, a very ample grant of privileges. It incorporated the inhabitants by the name of the Governor and Company of the Colony of Connecticut in New-England, in America. It ordained, that two general assemblies shall be annually held; and that the assembly shall consist of a governor, deputy governor, twelve assistants, and two deputies, from every town or city, to be chosen by the freemen, (the charter nominating the first governor and assistants.) The general assembly had authority to appoint judicatories, make freemen, elect officers, establish laws, and ordinances "not contrary to the laws of this realm of England," to punish offences "according to the course of other corporations within this our kingdom of England," to assemble the inhabitants in martial array for the common defence, and to exercise martial law in cases of necessity. The lands were to be holden as of the manor of East Greenwich, in free and common soccage. The inhabitants and their children born there were to enjoy and possess all the liberties and immunities of free, natural-born subjects, in the same manner, as if born within the realm. The right of general fishery on the coasts was reserved to all subjects; and finally the territory bounded on the east by the Narraganset river, {36} where it falls into the sea, and on the north by Massachusetts, and on the south by the sea, and in longitude, as the line of the Massachusetts colony running from east to west, that from Narraganset bay to the South sea, was granted and confirmed to the colony. The charter is silent in regard to religious rights and privileges.

§ 37. In 1685, a *quo warranto* was issued by king James against the colony for the repeal of the charter. No judgment appears to have been rendered upon it; but the colony offered its submission to the will of the crown; and Sir Edmund Andros, in 1687, went to Hartford, and in the name of the crown, declared the government dissolved. They did not, however, surrender the charter; but secreted it in an oak, which is still venerated; and immediately after the revolution of 1688, they resumed the exercise of all its powers. The successors of the Stuarts silently suffered them to retain it until the American Revolution, without any struggle or resistance. The charter continued to be maintained, as a fundamental law of the State, until the year 1818, when a new constitution of government was framed and adopted by the people.

CHAPTER VIII.

RHODE ISLAND.

§ 38. RHODE ISLAND was originally settled by emigrants from Massachusetts, fleeing thither to escape from religious persecution; and it still boasts of Roger Williams, as its founder, and as the early defender of religious freedom and the rights of conscience. One body of them purchased the island, which has given the name to the State, and another the territory of the Providence Plantations from the Indians, and began their settlements in both places nearly at the same period, viz. in 1636 and 1638. They entered into separate voluntary associations of government. But finding their associations not sufficient to protect them against the encroachments of Massachusetts, and having no title under any of the royal patents, they sent Roger Williams to England, in 1643, to procure a surer foundation both of title and government. He succeeded in obtaining from the Earl of Warwick (in 1643) a charter of incorporation of Providence Plantations; and also, in 1644, a charter from the two houses of parliament (Charles the First being then driven from his capital) for the incorporation of the towns of Providence, Newport, and Portsmouth, for the absolute government of themselves, but according to the laws of England.

§ 39. Under this charter an assembly was convened, in 1647, consisting of the collective freemen of the various plantations. The council of state of the commonwealth soon afterwards interfered to suspend their government; but the distractions at home prevented any serious interference by parliament in the administration {38} of their affairs; and they continued to act under their former government until the restoration of Charles the Second. That event seems to have given great satisfaction to these plantations. They immediately proclaimed the king, and sent an agent to England; and in July, 1663, after some opposition they succeeded in obtaining a charter from the crown.

§ 40. That charter incorporated the inhabitants by the name of the Governor and Company of the English Colony of Rhode Island and Providence Plantations in New-England in America, conferring on them the usual powers of corporations. The executive power was lodged in a governor, deputy governor, and ten assistants, chosen by the freemen. The supreme legislative authority was vested in a general assembly, consisting of a governor, deputy governor, ten assistants, and deputies from the respective towns; chosen by the freemen, (six for Newport, four for Providence, Portsmouth, and Warwick, and two for other towns,) the governor or deputy and six assistants being always present. The general assembly were authorized to admit freemen, choose officers, make laws and ordinances, so as that they were "not contrary and repugnant unto, but as near as may be agreeable to, the laws of this our realm of England, considering the nature and constitution of

25

the place and people; to create and organize courts; to punish offences according to the course of other corporations in England;" to array the martial force of the colony for the common defence, and enforce martial law; and to exercise other important powers and prerogatives. It further provided for a free fishery on the coasts; and that all the inhabitants and children born there should enjoy all the liberties and immunities of free and natural subjects born within the {39} realm of England. It then granted and confirmed unto them all that part of the king's dominions in New-England containing the Narraganset bay and the countries and parts adjacent, bounded westerly, to the middle of Pawcatuck river, and so along the river northward to the head thereof, thence by a straight line due north, until it meet the south line of Massachusetts, extending easterly three English miles to the most eastern and northeastern parts of Narraganset bay, as the bay extendeth southerly unto the mouth of the river running towards Providence, and thence along the easterly side or bank of the said river up to the falls, called Patucket Falls, and thence in a straight line due north till it meets the Massachusetts line. The territory was to be holden as of the manor of East Greenwich in free and common soccage. It further secured a free trade with all the other colonies.

§ 41. It is said, that the general conduct of Rhode Island seems to have given entire satisfaction to Charles the Second during the residue of his reign. Upon the accession of James, the inhabitants were among the first to offer their congratulations; and to ask protection for their chartered rights. That monarch however disregarded their request. They were accused of a violation of their charter, and a *quo warranto* was filed against them. They immediately resolved, without much hesitation, not to contend with the crown, but to surrender their charter; and passed an act for that purpose, which was afterwards suppressed. In December, 1686, Sir Edmund Andros, agreeably to his orders, dissolved their government, and assumed the administration of the colony. The revolution of 1688 put an end to his power; and the colony immediately afterwards resumed its charter, and, though not without some interruptions, {40} continued to maintain and exercise its powers down to the period of the American Revolution. It still continues to act under the same charter, as a fundamental law, it being the only state in the Union, which has not formed a new constitution of government. It seems, that until the year 1696 the governor, assistants, and deputies of the towns sat together. But by a law then passed they were separated, and the deputies acted as a lower house, and the governor and assistants as an upper house.

§ 42. We have now finished our review of all the successive colonies established in New-England. The remark of Chalmers is in general well founded: "Originally settled (says he) by the same kind of people, a similar policy naturally rooted in all the colonies of New-England. Their forms of government, their laws, their courts of justice, their manners, and their religious tenets, which gave birth to all these, were nearly the same." Still, however, the remark is subject to many local qualifications.

CHAPTER IX.

MARYLAND.

§ 43. THE province of Maryland was included originally in the patent of the Southern or Virginia company; and upon the dissolution of that company it reverted to the crown. King Charles the First, on the 20th June, 1632, granted it by patent to Cecilius Calvert Lord Baltimore, the son of George Calvert Lord Baltimore, to whom the patent was intended to have been made, but he died before it was executed. By the charter, the king erected it into a province, and gave it the name of Maryland, in honor of his Queen, Henrietta Maria, the daughter of Henry the Fourth of France, to be held of the crown of England, he yearly, for ever, rendering two Indian arrows. The territory was bounded by a right line drawn from Watkins's Point, on Chesapeake bay, to the ocean on the east, thence to that part of the estuary of Delaware on the north, which lieth under the 40th degree, where New-England is terminated; thence in a right line by the degree aforesaid to the meridian of the fountain of Potomac; thence following its course by the further bank to its confluence with the Chesapeake, and thence to Watkins's Point.

§ 44. The territory thus severed from Virginia, was made immediately subject to the crown, and was granted in full and absolute propriety to Lord Baltimore and his heirs, saving the allegiance and sovereign dominion to the crown, with all the rights, regalities, and prerogatives, which the Bishop of Durham enjoyed in that palatinate, to be held of the crown as of Windsor Castle, {42} in the county of Berks, in free and common soccage, and not in *capite*, or by knights' service. The charter further provided, that the proprietary should have authority by and with the consent of the freemen, or their delegates assembled for that purpose, to make all laws for the province, "so that such laws be consonant to reason, and not repugnant or contrary, but, as far as conveniently might be, agreeable to the laws, statutes, customs, and rights of this our realm of England." The proprietary was also vested with full executive power; and the establishment of courts of justice was provided for. The proprietary was also authorized to levy subsidies with the assent of the people in assembly. The inhabitants and their children were to enjoy all the rights, immunities, and privileges of subjects born in England. The right of the advowsons of the churches, according to the establishment of England, and the right to create manors and courts baron, to confer titles of dignity, to erect ports, and other regalities, were expressly given to the proprietary. An exemption of the colonists from all talliages on their goods and estates, to be imposed by the crown, was expressly covenanted for in perpetuity; an exemption, which had been conferred on other colonies for years only. License was granted to all subjects to transport themselves to the province; and is products were to be imported into England and Ireland under such taxes only, as were paid by other subjects. And the usual powers in other charters to repel invasions, to suppress rebellions, &c. were also conferred on the proprietary.

§ 45. Such is the substance of the patent. And Chalmers has with some pride asserted, that "Maryland {43} has always enjoyed the unrivalled honour of being the first colony, which was erected into a province of the English empire, and governed regularly by laws enacted in a provincial legislature."

CHAPTER X.

NEW-YORK.

§ 46. NEW-YORK was originally settled by emigrants from Holland. But the English government seems at all times to have disputed the right of the Dutch to make any settlement in America; and the territory occupied by them was unquestionably within the chartered limits of New-England as granted to the council of Plymouth. Charles the Second, soon after his restoration, instigated as much by personal antipathy, as by a regard for the interest of the crown, determined to maintain his right, and in March, 1664, granted a patent to his brother, the Duke of York and Albany, by which he conveyed to him the region extending from the western bank of Connecticut to the eastern shore of the Delaware, together with Long Island, and conferred on him the powers of government, civil and military. Authority was given (among other things) to correct, punish, pardon, govern, and rule all subjects, that should inhabit the territory according to such laws, ordinances, &c. as the Duke should establish, so always that the same "were not contrary, but as near as might be agreeable to the laws and statutes and government of the realm of England," saving to the crown a right to hear and determine all appeals. The usual authority was also given to use and exercise martial law in cases of rebellion, insurrection, mutiny, and invasion. A part of this tract was afterwards conveyed by the Duke, by deed of lease and release, in June, of the same year, to Lord Berkeley and Sir George Carteret. By this latter grant they were entitled to all the tract adjacent to {45} New-England, lying westward of Long Island, and bounded on the east by the main sea and partly by Hudson's river, and upon the west by Delaware bay or river, and extending southward to the main ocean as far as Cape May at the mouth of Delaware bay, and to the northward as far as the northernmost branch of Delaware bay or river, which is 41 degrees 40 minutes latitude; which tract was to be called by the name of Nova Cæsarea, or New-Jersey. So that the territory then claimed by the Dutch as the New-Netherlands was divided into the colonies of New-York and New-Jersey.

§ 47. In September, 1664, the Dutch colony was surprised by a British armament, which arrived on the coast, and was compelled to surrender to its authority. By the terms of the capitulation the inhabitants were to continue free denizens, and to enjoy their property. The Dutch inhabitants were to enjoy the liberty of their conscience in divine worship and church discipline; and their own customs concerning their inheritances. The government was instantly assumed by right of conquest in behalf of the Duke of York, the proprietary, and the territory was called New-York. Liberty of conscience was granted to all settlers. No laws contrary to those of England were allowed; and taxes were to be levied by authority of a general assembly. The peace of Breda, in 1667, confirmed the title in the conquerors by the rule of *uti possidetis*. In the next Dutch war the colony was reconquered; but it was restored to the Duke of York upon the succeeding peace of 1674.

§ 48. As the validity of the original grant to the Duke of York, while the Dutch were in quiet possession of the country, was deemed questionable, he thought it {46} prudent to ask, and he accordingly obtained, a new grant from the crown in June, 1674. It confirmed the former grant, and empowered him to govern the inhabitants by such ordinances, as he or his assigns should establish. It authorized him to administer justice according to the laws of England, allowing an appeal to the king in council. It prohibited trade thither without his permission; and allowed the colonists to import merchandize upon paying customs according to the laws of the realm. Under this charter he ruled the province until his accession to the throne. No general assembly was called for several years; and the people having become clamorous for the privileges enjoyed by other colonists, the governor was, in 1682, authorized to call an assembly, which was empowered to make laws for the general regulation of the state, which, however, were of no force without the ratification of the proprietary. Upon the revolution of 1688, the people of New-York immediately took side in favour of the Prince of Orange. From this era they were deemed entitled to all the privileges of British subjects, inhabiting a dependent province of the state. No charter was subsequently granted to them by the crown; and therefore they derived no peculiar privileges from that source.

CHAPTER XI.

NEW-JERSEY.

§ 49. NEW-JERSEY, as we have already seen, was a part of the territory granted to the Duke of York, and was by him granted, in June, 1664, to Lord Berkeley and Sir George Carteret, with all the rights, royalties, and powers of government, which he himself possessed. The proprietors, for the better settlement of the territory, agreed in February, 1664-1665, upon a constitution or concession of government, which was so much relished, that the eastern part of the province soon contained a considerable population.

§ 50. This constitution continued until the province was divided, in 1676, between the proprietors. By that division East New-Jersey was assigned to Carteret; and West New-Jersey to William Penn and others, who had purchased of Lord Berkeley. Carteret then explained and confirmed the former concessions for the territory thus exclusively belonging to himself. The proprietors also of West Jersey drew up another set of concessions for the settlers within that territory. They contain very ample privileges to the people.

§ 51. Whether these concessions became the general law of the province seems involved in some obscurity. There were many difficulties and contests for jurisdiction between the governors of the Duke of York and the proprietors of the Jerseys; and these were not settled, until after the Duke, in 1680, finally surrendered all right to both by letters patent granted to the respective proprietors. In 1681, the governor of the proprietors of West Jersey, with the consent of the general {48} assembly, made a frame of government embracing some of the fundamentals in the former concessions.

§ 52. Carteret died in 1679, and being sole proprietor of East Jersey, by his will he ordered it to be sold for payment of his debts; and it was accordingly sold to William Penn and eleven others, who were called the Twelve Proprietors. They afterwards took twelve more into the proprietaryship; and to the twenty-four thus formed, the Duke of York, in March, 1682, made his third and last grant of East Jersey. Very serious dissensions soon arose between the two provinces themselves, as well as between them and New-York; which banished moderation from their councils, and threatened the most serious calamities. A *quo warranto* was ordered by the crown in 1686, to be issued against both provinces. East Jersey immediately offered to be annexed to West Jersey, and to submit to a governor appointed by the crown. Soon afterwards the crown ordered the Jerseys to be annexed to New-England; and the proprietors of East-Jersey made a formal surrender of its patent, praying only for a new grant, securing their right of soil. Before this request could be granted, the revolution of 1688 took place, and they passed under the allegiance of a new sovereign.

31

§ 53. From this period both of the provinces were in a state of great confusion, and distraction; and remained so, until the proprietors of both made a formal surrender of all their powers of government, but not of their lands, to Queen Anne, in April, 1702. The Queen immediately reunited both provinces into one province; and by commission appointed a governor over them. He was thereby authorized to govern with the assistance of a council, and to call general assemblies of {49} representatives of the people to be chosen by the freeholders, who were required to take the oath of allegiance and supremacy, and the test provided by the acts of Parliament. The general assembly, with the consent of the governor and council, were authorized to make laws and ordinances for the welfare of the people "not repugnant, but, as near as may be, agreeable unto the laws and statutes of this our kingdom of England;" which laws were, however, to be subject to the approbation or dissent of the crown. The governor, with the consent of the council, was to erect courts of justice; to appoint judges and other officers; to collate to churches and benefices; and to command the military force. Liberty of conscience was allowed to all persons but Papists.

§ 54. From this time to the American Revolution the province was governed without any charter under royal commissions, substantially in the manner pointed out in the first. The people always strenuously contended for the rights and privileges guaranteed to them by the former concessions; and many struggles occurred from time to time between their representatives, and the royal governors on this subject.

CHAPTER XII.

PENNSYLVANIA.

§ 55. PENNSYLVANIA was originally settled by different detachments of planters under various authorities, Dutch, Swedes, and others, which at different times occupied portions of land on South or Delaware river. The ascendency was finally obtained over these settlements by the governors of New-York, acting under the charter of 1664, to the Duke of York. Chalmers, however, does not scruple to say, that "it is a singular circumstance in the history of this [then] inconsiderable colony, that it seems to have been at all times governed by usurpers, because their titles were defective." It continued in a feeble state, until the celebrated William Penn, in March, 1681, obtained a patent from Charles the Second, by which he became the proprietary of an ample territory, which in honor of his father was called Pennsylvania. The boundaries described in the charter were on the East by Delaware river from twelve miles' distance northwards of New-Castle town to the 43d degree of north latitude, if the said river doth extend so far northward; but if not, then by said river so far as it doth extend; and from the head of the river the eastern bounds are to be determined by a meridian line to be drawn from the head of said river unto the said 43d degree of north latitude. The said lands to extend westward five degrees in longitude, to be computed from the said eastern bounds, and the said lands to be bounded on the north by the beginning of the 43d degree of north latitude; and on the south by a circle drawn at twelve miles' distance from New-Castle, {51} northward and westward, to the beginning of the 40th degree of northern latitude; and then by a straight line westward to the limits of the longitude above mentioned.

§ 56. The charter constituted Penn the true and absolute proprietary of the territory thus described, (saving to the crown the sovereignty of the country, and the allegiance of the proprietary and the inhabitants,) to be holden of the crown as of the castle of Windsor in Berks, in free and common soccage, and not in *capite*, or by knight service; and erected it into a province and seignory by the name of Pennsylvania. It authorized the proprietary and his heirs and successors to make all laws for raising money and other purposes, with the assent of the freemen of the country, or their deputies assembled for the purpose. But "the same laws were to be consonant to reason, and not repugnant or contrary, but, as near as conveniently may be, agreeable to law and statutes and rights of this our kingdom of England." The laws for the descent and enjoyment of lands, and succession to goods, and of felonies, to be according to the course in England, until altered by the assembly. All laws were to be sent to England within five years after the making of them, and, if disapproved of by the crown within six months, to become null and void. It also authorized the proprietary to appoint judges and other officers;

to pardon and reprieve criminals; to establish courts of justice, with a right of appeal to the crown from all judgments; to create cities and other corporations; to erect ports, and manors, and courts baron in such manors. Liberty was allowed to subjects to transport themselves and their goods to the province; and to import the products of the province into England; and to export them from {52} thence within one year, the inhabitants observing the acts of navigation, and all other laws in this behalf made. It was further stipulated, that the crown should levy no tax, custom, or imposition upon the inhabitants, or their goods, unless by the consent of the proprietary or assembly, "or by act of Parliament in England." Such are, the most important clauses of this charter, which has been deemed one of the best drawn of the colonial charters, and which underwent the revision, not merely of the law officers of the crown, but of the then Lord Chief Justice (North) of England. It has been remarked, as a singular omission in this charter, that there is no provision, that the inhabitants and their children shall be deemed British subjects, and entitled to all the liberties and immunities thereof, such a clause being found in every other charter. Chalmers has observed, that the clause was wholly unnecessary, as the allegiance to the crown was reserved; and the common law thence inferred, that all the inhabitants were subjects, and of course were entitled to all the privileges of Englishmen.

§ 57. Penn immediately invited emigration to his province, by holding out concessions of a very liberal nature to all settlers; and under his benign and enlightened policy a foundation was early laid for the establishment of a government and laws, which have been justly celebrated for their moderation, wisdom, and just protection of the rights and liberties of the people.

§ 58. It was soon found that the original frame of government, drawn up before any settlements were made, was ill adapted to the state of things in an infant colony. Accordingly it was laid aside, and a new frame of government was, with the consent of the General Assembly, established in 1683. In 1692 Penn was {53} deprived of the government of Pennsylvania by William and Mary; but it was again restored to him in the succeeding year. A third frame of government was established in 1696. This again was surrendered, and a new final charter of government was, in October, 1701, with the consent of the General Assembly, established, under which the province continued to be governed down to the period of the American Revolution. It provided for full liberty of conscience and worship; and for the right of all persons, professing to believe in Jesus Christ, to serve the government in any capacity. An annual assembly was to be chosen of delegates from each county, and to have the usual legislative authority of other colonial assemblies, and also power to nominate certain persons for office to the governor. The laws were to be subject to the approbation of the governor, who had a council of state to assist him in the government. Provision was made in the same charter, that if the representatives of the province, and territories, (meaning, by territories, the three counties of Delaware,) should not agree to join together in legislation, they should be represented in distinct assemblies.

CHAPTER XIII.

DELAWARE.

{54}

§ 59. AFTER Penn had become proprietary of Pennsylvania, he purchased of the Duke of York, in 1682, all his right and interest in the territory, afterwards called the Three Lower Counties of Delaware, extending from the south boundary of the Province, and situated on the western side of the river and bay of Delaware to Cape Henlopen, beyond or south of Lewistown; and the three counties took the names of New-Castle, Kent, and Sussex. At this time they were inhabited principally by Dutch and Swedes; and seem to have constituted an appendage to the government of New-York.

§ 60. In the same year, with the consent of the people, an act of union with the province of Pennsylvania was passed, and an act of settlement of the frame of government in a general assembly, composed of deputies from the counties of Delaware and Pennsylvania. By this act the three counties were, under the name of the territories, annexed to the province; and were to be represented in the General Assembly, governed by the same laws, and to enjoy the same privileges as the inhabitants of Pennsylvania. Difficulties soon afterwards arose between the deputies of the Province and those of the Territories; and after various subordinate arrangements, a final separation took place between them, with the consent of the proprietary, in 1703. From that period down to the American {55} Revolution, the territories were governed by a separate legislature of their own, pursuant to the liberty reserved to them by a clause in the original charter or frame of government.

CHAPTER XIV.

NORTH AND SOUTH CAROLINA.

§ 61. WE next come to the consideration of the history of the political organization of the Carolinas. That level region, which stretches from the 36th degree of north latitude to Cape Florida, afforded an ample theatre for the early struggles of the three great European powers, Spain, France, and England, to maintain, or acquire an exclusive sovereignty. Various settlements were made under the auspices of each of the rival powers, and a common fate seemed for a while to attend them all. In March, 1662, [April, 1663,] Charles the Second made a grant to Lord Clarendon and others of the territory lying on the Atlantic ocean, and extending from the north end of the island, called Hope-Island, in the South Virginian seas, and within 36 degrees of north latitude; and to the west as far as the South Seas; and so respectively as far as the river Mathias upon the coast of Florida, and within 31 degrees of north latitude; and so west in a direct line to the South seas; and erected it into a province, by the name of Carolina, to be holden as of the manor of East-Greenwich in Kent, in free and common soccage, and not in *capite*, or by knight service, subject immediately to the crown, as a dependency, for ever.

§ 62. In 1665, the proprietaries obtained from Charles the Second a second charter, with an enlargement of boundaries. It recited the grant of the former charter, and declared the limits to extend north and eastward as far as the north end of Currituck river or inlet, upon a straight westerly line to Wyonoak creek, which {57} lies within or about 36 degrees 30 minutes of north latitude; and so west in a direct line as far as the South seas; and south and westward as far as the degrees of 29 inclusive of northern latitude, and so west in a direct line as far as the South seas. It then proceeded to constitute the proprietaries absolute owners and lords of the province, saving the faith, allegiance, and sovereign dominion of the crown, to hold the same as of the manor of East-Greenwich in Kent, in free and common soccage, and not in *capite*, or by knight service; and to possess in the same all the royalties, jurisdictions, and privileges of the Bishop of Durham in his diocese.

§ 63. In the year 1669, the proprietaries, dissatisfied with the systems already established within the province, signed a fundamental constitution for the government thereof the object of which is declared to be, "that we may establish a government agreeable to the monarchy, of which Carolina is a part, that we may avoid making too numerous a democracy." This constitution was drawn up by the celebrated John Locke; and his memory has been often reproached with the illiberal character of some of the articles, the oppressive servitude of others, and the general disregard of some of those maxims of religious and political liberty, for which he has in his treatises of government and other writings contended with so much ability and success. Probably there were many circumstances attending this

36

transaction, which are now unknown, and which might well have moderated the severity of the reproach, and furnished, if not a justification, at least some apology for this extraordinary instance of unwise and visionary legislation.

§ 64. It is easy to perceive that this celebrated constitution was ill adapted to the feelings, the wants, and {58} the opinions of the colonists. The introduction of it, therefore, was resisted by the people, as much as it could be; and indeed, in some respects, it was found impracticable. Public dissatisfaction daily increased; and after a few years' experience of its ill arrangements, and its mischievous tendency, the proprietaries, upon the application of the people, (in 1693,) abrogated the constitution, and restored the ancient form of government. Thus perished the labours of Mr. Locke; and thus perished a system, under the administration of which, it has been remarked, the Carolinians had not known one day of real enjoyment, and that introduced evils and disorders, which ended only with the dissolution of the proprietary government. Perhaps in the annals of the world there is not to be found a more wholesome lesson of the utter folly of all efforts to establish forms of governments upon mere theory; and of the dangers of legislation without consulting the habits, manners, feelings, and opinions of the people, upon which they are to operate.

§ 65. After James the Second came to the throne, the same general course was adopted of filing a *quo warranto* against the proprietaries, as had been successful in respect to the colonies. The proprietaries, with a view to elude the storm, prudently offered to surrender their charter, and thereby gained time. Before any thing definitive took place, the revolution of 1688 occurred, which put an end to the hostile proceedings. In April, 1698, the proprietaries made another system of fundamental constitutions, which embraced many of those propounded in the first, and, indeed, was manifestly a mere amendment of them.

§ 66. These constitutions (for experience does not seem to have imparted more wisdom to the proprietaries {59} on this subject) contained the most objectionable features of the system of government, of the former constitutions, and shared a common fate.

§ 67. There was at this period a space of three hundred miles between the Southern and Northern settlements of Carolina; and though the whole province was owned by the same proprietaries, the legislation of the two great settlements had been hitherto conducted by separate and distinct assemblies, sometimes under the same governor, and sometimes under different governors. The legislatures continued to remain distinct down to the period, when a final surrender of the proprietary charter was made to the crown in 1729. The respective territories were designated by the name of North Carolina and South Carolina, and the laws of each obtained a like appellation. Cape Fear seems to have been commonly deemed, in the commissions of the governor, the boundary between the two colonies.

§ 68. By the surrender of the charter, the whole government of the territory was vested in the crown; (it had been in fact exercised by the crown ever since the overthrow of the proprietary government in 1720;) and henceforward it became a royal province; and was governed by commission under a form of government substantially like that established in the other royal provinces. This change of government was very acceptable to the people, and gave a new impulse to their industry and enterprise. At a little later period [1732], for the convenience of the inhabitants, the province was divided; and the divisions were distinguished by the names of North Carolina and South Carolina. {60}

§ 69. The form of government conferred on Carolina, when it became a royal province, was in substance this. It consisted of a governor and council appointed by the crown, and an assembly chosen by the people, and these three branches constituted the legislature. The governor convened, prorogued, and dissolved the legislature, and had a negative upon the laws, and exercised the executive authority. He possessed also the powers of the court of chancery, of the admiralty, of supreme ordinary, and of appointing magistrates and militia officers. All laws were subject to the royal approbation or dissent; but were in the mean time in full force.

CHAPTER XV.

GEORGIA.

§ 70. IN the same year, in which Carolina was divided [1732], a project was formed for the settlement of a colony upon the unoccupied territory between the rivers Savannah and Altamaha. The object of the projectors was to strengthen the province of Carolina, to provide a maintenance for the suffering poor of the mother country, and to open an asylum for the persecuted protestants in Europe; and in common with all the other colonies to attempt the conversion and civilization of the natives. Upon application, George the Second granted a charter to the company, (consisting of Lord Percival and twenty others, among whom was the celebrated Oglethorpe,) and incorporated them by the name of the Trustees for establishing the Colony of Georgia in America.

§ 71. The charter was obviously intended for a temporary duration only; and the first measures adopted by the trustees, granting lands in tail male, to be held by a sort of military service, and introducing other restrictions, were not adapted to aid the original design, or foster the growth of the colony. It continued to languish, until at length the trustees, wearied with their own labours, and the complaints of the people, in June, 1751, surrendered the charter to the crown. Henceforward it was governed as a royal province, enjoying the same liberties and immunities as other royal provinces; and in process of time it began to flourish, and at the period of the American Revolution, it had attained considerable importance among the colonies.

CHAPTER XVI.

GENERAL REVIEW OF THE COLONIES.

§ 72. We have now finished our brief survey of the origin and political history of the colonies; and here we may pause for a short time for the purpose of some general reflections upon the subject.

§ 73. Plantations or colonies in distant countries are either, such as are acquired by occupying and peopling desert and uncultivated regions by emigrations from the mother country; or such as, being already cultivated and organized, are acquired by conquest or cession under treaties. There is, however, a difference between these two species of colonies in respect to the laws, by which they are governed, at least according to the jurisprudence of the common law. If an uninhabited country is discovered and planted by British subjects, the English laws are said to be immediately in force there; for the law is the birthright of every subject. So that wherever they go, they carry their laws with them; and the new found country is governed by them.

§ 74. This proposition, however, though laid down in such general terms by very high authority, requires many limitations, and is to be understood with many restrictions. Such colonists do not carry with them the whole body of the English laws, as they then exist; for many of them must, from the nature of the case, be wholly inapplicable to their situation, and inconsistent with their comfort and prosperity. There is, therefore, this necessary limitation implied, that {63} they carry with them all the laws applicable to their situation, and not repugnant to the local and political circumstances, in which they are placed.

§ 75. Even as thus stated, the proposition is full of vagueness and perplexity; for it must still remain a question of intrinsic difficulty to say, what laws are, or are not applicable to their situation; and whether they are bound by the present state of things, or are at liberty to apply them in future by adoption, as the growth or interests of the colony may dictate. The English rules of inheritance, and of protection from personal injuries, the rights secured by Magna Charta, and the remedial course in the administration of justice, are examples as clear perhaps as any, which can be stated, as presumptively adopted, or applicable. And yet in the infancy of a colony some of these very rights, and privileges, and remedies, and rules, may be in fact inapplicable, or inconvenient, and impolitic. It is not perhaps easy to settle, what parts of the English laws are, or are not in force in any such colony, until either by usage, or judicial determination, they have been recognized as of absolute force.

§ 76. In respect to conquered and ceded countries, which have already laws of their own, a different rule prevails. In such cases the crown has a right to abrogate the former laws, and institute new ones. But until such new laws are promulgated,

40

the old laws and customs of the country remain in full force, unless so far as they are contrary to our religion, or enact any thing, that is *malum in se*; for in all such cases the laws of the conquering or acquiring country shall prevail. This qualification of the rule arises from the presumption, that the crown could never intend to sanction laws contrary to religion or sound morals. But {64} although the king has thus the power to change the laws of ceded and conquered countries, the power is not unlimited. His legislation is subordinate to the authority of parliament. He cannot make any new change contrary to fundamental principles; he cannot exempt an inhabitant from that particular dominion, as for instance from the laws of trade, or from the power of parliament; and he cannot give him privileges exclusive of other subjects.

§ 77. Mr. Justice Blackstone, in his Commentaries, insists, that the American colonies are principally to be deemed conquered, or ceded countries. His language is, "Our American Plantations are principally of this latter sort, [i. e. ceded or conquered countries,] being obtained in the last century either by right of conquest and driving out the natives, (with what natural justice I shall not at present inquire,) or by treaties. And, therefore, the common law of England, as such, has no allowance or authority there; they being no part of the mother country, but distinct, though dependent dominions."

§ 78. The doctrine of Mr. Justice Blackstone, may well admit of serious doubt upon general principles. But it is manifestly erroneous, so far as it is applied to the colonies and plantations composing our Union. In the charters, under which all these colonies were settled, with a single exception, there is, an express declaration, that all subjects and their children inhabiting therein shall be deemed natural-born subjects, and shall enjoy all the privileges and immunities thereof; and that the laws of England, so far as they are applicable, shall be in force there; and no laws shall be made, which are repugnant to, but as near as may be conveniently, shall conform to the laws of England. {65} Now this declaration, even if the crown previously possessed a right to establish what laws it pleased over the territory, as a conquest from the natives, being a fundamental rule of the original settlement of the colonies, and before the emigrations thither, was conclusive, and could not afterwards be abrogated by the crown. It was an irrevocable annexation of the colonies to the mother country, as dependencies governed by the same laws, and entitled to the same rights.

§ 79. And so has been the uniform doctrine in America ever since the settlement of the colonies. The universal principle (and the practice has conformed to it) has been, that the common law is our birthright and inheritance, and that our ancestors brought hither with them upon their emigration all of it, which was applicable to their situation. The whole structure of our present jurisprudence stands upon the original foundations of the common law.

§ 80. We thus see in a very clear light the mode, in which the common law was first introduced into the colonies; as well as the true reason of the exceptions to it to be found in our colonial usages and laws. It was not introduced, as of original and universal obligation in its utmost latitude; but the limitations contained in the bosom of the common law itself, and indeed constituting a part of the law of nations, were affirmatively settled and recognised in the respective charters of settlement. Thus limited and defined, it has become the guardian of our political and civil rights; it has protected our infant liberties; it has watched over our maturer growth; it has expanded with our wants; it has nurtured that spirit of independence, which checked the first approaches of arbitrary power; it has enabled us to triumph in the midst of difficulties and dangers {66} threatening our political existence; and by the goodness of God, we are now enjoying, under its bold and manly principles, the blessings of a free, independent, and united government.

CHAPTER XVII.

GENERAL REVIEW OF THE COLONIES.

§ 81. IN respect to their interior polity, the colonies have been very properly divided by Mr. Justice Blackstone into three sorts; viz. Provincial, Proprietary, and Charter Governments. *First*, Provincial Establishments. The constitutions of these depended on the respective commissions issued by the crown to the governors, and the instructions, which usually accompanied those commissions. These commissions were usually in one form, appointing a governor as the king's representative or deputy, who was to be governed by the royal instructions, and styling him Captain General and Governor-in-Chief over the Province, and Chancellor, Vice-Admiral, and Ordinary of the same. The crown also appointed a council, who, besides their legislative authority, were to assist the governor in the discharge of his official duties; and power was given him to suspend them from office, and, in case of vacancies, to appoint others, until the pleasure of the crown should be known. The commissions also contained authority to convene a general assembly of representatives of the freeholders and planters; and under this authority provincial assemblies, composed of the governor, the council, and the representatives, were constituted; (the council being a separate branch or upper house, and the governor having a negative upon all their proceedings, and also the right of proroguing and dissolving them;) which assemblies had the power of making local laws and ordinances, not repugnant to the laws of England, but {68} as near as may be agreeable thereto, subject to the ratification and disapproval of the crown. The governors also had power, with advice of council, to establish courts, and to appoint judges and other magistrates, and officers for the province; to pardon offences, and to remit fines and forfeitures; to collate to churches and benefices; to levy military forces for defence; and to execute martial law in time of invasion, war, and rebellion. Appeals lay to the king in council from the decisions of, the highest courts of judicature of the province, as indeed they did from all others of the colonies. Under this form of government the provinces of New-Hampshire, New-York, New-Jersey, Virginia, the Carolinas; and Georgia, were governed (as we have seen) for a long period, and some of them from an early period after their settlement.

§ 82. *Secondly*, Proprietary Governments. These (as we have seen) were granted out by the crown to individuals, in the nature of feudatory principalities, with all the inferior royalties, and subordinate powers of legislation, which formerly belonged to the owners of counties palatine. Yet still there were these express conditions, that the ends, for which the grant was made, should be substantially pursued; and that nothing should be done or attempted, which might derogate from the sovereignty of the mother country. In the proprietary government the governors were appointed by the proprietaries, and legislative assemblies were assembled under their authority; and indeed all the usual prerogatives were exercised, which in provincial governments belonged to the crown. Three only existed at the period of the American Revolution; viz. the proprietary governments of Maryland, Pennsylvania, and Delaware. The former had this peculiarity in its {69} charter, that its laws were not subject to the supervision and control of the crown; whereas in both the latter such a supervision and control were expressly or impliedly provided for.

§ 83. *Thirdly*, Charter Governments. Mr. Justice Blackstone describes them, (1 Comm. 108,) as "in the nature of civil corporations with the power of making by-laws for their own internal regulation, not contrary to the laws of England; and with such rights and authorities as are specially given them in their several charters of incorporation. They have a governor named by the king, (or, in some proprietary colonies, by, the proprietor,) who is his representative or deputy. They have courts of justice of their own, from whose decisions an appeal lies to the king and council here in England. Their general assemblies, which are their house of commons, together with their council of State, being their upper house, with the concurrence of the king, or his representative the governor, make laws suited to their own emergencies." This is by no means a just or accurate description of the charter governments. They could not be justly considered, as mere civil corporations of the realm, empowered to pass bylaws; but rather as great political establishments or colonies, possessing the general powers of government, and rights of sovereignty, dependent, indeed, and subject to the realm of England; but still possessing within their own territorial limits the general powers of legislation and taxation. The only charter governments existing at the period of the American Revolution were those of Massachusetts, Rhode-Island, and Connecticut. The first charter of Massachusetts might be open to the objection, that it provided only for a civil corporation within the realm, and did not justify the assumption {70} of the extensive executive, legislative, and judicial powers, which were afterwards exercised upon the removal of that charter to America. And a similar objection might be urged against the charter of the Plymouth colony. But the charter of William and Mary, in 1691, was obviously upon a broader foundation, and was in the strictest sense a charter for general political government, a constitution for a state, with sovereign powers and prerogatives, and not for a mere municipality. By this last charter the organization of the different departments of the government was, in some respects, similar to that in the provincial governments; the governor was appointed by the crown; the council annually chosen by the General Assembly; and the House of Representatives by the people. But in Connecticut and Rhode-Island the charter governments were organized altogether upon popular and democratical principles; the governor, council, and assembly being annually chosen by the freemen of the colony, and all other officers appointed by their authority. By the statutes of 7 & 8 William 3, (ch. 22, § 6,) it was indeed required, that all governors appointed in charter and proprietary governments should be approved of by the crown, before entering upon the duties of their office; but this statute was, if at all, ill observed, and seems to have produced no essential change in the colonial policy.

§ 84. The circumstances, in which the colonies were generally agreed, notwithstanding the diversities of their organization into provincial, proprietary, and charter governments, were the following.

§ 85. (1.) They enjoyed the rights and privileges of British born subjects; and the benefit of the common laws of England; and all their laws were required {71} to be not repugnant unto, but, as near as might be, agreeable to the laws and statutes of England. This, as we have seen, was a limitation upon the legislative power contained in an express clause of all the charters; and could not be transcended without a clear breach of their fundamental conditions. A very liberal exposition of this clause seems, however, always to have prevailed, and to have been acquiesced in, if not adopted by the crown. Practically speaking, it seems to have been left to the judicial tribunals in the colonies to ascertain, what part of the common law was applicable to the situation of the colonies; and of course, from a difference of interpretation, the common law, as actually administered, was not in any two of the colonies exactly the same. The general foundation of the local jurisprudence was confessedly composed of the same materials; but in the actual superstructure they were variously combined, and modified, so as to present neither a general symmetry of design, nor an unity of execution.

§ 86. In regard to the legislative power, there was a still greater latitude allowed; for notwithstanding the cautious reference in the charters to the laws of England, the assemblies actually exercised the authority to abrogate every part of the common law, except that, which united the colonies to the parent state by the general ties of allegiance and dependency; and every part of the statute law, except those acts of Parliament, which expressly prescribed rules for the colonies, and necessarily bound them, as integral parts of the empire, in a general system, formed for all, and for the interest of all. To guard this superintending authority with more effect, it was enacted by Parliament in 7 & 8 William 3, (ch. 22,) "that all laws, by-laws, usages, and {72} customs, which should be in practice in any of the plantations, repugnant to any law made, or to be made in this kingdom relative to the said plantations, shall be utterly void and of none effect."

§ 87. It was under the consciousness of the full possession of the rights, liberties, and immunities of British subjects, that the colonists in almost all the early legislation of their respective assemblies insisted upon a declaratory act, acknowledging and confirming them. And for the most part they thus succeed in obtaining a real and effective magna charta of their liberties. The trial by jury in all cases, civil and criminal, was as firmly, and as universally established in the colonies, as in the mother country.

§ 88. (2.) In all the colonies local legislatures were established, one branch of which consisted of representatives of the people freely chosen, to represent and defend their interests, and possessing a negative upon all laws. We have seen, that in the original structure of the charters of the early colonies, no provision was made for such a legislative body. But accustomed as the colonists had been to possess the rights and privileges of Englishmen, and valuing as they did, above all others, the right of representation in Parliament, as the only real security for their political and civil liberties, it was easy to foresee, that they would not long endure the exercise of any arbitrary power; and that they would insist upon some share in framing the laws, by which they were, to be governed. We find accordingly, that at an early period [1619] a house of burgesses was forced upon the then proprietors of Virginia. In Massachusetts, Connecticut, New-Hampshire, and Rhode-Island, the same course was pursued. And Mr. Hutchinson has correctly observed, that all the colonies before {73} the reign of Charles the Second, (Maryland alone excepted, whose charter contained an express provision on the subject,) settled a model of government for themselves, in which the people had a voice, and representation in framing the laws, and in assenting to burthens to be imposed upon themselves. After the restoration, there was no instance of a colony without a representation of the people, nor any attempt to deprive the colonies of this privilege, except during the brief and arbitrary reign of King James the Second.

§ 89. (5.) All the colonies considered themselves, not as parcel of the realm of Great Britain, but as dependencies of the British crown, and owing allegiance thereto, the king being their supreme and sovereign lord. In virtue of its general superintendency the crown constantly claimed, and exercised the right of entertaining appeals from the courts of the last resort in the colonies; and these appeals were heard and finally adjudged by the king in council. This right of appeal was secured by express reservation in most of the colonial charters. It was expressly provided for by an early provincial law in New-Hampshire, when the matter in difference exceeded the true value or sum of £300 sterling. So, a like colonial law of Rhode-Island was enacted by its local legislature in 1719. It was treated by the crown, as an inherent right of the subject, independent of any such reservation. And so in divers cases it was held by the courts of England. The reasons given for the opinion, that writs of error [and appeals] lie to all the dominions belonging to England upon the ultimate judgments given there, are, (1.) That, otherwise, the law appointed, or permitted to such inferior dominion might be considerably changed without the assent of the superior {74} dominion; (2.) Judgments might be given to the disadvantage or lessening of the superiority, or to make the superiority of the king only, and not of the crown of England; and (3.) That the practice has been accordingly.

§ 90. (6.) Though the colonies had a common origin, and owed a common allegiance, and the inhabitants of each were British subjects, they had no direct political connexion with each other. Each was independent of all the others; each, in a limited sense, was sovereign within its own territory. There was neither alliance, nor confederacy between them. The assembly of one province could not make laws for another; nor confer privileges, which were to be enjoyed or exercised in another, farther than they could be in any independent foreign state. As colonies, they were also excluded from all connexion with foreign states. They were known only as dependencies; and they followed the fate of the parent country both in peace and war, without having assigned to them, in the intercourse or diplomacy of nations, any distinct or independent existence. They did not possess the power of forming any league or treaty among themselves, which should acquire an obligatory force without the assent of the parent state. And though their mutual wants and necessities often induced them to associate for common purposes of defence, these confederacies were of a casual and temporary nature, and were allowed as an indulgence, rather than as a right. They made several efforts to procure the establishment of some general superintending government over them all; but their own differences of opinion, as well as the jealousy of the crown, made these efforts abortive. These efforts, however, prepared their minds for the gradual reconciliation {75} of their local interests, and for the gradual developement of the principles, upon which a union ought to rest, rather than brought on an immediate sense of the necessity, or the blessings of such a general government.

§ 91. But although the colonies were independent of each other in respect to their domestic concerns, they were not wholly alien to each other. On the contrary, they were fellow subjects, and for many purposes one people. Every colonist had a right to inhabit, if he pleased, in any other colony; and, as a British subject, he was capable of inheriting lands by descent in every other colony. The commercial intercourse of the colonies, too, was regulated by the general laws of the British empire; and could not be restrained, or obstructed by colonial legislation. The remarks of Mr. Chief Justice Jay on this subject are equally just and striking. "All the people of this country were then subjects of the king of Great Britain, and owed allegiance to him; and all the civil authority then existing, or exercised here, flowed from the head of the British empire. They were, in a strict sense, *fellow* subjects, and in a variety of respects *one people*. When the Revolution commenced, the patriots did not assert, that only the same affinity and social connexion subsisted between the people of the colonies, which subsisted between the people of Gaul, Britain, and Spain, while Roman provinces, to wit, only that affinity and social connexion, which result from the mere circumstance of being governed by the same prince." Different ideas prevailed, and gave occasion to the Congress of 1774 and 1775.

§ 92. In respect to the political relations of the colonies with the parent country, it is not easy to state the exact limits of the dependency, which was admitted, {76} and the extent of sovereignty, which might be lawfully exercised over them, either by the crown, or by parliament. In regard to the crown, all of the colonies admitted, that they owed allegiance to the crown, as their sovereign liege lord, though the nature of the powers, which he might exercise, as sovereign, were still undefined.

§ 93. In the silence of express declarations we may resort to the doctrines maintained by the crown-writers, as furnishing, if not an exact, at least a comprehensive view of the claims of the royal prerogative over the colonial establishments. They considered it not necessary to maintain, that all the royal prerogatives, exercisable in England, were of course exercisable in the colonies; but only such fundamental rights and principles, as constituted the basis of the throne and its authority, and without which the king would cease to be sovereign in all his dominions. Hence the attributes of sovereignty, perfection, perpetuity, and irresponsibility, which were inherent in the political capacity of the king, belonged to him in all the territories subject to the crown, whatever were the nature of their laws, and government in other respects. Every where he was the head of the church, and the fountain of justice; every where he was entitled to a share in the legislation, (except where he had expressly renounced it;) every where he was generalissimo of all forces, and entitled to make peace or war. But minor prerogatives might be yielded, where they were inconsistent with the laws or usages of the place, or were inapplicable to the condition of the people. In every question, that respected the royal prerogatives in the colonies, where they were not of a strictly fundamental nature, the first thing to be considered was, whether the charter of the {77} particular colony contained any express provision on the subject. If it did, that was the guide. If it was silent, then the royal prerogatives were in the colony precisely the same, as in the parent country; for in such cases the common law of England was the common law of the colonies for such purposes. Hence, if the colonial charter contained no peculiar grant to the contrary, the king might erect courts of justice and exchequer therein; and the colonial judicatories, in point of law, were deemed to emanate from the crown, under the modifications made by the colonial assemblies under their charters. The king also might extend the privilege of sending representatives to new towns in the colonial assemblies. He might control, and enter a *nolle prosequi* in criminal prosecutions, and pardon crimes, and release forfeitures. He might present to vacant benefices; and he was entitled to royal mines, treasure-trove, escheats, and forfeitures. No colonial assemblies had a right to enact laws, except with the assent of the crown by charter, or commission, or otherwise; and if they exceeded the authority prescribed by the crown, their acts were void. The king might alter the constitution and form of the government of the colony, where there was no charter, or other confirmatory act by the colonial assembly with the assent of the crown; and it rested merely on the instructions and commissions given, from time to time, by the crown to its governors. The king had power also to vest in the royal governors in the colonies, from time to time, such of his prerogatives, as he should please; such as the power to prorogue, adjourn, and dissolve the colonial assemblies; to confirm acts and laws; to pardon offences; to act as captain general of the public forces; to appoint public officers; to act as chancellor and supreme ordinary; to {78} sit in the highest court of appeals and errors; to exercise the duties of vice-admiral, and to grant commissions to privateers. These last and some other of the prerogatives of the king, were commonly exercised by the royal governors without objection.

§ 94. The colonial assemblies were not considered as standing on the same footing, as parliament, in respect to rights, powers, and privileges; but as deriving all their energies from the crown, and limited by the respective charters, or other confirmatory acts of the crown, in all their proceedings. The king might, in respect to a colonial assembly, assent to an act of assembly, before it met, or ratify it, or dissent from it, after the session was closed. He might accept a surrender of a colonial charter, subject to the rights of third persons previously acquired; and give the colony a new charter, or otherwise institute therein a new form of government. And it has been even contended, that the king might, in cases of extraordinary necessity or emergency, take away a charter, where the defence or protection of the inhabitants required it, leaving them in possession of their civil rights.

§ 95. Such are some of the royal prerogatives, which were supposed to exist by the crown-writers in the colonial establishments, when not restrained by any positive charter or bill of rights. Of these, many were undisputed; but others were resisted with pertinacity and effect in the colonial assemblies.

§ 96. In regard to the authority of parliament to enact laws, which should be binding upon them, there was quite as much obscurity, and still more jealousy

spreading over the whole subject. The government of Great Britain always maintained the doctrine, that the parliament had authority to bind the colonies in all
cases {79} whatsoever. No acts of parliament, however, were understood to bind
the colonies, unless expressly named therein. But in America, at different times
and in different colonies, different opinions were entertained on the subject. In
fact it seemed to be the policy of the colonies, as much as possible, to withdraw
themselves from any acknowledgment of such authority, except so far as their necessities, from time to time, compelled them to acquiesce in the parliamentary
measures expressly extending to them. We have already seen, that they resisted
the imposition of taxes upon them, without the consent of their local legislatures,
from a very early period.

§ 97. But it was by no means an uncommon opinion in some of the colonies,
especially in the proprietary and charter governments, that no act of parliament
whatsoever could bind them without their own consent. An extreme reluctance
was shown by Massachusetts to any parliamentary interference as early as 1640;
and the famous navigation acts of 1651 and 1660 were perpetually evaded, even
when their authority was no longer denied, throughout the whole of New-England. Massachusetts, in 1679, in an address to the crown, declared, that she "apprehended them to be an invasion of the rights, liberties, and properties of the
subjects of his majesty in the colony, they not being represented in parliament;
and, according to the usual sayings of the learned in the law, the laws of England
were bounded within the four seas, and did not reach America." However, Massachusetts, as well as the other New-England colonies, finally acquiesced in the
authority of parliament to regulate trade and commerce; but denied it in regard to
taxation and internal regulation of the colonies. As late as 1757, the general court
of Massachusetts {80} admitted the constitutional authority of parliament in the
following words: — "The authority of all acts of parliament, which concern the
colonies, and extend to them, is ever acknowledged in all the courts of law, and
made the rule of all judicial proceedings in the province. There is not a member
of the general court, and we know no inhabitant within the bounds of the government, that ever questioned this authority." And in another address in 1761, they
declared, that "every act we make, repugnant to an act of parliament extending
to the plantations, is *ipso facto* null and void." And at a later period, in 1768, in a
circular address to the other colonies, they admitted, "that his majesty's high court
of Parliament is the supreme legislative power over the whole empire;" contending, however, that as British subjects they could not be taxed without their own
consent.

§ 98. "In the middle and southern provinces," (we are informed by a most respectable historian,) "no question respecting the supremacy of parliament in matters of general legislation existed. The authority of such acts of internal regulation,
as were made for America, as well as those for the regulation of commerce, even
by the imposition of duties, provided these duties were imposed for the purpose of
regulation, had been at all times admitted. But these colonies, however they might
acknowledge the supremacy of parliament in other respects, denied the right of
that body to tax them internally." If there were any exceptions to the general accuracy of this statement, they seem to have been too few and fugitive to impair the

general result. In the charter of Pennsylvania, an express reservation was made of the power of taxation by an act of parliament, {81} though this was argued not to be a sufficient foundation for the exercise of it.

§ 99. Perhaps the best general summary of the rights and liberties asserted by all the colonies is contained in the celebrated declaration drawn up by the Congress of the Nine Colonies, assembled at New-York, in October, 1765. That declaration asserted, that the colonists "owe the same allegiance to the crown of Great Britain, that is owing from his subjects born within the realm, and all due subordination to that august body, the parliament of Great Britain." That the colonists "are entitled to all the inherent rights and liberties of his [the king's] natural born subjects within the kingdom of Great Britain." "That it is inseparably essential to the freedom of a people, and the undoubted right of Englishmen, that no taxes be imposed on them, but with their own consent, given personally, or by their representatives." That the people of the "colonies are not, and from their local circumstances cannot be represented in the house of commons of Great Britain. That the only representatives of these colonies are persons chosen therein by themselves; and that no taxes ever have been, or can be, constitutionally imposed upon them, but by their respective legislatures. That all supplies of the crown being free gifts from the people, it is unreasonable and inconsistent with the principles and spirit of the British constitution for the people of Great Britain to grant to his majesty the property of the colonies. And that the trial by jury is the inherent and invaluable right of every British subject in these colonies."

§ 100. But after the passage of the stamp act, in 1765, many of the colonies began to examine this subject with more care and to entertain very different opinions, {82} as to parliamentary authority. The doctrines maintained in debate in parliament, as well as the alarming extent to which a practical application of those doctrines might lead, in drying up the resources, and prostrating the strength and prosperity of the colonies, drove them to a more close and narrow survey of the foundation of parliamentary supremacy. Doubts were soon infused into their minds; and from doubts they passed by an easy transition to a denial, first of the power of taxation, and next of all authority whatever to bind them by its laws. One of the most distinguished of our writers during the contest admits, that he entered upon the inquiry "with a view and expectation of being able to trace some constitutional line between those cases, in which we ought, and those, in which we ought not to acknowledge the power of parliament over us. In the prosecution of his inquiries he became fully convinced, that such a line does not exist; and that there can be no medium between acknowledging and denying that power in all cases."

§ 101. If other colonies did not immediately arrive at the same conclusion, it was easy to foresee, that the struggle would ultimately be maintained upon the general ground; and that a common interest, and a common desire of security, if not of independence, would gradually bring all the colonies to feel the absolute necessity of adhering to it, as their truest and safest defence. In 1773, Massachusetts found no difficulty in contending in the broadest terms for an unlimited independence of parliament; and in a bold and decided tone denied all its of legislation over them. A distinction was taken between subjection to parliament, and allegiance to the crown. The latter was admitted; but the former was resolutely opposed. It is remarkable, that {83} the Declaration of Independence, which sets forth our grievances in such warm and glowing colors, does not once mention parliament, or allude to our connexion with it; but treats the acts of oppression therein referred to, as acts of the king, in combination "with others," for the overthrow of our liberties.

§ 102. The stamp act was repealed; but within a few years afterwards duties of another sort were laid, the object of which was to raise a revenue from importations into the colonies. These of course became as offensive to the colonies as the prior attempt at internal taxation; and were resisted upon the same grounds of unconstitutionality. It soon became obvious, that the great struggle in respect to colonial and parliamentary rights could scarcely be decided otherwise, than by an appeal to arms. Great Britain was resolutely bent upon enforcing her claims by an open exercise of military power; and on the other hand, America scarcely saw any other choice left to her, but unconditional submission, or bold and unmeasured resistance.

BOOK II.

**HISTORY OF THE REVOLUTION
AND OF THE CONFEDERATION.**

CHAPTER I.

THE REVOLUTION.

§ 103. WE are next to proceed to an historical review of the origin of that union of the colonies, which led to the declaration of independence; of the effects of that event, and of the subsequent war upon the political character and rights of the colonies; of the formation and adoption of the articles of confederation; of the sovereign powers antecedently exercised by the continental congress; of the causes of the decline and fall of the confederation; and finally, of the establishment of the present constitution of the United States.

No redress of grievances having followed upon the many appeals made to the king, and to parliament, by and in behalf of the colonies, either conjointly or separately, it became obvious to them, that a closer union and co-operation were necessary to vindicate their rights, and protect their liberties. If a resort to arms should be indispensable, it was impossible to hope {85} for success, but in united efforts. If peaceable redress was to be sought, it was as clear, that the voice of the colonies must be heard, and their power felt in a national organization. In 1774 Massachusetts recommended the assembling of a continental congress to deliberate upon the state of public affairs; and according to her recommendation, delegates were appointed by the colonies for a congress, to be held in Philadelphia in the autumn of the same year. In some of the legislatures of the colonies, which were then in session, delegates were appointed by the popular, or representative branch; and in other cases they were appointed by conventions of the people in the colonies. The congress of delegates (calling themselves in their more formal acts "the delegates appointed by the *good people* of these colonies") assembled on the 4th of September, 1774; and having chosen officers, they adopted certain fundamental rules for their proceedings.

§ 105. Thus was organized under the auspices, and with the consent of the people, acting directly in their primary, sovereign capacity, and without the intervention of the functionaries, to whom the ordinary powers of government were delegated in the colonies, the first general or national government, which has been very aptly called "the revolutionary government," since in its origin and progress it was wholly conducted upon revolutionary principles. The congress thus assembled, exercised *de facto* and *de jure* a sovereign authority; not as the delegated agents of the governments *de facto* of the colonies, but in virtue of original powers derived from the people. The revolutionary government, thus formed, terminated only, when it was regularly superceded by the confederated government under the articles finally ratified, as we shall hereafter see, in 1781. {86}

§ 106. The first and most important of their acts was a declaration, that in determining questions in this congress, each colony or province should have one vote; and this became the established course during the revolution. They adopted a declaration of rights, not differing in substance from that of the congress of 1765, and affirming, that the respective colonies are entitled to the common law of England and the benefit of such English statutes, as existed at the time of their colonization, and which they have by experience respectively found to be applicable to their local and other circumstances. They also adopted addresses to the people of England, to the neighbouring British colonies, and to the king, explaining their grievances, and requesting aid and redress.

§ 107. In May, 1775, a second congress of delegates met from all the states. These delegates were chosen, as the preceding had been, partly by the popular branch of the state legislatures, when in session; but principally by conventions of the people in the various states. In a few instances the choice by the legislative body was confirmed by that of a convention, and *e converso*. They authorized the raising of continental troops, and appointed General Washington commander in chief, to whom they gave a commission in the name of the delegates of the united colonies. They had previously authorized certain military measures, and especially the arming of the militia of New-York, and the occupation of Crown Point and Ticonderoga. They authorized the emission of two millions of dollars in bills of credit, pledging the colonies to the redemption thereof. They framed rules for the government of the army. They published a solemn declaration of the causes of their taking up arms, an address to the king, {87} entreating a change of measures, and an address to the people of Great Britain, requesting their aid, and admonishing them of the threatening evils of a separation. They erected a general post-office, and organized the department for all the colonies. They apportioned the quota, that each colony should pay of the bills emitted by congress.

§ 108. At a subsequent adjournment, they authorized the equipment of armed vessels to intercept supplies to the British, and the organization of a marine corps. They authorized the grant of commissions to capture armed vessels and transports in the British service; and recommended the creation of prize courts in each colony, reserving a right of appeal to congress. They adopted rules for the regulation of the navy, and for the division of prizes and prize money. They denounced, as enemies, all, who should obstruct or discourage the circulation of bills of credit. They authorized further emissions of bills of credit, and created two military departments for the middle and southern colonies. They authorized general reprisals, and the equipment of private armed vessels against British vessels and property. They organized a general treasury department. They authorized the exportation and importation of all goods to and from foreign countries, not subject to Great Britain, with certain exceptions; and prohibited the importation of slaves; and declared a forfeiture of all prohibited goods. They recommended to the respective assemblies and conventions of the colonies, where no government, sufficient to the exigencies, had been established, to adopt such government, as in the opinion of the representatives should best conduce to the happiness and safety of their constituents in particular, and America in general, and {88} adopted a preamble, which stated, "that the exercise of every kind of authority under the crown of Great Britain should be totally suppressed."

§ 109. These measures, all of which progressively pointed to a separation from the mother country, and evinced a determination to maintain, at every hazard, the liberties of the colonies, were soon followed by more decisive steps. On the 7th of June, 1776, certain resolutions respecting independency were moved, which were referred to a committee of the whole. On the 10th of June it was resolved, that a committee be appointed to prepare a declaration, "that these united colonies are, and of right ought to be, free and independent states; that they are absolved from all allegiance to the British crown; and that all political connexion between them and the state of Great Britain is, and ought to be, dissolved." On the 11th of June a committee was appointed to prepare and digest the form of a confederation to be entered into between the colonies, and also a committee to prepare a plan of treaties to be proposed to foreign powers. On the 28th of June the committee appointed to prepare a Declaration of Independence brought in a draft. On the 2d of July, congress adopted the resolution for Independence; and on the 4th of July they adopted the Declaration of Independence; and thereby solemnly published and declared, "That these united colonies are, and of right ought to be, free and independent states; that they are absolved from all allegiance to the British crown; and that all political connexion between them and the state of Great Britain is, and ought to be, totally dissolved; and that, as free and independent states, they have full power to levy war, conclude peace, contract alliances, establish commerce, and to do all {89} other acts and things, which independent states may of right do."

§ 110. From the moment of the declaration of independence, if not for most purposes at an antecedent period, the united colonies must be considered as being a nation *de facto*, having a general government over it created, and acting by the general consent of the people of all the colonies. The powers of that government were not, and indeed could not be well defined. But still its exclusive sovereignty, in many cases, was firmly established; and its controlling power over the states was in most, if not in all national measures, universally admitted. The articles of confederation, of which we shall have occasion to speak more hereafter, were not prepared or adopted by congress until November, 1777; they were not signed or ratified by any of the states until July, 1778; and they were not ratified, so as to become obligatory upon all the states, until March, 1781. In the intermediate time, congress continued to exercise the powers of a general government, whose acts were binding on all the states. And though they constantly admitted the states to be "sovereign and independent communities;" yet it must be obvious, that the terms were used in the subordinate and limited sense already alluded to; for it was impossible to use them in any other sense, since a majority of the states could by their public acts in congress control and bind the minority. Among the exclusive powers exercised by congress, were the power to declare war and make peace; to authorize captures; to institute appellate prize courts; to direct and control all national, military, and naval operations; to form alliances, and make treaties; to contract debts, and issue bills of credit upon national {90} account. In respect to foreign governments, we were politically known as the United States only; and it was in our national capacity, as such, that we sent and received ambassadors, entered into treaties and alliances, and were admitted into the general community of nations, who might exercise the right of belligerents, and claim an equality of sovereign powers and prerogatives.

§ 111. In respect to the powers of the continental congress exercised before the adoption of the articles of confederation, few questions were judicially discussed during the revolutionary contest; for men had not leisure in the heat of war nicely to scrutinize or weigh such subjects; *inter arma silent leges*. The people, relying on the wisdom and patriotism of congress, silently acquiesced in whatever authority they assumed. But soon after the organization of the present government, the question was most elaborately discussed before the Supreme Court of the United States, in a case calling for an exposition of the appellate jurisdiction of congress in prize causes before the ratification of the confederation. The result of that examination was, that congress, before the confederation, possessed, by the consent of the people of the United States, sovereign and supreme powers for national purposes; and among others, the supreme powers of peace and war, and, as an incident, the right of entertaining appeals in the last resort in prize causes, even in opposition to state legislation. And that the actual powers exercised by congress, in respect to national objects, furnished the best exposition of its constitutional authority, since they emanated from the representatives of the people, and were acquiesced in by the people.

CHAPTER II.

ORIGIN OF THE CONFEDERATION.

§ 112. THE union, thus formed, grew out of the exigences of the times; and from its nature and objects might be deemed temporary, extending only to the maintenance of the common liberties and independence of the states, and to terminate with the return of peace with Great Britain, and the accomplishment of the ends of the revolutionary contest. It was obvious to reflecting minds, that such a future separation of the states into absolute, independent communities with no mutual ties, or controlling national government, would be fraught with the most imminent dangers to their common safety and peace, and expose them not only to the chance of re-conquest by Great Britain, after such separation in detached contests, but also to all the hazards of internal warfare and civil dissensions. So, that those, who had stood side by side in the common cause against Great Britain, might then, by the intrigues of their enemies, and the jealousies always incident to neighbouring nations, become instruments, in the hands of the ambitious abroad, or the corrupt at home, to aid in the mutual destruction of each other; and thus all sucessively fall, the victims of a domestic or foreign tyranny. Such considerations could not but have great weight with all honest and patriotic citizens, independent of the real blessings, which a permanent union could not fail to secure throughout all the states.

§ 113. It will be an instructive and useful lesson to us to trace historically the steps, which led to the formation and final adoption of the articles of confederation {92} and perpetual union between the United States. It will be instructive by disclosing the real difficulties attendant upon such a plan, even in times, when the necessity of it was forced upon the minds of men not only by common dangers, but by common protection, by common feelings of affection, and by common efforts of defence. It will be useful, by moderating the ardour of inexperienced minds, which are apt to imagine, that the theory of government is too plain, and the principles, on which it should be formed, too obvious, to leave much doubt for the exercise of the wisdom of statesmen, or the ingenuity of speculatists. Nothing is indeed more difficult to foresee, than the practical operation of given powers, unless it be the practical operation of restrictions, intended to control those powers.

§ 114. On the 11th of June, 1776, the same day, on which the committee for preparing the declaration of independence was appointed, congress resolved, that "a committee be appointed to prepare and digest the form of a confederation to be entered into between these colonies;" and on the next day a committee was accordingly appointed, consisting of a member from each colony. Nearly a year before this period, (viz. on the 21st of July, 1775,) Dr. Franklin had submitted to congress a sketch of articles of confederation, which does not, however, appear to have been acted on. These articles contemplated a union, until a reconciliation with Great Britain, and on failure thereof, the confederation to be perpetual.

§115. On the 12th of July, 1776, the committee, appointed to prepare articles of confederation, presented a draft, which was in the hand-writing of Mr. Dickinson, one of the committee, and a delegate from {93} Pennsylvania. The draft, so reported, was debated from the 22d to the 31st of July, and on several days between the 5th and 20th of August, 1776. On this last day, congress, in committee of the whole, reported a new draft, which was ordered to be printed for the use of the members.

§ 116. The subject seems not again to have been touched until the 8th of April, 1777, and the articles were debated at several times between that time and the 15th of November of the same year. On this last day the articles were reported with sundry amendments, and finally adopted by congress. A committee was then appointed to draft, and they accordingly drafted, a circular letter, requesting the states respectively to authorize their delegates in congress to subscribe the same in behalf of the state.

§ 117. Notwithstanding the strong and eloquent appeal made to the states in this letter it carried conviction very slowly to the minds of the local legislatures. Many objections were stated; and many amendments were proposed. All of them, however, were rejected by congress, not probably because they were all deemed inexpedient or improper in themselves; but from the danger of sending the instrument back again to all the states, for reconsideration. Accordingly on the 26th of June, 1778, a copy, engrossed for ratification, was prepared, and the ratification begun on the 9th day of July following. It was ratified by all the states, except Delaware and Maryland, in 1778; by Delaware in 1779, and by Maryland on the first of March, 1781, from which last date its final ratification took effect, and was joyfully announced by congress.

CHAPTER III.

DECLINE AND FALL OF THE CONFEDERATION.

§ 118. ANY survey, however slight, of the confederation will impress the mind with the intrinsic difficulties which attended the formation of its principal features. It is well known, that upon three important points, touching the common rights and interests of the several states, much diversity of opinion prevailed, and many animated discussions took place. The first was, as to the mode of voting in congress, whether it should be by states, or according to wealth, or population. The second, as to the rule, by which the expenses of the Union should be apportioned among the states. And the third, relative to the disposal of the vacant and unappropriated lands in the western territory.

§ 119. The leading defects of the confederation may be enumerated under the following heads:

In the first place, there was an utter want of all coercive authority to carry into effect its own constitutional measures. This, of itself, was sufficient to destroy its whole efficiency, as a superintending government, if that may be called a government, which possessed no one solid attribute of power. It has been justly observed, that "a government authorized to declare war, but relying on independent states for the means of prosecuting it; capable of contracting debts, and of pledging the public faith for their payment; but depending on thirteen distinct sovereignties for the preservation of that faith; could only be rescued from ignominy and contempt by finding those sovereignties administered by men exempt from the passions incident {95} to human nature." That is, by supposing a case, in which all human governments would become unnecessary, and all differences of opinion would become impossible. In truth, congress possessed only the power of recommendation.

§ 120. The fact corresponded with the theory. Even during the revolution, while all hearts and bands were engaged in the common cause, many of the measures of congress were defeated by the inactivity of the states; and in some instances the exercise of its powers were resisted. But after the peace of 1783, such opposition became common, and gradually extended its sphere of activity, until, in the expressive language already quoted, "the confederation became a shadow without the substance." There were no national courts having original or appellate jurisdiction over cases regarding the powers of the union; and if there had been, the relief would have been but of a very partial nature, since, without some act of state legislation, many of those powers could not be brought into life.

§ 121. A striking illustration of these remarks may be found in our juridical history. The power of appeal in prize causes, as an incident to the sovereign powers of peace and war, was asserted by congress after the most elaborate consideration, and supported by the voice of ten states, antecedent to the ratification of the articles of confederation. The exercise of that power was, however, resisted by the state courts, notwithstanding its immense importance to the preservation of the rights of independent neutral nations. The confederation gave, in express terms, this right of appeal. The decrees of the court of appeals were equally resisted; and in fact, they remained a dead letter, until {96} they were enforced by the courts of the United States under the present constitution.

§ 122. A farther illustration of this topic may be gathered from the palpable defect in the confederation, of any power to give a *sanction* to its laws. Congress had no power to exact obedience, or punish disobedience to its ordinances. They could neither impose fines, nor direct imprisonment, nor divest privileges, nor declare forfeitures, nor suspend refractory officers. There was in the confederation no *express* authority to exercise force; and though it might ordinarily be implied, as an incident, the right to make such implication was prohibited, for each state was to "retain every power, right, and jurisdiction, not *expressly* delegated to congress." The consequence naturally was, that the resolutions of congress were disregarded, not only by states but by individuals. Men followed their interests more than their duties; they cared little for persuasions, which came without force; or for recommendations, which appealed only to their consciences or their patriotism. Indeed it seems utterly preposterous to call that a government, which has no power to pass laws; or those enactments laws, which are attended with no sanction, and have no penalty or punishment annexed to the disobedience of them.

§ 123. But a still more striking defect was the total want of power to lay and levy taxes, or to raise revenue to defray the ordinary expenses of government. The whole power, confided to congress upon this head, was the power "to ascertain the sums necessary to be raised for the service of the United States;" and to apportion the quota or proportion on each state. But the power was expressly reserved to the states to lay and levy the taxes, and of course the time, as well as {97} the mode of payment, was extremely uncertain. The evils resulting from this source, even during the revolutionary war, were of incalculable extent; and, but for the good fortune of congress in obtaining foreign loans, it is far from being certain, that they would not have been fatal. The principle, which formed the basis of the apportionment, was sufficiently objectionable, as it took a standard extremely unequal in its operation upon the different states. The value of its lands was by no means a just representative of the proportionate contributions, which each state ought to make towards the discharge of the common burthens.

§ 124. But this consideration sinks into utter insignificance, in comparison with others. Requisitions were to be made upon thirteen independent states; and it depended upon the good will of the legislature of each state, whether it would comply at all; or if it did comply, at what time, and in what manner. The very tardiness of such an operation, in the ordinary course of things, was sufficient to involve the government in perpetual financial embarrassments, and to defeat many of its best measures, even when there was the utmost good faith and promptitude on the part of the states in complying with the requisitions. But many reasons concurred to produce a total want of promptitude on the part of the states, and, in numerous instances, a total disregard of the requisitions. Indeed, from the moment, that the peace of 1783 secured the country from the distressing calamities of war, a general relaxation took place; and many of the states successively found apologies for their gross neglect in evils common to all, or complaints listened to by all. Many solemn and affecting appeals were, from time to time, made by congress to the states; but they were attended with no {98} salutary effect. Many measures were devised to obviate the difficulties, nay, the dangers, which threatened the Union; but they failed to produce any amendments in the confederation. An attempt was made by congress, during the war, to procure from the states an authority to levy an impost of five per cent. upon imported and prize goods; but the assent of all the states could not be procured. The treasury was empty; the credit of the confederacy was sunk to a low ebb; the public burthens were increasing; and the public faith was prostrate.

§ 125. In February, 1786, congress determined to make another and last appeal to the states upon the subject. The report adopted upon that occasion contains a melancholy picture of the state of the nation. "In the course of this inquiry (said the report) it most clearly appeared, that the requisitions of congress for eight years past have been so irregular in their operation, so uncertain in their collection, and so evidently unproductive, that a reliance on them in future, as a source, from whence monies are to be drawn to discharge the engagements of the confederation, definite as they are in time and amount, *would be no less dishonourable to the understandings of those, who entertained such confidence*, than it would be dangerous to the welfare and peace of the Union." "It has become the duty of congress to declare most explicitly, that the crisis has arrived, when the people of these United States, by whose will and for whose benefit the federal government was instituted, must decide, whether they will support their rank, as a nation, by maintaining the public faith at home or abroad; or whether, for want of a timely exertion in establishing a general revenue, and thereby giving strength to the confederacy, they will {99} hazard, not only the existence of the Union, but of those great and invaluable privileges, for which they have so arduously and so honourably contended." After the adoption of this report, three states, which had hitherto stood aloof, came into the measure. New-York alone refused to comply with it; and after a most animated debate in her legislature, she remained inflexible, and the fate of the measure was sealed forever by her solitary negative.

§ 126. Independent, however, of this inability to lay taxes, or collect revenue, the want of any power in congress to regulate foreign or domestic commerce was deemed a leading defect in the confederation. This evil was felt in a comparatively slight degree during the war. But when the return of peace restored the country to its ordinary commercial relations, the want of some uniform system to regulate them was early perceived; and the calamities, which followed our shipping and navigation, our domestic, as well as our foreign trade, convinced the reflecting, that ruin impended upon these and other vital interests, unless a national remedy could be devised. We accordingly find the public papers of that period crowded with complaints on this subject. It was, indeed, idle and visionary to suppose, that while thirteen independent states possessed the exclusive power of regulating commerce, there could be found any uniformity of system, or any harmony and cooperation for the general welfare. Measures of a commercial nature, which were adopted in one state from a sense of its own interests, would be often countervailed, or rejected by other states from similar motives. If one state should deem a navigation act favourable to its own growth, the efficacy of such a measure might be defeated by the jealousy or policy of a neighbouring {100} state. If one should levy duties to maintain its own government and resources, there were many temptations for its neighbours to adopt the system of free trade, to draw to itself a larger share of foreign and domestic commerce. The agricultural states might easily suppose, that they had not an equal interest in a restrictive system with the navigating states. And, at all events, each state would legislate according to its estimate of its own interests, the importance of its own products, and the local advantages or disadvantages of its position in a political or commercial view. To do otherwise would be to sacrifice its immediate interests, without any adequate or enduring consideration; to legislate for others, and not for itself; to dispense blessings abroad, without regarding the security of those at home.

§ 127. These evils were aggravated by the situation of our foreign commerce. During the war, our commerce was nearly annihilated by the superior naval power of the enemy; and the return of peace enabled foreign nations, and especially Great Britain, in a great measure to monopolize all the benefits of our home trade. In the first place, our navigation, having no protection, was unable to engage in competition with foreign ships. In the next place, our supplies were almost altogether furnished by foreign importers or on foreign account. We were almost flooded with foreign manufactures, while our own produce bore but a reduced price. It was easy to foresee, that such a state of things must soon absorb all our means; and as our industry had but a narrow scope, would soon reduce us to absolute poverty. Our trade in our own ships with foreign nations was depressed in an equal degree; for it was loaded with heavy restrictions in their ports. {101} While, for instance, British ships with their commodities had free admission into our ports, American ships and exports were loaded with heavy exactions, or prohibited from entry into British ports. We were, therefore, the victims of our own imbecility, and reduced to a complete subjection to the commercial regulations of other countries, notwithstanding our boasts of freedom and independence. Congress had been long sensible of the fatal effects flowing from this source; but their efforts to ward off the mischiefs had been unsuccessful. Being invested by the articles of confederation with a limited power to form commercial treaties, they endeavoured to enter into treaties with foreign powers upon principles of reciprocity. But these negotiations were, as might be anticipated, unsuccessful, for the parties met upon very unequal terms. Foreign nations, and especially Great Britain, felt secure in the possession of their present command of our trade, and had not the least inducement to part with a single advantage. It was further pressed upon us, with a truth equally humiliating and undeniable, that congress possessed no effectual power to guaranty the faithful observance of any commercial regulations; and there must in such cases be reciprocal obligations.

§ 128. There were other defects seriously urged against the confederation, which, although not of such a fatal tendency, as those already enumerated, were deemed of sufficient importance to justify doubts, as to its efficacy as a bond of union, or an enduring scheme of government. It is not necessary to go at large into a consideration of them. It will suffice for the present purpose to enumerate the principal heads. (1.) The principle of regulating the contributions of the states into the common treasury by quotas, apportioned according {102} to the value of lands, which (as has been already suggested) was objected to, as unjust, unequal, and inconvenient in its operation. (2.) That want of a mutual guaranty of the state governments, so as to protect them against domestic insurrections, and usurpations destructive of their liberty. (3.) The want of a direct power to raise armies, which was objected to, as unfriendly to vigour and promptitude of action, as well as to economy and a just distribution of the public burthens. (4.) The right of equal suffrage among all the states, so that the least in point of wealth, population, and means stood equal in the scale of representation with those, which were the largest. From this circumstance it might, nay it must happen, that a majority of the states, constituting a third only of the people of America, could control the rights and interests of the other two thirds. Nay, it was constitutionally, not only possible, but true in fact, that even the votes of nine states might not comprehend a majority of the people in the Union. The minority, therefore, possessed a negative upon the majority. (5.) The organization of the whole powers of the general government in a single assembly, without any separate or distinct distribution of the executive, judicial, and legislative functions. It was objected, that either the whole superstructure would thus fall, from its own intrinsic feebleness; or, engrossing all the attributes of sovereignty, entail upon the country a most execrable form of government in the shape of an irresponsible aristocracy. (6.) The want of an *exclusive* power in the general government to issue paper money; and thus to prevent the inundation of the country with a base currency, calculated to destroy public faith, as well as private morals. (7.) The too frequent rotation required by {103} the confederation in the office of members of congress, by which the advantages, resulting from long experience and knowledge in the public affairs, were lost to the public councils. (8.) The want of judiciary power co-extensive with the powers of the general government.

§ 129. The last defect, which seems worthy of enumeration, is, that the confederation never had a ratification of the PEOPLE. Upon this objection, it will be sufficient to quote a single passage from the Federalist, as it affords a very striking commentary upon some extraordinary doctrines recently promulgated. "Resting on no better foundation than the consent of the state legislatures, it [the confederation] has been exposed to frequent and intricate questions concerning the validity of its powers; and has, in some instances, given birth to the enormous doctrine of a right of legislative repeal. Owing its ratification to a law of a state, it has been contended, that the same authority might repeal the law, by which it was ratified. However gross a heresy it may be to maintain, that a party to a compact has a right to revoke that compact, the doctrine itself has had respectable advocates. The possibility of a question of this nature proves the necessity of laying the foundations of our national government deeper, than in the mere sanction of delegated authority. The fabric of American empire ought to rest on the solid basis of the CONSENT OF THE PEOPLE. The streams of national power ought to flow immediately from that pure, original fountain of all legitimate authority."

§ 130. Whatever may be thought as to some of these enumerated defects, whether they were radical deficiencies or not, there cannot be a doubt, that others of {104} them went to the very marrow and essence of government. There had been, and in fact then were, different parties in the several states, entertaining opinions hostile, or friendly to the existence of a general government. The former would naturally cling to the state governments with a close and unabated zeal, and deem the least possible delegation of power to the Union sufficient, (if any were to be permitted,) with which it could creep on in a semi-animated state. The latter would as naturally desire, that the powers of the general government should have a real, and not merely a suspended vitality; that it should act, and move, and guide, and not merely totter under its own weight, or sink into a drowsy decrepitude, powerless and palsied. But each party must have felt, that the confederation had at last totally failed, as an effectual instrument of government; that its glory was departed, and its days of labour done; that it stood the shadow of a mighty name; that it was seen only, as a decayed monument of the past, incapable of any enduring record; that the steps of its decline were numbered and finished; and that it must soon be gathered to the perishable fragments of other ages.

BOOK III.

THE CONSTITUTION OF THE UNITED STATES.

CHAPTER I.

ORIGIN AND ADOPTION OF THE CONSTITUTION.

§ 131. IN this state of things, commissioners were appointed by the legislatures of Virginia and Maryland early in 1785, to form a compact relative to the navigation of the rivers Potomac and Pocomoke, and the Chesapeake Bay. The commissioners having met in March, in that year, felt the want of more enlarged powers, and particularly of powers to provide for a local naval force, and a tariff of duties upon imports. Upon receiving their recommendation, the legislature of Virginia passed a resolution for laying the subject of a tariff before all the states composing the Union. Soon afterwards, in January, 1786, the legislature adopted another resolution, appointing commissioners, "who were to meet such, as might be appointed by the other states in the Union, at a time and place to be agreed on, to take into consideration the trade of the United States; to examine the relative situation and trade of the states; to consider how far a uniform system in their commercial relations may be necessary to their {106} common interest, and their permanent harmony; and to report to the several states such an act, relative to this great object, as, when unanimously ratified by them, will enable the United States in congress assembled to provide for the same."

§ 132. These resolutions were communicated to the states, and a convention of commissioners from five states only, viz. New-York, New-Jersey, Pennsylvania, Delaware, and Virginia, met at Annapolis, in September, 1786. After discussing the subject, they deemed more ample powers necessary, and as well from this consideration, as because a small number only of the states was represented, they agreed to come to no decision, but to frame a report to be laid before the several states, as well as before congress. In this report they recommended the appointment of commissioners from all the states, "to meet at Philadelphia, on the second Monday of May, then next, to take into consideration the situation of the United States; to devise such further provisions, as shall appear to them necessary, to render the constitution of the federal government adequate to the exigencies of the Union; and to report such an act for that purpose to the United States in congress assembled, as when agreed to by them, and afterwards confirmed by the legislature of every state, will effectually provide for the same."

§ 133. On receiving this report, the legislature of Virginia passed an act for the appointment of delegates to meet such, as might be appointed by other states, at Philadelphia. The report was also received in congress. But no step was taken, until the legislature of New-York instructed its delegation in congress to move a resolution, recommending to the several states to appoint deputies to meet in convention for the purpose {107} of revising and proposing amendments to the federal constitution. On the 21st of February, 1787, a resolution was accordingly moved and carried in congress, recommending a convention to meet in Philadelphia, on the second Monday of May ensuing, "for the purpose of revising the articles of confederation, and reporting to congress, and the several legislatures, such alterations and provisions therein, as shall, when agreed to in congress, and confirmed by the states, render the federal constitution adequate to the exigencies of government, and the preservation of the Union." The alarming insurrection then existing in Massachusetts, without doubt, had no small share in producing this result. The report of congress, on that subject, at once demonstrates their fears, and their political weakness.

§ 184. At the time and place appointed, the representatives of twelve states assembled. Rhode-Island alone declined to appoint any on this momentous occasion. After very protracted deliberations, the convention finally adopted the plan of the present constitution, on the 17th of September, 1787; and by a contemporaneous resolution, directed it to be "laid before the United States in congress assembled," and declared their opinion, "that it should afterwards be submitted to a convention of delegates chosen in each state by the *people* thereof, under a recommendation of its legislature, for their *assent* and *ratification;*" and that each convention, assenting to and ratifying the same, should give notice thereof to congress. The convention by a further resolution declared their opinion, that as soon as nine states had ratified the constitution, congress should fix a day, on which electors should be appointed by the states, which should have ratified the same, {108} and a day, on which the electors should assemble and vote for the president, and the time and place of commencing proceedings under the constitution; and that after such publication, the electors should be appointed, and the senators and representatives elected. The same resolution contained further recommendations for the purpose of carrying the constitution into effect.

§ 135. Congress, having received the report of the convention, on the 28th of September, 1787, unanimously resolved, "that the said report, with the resolutions and letter accompanying the same, be transmitted to the several legislatures in order to be submitted to a *convention of delegates chosen in each state by the people thereof*, in conformity to the resolves of the convention, made and provided in that case."

§ 136. Conventions in the various states, which had been represented in the general convention, were accordingly called by their respective legislatures; and the constitution having been ratified by eleven out of the twelve states, congress, on the 13th of September, 1788, passed a resolution appointing the first Wednesday in January following, for the choice of electors of president; the first Wednesday of February following, for the assembling of the electors to vote for a president; and the first Wednesday of March following, at the then seat of congress [New-York] the time and place for commencing proceedings under the constitution. Electors were accordingly appointed in the several states, who met and gave their votes for a president; and the other elections for senators and representatives having been duly made, on Wednesday, the 4th of March, 1789, congress assembled under the new constitution, and commenced proceedings under it. A {109} quorum of both houses, however, did not assemble until the 6th of April, when the votes for president being counted, it was found that George Washington was unanimously elected president, and John Adams was elected vice-president. On the 30th of April, president Washington was sworn into office, and the government then went into full operation in all its departments.

§ 137. North-Carolina had not, as yet, ratified the constitution. The first convention called in that state, in August, 1788, refused to ratify it without some previous amendments, and a declaration of rights. In a second convention, however, called in November, 1789, this state adopted the constitution. The state of Rhode-Island had declined to call a convention; but finally, by a convention held in May, 1790, its assent was obtained; and thus all the thirteen original states became parties to the new government.

§ 138. Thus was achieved another, and still more glorious triumph in the cause of national liberty, than even that, which separated us from the mother country. By it we fondly trust, that our republican institutions will grow up, and be nurtured into more mature strength and vigour; our independence be secured against foreign usurpation and aggression; our domestic blessings be widely diffused, and generally felt; and our union, as a people, be perpetuated, as our own truest glory and support, and as a proud example of a wise and beneficent government, entitled to the respect, if not to the admiration of mankind.

CHAPTER II.

OBJECTIONS TO THE CONSTITUTION.

{110}

§ 139. LET it not, however, be supposed, that a constitution, which is now looked upon with such general favour and affection by the people, had no difficulties to encounter at its birth. The history of those times is full of melancholy instruction on this subject, at once to admonish us of past dangers, and to awaken us to a lively sense of the necessity of future vigilance. The constitution was adopted unanimously by Georgia, New-Jersey, and Delaware. It was supported by large majorities in Pennsylvania, Connecticut, Maryland, and South-Carolina. It was carried in the other states by small majorities, and especially in Massachusetts, New-York, and Virginia, by little more than a preponderating vote.

§ 140. Some of the objections were to the supposed defects and omissions in the instrument; others were to the nature and extent of the powers conferred by it; and others again to the fundamental plan or scheme of its organization.

(1.) It was objected in the first place, that the scheme of government was radically wrong, because it was not a confederation of the states; but a government over individuals. It was said, that the federal form, which regards the Union, as a confederation of sovereign states, ought to have been preserved; instead of which the convention had framed a national government, which regards the Union, as a consolidation of states. This objection was far from being universal; {111} for many admitted, that there ought to be a government over individuals to a certain extent, but by no means to the extent proposed. It is obvious, that this objection, pushed to its full extent, went to the old question of the confederation; and was but a re-argument of the point, whether there should exist a national government adequate to the protection and support of the Union. In its mitigated form it was a mere question, as to the extent of powers to be confided to the general government, and was to be classed accordingly. It was urged, however, with no inconsiderable force and emphasis; and its supporters predicted with confidence, that a government so organized would soon become corrupt and tyrannical, "and absorb the legislative, executive, and judicial powers of the several states, and produce from their ruins one consolidated government, which, from the nature of things, would be an iron-handed despotism."

§ 141. But the friends of the constitution met the objection by asserting the indispensable necessity of a form of government, like that proposed, and demonstrating the utter imbecility of a mere confederation, without powers acting directly upon individuals. They considered, that the constitution was partly federal, and partly national in its character, and distribution of powers. In its origin and establishment it was federal. In some of its relations it was federal; in others, national. In the senate it was federal; in the house of representatives it was national;

in the executive it was of a compound character; in the operation of its powers it was national; in the extent of its powers, federal. It acted on individuals, and not on states merely. But its powers were limited, and left a large mass of sovereignty in the states. In making amendments, {112} it was also of a compound character, requiring the concurrence of more than a majority, and less than the whole of the states. So, that on the whole their conclusion was, that "the constitution is, in strictness, neither a national nor a federal constitution, but a composition of both. In its foundation it is federal, not national; in the sources, from which the ordinary powers of the government are drawn, it is partly federal and partly national; in the operation of these powers it is national, not federal; in the extent of them again it is federal, not national; and, finally, in the authoritative mode of introducing amendments it is neither wholly federal, nor wholly national."

§ 142. If the original structure of the government was, as has been shown, a fertile source of opposition, another objection of a more wide and imposing nature was drawn from the nature and extent of its powers. This, indeed, like the former, gave rise to most animated discussions, in which reason was employed to demonstrate the mischiefs of the system, and imagination to portray them in all the exaggerations, which fear and prophesy could invent. Looking back, indeed, to that period with the calmness, with which we naturally review events and occurrences, which are now felt only as matters of history, one is surprised at the futility of some of the objections, the absurdity of others, and the overwrought colouring of almost all, which were urged on this head against the constitution. That some of them had a just foundation, need not be denied or concealed; for the system was human, and the result of compromise and conciliation, in which something of the correctness of theory was yielded to the interests or prejudices of particular states, and something of inequality of benefit borne for the common good. {113}

§ 143. The objections from different quarters were not only of different degrees and magnitude, but often of totally opposite natures. With some persons the mass of the powers was a formidable objection; with others, the distribution of those powers. With some the equality of vote in the senate was exceptionable; with others the inequality of representation in the house. With some the power of regulating the times and places of elections was fatal; with others the power of regulating commerce by a bare majority. With some the power of *direct* taxation was an intolerable grievance; with others the power of *indirect* taxation by duties on imports. With some the restraint of the state legislatures from laying duties upon exports, and passing *ex post facto* laws, was incorrect; with others the lodging of the executive power in a single magistrate. With some the term of office of the senators and representatives was too long; with others the term of office of the president was obnoxious to a like censure, as well as his re-eligibility. With some the intermixture of the legislative, executive, and judicial functions in the senate was a mischievous departure from all ideas of regular government; with others the non-participation of the house of representatives in the same functions was the alarming evil. With some the powers of the president were alarming and dangerous to liberty; with others the participation of the senate in some of those powers. With some the powers of the judiciary were far too extensive; with others the power to make treaties even with the consent of two thirds of the senate. With some the power to keep up a standing army was a sure introduction to despotism; with others the power over the militia. With some the paramount authority of the constitution, treaties, and laws of the {114} United States was a dangerous feature; with others the small number composing the senate and the house of representatives was an alarming and corrupting evil.

§ 144. Another class of objections urged against the constitution was founded upon its deficiencies and omissions. It cannot be denied, that some of the objections on this head were well taken, and that there was a fitness in incorporating some provision on the subject into the fundamental articles of a free government. There were others again, which might fairly enough be left to the legislative discretion, and to the natural influences of the popular voice in a republican form of government. There were others again so doubtful, both in principle and policy, that they might properly be excluded from any system aiming at permanence in its securities as well as in its foundations.

§ 145. Among the defects which were enumerated, none attracted more attention, or were urged with more zeal, than the want of a distinct bill of rights, which should recognise the fundamental principles of a free republican government, and the right of the people to the enjoyment of life, liberty, property, and the pursuit of happiness.

§ 146. Besides these, there were other defects relied on, such as the want of a suitable provision for a rotation in office, to prevent persons enjoying them for life; the want of an executive council for the president; the want of a provision limiting the duration of standing armies; the want of a clause securing to the people the enjoyment of the common law; the want of security for proper elections of public officers; the want of a prohibition of members of congress holding any public offices, and of judges holding any other offices; and {115} finally the want of drawing a clear and direct line between the powers to be exercised by congress and by the states.

§ 147. Many of these objections found their way into the amendments, which, simultaneously with the ratification, were adopted in many of the state conventions. With the view of carrying into effect the popular will, and also of disarming the opponents of the constitution of all reasonable grounds of complaint, congress, at its very first session, took into consideration the amendments so proposed; and by a succession of supplementary articles provided, in substance, a bill of rights, and secured by constitutional declarations most of the other important objects thus suggested. These articles (in all, twelve) were submitted by congress to the states for their ratification; and ten of them were finally ratified by the requisite number of states; and thus became incorporated into the constitution. It is a curious fact, however, that although the necessity of these amendments had been urged by the enemies of the constitution, and denied by its friends, they encountered scarcely any other opposition in the state legislatures, than what was given by the very party, which had raised the objections. The friends of the constitution generally supported them upon the ground of a large public policy, to quiet jealousies, and to disarm resentments.

CHAPTER III.

NATURE OF THE CONSTITUTION — WHETHER A COMPACT.

{116}

§ 148. HAVING thus sketched out a general history of the origin and adoption of the constitution of the United States, and a summary of the principal objections and difficulties, which it had to encounter, we are at length arrived at the point, at which it may be proper to enter upon the consideration of the actual structure, organization, and powers, which belong to it.

§ 149. Before doing this, however, it seems necessary, in the first place, to bestow some attention upon several points, which have attracted a good deal of discussion, and which are preliminary in their own nature; and in the next place to consider, what are the true rules of interpretation belonging to the instrument.

§ 150. In the first place, what is the true nature and import of the instrument? Is it a treaty, a convention, a league, a contract, or a compact? Who are the parties to it? By whom was it made? By whom was it ratified? What are its obligations? By whom, and in what manner may it be dissolved? Who are to determine its validity and construction? Who are to decide upon the supposed infractions and violations of it? These are questions often asked, and often discussed, not merely for the purpose of theoretical speculation; but as matters of practical importance, and of earnest and even of vehement debate. The answers given to them by statesmen and jurists are {117} often contradictory, and irreconcilable with each other; and the consequences, deduced from the views taken of some of them, go very deep into the foundations of the government itself, and expose it, if not to utter destruction, at least to evils, which threaten its existence, and disturb the just operation of its powers.

§ 151. In what light, then, is the constitution of the United States to be regarded? Is it a mere compact, treaty, or confederation of the states composing the Union, or of the people thereof, whereby each of the several states, and the people thereof, have respectively bound themselves to each other? Or is it a form of government, which, having been ratified by a majority of the people in all the states, is obligatory upon them, as the prescribed rule of conduct of the sovereign power, to the extent of its provisions?

§ 152. Let us consider, in the first place, whether it is to be deemed a compact. By this, we do not mean an act of solemn assent by the people to it, as a form of government, (of which there is no room for doubt;) but a contract imposing mutual obligations, and contemplating the permanent subsistence of parties having an independent right to construe, control, and judge of its obligations. If in this latter sense it is to be deemed a compact, it must be, either because it contains on its face stipulations to that effect, or because it is necessarily implied from the nature and objects of a frame of government.

§ 153. There is nowhere found upon the face of the constitution any clause, intimating it to be a compact, or in anywise providing for its interpretation, as such. On the contrary, the preamble emphatically speaks of it, as a solemn ordinance and establishment of government. {118} The language is, "We, the people of the United States, do *ordain* and *establish* this *constitution* for the United States of America." *The people* do *ordain* and *establish*, not contract and stipulate with each other. The people of the *United States*, not the distinct people of a *particular state* with the people of the other states. The people ordain and establish a "*constitution*," not a "*confederation*." The distinction between a constitution and a confederation is well known, and understood. The latter, or at least a pure confederation, is a mere treaty or league between independent states, and binds no longer, than during the good pleasure of each. It rests forever in articles of compact, where each is, or may be the supreme judge of its own rights and duties. The former is a permanent form of government, where the powers, once given, are irrevocable, and cannot be resumed or withdrawn at pleasure. Whether formed by a single people, or by different societies of people, in their political capacity, a constitution, though originating in consent, becomes, when ratified, obligatory, as a fundamental ordinance or law. The constitution of a confederated republic, that is, of a national republic, formed of several states, is, or at least may be, not less an irrevocable form of government, than the constitution of a state formed and ratified by the aggregate of the several counties of the state.

§ 154. If it had been the design of the framers of the constitution or of the people, who ratified it, to consider it a mere confederation, resting on treaty stipulations, it is difficult to conceive, that the appropriate terms should not have been found in it. The United States were no strangers to compacts of this nature. They had subsisted to a limited extent before the revolution. The articles of confederation, though in some few respects {119} national, were mainly of a pure federative character, and were treated as stipulations between states, for many purposes independent and sovereign. And yet, (as has been already seen,) it was deemed a political heresy to maintain, that under it any state had a right to withdraw from it at pleasure, and repeal its operation; and that a party to the compact had a right to revoke that compact.

§ 155. But that, which would seem conclusive on the subject, (as has been already stated,) is the very language of the constitution itself, declaring it to be a supreme fundamental law, and to be of judicial obligation, and recognition in the administration of justice. "This constitution," says the sixth article, "and the laws of the United States, which shall be made in pursuance thereof, and all treaties made, or which shall be made under the authority of the United States, *shall be the supreme law of the land*; and the *judges* in every state shall be bound thereby, *any thing in the constitution or laws* of any state to the contrary notwithstanding." If it is the supreme law, how can the people of any state, either by any form of its own constitution, or laws, or other proceedings, repeal, or abrogate, or suspend it?

§ 156. But if the language of the constitution were less explicit and irresistible, no other inference could be correctly deduced from a view of the nature and objects of the instrument. The design is to establish a form of government. This, of itself, imports legal obligation, permanence, and uncontrollability by any, but the authorities authorized to alter, or abolish it. The object was to secure the blessings of liberty to the people, and to their posterity. The avowed intention was to supercede the old confederation, and substitute {120} in its place a new form of government. We have seen, that the inefficiency of the old confederation forced the states to surrender the league then existing, and to establish a national constitution. The convention also, which framed the constitution, declared this in the letter accompanying it. "It is obviously impracticable in the federal government of these states," says that letter, "to secure all rights of independent sovereignty to each, and yet provide for the interest and safety of all. Individuals entering into society must give up a share of liberty to preserve the rest." "In all our deliberations on this subject, we kept steadily in our view that, which appeared to us the greatest interest of every true American, the *consolidation of our Union*, in which is involved our prosperity, felicity, safety, perhaps our national existence." Could this be attained consistently with the notion of an existing treaty or confederacy, which each at its pleasure was at liberty to dissolve?

§ 157. It is also historically known, that one of the objections taken by the opponents of the constitution was, "that it is not a *confederation* of the states, but a *government* of individuals." It was, nevertheless, in the solemn instruments of ratification by the people of the several states, assented to, as a constitution. And although many declarations of rights, many propositions of amendments, and many protestations of reserved powers, are to be found accompanying the ratifications of the various conventions, sufficiently evincive of the extreme caution and jealousy of those bodies, and of the people at large, it is remarkable, that there is nowhere to be found the slightest allusion to the instrument, as a confederation or compact of states in their sovereign capacity, and no reservation of any right, on {121} the part of any state, to dissolve its connexion, or to abrogate its assent, or to suspend the operations of the constitution, as to itself.

§ 158. So that there is very strong negative testimony against the notion of its being a compact or confederation, founded upon the known history of the times, and the acts of ratification, as well as upon the antecedent articles of confederation. The latter purported on their face to be a mere confederacy. The language of the third article was, "The said states hereby severally enter into a firm *league* of friendship with each other for their common defence, &c. binding themselves to assist each other." And the ratification was by delegates of the state legislatures, who solemnly plighted and engaged the *faith* of their respective constituents, that they should abide by the determination of the United States in congress assembled on all questions, which by the said confederation, are submitted to them; and that the articles thereof should be inviolably observed by the states they respectively represented.

§ 159. It is not unworthy of observation, that in the debates of the various conventions called to examine and ratify the constitution, this subject did not pass without discussion. The opponents, on many occasions, pressed the objection, that it was a consolidated government, and contrasted it with the confederation. None of its advocates pretended to deny, that its design was to establish a national government, as contra-distinguished from a mere league or treaty, however they might oppose the suggestion, that it was a consolidation of the states.

§ 160. The cardinal conclusion, for which this doctrine of a compact has been, with so much ingenuity {122} and ability, forced into the language of the constitution, (for the latter no where alludes to it,) is avowedly to establish, that in construing the constitution, there is no common umpire; but that each state, nay each department of the government of each state, is the supreme judge for itself, of the powers, and rights, and duties, arising under that instrument.

§ 161. But if it were admitted, that the constitution is a compact, the conclusion, that there is no common arbiter, would neither be a necessary, nor a natural conclusion from that fact standing alone. To decide upon the point, it would still behove us to examine the very terms of the constitution, and the delegation of powers under it. It would be perfectly competent even for confederated states to agree upon, and delegate authority to construe the compact to a common arbiter. The people of the United States had an unquestionable right to confide this power to the government of the United States, or to any department thereof, if they chose so to do. The question is, whether they have done it. If they have, it becomes obligatory and binding upon all the states.

§ 162. It is not, then, by artificial reasoning founded upon theory, but upon a careful survey of the language of the constitution itself, that we are to interpret its powers, and its obligations. We are to treat it, as it purports on its face to be, as a CONSTITUTION of government; and we are to reject all other appellations, and definitions of it, such, as that it is a compact, especially as they may mislead us into false constructions and glosses, and can have no tendency to instruct us in its real objects.

CHAPTER IV.

WHO IS THE FINAL JUDGE OR INTERPRETER IN CONSTITUTIONAL CONTROVERSIES.

§ 163. THE consideration of the question, whether the constitution has made provision for any common arbiter to construe its powers and obligations, would properly find a place in the analysis of the different clauses of that instrument. But, as it is immediately connected with the subject before us, it seems expedient in this place to give it a deliberate attention.

§ 164. In order to clear the question of all minor points, which might embarrass us in the discussion, it is necessary to suggest a few preliminary remarks. The constitution, contemplating the grant of limited powers, and distributing them among various functionaries, and the state governments, and their functionaries, being also clothed with limited powers, subordinate to those granted to the general government, whenever any question arises, as to the exercise of any power by any of these functionaries under the state, or federal government, it is of necessity, that such functionaries must, in the first instance, decide upon the constitutionality of the exercise of such power. It may arise in the course of the discharge of the functions of any one, or of all, of the great departments of government, the executive, the legislative, and the judicial. The officers of each of these departments are equally bound by their oaths of office to support the constitution of the United States, and are therefore conscientiously bound to abstain from all acts, which are inconsistent with it. Whenever, therefore, they are required to act in a case, {124} not hitherto settled by any proper authority, these functionaries must, in the first instance, decide, each for himself, whether, consistently with the constitution, the act can be done. If, for instance, the president is required to do any act, he is not only authorized, but required, to decide for himself, whether, consistently with his constitutional duties, he can do the act. So, if a proposition be before congress, every member of the legislative body is bound to examine, and decide for himself, whether the bill or resolution is within the constitutional reach of the legislative powers confided to congress. And in many cases the decisions of the executive and legislative departments, thus made, become final and conclusive, being from their very nature and character incapable of revision. Thus, in measures exclusively of a political, legislative, or executive character, it is plain, that as the supreme authority, as to these questions, belongs to the legislative and executive departments, they cannot be reexamined elsewhere. Thus, congress having the power to declare war, to levy taxes, to appropriate money, to regulate intercourse and commerce with foreign nations, their mode of executing these powers can never become the subject of re-examination in any other tribunal. So the power to make treaties being confided to the president and senate, when a treaty is properly ratified, it becomes the law of the land, and no other tribunal can gainsay its stipulations. Yet cases may readily be imagined, in which a tax may be laid, or a treaty made, upon motives and grounds wholly beside the intention of the constitution. The remedy, however, in such cases is solely by an appeal to the people at the elections; or by the salutary power of amendment, provided by the constitution itself. {125}

§ 165. But, where the question is of a different nature, and capable of judicial inquiry and decision, there it admits of a very different consideration. The decision then made, whether in favour, or against the constitutionality of the act, by the state, or by the national authority, by the legislature, or by the executive, being capable, in its own nature, of being brought to the test of the constitution, is subject to judicial revision. It is in such cases, as we conceive, that there is a final and common arbiter provided by the constitution itself, to whose decisions all others are subordinate; and that arbiter is the supreme judicial authority of the courts of the Union.

§ 166. Let us examine the grounds, on which this doctrine is maintained. The constitution declares, (Art. 6,) that "*This constitution*, and the *laws* of the United States, which shall be made in pursuance thereof, and all *treaties*, &c. shall be the *supreme law* of the land." It also declares, (Art. 3,) that "The judicial power shall extend to all cases in law and equity, arising under this constitution, the laws of the United States and treaties made, and which shall be made under their authority." It further declares, (Art. 3,) that the judicial power of the United States "shall be vested in one Supreme Court, and in such inferior courts, as the congress may, from time to time, ordain and establish." Here, then, we have express, and determinate provisions upon the very subject. Nothing is imperfect, and nothing is left to implication. The constitution is the supreme law; the judicial power extends to all cases arising in law and equity under it; and the courts of the United States are, and, in the last resort, the Supreme Court of the United States is, to be vested with this judicial power. No man can {126} doubt or deny, that the power to construe the constitution is a judicial power. The power to construe a treaty is clearly so, when the case arises in judgment in a controversy between individuals. The like principle must apply, where the meaning of the constitution arises in a judicial controversy; for it is an appropriate function of the judiciary to construe laws. If, then, a case under the constitution does arise, if it is capable of judicial examination and decision, we see, that the very tribunal is appointed to make the decision. The only point left open for controversy is, whether such decision, when made, is conclusive, and binding upon the states, and the people of the states. The reasons, why it should be so deemed, will now be submitted.

§ 167. In the first place, the judicial power of the United States rightfully extending to all such cases, its judgment becomes *ipso facto* conclusive between the parties before it, in respect to the points decided, unless some mode be pointed out by the constitution, in which that judgment may be revised. No such mode is pointed out. Congress is vested with ample authority to provide for the exercise by the Supreme Court of appellate jurisdiction from the decisions of all inferior tribunals, whether state or national, in cases within the purview of the judicial power of the United States; but no mode is provided, by which any superior tribunal can re-examine, what the Supreme Court has itself decided. Ours is emphatically a government of laws, and not of men; and judicial decisions of the, highest tribunal, by the known course of the common law, are considered, as establishing the true construction of the laws, which are brought into controversy before it. The case is not alone considered {127} as decided and settled; but the principles of the decision are held, as precedents and authority, to bind future cases of the same nature. This is the constant practice under our whole system of jurisprudence. Our ancestors brought it with them, when they first emigrated to this country; and it is, and always has been considered, as the great security of our rights, our liberties, and our property. It is on this account, that our law is justly deemed certain, and founded in permanent principles, and not dependent upon the caprice, or will of particular judges. A more alarming doctrine could not be promulgated by any American court, than that it was at liberty to disregard all former rules and decisions, and to decide for itself, without reference to the settled course of antecedent principles.

§ 168. This known course of proceeding, this settled habit of thinking, this conclusive effect of judicial adjudications, was in the full view of the framers of the constitution. It was recognized, and enforced in every state in the Union; and a departure from it would have been justly deemed an approach to tyranny and arbitrary power, to the exercise of mere discretion, and to the abandonment of all the just checks upon judicial authority. It would seem impossible, then, to presume, if the people intended to introduce a new rule in respect to the decisions of the Supreme Court, and to limit the nature and operations of their judgments in a manner wholly unknown to the common law, and to our existing jurisprudence, that some indication of that intention should not be apparent on the face of the constitution. We find, (Art. 4.) that the constitution has declared, that full faith and credit shall be given in each state to the judicial proceedings of every other {128} state. But no like provision has been made in respect to the judgments of the courts of the United States, because they were plainly supposed to be of paramount and absolute obligation throughout all the states. If the judgments of the Supreme Court upon constitutional questions are conclusive and binding upon the citizens at large, must they not be equally conclusive upon the states? If the states are parties to that instrument, are not the people of the states also parties?

§ 169. In the next place, as the judicial power extends to all cases arising under the constitution, and that constitution is declared to be the supreme law, that supremacy would naturally be construed to extend, not only over the citizens, but over the states. This, however, is not left to implication, for it is declared to be the supreme law of the land, "anything in the constitution or laws of any state to the contrary notwithstanding." The people of any state cannot, then, by any alteration of their state constitution, destroy, or impair that supremacy. How, then, can they do it in any other less direct manner? Now, it is the proper function of the judicial department to interpret laws, and by the very terms of the constitution to interpret the supreme law. Its interpretation, then, becomes obligatory and conclusive upon all the departments of the federal government, and upon the whole people, so far as their rights and duties are derived from, or affected by that constitution. If then all the departments of the national government may rightfully exercise all the powers, which the judicial department has, by its interpretation, declared to be granted by the constitution; and are prohibited from exercising those, which are thus declared not to be granted by it, would it not be a solecism to hold, notwithstanding, that such {129} rightful exercise should not be deemed the supreme law of the land, and such prohibited powers should still be deemed granted? It would seem repugnant to the first notions of justice, that in respect to the same instrument of government, different powers, and duties, and obligations should arise, and different rules should prevail, at the same time among the governed, from a right of interpreting the same words (manifestly used in one sense only) in different, nay, in opposite senses. If there ever was a case, in which uniformity of interpretation might well be deemed a necessary postulate, it would seem to be that of a fundamental law of a government. It might otherwise follow, that the same individual, as a magistrate, might be bound by one rule, and in his private capacity by another, at the very same moment.

§ 170. There would be neither wisdom nor policy in such a doctrine; and it would deliver over the constitution to interminable doubts, founded upon the fluctuating opinions and characters of those, who should, from time to time, be called to administer it. Such a constitution could, in no just sense, be deemed a law, much less a supreme or fundamental law. It would have none of the certainty or universality, which are the proper attributes of such a sovereign rule. It would entail upon us all the miserable servitude, which has been deprecated, as the result of vague and uncertain jurisprudence. *Misera est servitus, ubi jus est vagum aut incertum.* It would subject us to constant dissensions, and perhaps to civil broils, from the perpetually recurring conflicts upon constitutional questions. On the other hand, the worst, that could happen from a wrong decision of the judicial department, would be, that it might require the interposition of congress, or, {130} in the last resort, of the amendatory power of the states, to redress the grievance.

§ 171. We find the power to construe the constitution expressly confided to the judicial department, without any limitation or qualification, as to its conclusiveness. Who, then, is at liberty, by general implications, not from the terms of the instrument, but from mere theory, and assumed reservations of sovereign right, to insert such a limitation or qualification? We find, that to produce uniformity of interpretation, and to preserve the constitution, as a perpetual bond of union, a supreme arbiter or authority of construing is, if not absolutely indispensable, at least, of the highest possible practical utility and importance. Who, then, is at liberty to reason down the terms of the constitution, so as to exclude their natural force and operation?

§ 172. We find, that it is the known course of the judicial department of the several states to decide in the last resort upon all constitutional questions arising in judgment; and that this has always been maintained as a rightful exercise of authority, and conclusive upon the whole state. As such, it has been constantly approved by the people, and never withdrawn from the courts by any amendment of their constitutions, when the people have been called to revise them. We find, that the people of the several states have constantly relied upon this last judicial appeal, as the bulwark of their state rights and liberties; and that it is in perfect consonance with the whole structure of the jurisprudence of the common law. Under such circumstances, is it not most natural to presume, that the same rule was intended to be applied to the constitution of the United States? And when we {131} find, that the judicial department of the United States is actually entrusted with a like power, is it not an irresistible presumption, that it had the same object, and was to have the same universally conclusive effect? Even under the confederation, an instrument framed with infinitely more jealousy and deference for state rights, the judgment of the judicial department appointed to decide controversies between states was declared to be final and conclusive; and the appellate power in other cases was held to overrule all state decisions and state legislation.

§ 173. If, then, reasoning from the terms of the constitution, and the known principles of our jurisprudence, the appropriate conclusion is, that the judicial department of the United States is, in the last resort, the final expositor of the constitution, as to all questions of a judicial nature; let us see, in the next place, how far this reasoning acquires confirmation from the past history of the constitution, and the practice under it.

§ 174. That this view of the constitution was taken by its framers and friends, and was submitted to the people before its adoption, is positively certain. The same doctrine was constantly avowed in the state conventions, called to ratify the constitution. With some persons it formed a strong objection to the constitution; with others it was deemed vital to its existence and value. So, that it is indisputable, that the constitution was adopted under a full knowledge of this exposition of the grant of power to the judicial department.

§ 175. This is not all. The constitution has now been in full operation more than forty years; and during this period the Supreme Court has constantly exercised this power of final interpretation in relation, not {132} only to the constitution, and laws of the Union, but in relation to state acts and state constitutions and laws, so far as they have affected the constitution, and laws, and treaties of the United States. Their decisions upon these grave questions have never been repudiated, or impaired by congress. No state has ever deliberately, or forcibly resisted the execution of the judgments founded upon them; and the highest state tribunals have, with scarcely a single exception, acquiesced in, and, in most instances, assisted in executing them. During the same period, eleven states have been admitted into the Union, under a full persuasion, that the same power would be exerted over them. Many of the states have, at different times within the same period, been called upon to consider, and examine the grounds, on which the doctrine has been maintained, at the solicitation of other states, which felt, that it operated injuriously, or might operate injuriously upon their interests. A great majority of the states, which have been thus called upon in their legislative capacities to express opinions, have maintained the correctness of the doctrine, and the beneficial effects of the power, as a bond of union, in terms of the most unequivocal nature. Whenever any amendment has been proposed to change the tribunal, and substitute another common umpire or interpreter, it has rarely received the concurrence of more than two or three states, and has been uniformly rejected by a great majority, either silently, or by an express dissent. And instances have occurred, in which the legislature of the same state has, at different times, avowed opposite opinions, approving at one time, what it had denied, or at least questioned at another. So, that it may be asserted with entire confidence, that for forty years {133} three fourths of all the states composing the Union have expressly assented to, or silently approved, this construction of the constitution, and have resisted every effort to restrict, or alter it.

§ 176. A weight of public opinion among the people for such a period, uniformly thrown into one scale so strongly, and so decisively, in the midst of all the extraordinary changes of parties, the events of peace and of war, and the trying conflicts of public policy and state interests, is perhaps unexampled in the history of all other free governments. It affords, as satisfactory a testimony in favor of the just and safe operation of the system, as can well be imagined; and, as a commentary upon the constitution itself, it is as absolutely conclusive, as any ever can be, and affords the only escape from the occurrence of civil conflicts, and the delivery over of the subject to interminable disputes.

§ 177. In this review of the power of the judicial department, upon a question of its supremacy in the interpretation of the constitution, it has not been thought necessary to rely on the deliberate judgments of that department in affirmance of it. But it may be proper to add, that the judicial department has not only constantly exercised this right of interpretation in the last resort; but its whole course of reasonings and operations has proceeded upon the ground, that, once made, the interpretation was conclusive, as well upon the states, as upon the people.

CHAPTER V.

RULES OF INTERPRETATION.

§ 178. IN our future commentaries upon the constitution we shall treat it, then, as it is denominated in the instrument itself, as a CONSTITUTION of government, ordained and established by the people of the United States for themselves and their posterity. They have declared it the supreme law of the land. They have made it a limited government. They have defined its authority. They have restrained it to the exercise of certain powers, and reserved all others to the states or to the people. It is a popular government. Those, who administer it, are responsible to the people. It is as popular, and just as much emanating from the people, as the state governments. It is created for one purpose; the state governments for another. It may be altered, and amended, and abolished at the will of the people. In short, it was made by the people, made for the people, and is responsible to the people.

§ 179. In this view of the matter, let us now proceed to consider the rules, by which it ought to be interpreted; for if these rules are correctly laid down, it will save us from many embarrassments in examining and defining its powers. Much of the difficulty, which has arisen in all the public discussions on this subject, has had its origin in the want of some uniform rules of interpretation, expressly or tacitly agreed on by the disputants. Very different doctrines on this point have been adopted by different commentators; and not unfrequently very different language held by the same parties at different periods. In short, the rules of interpretation {135} have often been shifted to suit the emergency; and the passions and prejudices of the day, or the favor and odium of a particular measure, have not unfrequently furnished a mode of argument, which would, on the one hand, leave the constitution crippled and inanimate, or, on the other hand, give it an extent and elasticity, subversive of all rational boundaries.

§ 180. Let us, then, endeavor to ascertain, what are the true rules of interpretation applicable to the constitution; so that we may have some fixed standard, by which to measure its powers, and limit its prohibitions, and guard its obligations, and enforce its securities of our rights and liberties.

§ 181. I. The first and fundamental rule in the interpretation of all instruments is, to construe them according to the sense of the terms, and the intention of the parties. Mr Justice Blackstone has remarked, that the intention of a law is to be gathered from the words, the context, the subject-matter, the effects and consequence, or the reason and spirit of the law. He goes on to justify the remark by stating, that words are generally to be understood in their usual and most known signification, not so much regarding the propriety of grammar, as their general and popular use; that if words happen to be dubious, their meaning may be established by the context, or by comparing them with other words and

85

sentences in the same instrument; that illustrations may be further derived from the subject-matter, with reference to which the expressions are used; that the effect and consequence of a particular construction is to be examined, because, if a literal meaning would involve a manifest absurdity, it ought not to be adopted; and that the reason and spirit of the law, or the causes, which led to its enactment, {136} are often the best exponents of the words, and limit their application.

§ 182. Where the words are plain and clear, and the sense distinct and perfect arising on them, there is generally no necessity to have recourse to other means of interpretation. It is only, when there is some ambiguity or doubt arising from other sources, that interpretation has its proper office. There may be obscurity, as to the meaning, from the doubtful character of the words used, from other clauses in the same instrument, or from an incongruity or repugnancy between the words, and the apparent intention derived from the whole structure of the instrument, or its avowed object. In all such cases interpretation becomes indispensable.

§ 183. II. In construing the constitution of the United States, we are, in the first instance, to consider, what are its nature and objects, its scope and design, as apparent from the structure of the instrument, viewed as a whole, and also viewed in its component parts. Where its words are plain, clear, and determinate, they require no interpretation; and it should, therefore, be admitted, if at all, with great caution, and only from necessity, either to escape some absurd consequence, or to guard against some fatal evil. Where the words admit of two senses, each of which is conformable to common usage, that sense is to be adopted, which, without departing from the literal import of the words, best harmonizes with the nature and objects, the scope and design of the instrument. Where the words are unambiguous, but the provision may cover more or less ground according to the intention, which is yet subject to conjecture; or where it may include in its general terms more or less, than might seem dictated by the general design, as that may be gathered {137} from other parts of the instrument, there is much more room for controversy; and the argument from inconvenience will probably have different influences upon different minds. Whenever such questions arise, they will probably be settled, each upon its own peculiar grounds; and whenever it is a question of power, it should be approached with infinite caution, and affirmed only upon the most persuasive reasons. In examining the constitution, the antecedent situation of the country, and its institutions, the existence and operations of the state governments, the powers and operations of the confederation, in short all the circumstances, which had a tendency to produce, or to obstruct its formation and ratification, deserve a careful attention. Much, also, may be gathered from contemporary history, and contemporary interpretation, to aid us in just conclusions.

§ 184. Contemporary construction is properly resorted to, to illustrate, and confirm the text, to explain a doubtful phrase, or to expound an obscure clause; and in proportion to the uniformity and universality of that construction, and the known ability and talents of those, by whom it was given, is the credit, to which it is entitled. It can never abrogate the text; it can never fritter away its obvious sense; it can never narrow down its limitations; it can never enlarge its natural boundaries.

§ 185. And, after all, the most unexceptionable source of collateral interpretation is from the practical expositions of the government itself in its various departments upon particular questions, discussed and settled upon their own single merits. These approach the nearest in their own nature to judicial expositions; and have the same general recommendation, that belongs {138} to the latter. They are decided upon solemn argument, *pro re natâ*, upon a doubt raised, upon a *lis mota*, upon a deep sense of their importance and difficulty, in the face of the nation, with a view to present action, in the midst of jealous interests, and by men capable of urging, or repelling the grounds of argument, from their exquisite genius, their comprehensive learning, or their deep meditation upon the absorbing topic. How light, compared with these means of instruction, are the private lucubrations of the closet, or the retired speculations of ingenious minds, intent on theory, or general views, and unused to encounter a practical difficulty at every step!

§ 186. But to return to the rules of interpretation, arising *ex directo* from the text of the constitution. And first the rules to be drawn from the nature of the instrument. (1.) It is to be construed, as a *frame*, or *fundamental law* of government, established by the PEOPLE of the United States, according to their own free pleasure and sovereign will. In this respect it is in no wise distinguishable from the constitutions of the state governments. Each of them is established by the people for their own purposes, and each is founded on their supreme authority. The powers, which are conferred, the restrictions, which are imposed, the authorities, which are exercised, the organization and distribution thereof, which are provided, are in each case for the same object, the common benefit of the governed, and not for the profit or dignity of the rulers.

§ 187. If this be the true view of the subject, the constitution of the United States is to receive as favorable a construction, as those of the states. Neither is to be construed alone; but each with a reference to {139} the other. Each belongs to the same system of government; each is limited in its powers; and within the scope of its powers each is supreme. Each, by the theory of our government, is essential to the existence and due preservation of the powers and obligations of the other. The destruction of either would be equally calamitous, since it would involve the ruin of that beautiful fabric of balanced government, which has been reared with so much care and wisdom, and in which the people have reposed their confidence, as the truest safeguard of their civil, religious, and political liberties. The exact limits of the powers, confided by the people to each, may not always be capable, from the inherent difficulty of the subject, of being defined, or ascertained in all cases with perfect certainty. But the lines are generally marked out with sufficient broadness and clearness; and in the progress of the developement of the peculiar functions of each, the part of true wisdom would seem to be, to leave in every practicable direction a wide, if not an unmeasured, distance between the actual exercise of the sovereignty of each. In every complicated machine slight causes may disturb the operations; and it is often more easy to detect the defects, than to apply a safe and adequate remedy.

§ 188. IV. From the foregoing considerations we deduce the conclusion, that as a frame or fundamental law of government, (2.) The constitution of the United States is to receive a reasonable interpretation of its language, and its powers, keeping in view the objects and purposes, for which those powers were conferred.

By a reasonable interpretation, we mean, that in case the words are susceptible of two different senses, the one strict, the other more enlarged, that should be adopted, which is most consonant with the {140} apparent objects and intent of the constitution; that which will give it efficacy and force, as a *government*, rather than that, which will impair its operations, and reduce it to a state of imbecility. Of course we do not mean, that the words for this purpose are to be strained beyond their common and natural sense; but keeping within that limit, the exposition is to have a fair and just latitude, so as on the one hand to avoid obvious mischief, and on the other hand to promote the public good.

§ 189. This consideration is of great importance in construing a frame of government; and *à fortiori* a frame of government, the free and voluntary institution of the people for their common benefit, security, and happiness. It is wholly unlike the case of a municipal charter, or a private grant, in respect both to its means and its ends. When a person makes a private grant of a particular thing, or of a license to do a thing, or of an easement for the exclusive benefit of the grantee, we naturally confine the terms, however general, to the objects clearly in the view of the parties. But even in such cases, doubtful words, within the scope of those objects, are construed most favorably for the grantee; because, though in derogation of the rights of the grantor, they are promotive of the general rights secured to the grantee. But, where the grant enures, solely and exclusively, for the benefit of the grantor himself, no one would deny the propriety of giving to the words of the grant a benign and liberal interpretation. In cases, however, of private grants, the objects generally are few; they are certain; they are limited; they neither require, nor look to a variety of means or changes, which are to control, or modify either the end, or the means. {141}

§ 190. But a constitution of government, founded by the people for themselves and their posterity, and for objects of the most momentous nature, for perpetual union, for the establishment of justice, for the general welfare, and for a perpetuation of the blessings of liberty, necessarily requires, that every interpretation of its powers should have a constant reference to these objects. No interpretation of the words, in which those powers are granted, can be a sound one, which narrows down their ordinary import, so as to defeat those objects. That would be to destroy the spirit, and to cramp the letter. It has been justly observed, by the Supreme Court, that "the constitution unavoidably deals in general language. It did not suit the purposes of the people, in framing this great charter of our liberties, to provide for minute specification of its powers, or to declare the means, by which those powers should be carried into execution. It was foreseen, that it would be a perilous, and difficult, if not an impracticable task. The instrument was not intended to provide merely for the exigencies of a few years; but was to endure through a long lapse of ages, the events of which were locked up in the inscrutable purposes of Providence. It could not be foreseen, what new changes and modifications of power might be indispensable to effectuate the general objects of the charter; and restrictions and specifications, which at the present might seem salutary, might in the end prove the overthrow of the system itself. Hence its powers are expressed in general terms, leaving the legislature, from time to time, to adopt its own means to effectuate legitimate objects, and to mould and model the exercise of its powers, as its own wisdom and the public interests should require." Language to the same effect will be found in other judgments of the same tribunal. {142}

§ 191. V. Where the power is granted in general terms, the power is to be construed, as co-extensive with the terms, unless some clear restriction upon it is deducible from the context. We do not mean to assert, that it is necessary, that such restriction should be expressly found in the context. It will be sufficient, if it arise by necessary implication. But it is not sufficient to show, that there was, or might have been, a sound or probable motive to restrict it. A restriction founded on conjecture is wholly inadmissible. The reason is obvious: the text was adopted by the people in its obvious, and general sense. We have no means of knowing, that any particular gloss, short of this sense, was either contemplated, or approved by the people; and such a gloss might, though satisfactory in one state, have been the very ground of objection in another. It might have formed a motive to reject it in one, and to adopt it in another. The sense of a part of the people has no title to be deemed the sense of the whole. Motives of state policy, or state interest, may properly have influence in the question of ratifying it; but the constitution itself must be expounded, as it stands; and not as that policy, or that interest may seem now to dictate. We are to construe, and not to frame the instrument.

§ 192. VI. A power, given in general terms, is not to be restricted to particular cases, merely because it may be susceptible of abuse, and, if abused, may lead to mischievous consequences. This argument is often used in public debate; and in its common aspect addresses itself so much to popular fears and prejudices, that it insensibly acquires a weight in the public mind, to which it is no wise entitled. The argument *ab inconvenienti is* sufficiently open to question, from, the {143} laxity of application, as well as of opinion, to which it leads. But the argument from a possible abuse of a power against its existence or use, is, in its nature, not only perilous, but, in respect to governments, would shake their very foundation. Every form of government unavoidably includes a grant of some discretionary powers. It would be wholly imbecile without them. It is impossible to foresee all the exigencies, which may arise in the progress of events, connected with the rights, duties, and operations of a government. If they could be foreseen, it would be impossible *ab ante* to provide for them. The means must be subject to perpetual modification, and change; they must be adapted to the existing manners, habits, and institutions of society, which are never stationary; to the pressure of dangers, or necessities; to the ends in view; to general and permanent operations, as well as to fugitive and extraordinary emergencies. In short, if the whole society is not to be revolutionized at every critical period, and remodeled in every generation, there must be left to those, who administer the government, a very large mass of discretionary powers, capable of greater or less actual expansion according to circumstances, and sufficiently flexible not to involve the nation in utter destruction from the rigid limitations imposed upon it by an improvident jealousy. Every power, however limited, as well as broad, is in its own nature susceptible of abuse. No constitution can provide perfect guards against it. Confidence must be reposed some where; and in free governments, the ordinary securities against abuse are found in the responsibility of rulers to the people, and in the just exercise of their elective franchise; and ultimately in the sovereign power of change belonging to them, in cases requiring extraordinary {146} remedies. Few cases are to be supposed, in which a power, however general, will be exerted for the permanent oppression of the people. And yet, cases may easily be put, in which a limitation upon such a power might be found in practice to work mischief; to incite foreign aggression; or encourage domestic disorder. The power of taxation, for instance, may be carried to a ruinous excess; and yet, a limitation upon that power might, in a given case, involve the destruction of the independence of the country.

§ 193. VII. On the other hand, a rule of equal importance is, not to enlarge the construction of a given power beyond the fair scope of its terms, merely because the restriction is inconvenient, impolitic, or even mischievous. If it be mischievous, the power of redressing the evil lies with the people by an exercise of the power of amendment. If they do not choose to apply the remedy, it may fairly be presumed, that the mischief is less than what would arise from a further extension of the power; or that it is the least of two evils. Nor should it ever be lost sight of, that the government of the United States is one of limited and enumerated powers; and that a departure from the true import and sense of its powers is, *pro tanto*, the establishment of a new constitution. It is doing for the people, what they have not chosen to do for themselves. It is usurping the functions of a legislator, and deserting those of an expounder of the law. Arguments drawn from impolicy or inconvenience ought here to be of no weight. The only sound principle is to declare, *ita lex scripta est*, to follow, and to obey. Nor, if a principle so just and conclusive could be overlooked, could there well be found a more unsafe guide in practice, than mere policy and {145} convenience. Men on such subjects complexionally differ from each other. The same men differ from themselves at different times. Temporary delusions, prejudices, excitements, and objects have irresistible influence in mere questions of policy, And the policy of one age may ill suit the wishes, or the policy of another. The constitution is not to be subject to such fluctuations. It is to have a fixed, uniform, permanent construction. It should be, so far at least as human infirmity will allow, not dependent upon the passions or parties of particular times, but the same yesterday, to-day, and for ever.

§ 194. VIII. No construction of a given power is to be allowed, which plainly defeats, or impairs its avowed objects. If, therefore, the words are fairly susceptible of two interpretations, according to their common sense and use, the one of which would defeat one, or all of the objects, for which it was obviously given, and the other of which would preserve and promote all, the former interpretation ought to be rejected, and the latter be held the true interpretation. This rule results from the dictates of mere common sense; for every instrument ought to be so construed, *ut magis valeat, quam pereat*. For instance, the constitution confers on congress the power to declare war. Now the word *declare* has several senses. It may mean to proclaim, or publish. But no person would imagine, that this was the whole sense, in which the word is used in this connexion. It should be interpreted in the sense, in which the phrase is used among nations, when applied to such a subject matter. A power to declare war is a power to make, and carry on war. It is not a mere power to make known an existing thing, but to give life and effect to the thing itself. The true doctrine {146} has been expressed by the Supreme Court: "If from the imperfection of human language there should be any serious doubts respecting the extent of any given power, the objects, for which it was given, especially when those objects are expressed in the instrument itself, should have great influence in the construction."

§ 195. IX. Where a power is remedial in its nature, there is much reason to contend, that it ought to be construed liberally. That was the doctrine of Mr Chief Justice Jay, in *Chisholm v. Georgia*; and it is generally adopted in the interpretation of laws. But this liberality of exposition is clearly inadmissible, if it extends beyond the just and ordinary sense of the terms.

§ 196. X. In the interpretation of a power, all the ordinary and appropriate means to execute it are to be deemed a part of the power itself. This results from the very nature and design of a constitution. In giving the power, it does not intend to limit it to any one mode of exercising it, exclusive of all others. It must be obvious, (as has been already suggested,) that the means of carrying into effect the objects of a power may, nay, must be varied, in order to adapt themselves to the exigencies of the nation at different times. A mode efficacious and useful in one age, or under one posture of circumstances, may be wholly vain, or even mischievous at another time. Government pre-supposes the existence of a perpetual mutability in its own operations on those, who are its subjects; and a perpetual flexibility in adapting itself to their wants, their interests, their habits, their occupations, and their infirmities.

§ 197. XI. And this leads us to remark, in the next place, that in the interpretation of the constitution there {147} is no solid objection to implied powers. Had the faculties of man been competent to the framing of a system of government, which would leave nothing to implication, it cannot be doubted, that the effort would have been made by the framers of our constitution. The fact, however, is otherwise. There is not in the whole of that admirable instrument a grant of powers, which does not draw after it others, not expressed, but vital to their exercise; not substantive and independent, indeed, but auxiliary and subordinate. There is no phrase in it, which, like the articles of confederation, excludes incidental and implied powers, and which requires, that every thing granted shall be expressly and minutely described. Even the tenth amendment, which was framed for the purpose of quieting the excessive jealousies, which had been excited, omits the word "expressly," (which was contained in the articles of confederation,) and declares only, that "the powers, not delegated to the United States, nor prohibited by it to the states, are reserved to the states respectively, or to the people;" thus leaving the question, whether the particular power, which may become the subject of contest, has been delegated to the one government, or prohibited to the other, to depend upon a fair construction of the whole instrument. The men, who drew and adopted this amendment, had experienced the embarrassments, resulting from the insertion of this word in the articles of confederation, and probably omitted it to avoid those embarrassments. A constitution, to contain an accurate detail of all the subdivisions, of which its great powers will admit, and of all the means, by which these may be carried into execution, would partake of the prolixity of a legal code, and could scarcely be embraced by the human mind. {148} It would probably never be understood by the public. Its nature, therefore, requires, that only its great outlines should be marked, its important objects designated, and the minor ingredients, which compose those objects, be deduced from the nature of those objects themselves. That this idea was entertained by the framers of the American constitution, is not only to be inferred from the nature of the instrument, but from the language. Why, else, were some of the limitations, found in the ninth section of the first article, introduced? It is also, in some degree, warranted, by their having omitted to use any restrictive term, which might prevent its receiving a fair and just interpretation. In considering this point, we should never forget, that it is a constitution we are expounding.

§ 198. XII. Another point, in regard to the interpretation of the constitution, requires us to advert to the rules applicable to cases of concurrent and exclusive powers. In what cases are the powers given to the general government exclusive, and in what cases may the states maintain a concurrent exercise? Upon this subject we have an elaborate exposition by the authors of the Federalist; and as it involves some of the most delicate questions growing out of the constitution, and those, in which a conflict with the states is most likely to arise, we cannot do better than to quote the reasoning.

§ 199. "An entire consolidation of the states into one complete national sovereignty, would imply an entire subordination of the parts; and whatever powers might remain in them, would be altogether dependent on the general will. But as the plan of the convention aims only at a partial union or consolidation, the state governments would clearly retain all the rights of sovereignty, {149} which they before had, and which were not, by that act, *exclusively* delegated to the United States. This exclusive delegation, or rather this alienation of state sovereignty, would only exist in three cases: where the constitution in express terms granted an exclusive authority to the Union; where it granted, in one instance, an authority to the Union, and in another, prohibited the states from exercising the like authority; and where it granted an authority to the Union, to which a similar authority in the states would be absolutely and totally *contradictory* and *repugnant*. I use these terms to distinguish this last case from another, which might appear to resemble it; but which would, in fact, be essentially different: I mean, where the exercise of a concurrent jurisdiction might be productive of occasional interferences in the *policy* of any branch of administration, but would not imply any direct contradiction or repugnancy in point of constitutional authority. These three cases of exclusive jurisdiction in the federal government, may be exemplified by the following instances. The last clause but one in the eighth section of the first article, provides expressly, that congress shall exercise '*exclusive legislation*' over the district to be appropriated as the seat of government. This answers to the first case. The first clause of the same section empowers congress '*to lay and collect taxes, duties, imposts, and excises;*' and the second clause of the tenth section of the same article declares, that '*no state shall*, without the consent of congress, *lay any imposts or duties on imports or exports*, except for the purpose of executing its inspection laws.' Hence would result an exclusive power in the Union to lay duties on imports and exports, with the particular exception mentioned. But {150} this power is abridged by another clause, which declares, that no tax or duty shall be laid on articles exported from any state; in consequence of which qualification, it now only extends to the *duties on imports*. This answers to the second case. The third will be found in that clause, which declares, that congress shall have power 'to establish an *uniform rule* of naturalization throughout the United States.' This must necessarily be exclusive; because, if each state had power to prescribe a *distinct rule*, there could be no *uniform rule*." The correctness of these rules of interpretation has never been controverted; and they have been often recognised by the Supreme Court.

§ 200. The two first rules are so completely self-evident, that every attempt to illustrate them would be vain, if it had not a tendency to perplex and confuse. The last rule, viz. that which declares, that the power is exclusive in the national government, where an authority is granted to the Union, to which a similar authority in the states would be absolutely and totally contradictory and repugnant, is that alone, which may be thought to require comment. This rule seems, in its own nature, as little susceptible of doubt, as the others, in reference to the constitution. For, since the constitution has declared, that the constitution and laws, and treaties in pursuance of it shall be the supreme law of the land; it would be absurd to say, that a state law, repugnant to it, might have concurrent operation and validity; and especially, as it is expressly added, anything in the constitution or laws of any state to the contrary notwithstanding. The repugnancy, then, being made out, it follows, that the state law is just as much void, as though it had been expressly declared to be void; or the power in congress {151} had been expressly declared to be exclusive. Every power given to congress is by the constitution necessarily supreme; and if, from its nature, or from the words of the grant, it is apparently intended to be exclusive, it is as much so, as if the states were expressly forbidden to exercise it.

§ 201. And this leads us to remark, that in the exercise of concurrent powers, if there be a conflict between the laws of the Union and the laws of the states, the former being supreme, the latter must of course yield. The possibility, nay the probability, of such a conflict was foreseen by the framers of the constitution, and was accordingly expressly provided for. If a state passes a law inconsistent with the constitution of the United States it is a mere nullity. If it passes a law clearly within its own constitutional powers, still if it conflicts with the exercise of a power given to congress, to the extent of the interference its operation is suspended; for in a conflict of laws, that which is supreme must govern. Therefore, it has often been adjudged, that if a state law is in conflict with a treaty, or an act of congress, it becomes *ipso facto* inoperative to the extent of the conflict.

§ 202. From this great rule, that the constitution and laws, made in pursuance thereof, are supreme; and that they control the constitutions and laws of the states, and cannot be controlled by them, from this, which may be deemed an axiom, other auxiliary corollaries may be deduced. In the first place, that, if a power is given to create a thing, it implies a power to preserve it. Secondly, that a power to destroy, if wielded by a different hand, is hostile to, and incompatible with this power to create and preserve. Thirdly, that where this repugnancy exists, the authority, {152} which is supreme, must control, and not yield to that, over which it is supreme. Consequently, the inferior power becomes a nullity.

§ 203. But a question of a still more delicate nature may arise; and that is, how far in the exercise of a concurrent power, the actual legislation of congress supersedes the state legislation, or suspends its operation over the subject matter. Are the state laws inoperative only to the extent of the actual conflict; or does the legislation of congress suspend the legislative power of the states over the *subject matter*? To such an inquiry, probably, no universal answer could be given. It may depend upon the nature of the power, the effect of the actual exercise, and the extent of the subject matter.

§ 204. It has been sometimes argued, that when a power is granted to congress to legislate in specific cases, for purposes growing out of the Union, the natural conclusion is, that the power is designed to be exclusive; that the power is to be exercised for the good of the whole, by the will of the whole, and consistently with the interests of the whole; and that these objects can no where be so clearly seen, or so thoroughly weighed, as in congress, where the whole nation is represented. But the argument proves too much; and pursued to its full extent, it would establish, that all the powers granted to congress are exclusive, unless where concurrent authority is expressly reserved to the states. For instance, upon this reasoning the power of taxation in congress would annul the whole power of taxation of the states; and thus operate a virtual dissolution of their sovereignty. Such a pretension has been constantly disclaimed. {153}

§ 205. On the other hand, it has been maintained with great pertinacity, that the states possess concurrent authority with congress in all cases, where the power is not expressly declared to be exclusive, or expressly prohibited to the states; and if, in the exercise of a concurrent power, a conflict arises, there is no reason, why each should not be deemed equally rightful. But it is plain, that this reasoning goes to the direct overthrow of the principle of supremacy; and, if admitted, it would enable the subordinate sovereignty to annul the powers of the superior. There is a plain repugnance in conferring on one government a power to control the constitutional measures of another, which other, with respect to these very measures, is declared to be supreme over that, which exerts the control. For instance, the states have acknowledgedly a concurrent power of taxation. But it is wholly inadmissible to allow that power to be exerted over any instrument employed by the general government to execute its own powers; for such a power to tax involves a power to destroy; and this power to destroy may defeat, and render useless the power to create. Thus, a state may not tax the mail, the mint, patent rights, customhouse papers, or judicial process of the courts of the United States. And yet there is no clause in the constitution, which prohibits the states from exercising the power; nor any exclusive grant to the United States. The apparent repugnancy creates, by implication, the prohibition.

§ 206. In considering, then, this subject, it would be impracticable to lay down any universal rule, as to what powers are, by implication, exclusive in the general government, or concurrent in the states; and in relation to the latter, what restrictions either on the {154} power itself, or on the actual exercise of the power, arise by implication. In some cases, as we have seen, there may exist a concurrent power, and yet restrictions upon it must exist in regards to objects. In other cases, the actual operations of the power only are suspended or controlled, when there arises a conflict with the actual operations of the Union. Every question of this sort must be decided by itself upon its own circumstances and reasons. Because the power to regulate commerce, from its nature and objects, is exclusive, it does not follow, that the power to pass bankrupt laws is exclusive.

§ 207. XIII. Another rule of interpretation deserves considerations in regard to the constitution. There are certain maxims, which have found their way, not only into judicial discussions, but into the business of common life, as founded in common sense, and common convenience. Thus, it is often said, that in an instrument a specification of particulars is an exclusion of generals; or the expression of one thing is the exclusion of another. Lord Bacon's remark, "that, as exception strengthens the force of a law in cases not excepted, so enumeration weakens it in cases not enumerated," has been perpetually referred to, as a fine illustration. These maxims, rightly understood, and rightly applied, undoubtedly furnish safe guides to assist us in the task of exposition. But they are susceptible of being applied, and indeed are often ingeniously applied, to the subversion of the text, and the objects of the instrument. Thus, it has been suggested, that an affirmative provision in a particular case excludes the existence of the like provision in every other case; and a negative provision in a particular case admits the existence of the same form in every other case. {155} Both of these deductions are, or rather may be, unfounded in solid reasoning. Thus, it was objected to the constitution that, having provided for the trial by jury in criminal cases, there was an implied exclusion of it in civil cases. As if there was not an essential difference between silence and abolition, between a positive adoption of it in one class of cases, and a discretionary right (it being clearly within the reach of the judicial power confided to the Union) to adopt, or reject it in all or any other cases. One might with just as much propriety hold, that, because congress have power "to declare war," but no power is expressly given to make peace, the latter is excluded; or that, because it is declared, that "no bill of attainder, or *ex post facto* law shall be passed" by congress, therefore congress possess in all other cases the right to pass any laws. The truth is, that in order to ascertain, how far and affirmative or negative provision excludes, or implies others, we must look to the nature of the provision, the subject matter, the objects, and the scope of the instruments. These, and these only, can properly determine the rule of construction. There can be no doubt, that an affirmative grant of powers in many cases will imply an exclusion of all others. As, for instance, the constitution declares, that the powers of congress shall extend to certain enumerated cases. This specification of particulars evidently excludes all pretensions to a general legislative authority. Why? Because an affirmative grant of special powers would be absurd, as well as useless, if a general authority were intended. In relation, then, to such a subject as a constitution, the natural and obvious sense of its provisions, apart from any technical or artificial rules, is the true criterion of construction. {156}

§ 208. XIV. Another rule of interpretation of the constitution, suggested by the foregoing, is, that the natural import of a single clause is not to be narrowed, so as to exclude implied powers resulting from its character, simply because there is another clause, which enumerates certain powers, which might otherwise be deemed implied powers within its scope; for in such cases we are not, as a matter of course, to assume, that the affirmative specification excludes all other implications. This rule has been put in a clear and just light by one of our most distinguished statesmen; and his illustration will be more satisfactory, perhaps, than any other, which can be offered. "The constitution," says he, "vests in congress, expressly, the power to lay and collect taxes, duties, imposts, and excises, and the power to regulate trade. That the former power, if not particularly expressed, would have been included in the latter, as one of the objects of a general power to regulate trade, is not necessarily impugned by its being so expressed. Examples of this sort cannot sometimes be easily avoided, and are to be seen elsewhere in the constitution. Thus, the power 'to define and punish offences against the law of nations' includes the power, afterwards particularly expressed, 'to make rules concerning captures,' &c. from offending neutrals. So, also, a power 'to coin money' would, doubtless, include that of 'regulating its value,' had not the latter power been expressly inserted. The term *taxes*, if standing alone, would certainly have included 'duties, imposts, and excises.' In another clause it is said, 'no tax or duty shall be laid on exports.' Here the two terms are used as synonymous. And in another clause, where it is said 'no state shall lay any imposts or duties,' &c. the {157} terms *imposts* and *duties* are synonymous. Pleonasms, tautologies, and the promiscuous use of terms and phrases, differing in their shades of meaning, (always to be expounded with reference to the context, and under the control of the general character and scope of the instrument, in which they are found,) are to be ascribed, sometimes to the purposes of greater caution, sometimes to the imperfection of language, and sometimes to the imperfection of man himself. In this view of the subject it was quite natural, however certainly the power to regulate trade might include a power to impose duties on it, not to omit it in a clause enumerating the several modes of revenue authorized by the construction. In few cases could the rule, *ex majori cautela*, occur with more claim to respect."

§ 209. We may close this view of some of the more important rules to be employed in the interpretation of the constitution, by adverting to a few belonging to mere verbal criticism, which are indeed but corollaries from what has been said, and have been already alluded to; but which, at the same time, it may be of some use again distinctly to enunciate.

§ 210. XV. In the first place, then, every word employed in the constitution is to be expounded in its plain, obvious, and common sense, unless the context furnishes some ground to control, qualify, or enlarge it. Constitutions are not designed for metaphysical or logical subtleties, for niceties of expression, for critical propriety, for elaborate shades of meaning, or for the exercise of philosophical acuteness, or juridical research. They are instruments of a practical nature, founded on the common business of human life, adapted to common wants, designed for common use, and fitted for common understandings. The people make {158} them; the people adopt them; the people must be supposed to read them, with the help of common sense; and cannot be presumed to admit in them any recondite meaning, or any extraordinary gloss.

§ 211. XVI. But, in the next place, words, from the necessary imperfection of all human language, acquire different shades of meaning, each of which is equally appropriate, and equally legitimate; each of which recedes in a wider or narrower degree from the others, according to circumstances; and each of which receives from its general use some indefiniteness and obscurity, as to its exact boundary and extent. We are, indeed, often driven to multiply commentaries from the vagueness of words in themselves; and perhaps still more often from the different manner, in which different minds are accustomed to employ them. They expand or contract, not only from the conventional modifications introduced by the changes of society; but also from the more loose or more exact uses, to which men of different talents, acquirements, and tastes, from choice or necessity apply them. No person can fail to remark the gradual deflections in the meaning of words from one age to another; and so constantly is this process going on, that the daily language of life in one generation sometimes requires the aid of a glossary in another. It has been justly remarked, that no language is so copious, as to supply words and phrases for every complex idea; or so correct, as not to include many, equivocally denoting different ideas. Hence it must happen, that however accurately objects may be discriminated in themselves, and however accurately the discrimination may be considered, the definition of them may be rendered inaccurate by the inaccuracy of the terms, in which it is delivered. We must resort then to the {159} context, and shape the particular meaning, so as to make it fit that of the connecting words, and agree with the subject matter.

§ 212. XVII. In the next place, where technical words are used, the technical meaning is to be applied to them, unless it is repelled by the context. But the same word often possesses a technical, and a common sense. In such a case the latter is to be preferred, unless some attendant circumstance points clearly to the former. No one would doubt, when the constitution has declared, that "the privilege of the writ of *habeas corpus* shall not be suspended," unless under peculiar circumstances, that it referred, not to every sort of writ, which has acquired that name; but to that, which has been emphatically so called, on account of its remedial power to free a party from arbitrary imprisonment. So, again, when it declares, that in suits at *common law*, &c. the right of trial by jury shall be preserved, though the phrase "common law" admits of different meanings, no one can doubt, that it is used in a technical sense. When, again, it declares, that congress shall have power to *provide* a navy, we readily comprehend, that authority is given to construct, prepare, or in any other manner to obtain a navy. But when congress is further authorized to *provide* for calling forth the militia, we perceive at once, that the word "provide" is used in a somewhat different sense.

§ 213. XVIII. And this leads us to remark, in the next place, that it is by no means a correct rule of interpretation to construe the same word in the same sense, wherever it occurs in the same instrument. It does not follow, either logically or grammatically, that because a word is found in one connexion in the constitution, with a definite sense, therefore the same {160} sense is to be adopted in every other connexion, in which it occurs. This would be to suppose, that the framers weighed only the force of single words, as philologists or critics, and not whole clauses and objects, as statesmen and practical reasoners. And yet nothing has been more common than to subject the constitution to this narrow and mischievous criticism. Men of ingenious and subtle minds, who seek for symmetry and harmony in language, having found in the constitution a word used in some sense, which falls in with their favourite theory of interpreting it, have made that the standard, by which to measure its use in every other part of the instrument.

They have thus stretched it, as it were, on the bed of Procustes, lopping of its meaning, when it seemed too large for their purposes, and extending it, when it seemed too short. They have thus distorted it to the most unnatural shapes, and crippled, where they have sought only to adjust its proportions according to their own opinions. It was very justly observed by the Supreme Court, "that the same words have not necessarily the same meaning attached to them, when found in different parts of the same instrument. Their meaning is controlled by the context. This is undoubtedly true. In common language, the same word has various meanings; and the peculiar sense, in which it is used in any sentence, is to be determined by the context." A very easy example of this sort will be found in the use of the word "establish," which is found in various places in the constitution. Thus, in the preamble, one object of the constitution is avowed to be "to establish justice," which seems here to mean to settle firmly, to fix unalterably, or rather, perhaps, as justice, abstractedly considered, {161} must be considered as for ever fixed and unalterable, to dispense or administer justice. Again, the constitution declares, that congress shall have power "to establish an uniform rule of naturalization, and uniform laws on the subject of bankruptcies," where it is manifestly used as equivalent to make, or form, and not to fix or settle unalterably and forever. Again, "congress shall have power to establish post-offices and post-roads," where the appropriate sense would seem to be to create, to found, and to regulate, not so much with a view to permanence of form, as to convenience of action. Again, it is declared, that "congress shall make no law respecting an establishment of religion," which seems to prohibit any laws, which shall recognise, found, confirm, or patronize any particular religion, or form of religion, whether permanent or temporary, whether already existing, or to arise in future. In this clause, establishment seems equivalent in meaning to settlement, recognition, or support. And again, in the preamble, it is said, "We, the people, &c. do ordain and establish this constitution," &c. where the most appropriate sense seems to be to create, to ratify, and to confirm. So, the word "state" will be found used in the constitution in all the various senses, to which it is commonly applied. It sometimes means, the separate sections of territory occupied by the political societies within each; sometimes the particular governments established by these societies; sometimes these societies as organized into these particular governments; and lastly, sometimes the people composing these political societies in their highest sovereign capacity.

§ 214. XIX. But the most important rule, in cases of this nature, is, that a constitution of government does not, and cannot, from its nature, depend in any {162} great degree upon mere verbal criticism, or upon the import of single words. Such criticism may not be wholly without use; it may sometimes illustrate, or unfold the appropriate sense; but unless it stands well with the context and subject-matter, it must yield to the latter. While, then, we may well resort to the meaning of single words to assist our inquiries, we should never forget, that it is an instrument of government we are to construe; and, as has been already stated, that must be the truest exposition, which best harmonizes with its design, its objects, and its general structure.

§ 215. The remark of Mr. Burke may, with a very slight change of phrase, be addressed as an admonition to all those, who are called upon to frame, or to interpret a constitution. Government is a practical thing made for the happiness of mankind, and not to furnish out a spectacle of uniformity to gratify the schemes of visionary politicians. The business of those, who are called to administer it, is to rule, and not to wrangle. It would be a poor compensation, that we had triumphed in a dispute, whilst we had lost an empire; that we had frittered down a power, and at the same time had destroyed the republic.

CHAPTER VI.

THE PREAMBLE.

§ 216. HAVING disposed of these preliminary inquiries, we are now arrived at that part of our labours, which involves a commentary upon the actual provisions of the constitution of the United States. It is proposed generally to take up the successive clauses in the order in which they stand in the instrument itself, so that the exposition may naturally flow from the terms of the text.

§ 217. We begin then with the preamble of the constitution. It is in the following words:

> "We, the people of the United States, in order to form a more perfect union, establish justice, insure domestic tranquillity, provide for the common defence, promote the general welfare, and secure the blessings of liberty to ourselves and our posterity, do ordain and establish this constitution for the United States of America."

§ 218. The importance of examining the preamble, for the purpose of expounding the language of a statute, has been long felt, and universally conceded in all juridical discussions. It is an admitted maxim in the ordinary course of the administration of justice, that the preamble of a statute is a key to open the mind of the makers, as to the mischiefs, which are to be remedied, and the objects, which are to be accomplished by the provisions of the statute. We find it laid down in some of our earliest authorities in the common law; and civilians are accustomed to a similar expression, *cessante legis præmio, cessat et ipsa lex.* {164}

§ 219. There does not seem any reason, why, in a fundamental law or constitution of government, an equal attention should not be given to the intention of the framers, as stated in the preamble. And accordingly we find, that it has been constantly referred to by statesmen and jurists to aid them in the exposition of its provisions.

§ 220. The language of the preamble of the constitution was probably in a good measure drawn from that of the third article of the confederation, which declares, that "The said states hereby severally enter into a firm *league* of friendship with each other, for their common defence, the security of their liberties, and their mutual and general welfare." And we accordingly find, that the first resolution offered in the convention, which framed the constitution, was, that the articles of the confederation ought to be so corrected and enlarged, as to accomplish the objects proposed by their institution, namely, common defence, security of liberty, and general welfare.

§ 221. And, here, we must guard ourselves against an error, which is too often allowed to creep into the discussions upon this subject. The preamble never can be resorted to, to enlarge the powers confided to the general government, or any of its departments. It cannot confer any power *per se*; it can never amount, by implication, to an enlargement of any power expressly given. It can never be the legitimate source of any implied power, when otherwise withdrawn from the constitution. Its true office is to expound the nature, and extent, and application of the powers actually conferred by the constitution, and not substantively to create them. For example, the preamble declares one object to be, "to provide for the common defence." {165} No one can doubt, that this does not enlarge the power of congress to pass any measures, which they may deem useful for the common defence. But, suppose the terms of a given power admit of two constructions, the one more restrictive, the other more liberal, and each of them is consistent with the words, but is, and ought to be, governed by the intent of the power; if one would promote, and the other defeat the common defence, ought not the former, upon the soundest principles of interpretation to be adopted? Are we at liberty, upon any principles of reason, or common sense, to adopt a restrictive meaning, which will defeat an avowed object of the constitution, when another equally natural, and more appropriate to the object, is before us? Would not this be to destroy an instrument by a measure of its words, which that instrument itself repudiates?

§ 222. The constitution having been in operation more than forty years, and being generally approved, it may, at first sight, seem unnecessary to enter upon any examination of the manner and extent, to which it is calculated to accomplish the objects proposed in the preamble, or the importance of those objects, not merely to the whole, in a national view, but also to the individual states. Attempts have, however, been made at different times, in different parts of the Union, to stir up a disaffection to the theory, as well as to the actual exercise of the powers of the general government; to doubt its advantages; to exaggerate the unavoidable inequalities of its operations; to accustom the minds of the people to contemplate the consequences of a division, as fraught with no dangerous evils; and thus to lead the way, if not designedly, at least insensibly, to a separation, as involving no necessary sacrifice of important {166} blessings, or principles, and, on the whole, under some circumstances, as not undesirable, or improbable.

§ 223. It is easy to see, how many different, and even opposite motives may, in different parts of the Union, at different times, give rise to, and encourage such speculations. Political passions and prejudices, the disappointments of personal ambition, the excitements and mortifications of party strife, the struggles for particular systems and measures, the interests, jealousies, and rivalries of particular states, the unequal local pressure of a particular system of policy, either temporary or permanent, the honest zeal of mere theorists and enthusiasts in relation to government, the real or imaginary dread of a national consolidation, the debasive and corrupt projects of mere demagogues; these, and many other influences of more or less purity and extent, may, and we almost fear, must, among a free people, open to argument, and eager for discussion, and anxious for a more perfect organization of society, for ever preserve the elements of doubt and discord, and bring into inquiry among many minds, the question of the value of the Union.

§ 224. Under these circumstances it may not be without some use to condense, in an abridged form, some of those reasons, which became, with reflecting minds, the solid foundation, on which the adoption of the constitution was originally rested, and which, being permanent in their nature, ought to secure its perpetuity, as the sheet anchor of our political hopes.

§ 225. The constitution, then, was adopted, first "to form a more perfect union." Why this was desirable has been in some measure anticipated in considering the defects of the confederation. When the constitution, however, was before the people for ratification, {167} suggestions were frequently made by those, who were opposed to it, that the country was too extensive for a single national government, and ought to be broken up into several distinct confederacies, or sovereignties; and some even went so far, as to doubt, whether it was not, on the whole, best, that each state should retain a separate, independent, and sovereign political existence. Those, who contemplated several confederacies, speculated upon a dismemberment into three great confederacies, one of the northern, another of the middle, and a third of the southern states. The greater probability, certainly, then was of a separation into two confederacies; the one composed of the northern and middle states, and the other of the southern. The reasoning of the Federalist on this subject seems absolutely irresistible. The progress of the population in the western territory since that period has materially changed the basis of all that reasoning. There could scarcely now exist, upon any dismemberment with a view to local interests, political associations, or public safety, less than three confederacies, and most probably four. And it is more than probable, that the line of division would be traced out by geographical boundaries, which would separate the slave-holding from the non-slave-holding states. Such a distinction in government is so fraught with causes of irritation and alarm, that no honest patriot could contemplate it without many painful and distressing fears.

§ 226. But the material consideration, which should be kept steadily in view, is, that under such circumstances a national government, clothed with powers at least equally extensive with those given by the constitution, would be indispensable for the preservation of each separate confederacy. Nay, it cannot be doubted, {168} that much larger powers, and much heavier expenditures would be necessary. No nation could long maintain its public liberties, surrounded by powerful and vigilant neighbours, unless it possessed a government clothed with powers of great efficiency, prompt to act, and able to repel every invasion of its rights. Nor would it afford the slightest security, that all the confederacies were composed of a people descended from the same ancestors, speaking the same language, professing the same religion, attached to the same principles of government, and possessing similar manners, habits, and customs. If it be true, that these circumstances would not be sufficient to hold them in a bond of peace and union, when forming one government, acting for the interests, and as the representatives of the rights of the whole; how could a better fate be expected, when the interests and the representation were separate; and ambition, and local interests, and feelings, and peculiarities of climate, and products, and institutions, and imaginary or real aggressions and grievances, and the rivalries of commerce, and the jealousies of dominion, should spread themselves over the distinct councils, which would regulate their concerns by independent legislation? The experience of the whole world is against any reliance for security and peace between neighbouring nations, under such circumstances. The Abbe Mably has forcibly stated in a single passage the whole result of human experience on this subject. "Neighbouring states," says he, "are naturally enemies of each other, unless their common weakness forces them to league in a confederative republic; and their constitution prevents the differences, that neighbourhood occasions, extinguishing that secret jealousy, which disposes all states to aggrandize themselves at {169} the expense of their neighbours." This passage, as has been truly observed, at the same time points out the evils, and suggests the remedy.

§ 227. The same reasoning would apply with augmented force to the case of a dismemberment, when each state should by itself constitute a nation. The very inequalities in the size, the revenues, the population, the products, the interests, and even in the institutions and laws of each, would occasion a perpetual petty warfare of legislation, of border aggressions and violations, and of political and personal animosities, which, first or last, would terminate in the subjugation of the weaker to the arms of the stronger. In our further observations on this subject, it is not proposed to distinguish the case of several confederacies from that of a complete separation of all the states; as in a general sense the remarks apply with irresistible, if not with uniform, force to each.

§ 228. Does, then, the extent of our territory offer any solid objection against forming "this more perfect union?" This question, so far as respects the original territory included within the boundaries of the United States by treaty of peace of 1783, seems almost settled by the experience of the last forty years. It is no longer a matter of conjecture, how far the government is capable (all other things being equal) of being practically applied to the whole of that territory. The distance between the utmost limits of our present population, and the diversity of interests among the whole, seem to have presented no obstacles under the beneficent administration of the general government, to the most perfect harmony and general advancement of all. Perhaps it has been demonstrated, (so far as our limited experience goes,) that the increased facilities of intercourse, {170} the uniformity of regulations and laws, the common protection, the mutual sacrifices of local interests, when incompatible with that of the nation, and the pride and confidence in a government, in which all are represented, and all are equal in rights and privileges; perhaps, we say, it has been demonstrated, that these effects of the Union have promoted, in a higher degree, the prosperity of every state, than could have been attained by any single state, standing alone, in the freest exercise of all its intelligence, its resources, and its institutions, without any check or obstruction during the same period. The great change, which has been made in our internal condition, as well as in our territorial power, by the acquisition of Louisiana and Florida, have, indeed, given rise to many serious reflections, whether such an expansion of our empire may not hereafter endanger the original system. But time alone can solve this question; and to time it is the part of wisdom and patriotism to leave it.

§ 229. The union of these states, "the more perfect union" is, then, and must for ever be invaluable to all, in respect both to foreign and domestic concerns. It will prevent some of the causes of war, that scourge of the human race, by enabling the general government, not only to negotiate suitable treaties for the protection of the rights and interests of all, but by compelling a general obedience to them, and a general respect for the obligations of the law of nations. It is notorious, that even under the confederation, the obligations of treaty stipulations were openly violated, or silently disregarded; and the peace of the whole confederacy was at the mercy of the majority of any single state. If the states were separated, they would, or might, form separate and independent treaties with different nations, {171} according to their peculiar interests. These treaties would, or might, involve jealousies and rivalries at home, as well as abroad, and introduce conflicts between nations struggling for a monopoly of the trade of each state. Retaliatory or evasive stipulations would he made, to counteract the injurious system of a neighbouring or distant state, and thus the scene be again acted over with renewed violence, which succeeded the peace of 1783, when the common interests were forgotten in the general struggle for superiority. It would manifestly be the interest of foreign nations to promote these animosities and jealousies, that in the general weakness the states might seek their protection by an undue sacrifice of their own interests, or fall an easy prey to their arms.

§ 230. The dangers, too, to all the states, in case of division, from foreign wars and invasion, must be imminent, independent of those from the neighbourhood of the colonies and dependencies of other governments on this continent. Their very weakness would invite aggression. The ambition of the European governments, to obtain a mastery of power in colonies and distant possessions, would be perpetually involving them in embarrassing negotiations or conflicts, however peaceable might be their own conduct, and however inoffensive their own pursuits and objects. America, as of old, would become the theatre of warlike operations, in which she had no interests; and with a view to their own security, the states would be compelled to fall back into a general colonial submission, or sink into dependencies of such of the great European powers, as might be most favorable to their interests, or most commanding over their resources. {172}

§ 231. There are also peculiar interests of some of the states, which would, upon a separation, be wholly sacrificed, or become the source of immeasurable calamities. The New-England states have a vital interest in the fisheries with their rivals, England and France; and how could New-England resist either of these powers in a struggle for the common right, if it should be attempted to be restrained or abolished? What would become of Maryland and Virginia, if the Chesapeake were under the dominion of different foreign powers *de facto*, though not in form? The free navigation of the Mississippi and the lakes, and it may be added, the exclusive navigation of them, seems indispensable to the security, as well as the prosperity of the western states. How otherwise than by a general union, could this be maintained or guarantied?

§ 232. And again, as to commerce, so important to the navigating states, and so productive to the agricultural states, it must be at once perceived, that no adequate protection could be given to either, unless by the strong and uniform operations of a general government. Each state by its own regulations would seek to promote its own interests, to the ruin or injury of those of others. The relative situation of these states; the number of rivers, by which they are intersected, and of bays, that wash their shores; the facility of communication in every direction; the affinity of language and manners; the familiar habits of intercourse; all these circumstances would conspire to render an illicit trade between them matter of little difficulty, and would insure frequent evasions of the commercial regulations of each other. All foreign nations would have a common interest in crippling us; and all the evils of colonial servitude, and commercial monopoly would be inflicted {173} upon us, by the hands of our own kindred and neighbours. But this topic, though capable of being presented in detail from our past experience in such glowing colours, as to startle the most incredulous into a conviction of the ultimate poverty, wretchedness, and distress, which would overwhelm every state, does not require to be more than hinted at. We have already seen in our former examination of the defects of the confederation, that every state was ruined in its revenues, as well as in its commerce, by the want of a more efficient government:

§ 233. Nor should it be imagined, that however injurious to commerce, the evils would be less in respect to domestic manufactures and agriculture. In respect to manufactures, the truth is so obvious, that it requires no argument to illustrate it. In relation to the agricultural states, however, an opinion has, at some times and in some sections of the country, been prevalent, that the agricultural interests would be equally safe without any general government. The following, among other considerations, may serve to show the fallacy of all such suggestions. A large and uniform market at home for native productions has a tendency to prevent those sudden rises and falls in prices, which are so deeply injurious to the farmer and the planter. The exclusive possession of the home market against all foreign competition gives a permanent security to investments, which slowly yield their returns, and encourages the laying out of capital in agricultural improvements. Suppose cotton, tobacco, and wheat were at all times admissible from foreign states without duty, would not the effect be permanently to check any cultivation beyond what at the moment seems sure of a safe sale? Would not foreign nations be perpetually {174} tempted to send their surplus here, and thus, from time to time, depress or glut the home market?

§ 234. Again; the neighbouring states would often engage in the same species of cultivation; and yet with very different natural, or artificial means of making the products equally cheap. This inequality would immediately give rise to legislative measures to correct the evil, and to secure, if possible, superior advantages over the rival state. This would introduce endless crimination and retaliation, laws for defence, and laws for offence. Smuggling would be every where openly encouraged, or secretly connived at. The vital interests of a state would lie in many instances at the mercy of its neighbours, who might, at the same time, feel, that their own interests were promoted by the ruin of their neighbours. And the distant states, knowing that their own wants and pursuits were wholly disregarded, would become willing auxiliaries in any plans to encourage cultivation and consumption elsewhere. Such is human nature! Such are the infirmities, which history severely instructs us belong to neighbours and rivals; to those, who navigate, and those, who plant; to those, who desire, and those, who repine at the prosperity of surrounding states.

§ 235. Again; foreign nations, under such circumstances, must have a common interest, as carriers, to bring to the agricultural states their own manufactures, at as dear a rate as possible, and to depress the market of the domestic products to the minimum price of competition. They must have a common interest to stimulate the neighbouring states to a ruinous jealousy; or by fostering the interests of one, with whom they can deal upon more advantageous terms, or over whom they have acquired a decisive influence, to subject to a {175} corresponding influence others, which struggle for an independent existence. This is not mere theory. Examples, and successful examples of this policy, may be traced throughout the period between the peace of 1783 and the adoption of the constitution.

§ 236. But not to dwell farther on these important inducements "to form a more perfect union," let us pass to the next object, which is to "establish justice." This must for ever be one of the great ends of every wise government; and even in arbitrary governments it must, to a great extent, be practised, at least in respect to private persons, as the only security against rebellion, private vengeance, and popular cruelty. But in a free government it lies at the very basis of all its institutions. Without justice being freely, fully, and impartially administered, neither our persons, nor our rights, nor our property, can be protected. And if these, or either of them, are regulated by no certain laws, and are subject to no certain principles, and are held by no certain tenure, and are redressed, when violated, by no certain remedies, society fails of all its value; and men may as well return to a state of savage and barbarous independence. No one can doubt, therefore, that the establishment of justice must be one main object of all our state governments. Why, then, may it be asked, should it form so prominent a motive in the establishment of the national government?

§ 237. This is now proposed to be shown in a concise manner. In the administration of justice, foreign nations, and foreign individuals, as well as citizens, have a deep stake; but the former have not always as complete means of redress as the latter; for it may be presumed, that the state laws will always provide adequate tribunals to redress the grievances and sustain {176} the rights of their own citizens. But this would be a very imperfect view of the subject. Citizens of contiguous states have a very deep interest in the administration of justice in each state; and even those, which are more distant, but belonging to the same confederacy, cannot but be affected by every inequality in the provisions, or in the actual operations of the laws of each other. While every state remains at full liberty to legislate upon the subject of rights, preferences, contracts, and remedies, as it may please, it is scarcely to be expected, that they will all concur in the same general system of policy. The natural tendency of every government is to favour its own citizens; and unjust preferences, not only in the administration of justice, but in the very structure of the laws, may reasonably be expected to arise. Popular prejudices, or passions, supposed or real injuries, the predominance of home pursuits and feelings over the comprehensive views of a liberal jurisprudence, will readily achieve the most mischievous projects for this purpose. And these, again, by a natural reaction, will introduce correspondent regulations, and retaliatory measures in other states.

§ 238. Now, exactly what this course of reasoning would lead us to presume as probable, has been demonstrated by experience to be true in respect to our own confederacy, during the short period of its existence, and under circumstances well calculated to induce each state to sacrifice many of its own objects for the general good. Nay, even when we were colonies, dependent upon the authority of the mother country, these inequalities were observable in the local legislation of several of the states, and produced heart-burnings and discontents, which were not easily appeased. {177}

§ 239. First, in respect to foreign nations. After the confederacy was formed, and we had assumed the general rights of war as a sovereign belligerent nation, authority to make captures, and to bring in ships and cargoes for adjudication naturally flowed from the proper exercise of these rights by the law of nations. The states respectively retained the power of appointing prize tribunals, to take cognizance of these matters in the first instance; and thus thirteen distinct jurisdictions were established, which acted entirely independent of each other. It is true, that the articles of confederation had delegated to the general government the authority of establishing courts for receiving and determining, finally, appeals in all cases of captures. Congress accordingly instituted proper appellate tribunals, to which the state courts were subordinate, and, upon constitutional principles, were bound to yield obedience. But it is notorious, that the decisions of the appellate tribunals were disregarded, and treated as mere nullities, for no power to enforce them was lodged in congress. They operated, therefore, merely by moral influence and requisition, and, as such, soon sunk into insignificance. Neutral individuals, as well as neutral nations, were left wholly without any adequate redress for the most inexcusable injustice, and the confederacy was subjected to imminent hazards. Until the constitution of the United States was established, no remedy was ever effectually administered. Treaties, too, were formed by congress with various nations; and above all, the treaty of peace of 1783, which gave complete stability to our independence against Great Britain. These treaties were, by the theory of the confederation, absolutely obligatory upon all the states. Yet their provisions were notoriously {178} violated both by state legislation and state judicial tribunals. The non-fulfilment of the stipulations of the British treaty on our part more than once threatened to involve the whole country again in war. And the provision in that treaty for the payment of British debts was practically disregarded in many, if not in all the state courts. These debts never were enforced, until the constitution gave them a direct and adequate sanction, independently of state legislation and state courts.

§ 240. Besides the debts due to foreigners, and the obligations to pay the same, the public debt of the United States was left utterly unprovided for; and the officers and soldiers of the revolution, who had achieved our independence, were, as we have had occasion to notice, suffered to languish in want, and their just demands evaded, or passed by with indifference. No efficient system to pay the public creditors was ever carried into operation, until the constitution was adopted; and, notwithstanding the increase of the public debt, occasioned by intermediate wars, it is now on the very eve of a total extinguishment.

§ 241. These evils, whatever might be their magnitude, did not create so universal a distress, or so much private discontent, as others of a more domestic nature, which were subversive of the first principles of justice. Independent of the unjustifiable preferences, which were fostered in favour of citizens of the state over those belonging to other states, which were not few, nor slight, there were certain calamities inflicted by the common course of legislation in most of the states, which went to the prostration of all public faith and all private credit. Laws were constantly made by the state legislatures violating, with more or less degrees {179} of aggravation, the sacredness of private contracts. Laws compelling the receipt of a depreciated and depreciating paper currency in payment of debts were generally, if not universally, prevalent. Laws authorizing the payment of debts by instalments, at periods differing entirely from the original terms of the contract; laws suspending, for a limited or uncertain period, the remedies to recover debts in the ordinary course of legal proceedings; laws authorizing the delivery of any sort of property, however unproductive or undesirable, in payment of debts upon an arbitrary or friendly appraisement; laws shutting up the courts for certain periods and under certain circumstances; were not infrequent upon the statute books of many of the states now composing the Union. In the rear of all these came the systems of general insolvent laws, some of which were of a permanent nature, and others again were adopted upon the spur of the occasion, like a sort of gaol delivery under the Lords' Acts in England, which had so few guards against frauds of every kind by the debtor, that in practice they amounted to an absolute discharge from every debt, without any thing more than a nominal dividend; and sometimes even this vain mockery was dispensed with. In short, by the operations of paper currency, tender laws, instalment laws, suspension laws, appraisement laws, and insolvent laws, contrived with all the dexterous ingenuity of men oppressed by debt, and popular by the very extent of private embarrassments, the states were almost universally plunged into a ruinous poverty, distrust, debility, and indifference to justice. The local tribunals were bound to obey the legislative will; and in the few instances, in which it was resisted, the independence of the judges was sacrificed to the temper of the times. {180} It is well known, that Shays's rebellion in Massachusetts took its origin from this source. The object was to prostrate the regular administration of justice by a system of terror, which should prevent the recovery of debts and taxes.

§ 242. So, that we see completely demonstrated by our own history the importance of a more effectual establishment of justice under the auspices of a national government.

§ 243. The next clause in the preamble is "to ensure domestic tranquillity." The illustrations appropriate to this head have been in a great measure anticipated in our previous observations. The security of the states against foreign influence, domestic dissensions, commercial rivalries, legislative retaliations, territorial disputes, and the petty irritations of a border warfare for privileges, exemptions, and smuggling, have been already noticed. The very habits of intercourse, to which the states were accustomed with each other during their colonial state, would, as has been justly remarked, give a keener edge to every discontent excited by any inequalities, preferences, or exclusions, growing out of the public policy of any of them. These, however, are not the only evils. In small communities domestic factions may well be expected to arise, which, when honest, may lead to the most pernicious public measures; and when corrupt, to domestic insurrections, and even to an overthrow of the government. The dangers to a republican government from this source have been dwelt upon by the advocates of arbitrary government with much exultation; and it must be confessed, that the history of free governments has furnished but too many examples to apologize for, though not to justify their arguments, urged not only {181} against the forms of republican government, but against the principles of civil liberty. They have pointed out the brief duration of republics, the factions, by which they have been rent, and the miseries, which they have suffered from distracted councils, and time-serving policy, and popular fury, and corruption, in a manner calculated to increase the solicitude of every well-wisher to the cause of rational liberty. And even those, who are most favourable in their views, seem to have thought, that the experience of the world had never yet furnished any conclusive proofs in its support. We know but too well, that factions have been the special growth of republics. By a faction, we are to understand a number of citizens, whether amounting to a minority or majority of the whole, who are united by some common impulse or passion, or interest, or party, adverse to the rights of the other citizens, or to the permanent and aggregate interests of the community.

§ 244. There are but two methods of curing the mischiefs of faction; the one, by removing its causes, which, in a free government, is impracticable without the destruction of liberty; the other, by controling its effects. If a faction be a minority, the majority may apply the proper corrective, by defeating or checking the violence of the minority in the regular course of legislation. In small states, however, this is not always easily attainable, from the difficulty of combining in a permanent form sufficient influence for this purpose. A feeble domestic faction will naturally avail itself, not only of all accidental causes of dissatisfaction at home, but also of all foreign aid and influence to carry its projects. And, indeed, in the gradual operations of factions, so many combinations are formed and dissolved, so many private resentments become embodied in public {182} measures, and success and triumph so often follow after defeat, that the remnants of different factions, which have had a brief sway, however hostile to each other, have an interest to unite in order to put down their rivals. But if the faction be a majority, and stand unchecked, except by its own sense of duty, or its own fears, the dangers are imminent to all those, whose principles, or interests, or characters stand in the way of its supreme dominion.

§ 245. These evils are felt in great states; but it has been justly observed, that in small states they are far more aggravated, bitter, cruel, and permanent. The most effectual means to control such effects seem to be in the formation of a confederate republic, consisting of several states. It will be rare, under such circumstances, if proper powers are confided to the general government, that the state line does not form the natural, as it will the jurisdictional boundary of the operations of factions. The authority of the general government will have a natural tendency to suppress the violence of faction, by diminishing the chances of ultimate success; and the example of the neighbouring states, who will rarely, at the same time, partake of the same feelings, or have the same causes to excite them into action, will mitigate, if it does not wholly disarm, the violence of the predominant faction.

§ 246. We now proceed to the next clause in the preamble, to "provide for the common defence." And many of the considerations already stated apply with still greater force under this head. One of the surest means of preserving peace is said to be, by being always prepared for war. But a still more sure means is the power to repel, with effect, every aggression. That power can scarcely be attained without a wide {183} extent of population, and at least a moderate extent of territory. A country, which is large in its limits, even if thinly peopled, is not easily subdued. Its variety of soil and climate, its natural and artificial defences, nay, its very poverty and scantiness of supplies, make it difficult to gain, or to secure a permanent conquest. It is far easier to overrun, than to subdue it. Armies must be divided, distant posts must be maintained, and channels of supplies kept constantly open. But where the territory is not only large, but populous, permanent conquest can rarely occur, unless (which is not our case) there are very powerful neighbours on every side, having a common interest to assist each other, and to subjugate their enemy. It is far otherwise, where there are many rival and independent states, having no common union of government or interests. They are half subdued by their own dissensions, jealousies, and resentments before the conflict is begun. They are easily made to act a part in the destruction of each other, or easily fall a prey for want of proper concert and energy of operations.

§ 247. Besides; — The resources of a confederacy must be far greater than those of any single state belonging to it, both for peace and war. It can command a wider range of revenue, of military power, of naval armaments, and of productive industry. It is more independent in its employments, in its capacities, and in its influences. In the present state of the world, a few great powers possess the command of commerce, both, on land and at sea. In war, they trample upon the rights of neutrals, who are feeble; for their weakness furnishes an excuse both for servility and disdain. In peace, they control the pursuits of the rest of the world, and force their trade into every channel by the {184} activity of their enterprise, their extensive navigation, and their flourishing manufactures. They little regard the complaints of those, who are subdivided into petty states with varying interests; and use them only as instruments to annoy or check the enterprise of each other. Such states are not formidable in peace or in war. To secure their rights and maintain their independence they must become a confederated nation, and speak with the force of numbers, as well as the eloquence of truth. The navy or army, which could be maintained by any single state in the Union, would be scarcely formidable to any second rate power in Europe. It would be a grievous public burthen, and exhaust the whole resources of the state. But a navy or army for all the purposes of home defence, or protection upon the ocean, is within the compass of the resources of the general government, without any severe exaction. And with the growing strength of the Union must be at once more safe for us, and more formidable to foreign nations. The means, therefore, to provide for the common defence are ample; and they can only be rendered inert and inadequate by a division among the states, and a want of unity of operations.

§ 248. We pass, in the next place, to the clause to "promote the general welfare." And it may be asked, as the state governments are formed for the same purpose by the people, why should this be set forth, as a peculiar or prominent object of the constitution of the United States? To such an inquiry two general answers may be given. (1.) The states, separately, would not possess the means. (2.) If they did possess the means, they would not possess the power to carry the appropriate measures into operation. {185}

§ 249. First, in respect to means. It is obvious from the local position and size of several of the states, that they must for ever possess but a moderate revenue, not more than what is indispensable for their own wants, and, in the strictest sense, for domestic improvements. In relation to others more favourably situated for commerce and navigation, the revenues from taxation may be larger; but the main reliance must be placed upon the taxation by way of imposts upon importations. Now, it is obvious, from the remarks already made, that no permanent revenue can be raised from this source, when the states are separated. The evasions of the laws, which will constantly take place from the rivalries, and various interests of the neighbouring states; the facilities afforded by the numerous harbours, rivers, and bays, which indent and intersect our coasts; the strong interest of foreigners to promote smuggling; the want of uniformity in the duties laid by the different states; the means of intercourse along the internal territorial boundaries of the commercial states; these, and many other causes, would inevitably lead to a very feeble administration of any local revenue system, and would make its returns moderate and unsatisfactory. What could New-York do with a single sea-port, surrounded on each side by jealous maritime neighbours with numerous ports? What could Massachusetts, or Connecticut do with the intermediate territory of Rhode-Island, running into the heart of these states by water communications admirably adapted for the security of illicit trade? What could Maryland, or Virginia do with the broad Chesapeake between them with its thousand landing places? What could Pennsylvania oppose to the keen resentments, or the facile policy of her weaker neighbour, Delaware? What could any {186} single state on the Mississippi do to force a steady trade for itself with adequate protecting duties? In short, turn to whichever part of the continent we may, the difficulties of maintaining an adequate system of revenue would be insurmountable, and the expenses of collecting it enormous. After some few struggles for uniformity, and co-operation for mutual support, each state would sink back into listless indifference or gloomy despondency; and rely, principally, upon direct taxation for its ordinary supplies. The experience of the few years succeeding the peace of 1783 fully justifies the worst apprehensions on this head.

§ 250. On the other hand, a general government, clothed with suitable authority over all the states, could easily guard the whole Atlantic coast, and make it the interest of all honourable merchants to assist in a regular and punctilious payment of duties. Vessels arriving at different ports of the Union would rarely choose to expose themselves to the perils of seizure, not in a single state only, but in every state, into which the goods might be successively imported. The dangers upon the coast, from the vigilant operations of the revenue officers and revenue vessels, would be great; and they would be much enhanced by the expenses of concealment after the goods were landed. And the fact has corresponded with the theory. Since the establishment of the national government, there has been comparatively little smuggling on our coasts; and the revenue from the duties upon importations has steadily increased with the developement of the other resources of the country.

§ 251. But the fact alone of an unlimited intercourse, without duty or restriction, between all the states, is of itself a blessing of almost inconceivable {187} value. It makes it an object with each permanently to look to the interests of all, and to withdraw its operations from the narrow sphere of its own exclusive territory. Without entering here into the inquiry, how far the general government possesses the power to make, or aid in the making of roads, canals, and other general improvements, which will properly arise in our future discussions, it is clear, that, if there were no general government, the interest of each state to undertake, or to promote in its own legislation any such project, would be far less strong, than it now is; since there would be no certainty, as to the value or duration of such improvements, looking beyond the boundaries of the state. The consciousness, that the Union of the states is permanent, and will not be broken up by rivalries, or conflicts of policy, that caprice, or resentment, will not divert any state from its proper duties, as a member of the Union, will give a solid character to all improvements. Independent of the exercise of any authority by the general government for this purpose, it was justly foreseen, that roads would be every where shortened and kept in better order; accommodations for travellers would be multiplied and meliorated; an interior navigation on our eastern side would be opened throughout the whole extent of our coast; and, by canals and improvements in river navigation, a boundless field opened to enterprise and emigration, to commerce and products, through the interior states, to the farthest limits of our western territories.

§ 252. Independent of these means of promoting the general welfare, we shall at once see, in our negotiations with foreign powers, the vast superiority of a nation combining numbers and resources over states of small extent, and divided by different interests. If we {188} are to negotiate for commercial or other advantages, the national government has more authority to speak, as well as more power to influence, than can belong to a single state. It has more valuable privileges to give in exchange, and more means of making those privileges felt by prohibitions, or relaxations of its commercial legislation. Is money wanted; how much more easy and cheap to borrow upon the faith of a nation competent to pay, than of a single state of fluctuating policy. Is confidence asked for the faithful fulfilment of treaty stipulations; how much more strong the guaranty of the Union with suitable authorities, than any pledge of an individual state. Is a currency wanted at once fixed on a solid basis, and sustained by adequate sanctions to enlarge public or private credit; how much more decisive is the legislation of the Union, than that of a single state, with a view to extent, or uniformity of operations.

§ 253. Thus we see, that the national government, suitably organized, has more efficient means, and more extensive jurisdiction to promote the general welfare, than can belong to any single state of the confederacy. And there is much truth in the suggestion, that it will generally be directed by a more enlightened policy, a more liberal justice, and more comprehensive wisdom, in the application of its means and its powers to their appropriate end. Generally speaking, it will be better administered; because it will command higher talents, more extensive experience, more practical knowledge, and more various information of the wants of the whole community, than can belong to smaller societies. The wider the sphere of action, the less reason there is to presume, that narrow views, or local prejudices will prevail in the public councils. The very diversities of {189} opinion in the different representatives of distant regions will have a tendency, not only to introduce mutual concession and conciliation, but to elevate the policy, and instruct the judgment of those, who are to direct the public measures.

§ 254. The last clause in the preamble is to "secure the blessings of liberty to ourselves and our posterity." And surely no object could be more worthy of the wisdom and ambition of the best men in any age. If there is any thing, which may justly challenge the admiration of all mankind, it is that sublime patriotism, which, looking beyond its own times, and its own fleeting pursuits, aims to secure the permanent happiness of posterity by laying the broad foundations of government upon immovable principles of justice. Our affections, indeed, may naturally be presumed to outlive the brief limits of our own lives, and to repose with deep sensibility upon our own immediate descendants. But there is a noble disinterestedness in that forecast, which disregards present objects for the sake of all mankind, and erect structures to protect, support, and bless the most distant generations. He, who founds a hospital, a college, or even a more private and limited charity, is justly esteemed a benefactor of the human race. How much more do they deserve our reverence and praise, whose lives are devoted to the formation of institutions, which, when they and their children are mingled in the common dust, may continue to cherish the principles and the practice of liberty in perpetual freshness and vigour.

§ 255. The grand design of the state governments is, doubtless, to accomplish this important purpose; and there can be no doubt, that they are, when well administered, well adapted to the end. But the question is {190} not so much, whether they conduce to the preservation of the blessings of liberty, as whether they of themselves furnish a complete and satisfactory security. If the remarks, which have been already offered, are founded in sound reasoning and human experience, they establish the position, that the state governments, *per se*, are incompetent and inadequate to furnish such guards and guaranties, as a free people have a right to require for the maintenance of their vital interests, and especially of their liberty. The inquiry then naturally presents itself, whether the establishment of a national government will afford more effectual and adequate securities.

§ 256. The fact has been already adverted to, that when the constitution was before the people for adoption, it was generally represented by its opponents, that its obvious tendency to a consolidation of the powers of government would subvert the state sovereignties, and thus prove dangerous to the liberties of the people. This indeed was a topic dwelt on with peculiar emphasis; and it produced so general an alarm and terror, that it came very nigh accomplishing the rejection of the constitution. And yet the reasoning, by which it was supported, was so vague and unsatisfactory; and the reasoning, on the other side, was so cogent and just, that it seems difficult to conceive, how, at that time, or at any later time, (for it has often been resorted to for the same purpose,) the suggestion could have had any substantial influence upon the public opinion.

§ 257. Let us glance at a few considerations, (some of which have been already hinted at,) which are calculated to suppress all alarm upon this subject. In the first place, the government of the United States is one of limited powers, leaving all residuary general powers in the state governments, or in the people thereof. The {191} jurisdiction of the general government is confined to a few enumerated objects, which concern the common welfare of all the states. The state governments have a full superintendence and control over the immense mass of local interests of their respective states, which connect themselves with the feelings, the affections, the municipal institutions, and the internal arrangements of the whole population. They possess, too, the immediate administration of justice in all cases, civil and criminal, which concern the property, personal rights, and peaceful pursuits of their own citizens. They must of course possess a large share of influence; and being independent of each other, will have many opportunities to interpose checks, as well as to combine a common resistance, to any undue exercise of power by the general government, independent of direct force.

§ 258. In the next place, the state governments are, by the very theory of the constitution, essential constituent parts of the general government. They can exist without the latter, but the latter cannot exist without them. Without the intervention of the state legislatures, the president of the United States cannot be elected at all; and the senate is exclusively and absolutely under the choice of the state legislatures. The representatives are chosen by the people of the states. So that the executive and legislative branches of the national government depend upon, and emanate from the states. Every where the state sovereignties are represented; and the national sovereignty, as such, has no representation. How is it possible, under such circumstances, that the national government can be dangerous to the liberties of the people, unless the states, and the people of the states, conspire together for their overthrow? If there should be such a conspiracy, {192} is not this more justly to be deemed an act of the states through their own agents, and by their own choice, rather than a corrupt usurpation by the general government?

§ 259. Besides; the perpetual organization of the state governments, in all their departments, executive, legislative, and judicial; their natural tendency to cooperation in cases of threatened danger to their common liberties; the perpetually recurring right of the elective franchise, at short intervals, must present the most formidable barriers against any deliberate usurpation, which does not arise from the hearty co-operation of the people of the states. And when such a general co-operation for usurpation shall exist, it is obvious, that neither the general, nor the state governments, can interpose any permanent protection. Each must submit to that public will, which created, and may destroy them.

§ 260. Another not unimportant consideration is, that the powers of the general government will be, and indeed must be, principally employed upon external objects, such as war, peace, negotiations with foreign powers, and foreign commerce. In its internal operations it can touch but few objects, except to introduce regulations beneficial to the commerce, intercourse, and other relations, between the states, and to lay taxes for the common good. The powers of the states, on the other hand, extend to all objects, which, in the ordinary course of affairs, concern the lives, and liberties, and property of the people, and the internal order, improvement, and prosperity of the state. The operations of the general government will be most extensive and important in times of war and danger; those of the state governments in times of peace and security. Independent {193} of all other considerations, the fact, that the states possess a concurrent power of taxation, and an exclusive power to regulate the descents, devise, and distribution of estates, (a power the most formidable to despotism, and the most indispensable in its right exercise to republicanism,) will for ever give them an influence, which will be as commanding, as, with reference to the safety of the Union, they could deliberately desire.

§ 261. Hitherto our experience has demonstrated the entire safety of the states, under the benign operations of the constitution. Each of the states has grown in power, in vigour of operation, in commanding influence, in wealth, revenue, population, commerce, agriculture, and general efficiency. No man will venture to affirm, that their power, relative to that of the Union, has been diminished, although our population has, in the intermediate period, passed from three to more than twelve millions. No man will pretend to say, that the affection for the state governments has been sensibly diminished by the operations of the general government. If the latter has become more deeply an object of regard and reverence, of attachment and pride, it is, because it is felt to be the parental guardian of our public and private rights, and the natural ally of all the state governments, in the administration of justice, and the promotion of the general prosperity. It is beloved, not for its power, but for its beneficence; not because it commands, but because it protects; not because it controls, but because it sustains the common interests, and the common liberties, and the common rights of the people.

§ 262. If, upon a closer survey of all the powers given by the constitution, and all the guards upon their {194} exercise, we shall perceive still stronger inducements to fortify this conclusion, and to increase our confidence in the constitution, may we not justly hope, that every honest American will concur in the dying expression of Father Paul, "Esto perpetua," *may it be perpetual.*

CHAPTER VII.

DISTRIBUTION OF POWERS.

§ 263. IN surveying the general structure of the constitution of the United States, we are naturally led to an examination of the fundamental principles, on which it is organized, for the purpose of carrying into effect the objects disclosed in the preamble. Every government must include within its scope, at least if it is to possess suitable stability and energy, the exercise of the three great powers, upon which all governments are supposed to rest, viz. the executive, the legislative, and the judicial powers. The manner and extent, in which these powers are to be exercised, and the functionaries, in whom they are to be vested, constitute the great distinctions, which are known in the forms of government. In absolute governments the whole executive, legislative, and judicial powers are, at least in their final result, exclusively confided to a single individual; and such a form of government is denominated a despotism, as the whole sovereignty of the state is vested in him. If the same powers are exclusively confided to a few persons, constituting a permanent sovereign council, the government may be appropriately denominated an absolute or despotic Aristocracy. If they are exercised by the people at large in their original sovereign assemblies, the government is a pure and absolute Democracy. But it is more common to find these powers divided, and separately exercised by independent functionaries, the executive power by one department, the legislative by another, and the judicial {196} by a third; and in these cases the government is properly deemed a mixed one; a mixed monarchy, if the executive power is hereditary in a single person; a mixed aristocracy, if it is hereditary in several chieftains or families; and a mixed democracy or republic, if it is delegated by election, and is not hereditary. In mixed monarchies and aristocracies some of the functionaries of the legislative and judicial powers are, or at least may be hereditary. But in a representative republic all power emanates from the people, and is exercised by their choice, and never extends beyond the lives of the individuals, to whom it is entrusted. It may be entrusted for any shorter period; and then it returns to them again, to be again delegated by a new choice.

§ 264. In the convention, which framed the constitution of the United States, the first resolution adopted by that body was, that "a national, government ought to be established, consisting of a supreme legislative, judiciary, and executive." And from this fundamental proposition sprung the subsequent organization of the whole government of the United States.

§ 265. In the establishment of free governments, the division of the three great powers of government, the executive, the legislative, and the judicial, among different functionaries, has been a favorite policy with patriots and statesmen. It has by many been deemed a maxim of vital importance, that these powers should for ever be kept separate and distinct. And accordingly we find it laid down with emphatic care in the bill of rights of several of the state constitutions.

§ 266. The general reasoning, by which the maxim is supported, independently of the just weight of the authority in its support, seems entirely satisfactory. {197} What is of far more value than any mere reasoning, experience has demonstrated it to be founded in a just view of the nature of government, and the safety and liberty of the people. And it is no small commendation of the constitution of the United States, that instead of adopting a new theory, it has placed this practical truth, as the basis of its organization. It has placed the legislative, executive, and judicial powers in different hands. It has, as we shall presently see, made their term of office and their organization different; and, for objects of permanent and paramount importance, has given to the judicial department a tenure of office during good behaviour; while it has limited each of the others to a term of years.

§ 267. But when we speak of a separation of the three great departments of government, and maintain, that that separation is indispensable to public liberty, we are to understand this maxim in a limited sense. It is not meant to affirm, that they must be kept wholly and entirely separate and distinct, and have no common link of connexion or dependence, the one upon the other, in the slightest degree. The true meaning is, that the whole power of one of these departments should not be exercised by the same hands, which possess the whole power of either of the other departments; and that such exercise of the whole would subvert the principles of a free constitution.

§ 268. How far the constitution of the United States, in the actual separation of these departments, and the occasional mixtures of some of the powers of each, has accomplished the objects of the great maxim, which we have been considering, will appear more fully, when a survey is taken of the particular powers confided to each department. But {198} the true and only test must, after all, be experience, which corrects at once the errors of theory, and fortifies and illustrates the eternal judgments of nature.

CHAPTER VIII.

THE LEGISLATURE.

§ 269. THE first article of the constitution contains the structure, organization, and powers, of the legislature of the Union. Each section of that article, and indeed, of every other article, will require a careful analysis, and distinct examination. It is proposed, therefore, to bring each separately under review, in the present commentaries, and to unfold the reasons, on which each is founded, the objections, which have been urged against it, and the interpretation, so far as it can be satisfactorily ascertained, of the terms, in which each is expressed.

§ 270. The first section of the first article is in the following words:

"All legislative powers herein granted shall be vested in a congress of the United States, which shall consist of a senate and house of representatives."

§ 271. This section involves, as a fundamental rule, the exercise of the legislative power by two distinct and independent branches. Under the confederation, the whole legislative power of the Union was vested in a single branch. Limited as was that power, the concentration of it in a single body was deemed a prominent defect of the confederation. But if a single assembly could properly be deemed a fit receptacle of the slender and fettered authorities, confided to the federal government by that instrument, it could scarcely be consistent with the principles of a good government to entrust it with the more enlarged and vigorous powers delegated in the constitution. {200}

§ 272. The utility of a subdivision of the legislative power into different branches, having a negative upon each other, is, perhaps, at the present time admitted by most persons of sound reflection. But it has not always found general approbation; and it is, even now, sometimes disputed by men of speculative ingenuity, and recluse habits. It has been justly observed, that there is scarcely in the whole science of politics a more important maxim, and one, which bears with greater influence upon the practical operations of government.

§ 273. It may not, therefore, be uninstructive to review some of the principal arguments, by which this division is vindicated. The first and most important ground is, that it forms a great check upon undue, hasty, and oppressive legislation. Public bodies, like private persons, are occasionally under the dominion of strong passions and excitements; and are impatient, irritable, and impetuous. The habit of acting together produces a strong tendency to what, for want of a better word, may be called the corporation spirit, or what is so happily expressed in a foreign phrase, *l'esprit du corps*. Certain popular leaders often acquire an extraordinary ascendency over the body, by their talents, their eloquence, their intrigues, or their cunning. Measures are often introduced in a hurry, and debated with little

118

care, and examined with less caution. The very restlessness of many minds produces an utter impossibility of debating with much deliberation, when a measure has a plausible aspect, and enjoys a momentary favour. Nor is it infrequent, especially in cases of this sort, to overlook well-founded objections to a measure, not only because the advocates of it have little desire to bring them in review, but because the opponents are often {201} seduced into a credulous silence. A legislative body is not ordinarily apt to mistrust its own powers, and far less the temperate exercise of those powers. As it prescribes its own rules for its own deliberations, it easily relaxes them, whenever any pressure is made for an immediate decision. If it feels no check but its own will, it rarely has the firmness to insist upon holding a question long enough under its own view, to see and mark it in all its bearings and relations on society.

§ 274. But it is not merely inconsiderate and rash legislation, which is to be guarded against, in the ordinary course of things. There is a strong propensity in public bodies to accumulate power in their own hands, to widen the extent of their own influence, and to absorb within their own circle the means, and the motives of patronage. If the whole legislative power is vested in a single body, there can be, practically, no restraint upon the fullest exercise of that power; and of any usurpation, which it may seek to excuse or justify, either from necessity, or a superior regard to the public good. It has been often said, that necessity is the plea of tyrants; but it is equally true, that it is the plea of all public bodies invested with power, where no check exists upon its exercise. Mr. Hume has remarked with great sagacity, that men are generally more honest in their private, than in their public capacity; and will go greater lengths to serve a party, than when their own private interest is alone concerned. Honour is a great check upon mankind. But where a considerable body of men act together, this check is in a great measure removed, since a man is sure to be approved of by his own party, for what promotes the common interest; and he soon learns to despise the clamours of adversaries. This is by no means an opinion peculiar to Mr. Hume. {202} It will be found lying at the foundation of the political reasonings of many of the greatest men in all ages, as the result of a close survey of the passions, and infirmities, of the history, and experience of mankind. With a view, therefore, to preserve the rights and liberties of the people against unjust encroachments, and to secure the equal benefits of a free constitution, it is of vital importance to interpose some check against the undue exercise of the legislative power, which in every government is the predominating, and almost irresistible power.

§ 275. The value, then, of a distribution of the legislative power, between two branches, each possessing a negative upon the other, may be summed up under the following heads. First: It operates directly as a security against hasty, rash, and dangerous legislation; and allows errors and mistakes to be corrected, before they have produced any public mischiefs. It interposes delay between the introduction, and final adoption of a measure; and thus furnishes time for reflection; and for the successive deliberations of different bodies, actuated by different motives, and organized upon different principles.

§ 276. In the next place, it operates indirectly as a preventive to attempts to carry private, personal, or party objects, not connected with the common good.

The very circumstance, that there exists another body clothed with equal power, and jealous of its own rights, and independent of the influence of the leaders, who favour a particular measure, by whom it must be scanned, and to whom it must be recommended upon its own merits, will have a silent tendency to discourage the efforts to carry it by surprise, or by intrigue, or by corrupt party combinations. It is far less easy to deceive, {203} or corrupt, or persuade two bodies into a course, subversive of the general good, than it is one; especially if the elements, of which they are composed, are essentially different.

§ 277. In the next place as legislation necessarily acts, or may act, upon the whole community, and involves interests of vast difficulty and complexity, and requires nice adjustments, and comprehensive enactments, it is of the greatest consequence to secure an independent review of it by different minds, acting under different, and sometimes opposite opinions and feelings; so, that it may be as perfect, as human wisdom can devise. An appellate jurisdiction, therefore, that acts, and is acted upon alternatively, in the exercise of an independent revisory authority, must have the means, and can scarcely fail to possess the will, to give it a full and satisfactory review. Every one knows, notwithstanding all the guards interposed to secure due deliberation, how imperfect all human legislation is; how much it embraces of doubtful principle, and of still more doubtful utility; how various, and yet how defective, are its provisions to protect rights, and to redress wrongs. Whatever, therefore, naturally and necessarily awakens doubt, solicits caution, attracts inquiry, or stimulates vigilance and industry, is of value to aid us against precipitancy in framing, or altering laws, as well as against yielding to the suggestions of indolence, the selfish projects of ambition, or the cunning devices of corrupt and hollow demagogues. For this purpose, no better expedient has, as yet, been found, than the creation of an independent branch of censors to revise the legislative enactments of others, and to alter, amend, or reject them at its pleasure, while, in return, its own are to pass through a like ordeal. {204}

§ 278. In the next place, there can scarcely be any other adequate security against encroachments upon the constitutional rights and liberties of the people. Algernon Sidney has said with great force, that the legislative power is always arbitrary, and not to be trusted in the hands of any, who are not bound to obey the laws they make. But it is not less true, that it has a constant tendency to overleap its proper boundaries, from passion, from ambition, from inadvertence, from the prevalence of faction, or from the overwhelming influence of private interests. Under such circumstances, the only effectual barrier against oppression, accidental or intentional, is to separate its operations, to balance interest against interest, ambition against ambition, the combinations and spirit of dominion of one body against the like combinations and spirit of another. And it is obvious, that the more various the elements, which enter into the actual composition of each body, the greater the security will be.

§ 279. Such is an outline of the general reasoning, by which the system of a separation of the legislative power into two branches has been maintained. Experience has shown, that if in all cases it has not been found a complete check to inconsiderate or unconstitutional legislation; yet, it has, upon many occasions, been found sufficient for the purpose. There is not probably at this moment a single state in the Union, which would consent to unite the two branches into one assembly; though there have not been wanting at all times minds of a high order, which have been led by enthusiasm, or a love of simplicity, or a devotion to theory, to vindicate such a union with arguments, striking and plausible, if not convincing. {205}

§ 280. Having considered the general reasoning, by which the division of the legislative power has been justified, it may be proper, in conclusion, to give a summary of those grounds, which were deemed most important, and which had most influence in settling the actual structure of the constitution of the United States. The question of course had reference altogether to the establishment of the senate; for no one doubted the propriety of establishing a house of representatives, as a depositary of the legislative power, however much any might differ, as to the nature of its composition.

§ 281. In order to justify the existence of a senate with co-ordinate powers, it was said, first, that it is a misfortune incident to republican governments, though in a less degree, than to other governments, that those, who administer it, may forget their obligations to their constituents, and prove unfaithful to their important trust. In this point of view, a senate, as a second branch of the legislative assembly, distinct from, and dividing the power with a first, must be in all cases a salutary check on the government. It doubles the security to the people by requiring the concurrence of two distinct bodies, in schemes of usurpation or perfidy; whereas the ambition or corruption of one would otherwise be sufficient. This precaution, it was added, is founded on such clear principles, and so well understood in the United States, that it is superfluous to enlarge on it. As the improbability of sinister combinations would be in proportion to the dissimilarity in the genius of the two bodies, it must be politic to distinguish them from each other by every circumstance, which would consist with a due harmony in all proper measures, and with the genuine principles of republican government. {206}

§ 282. Secondly. The necessity of a senate is not less indicated by the propensity of all single and numerous assemblies to yield to the impulse of sudden and violent passions, and to be seduced by factious leaders into intemperate and pernicious resolutions. Examples of this sort might be cited without number, and from proceedings in the United States, as well as from the history of other nations. A body, which is to correct this infirmity, ought to be free from it, and consequently ought to be less numerous, and to possess a due degree of firmness, and a proper tenure of office.

§ 283. Thirdly. Another defect to be supplied by a senate lies in the want of a due acquaintance with the objects and principles of legislation. A good government implies two things; first, fidelity to the objects of the government; secondly, a knowledge of the means, by which those objects can be best attained. It was suggested, that in the American governments too little attention had been paid to the last; and that the establishment of a senate upon a proper basis would greatly increase the chances of fidelity, and of wise and safe legislation. What (it was asked) are all the repealing, explaining, and amending laws, which fill and disgrace our voluminous codes, but so many monuments of deficient wisdom; so many impeachments exhibited by each succeeding, against each preceding session; so many admonitions to the people of the value of those aids, which may be expected from a well-constituted senate?

§ 284. Fourthly. Such a body would prevent too great a mutability in the public councils, arising from a rapid succession of new members; for from a change of men there must proceed a change of opinions, and from {207} a change of opinions, a change of measures. Such instability in legislation has a tendency to diminish respect and confidence abroad, as well as safety and prosperity at home. It has a tendency to damp the ardour of industry and enterprise; to diminish the security of property; and to impair the reverence and attachment, which are indispensable to the permanence of every political institution.

§ 285. Fifthly. Another ground, illustrating the utility of a senate, was suggested to be the keeping alive of a due sense of national character. In respect to foreign nations, this is of vital importance; for in our intercourse with them, if a scrupulous and uniform adherence to just principles is not observed, it must subject us to many embarrassments and collisions. It is difficult to impress upon a single body, which is numerous and changeable, a deep sense of the value of national character. A small portion of the praise, or blame of any particular measure can fall to the lot of any particular person; and the period of office is so short, that little responsibility is felt, and little pride is indulged, as to the course of the government.

§ 286. Sixthly. It was urged, that, paradoxical, as it might seem, the want in some important cases of a due responsibility in the government arises from that very frequency of elections, which in other cases produces such responsibility. In order to be reasonable, responsibility must be limited to objects within the power of the responsible party; and in order to be effectual, it must relate to operations of that power, of which a ready and proper judgment can be formed by the constituents. Some measures have singly an immediate and sensible operation; others again depend {208} on a succession of well conducted schemes, and have a gradual, and perhaps unobserved operation. If, therefore, there be but one assembly, chosen for a short period, it will be difficult to keep up the train of proper measures, or to preserve the proper connexion between the past and the future. And the more numerous the body, and the more changeable its component parts, the more difficult it will be to preserve the personal responsibility, as well, as the uniform action, of the successive members to the great objects of the public welfare.

§ 287. Lastly. A senate duly constituted would not only operate, as a salutary check upon the representatives, but occasionally upon the people themselves, against their own temporary delusions and errors. The cool, deliberate sense of the community ought in all governments, and actually will in all free governments, ultimately prevail over the views of their rulers. But there are particular moments in public affairs, when the people, stimulated by some irregular passion, or some illicit advantage, or misled by the artful misrepresentations of interested men, may call for measures, which they themselves will afterwards be the most ready to lament and condemn. In these critical moments, how salutary will be the interference of a body of respectable citizens, chosen without reference to the exciting cause, to check the misguided career of public opinion, and to suspend the blow, until reason, justice, and truth can regain their authority over the public mind.

It was thought to add great weight to all these considerations, that history has informed us of no long-lived republic, which had not a senate. Sparta, Rome, Carthage were, in fact, the only states, to whom that character can be applied. {209}

§ 288. It will be observed, that some parts of the foregoing reasoning apply to the fundamental importance of an actual division of the legislative power; and other parts to the true principles, upon which that division should be subsequently organized, in order to give full effect to the constitutional check. Some parts go to show the value of a senate; and others, what should be its structure, in order to ensure wisdom, experience, fidelity, and dignity in its members. All of it, however, instructs us, that, in order to give it fair play and influence, as a co-ordinate branch of government, it ought to be less numerous, more select, and more durable, than the other branch; and be chosen in a manner, which should combine, and represent different interests with a varied force. How far these objects are attained by the constitution will be better seen, when the details belonging to each department are successively examined.

CHAPTER IX.

HOUSE OF REPRESENTATIVES.

§ 289. THE second section of the first article contains the structure and organization of the house of representatives. The first clause is as follows:

> "The house of representatives shall be composed of members chosen every second year by the people of the several states; and the electors in each state shall have the qualifications requisite for electors of the most numerous branch of the state legislature."

§ 290. As soon as it was settled, that the legislative power should be divided into two separate and distinct branches, a very important consideration arose in regard to the organization of those branches respectively. It is obvious, that the organization of each is susceptible of very great diversities and modifications, in respect to the principles of representation; the qualification of the electors, and the elected; the term of, service of the members; the ratio of representation; and the number, of which the body should be composed.

§ 291. First; the principle of representation. The American people had long been in the enjoyment of the privilege of electing, at least, one branch of the legislature; and, in some of the colonies, of electing all the branches composing the legislature. A house of representatives, under various denominations, such as a house of delegates, a house of commons, or, simply, a house of representatives, emanating directly from, and responsible to the people, and possessing a distinct and independent legislative authority, was familiar to all the colonies, and was held by them in the highest reverence {211} and respect. They justly thought, that as the government in general should always have a common interest with the people, and be administered for their good; so it was essential to their rights and liberties, that the most numerous branch should have an immediate dependence upon, and sympathy with the people. There was no novelty in this view. It was not the mere result of a state of colonial dependence, in which their jealousy was awake to all the natural encroachments of power in a foreign realm. They had drawn their opinions and principles from the practice of the parent country. They knew the inestimable value of the house of commons, as a component branch of the British parliament; and they believed, that it had at all times furnished the best security against the oppressions of the crown, and the aristocracy. While the power of taxation, of revenue, and of supplies, remained in the hands of a popular branch, it was difficult for usurpation to exist for any length of time without check; and prerogative must yield to that necessity, which controlled at once the sword and the purse. No reasoning, therefore, was necessary to satisfy the American people of the advantages of a house of representatives, which should emanate directly from themselves; which should guard their interests, support their rights, express their opinions, make known their wants, redress their grievances, and introduce a pervading popular influence throughout all the operations of the government. Experience, as well as theory, had settled it in their minds, as a fundamental principle of a free government, and especially of a republican government, that no laws ought to be passed without the co-operation and consent of the representatives of the people; and that these representatives should be chosen by themselves, {212} without the intervention of any other functionaries to intercept, or vary their responsibility.

§ 292. We accordingly find, that in the section under consideration, the house of representatives is required to be composed of representatives chosen by the people of the several states. The choice, too, is to be made immediately by them; so that the power is direct; the influence direct; and the responsibility direct. If any intermediate agency had been adopted, such as a choice through an electoral college, or by official personages, or by select and specially qualified functionaries *pro hac vice*, it is obvious, that the dependence of the representatives upon the people, and the responsibility to them, would have been far less felt, and far more obstructed. Influence would have naturally grown up with patronage; and here, as in many other cases, the legal maxim would have applied, *causa proxima, non remota, spectatur*. The select body would have been at once the patrons and the guides of the representative; and the people themselves would have become the instrument of subverting their own rights and power.

§ 293. But this fundamental principle of an immediate choice by the people, however important, would alone be insufficient for the public security, if the right of choice had not had many auxiliary guards and accompaniments. It was indispensable, secondly, to provide for the qualifications of the electors. It is obvious, that even when the principle is established, that the popular branch of the legislature shall emanate directly from the people, there still remains a very serious question; by whom and in what manner the choice shall be made. It is a question vital to the system, and in a practical sense decisive, as to the durability and efficiency of the powers of government. Here, there is much room for {213} doubt, and ingenious speculation, and theoretical inquiry; upon which different minds may arrive, and indeed have arrived, at very different results. To whom ought the right of suffrage, in a free government, to be confided? Or, in other words, who ought to be permitted to vote in the choice of the representatives of the people? Ought the right of suffrage to be absolutely universal? Ought it to be qualified and restrained? Ought it to belong to many, or few? If there ought to be restraints and qualifications, what are the true boundaries and limits of such restraints and qualifications?

§ 294. These questions are sufficiently perplexing and disquieting in theory; and in the practice of different states, and even of free states, ancient as well as modern, they have assumed almost infinite varieties of form and illustration. Perhaps they do not admit of any general, much less of any universal answer, so as to furnish an unexceptionable and certain rule for all ages and all nations. The manners, habits, institutions, characters, and pursuits of different nations; the local position of the territory, in regard to other nations; the actual organizations and classes of society; the influences of peculiar religious, civil, or political institutions; the dangers, as well as the difficulties, of the times; the degrees of knowledge or ignorance pervading the mass of society; the national temperament, and even the climate and products of the soil; the cold and thoughtful gravity of the north; and the warm and mercurial excitability of tropical or southern regions; all these may, and probably will, introduce modifications of principle, as well as of opinion, in regard to the right of suffrage, which it is not easy either to justify, or to overthrow. {214}

§ 295. Without laying any stress upon theoretical reasoning on this subject, it may be proper to state, that every civilized society has uniformly fixed, modified, and regulated the right of suffrage for itself, according to its own free will and pleasure. Every constitution of government in these United States has assumed, as a fundamental principle, the right of the people of the state to alter, abolish, and modify the form of its own government, according to the sovereign pleasure of the people. In fact, the people of each state have gone much farther, and settled a far more critical question, by deciding, who shall be the voters, entitled to approve and reject the constitution framed by a delegated body under their direction. In the adoption of no state constitution has the assent been asked of any, but the qualified voters; and women, and minors, and other persons, not recognised as voters by existing laws, have been studiously excluded. And yet the constitution has been deemed entirely obligatory upon them, as well as upon the minority, who voted against it. From this it will be seen, how little, even in the most free of republican governments, any abstract right of suffrage, or any original and indefeasible privilege, has been recognised in practice. If this consideration does not satisfy our minds, it at least will prepare us to presume, that there may be an almost infinite diversity in the established right of voting, without any state being able to assert, that its own mode is exclusively founded in natural justice, or is most conformable to sound policy, or is best adapted to the public security. It will teach us, that the question is necessarily complex and intricate in its own nature, and is scarcely susceptible of any simple solution, which shall rigidly {215} apply to the circumstances and conditions, the interests and the feelings, the institutions and the manners of all nations. What may best promote the public weal, and secure the public liberty, and advance the public prosperity in one age or nation, may totally fail of similar results under local, physical, or moral predicaments essentially different.

§ 296. It would carry us too far from the immediate objects of these Commentaries to take a general survey of the various modifications, under which the right of suffrage, either in relation to laws, or magistracy, or even judicial controversies, has appeared in different nations in ancient and modern times. The examples of Greece and Rome in ancient times, and of England in modern times, will be found most instructive. In England, the qualifications of voters, as also the modes of representation, are various, and framed upon no common principle. The counties are represented by knights, elected by the proprietors of lands, who are freeholders; the boroughs and cities are represented by citizens and burgesses, or others chosen by the citizens or burgesses, according to the qualifications prescribed by custom, or by the respective charters and by-laws of each borough, or city. In these, the right of voting is almost infinitely varied and modified. In the American colonies, under their charters and laws, no uniform rules in regard to the right of suffrage existed. In some of the colonies the course of the parent country was closely followed, so that freeholders alone were voters; in others a very near approach was made to universal suffrage among the males of competent age; and in others, again, a middle principle was adopted, which made taxation and voting dependent upon each other, or annexed to it the qualification {216} of holding some personal estate, or the privilege of being a freeman, or the eldest son of a freeman of the town or corporation. When the revolution brought about the separation of the colonies, and they formed themselves into independent states, a very striking diversity was observable in the original constitutions adopted by them; and a like diversity has pervaded all the constitutions of the new states, which have since grown up, and all the revised constitutions of the old states, which have received the final ratification of the people. In some of the states the right of suffrage depends upon a certain length of residence, and payment of taxes; in others, upon mere citizenship and residence; in others, upon the possession of a freehold, or some estate of a particular value, or upon the payment of taxes, or performance of some public duty, such as service in the militia, or on the highways. In no two of these state constitutions will it be found, that the qualifications of the voters are settled upon the same uniform basis. So that we have the most abundant proofs, that among a free and enlightened people, convened for the purpose of establishing their own forms of government, and the rights of their own voters, the question, as to the due regulation of the qualifications, has been deemed a matter of mere state policy, and varied to meet the wants, to suit the prejudices, and to foster the interests of the majority. An absolute, indefeasible right to elect, or be elected, seems never to have been asserted on one side, or denied on the other; but the subject has been freely canvassed, as one of mere civil polity, to be arranged upon such a basis, as the majority might deem expedient with reference to the moral, physical, and intellectual condition of the particular state. {217}

§ 297. It was under this known diversity of constitutional provisions in regard to state elections, that the convention, which framed the constitution of the Union, was assembled. The definition of the right of suffrage is very justly regarded, as a fundamental article of a republican government. It was incumbent on the convention, therefore, to define and establish this right in the constitution. To have left it open for the occasional regulation of congress would have been improper, for the reason just mentioned. To have submitted it to the legislative discretion of the states would have been improper for the same reason, and for the additional reason, that it would have rendered too dependent on the state governments that branch of the federal government, which ought to be dependent on the people alone. Two modes of providing for the right of suffrage in the choice of representatives were presented to the consideration of that body. One was to devise some plan, which should operate uniformly in all the states, on a common principle; the other was to conform to the existing diversities in the states, thus creating a mixed mode of representation. In favour of the former course, it might be urged, that all the states ought, upon the floor of the house of representatives, to be represented equally; that this could be accomplished only by the adoption of a uniform qualification of the voters, who would thus express the same public opinion of the same body of citizens throughout the Union; that, if freeholders alone in one state chose the representatives, and in another all male citizens of competent age, and in another all freemen of particular towns or corporations, and in another all taxed inhabitants, it would be obvious, that different interests and classes would obtain exclusive representations {218} in different states; and thus the great object of the constitution, the promotion of the general welfare and common defence, might be unduly checked and obstructed; that a uniform principle would at least have this recommendation, that it could create no well-founded jealousies among the different states, and would be most likely to satisfy the body of the people by its perfect fairness, its permanent equality of operation, and its entire independence of all local legislation, whether in the shape of state laws, or of amendments to state constitutions.

§ 298. On the other hand, it might be urged in favour of the latter course, that the reducing of the different qualifications, already existing in the different states, to one uniform rule, would have been a very difficult task, even to the convention itself, and would be dissatisfactory to the people of different states. It would not be very easy for the convention to frame any rule, which would satisfy the scruples, the prejudices, or the judgments of a majority of its own members. It would not be easy to induce Virginia to give up the exclusive right of freeholders to vote; or Rhode-Island, or Connecticut, the exclusive right of freemen to vote; or Massachusetts, the right of persons possessing a given value of personal property to vote; or other states, the right of persons paying taxes, or having a fixed residence, to vote. The subject itself was not susceptible of any very exact limitations upon any general reasoning. The circumstances of different states might create great diversities in the practical operation of any uniform system. And the natural attachments, which long habit and usage had sanctioned, in regard to the exercise of the right, would enlist all the feelings, and interests, and opinions of every state against any substantial change {219} in its own institutions. A great embarrassment would be thus thrown in the way of the adoption of the constitution itself, which perhaps would thus be put at hazard, upon the mere ground of theoretical propriety.

§ 299. In the judgment of the convention, this latter reasoning seems to have obtained a decisive influence, and to have established the final result; and it was accordingly declared, in the clause under consideration, that "the electors in each state shall have the qualifications requisite for electors of the most numerous branch of the state legislature." Upon this clause (which was finally adopted by a unanimous vote) the Federalist has remarked, "the provision made by the convention appears to be the best, that lay within their option. It must be satisfactory to every state, because it is conformable to the standard already established by the state itself. It will be safe to the United States, because, being fixed by the state constitutions, it is not alterable by the state governments; and it cannot be feared, that the people of the states will alter this part of their constitutions in such a manner, as to abridge the rights secured to them by the federal constitution."

§ 300. In the third place, the term of service of representatives. In order to ensure permanent safety to the liberties of the people, other guards are indispensable, besides those, which are derived from the exercise of the right of suffrage and representation. If, when the legislature is once chosen, it is perpetual, or may last during the life of the representatives; and in case of death, or resignation only, the vacancy is to be supplied by the election of new representatives; it is easy to perceive, that in such cases there will be but a very slight check upon their acts, on the part of the people. In such cases, if the legislative body should be once corrupted, the evil {220} would be past all remedy, at least without some violent revolution, or extraordinary calamity. But, when different legislative bodies are to succeed each other at short intervals, if the people disapprove of the present, they may rectify its faults, by the silent exercise of their power in the succeeding election. Besides; a legislative assembly, which is sure to be separated again, and its members soon return to private life, will feel its own interests, as well as duties, bound up with those of the community at large. It may, therefore, be safely laid down as a fundamental axiom of republican governments, that there must be a dependence on, and responsibility to, the people, on the part of the representative, which shall constantly exert an influence upon his acts and opinions, and produce a sympathy between him and his constituents. If, when he is once elected, he holds his place for life, or during good behaviour, or for a long period of years, it is obvious, that there will be little effective control exercised upon him; and he will soon learn to disregard the wishes, the interests, and even the rights of his constituents, whenever they interfere with his own selfish pursuits and objects. When appointed, he may not, indeed, consider himself, as exclusively their representative, bound by their opinions, and devoted to their peculiar local interests, although they may be wholly inconsistent with the good of the Union. He ought rather to deem himself a representative of the nation, and bound to provide for the general welfare, and to consult for the general safety. But still in a just sense, he ought to feel his responsibility to them, and to act for them in common with the rest of the people; and to deem himself, in an emphatic manner, their defender, and their friend. {221}

§ 301. Frequent elections are unquestionably the soundest, if not the sole policy, by which this dependence and sympathy and responsibility can be effectually secured. But the question, what degree of frequency is best calculated to accomplish that object, is not susceptible of any precise and universal answer, and must essentially depend upon very different considerations in different nations, and vary with their size, their age, their condition, their institutions, and their local peculiarities.

§ 302. Without pretending to go into a complete survey of the subject in all its bearings, the frequency of elections may be materially affected, as matter of policy, by the extent of the population and territory of a country, the concentration or sparseness of the population, the nature of the pursuits, and employments, and engagements of the people; and by the local and political situation of the nation in regard to contiguous nations. If the government be of small extent, or be concentrated in a single city, it will be far more easy for the citizens to choose their rulers frequently, and to change them without mischief, than it would be, if the territory were large, the population sparse, and the means of intercourse few, and liable to interruption. If all the inhabitants, who are to vote, reside in towns and villages, there will be little inconvenience in assembling them together at a short notice to make a choice. It will be far otherwise, if the inhabitants are scattered over a large territory, and are engaged in agricultural pursuits, like the planters and farmers of the southern and western states, who must meet at a distance from their respective homes, and at some common place of assembling. In cases of this sort, the sacrifice of time necessary to accomplish the object, the expenses of the journey, the imperfect {222} means of communication, the slow progress of interchanges of opinion, would naturally diminish the exercise of the right of suffrage. There would be great danger, under such circumstances, that there would grow up a general indifference or inattention to elections, if they were frequent, since they would create little interest, and would involve heavy charges and burthens. The nature of the pursuits and employments of the people must also have great influence in settling the question. If the mass of the citizens are engaged in employments, which take them away for a long period from home, such as employment in the whale and cod fisheries, in the fur-trade, in foreign and distant commerce, in periodical caravans, or in other pursuits, which require constant attention, or long continued labours at particular seasons; it is obvious, that frequent elections, which should interfere with their primary interests and objects, would be at once inconvenient, oppressive, and unequal. They would enable the few to obtain a complete triumph and ascendency in the affairs of the state over the many. Besides; the frequency of elections must be subject to other considerations, affecting the general comfort and convenience, as well of rulers, as of electors. In the bleak regions of Lapland, and the farther north, and in the sultry and protracted heats of the south, a due regard must be had to the health of the inhabitants, and to the ordinary means of travelling. If the territory be large, the representatives must come from great distances, and are liable to be retarded by all the varieties of climate, and geological features of the country; by drifts of impassable snows; by sudden inundations; by chains of mountains; by extensive prairies; by numerous streams; by sandy deserts. {223}

§ 303. The task of legislation, too, is exceedingly different in a small state, from what it is in a large one; in a state engaged in a single pursuit, or living in pastoral simplicity, from what it is in a state engaged in the infinitely varied employments of agriculture, manufacture, and commerce, where enterprise and capital rapidly circulate and new legislation is constantly required by the new fortunes of society. A single week might suffice for the ordinary legislation of a state of the territorial extent of Rhode-Island; while several months would scarcely suffice for that of New-York. In Great-Britain a half year is consumed in legislation for its diversified interests and occupations; while a week would accomplish all, that belongs to that of Lapland or of Greenland, of the narrow republic of Geneva, or of the subordinate principalities of Germany. Athens might legislate, without obstructing the daily course of common business, for her own meagre territory; but when Rome had become the mistress of the world, the year seemed too short for all the exigencies of her sovereignty. When she deliberated for a world, she felt, that legislation, to be wise or safe, must be slow and cautious; that knowledge, as well as power, was indispensable for the just government of her provinces.

§ 304. Again; the local position of a nation in regard to other nations may require very different courses of legislation, and very different intervals of elections, from what would be dictated by a sense of its own interest and convenience under other circumstances. If it is surrounded by powerful and warlike neighbours, its own government must be invested with proportionately prompt means to act, and to legislate, in order to repel aggressions, and secure its own rights. Frequent {224} changes in the public councils might not only leave it exposed to the hazard of having no efficient body in existence to act upon any sudden emergency, but also, by the fluctuations of opinion, necessarily growing out of these changes, introduce imbecility, irresolution, and the want of due information into those councils. Men, to act with vigour and effect, must have time to mature measures, and judgment and experience, as to the best method of applying them. They must not be hurried on to their conclusions by the passions, or the fears of the multitude. They must deliberate, as well as resolve. If the power drops from their hands before they have an opportunity to carry any system into full effect, or even to put it on its trial, it is impossible, that foreign nations should not be able, by intrigues, by false alarms, and by corrupt influences, to defeat the wisest measures of the best patriots.

§ 305. One other consideration of a general nature deserves attention. It is, that while, on the one hand, constantly recurring elections afford a great security to public liberty, they are not, on the other hand, without some dangers and inconveniences of a formidable nature. The very frequency of elections has a tendency to create agitations and dissensions in the public mind; to nourish factions, and encourage restlessness; to favour rash innovations in domestic legislation and public policy; and to produce violent and sudden changes in the administration of public affairs, founded upon temporary excitements and prejudices.

§ 306. It is plain, that some of the considerations, which have been stated, must apply with very different force to the condition and interests of different states; and they demonstrate, if not the absurdity, at least the impolicy of laying down any general maxim, as to the {225} frequency of elections to legislative, or other offices. There is quite as much absurdity in laying down, as a general rule, that where annual elections end, tyranny begins, as there is in saying, that the people are free, only while they are choosing their representatives, and slaves during the whole period of their service.

§ 307. The reasons, which finally prevailed in the convention and elsewhere in favour of biennial elections in preference to any other period, may be arranged under the following heads:

§ 308. In the first place, an argument may properly be drawn from the extent of the country to be governed. The territorial extent of the United States will require the representatives to travel from great distances; and the arrangements, rendered necessary by that circumstance, will furnish much more serious objections with men fit for this service, if limited to a single year, than if extended to two years. Annual elections might be very well adapted to the state legislatures from the facility of convening the members, and from the familiarity of the people with all the general objects of local legislation, when they would be highly inconvenient for the legislature of the Union. If, when convened, the term of congress were of short duration, there would scarcely be time properly to examine and mature measures. A new election might intervene before there had been an opportunity to interchange opinions and acquire the information indispensable for wise and salutary action. Much of the business of the national legislature must necessarily be postponed beyond a single session; and if new men are to come every year, a great part of the information already accumulated will be lost, or be unavoidably open for reexamination before any vote can be properly had. {226}

§ 309. In the next place, however well founded the maxim may be, that where no other circumstances affect the case, the greater the power is, the shorter ought to be its duration; and conversely, the smaller the power, the more safely its duration may be protracted; that maxim, if it applies at all to the government of the Union, is favorable to the extension of the period of service beyond that of the state legislatures. The powers of congress are few and limited, and of a national character; those of the state legislatures are general, and have few positive limitations if annual elections are safe for a state; biennial elections would not be less safe for the United States. No just objection, then, could arise from this source, upon any notion, that there would be a more perfect security for public liberty in annual than in biennial elections.

§ 310. But a far more important consideration grows out of the nature and objects of the powers of congress. The aim of every political constitution is, or ought to be, first, to obtain for rulers men, who possess most wisdom to discern, and most virtue to pursue, the common good of society; and, in the next place, to take the most effectual precautions for keeping them virtuous, whilst they continue to hold their public trust. Frequent elections have, without question, a tendency to accomplish the latter object. But too great a frequency will, almost invariably, defeat the former object, and, in most cases, put at hazard the latter. As has been already intimated, it has a tendency to introduce faction, and rash counsels, and passionate appeals to the prejudices, rather than to the sober judgment of the people. And we need not to be reminded, that faction and enthusiasm are the instruments, by which popular governments are destroyed. It operates also, {227} as a great discouragement upon suitable candidates offering themselves for the public service. They can have little opportunity to establish a solid reputation, as statesmen or patriots, when their schemes are liable to be suddenly broken in upon by demagogues, who may create injurious suspicions, and even displace them from office, before their measures are fairly tried. And they are apt to grow weary of continued appeals to vindicate their character and conduct at the polls, since success, however triumphant, is of such short duration, and confidence is so easily loosened. These considerations, which are always of some weight, are especially applicable to services in a national legislature, at a distance from the constituents, and in cases, where a great variety of information, not easily accessible, is indispensable to a right understanding of the conduct and votes of representatives.

§ 311. But the very nature and objects of the national government require far more experience and knowledge, than what may be thought requisite in the members of a state legislature. For the latter a knowledge of local interests and opinions may ordinarily suffice. But it is far different with a member of congress. He is to legislate for the interest and welfare, not of one state only, but of all the states. It is not enough, that he comes to the task with an upright intention and sound judgment, but he must have a competent degree of knowledge of all the subjects, on which he is called to legislate; and he must have skill, as to the best mode of applying it. The latter can scarcely be acquired, but by long experience and training in the national councils. The period of service ought, therefore, to bear some proportion to the variety of knowledge and practical skill, which the duties of the station demand. {228}

§ 312. And this leads us naturally to another remark; and that is, that a due exercise of some of the powers confided to the house of representatives, even in its most narrow functions, require, that the members should at least be elected for a period of two years. The power of impeachment could scarcely be exerted with effect by any body, which had not a legislative life of such a period. It would scarcely be possible, in ordinary cases, to begin and end an impeachment at a single annual session. And the effect of a change of members during its prosecution would be attended with no inconsiderable embarrassment and inconvenience. If the power is ever to be exerted, so as to bring great offenders to justice, there must be a prolonged legislative term of office, so as to meet the exigency. One year will not suffice to detect guilt, and to pursue it to conviction.

§ 313. Again; the house of representatives is to be the sole judge of the elections of its own members. Now, if but one legislative session is to be held in a year, and more than one cannot ordinarily be presumed convenient or proper, spurious elections cannot be investigated and annulled in time to have a due effect. The sitting member must either hold his seat during the whole period of the investigation, or he must be suspended during the same period. In either case the public mischief will be very great. The uniform practice has been to allow the member, who is returned, to hold his seat and vote, until he is displaced by the order of the house, after full investigation. If, then, a return can be obtained, no matter by what means, the irregular member is sure of holding his seat, until a long period has elapsed, (for that is indispensable to any thorough investigation of facts arising at great distances;) {229} and thus a very pernicious encouragement is given to the use of unlawful means for obtaining irregular returns, and fraudulent elections.

§ 314. There is one other consideration, not without its weight in all questions of this nature. Where elections are very frequent, a few of the members, as happens in all such assemblies, will possess superior talents; will, by frequent re-elections, become members of long standing; will become thoroughly masters of the public business; and thus will acquire a preponderating and undue influence, of which they will naturally be disposed to avail themselves. The great bulk of the house will be composed of new members, who will necessarily be inexperienced, diffident, and undisciplined, and thus be subjected to the superior ability and information of the veteran legislators. If biennial elections would have no more cogent effect, than to diminish the amount of this inequality; to guard unsuspecting confidence against the snares, which may be set for it; and to stimulate a watchful and ambitious responsibility, it would have a decisive advantage over mere annual elections.

§ 315. Such were some of the reasons, which produced, on the part of the framers of the constitution, and ultimately of the people themselves, an approbation of biennial elections. Experience has demonstrated the sound policy and wisdom of the provision. But looking back to the period, when the constitution was upon its passage, one cannot but be struck with the alarms, with which the public mind was on this subject attempted to be disturbed. It was repeatedly urged in and out of the state conventions, that biennial elections were dangerous to the public liberty; and that congress might perpetuate itself, and reign with absolute power over the nation. {230}

§ 316. In the next place, as to the qualifications of the elected. The constitution on this subject is as follows:

> "No person shall be a representative, who shall not have attained to the age of twenty-five years, and been seven years a citizen of the United States; and who shall not, when elected, be an inhabitant of that state, in which he shall be chosen."

§ 317. It is obvious, that the inquiry, as to the due qualifications of representatives, like that, as to the due qualifications of electors in a government, is susceptible, in its own nature, of very different answers, according to the habits, institutions, interests, and local peculiarities of different nations. It is a point, upon which we can arrive at no universal rule, which will accomodate itself to the welfare and wants of ever people, with the same proportionate advantages. The great objects are, or ought to be, to secure, on the part of the representatives, fidelity, sound judgment, competent information, and incorruptible independence. The best modes, by which these objects can be attained, are matters of discussion and reasoning, and essentially dependent upon a large and enlightened survey of the human character and passions, as developed in the different stages of civilized society. There is great room, therefore, for diversities of judgment and opinion upon a subject so comprehensive and variable in its elements. It would be matter of surprise, if doctrines essentially different, nay, even opposite to each other, should not, under such circumstances, be maintained by political writers, equally eminent and able. Upon questions of civil policy, and the fundamental structure of governments, there has hitherto been too little harmony of opinion among the greatest men to encourage any hope, that the future will be less fruitful in dissonances, than the {231} past. In the practice of governments, a very great diversity of qualifications has been insisted on, as prerequisites of office; and this alone would demonstrate, that there is not admitted to exist any common standard of superior excellence, adapted to all ages, and all nations.

§ 318. Among the American colonies antecedent to the revolution, a great diversity of qualifications existed; and the state constitutions, subsequently formed, by no means lessen that diversity. Some insist upon a freehold, or other property, of a certain value; others require a certain period of residence, and citizenship only; others require a freehold only; others a payment of taxes, or an equivalent; others, again, mix up all the various qualifications of property, residence, citizenship, and taxation, or substitute some of these, as equivalents for others.

§ 319. The existing qualifications in the states being then so various, it may be thought, that the best course would have been, to adopt the rules of the states respectively, in regard to the most numerous branch of their own legislatures. And this course might not have been open to serious objections. But, as the qualifications of members were thought to be less carefully defined in the state constitutions, and more susceptible of uniformity, than those of the electors, the subject was thought proper for regulation by the convention. And it is observable, that the positive qualifications are few and simple. They respect only age, citizenship, and inhabitancy.

§ 320. First, in regard to age. The representative must have attained twenty-five years. And certainly to this no reasonable objection can be made. If experience, or wisdom, or knowledge, be of value in the national {232} councils, it can scarcely be pretended, that an earlier age could afford a certain guaranty for either. That some qualification of age is proper, no one will dispute. No one will contend, that persons, who are minors, ought to be eligible; or, that those, who have not attained manhood, so as to be entitled by the common law to dispose of their persons, or estates, at their own will, would be fit depositaries of the authority to dispose of the rights, persons, and property of others. Would the mere attainment of twenty-one years of age be a more proper qualification? All just reasoning would be against it. The characters and passions of young men can scarcely be understood at the moment of their majority. They are then new to the rights of self-government; warm in their passions; ardent in their expectations; and, just escaping from pupilage, are strongly tempted to discard the lessons of caution, which riper years inculcate. What they will become, remains to be seen; and four years beyond that period is but a very short space, in which to try their virtues, develope their talents, enlarge their resources, and give them a practical insight into the business of life adequate to their own immediate wants and duties. Can the interests of others be safely confided to those, who have yet to learn, how to take care of their own? The British constitution has, indeed, provided only for the members of the house of commons not being minors; and illustrious instances have occurred to show, that great statesmen may be formed even during their minority. But such instances are rare; they are to be looked at as prodigies, rather than as examples; as the extraordinary growth of a peculiar education and character, and a hot-bed precocity, in a monarchy, rather than as the sound and thrifty growth of the open air, {233} and the bracing hardihood of a republic. In the convention this qualification, as to age, did not pass without a struggle. It was originally carried by a vote of seven states against three, one being divided; though it was ultimately adopted without a division. In the state conventions it does not seem to have formed any important topic of debate.

§ 321. Secondly, in regard to citizenship. It is required, that the representative shall have been a citizen of the United States seven years. Upon the propriety of excluding aliens from eligibility, there could scarcely be any room for debate; for there could be no security for a due administration of any government by persons, whose interests and connexions were foreign, and who owed no permanent allegiance to it, and had no permanent stake in its measures or operations. Foreign influence, of the most corrupt and mischievous nature, could not fail to make its way into the public councils, if there were no guard against the introduction of alien representatives. It has accordingly been a fundamental policy of most, if not of all free states, to exclude all foreigners from holding offices in the state. The only practical question would seem to be, whether foreigners, even after naturalization, should be eligible as representatives; and if so, what is a suitable period of citizenship for the allowance of the privilege. In England, all aliens born, unless naturalized, were originally excluded from a seat in parliament; and now, by positive legislation, no alien, though naturalized, is capable of being a member of either house of parliament. A different course, naturally arising from the circumstances of the country, was adopted in the American colonies antecedent to the revolution, with a view to invite emigrations, and settlements, and thus to facilitate {234} the cultivation of their wild and waste lands. A similar policy had since pervaded the state governments, and had been attended with so many advantages, that it would have been impracticable to enforce any total exclusion of naturalized citizens from office. In the convention it was originally proposed, that three years' citizenship should constitute a qualification; but that was exchanged for seven years by a vote of ten states to one. No objection seems even to have been suggested against this qualification; and hitherto it has obtained a general acquiescence or approbation. It certainly subserves two important purposes. 1. That the constituents have a full opportunity of knowing the character and merits of their representative. 2. That the representative has a like opportunity of learning the character, and wants, and opinions of his constituents.

§ 322. Thirdly, in regard to inhabitancy. It is required, that the representative shall, when elected, be an inhabitant of the state, in which he shall be chosen. The object of this clause, doubtless, was to secure an attachment to, and a just representation of, the interests of the state in the national councils. It was supposed, that an inhabitant would feel a deeper concern, and possess a more enlightened view of the various interests of his constituents, than a mere stranger. And, at all events, he would generally possess more entirely their sympathy and confidence. It is observable, that the inhabitancy required is within the state, and not within any particular district of the state, in which the member is chosen. In England, in former times, it was required, that all the members of the house of commons should be inhabitants of the places, for which they were chosen. But this was for a long time wholly {235} disregarded in practice, and was at length repealed by statute of 14 Geo. 3, ch. 58. This circumstance is not a little remarkable in parliamentary history; and it establishes, in a very striking manner, how little mere theory can be regarded in matters of government. It was found by experience, that boroughs and cities were often better represented by men of eminence, and known patriotism, who were strangers to them, than by those chosen from their own vicinage. And to this very hour some of the proudest names in English history, as patriots and statesmen, have been the representatives of obscure, and, if one may so say, of ignoble boroughs.

§ 323. It has been justly observed, that under the reasonable qualifications established by the constitution, the door of this part of the federal government is open to merit of every description, whether native or adoptive, whether young or old, and without regard to poverty or wealth, or any particular profession of religious faith.

§ 324. The next clause of the second section of the first article respects the apportionment of the representatives among the states. It is as follows:

"Representatives and direct taxes shall be apportioned among the several states, which may be included in this Union, according to their respective numbers, which shall be determined by adding to the whole number of free persons, including those bound to service for a term of years, and excluding Indians not taxed, three-fifths of all other persons. The actual enumeration shall be made within three years after the first meeting of the congress of the United States, and within every subsequent term of ten years, in such manner as they shall, by law, direct. The number of representatives {236} shall not exceed one for every thirty thousand; but each state shall have at least one representative. And until such enumeration shall be made, the state of New-Hampshire shall be entitled to choose three, Massachusetts eight, Rhode-Island and Providence Plantations one, Connecticut five, New-York six, New-Jersey four, Pennsylvania eight, Delaware one, Maryland six, Virginia ten, North-Carolina five, South-Carolina five, and Georgia three."

§ 325. The first apportionment thus made, being of a temporary and fugacious character, requires no commentary. The basis assumed was probably very nearly the same, which the constitution pointed out for all future apportionments, or, at least, of all the free persons in the states.

It is obvious, that the question, how the apportionment should be made, was one, upon which a considerable diversity of judgment might, and probably would, exist. Three leading principles of apportionment would, at once, present themselves. One was to adopt the rule already existing under the confederation; that is, an equality of representation and vote by each state, thus giving each state a right to send not less than two, nor more than seven representatives, and in the determination of questions, each state to have one vote. This would naturally receive encouragement from all those, who were attached to the confederation, and preferred a mere league of states, to a government in any degree national. And accordingly it formed, as it should seem, the basis of what was called the New-Jersey Plan. This rule of apportionment met, however, with a decided opposition, and was negatived in the convention at an early period, seven states voting against it, three being in its favour, and one being divided. {237}

§ 326. Another principle might be, to apportion the representation of the states according to the relative property of each, thus making property the basis of representation. This might commend itself to some persons, because it would introduce a salutary check into the legislature in regard to taxation, by securing, in some measure, an equalization of the public burthens, by the voice of those, who were called to give most towards the common contributions. That taxation ought to go hand in hand with representation had been a favourite theory of the American people. Under the confederation, all the common expenses were required to be borne by the states in proportion to the value of the land within each state. But it has been already seen, that this mode of contribution was extremely difficult and embarrassing, and unsatisfactory in practice, under the confederation. There do not, indeed, seem to be any traces in the proceedings of the convention, that this scheme had an exclusive influence with any persons in that body. It mixed itself up with other considerations, without acquiring any decisive preponderance. In the first place, it was easy to provide a remedial check upon undue direct taxation, the only species, of which there could be the slightest danger of unequal and oppressive levies. And it will be seen, that this was sufficiently provided for, by declaring, that representatives and direct taxes should be apportioned by the same ratio.

§ 327. In the next place, although property may not be directly aimed at, as a basis in the representation, provided for by the constitution, it cannot, on the other hand, be deemed to be totally excluded, as will presently be seen. In the next place, it is not admitted, that property alone can, in a free government, safely be relied {238} on, as the sole basis of representation. It may be true, and probably is, that, in the ordinary course of affairs, it is not the interest, or policy of those, who possess property, to oppress those, who want it. But, in every well-ordered commonwealth, persons, as well as property, should possess a just share of influence. The liberties of the people are too dear, and too sacred, to be entrusted to any persons, who may not, at all times, have a common sympathy and common interest with the people in the preservation of their public rights, privileges, and liberties. Checks and balances, if not indispensable to, are at least a great conservative in, the operations of all free governments. And, perhaps, upon mere abstract theory, it cannot be justly affirmed, that either persons or property, numbers or wealth, can safely be trusted, as the final repositaries of the delegated powers of government. By apportioning influence among each, vigilance, caution, and mutual checks are naturally introduced, and perpetuated.

§ 328. The third and remaining principle was, to apportion the representatives among the states according to their relative numbers. This had the recommendation of great simplicity and uniformity in its operation, of being generally acceptable to the people, and of being less liable to fraud and evasion, than any other, which could be devised. Besides; although wealth and property cannot be affirmed to be in different states exactly in proportion to the numbers; they are not so widely separated from it, as, at a hasty glance, might be imagined. There is, if not a natural, at least a very common connexion between them; and, perhaps, an apportionment of taxes according to numbers is as equitable a rule for contributions according to relative wealth, as any, which can be practically obtained. {239}

§ 329. The scheme, therefore, under all the circumstances, of making numbers, the basis of the representation of the Union, seems to have obtained more general favour, than any other in the convention, because it had a natural and universal connexion with the rights and liberties of the whole people.

§ 330. But here a difficulty of a very serious nature arose. There were other persons in several of the states, than those, who were free. There were some persons, who were bound to service for a term of years; though these were so few, that they would scarcely vary the result of the general rule, in any important degree. There were Indians, also, in several, and probably in most, of the states at that period, who were not treated as citizens, and yet, who did not form a part of independent communities or tribes, exercising general sovereignty and powers of government within the boundaries of the states. It was necessary, therefore, to provide for these cases, though they were attended with no practical difficulty. There seems not to have been any objection to including, in the ratio of representation, persons bound to service for a term of years, and to excluding Indians not taxed. The real (and it was a very exciting) controversy was in regard to slaves, whether they should be included in the enumeration, or not.

§ 331. The truth is, that the arrangement adopted by the constitution was a matter of compromise and concession, confessedly unequal in its operation, but a necessary sacrifice to that spirit of conciliation, which was indispensable to the union of states having a great diversity of interests, and physical condition, and political institutions. It was agreed, that slaves should be represented under the mild appellation of "other persons," {240} not as free persons, but only in the proportion of three fifths. In order to reconcile the non-slave-holding states to this provision, another clause was inserted, that direct taxes should be apportioned in the same manner as representatives. So, that, theoretically, representation and taxation might go *pari passu*. This provision, however, is more specious than solid; for while, in the levy of direct taxes, it apportions them on three fifths of persons not free, it, on the other hand, really exempts the other two fifths from being taxed at all, as property. Whereas, if direct taxes had been apportioned, as upon principle they ought to be, according to the real value of property within the state, the whole of the slaves would have been taxable, as property. But a far more striking inequality has been disclosed by the practical operations of the government. The principle of representation is constant, and uniform; the levy of direct takes is occasional, and rare. In the course of forty years, no more than three direct taxes have been levied; and those only under very extraordinary and pressing circumstances. The ordinary expenditures of the government are, and always have been, derived from other sources. Imposts upon foreign importations have supplied, and will generally supply, all the common wants; and if these should not furnish an adequate revenue, excises are next resorted to, as the surest and most convenient mode of taxation. Direct taxes constitute the last resort; and (as might have been foreseen) would never be laid, until other resources had failed.

§ 332. Viewed in its proper light, as a real compromise, in a case of conflicting interests, for the common good, the provision is entitled to great praise for its moderation, its aim at practical utility, and its tendency {241} to satisfy the people, that the Union, framed by all, ought to be dear to all, by the privileges it confers, as well as the blessings it secures. It had a material influence in reconciling the southern states to other provisions in the constitution, and especially to the power of making commercial regulations by a mere majority, which was thought peculiarly to favour the northern states. It has sometimes been complained of, as a grievance; but he, who wishes well to his country, will adhere steadily to it, as a fundamental policy, which extinguishes some of the most mischievous sources of all political divisions, — those founded on geographical positions, and domestic institutions.

§ 333. Another part of the clause regards the periods, at which the enumeration or census of the inhabitants of the United States shall be taken, in order to provide for new apportionments of representatives, according to the relative increase of the population of the states. Various propositions for this purpose were laid, at different times, before the convention. It was proposed to have the census taken once in fifteen years, and in twenty years; but the vote finally prevailed in favour of ten. The importance of this provision for a decennial census can scarcely be overvalued. It is the only effectual means, by which the relative power of the several states could be justly represented. If the system first established had been unalterable, very gross inequalities would soon have taken place among the states, from the very unequal increase of their population. The representation would soon have exhibited a system very analogous to that of the house of commons, in Great-Britain, where old and decayed boroughs send representatives, not only wholly disproportionate to their importance, but in some cases, with scarcely a single {242} inhabitant, they match the representatives of the most populous counties.

§ 334. In regard to the United States, the slightest examination of the apportionment made under the first three censuses will demonstrate this conclusion in a very striking manner. The representation of Delaware remains, as it was at the first apportionment; that of New-Hampshire, Rhode-Island, Connecticut, New-Jersey, and Maryland has had but a small comparative increase; whilst that of Massachusetts (including Maine) has swelled from eight to twenty; that of New-York, from six to thirty-four; and that of Pennsylvania, from eight to twenty-six. In the mean time, the new states have sprung into being; and Ohio, which in 1803 was only entitled to one, now counts fourteen representatives. The census of 1831 exhibits still more striking results. In 1790, the whole population of the United States was about three millions nine hundred and twenty-nine thousand; and in 1830, it was about twelve millions eight hundred and fifty-six thousand. Ohio, at this very moment, contains at least one million, and New-York two millions of inhabitants. These facts show the wisdom of the provision for a decennial apportionment; and, indeed, it would otherwise have happened, that the system, however sound at the beginning, would by this time have been productive of gross abuses, and probably have engendered feuds and discontents, of themselves sufficient to have occasioned a dissolution of the Union. We probably owe this provision to those in the convention, who were in favour of a national government, in preference to a mere confederation of states.

§ 335. The next part of the clause relates to the total number of the house of representatives. It declares, {243} that "the number of representatives shall not exceed one for every thirty thousand." This was a subject of great interest; and it has been asserted, that scarcely any article of the whole constitution seems to be rendered more worthy of attention by the weight of character, and the apparent force of argument, with which it was originally assailed. The number fixed by the constitution to constitute the body in the first instance, and until a census was taken, was sixty-five.

§ 336. Several objections were urged against the provision. First, that so small a number of representatives would be an unsafe depositary of the public interests. Secondly, that they would not possess a proper knowledge of the local circumstances of their numerous constituents. Thirdly, that they would be taken from that class of citizens, which would sympathize least with the feelings of the people, and be most likely to aim at a permanent elevation of the few, on the depression of the many. Fourthly, that defective, as the number in the first instance would be, it would be more and more disproportionate by the increase of the population, and the obstacles, which would prevent a correspondent increase bf the representatives.

§ 337. Time and experience have demonstrated the fallacy of some, and greatly impaired, if they have not utterly destroyed, the force of all of these objections. The fears, which were at that period so studiously cherished; the alarms, which were so forcibly spread; the dangers to liberty, which were so strangely exaggerated; and the predominance of aristocratical and exclusive power, which were so confidently predicted, have all vanished into air, into thin air. {244}

§ 338. It remains only to take notice of two qualifications of the general principle of representation, which are engrafted on the clause. One is, that each state shall have at least one representative; the other is that already quoted, that the number of representatives shall not exceed one for every 30,000. The former was indispensable in order to secure to each state a just representation in each branch of the legislature; which, as the powers of each branch were not exactly co-extensive, and especially, as the power of originating taxation was exclusively vested in the house of representatives, was indispensable to preserve the equality of the small states, and to reconcile them to a surrender of their sovereignty. This proviso was omitted in the first draft of the constitution, though proposed in one of the preceding resolutions. But it was adopted without resistance, when the draft passed under the solemn discussion of the convention. The other was a matter of more controversy. The original limitation proposed was 40,000; and it was not until the very last day of the session of the convention, that the number was reduced to 30,000. The object of fixing some limitation was to prevent the future existence of a very numerous and unwieldy house of representatives. The friends of a national government had no fears, that the body would ever become too small for real, effective, protecting service. The danger was, that from the natural impulses of the popular will, and the desire of ambitious candidates to attain office, the number would be soon swollen to an unreasonable size, so that it would at once generate, and combine factions, obstruct deliberations, and introduce and perpetuate turbulent and rash counsels. {245}

§ 339. There yet remain two practical questions of no inconsiderable importance, connected with the clause of the constitution now under consideration. One is, what are to be deemed direct taxes within the meaning of the clause. The other is, in what manner the apportionment of representatives is to be made. The first will naturally come under review in examining the powers of congress, and the constitutional limitations upon those powers; and may therefore, for the present, be passed over. The other was a subject of much discussion at the time, when the first apportionment was before congress after the first census was taken; and has been recently revived with new and increased interest and ability. It deserves, therefore, a very deliberate examination.

§ 340. The language of the constitution is, that

"representatives and direct taxes shall be apportioned among the several states, &c. according to their respective numbers;"

and at the first view it would not seem to involve the slightest difficulty. A moment's reflection will dissipate the illusion, and teach us, that there is a difficulty intrinsic in the very nature of the subject. In regard to direct taxes, the natural course would he to assume a particular sum to be raised, as three millions of dollars; and to apportion it among the states according to their relative numbers. But even here, there will always be a very small fractional amount incapable of exact distribution, since the numbers in each state will never exactly coincide with any common divisor, or give an exact aliquot part for each state without any remainder. But, as the amount may be carried through a long series of descending money fractions, it may be ultimately reduced to the smallest fraction of any existing, or even imaginary coin. {246}

§ 341. But the difficulty is far otherwise in regard to representatives. Here, there can be no subdivision of the unit; each state must be entitled to an entire representative, and a fraction of a representative is incapable of apportionment. Yet it will be perceived at once, that it is scarcely possible, and certainly is wholly improbable, that the relative numbers in each state should bear such an exact proportion to the aggregate, that there should exist a common divisor for all, which should leave no fraction in any state. Such a case never yet has existed; and in all human probability it never will. Every common divisor, hitherto applied, has left a fraction greater, or smaller in every state; and what has been in the past must continue to be for the future. Assume the whole population to be three, or six, or nine, or twelve millions, or any other number; if you follow the injunctions of the constitution, and attempt to apportion the representatives according to the numbers in each state, it will be found to be absolutely impossible. The theory, however true, becomes practically false in its application. Each state may have assigned a relative proportion of representatives up to a given number, the whole being divisible by some common divisor; but the fraction of population belonging to each beyond that point is left unprovided for. So that the apportionment is, at best, only an approximation to the rule laid down by the constitution, and not a strict compliance with the rule. The fraction in one state may be ten times as great, as that in another; and so may differ in each state in any assignable mathematical proportion. What then is to be done? Is the constitution to be wholly disregarded on this point? Or is it to be followed out in its true spirit, though unavoidably differing from the letter, by {247} the nearest approximation to it? If an additional representative can be assigned to one state beyond its relative proportion to the whole population, it is equally true, that it can be assigned to all, that are in a similar predicament. If a fraction admits of representation in any case, what prohibits the application of the rule to all fractions? The only constitutional limitation seems to be, that no state shall have more than one representative for every thirty thousand persons. Subject to this, the truest rule seems to be, that the apportionment ought to be the nearest practical approximation to the terms of the constitution; and the rule ought to be such, that it shall always work the same way in regard to all the states, and be as little open to cavil, or controversy, or abuse, as possible.

§ 342. But it may be asked, what are the first steps to be taken in order to arrive at a constitutional apportionment? Plainly, by taking the aggregate of population in all the states, (according to the constitutional rule,) and then ascertain the relative proportion of the population of each state to the population of the whole. This is necessarily so in regard to direct taxes; and there is no reason to say, that it can, or ought to be otherwise in regard to representatives; for that would be to contravene the very injunctions of the constitution, which require the like rule of apportionment in each case. In the one, the apportionment may be run down below unity; in the other, it cannot. But this does not change the nature of the rule, but only the extent of its application.

§ 343. The next clause of the second section of the first article, is:

"When vacancies happen in the representation of any state, the executive authority thereof shall issue writs of election to fill such vacancies." {248}

§ 344. The propriety of adopting this clause does not seem to have furnished any matter of discussion, either in, or out of the convention. It was obvious, that the power ought to reside somewhere; and must be exercised, either by the state or national government, or by some department thereof. The friends of state powers would naturally rest satisfied with leaving it with the state executive; and the friends of the national government would acquiesce in that arrangement, if other constitutional provisions existed sufficient to preserve its due execution. The provision, as it stands, has the strong recommendation of public convenience, and facile adaptation to the particular local circumstances of each state. Any general regulation would have worked with some inequality.

§ 345. The next clause is, that

> "the house of representatives shall choose their speaker, and other officers, and shall have the sole power of impeachment."

§ 346. Each of these privileges is of great practical value and importance. In Great Britain the house of commons elect their own speaker; but he must be approved by the king. This approval is now altogether a matter of course; but anciently, it seems, the king intimated his wish previously, in order to avoid the necessity of a refusal; and it was acceded to. The very language used by the speakers in former times, in order to procure the approval of the crown, was such as would not now be tolerated; and indicated, at least, a disposition to undue subserviency. A similar power of approval existed in the royal governors in many of the colonies before the revolution. The exclusive right of choosing a speaker, without any appeal to, or approval by any other department of the government, {249} is an improvement upon the British system. It secures a more independent and unlimited choice on the part of the house, according to the merits of the individual, and their own sense of duty. It avoids those inconveniences and collisions, which might arise from the interposition of a negative in times of high party excitement. It extinguishes a constant source of jealousy and heart-burning; and a disposition on one side to exert an undue influence, and on the other to assume a hostile opposition. It relieves the executive department from all the embarrassments of opposing the popular will; and the house from all the irritation of not consulting the cabinet wishes.

§ 347. The other power, the sole power of impeachment, has a far wider scope and operation. An impeachment, as described in the common law of England, is a presentment by the house of commons, the most solemn grand inquest of the whole kingdom, to the house of lords, the most high and supreme court of criminal jurisdiction of the kingdom. The articles of impeachment are a kind of bill of indictment found by the commons, and tried by the lords, who are, in cases of misdemeanors, considered, not only as their own peers, but as the peers of the whole nation. The origin and history of the jurisdiction of parliament, in cases of impeachment, are summarily given by Mr. Woodeson; but little can be gathered from it, which is now of much interest, and, like most other legal antiquities, it is involved in great obscurity. To what classes of offenders it applies, will be more properly an inquiry hereafter. In the constitution of the United States, the house of representatives exercises the functions of the house of commons in regard to impeachments; and the senate (as we shall hereafter see) the {250} functions of the house of lords in relation to the trial of the party accused. The principles of the common law, so far as the jurisdiction is to be exercised, are deemed of primary obligation and government. The object of prosecutions of this sort in both countries is to reach high and potent offenders, such as might be presumed to escape punishment in the ordinary tribunals, either from their own extraordinary influence, or from the imperfect organization and powers of those tribunals. These prosecutions are, therefore, conducted by the representatives of the nation, in their public capacity, in the face of the nation, and upon a responsibility, which is at once felt, and reverenced by the whole community. The notoriety of the proceedings; the solemn manner, in which they are conducted; the deep extent, to which they affect the reputation of the accused; the ignominy of a conviction, which is to be known through all time; and the glory of an acquittal, which ascertains and confirms innocence; — these are all calculated to produce a vivid and lasting interest in the public mind; and to give to such prosecutions, when necessary, a vast importance, both as a check to crime, and an incitement to virtue.

§ 348. This subject will be resumed hereafter, when the other provisions of the constitution, in regard to impeachments, come under review. It does not appear, that the vesting of the power of impeachment in the house of representatives was deemed a matter of serious doubt or question, either in the convention, or with the people. If the true spirit of the constitution is consulted, it would seem difficult to arrive at any other conclusion, than of its fitness. It is designed, as a method of national inquest into the conduct of public men. If such is the design, who can so properly be the {251} inquisitors for the nation, as the representatives of the people themselves? They must be presumed to be watchful of the interests, alive to the sympathies, and ready to redress the grievances, of the people. If it is made their duty to bring official delinquents to justice, they can scarcely fail of performing it without public denunciation, and political desertion, on the part of their constituents.

CHAPTER X.

THE SENATE.

§ 349. THE third section of the first article relates to the organization and powers of the senate.

§ 350. In considering the organization of the senate, our inquiries naturally lead us to ascertain; first, the nature of the representation and vote of the states therein; secondly, the mode of appointment; thirdly, the number of the senators; fourthly, their term of service; and fifthly, their qualifications.

§ 351. The first clause of the third section is in the following words:

> "The senate of the United States shall he composed of two senators from each state, chosen by the legislature thereof for six years; and each senator shall have one vote."

§ 352. In the first place, the nature of the representation and vote in the senate. Each state is entitled to two senators; and each senator is entitled to one vote. This, of course, involves in the very constitution of this branch of the legislature a perfect equality among all the states, without any reference to their respective size, population, wealth, or power. In this respect there is a marked contrast between the senate and the house of representatives. In the latter, there is a representation of the people according to the relative population of each state upon a given basis; in the former, each state in its political capacity is represented upon a footing of perfect equality, like a congress of sovereigns, or ambassadors, or like an assembly of peers. The only difference between it and the continental congress under the old confederation is, that in this {253} the vote was by states; in the senate, each senator has a single vote. So that, though they represent states, they vote as individuals. The vote of the senate thus may, and often does, become a mixed vote, embracing a part of the senators from some of the states on one side, and another part on the other.

§ 353. It is obvious, that this arrangement could only arise from a compromise between independent states; and it must have been less the result of theory, than "of a spirit of amity, and of mutual deference and concessions, which the peculiarity of the situation of the United States rendered indispensable." It constituted one of the great struggles between the large and the small states, which was constantly renewed in the convention, and impeded it in every step of its progress in the formation of the constitution. The struggle applied to the organization of each branch of the legislature. The small states insisted upon an equality of vote and representation in each branch; and the large states upon a vote in proportion to their relative importance and population. Upon this vital question there was so near a balance of the states, that a union in any form of government, which provided either for a perfect equality or inequality of the states in both branches of the legislature, became utterly hopeless. If the basis of the senate was an equality of representation, the basis of the house must be in proportion to the relative population of the states. A compromise was, therefore, indispensable, or the convention must be dissolved. The small states at length yielded the point, as to an equality of representation in the house, and acceded to a representation proportionate to the federal numbers. But they insisted upon an equality in the senate. To this the large states were unwilling to assent; and for a {254} time the states were; on this point, equally divided. Finally, the subject was referred to a committee, who reported a scheme, which became, with some amendments, the basis of the representation, as it now stands.

§ 354. Whatever may now be thought of the reasoning of the contending parties, no person, who possesses a sincere love of country, and wishes for the permanent union of the states, can doubt, that the compromise actually made was well founded in policy, and may now be fully vindicated upon the highest principles of political wisdom, and the true nature of the government, which was intended to be established.

§ 355. No system could be more admirably contrived to ensure due deliberation and inquiry, and just results in all matters of legislation. No law or resolution can be passed without the concurrence, first of a majority of the people, and then of a majority of the states. The interest, and passions, and prejudices of a district are thus checked by the influence of a whole state; the like interests, and passions, and prejudices of a state, or of a majority of the states, are met and controlled by the voice of the people of the nation. It may be thought, that this complicated system of checks may operate, in some instances, injuriously, as well as beneficially. But if it should occasionally work unequally, or injuriously, its general operation will be salutary and useful. The disease most incident to free governments is the facility and excess of law-making; and while it never can be the permanent interest of either branch to interpose any undue restraint upon the exercise of all fit legislation, a good law had better occasionally fail, rather than bad laws be multiplied with a heedless and mischievous frequency. Even reforms, to be safe, must, in general, be slow; and there can be {255} little danger, that public opinion will not sufficiently stimulate all public bodies to changes, which are at once desirable, and politic. All experience proves, that the human mind is more eager and restless for changes, than tranquil and satisfied with existing institutions. Besides; the large states will always be able, by their power over the supplies, to defeat any unreasonable exertions of this prerogative by the smaller states.

§ 356. This reasoning, which theoretically seems entitled to great weight, has in the progress of the government, been fully realized. It has not only been demonstrated, that the senate, in its actual organization, is well adopted to the exigencies of the nation; but that it is a most important and valuable part of the system, and the real balance-wheel, which adjusts, and regulates its movements. The other auxiliary provisions in the same clause, as to the mode of appointment and duration of office, will be found to conduce very largely to the same beneficial end.

§ 357. Secondly; the mode of appointment of the senators. They are to be chosen by the legislature of each state. Three schemes presented themselves, as to the mode of appointment; one was by the legislature of each state; another was by the people thereof; and a third was by the other branch of the national legislature, either directly, or out of a select nomination. The last scheme was proposed in the convention, in what was called the Virginia scheme, one of the resolutions, declaring, "that the members of the *second* branch (the Senate) ought to be elected by those of the *first* (the house of representatives) out of a proper number nominated by the individual legislatures" (of the states.) It met, however, with no decided support, and was negatived, no state voting in its favour, nine {256} states voting against it, and one being divided. The second scheme, of an election by the people in districts, or otherwise, seems to have met with as little favour. The first scheme, that of an election by the legislature, finally prevailed by a unanimous vote.

§ 358. The constitution has not provided for the manner, in which the choice shall be made by the state legislatures, whether by a joint, or by a concurrent vote; the latter is, where both branches form one assembly, and give a united vote numerically; the former is, where each branch gives a separate and independent vote. As each of the state legislatures now consists of two branches, this is a very important practical question. Generally, but not universally, the choice of senators is made by a concurrent vote. Another question might be suggested, whether the executive constitutes a part of the legislature for such a purpose, in cases where the state constitution gives him a qualified negative upon the laws. But this has been silently and universally settled against the executive participation in the appointment.

§ 359. Thirdly; the number of senators. Each state is entitled to two senators. It is obvious, that to ensure competent knowledge and ability to discharge all the functions entrusted to the senate, (of which more will be said hereafter,) it is indispensable, that it should consist of a number sufficiently large to ensure a sufficient variety of talents, experience, and practical skill, for the discharge of all their duties. The legislative power alone, for its enlightened and prudent exercise, requires (as has been already shown) no small share of patriotism, and knowledge, and ability. In proportion to the extent and variety of the labours of legislation, there should be members, who should share {257} them, in order, that there may be a punctual and perfect performance of them. If the number be very small, there is danger, that some of the proper duties will be overlooked, or neglected, or imperfectly attended to. No human genius, or industry, is adequate to all the vast concerns of government, if it be not aided by the power and skill of numbers. The senate ought, therefore, on this account alone, to be somewhat numerous, though it need not, and indeed ought not for other reasons, to be as numerous, as the house. Besides; numbers are important to give to the body a sufficient firmness to resist the influence, which the popular branch will ever be solicitous to exert over them. A very small body is more easily overawed, and intimidated, and controlled by external influences, than one of a reasonable size, embracing weight of character, and dignity of talents. Numbers alone, in many cases, confer power; and what is of not less importance, they present more resistance to corruption and intrigue. A body of five may be bribed, or overborne, when a body of fifty would be an irresistible barrier to usurpation.

§ 360. In addition to this consideration, it is desirable, that a state should not be wholly unrepresented in the national councils by mere accident, or by the temporary absence of its representative. If there be but a single representative, sickness or casualty may deprive the state of its vote on the most important occasions. It was on this account, (as well as others) that the confederation entitled each state to send not less than *two*, nor more than *seven* delegates. In critical cases, too, it might be of great importance to have an opportunity of consulting with a colleague or colleagues, having a common interest and feeling for the {258} state. And if it be not always in the strictest sense true, that in the multitude of counsel there is safety; there is a sufficient foundation in the infirmity, of human nature to make it desirable to gain the advantage of the wisdom, and information, and reflection of other independent minds, not labouring under the suspicion of any unfavourable bias. These reasons may be presumed to have had their appropriate weight in the deliberations of the convention. If more than one representative of a state was to be admitted into the senate, the least practicable ascending number was that adopted. At that time a single representative of each state would have made the body too small for all the purposes of its institution, and all the objects before explained. It would have been composed but of thirteen; and supposing no absences, which could not ordinarily be calculated upon, seven would constitute a majority to decide all the measures. Twenty-six was not, at that period, too large a number for dignity, independence, wisdom, experience, and efficiency. And, at the present moment, when the states have grown to twenty-four, it is found, that forty-eight is a number quite small enough to perform the great national functions confided to it, and to embody the requisite skill and ability to meet the increased exigencies, and multiplied duties of the office. There is probably no legislative body on earth, whose duties are more various, and interesting, and important to the public welfare; and none, which calls for higher talents, and more comprehensive attainments, and more untiring industry, and integrity.

§ 361. Fourthly; the term of service of the senators. It is for six years; although, as will be presently seen, another element in the composition of that body is, that one third of it is changed every two years. {259}

What would be the most proper period of office for senators, was an inquiry, admitting of a still wider range of argument and opinion, than what would be the most proper for the members of the house of representatives. The subject was confessedly one full of intricacy, and doubt, upon which the wisest statesmen might well entertain very different views, and the best patriots might well ask for more information, without, in the slightest degree, bringing into question their integrity, their love of liberty, or their devotion to a republican government.

§ 362. The objections to the senatorial term of office all resolve themselves into a single argument, however varied in its forms, or illustrations. That argument is, that political power is liable to be abused; and that the great security for public liberty consists in bringing home responsibility, and dependence in those, who are entrusted with office; and these are best attained by short periods of office, and frequent expressions of public opinion in the choice of officers. If the argument is admitted in its most ample scope, it still leaves the question open to much discussion, what is the proper period of office, and how frequent the elections should be. This question must, in its nature, be complicated; and may admit, if it does not absolutely require, different answers, as applicable to different functionaries. Without wandering into ingenious speculations upon the topic in its most general form, our object will be to present the reasons, which have been, or may be relied on, to establish the sound policy and wisdom of the duration of office of the senators as fixed by the constitution.

§ 363. In the first place, then, all the reasons, which apply to the duration of the legislative office generally, {260} founded upon the advantages of various knowledge, and experience in the principles and duties of legislation, may be urged with increased force in regard to the senate. A good government implies two things; first, fidelity to the object of government, which is the happiness of the people; secondly, a knowledge of the means, by which that object is to be attained. Some governments are deficient in both these qualities; most are deficient in the first. Some of our wisest statesmen have not scrupled to assert, that in the American governments too little attention has been paid to the latter.

§ 364. A well constituted senate, then, which should interpose some restraints upon the sudden impulses of a more numerous branch, would, on this account, be of great value. But its value would be incalculably increased by making its term of office such, that with moderate industry, talents, and devotion to the public service, its members could scarcely fail of having the reasonable information, which would guard them against gross errors, and the reasonable firmness, which would enable them to resist visionary speculations, and popular excitements. If public men know, that they may safely wait for the gradual action of a sound public opinion, to decide upon the merit of their actions and measures, before they can be struck down, they will be more ready to assume responsibility, and pretermit present popularity for future solid reputation. If they are designed, by the very structure of the government, to secure the states against encroachments upon their rights and liberties, this very permanence of office adds new means to effectuate the object. Popular opinion, may, perhaps, in its occasional extravagant sallies, at the instance of a fawning demagogue, or a favorite {261} chief, incline to overleap the constitutional barriers, in order to aid their advancement, or gratify their ambition. But the solid judgment of a senate may stay the evil, if its own duration of power exceeds that of the other branches of the government, or if it combines the joint durability of both. In point of fact, the senate has this desirable limit. It combines the period of office of the executive with that of the members of the house; while at the same time, from its own biennial changes, (as we shall presently see,) it is silently subjected to the deliberate voice of the states.

§ 365. In the next place, mutability in the public councils, arising from a rapid succession of new members, is found by experience to work, even in domestic concerns, serious mischiefs. It is a known fact in the history of the states, that every new election changes nearly or quite one half of its representatives; and in the national government changes less frequent, or less numerous can scarcely be expected. From this change of men, there must unavoidably arise a change of opinions; and with this change of opinions a correspondent change of measures. Now experience demonstrates, that a continual change, even of good measures for good, is inconsistent with every rule of prudence and every prospect of success. In all human affairs, time is required to consolidate the elements of the best concerted measures, and to adjust the little interferences, which are incident to all legislation. Perpetual changes in public institutions not only occasion intolerable controversies, and sacrifices of private interests; but check the growth of that steady industry and enterprise, which, by wise forecast, lays up the means of future prosperity.

§ 366. But the ill effects of a mutable government are still more strongly felt in the intercourse with foreign {262} nations. It forfeits the respect and confidence of foreign nations, and all the advantages connected with national character. It not only lays its measures open to the silent operations of foreign intrigue and management; but it subjects its whole policy to be counteracted by the wiser and more stable policy of its foreign rivals and adversaries. One nation is to another, what one individual is to another, with this melancholy distinction perhaps, that the former, with fewer benevolent emotions than the latter, are under fewer restraints also from taking undue advantages of the indiscretions of each other. If a nation is perpetually fluctuating in its measures, as to the protection of agriculture, commerce, and manufactures, it exposes all its infirmities of purpose to foreign nations; and the latter with a systematical sagacity will sap all the foundations of its prosperity.

§ 367. Further; foreign governments can never safely enter into any permanent arrangements with one, whose councils and government are perpetually fluctuating. It was not unreasonable, therefore, for them to object to the continental congress, that they could not guaranty the fulfilment of any treaty; and therefore it was useless to negotiate any. To secure the respect of foreign nations, there must be power to fulfil engagements; confidence to sustain them; and durability to ensure their execution on the part of the government. National character in cases of this sort is inestimable. It is not sufficient, that there should be a sense of justice, and disposition to act right; but there must be an enlightened permanency in the policy of the government.

§ 368. Considering, then, the various functions of the senate, the qualifications of skill, experience, and {263} information, which are required to discharge them, and the importance of interposing, not a nominal, but a real check, in order to guard the states from usurpations upon their authority, and the people from becoming the victims of violent paroxysms in legislation; the term of six years would seem to hit the just medium between a duration of office, which would too much resist, and a like duration, which would too much invite those changes of policy, foreign and domestic, which the best interests of the country may require to be deliberately weighed, and gradually introduced, if the state governments are found tranquil, and prosperous, and safe, with a senate of two, three, four, and five years' duration, it would seem impossible for the Union to be in danger from a term of service of six years.

§ 369. But, in order to quiet the last lingering scruples of jealousy, the succeeding clause of the constitution has interposed an intermediate change in the elements of the body, which would seem to make it absolutely above exception, if reason, and not fear, is to prevail; and if government is to be a reality, and not a vision.

§ 370. It declares,

"Immediately after they (the senators) shall be assembled, in consequence of the first election, they shall be divided, as equally as may be, into three classes. The seats of the senators of the first class shall be vacated at the expiration of the second year; of the second class, at the expiration of the fourth year; and of the third class, at the expiration of the sixth year, so that one third may be chosen every second year."

A proposition was made in the convention, that the senators should be chosen for nine years, one third to go out biennially, and was {264} lost, three states voting in the affirmative, and eight in the negative; and then the present limitation was adopted by a vote of seven states against four. Here, then, is a clause, which, without impairing the efficiency of the senate for the discharge of its high functions, gradually changes its members, and introduces a biennial appeal to the states, which must for ever prohibit any permanent combination for sinister purposes. No person would probably propose a less duration of office for the senate, than double the period of the house. In effect, this provision changes the composition of two thirds of that body within that period.

§ 371. As vacancies might occur in the senate during the recess of the state legislature, it became indispensable to provide for that exigency. Accordingly the same clause proceeds to declare:

"And if vacancies happen by resignation, or otherwise, during the recess of the legislature of any state, the executive thereof may make temporary appointments until the next meeting of the legislature, which shall then fill such vacancies."

It does not appear, that any strong objection was urged in the convention against this proposition, although it was not adopted without some opposition. There seem to have been three courses presented for the consideration of the convention; either to leave the vacancies unfilled, until the meeting of the state legislature; or to allow the state legislatures to provide at their pleasure prospectively for the occurrence; or to confide a temporary appointment to some select state functionary or body. The latter was deemed the most satisfactory and convenient course. Confidence might justly be reposed in the state executive, as representing at once the interests and wishes of the state, and enjoying all the proper {265} means of knowledge and responsibility, to ensure a judicious appointment.

§ 372. Fifthly; the qualifications of senators. The constitution declares, that

"No person shall be a senator, who shall not have attained the age of thirty years, and been nine years a citizen of the United States, and who shall not, when elected, be an inhabitant of that state, for which he shall be chosen."

As the nature of the duties of a senator require more experience, knowledge, and stability of character, than those of a representative, the qualification in point of age is raised. A person may be a representative at twenty-five; but he cannot be a senator until thirty. A similar qualification of age was required of the members of the Roman senate. It would have been a somewhat singular anomaly in the history of free governments, to have found persons actually exercising the highest functions of government, who, in some enlightened and polished countries, would not be deemed to have arrived at an age sufficiently mature to be entitled to all the private and municipal privileges of manhood. In Rome persons were not deemed at full age until twenty-five; and that continues to be the rule in France, and Holland, and other civil law countries; and in France, by the old law, in regard to marriage full age was not attained until thirty. It has since been varied, and the term diminished.

§ 373. The age of senators was fixed in the constitution at first by a vote of seven states against four; and finally, by an unanimous vote. Perhaps no one, in our day, is disposed to question the propriety of this limitation; and it is, therefore, useless to discuss a point, which is so purely speculative if counsels are to be wise, the ardour, and impetuosity, and confidence {266} of youth must be chastised by the sober lessons of experience; and if knowledge, and solid judgment, and tried integrity, are to be deemed indispensable qualifications for senatorial service, it would be rashness to affirm, that thirty years is too long a period for a due maturity and probation.

§ 374. The next qualification is citizenship. The propriety of some limitation upon admissions to office, after naturalization, cannot well be doubted. The senate is to participate largely in transactions with foreign governments; and it seems indispensable, that time should have elapsed sufficient to wean a senator from all prejudices, resentments, and partialities, in relation to the land of his nativity, before he should be entrusted with such high and delicate functions. Besides; it can scarcely be presumed, that any foreigner can have acquired a thorough knowledge of the institutions and interests of a country, until he has been permanently incorporated into its society, and has acquired by the habits and intercourse of life the feelings and the duties of a citizen. And if he has acquired the requisite knowledge, he can scarcely feel that devoted attachment to them, which constitutes the great security for fidelity and promptitude in the discharge of official duties. If eminent exceptions could be stated, they would furnish no safe rule; and should rather teach us to fear our being misled by brilliancy of talent, or disinterested patriotism, into a confidence, which might betray, or an acquiescence, which might weaken, that jealousy of foreign influence, which is one of the main supports of republics. In the convention it was at first proposed, that the limitation should be four years; and it was finally altered by a vote of six states against four, one being divided, {267} which was afterwards confirmed by a vote of eight states to three. This subject has been already somewhat considered in another place; and it may be concluded, by adopting the language of the Federalist on the same clause. "The term of nine years appears to be a prudent mediocrity between a total exclusion of adopted citizens, whose merit and talents may claim a share in the public confidence, and an indiscriminate and hasty admission of them, which might create a channel for foreign influence in the national councils."

§ 375. The only other qualification is, that every senator shall, when elected, be an inhabitant of the state, for which he is chosen. This scarcely requires any comment; for it is manifestly proper, that a state should be represented by one, who, besides an intimate knowledge of all its wants and wishes, and local pursuits, should have a personal and immediate interest in all measures touching its sovereignty, its rights, or its influence. The only surprise is, that provision was not made for his ceasing to represent the state in the senate, as soon as he should cease to be an inhabitant. There does not seem to have been any debate in the convention on the propriety of inserting the clause, as it now stands.

§ 376. In concluding this topic, it is proper to remark, that no qualification whatsoever of property is established in regard to senators, as none had been established in regard to representatives. Merit, therefore, and talent have the freest access open to them into every department of office under the national government. Under such circumstances, if the choice of the people is but directed by a suitable sobriety of judgment, the senate cannot fail of being distinguished for wisdom, for learning, for exalted patriotism, for incorruptible integrity, and for inflexible independences. {268}

§ 377. The next clause of the third section of the first article respects the person, who shall preside in the senate. It declares, that

"the Vice President of the United States shall be president of the senate; but shall have no vote, unless they be equally divided;"

and the succeeding clause, that

"the senate shall choose their other officers, and also a president pro tempore, in the absence of the vice president, or when he shall exercise the office of president of the United States."

§ 378. The original article, as first reported, authorized the senate to choose its own president, and other officers; and this was adopted in the convention. But the same draft authorized the president of the senate, in case of the removal, death, resignation, or disability of the president, to discharge his duties. When at a late period of the convention it was deemed advisable, that there should be a vice president, the propriety of retaining him, as presiding officer of the senate, seems to have met with general favour, eight states voting in the affirmative, and two only in the negative.

§ 379. The propriety of creating the office of vice president will be reserved for future consideration, when, in the progress of these commentaries, the constitution of the executive department comes under review. The reasons, why he was authorized to preside in the senate, belong appropriately to this place.

§ 380. There is no novelty in the appointment of a person to preside, as speaker, who is not a constituent member of the body, over which he is to preside. In the house of lords in England the presiding officer is the lord chancellor, or lord keeper of the great seal, or other person appointed by the king's commission; and if none such be so appointed, then it is said, that {269} the lords may elect. But it is by no means necessary, that the person appointed by the king should be a peer of the realm, or lord of parliament. Nor has this appointment by the king ever been complained of, as a grievance, nor has it operated with inconvenience or oppression in practice. It is on the contrary deemed an important advantage, both to the officer, and to the house of peers, adding dignity and weight to the former, and securing great legal ability and talent in aid of the latter. This consideration alone might have had some influence in the convention. The vice president being himself chosen by the states, might well be deemed, in point of age, character, and dignity, worthy to preside over the deliberations of the senate, in which the states were all assembled, and represented. His impartiality in the discharge of its duties might be fairly presumed; and the employment would not only bring his character in review before the public; but enable him to justify the public confidence, by performing his public functions with independence, and firmness, and sound discretion. A citizen, who was deemed worthy of being one of the competitors for the presidency, could scarcely fail of being distinguished by private virtues, by comprehensive acquirements, and by eminent services. In all questions before the senate he might safely be appealed to, as a fit arbiter upon an equal division, in which case alone he is entrusted with a vote.

§ 381. But the strong motive for this appointment was of another sort, founded upon state jealousy, and state equality in the senate. If the speaker of the senate was to be chosen from its own members, the state, upon whom the choice would fall, might possess either more or less, than its due share of influence. If {270} the speaker were not allowed to vote, except when there was an equal division, independent of his own vote, then the state might lose its own voice; if he were allowed to give his vote, and also a casting vote, then the state might, in effect, possess a double vote. Either alternative would of itself present a predicament sufficiently embarrassing. On the other hand, if no casting vote were allowed in any case, then the indecision and inconvenience might be very prejudicial to the public interests, in case of an equality of votes. It might give rise to dangerous feuds, or intrigues, and create sectional and state agitations. The smaller states might well suppose, that their interests were less secure, and less guarded, than they ought to be. Under such circumstances, the vice president would seem to be the most fit arbiter to decide, because he would be the representative, not of one state only, but of all; and must be presumed to feel a lively interest in promoting all measures for the public good. This reasoning appears to have been decisive in the convention, and satisfactory to the people. It establishes, that there was a manifest propriety in making the arrangement, conducive to the harmony of the states, and the dignity of the general government. And as the senate possesses the power to make rules for its own proceedings, there is little danger, that there can ever arise any abuse of the presiding power. The danger, if any, is rather the other way, that the presiding power will be either silently weakened, or openly surrendered, so as to leave the office little more, than the barren honour of a place, without influence and without action.

§ 382. The propriety of entrusting the senate with the choice of its other officers, and also of a president {271} pro tempore in the absence of the vice president, or when he exercises the office of president, seems never to have been questioned; and indeed is so obvious, that it is wholly unnecessary to vindicate it. Confidence between the senate and its officers, and the power to make a suitable choice, and to secure a suitable responsibility for the faithful discharge of the duties of office, are so indispensable for the public good, that the provision will command universal assent, as soon as it is mentioned. It has grown into a general practice for the vice president to vacate the senatorial chair a short time before the termination of each session, in order to enable the senate to choose a president pro tempore, who might already be in office, if the vice president in the recess should be called to the chair of state. The practice is founded in wisdom and sound policy, as it immediately provides for an exigency, which may well be expected to occur at any time; and prevents the choice from being influenced by temporary excitements or intrigues, arising from the actual existence of a vacancy. As it is useful in peace to provide for war; so it is likewise useful in times of profound tranquillity to provide for political agitations, which may disturb the public harmony.

§ 383. The next clause of the third section of the first article respects the subject of impeachment. It is as follows:

> "The senate shall have the sole power to try all impeachments. When sitting for that purpose, they shall be on oath or affirmation. When the president of the United States is tried, the chief justice shall preside. And no person shall be convicted without the concurrence of two thirds of the members present."

§ 384. The great objects, to be attained in the selection {272} of a tribunal for the trial of impeachments, are, impartiality, integrity, intelligence, and independence. If either of these is wanting, the trial must be radically imperfect. To ensure impartiality, the body must be in some degree removed from popular power and passions, from the influence of sectional prejudice, and from the more dangerous influence of mere party spirit. To secure integrity, there must be a lofty sense of duty, and a deep responsibility to future times, as well as to God. To secure intelligence, there must be age, experience, and high intellectual powers, as well as attainments. To secure independence, there must be numbers, as well as talents, and a confidence resulting at once from permanency of place, and dignity of station, and enlightened patriotism. Does the senate combine, in a suitable degree, all these qualifications? Does it combine them more perfectly, than any other tribunal, which could be constituted? What other tribunal could be entrusted with the authority? These are questions of the highest importance, and of the most frequent occurrence. They arose in the convention, and underwent a full discussion there. They were again deliberately debated in the state conventions; and they have been at various times since agitated by jurists and statesmen, and political bodies. Few parts of the constitution have been assailed with more vigour; and few have been defended with more ability.

§ 385. The subject is itself full of intrinsic difficulty in a government purely elective. The jurisdiction is to be exercised over offences, which are committed by public men in violation of their public trust and duties. Those duties are, in many cases, political; and, indeed, in other cases, to which the power of impeachment will {273} probably be applied, they will respect functionaries of a high character, where the remedy would otherwise be wholly inadequate, and the grievance be incapable of redress. Strictly speaking, then, the power partakes of a political character, as it respects injuries to the society in its political character; and, on this account, it requires to be guarded in its exercise against the spirit of faction, the intolerance of party, and the sudden movements of popular feeling. The prosecution will seldom fail to agitate the passions of the whole community, and to divide it into parties, more or less friendly, or hostile to the accused. The press, with its unsparing vigilance, will arrange itself on either side, to control, and influence public opinion; and there will always be some danger, that the decision will be regulated more by the comparative strength of parties, than by the real proofs of innocence or guilt.

§ 386. On the other hand, the delicacy and magnitude of a trust, which so deeply concerns the political existence and reputation of every man engaged in the administration of public affairs, cannot be overlooked. It ought not to be a power so operative and instant, that it may intimidate a modest and conscientious statesman, or other functionary from accepting office; nor so weak and torpid, as to be capable of lulling offenders into a general security and indifference. The difficulty of placing it rightly in a government, resting entirely on the basis of periodical elections, will be more strikingly perceived, when it is considered, that the ambitious and the cunning will often make strong accusations against public men the means of their own elevation to office; and thus give an impulse to the power of impeachment, by pre-occupying the public opinion. The convention appears to have been very {274} strongly impressed with the difficulty of constituting a suitable tribunal; and finally came to the result, that the senate was the most fit depositary of this exalted trust. In so doing, they had the example before them of several of the best considered state constitutions; and the example, in some measure, of Great Britain. The most strenuous opponent cannot, therefore, allege, that it is a rash and novel experiment; the most unequivocal friend must, at the same time, admit, that it is not free from all plausible objections.

§ 387. The conclusion, to which, upon a large survey of the whole subject, our judgments are naturally led, is, that the power has been wisely deposited with the senate. In the language of a learned commentator, it may be said, that of all the departments of the government, "none will be found more suitable to exercise this peculiar jurisdiction, than the senate. Although, like their accusers, they are representatives of the people; yet they are so by a degree more removed, and hold their stations for a longer term. They are, therefore, more independent of the people, and being chosen with the knowledge, that they may, while in office, be called upon to exercise this high function, they bring with them the confidence of their constituents, that they will faithfully execute it, and the implied compact on their own part, that it shall be honestly discharged. Precluded from ever becoming accusers themselves, it is their duty not to lend themselves to the animosities of party, or the prejudices against individuals, which may sometimes unconsciously induce the house of representatives to the acts of accusation. Habituated to comprehensive views of the great political relations of the country, they are naturally the best qualified to decide on those charges, which may have any connexion {275} with transactions abroad, or great political interests at home. And although we cannot say, that, like the English house of lords, they form a distinct body, wholly uninfluenced by the passions, and remote from the interests, of the people; yet we can discover in no other division of the government a greater probability of impartiality and independence."

§ 388. The remaining parts of the clause of the constitution now under consideration will not require an elaborate commentary. The first is, that the senate, when sitting as a court of impeachment, "shall be on oath or affirmation;" a provision, which, as it appeals to the conscience and integrity of the members by the same sanction, which applies to judges and jurors, who sit in other trials, will commend itself to all persons, who deem the highest trusts, rights, and duties, worthy of the same protection and security, at least, as those of the humblest order. It would, indeed, be a monstrous anomaly, that the highest officers might be convicted of the worst crimes, without any sanction being interposed against the exercise of the most vindictive passions; while the humblest individual has a right to demand an oath of fidelity from those, who are his peers, and his triors. In England, however, upon the trial of impeachments, the house of lords are not under oath; but only make a declaration upon their honour. This is a strange anomaly, as in all civil and criminal trials by a jury, the jurors are under oath; and there seems no reason, why a sanction equally obligatory upon the consciences of the triors should not exist in trials for capital or other offences before every other tribunal. What is there in the honour of a peer, which necessarily raises it above the honour of a commoner? The anomaly is rendered still more glaring {276} by the fact, that a peer cannot give testimony, as a witness, except on oath; for, here, his honour is not trusted. The maxim of the law, in such a case, is *in judicio non creditur, nisi juratis.* Why should the obligation of a judge be less solemn, than the obligation of a witness? The truth is, that it is a privilege of power, conceded in barbarous times, and founded on feudal sovereignty, more than on justice, or principle.

§ 389. The next provision is:

"When the president of the United States is tried, the chief justice shall preside."

The reason of this clause has been already adverted to. It is to preclude the vice president, who might be supposed to have a natural desire to succeed to the office, from being instrumental in procuring the conviction of the chief magistrate. Under such circumstances, who could be deemed more suitable to preside, than the highest judicial magistrate of the Union. His impartiality and independence could be as little suspected, as those of any person in the country. And the dignity of his station might well be deemed an adequate pledge for the possession of the highest accomplishments.

§ 390. It is added,

"And no person shall be convicted without the concurrence of two thirds of the members present."

Although very numerous objections were taken to the constitution, none seems to have presented itself against this particular quorum required for a conviction; and yet it might have been fairly thought to be open to attack on various sides from its supposed theoretical inconvenience and incongruity. It might have been said with some plausibility, that it deserted the general principles even of courts of justice, where a mere majority make the decision; {277} and, of all legislative bodies, where a similar rule is adopted; and, that the requisition of two thirds would reduce the power of impeachment to a mere nullity. Besides; upon the trial of impeachments in the house of lords the conviction or acquittal is by a mere majority; so that there is a failure of any analogy to support the precedent.

§ 391. It does not appear from any authentic memorials, what were the precise grounds, upon which this limitation was interposed. But it may well be conjectured, that the real grounds were, to secure an impartial trial, and to guard public men from being sacrificed to the immediate impulses of popular resentment or party predominance. In England, the house of lords, from its very structure and hereditary independence, furnishes a sufficient barrier against such oppression and injustice. Mr. Justice Blackstone has remarked, with manifest satisfaction, that the nobility "have neither the same interests, nor the same passions, as popular assemblies;" and, that "it is proper, that the nobility should judge, to insure justice to the accused; as it is proper, that the people should accuse, to insure justice to the commonwealth." Our senate is, from the very theory of the constitution, founded upon a more popular basis; and it was desirable to prevent any combination of a mere majority of the states to displace, or to destroy a meritorious public officer. If a mere majority were sufficient to convict, there would be danger, in times of high popular commotion or party spirit, that the influence of the house of representatives would be found irresistible. The only practicable check seemed to be, the introduction of the clause of two thirds, which would thus require a union of opinion and interest, rare, except in cases, {278} where guilt was manifest, and innocence scarcely presumable. Nor could the limitation be justly complained of; for, in common cases, the law not only presumes every man innocent, until he is proved guilty; but unanimity in the verdict of the jury is indispensable. Here, an intermediate scale is adopted between unanimity, and a mere majority. And if the guilt of a public officer cannot be established to the satisfaction of two thirds of a body of high talents and acquirements, which sympathizes with the people, and represents the states, after a full investigation of the facts, it must be, that the evidence is too infirm, and too loose to justify a conviction. Under such circumstances, it would be far more consonant to the notions of justice in a republic, that a guilty person should escape, than that an innocent person should become the victim of injustice from popular odium, or party combinations.

§ 392. The next clause is, that

"Judgment in cases of impeachment shall not extend further, than to removal from office, and disqualification to hold and enjoy any office of honour, trust, or profit, under the United States. But the party convicted shall nevertheless be liable and subject to indictment, trial, judgment, and punishment, according to law."

§ 393. It is obvious, that, upon trials on impeachments, one of two courses must be adopted in case of a conviction; either for the court to proceed to pronounce a full and complete sentence of punishment for the offence according to the law of the land in like cases, pending in the common tribunals of justice, superadding the removal from office, and the consequent disabilities; or, to confine its sentence to the removal from office and other disabilities. If the former duty {279} be a part of the constitutional functions of the court, then, in case of an acquittal, there cannot be another trial of the party for the same offence in the common tribunals of justice, because it is repugnant to the whole theory of the common law, that a man should be brought into jeopardy of life or limb more than once for the same offence. A plea of acquittal is, therefore, an absolute bar against any second prosecution for the same offence. If the court of impeachments is merely to pronounce a sentence of removal from office and the other disabilities; then it is indispensable, that provision should be made, that the common tribunals of justice should be at liberty to entertain jurisdiction of the offence, for the purpose of inflicting the common punishment applicable to unofficial offenders. Otherwise, it might be matter of extreme doubt, whether, consistently with the great maxim above mentioned, established for the security of the life and limbs and liberty of the citizen, a second trial for the same offence could be had, either after an acquittal, or a conviction in the court of impeachments. And if no such second trial could be had, then the grossest official offenders might escape without any substantial punishment, even for crimes, which would subject their fellow citizens to capital punishment.

§ 394. The constitution, then, having provided, that judgment upon impeachments shall not extend further, than to removal from office, and disqualification to hold office, (which, however afflictive to an ambitious and elevated mind, would be scarcely felt, as a punishment, by the profligate and the base,) has wisely subjected the party to trial in the common criminal tribunals, for the purpose of receiving such punishment, as ordinarily belongs to the offence. Thus, for instance, {280} treason, which by our laws is a capital offence, may receive its appropriate punishment; and bribery in high officers, which otherwise would be a mere disqualification from office, may have the measure of its infamy dealt out to it with the same unsparing severity, which attends upon other and humbler offenders.

§ 395. In England, the judgment upon impeachments is not confined to mere removal from office; but extends to the whole punishment attached by law to the offence. The house of lords, therefore, upon a conviction, may, by its sentence, inflict capital punishment; or perpetual banishment; or forfeiture of goods and lands; or fine and ransom; or imprisonment; as well as removal from office, and incapacity to hold office, according to the nature and aggravation of the offence.

§ 396. As the offences, to which the remedy of impeachment has been, and will continue to be principally applied, are of a political nature, it is natural to suppose, that they will be often exaggerated by party spirit, and the prosecutions be sometimes dictated by party resentments, as well as by a sense of the public good. There is danger, therefore, that in cases of conviction the punishment may be wholly out of proportion to the offence, and pressed as much by popular odium, as by aggravated crime. From the nature of such offences, it is impossible to fix any exact grade, or measure, either in the offences, or the punishments; and a very large discretion must unavoidably be vested in the court of impeachments, as to both. Any attempt to define the offences, or to affix to every grade of distinction its appropriate measure of punishment, would probably tend to more injustice and inconvenience, than it would correct; and perhaps would {281} render the power at once inefficient and unwieldly. The discretion, then, if confided at all, being peculiarly subject to abuse, and connecting itself with state parties, and state contentions, and state animosities, it was deemed most advisable by the convention, that the power of the senate to inflict punishment should merely reach the right and qualifications to office; and thus take away the temptation in factious times to sacrifice good and great men upon the altar of party. History had sufficiently admonished them, that the power of impeachment had been thus mischievously and inordinately applied in other ages; and it was not safe to disregard those lessons, which it had left for our instruction, written not unfrequently in blood. Lord Strafford, in the reign of Charles the First, and Lord Stafford, in the reign of Charles the Second, were both convicted, and punished capitally by the house of Lords; and both have been supposed to have been rather victims to the spirit of the times, than offenders meriting such high punishments. And other cases have occurred, in which, whatever may have been the demerits of the accused, his final overthrow has been the result of political resentments and hatreds, far more than of any desire to promote public justice.

§ 397. There is wisdom, and sound policy, and intrinsic justice in this separation of the offence, at least so far as the jurisdiction and trial are concerned, into its proper elements, bringing the political part under the power of the political department of the government, and retaining the civil part for presentment and trial in the ordinary forum. A jury might well be entrusted with the latter; while the former should meet its appropriate trial and punishment before the senate. If it should be asked, why separate trials should thus {282} be successively had; and why, if a conviction should take place in a court of law, that court might not be entrusted with the power to pronounce a removal from office, and the disqualification to office, as a part of its sentence, the answer has been already given in the reasoning against vesting any court of law with merely political functions. In the ordinary course of the administration of criminal justice, no court is authorized to remove, or disqualify an offender, as a part of its regular judgment. If it results at all, it results as a consequence, and not as a part of the sentence. But it may be properly urged, that the vesting of such a high and delicate power, to be exercised by a court of law at its discretion, would, in relation to the distinguished functionaries of the government, be peculiarly unfit and inexpedient. What could be more embarrassing, than for a court of law to pronounce for a removal upon the mere ground of political usurpation, or malversation in office, admitting of endless varieties, from the slightest guilt up to the most flagrant corruption? Ought a president to be removed from office at the mere will of a court for political misdemeanours? Is not a political body, like the senate, from its superior information in regard to executive functions, far better qualified to judge, how far the public weal might be promoted by such a punishment in a given case, than a mere juridical tribunal? Suppose the senate should still deem the judgment irregular, or unjustifiable, how is the removal to take effect, and how is it to be enforced? A separation of the removing power altogether from the appointing power might create many practical difficulties, which ought not, except upon the most urgent reasons, to be introduced into matters of government. Without attempting to maintain, that the {283} difficulties would be insuperable, it is sufficient to show, that they might be highly inconvenient in practice.

§ 398. In order to complete our review of the constitutional provisions on the subject of impeachments, it is necessary to ascertain, who are the persons liable to be impeached; and what are impeachable offences. By some strange inadvertence, this part of the constitution has been taken from its natural connexion, and with no great propriety arranged under that head, which embraces the organization, and rights, and duties of the executive department. To prevent the necessity of again recurring to this subject, the general method prescribed in these commentaries will, in this instance, be departed from, and the only remaining provision on impeachments be here introduced.

§ 399. The fourth section of the second article is as follows:

"The president, vice-president, and all civil officers of the United States, shall be removed from office on impeachment for, and conviction of, treason, bribery, or other high crimes and misdemeanours."

§ 400. From this clause it appears, that the remedy by impeachment is strictly confined to civil officers of the United States, including the president and vice-president. In this respect, it differs materially from the law and practice of Great-Britain. In that kingdom, all the king's subjects, whether peers or commoners, are impeachable in parliament; though it is asserted, that commoners cannot now be impeached for capital offences, but for misdemeanors only. Such kinds of misdeeds, however, as peculiarly injure the commonwealth by the abuse of high offices of trust, are the most proper, and have been the most usual ground for this kind of prosecution in parliament. There seems a peculiar propriety, in a republican government at least, in {284} confining the impeaching power to persons holding office. In such a government all the citizens are equal, and ought to have the same security of a trial by jury, for all crimes and offences laid to their charge, when not holding any official character. To subject them to impeachment would not only be extremely oppressive and expensive, but would endanger their lives and liberties, by exposing them against their wills to persecution for their conduct in exercising their political rights and privileges. Dear as the trial by jury justly is in civil cases, its value, as a protection against the resentment and violence of rulers and factions, in criminal prosecutions makes it inestimable. It is there, and there only, that a citizen, in the sympathy, the impartiality, the intelligence, and incorruptible integrity of his fellows, empanelled to try the accusation, may indulge a well-founded confidence to sustain and cheer him. If should choose to accept office, he would voluntarily incur all the additional responsibility growing out of it. If impeached for his conduct, while in office, he could not justly complain, since he was placed in that predicament by his own choice; and in accepting office he submitted to all the consequences. Indeed, the moment it was decided, that the judgment upon impeachments should be limited to removal and disqualification from office, it followed as a natural result, that it ought not to reach any but officers of the United States. It seems to have been the original object of the friends of the national government to confine it to these limits; for in the original resolutions proposed to the convention, and in all the subsequent proceedings, the power was expressly limited to national officers.

§ 401. Who are "civil officers," within the meaning of this constitutional provision, is an inquiry, which naturally {285} presents itself; and the answer cannot, perhaps, be deemed settled by any solemn adjudication. The term "civil" has various significations. It is sometimes used in contradistinction to *barbarous*, or *savage*, to indicate a state of society reduced to order and regular government. Thus, we speak of civil life, civil society, civil government, and civil liberty; in which it is nearly equivalent in meaning to *political*. It is sometimes used in contradistinction to *criminal*, *to* indicate the private rights and remedies of men, as members of the community, in contrast to those, which are public, and relate to the government. Thus, we speak of civil process and criminal process, civil jurisdiction and criminal jurisdiction. It is sometimes used in contradistinction to *military* or *ecclesiastical*, to *natural* or *foreign*. Thus, we speak of a civil station, as opposed to a military or ecclesiastical station; a civil death, as opposed to a natural death;

a civil war, as opposed to a foreign war. The sense, in which the term is used in the constitution, seems to be in contradistinction to military, to indicate the rights and duties relating to citizens generally, in contradistinction to those of persons engaged in the land or naval service of the government. It is in this sense, that Blackstone speaks of the laity in England, as divided into three distinct states; the civil, the military, and the maritime; the two latter embracing the land and naval forces of the government. And in the same sense the expenses of the civil list of officers are spoken of, in contradistinction to those of the army and navy.

§ 402. All officers of the United States, therefore, who hold their appointments under the national government, whether their duties are executive or judicial, in the highest or in the lowest departments of the government, {286} with the exception of officers in the army and navy, are properly civil officers within the meaning of the constitution, and liable to impeachment. The reason for excepting military and naval officers is, that they are subject to trial and punishment according to a peculiar military code, the laws, rules, and usages of war. The very nature and efficiency of military duties and discipline require this summary and exclusive jurisdiction; and the promptitude of its operations are not only better suited to the notions of military men; but they deem their honor and their reputation more safe in the hands of their brother officers, than in any merely civil tribunals. Indeed, in military and naval affairs it is quite clear, that the senate could scarcely possess competent knowledge or experience to decide upon the acts of military men; so much are these acts to be governed by mere usage, and custom, by military discipline, and military discretion, that the constitution has wisely committed the whole trust to the decision of courts-martial.

§ 403. The next inquiry is, what are impeachable offences? They are "treason, bribery, or other high crimes and misdemeanours." For the definition of treason, resort may be had to the constitution itself; but for the definition of bribery, resort is naturally and necessarily had to the common law; for that, as the common basis of our jurisprudence, can alone furnish the proper exposition of the nature and limits of this offence. The only practical question is, what are to be deemed high crimes and misdemeanours? Now, neither the constitution, nor any statute of the United States, has in any manner defined any crimes, except treason and bribery, to be high crimes and misdemeanours, and as such impeachable. In what manner, then, are they to {287} be ascertained? Is the silence of the statute book to be deemed conclusive in favour of the party, until congress have made a legislative declaration and enumeration of the offences, which shall be deemed high crimes and misdemeanors? If so, then, as has been truly remarked, the power of impeachment, except as to the two expressed cases, is a complete nullity; and the party is wholly dispunishable, however enormous may be his corruption or criminality. It will not be sufficient to say, that in the cases, where any offence is punished by any statute of the United States, it may, and ought to be, deemed an impeachable offence. It is not every offence, that by the constitution is so impeachable. It must not only be an offence, but a *high* crime and misdemeanour. Besides; there are many most flagrant offences, which, by the statutes of the United States, are punishable only, when committed in special places, and within peculiar jurisdictions, as, for instance, on the high seas, or in forts, navy-yards, and arsenals, ceded to the United States. Suppose the offence is committed in some other, than these privileged places, or under circumstances not reached by any statute of the United States, would it be impeachable?

§ 404. Again, there are many offences, purely political, which have been held to be within the reach of parliamentary impeachments, not one of which is in the slightest manner alluded to in our statute book. And, indeed, political offences are of so various and complex a character, so utterly incapable of being defined, or classified, that the task of positive legislation would be impracticable, if it were not almost absurd to attempt it. What, for instance, could positive legislation do in cases of impeachment, like the charges against Warren Hastings, in 1788? Resort, then, must be had either {288} to parliamentary practice, and the common law, in order to ascertain, what are high crimes and misdemeanours; or the whole subject must be left to the arbitrary discretion of the senate, for the time being. The latter is so incompatible with the genius of our institutions, that no lawyer or statesman would be inclined to countenance so absolute a despotism of opinion and practice, which might make that a crime at one time, or in one person, which would be deemed innocent at another time, or in another person. The only safe guide in such cases must be the common law, which is the guardian at once of private rights and public liberties.

§ 405. Congress have unhesitatingly adopted the conclusion, that no previous statute is necessary to authorize an impeachment for any official misconduct; and the rules of proceeding, and the rules of evidence, as well as the principles of decision, have been uniformly regulated by the known doctrines of the common law and parliamentary usage. In the few cases of impeachment, which have hitherto been tried, no one of the charges has rested upon any statutable misdemeanour. It seems, then, to be the settled doctrine of the high court of impeachment, that though the common law cannot be a foundation of a jurisdiction not given by the constitution, or laws, that jurisdiction, when given, attaches, and is to be exercised according to the rules of the common law; and that, what are, and what are not high crimes and misdemeanours, is to be ascertained by a recurrence to that great basis of American jurisprudence.

§ 406. As it is declared in one clause of the constitution, that

> "judgment, in cases of impeachment, shall not extend further, than a removal from office, and disqualification to hold any office of {289} honour, trust, or profit, under the United States;"

and in another clause, that

> "the president, vice-president, and all civil officers of the United States, shall be removed from office on impeachment for, and conviction of, treason, bribery, or other high crimes or misdemeanours;"

it would seem to follow, that the senate, on the conviction, were bound, in all cases, to enter a judgment of removal from office, though it has a discretion, as to inflicting the punishment of disqualification. If, then, there must be a judgment of removal from office, it would seem to follow, that the constitution contemplated, that the party was still in office at the time of the impeachment. If he was not, his offence was still liable to be tried and punished in the ordinary tribunals of justice.

And it might be argued with some force, that it would be a vain exercise of authority to try a delinquent for an impeachable offence, when the most important object, for which the remedy was given, was no longer necessary, or attainable. And although a judgment of disqualification might still be pronounced, the language of the constitution may create some doubt, whether it can be pronounced without being coupled with a removal from office. There is also much force in the remark, that an impeachment is a proceeding purely of a political nature. It is not so much designed to punish an offender, as to secure the state against gross official misdemeanors. It touches neither his person, nor his property; but simply divests him of his political capacity.

§ 407. Having thus gone through the subject of impeachments, it only remains to observe, that a close survey of the system, unless we are egregiously deceived, will completely demonstrate the wisdom of the arrangements made in every part of it. The jurisdiction {290} to impeach is placed, where it should be, in the possession and power of the immediate representatives of the people. The trial is before a body of great dignity, and ability, and independence, possessing the requisite knowledge and firmness to act with vigour, and to decide with impartiality upon the charges. The persons subjected to the trial are officers of the national government; and the offences are such, as may affect the rights, duties, and relations of the party accused to the public in his political or official character, either directly or remotely. The general rules of law and evidence, applicable to common trials, are interposed, to protect the party against the exercise of wanton oppression, and arbitrary power. And the final judgment is confined to a removal from, and disqualification for, office; thus limiting the punishment to such modes of redress, as are peculiarly fit for a political tribunal to administer, and as will secure the public against political injuries. In other respects the offence is left to be disposed of by the common tribunals of justice, according to the laws of the land, upon an indictment found by a grand jury, and a trial by jury of peers, before whom the party is to stand for his final deliverance, like his fellow citizens.

CHAPTER XI.

ELECTIONS AND MEETINGS OF CONGRESS.

{291}

§ 408. THE first clause of the fourth section of the first article is as follows:

"The times, places, and manner of holding elections for senators and representatives shall be prescribed in each state by the legislature thereof. But the congress may, at any time, by law, make or alter such regulations, except as to the place of choosing senators."

§ 409. This clause does not appear to have attracted much attention, or to have encountered much opposition in the convention, at least as far, as can be gathered from the journal of that body. But it was afterwards assailed by the opponents of the constitution, both in and out of the state conventions, with uncommon zeal and virulence. The objection was not to that part of the clause, which vests in the state legislatures the power of prescribing the times, places, and manner of holding elections; for, so far, it was a surrender of power to the state governments. But it was, to the superintending power of congress to make, or alter such regulations. It was said, that such a superintending power would be dangerous to the liberties of the people, and to a just exercise of their privileges in elections. Congress might prescribe the times of election so unreasonably, as to prevent the attendance of the electors; or the place at so inconvenient a distance from the body of the electors, as to prevent a due exercise of the right of choice. And congress might contrive the *manner* of holding elections, so as to exclude all but their own favourites from office. They might modify the right of {292} elections, as they should please; they might regulate the number of votes by the quantity of property, without involving any repugnancy to the constitution. These, and other suggestions of a similar nature, calculated to spread terror and alarm among the people, were dwelt upon with peculiar emphasis.

§ 410. In answer to all such reasoning, it was urged, that there was not a single article in the whole system more completely defensible. Its propriety rested upon this plain proposition, that every government ought to contain in itself the means of its own preservation. If, in the constitution, there were some departures from this principle, (as it might be admitted there were,) they were matters of regret, and dictated by a controlling moral or political necessity; and they ought not to be extended. It was obviously impracticable to frame, and insert in the constitution an election law, which would be applicable to all possible changes in the situation of the country, and convenient for all the states. A discretionary power over elections must be vested somewhere. There seemed but three ways, in which it could be reasonably organized. It might be lodged either wholly in the national legislature; or wholly in the state legislatures; or primarily in the latter, and ultimately in the former. The last was the mode adopted by the convention. The regulation of elections is submitted, in the first instance, to the local governments, which, in ordinary cases, and when no improper views prevail, may both conveniently and satisfactorily be by them exercised. But, in extraordinary circumstances, the power is reserved to the national government; so that it may not be abused, and thus hazard the safety and permanence of the Union. Nor let it be thought, that such an occurrence is wholly imaginary. {293} It is a known fact, that, under the confederation, Rhode-Island, at a very critical period, withdrew her delegates from congress; and thus prevented some important measures from being carried.

§ 411. The objections, then, to the provision are not sound, or tenable. The reasons in its favour are, on the other hand, of great force and importance. In the first place, the power may be applied by congress to correct any negligence in a state in regard to elections, as well as to prevent a dissolution of the government by designing and refractory states, urged on by some temporary excitements. In the next place, it will operate as a check in favour of the people against any designs of a federal senate, and their constituents, to deprive the people of the state of their right to choose representatives. In the next place, it provides a remedy for the evil, if any state, by reason of invasion, or other cause, cannot have it in its power to appoint a place, where the citizens can safely meet to choose representatives. In the last place, (as the plan is but an experiment,) it may hereafter become important, with a view to the regular operations of the general government, that there should be a uniformity in the time and manner of electing representatives and senators, so as to prevent vacancies, when there may be calls for extraordinary sessions of congress. If such a time should occur, or such a uniformity be hereafter desirable, congress is the only body possessing the means to produce it.

§ 412. It remains only to notice an exception to the power of congress in this clause. It is, that congress cannot alter, or make regulations, "as to the place of choosing senators." This exception is highly reasonable. The choice is to be made by the state legislature; {294} and it would not be either necessary, or becoming in congress, to prescribe the place, where it should sit. This exception was not in the revised draft of the constitution; and was adopted almost at the close of the convention; not, however, without some opposition, for nine states were in its favour, one against it, and one was divided.

§ 413. The second clause of the fourth section of the first article is as follows:

"The congress shall assemble at least once in every year; and such meeting shall be on the first Monday in December, unless they shall by law appoint a different day."

This clause, for the first time, made its appearance in the revised draft of the constitution near the close of the convention; and was silently adopted, and, so far as can be perceived, without opposition. Annual parliaments had been long a favourite opinion and practice with the people of England; and in America, under the colonial governments, they were justly deemed a great security to public liberty. The present provision could hardly be overlooked by a free people, jealous of their rights; and therefore the constitution fixed a constitutional period, at which congress should assemble in every year, unless some other day was specially prescribed. Thus, the legislative discretion was necessarily bounded; and annual sessions were placed equally beyond the power of faction, and of party, of power, and of corruption. In two of the states a more frequent assemblage of the legislature was known to exist. But it was obvious, that from the nature of their duties, and the distance of their abodes, the members of congress ought not to be brought together at shorter periods, unless upon the most pressing exigencies. A provision, {295} so universally acceptable, requires no vindication, or commentary.

§ 414. The fifth section of the first article embraces provisions principally applicable to the powers, rights, and duties of each house in its separate corporate character. These will not require much illustration or commentary, as they are such, as are usually delegated to all legislative bodies in free governments; and were in practice in Great-Britain at the time of the emigration of our ancestors; and were exercised under the colonial governments; and have been secured and recognised in the present state constitutions.

§ 415. The first clause declares, that

"each house shall be the judge of the elections, returns, and qualifications of its own members, and a majority of each shall constitute a quorum to do business; but a smaller number may adjourn from day to day, and may be authorized to compel the attendance of absent members, in such manner, and under such penalties, as each house may provide."

§ 416. It is obvious, that a power must be lodged somewhere to judge of the elections, returns, and qualifications of the members of each house composing the legislature; for otherwise there could be no certainty, as to who were legitimately chosen members, and any intruder, or usurper, might claim a seat, and thus trample upon the rights, and privileges, and liberties of the people. Indeed, elections would become, under such circumstances, a mere mockery; and legislation the exercise of sovereignty by any self-constituted body. The only possible question on such a subject is, as to the body, in which such a power shall be lodged. If lodged in any other, than the legislative body itself, its independence, its purity, and even its existence and {296} action may be destroyed, or put into imminent danger. No other body, but itself, can have the same motives to preserve and perpetuate these attributes; no other body can be so perpetually watchful to guard its own rights and privileges from infringement, to purify and vindicate its own character, and to preserve the rights, and sustain the free choice of its constituents. Accordingly, the power has always been lodged in the legislative body by the uniform practice of England and America.

§ 417. The propriety of establishing a rule for a quorum for the despatch of business is equally clear; since otherwise the concerns of the nation might be decided by a very small number of the members of each body. In England, where the house of commons consists of nearly six hundred members, the number of forty-five constitutes a quorum to do business. In some of the state constitutions a particular number of the members constitutes a quorum to do business; in others, a majority is required. The constitution of the United States has wisely adopted the latter course; and thus, by requiring a majority for a quorum, has secured the public from any hazard of passing laws by surprise, or against the deliberate opinion of a majority of the representative body.

§ 418. But, as a danger of an opposite sort required equally to be guarded against, a smaller number is authorized to adjourn from day to day, thus to prevent a legal dissolution of the body, and also to compel the attendance of absent members. Thus, the interests of the nation, and the despatch of business, are not subject to the caprice, or perversity, or negligence of the minority. It was a defect in the articles of confederation, sometimes productive of great public mischief that {297} no vote, except for an adjournment, could be determined, unless by the votes of a majority of the states; and no power of compelling the attendance of the requisite number existed.

CHAPTER XII.

PRIVILEGES AND POWERS OF BOTH HOUSES
OF CONGRESS.

§ 419. THE next clause is,

> "each house may determine the rules of its proceedings, punish its members for disorderly behaviour, and, with the concurrence of two thirds, expel a member."

No person can doubt the propriety of the provision authorizing each house to determine the rules of its own proceedings. If the power did not exist, it would be utterly impracticable to transact the business of the nation, either at all, or at least with decency, deliberation, and order. The humblest assembly of men is understood to possess this power; and it would be absurd to deprive the councils of the nation of a like authority. But the power to make rules would be nugatory, unless it was coupled with a power to punish for disorderly behaviour, or disobedience to those rules. And as a member might be so lost to all sense of dignity and duty, as to disgrace the house by the grossness of his conduct, or interrupt its deliberations by perpetual violence or clamour, the power to expel for very aggravated misconduct was also indispensable, not as a common, but as an ultimate redress for the grievance. But such a power, so summary, and at the same time so subversive of the rights of the people, it was foreseen, might be exerted for mere purposes of faction or party, to remove a patriot, or to aid a corrupt measure; and it has therefore been wisely guarded, by the restriction, that there shall be a concurrence of two thirds of the members, to justify {299} an expulsion. This clause, requiring a concurrence of two thirds, was not in the original draft of the constitution, but it was inserted by a vote of ten states, one being divided. A like general authority to expel, exists in the British house of commons; and in the legislative bodies of many of the states composing the Union.

§ 420. The next clause is,

> "each house shall keep a journal of its proceedings, and from time to time publish the same, except such parts, as may in their judgment require secrecy. And the yeas and nays of the members of either house on any question shall, at the desire of one fifth of those present, be entered on the journal."

§ 421. This clause in its actual form did not pass in the convention without some struggle and some propositions of amendment. The object of the whole clause is to ensure publicity to the proceedings of the legislature, and a correspondent responsibility of the members to their respective constituents. And it is founded in sound policy and deep political foresight. Intrigue and cabal are thus deprived of some of their main resources, by plotting and devising measures in secrecy. The public mind is enlightened by an attentive examination of the public measures; patriotism, and integrity, and wisdom obtain their due reward; and votes are ascertained, not by vague conjecture, but by positive facts.

§ 422. The restriction of calls of the yeas and nays to one fifth is founded upon the necessity of preventing too frequent a recurrence to this mode of ascertaining the votes, at the mere caprice of an individual. A call consumes a great deal of time, and often embarasses the just progress of beneficial measures. It is said to {300} have been often used to excess in the congress under the confederation; and even under the present constitution it is notoriously used, as an occasional annoyance, by a dissatisfied minority, to retard the passage of measures, which are sanctioned by the approbation of a strong majority. The check, therefore, is not merely theoretical; and experience shows, that it has been resorted to, at once to admonish members, and to control them in this abuse of the public patience and the public indulgence.

§ 423. The next clause is,

"neither house, during the session of congress, shall, without the consent of the other, adjourn for more than three days, nor to any other place, than that, in which the two houses shall be sitting."

It is observable, that the duration of each session of congress, (subject to the constitutional termination of their official agency,) depends solely upon their own will and pleasure, with the single exception, as will be presently seen, of cases, in which the two houses disagree in respect to the time of adjournment. In no other case is the president allowed to interfere with the time and extent of their deliberations. And thus their independence is effectually guarded against any encroachment on the part of the executive. Very different is the situation of parliament under the British constitution; for the king may, at any time, put an end to a session by a prorogation of parliament, or terminate the existence of parliament by a dissolution, and a call of a new parliament. It is true, that each house has authority to adjourn itself separately; and this is commonly done from day to day, and sometimes for a week or a month together, as at Christmas and Easter, or upon other particular occasions. But the adjournment of one house is not the adjournment of the {301} other. And it is usual, when the king signifies his pleasure, that both, or either of the houses should adjourn themselves to a certain day, to obey the king's pleasure, and adjourn accordingly; for otherwise a prorogation would certainly follow.

§ 424. Under the colonial governments, the undue exercise of the same power by the royal governors constituted a great public grievance, and was one of the numerous cases of misrule, upon which the declaration of independence strenuously relied. It was there solemnly charged against the king, that he had called together legislative [colonial] bodies at places unusual, uncomfortable, and distant from the repository of the public records; that he had dissolved representative bodies, for opposing his invasions of the rights of the people; and after such dissolutions, he had refused to reassemble them for a long period of time. It was natural, therefore, that the people of the United States should entertain a strong jealousy on this subject, and should interpose a constitutional barrier against any such abuse by the prerogative of the executive. The state constitutions generally contain some provision on the same subject, as a security to the independence of the legislature.

§ 425. These are all the powers and privileges, which are expressly vested in each house of congress by the constitution. What further powers and privileges they incidentally possess has been a question much discussed, and may hereafter be open, as new cases arise, to still further discussion. It is remarkable, that no power is conferred to punish for any contempts committed against either house; and yet it is obvious, that, unless such a power, to some extent, exists by implication, it is utterly impossible for either house to perform {302} its constitutional functions. For instance, how is either house to conduct its own deliberations, if it may not keep out, or expel intruders? If it may not require, and enforce upon strangers silence and decorum in its presence? If it may not enable its own members to have free ingress, egress, and regress to its own hall of legislation? And if the power exists, by implication, to require the duty, it is wholly nugatory, unless it draws after it the incidental authority to compel obedience, and to punish violations of it.

§ 426. This subject has of late undergone a great deal of discussion both in England and America; and has finally received the adjudication of the highest judicial tribunals in each country. In each country upon the fullest consideration the result was the same, viz. that the power did exist, and that the legislative body was the proper and exclusive forum to decide, when the contempt existed, and when there was a breach of its privileges; and, that the power to punish followed, as a necessary incident, to the power to take cognizance of the offence.

§ 427. The power to punish for contempts, thus asserted both in England and America, is confined to punishment during the session of the legislative body, and cannot be extended beyond it. It seems, that the power of congress to punish cannot, in its utmost extent, proceed beyond imprisonment; and then it terminates with the adjournment, or dissolution of that body.

§ 428. The sixth section of the first article contains an enumeration of the rights, privileges, and disabilities of the members of each house in their personal and individual characters, as contradistinguished from the rights, privileges, and disabilities of the body, of which {303} they are members. It may here, again, be remarked, that these rights and privileges are, in truth, the rights and privileges of their constituents, and for their benefit and security, rather than the rights and privileges of the member for his own benefit and security. In like manner, the disabilities imposed are founded upon the same comprehensive policy; to guard the powers of the representative from abuse, and to secure a wise, impartial, and uncorrupt administration of his duties.

§ 429. The first clause is as follows:

> "The senators and representatives shall receive a compensation for their services, to be ascertained by law, and paid out of the treasury of the United States. They shall, in all cases, except treason, felony, and breach of the peace, be privileged from arrest during their attendance at the session of their respective houses, and in going to, and returning from, the same. And for any speech or debate in either house they shall not be questioned in any other place."

§ 430. Whether it is, on the whole, best to allow to members of legislative bodies a compensation for their services, or whether their services should be considered merely honorary, is a question admitting of much argument on each side;

and it has accordingly found strenuous advocates, and opponents, not only in speculation, but in practice. It is well known, that in England none is now allowed, or claimed; and there can be little doubt, that public opinion there is altogether in favour of their present course. On the other hand, in America an opposite opinion prevails among those, whose influence is most impressive with the people on such subjects. It is not surprising, that under such circumstances, there should have been a considerable diversity of opinion manifested in the convention itself. {304}

§ 431. The principal reasons in favour of a compensation may be presumed to have been the following. In the first place, the advantage is secured of commanding the first talents of the nation in the public councils, by removing a virtual disqualification, that of poverty, from that large class of men, who, though favoured by nature, might not be favoured by fortune. It could hardly be expected, that such men would make the necessary sacrifices in order to gratify their ambition for a public station; and if they did, there was a corresponding danger, that they might be compelled by their necessities, or tempted by their wants, to yield up their independence, and perhaps their integrity, to the allurements of the corrupt, or the opulent. In the next place, it would, in a proportionate degree, gratify the popular feeling by enlarging the circle of candidates, from which members might be chosen, and bringing the office within the reach of persons in the middle ranks of society, although they might not possess shining talents; a course best suited to the equality found, and promulgated in a republic. In the next place, it would make a seat in the national councils, as attractive, and perhaps more so, than in those of the state by the superior emoluments of office. And in the last place it would be in conformity to a long and well settled practice, which embodied public sentiment, and had been sanctioned by public approbation.

§ 432. On the other hand, it might be, and it was, probably, urged against it, that the practice of allowing compensation was calculated to make the office rather more a matter of bargain and speculation, than of high political ambition. It would operate, as an inducement to vulgar and grovelling demagogues, of little talent, and narrow means, to defeat the claims of higher candidates, {305} than themselves; and with a view to the compensation alone to engage in all sorts of corrupt intrigues to procure their own election. It would thus degrade these high trusts from being deemed the reward of distinguished merit, and strictly honorary, to a mere traffic for political office, which would first corrupt the people at the polls, and then subject their liberties to be bartered by their venal candidate. Men of talents in this way would be compelled to degradation, in order to acquire office, or would be excluded by more unworthy, or more cunning candidates, who would feel, that the labourer was worthy of his hire. There is no danger, that the want of compensation would deter men of suitable talents and virtues, even in the humbler walks of life, from becoming members; since it could scarcely be presumed, that the public gratitude would not, by other means, aid them in their private business, and increase their just patronage. And if, in a few cases, it should be otherwise, it should not be forgotten, that one of the most, wholesome lessons to be taught in republics is, that men should learn suitable economy and prudence in their private affairs; and that profusion and poverty are, with a few splendid exceptions, equally unsafe to be entrusted with the public rights and interests, since, if they do not betray, they can hardly be presumed willing to protect them. The practice of England abundantly showed, that compensation was not necessary to bring into public life the best talents and virtues of the nation. In looking over her list of distinguished statesmen, of equal purity and patriotism, it would be found, that comparatively few had possessed opulence; and many had struggled through life with the painful pressure of narrow resources, the *res augustæ domi.* {306}

§ 433. If it be proper to allow a compensation for services to the members of congress, there seems the utmost propriety in its being paid out of the public treasury of the United States. The labour is for the benefit of the nation, and it should properly be remunerated by the nation. Besides; if the compensation were to be allowed by the states, or by the constituents of the members, if left to their discretion, it might keep the latter in a state of slavish dependence, and might introduce great inequalities in the allowance. And if it were to be ascertained by congress, and paid by the constituents, there would always be danger, that the rule would be fixed to suit those, who were the least enlightened, and the most parsimonious, rather than those, who acted upon a high sense of the dignity and the duties of the station. Fortunately, it is left for the decision of congress. The compensation is "to be ascertained by law;" and never addresses itself to the pride, or the parsimony, the local prejudices, or local habits of any part of the Union. It is fixed with a liberal view to the national duties, and is paid from the national purse. If the compensation had been left, to be fixed by the state legislature, the general government would have become dependent upon the governments of the states; arid the latter could almost, at their pleasure, have dissolved it. Serious evils were felt from this source under the confederation, by which each state was to maintain its own delegates in congress; for it was found, that the states too often were operated upon by local considerations, as contradistinguished from general and national interests.

§ 434. The only practical question, which seems to have been farther open upon this head, is, whether the compensation should have been ascertained by the constitution {307} itself, or left, (as it now is,) to be ascertained from time to time by congress. If fixed by the constitution, it might, from the change of the value of money, and the modes of life, have become too low, and utterly inadequate. Or it might have become too high in consequence of serious changes in the prosperity of the nation. It is wisest, therefore, to have it left, where it is, to be decided by congress from time to time, according to their own sense of justice, and a large view of the national resources.

§ 435. The next part of the clause regards the privilege of the members from arrest, except for crimes, during their attendance at the sessions of congress, and their going to, and returning from them. This privilege is conceded by law to the humblest suitor and witness in a court of justice; and it would be strange, indeed, if it were denied to the highest functionaries of the state in the discharge of their public duties. It belongs to congress in common with all other legislative bodies, which exist, or have existed in America, since its first settlement, under every variety of government; and it has immemorially constituted a privilege of both houses of the British parliament. It seems absolutely indispensable for the just exercise of the legislative power in every nation, purporting to possess a free constitution of government; and it cannot be surrendered without endangering the public liberties, as well as the private independence of the members.

§ 436. The effect of this privilege is, that the arrest of the member is unlawful, and a trespass *ab initio*, for which he may maintain an action, or proceed against the aggressor by way of indictment. He may also be discharged by motion to a court of justice, or upon a writ {308} of *habeas corpus*; and the arrest may also be punished, as a contempt of the house.

§ 437. In respect to the time of going and returning, the law is not so strict in point of time, as to require the party to set out immediately on his return; but allows him time to settle his private affairs, and to prepare for his journey. Nor does it nicely scan his road, nor is his protection forfeited, by a little deviation from that, which is most direct; for it is supposed, that some superior convenience or necessity directed it. The privilege from arrest takes place by force of the election, and before the member has taken his seat, or is sworn.

§ 438. The exception to the privilege is, that it shall not extend to "treason, felony, or breach of the peace." These words are the same as those, in which the exception to the privilege of parliament is usually expressed at the common law, and was doubtless borrowed from that source. Now, as all crimes are offences against the peace, the phrase "breach of the peace" would seem to extend to all indictable offences, as well those, which are, in fact, attended with force and violence, as those, which are only constructive breaches of the peace of the government, inasmuch as they violate its good order. And so in truth it was decided in parliament, in the case of a seditious libel, published by a member, (Mr. Wilkes,) against the opinion of Lord Camden and the other judges of the Court of Common Pleas; and, as it will probably now be thought, since the party spirit of those times has subsided, with entire good sense, and in furtherance of public justice. It would be monstrous, that any member should protect himself from arrest, or punishment for a libel, often a crime of the deepest malignity and mischief, while he {309} would be liable to arrest for the pettiest assault, or the most insignificant breach of the peace.

§ 439. The next great and vital privilege is the freedom of speech and debate, without which all other privileges would be comparatively unimportant, or ineffectual. This privilege also is derived from the practice of the British parliament, and was in full exercise in our colonial legislatures, and now belongs to the legislature of every state in the Union, as matter of constitutional right. In the British parliament it is a claim of immemorial right, and is now farther fortified by an act of parliament; and it is always particularly demanded of the king in person by the speaker of the house of commons, at the opening of every new parliament. But this privilege is strictly confined to things done in the course of parliamentary proceedings, and does not cover things done beyond the place and limits of duty. Therefore, although a speech delivered in the house of commons is privileged, and the member cannot be questioned respecting it elsewhere; yet, if he publishes his speech, and it contains libellous matter, he is liable to an action and prosecution therefor, as in common cases of libel. And the same principles seem applicable to the privilege of debate and speech in congress. No man ought to have a right to defame others under colour of a performance of the duties of his office. And if he does so in the actual discharge of his duties in congress, that furnishes no reason, why he should be enabled through the medium of the press to destroy the reputation, and invade the repose of other citizens. It is neither within the scope of his duty, nor in furtherance of public rights, or public policy. Every citizen has as good a right to be protected by the laws from malignant scandal, and false charges, and defamatory {310} imputations, as a member of congress has to utter them in his seat. If it were otherwise, a man's character might be taken away without the possibility of redress, either by the malice, or indiscretion, or overweaning self-conceit of a member of congress. It is proper, however, to apprise the learned reader, that it has been recently denied in congress by very distinguished lawyers, that the privilege of speech and debate in congress does not extend to publication of his speech. And they ground themselves upon an important distinction arising from the actual differences between English and American legislation. In the former, the publication of the debates is not strictly lawful, except by license of the house. In the latter, it is a common right, exercised and supported by the direct encouragement of the body. This reasoning deserves a very attentive examination.

§ 440. The next clause regards the disqualifications of members of congress; and is as follows:

> "No senator or representative shall, during the time, for which he was elected, be appointed to any civil office under the authority of the United States, which shall have been created, or the emoluments whereof shall have been increased, during such time. And no person, holding any office under the United States, shall be a member of either house of congress during his continuance in office."

This clause does not appear to have met with any opposition in the convention, as to the propriety of some provision on the subject, the principal question being, as to the best mode of expressing the disqualifications. It has been deemed by one commentator an admirable provision against venality, though not perhaps sufficiently guarded to prevent evasion. And it has been elaborately vindicated by {311} another with uncommon earnestness. The reasons for excluding persons from offices, who have been concerned in creating them, or increasing their emoluments, are, to take away, as far as possible, any improper bias in the vote of the representative, and to secure to the constituents some solemn pledge of his disinterestedness. The actual provision, however, does not go to the extent of the principle; for his appointment is restricted only "during the time, for which he was elected;" thus leaving in full force every influence upon his mind, if the period of his election is short, or the duration of it is approaching its natural termination. It has sometimes been matter of regret, that the disqualification had not been made co-extensive with the supposed mischief; and thus to have for ever excluded members from the possession of offices created, or rendered more lucrative, by themselves. Perhaps there is quite as much wisdom in leaving the provision, where it now is.

§ 441. The other part of the clause, which disqualifies persons holding any office under the United States from being members of either house during their continuance in office, has been still more universally applauded; and has been vindicated upon the highest grounds of public policy. It is doubtless founded in a deference to state jealousy, and a sincere desire to obviate the fears, real or imaginary, that the general government would obtain an undue preference over the state governments. It has also the strong recommendation, that it prevents any undue influence from office, either upon the party himself, or those, with whom he is associated in legislative deliberations. The universal exclusion of all persons holding office is (it must be admitted) attended with some inconveniences. The {312} heads of the departments are, in fact, thus precluded from proposing, or vindicating their own measures in the face of the nation in the course of debate; and are compelled to submit them to other men, who are either imperfectly acquainted with the measures, or are indifferent to their success or failure. Thus, that open and public responsibility for measures, which properly belongs to the executive in all governments, and especially in a republican government, as its greatest security and strength, is completely done away. The executive is compelled to resort to secret and unseen influence, to private interviews, and private arrangements, to accomplish its own appropriate purposes; instead of proposing and sustaining its own duties and measures by a bold and manly appeal to the nation in the face of its representatives. One consequence of this state of things is, that there never can be traced home to the executive any responsibility for the measures, which are planned, and carried at its suggestion. Another consequence will be, (if it has not yet been,) that measures will be adopted, or defeated by private intrigues, political combinations, irresponsible recommendations, and all the blandishments of office, and all the deadening weight of silent patronage. The executive will never be compelled to avow, or to support any opinions. His ministers may conceal, or evade any expression of their opinions. He will seem to follow, when in fact he directs, the opinions of congress. He will assume the air of a dependent instrument, ready to adopt the acts of the legislature, when in fact his spirit and his wishes pervade the whole system of legislation. If corruption ever eats its way silently into the vitals of this republic, it will be, because the people are unable to bring responsibility home to the executive through {313} his chosen ministers. They will be betrayed, when their suspicions are most lulled by the executive, under the disguise of an obedience to the will of congress. If it would not have been safe to trust the heads of departments, as representatives, to the choice of the people, as their constituents, it would have been at least some gain to have allowed them a seat, like territorial delegates, in the house of representatives, where they might freely debate without a title to vote. In such an event, their influence, whatever it would be, would be seen, and felt, and understood, and on that account would have involved little danger, and more searching jealousy and opposition; whereas, it is now secret and silent, and from that very cause may become overwhelming.

§ 442. One other reason in favour of such a right is, that it would compel the executive to make appointments for the high departments of government, not from personal or party favourites, but from statesmen of high public character, talents, experience, and elevated services; from statesmen, who had earned public favour, and could command public confidence. At present, gross incapacity may be concealed under official forms, and ignorance silently escape by shifting the labours upon more intelligent subordinates in office. The nation would be, on the other plan, better served; and the executive sustained by more masculine eloquence, as well as more liberal learning.

§ 443. Such is the reasoning, by which many enlightened statesmen have not only been led to doubt, but even to deny the value of this constitutional disqualification. And even the most strenuous advocates of it are compelled so far to admit its force, as to concede, that the measures of the executive government, {314} so far as they fall within the immediate department of a particular officer, might be more directly and fully explained on the floor of the house. Still, however, the reasoning from the British practice has not been deemed satisfactory by the public; and the guard interposed by the constitution has been received with general approbation, and has been thought to have worked well during our experience under the national government. Indeed, the strongly marked parties in the British parliament, and their consequent dissensions, have been ascribed to the non-existence of any such restraints; and the progress of the influence of the crown, and the supposed corruptions of legislation, have been by some writers traced back to the same original blemish. Whether these inferences are borne out by historical facts, is a matter, upon which different judgments may arrive at different conclusions; and a work, like the present, is not the proper place to discuss them.

CHAPTER XIII.

MODE OF PASSING LAWS. PRESIDENT'S NEGATIVE.

§ 444. THE seventh section of the first article treats of two important subjects, the right of originating revenue bills, and the nature and extent of the president's negative upon the passing of laws.

§ 445. The first clause declares —

> "All bills for raising revenue shall originate in the house of representatives; but the senate may propose, or concur with amendments, as on other bills."

This provision, so far as it regards the right to originate what are technically called "money bills," is, beyond all question, borrowed from the British house of commons, of which it is the ancient and indisputable privilege and right, that all grants of subsidies and parliamentary aids shall begin in their house, and are first bestowed by them, although their grants are not effectual to all intents and purposes, until they have the assent of the other two branches of the legislature. The general reason given for this privilege of the house of commons is, that the supplies are raised upon the body of the people; and therefore it is proper, that they alone should have the right of taxing themselves. And Mr. Justice Blackstone has very correctly remarked, that this reason would be unanswerable, if the commons taxed none but themselves. But it is notorious, that a very large share of property is in possession of the lords; that this property is equally taxed, as the property of the commons; and therefore the commons, not being the sole persons taxed, this cannot be the reason of their having the sole right of raising and modelling the supply. The {316} true reason seems to be this. The lords being a permanent hereditary body, created at pleasure by the king, are supposed more liable to be influenced by the crown, and when once influenced, more likely to continue so, than the commons, who are a temporary elective body, freely nominated by the people. It would, therefore, be extremely dangerous to give the lords any power of framing new taxes for the subject. It is sufficient, that they have a power of rejecting, if they think the commons too lavish or improvident in their grants.

§ 446. It will be at once perceived, that the same reasons do not exist in the same extent, for the same exclusive right in our house of representatives in regard to money bills, as exist for such right in the British house of commons. It may be fit, that it should possess the exclusive right to originate money bills; since it may be presumed to possess more ample means of local information, and it more directly represents the opinions, feelings, and wishes of the people. And, being directly dependent upon them for support, it will be more watchful and cautious in the imposition of taxes, than a body, which emanates exclusively from the states in their sovereign political capacity. But, as the senators are in a just sense

178

equally representatives of the people, and do not hold their offices by a permanent or hereditary title, but periodically return to the common mass of citizens; and above all, as direct taxes are, and must be, apportioned among the states according to their federal population; and as all the states have a distinct local interest, both as to the amount and nature of all taxes of every sort, which are to be levied, there seems a peculiar fitness in giving to the senate a power to alter and amend, as well as to {317} concur with, or reject all money bills. The due influence of all the states is thus preserved; for otherwise it might happen, from the overwhelming representation of some of the large states, that taxes might be levied, which would bear with peculiar severity upon the interests, either agricultural, commercial, or manufacturing, of others being the minor states; and thus the equilibrium intended by the constitution, as well of power, as of interest, and influence, might be practically subverted.

§ 447. There would also be no small inconvenience in excluding the senate from the exercise of this power of amendment and alteration; since if any, the slightest modification were required in such a bill to make it either palatable or just, the senate would be compelled to reject it, although an amendment of a single line might make it entirely acceptable to both houses. Such a practical obstruction to the legislation of a free government would far outweigh any supposed theoretical advantages from the possession or exercise of an exclusive power by the house of representatives. Infinite perplexities, and misunderstandings, and delays would clog the most wholesome legislation. Even the annual appropriation bills might be in danger of a miscarriage on these accounts; and the most painful dissensions might be introduced.

§ 448. The next clause respects the power of the president to approve, and negative laws. In the convention there does not seem to have been much diversity of opinion on the subject of the propriety of giving to the president a negative on the laws. The principal points of discussion seem to have been, whether the negative should be absolute, or qualified; and if the latter, by what number of each house the bill should be {318} subsequently passed, in order to become a law; and whether the negative should in either case be exclusively vested in the president alone, or in him jointly with some other department of the government.

§ 449. Two points may properly arise upon this subject. First, the propriety of vesting the power in the president; and secondly, the extent of the legislative check, to prevent an undue exercise of it. The former also admits of a double aspect, viz. whether the negative should be absolute, or should be qualified. An absolute negative on the legislature appears, at first, to be the natural defence, with which the executive magistrate should be armed. But in a free government, it seems not altogether safe, nor of itself a sufficient defence. On ordinary occasions, it may not be exerted with the requisite firmness; and on extraordinary occasions, it may be perfidiously abused. It is true, that the defect of such an absolute negative has a tendency to weaken the executive department. But this may be obviated, or at least counterpoised, by other arrangements in the government; such as a qualified connexion with the senate in making treaties and appointments, by which the latter, being a stronger department, may be led to support the constitutional rights of the former, without being too much detached from its own legislative functions. And the patronage of the executive has also some tendency to create a counteracting influence in aid of his independence. It is true, that in England an absolute negative is vested in the king, as a branch of the legislative power; and he possesses the absolute power of rejecting, rather than of resolving. And this is thought by Mr. Justice Blackstone and others, to be a most important, and indeed indispensable part of the royal prerogative, to guard it {319} against the usurpations of the legislative authority. Yet in point of fact this negative of the king has not been once exercised since the year 1692; a fact, which can only be accounted for upon one of two suppositions, either that the influence of the crown has prevented the passage of objectionable measures, or that the exercise of the prerogative has become so odious, that it has not been deemed safe to exercise it, except upon the most pressing emergencies. Probably both motives have alternately prevailed in regard to bills, which were disagreeable to the crown; though, for the last half century, the latter has had the most uniform and decisive operation. As the house of commons becomes more and more the representative of the popular opinion, the crown will have less and less inducement to hazard its own influence by a rejection of any favourite measure of the people. It will be more likely to take the lead, and thus guide and moderate, instead of resisting the commons. And, practically speaking, it is quite problematical, whether a qualified negative may not hereafter in England become a more efficient protection of the crown, than an absolute negative, which makes no appeal to the other legislative bodies, and consequently compels the crown to bear the exclusive odium of a rejection. Be this as it may, the example of England furnishes, on this point, no sufficient authority for America. The whole structure of our government is so entirely different, and the elements, of which it is composed, are so dissimilar from that of England, that no argument can be drawn from the practice of the latter, to assist us in a just arrangement of the executive authority.

§ 450. The reasons why the president should possess a qualified negative, if they are not quite obvious, {320} are, at least, when fairly expounded, entirely satisfactory. In the first place, there is a natural tendency in the legislative department to intrude upon the rights, and to absorb the powers of the other departments of government. A mere parchment delineation of the boundaries of each is wholly insufficient for the protection of the weaker branch, as the executive unquestionably is; and hence there arises a constitutional necessity of arming it with powers for its own defence. If the executive did not possess this qualified negative, he would gradually be stripped of all his authority, and become, what it is well known the governors of some states are, a mere pageant and shadow of magistracy.

§ 451. In the next place, the power is important, as an additional security against the enactment of rash, immature, and improper laws. It establishes a salutary check upon the legislative body, calculated to preserve the community against the effects of faction, precipitancy, unconstitutional legislation, and temporary excitements, as well as political hostility. It may, indeed, be said, that a single man, even though he be president, cannot be presumed to possess more wisdom, or virtue, or experience, than what belongs to a number of men. But this furnishes no answer to the reasoning. The question is not, how much wisdom, or virtue, or experience, is possessed by either branch of the government, (though the executive magistrate may well be presumed to be eminently distinguished in all these respects, and therefore the choice of the people;) but whether the legislature may not be misled by a love of power, a spirit of faction, a political impulse, or a persuasive influence, local or sectional, which, at the same time, may not, from the difference in the election {321} and duties of the executive, reach him at all, or not reach him in the same degree. He will always have a primary inducement to defend his own powers; the legislature may well be presumed to have no desire to favour them. He will have an opportunity soberly to examine the acts and resolutions passed by the legislature, not having partaken of the feelings or combinations, which have procured their passage, and thus to correct, what will sometimes be wrong from haste and inadvertence, as well as design. His view of them, if not more wise, or more elevated, will, at least, be independent, and under an entirely different responsibility to the nation, from what belongs to them. He is the representative of the whole nation in the aggregate; they are the representatives only of distinct parts; and sometimes of little more than sectional or local interests.

§ 452. Nor is there any solid objection to this qualified power. If it should be objected, that it may sometimes prevent the passage of good laws, as well as of bad laws, the objection is entitled to but little weight. In the first place, it can never be effectually exercised if two thirds of both houses are in favour of the law; and if they are not, it is not so easily demonstrable, that the law is either wise or salutary. The presumption would rather be the other way; or, at least, that the utility of it is not unquestionable, or it would receive the requisite support. In the next place, the great evil of all free governments is a tendency to over-legislation; and the mischief of inconstancy and mutability in the laws forms a great blemish in the character and genius of all free governments. The injury, which may possibly arise from the postponement of a salutary law, is far less, than from the passage of a mischievous one, {322} or from a redundant and vacillating legislation. In the next place, there is no practical danger, that this power will be much, if any, abused by the president. The superior weight and influence of the legislative body in a free government, and the hazard to the weight and influence of the executive in a trial of strength, afford a satisfactory security, that the power will generally be employed with great caution; and that there will be more often room for a charge of timidity, than of rashness in its exercise. It has been already seen, that the British king, with all his sovereign attributes, has rarely interposed this high prerogative, and that more than a century has elapsed since its actual application. If from the offensive nature of the power a royal hereditary executive thus indulges serious scruples in its actual exercise, surely a republican president, chosen for four years, may be presumed to be still more unwilling to exert it.

§ 453. It has this additional recommendation, as a qualified negative, that it does not, like an absolute negative, present a categorical and harsh resistance to the legislative will, which is so apt to engender strife, and nourish hostility. It assumes the character of a mere appeal to the legislature itself, and asks a revision of its own judgment. It is in the nature, then, merely of a rehearing, or a reconsideration, and involves nothing to provoke resentment, or rouse pride. A president, who might hesitate to defeat a law by an absolute veto, might feel little scruple to return it for reconsideration upon reasons and arguments suggested on the return. If these were satisfactory to the legislature, he would have the cheering support of a respectable portion of the body in justification of his conduct. If, on the other hand, they should not be satisfactory, the concurrence {323} of two thirds would secure the ultimate passage of the law, without exposing him to undue censure or reproach. Even in such cases his opposition would not be without some benefit. His observations would be calculated to excite public attention and discussion, to lay bare the grounds, and policy, and constitutionality of measures; and to create a continued watchfulness, as to the practical effects of the laws thus passed, so as that it might be ascertained by experience, whether his sagacity and judgment were safer, than those of the legislature. Nothing but a gross abuse of the power upon frivolous, or party pretences, to secure a petty triumph, or to defeat a wholesome restraint, would bring it into contempt, or odium. And then, it would soon be followed by that remedial justice from the people, in the exercise of the right of election, which, first or last, will be found to follow with reproof, or cheer with applause, the acts of their rulers, when passion and prejudice have removed the temporary bandages, which have blinded their judgment.

§ 454. The other point of inquiry is, as to the extent of the legislative check upon the negative of the executive. It was originally proposed, that a concurrence of two thirds of each house should be required; this was subsequently altered to three fourths; and was finally brought back again to the original number. One reason against the three fourths seems to have been, that it would afford little security for any effectual exercise of the power. The larger the number required to overrule the executive negative, the more easy it would be for him to exert a silent and secret influence to detach the requisite number in order to carry his object. Another reason was, that even, supposing no such influence to be exerted, still, in a great variety of {324} cases of a political nature, and especially such, as touched local or sectional interests, the pride or the power of states, it would be easy to defeat the most salutary measures, if a combination of a few states could produce such a result. And the executive himself might, from his local attachments or sectional feelings, partake of this common bias. In addition to this, the departure from the general rule, of the right of a majority to govern, ought not to be allowed but upon the most urgent occasions. And an expression of opinion by two thirds of both houses in favour of a measure certainly affords all the just securities, which any wise, or prudent people ought to demand in the ordinary course of legislation; for all laws thus passed may, at any time, be repealed at the mere will of the majority. It was also no small recommendation of the lesser number, that it offered fewer inducements to improper combinations, either of the great states, or the small states, to accomplish particular objects. There could be but one of two rules adopted in all governments, either, that the majority should govern, or the minority should govern. The president might be chosen by a bare majority of electoral votes, and this majority might be by the combination of a few large states, and by a minority of the whole people. Under such circumstances, if a vote of three fourths were required to pass a law, the voice of two thirds of the people might be permanently disregarded during a whole administration. The case put may seem strong; but it is not stronger, than the supposition, that two thirds of both houses would be found ready to betray the solid interests of their constituents by the passage of injurious or unconstitutional laws. The provision, therefore, as it stands, affords all reasonable security; and pressed farther, it would endanger {325} the very objects, for which it is introduced into the constitution.

§ 455. But the president might effectually defeat the wholesome restraint, thus intended, upon his qualified negative, if he might silently decline to act, after a bill was presented to him for approval or rejection. The constitution, therefore, has wisely provided, that

> "if any bill shall not be returned by the president within ten days (Sundays excepted) after it shall have been presented to him, it shall be a law, in like manner, as if he had signed it."

But if this clause stood alone, congress might, in like manner, defeat the due exercise of his qualified negative by a termination of the session, which would render it impossible for the president to return the bill. It is therefore added,

> "unless the congress, by their adjournment, prevent its return, in which case it shall not be a law."

§ 456. The remaining clause merely applies to *orders, resolutions, and votes,* to which the concurrence of both houses may be necessary; and as to these, with a single exception, the same rule is applied, as is by the preceding clause applied to *bills.* If this provision had not been made, congress, by adopting the form of an order or resolution, instead of a bill, might have effectually defeated the president's qualified negative in all the most important portions of legislation.

§ 457. A review of the forms and modes of proceeding in the passing of laws cannot fail to impress upon every mind the cautious steps, by which legislation is guarded, and the solicitude to conduct business without precipitancy, rashness, or irregularity. Frequent opportunities are afforded to each house to review their own proceedings; to amend their own errors; to correct their own inadvertences; to recover {326} from the results of any passionate excitement; and to reconsider the votes, to which persuasive eloquence, or party spirit, has occasionally misled their judgments. Under such circumstances, if legislation be unwise, or loose, or inaccurate, it belongs to the infirmity of human nature in general, or to that personal carelessness and indifference, which is sometimes the foible of genius, as well as the accompaniment of ignorance and prejudice.

§ 458. The structure and organization of the several branches, composing the legislature, have also (unless my judgment has misled me) been shown by the past review to be admirably adapted to preserve a wholesome and upright exercise of their powers. All the checks, which human ingenuity has been able to devise, (at least all, which, with reference to our habits, institutions, and local interests, seem practicable, or desirable,) to give perfect operation to the machinery of government; to adjust all its movements; to prevent its eccentricities; and to balance its forces; — all these have been introduced, with singular skill, ingenuity, and wisdom, into the structure of the constitution.

§ 459. Yet, after all, the fabric may fall; for the work of man is perishable, and must for ever have inherent elements of decay. Nay; it must perish, if there be not that vital spirit in the people, which alone can nourish, sustain, and direct all its movements. It will be in vain, that statesmen shall form plans of government, in which the beauty and harmony of a republic shall be embodied in visible order, shall be built up on solid substructions, and adorned by every useful ornament, if the inhabitants suffer the silent power of time to dilapidate its walls, or crumble its massy supporters into dust; if the assaults from without are never resisted, {327} and the rottenness and mining from within are never guarded against. Who can preserve the rights and liberties of the people, when they are abandoned by themselves? Who shall keep watch in the temple, when the watchmen sleep at their posts? Who shall call upon the people to redeem their possessions, and revive the republic, when their own hands have deliberately and corruptly surrendered them to the oppressor, and have built the prisons, or dug the graves of their own friends? Aristotle, in ancient times, upon a large survey of the republics of former days, and of the facile manner, in which they had been made the instruments of their own destruction, felt himself compelled to the melancholy reflection, which has been painfully repeated by one of the greatest statesmen of modern times, that a democracy has many striking points of resemblance with a tyranny. "The ethical character," says he, "is the same; both exercise despotism over the better class of citizens; and the decrees are in the one, what ordinances and arrets are in the other. *The demagogue, too, and the court favourite are not unfrequently the same identical men, and always bear a close analogy.* And these have the principal power, each in their respective governments, favourites with the absolute monarch, and demagogues with a people, such as I have described."

§ 460. This dark picture, it is to be hoped, will never be applicable to the republic of America. And yet it affords a warning, which, like all the lessons of past experience, we are not permitted to disregard. America, free, happy, and enlightened, as she is, must rest the preservation of her rights and liberties upon the virtue, independence, justice, and sagacity of the people. If either fail, the republic is gone. Its shadow {328} may remain with all the pomp, and circumstance, and trickery of government; but its vital power will have departed. In America, the demagogue may arise, as well as elsewhere. He is the natural, though spurious growth of republics; and like the courtier he may, by his blandishments, delude the ears, and blind the eyes of the people to their own destruction. If ever the day shall arrive, in which the best talents and the best virtues shall be driven from office by intrigue or corruption, by the ostracism of the press, or the still more unrelenting persecution of party, legislation will cease to be national. It will be wise by accident, and bad by system.

CHAPTER XIV.

POWERS OF CONGRESS.

§ 461. WE have now arrived, in the course of our inquiries, at the eighth section of the first article of the constitution, which contains an enumeration of the principal powers of legislation confided to congress. A consideration of this most important subject will detain our attention for a considerable time; as well, because of the variety of topics, which it embraces, as of the controversies, and discussions, to which it has given rise. It has been, in the past time, it is in the present time, and it will probably in all future time continue to be, the debateable ground of the constitution, signalized, at once, by the victories, and the defeats of the same parties.

§ 462. The first clause of the eighth section is in the following words:

> "The congress shall have power to lay and collect taxes, duties, imposts, and excises, to pay the debts and provide for the common defence, and general welfare of the United States; but all duties, imposts, and excises, shall be uniform throughout the United States."

§ 463. Before proceeding to consider the nature and extent of the power conferred by this clause, and the reasons, on which it is founded, it seems necessary to settle the grammatical construction of the clause, and to ascertain its true reading. Do the words, "to lay and collect taxes, duties, imposts, and excises," constitute a distinct, substantial power; and the words, "to pay debts, and provide for the common defence, and general welfare of the United States," constitute {330} another distinct and substantial power? Or are the latter words connected with the former, so as to constitute a qualification upon them? This has been a topic of political controversy; and has furnished abundant materials for popular declamation and alarm. If the former be the true interpretation, then it is obvious, that under colour of the generality of the words to "provide for the common defence and general welfare," the government of the United States is, in reality, a government of general and unlimited powers, notwithstanding the subsequent enumeration of specific powers; if the latter be the true construction, then the power of taxation only is given by the clause, and it is limited to objects of a national character, "for "the common defence and the general welfare."

§ 464. The former opinion has been maintained by some minds of great ingenuity, and liberality of views. The latter has been the generally received sense of the nation, and seems supported by reasoning at once solid and impregnable. The reading, therefore, which will be maintained in these commentaries, is that, which makes the latter words a qualification of the former; and this will be best illustrated by supplying the words, which are necessarily to be understood in this interpretation. They will then stand thus:

"The congress shall have power to lay and collect taxes, duties, imposts, and excises, *in order* to pay the debts, and to provide for the common defence and general welfare of the United States;"

that is, for the purpose of paying the public debts, and providing for the common defence and general welfare of the United States. In this sense, congress has not an unlimited power of taxation; but it is limited to specific objects, — the payment of the public debts, {331} and providing for the common defence and general welfare. A tax, therefore, laid by congress for neither of these objects, would be unconstitutional, as an excess of its legislative authority. In what manner this is to be ascertained, or decided, will be considered hereafter. At present, the interpretation of the words only is before us.

§ 465. Having thus disposed of the question, what is the true interpretation of the clause, as it stands in the text of the constitution, and ascertained, that the power of taxation, though general, as to the subjects, to which it may be applied, is yet restrictive, as to the purposes, for which it may be exercised; it next becomes matter of inquiry, what were the reasons, for which this power was given, and what were the objections, to which it was deemed liable.

§ 466. That the power of taxation should be, to some extent, vested in the national government, was admitted by all persons, who sincerely desired to escape from the imbecilities, as well as the inequalities of the confederation. Without such a power it would not be possible to provide for the support of the national forces by land or sea, or the national civil list, or the ordinary charges and expenses of government. For these purposes at least, there must be a constant and regular supply of revenue. If there should be a deficiency, one of two evils must inevitably ensue; either the people must be subjected to continual arbitrary plunder; or the government must sink into a fatal atrophy. The former is the fate of Turkey under its sovereigns: the latter was the fate of America under the confederation.

§ 467. If, then, there is to be a real, effective national government, there must be a power of taxation {332} co-extensive with its powers, wants, and duties. The only inquiry properly remaining is, whether the resources of taxation should be specified and limited; or, whether the power in this respect should be general, leaving a full choice to the national legislature. The opponents of the constitution strenuously contended, that the power should be restricted; its friends, as strenuously contended, that it was indispensable for the public safety, that it should be general.

§ 468. The general reasoning, by which an unlimited power was sustained, was to the following effect. Every government ought to contain within itself every power requisite to the full accomplishment of the objects committed to its care, and the complete execution of the trusts, for which it is responsible, free from every other control, but a regard to the public good, and to the security of the people. In other words, every power ought to be proportionate to its object. The duties of superintending the national defence, and of securing the public peace against foreign or domestic violence, involve a provision for casualties and dangers, to which no possible limits can be assigned; and therefore the power of making that provision ought to know no other bounds, than the exigencies of the nation, and the resources of the community. Revenue is the essential engine, by which the means of answering the national exigencies must be procured; and therefore the power of procuring it must necessarily be comprehended in that of providing for those exigencies. Theory, as well as practice, the past experience of other nations, as well as our own sad experience under the confederation, conspire to prove, that the power of procuring revenue is unavailing, and a mere mockery, when exercised over states in their {333} collective capacities. If, therefore, the federal government was to be of any efficiency, and a bond of union, it ought to be invested with an unqualified power of taxation for all national purposes. In the history of mankind it has ordinarily been found, that in the usual progress of things the necessities of a nation in every stage of its existence are at least equal to its resources. But, if a more favourable state of things should exist in our own government, still we must expect reverses, and ought to provide against them. It is impossible to foresee all the various changes in the posture, relations, and power of different nations, which may affect the prosperity and safety of our own. We may have formidable foreign enemies. We may have internal commotions. We may suffer from physical, as well as moral calamities; from plagues, famine, and earthquakes; from political convulsions, and rivalries; from the gradual decline of particular sources of industry; and from the necessity of changing our own habits and pursuits, in consequence of foreign improvements and competitions, and the variable nature of human wants and desires. A source of revenue, adequate in one age, may wholly or partially fail in another. Commerce, or manufactures, or agriculture may thrive under a tax in one age, which would destroy them in another. The power of taxation, therefore, to be useful, must not only be adequate to all the exigencies of the nation, but it must be capable of reaching from time to time all the most productive sources. It has been observed with no less truth, than point, that "in political arithmetic two and two do not always make four." Constitutions of government are not to be framed upon a calculation of existing exigencies; but upon a combination {334} of these with the probable exigencies of ages, according to the natural and tried course of human affairs. There ought to be a capacity to provide for future contingencies, as they may happen; and as these are (as has been already suggested) illimitable in their nature, so it is impossible safely to limit that capacity.

§ 469. In regard to other objections it was urged, that it was impossible to rely (as the history of the government under the confederation abundantly proved) upon requisitions upon the states. Direct taxes were exceedingly unequal, and difficult to adjust; and could not safely be relied on, as an adequate or satisfactory source of revenue, except as a final resort, when others, more eligible, failed. The distinction between external and internal taxation was indeed capable of being reduced to practice. But in many emergencies it might leave the national government without any adequate resources, and compel it to a course of taxation ruinous to our trade and industry, and the solid interests of the country. No one of due reflection can contend, that commercial imports are, or could be, equal to all future exigencies of the Union; and indeed ordinarily they may not be found equal to them. Suppose they are equal to the ordinary expenses of the Union; yet, if war should come, the civil list must be entirely overlooked, or the military left without any adequate supply. How is it possible, that a government half supplied and half necessitous can fulfil the purposes of its institution, or can provide for the security, advance the prosperity, or support the reputation of the commonwealth? How can it ever possess either energy or stability, dignity or credit, confidence at home, or respectability abroad? How can its administration be any thing else, than a succession of expedients, {335} temporary, impotent, and disgraceful? How will it be able to avoid a frequent sacrifice of its engagements to immediate necessity? How can it undertake, or execute any liberal or enlarged plans of public good? Who would lend to a government, incapable of pledging any permanent resources to redeem its debts? It would be the common case of needy individuals, who must borrow upon onerous conditions and usury, because they cannot promise a punctilious discharge of their engagements. It would, therefore, not only not be wise, but be the extreme of folly to stop short of adequate resources for all emergencies, and to leave the government entrusted with the care of the national defence in a state of total, or partial incapacity to provide for the protection of the community against future invasions of the public peace by foreign war, or domestic convulsions. If, indeed, we are to try the novel, not to say absurd, experiment in politics, of tying up the hands of government from protective and offensive war, founded upon reasons of state, we ought certainly to be able to compel foreign nations to abstain from all measures, which shall injure, or cripple us. We must be able to repress their ambition, and disarm their enmity; to conquer their prejudices, and destroy their rivalries and jealousies. Who is so visionary, as to dream of such a moral influence in a republic over the whole world? It should never be forgotten, that the chief sources of expense in every government have ever arisen from wars and rebellions, from foreign ambition and enmity, or from domestic insurrections and factions. And it may well be presumed, that what has been in the past, will continue to be in the future.

§ 470. The states, with a concurrent power, will {336} be entirely safe, and have ample resources to meet all their wants, whatever they may be, although few public expenses, comparatively speaking, will fall to their lot to provide for. They will be chiefly of a domestic character, and affecting internal polity; whereas, the resources of the Union will cover the vast expenditures, occasioned by foreign intercourse, wars, and other charges necessary for the safety and prosperity of the Union. The mere civil list of any country is always small; the expenses of armies, and navies, and foreign relations unavoidably great. There is no sound reason, why the states should possess any *exclusive* power over sources of revenue, not required by their wants. But there is the most urgent propriety in conceding to the Union all, which may be commensurate to their wants. Any attempt to discriminate between the sources of revenue would leave too much, or too little to the states. If the exclusive power of external taxation were given to the Union, and of internal taxation to the states, it would, at a rough calculation, probably give to the states a command of two thirds of the resources of the community, to defray from a tenth to a twentieth of its expenses; and to the Union, one third of the resources of the community, to defray from nine tenths to nineteen twentieths of its expenses. Such an unequal distribution is wholly indefensible. And it may be added, that the resources of the Union would, or might be diminished exactly in proportion to the increase of demands upon its treasury; for (as has been already seen) war, which brings the great expenditures, narrows, or at least may narrow the resources of taxation from duties on imports to a very alarming degree. If we enter any other line of discrimination, it will be equally difficult to adjust the {337} proper proportions; for the inquiry itself, in respect to the future wants, as well of the states, as of the Union, and their relative proportion, must involve elements, for ever changing, and incapable of any precise ascertainment. Too much, or too little would for ever be found to belong to the states; and the states, as well as the Union, might be endangered by the very precautions to guard against abuses of power. Any separation of the subjects of revenue, which could have been fallen upon, would have amounted to a sacrifice of the interests of the Union to the power of the individual states; or of a surrender of important functions by the latter, which would have removed them to a mean provincial servitude, and dependence.

§ 471. The language of the constitution is,

"Congress shall have power to lay and collect taxes, duties, imposts, and excises," &c.

"But all *duties*, *imposts*, and *excises* shall be uniform throughout the United States."

A distinction is here taken between taxes, and duties, imposts, and excises; and, indeed, there are other parts of the constitution respecting the taxing power, (as will presently be more fully seen,) such as the regulations respecting direct taxes, the prohibition of taxes or duties on exports by the United States, and the prohibition of imposts or duties by the states on imports or exports, which require an attention to this distinction.

§ 472. In a general sense, all contributions imposed by the government upon individuals for the service of the state, are called taxes, by whatever name they may be known, whether by the name of tribute, tythe, talliage, impost, duty, gabel, custom, subsidy, aid, supply, excise, or other name. In this sense, they are usually divided into two great classes, those, which {338} are direct, and those, which are indirect. Under the former denomination are included taxes on land, or real property, and under the latter, taxes on articles of consumption. The constitution, by giving the power to lay and collect taxes in general terms, doubtless meant to include all sorts of taxes, whether direct or indirect. But, it may be asked, if such was the intention, why were the subsequent words, *duties*, *imposts* and *excises*, added in the clause? Two reasons may be suggested; the first, that it was done to avoid all possibility of doubt in the construction of the clause, since, in common parlance, the word *taxes* is sometimes applied in contradistinction to duties, imposts, and excises, and, in the delegation of so vital a power, it was desirable to avoid all possible misconception of this sort; and, accordingly, we find, in the very first draft of the constitution, these explanatory words are added. Another reason was, that the constitution prescribed different rules of laying taxes in different cases, and, therefore, it was indispensable to make a discrimination between the classes, to which each rule was meant to apply.

§ 473. The second section of the first article, which has been already commented on for another purpose, declares, that "*direct* taxes shall be apportioned among the several states, which may be included within this Union, according to their respective numbers."

The fourth clause of the ninth section of the same article (which would regularly be commented on in a future page) declares, that

"no capitation, or other direct tax, shall be laid, unless in proportion to the census or enumeration herein before directed to be taken;"

and the clause now under consideration, that

"all duties, imposts, and excises shall be uniform throughout {339} the United States."

Here, then, two rules are prescribed, the rule of apportionment (as it is called) for *direct* taxes, and the rule of uniformity for *duties*, *imposts*, and *excises*. If there are any other kinds of taxes, not embraced in one or the other of these two classes, (and it is certainly difficult to give full effect to the words of the constitution without supposing them to exist,) it would seem, that congress is left at full liberty to levy the same by either rule, or by a mixture of both rules, or perhaps by any other rule, not inconsistent with the general purposes of the constitution. It is evident, that "duties, imposts, and excises" are indirect taxes in the sense of the constitution. But the difficulty still remains, to ascertain what taxes are comprehended under this description; and what under the description of *direct* taxes.

§ 474. The word "duties" has not, perhaps, in all cases a very exact signification, or rather it is used sometimes in a larger, and sometimes in a narrower sense. In its large sense, it is very nearly an equivalent to taxes, embracing all impositions or charges levied on persons or things. In its more restrained sense, it is often used as equivalent to "customs," which appellation is usually applied to those taxes, which are payable upon goods and merchandise imported, or exported, and was probably given on account of the usual and constant demand of them for the use of kings, states, and governments. In this sense, it is nearly synonymous with "imposts," which is sometimes used in the large sense of taxes, or duties, or impositions, and sometimes in the more restrained sense of a duty on imported goods and merchandise.

§ 475. "Excises" are generally deemed to be of an opposite nature to "imposts," in the restrictive sense {340} of the latter term, and are defined to be an inland imposition, paid sometimes upon the consumption of the commodity, or frequently upon the retail sale, which is the last stage before the consumption.

§ 476. But the more important inquiry is, what are direct taxes in the sense of the constitution, since they are required to be laid by the rule of apportionment, and all indirect taxes, whether they fall under the head of "duties, imposts, or excises," or under any other description, may be laid by the rule of uniformity. It is clear, that capitation taxes, or, as they are more commonly called, poll taxes, that is, taxes upon the polls, heads, or persons, of the contributors, are direct taxes, for the constitution has expressly enumerated them, as such. "No capitation, or *other direct* tax, shall be laid," &c. is the language of that instrument.

§ 477. Taxes on lands, houses, and other permanent real estate, or on parts or appurtenances thereof, have always been deemed of the same character, that is, direct taxes. It has been seriously doubted, if, in the sense of the constitution, any taxes are direct taxes, except those on polls or on lands.

§ 478. In the year 1794, congress passed an act, laying duties upon carriages for the conveyance of persons, which were kept by or for any person, for his own use, or to be let out to hire, or for the conveying of passengers, to wit, for every coach the yearly sum of ten dollars, &c. &c.; and made the levy uniform throughout the United States, The constitutionality of the act was contested, upon the ground, that it was a direct tax, and so ought to be *apportioned* among the states according to their numbers. After solemn argument, the Supreme Court decided, that it was not a direct tax within the meaning of {341} the constitution. The grounds of this decision, as stated in the various opinions of the judges, were; first, the doubt, whether any taxes were direct in the sense of the constitution, but capitation and land taxes, as has been already suggested; secondly, that in cases of doubt, the rule of apportionment ought not to be favoured, because it was matter of compromise, and in itself radically indefensible and wrong; thirdly, the monstrous inequality and injustice of the carriage tax, if laid by the rule of apportionment, which would show, that no tax of this sort could have been contemplated by the convention, as within the rule of apportionment; fourthly, that the terms of the constitution were satisfied by confining the clause, respecting direct taxes, to capitation and land taxes; fifthly, that, accurately speaking, all taxes on expenses or consumption are *indirect* taxes, and a tax on carriages is of this kind; and, sixthly, (what is probably of most cogency and force, and of itself decisive,) that no tax could be a direct one in the sense of the constitution, which was not capable of apportionment according to the rule laid down in the constitution.

§ 479. Having endeavoured to point out the and distinctions between direct and indirect taxes, and that duties, imposts, and excises, in the sense of the constitution, belong to the latter class, the order of the subject would naturally lead us to the inquiry, why direct taxes are required to be governed by the rule of apportionment; and why "duties, imposts, and excises" are required to be uniform throughout the United States. The answer to the former will be given, when we come to the farther examination of certain prohibitory and restrictive clauses of the constitution on the subject of taxation. The answer to the latter may be given in a {342} few words. It was to cut off all undue preferences of one state over another in the regulation of subjects affecting their common interests. Unless duties, imposts, and excises were uniform, the grossest and most oppressive inequalities, vitally affecting the pursuits and employments of the people of different states, might exist. The agriculture, commerce, or manufactures of one state might be built up on the ruins of those of another; and a combination of a few states in congress might secure a monopoly of certain branches of trade and business to themselves, to the injury, if not to the destruction, of their less favoured neighbors. The constitution throughout all its provisions is an instrument of checks, and restraints, as well as of powers. It does not rely on confidence in the general government to preserve the interests of all the states. It is founded in a wholesome and strenuous jealousy, which, foreseeing the possibility of mischief, guards with solicitude against any exercise of power, which may endanger the states, as far as it is practicable. If this provision, as to uniformity of duties, had been omitted, although the power might never have been abused to the injury of the feebler states of the Union, (a presumption, which history does not justify us in deeming quite safe or certain;) yet it would, of itself, have been sufficient to demolish, in a practical sense, the value of most of the other restrictive clauses in the constitution. New York and Pennsylvania might, by an easy combination with the Southern states, have destroyed the whole navigation of New England. A combination of a different character, between the New England and the Western states, might have borne down the agriculture of the South; and a combination of a yet different character might have struck at the {343} vital interests of manufactures. So that the general propriety of this clause is established by its intrinsic political wisdom, as well as by its tendency to quiet alarms, and suppress discontents.

§ 480. Two practical questions of great importance have arisen upon the construction of this clause, either standing alone, or in connexion with other clauses, and incidental powers, given by the constitution. One is, whether the government has a right to lay taxes for any other purpose than to raise revenue, however much that purpose may be for the common defence, or general welfare. The other is, whether the money, when raised, can be appropriated to any other purposes, than such, as are pointed out in the other enumerated powers of congress. The former involves the question, whether congress can lay taxes to protect and encourage domestic manufactures; the latter, whether congress can appropriate money to internal improvements. Each of these questions has given rise to much animated controversy; each has been affirmed and denied, with great pertinacity, zeal, and eloquent reasoning; each has become prominent in the struggles of party; and defeat in each has not hitherto silenced opposition, or given absolute security to victory. The contest is often renewed; and the attack and defence maintained with equal ardour.

§ 481. It is unnecessary to consider the argument at present, so far as it bears upon the constitutional authority of congress to protect or encourage manufactures; because that subject will more properly come under review, in all its bearings, under another head, viz. the power to regulate commerce, to which it is nearly allied, and from which it is more usually derived. Stripping the argument against the power of this adventitious {344} circumstance, it resolves itself into this statement. The power to lay taxes is a power exclusively given to raise revenue, and it can constitutionally be applied to no other purposes. The application for other purposes is an abuse of the power; and, in fact, however it may be in *form* disguised, it is a premeditated usurpation of authority. Whenever money or revenue is wanted for constitutional purposes, the power to lay taxes may be applied to obtain it. Whenever money or revenue is not so wanted, it is not a proper means for any constitutional end.

§ 482. The argument in favour of the constitutional authority is grounded upon the terms and the intent of the constitution. It seeks for the true meaning and objects of the power according to the obvious sense of the language, and the nature of the government proposed to be established by that instrument. It relies upon no strained construction of words; but demands a fair and reasonable interpretation of the clause, without any restrictions not naturally implied in it, or in the context. It will not do to assume, that the clause was intended solely for the purposes of raising revenue; and then argue, that being so, the power cannot be constitutionally applied to any other purposes. The very point in controversy is, whether it is restricted to purposes of revenue. That must be proved; and cannot be assumed, as the basis of reasoning.

§ 483. The language of the constitution is,

"Congress shall have power to lay and collect taxes, duties, imposts, and excises."

If the clause had stopped here, and remained in this absolute form, (as it was in fact, when reported in the first draft in the convention,) there could not have been the slightest doubt on the subject. The absolute power to lay taxes includes {345} the power in every form, in which it may be used, and for every purpose, to which the legislature may choose to apply it. This results from the very nature of such an unrestricted power. *A fortiori* it might be applied by congress to purposes, for which nations have been accustomed to apply it. Now, nothing is more clear, from the history of commercial nations, than the fact, that the taxing power is often, very often, applied for other purposes, than revenue. It is often applied, as a regulation of commerce. It is often applied, as a virtual prohibition upon the importation of particular articles, for the encouragement and protection of domestic products, and industry; for the support of agriculture, commerce, and manufactures; for retaliation upon foreign monopolies and injurious restrictions; for mere purposes of state policy, and domestic economy; sometimes to banish a noxious article of consumption; sometimes, as a bounty upon an infant manufacture, or agricultural product; sometimes, as a temporary restraint of trade; sometimes, as a suppression of particular employments; sometimes, as a prerogative power to destroy competition, and secure a monopoly to the government!

§ 484. If, then, the power to lay taxes, being general, may embrace, and in the practice of nations does embrace, all these objects, either separately, or in combination, upon what foundation does the argument rest, which assumes one object only, to the exclusion of all the rest? which insists, in effect, that because revenue may be one object, therefore it is the sole object of the power? which assumes its own construction to be correct, because it suits its own theory, and denies the same right to others, entertaining a different theory? If the power is general in its terms, {346} is it not an abuse of all fair reasoning to insist, that it is particular? to desert the import of the language and to substitute other and different language? Is this allowable in regard to any instrument? Is it allowable in an especial manner, as to constitutions of government, growing out of the rights, duties, and exigencies of nations, and looking to an infinite variety of circumstances, which may require very different applications of a given power?

§ 485. The other question is, whether congress has any power to appropriate money, raised by taxation or otherwise, for any other purposes, than those pointed out in the enumerated powers, which follow the clause respecting taxation. It is said, "raised by taxation or otherwise;" for there may be, and in fact are, other sources of revenue, by which money may, and does come into the treasury of the United States otherwise, than by taxation; as, for instance, by fines, penalties, and forfeitures; by sales of the public lands, and interests and dividends on bank stocks; by captures and prize in times of war; and by other incidental profits and emoluments growing out of governmental transactions and prerogatives. But, for all the common purposes of argument, the question may be treated, as one growing out of levies by taxation.

§ 486. The reasoning, upon which the opinion, adverse to the authority of congress to make appropriations not within the scope of the enumerated powers, is maintained, has been already, in a great measure, stated in the preceding examination of the grammatical construction of the clause, giving the power to lay taxes. The controversy is virtually at an end, if it is once admitted, that the words, "to provide for the common defence and general welfare," are a part and {347} qualification of the power to lay taxes; for then, congress has certainly a right to appropriate money to any purposes, or in any manner, conducive to those ends. The whole stress of the argument is, therefore, to establish, that the words, "to provide for the common defence and general welfare," do not form an independent power, nor any qualification of the power to lay taxes. And the argument is, that they are mere general terms, explained and limited by the subjoined specifications." It is attempted to be fortified by a recurrence to the history of the confederation; to the successive reports and alterations of the tax clause in the convention; to the inconveniencies of such a large construction; and to the supposed impossibility, that a power to make such appropriations for the common defence and general welfare, should not have been, at the adoption of the constitution, a subject of great alarm, and jealousy; and as such, resisted in and out of the state conventions.

§ 487. The argument in favour of the power is derived, in the first place, from the language of the clause, conferring the. power, (which it is admitted in its literal terms covers it;) secondly, from the nature of the power, which renders it in the highest degree, expedient, if not indispensable for the due operations of the national government; thirdly, from the early, constant and decided maintenance of it by the government and its functionaries, as well as by many of our ablest statesmen from the very commencement of the constitution. So, that it has the language and intent of the text, and the practice of the government to sustain it against an artificial doctrine, set up on the other side.

§ 488. The argument derived from the words and {348} intent has been so fully considered already, that it cannot need repetition. It is summed up with great force in the report of the secretary of the treasury on manufactures, in 1791. "The national legislature," says he, "has express authority to lay and collect taxes, duties, imposts, and excises; to pay the debts and provide for the common defence and general welfare, with no other qualifications, than that all other duties, imposts, and excises, shall be uniform throughout the United States; that no capitation or other direct tax shall be laid, unless in proportion to numbers ascertained by a census, or enumeration taken on the principle prescribed in the constitution; and that no tax or duty shall be laid on articles exported from any state. These three qualifications excepted, the power to raise money is plenary and indefinite. And the objects, to which it may be appropriated, are no less comprehensive, than the payment of the public debts, and the providing for the common defence and general welfare. The terms 'general welfare' were doubtless intended to signify more, than was expressed or imported in those, which preceded; otherwise numerous exigencies, incident to the affairs of the nation, would have been left without a provision. The phrase is as comprehensive, as any, that could have been used; because it was not fit, that the constitutional authority of the Union to appropriate its revenues should have been restricted within narrower limits, than the general welfare; and because this necessarily embraces a vast variety of particulars, which are susceptible neither of specification, nor of definition. It is, therefore, of necessity left to the discretion of the national legislature to pronounce upon the objects, which concern the general welfare, and for which, under that description, {349} an appropriation of money is requisite and proper. And there seems no room for a doubt, that whatever concerns the general interests of learning, of agriculture, of manufactures, and of commerce, are within the sphere of the national councils, *so far as regards an application of money.* The only qualification of the generality of the phrase in question, which seems to be admissible, is this; that the object, to which an appropriation of money is to be made, must be *general*, and not *local*; its operation extending in fact, or by possibility, throughout the Union, and not being confined to a particular spot. No objection ought to arise to this construction from a supposition, that it would imply a power to do, whatever else should appear to congress conducive to the general welfare. A power *to appropriate money* with this latitude, which is granted in express terms, would not carry a power to do any other thing, not authorized in the constitution either expressly, or by fair implication."

§ 489. In regard, to the practice of the government, it has been entirely in conformity to the principles here laid down. Appropriations have never been limited by congress to cases falling within the specific powers enumerated in the constitution, whether those powers be construed in their broad, or their narrow sense. And in an especial manner appropriations have been made to aid internal improvements of various sorts, in our roads, our navigation, our streams, and other objects of a national character and importance. In some cases, not silently, but upon discussion, congress has gone the length of making appropriations to aid destitute foreigners, and cities labouring under severe calamities; as in the relief of the St. Domingo refugees, in 1794, and the citizens of Venezuela, who suffered {350} from an earthquake in 1812. An illustration, equally forcible, of a domestic character, is in the bounty given in the cod-fisheries, which was strenuously resisted on constitutional grounds in 1792; but which still maintains its place in the statute book of the United States.

§ 490. In order to prevent the necessity of recurring again to the subject of taxation, it seems desirable to bring together, in this connexion, all the remaining provisions of the constitution on this subject, though they are differently arranged in that instrument. The first one is,

> "no capitation or other direct tax shall be laid, unless in proportion to the census, or enumeration, herein before directed to be taken."

This includes poll taxes, and land taxes, as has been already remarked.

§ 491. The object of this clause doubtless is, to secure the Southern states against any undue proportion of taxation; and, as nearly as practicable, to overcome the necessary inequalities of a direct tax. The South have a very large slave population; and consequently a poll tax, which should be laid by the rule of uniformity, would operate with peculiar severity on them. It would tax their property beyond its supposed relative value, and productiveness to white labour. Hence, a rule is adopted, which, in effect, in relation to poll taxes, exempts two fifths of all slaves from taxation; and thus is supposed to equalize the burthen with the white population.

§ 492. In respect to direct taxes on land, the difficulties of making a due apportionment, so as to equalize the burthens and expenses of the Union according to the relative wealth and ability of the states, was felt as a most serious evil under the confederation. {351} By that instrument, (it will be recollected,) the apportionment was to be among the states according to the value of all land within each state, granted or surveyed for any person, and the buildings and improvements thereon, to be estimated in such mode, as congress should prescribe. The whole proceedings to accomplish such an estimate were so operose and inconvenient, that congress, in April, 1783, recommended, as a substitute for the article, an apportionment, founded on the basis of population, adding to the whole number of white and other free citizens and inhabitants, including those bound to service for a term of years, three fifths of all other persons, &c. in each state; which is precisely the rule adopted in the constitution.

§ 493. Those, who are accustomed to contemplate the circumstances, which produce and constitute national wealth, must be satisfied, that there is no common standard, by which the degrees of it can be ascertained. Neither the value of lands, nor the numbers of the people, which have been successively proposed, as the rule of state contributions, has any pretension to being deemed a just representative of that wealth. If we compare the wealth of the Netherlands with that of Russia or Germany, or even of France, and at the same time compare the total value of the lands, and the aggregate population of the contracted territory of the former, with the total value of the lands, and the aggregate population of the immense regions of either of the latter kingdoms, it will be at once discovered, that there is no comparison between the proportions of these two subjects, and that of the relative wealth of those nations. If a like parallel be run between the American states, it will furnish a similar result. Let Virginia be contrasted with Massachusetts, {352} Pennsylvania with Connecticut, Maryland with Virginia, Rhode-Island with Ohio, and the disproportion will be at, once perceived. The wealth of neither will be found to be, in proportion to numbers, or the value of lands.

§ 494. The truth is, that the wealth of nations depends upon an infinite variety of causes. Situation, soil, climate; the nature of the productions; the nature of the government; the genius of the citizens; the degree of information they possess; the state of commerce, of arts, and industry; the manners and habits of the people; these, and many other circumstances, too complex, minute, and adventitious to admit of a particular enumeration, occasion differences, hardly conceivable, in the relative opulence and riches of different countries. The consequence is, that there can be no common measure of national wealth; and, of course, no general rule, by which the ability of a state to pay taxes can be determined. The estimate, however fairly or deliberately made, is open to many errors and inequalities, which become the fruitful source of discontents, controversies, and heart-burnings. These are sufficient, in themselves, to shake the foundations of any national government,

when no common artificial rule is adopted to settle permanently the apportionment; and every thing is left open for debate, as often as a direct tax is to be imposed. Even in those states, where direct taxes are constantly resorted to, every
new valuation or apportionment is found, practically, to be attended with great
inconvenience, and excitements. In short, it may be affirmed without fear of contradiction, that some artificial rule of apportionment of a fixed nature is indispensable to the public repose; and considering the {353} peculiar situation of the
American states, and especially of the slave and agricultural states, it is difficult
to find any rule of greater equality or justice, than that, which the constitution has
adopted.

§ 495. The next clause in the constitution is:

"No tax or duty shall be laid on articles exported from any state. No preference
shall be given by any regulation of commerce, or revenue, to the ports of one
state over those of another; nor shall vessels bound to, or from one state he
obliged to enter, clear, or pay duties in another."

§ 496. The obvious object of these provisions is, to prevent any possibility of
applying the power to lay taxes, or regulate commerce, injuriously to the interests
of any one state, so as to favour or aid another. If congress were allowed to lay a
duty on exports from any one state it might unreasonably injure, or even destroy,
the staple productions, or common articles of that state. The inequality of such a
tax would be extreme. In some of the states, the whole of their means result from
agricultural exports. In others, a great portion is derived from other sources; from
external fisheries; from freights; and from the profits of commerce in its largest
extent. The burthen of such a tax would, of course, be very unequally distributed.
The power to intermeddle with the subject of exports is, therefore, wholly taken
away. On the other hand, preferences might be given to the ports of one state by
regulations, either of commerce or revenue, which might confer on them local
facilities or privileges in regard to commerce, or revenue. And such preferences
might be equally fatal, if indirectly given under the milder form of requiring an
entry, clearance, or payment of duties in the ports of any {354} state, other than
the ports of the state, to or from which the vessel was bound. The last clause,
therefore, does not prohibit congress from requiring an entry or clearance, or payment of duties at the custom-house, on importations in any port of a state, to or
from which the vessel is bound; but it cuts off the right to require such acts to be
done in other states, to which the vessel is not bound. In other words, it cuts off
the power to require that circuitry of voyage, which, under the British colonial system, was employed to interrupt the American commerce before the revolution. No
American vessel could then trade with Europe, unless through a circuitous voyage
to and from a British port.

§ 497. The next clause contains a prohibition on the states for the, like objects
and purposes.

"No state shall, *without the consent of congress*, lay any imposts, or duties on
imports or exports, except what may he absolutely necessary for executing its
inspection laws; and the net produce of all duties and imposts laid by any state
on imports and exports shall be for the use of the treasury of the United States;
and all such laws shall be subject to the revision and control of congress. No

state shall, without the consent of congress, lay any tonnage duty."

If there is wisdom and sound policy in restraining the United States from exercising the power of taxation unequally in the states, there is, at least, equal wisdom and policy in restraining the states themselves from the exercise of the same power injuriously to the interests of each other. A petty warfare of regulation is thus prevented, which would rouse resentments, and create dissensions, to the ruin of the harmony and amity of the states. The power to enforce their inspection laws is still retained, subject to {355} the revision and control of congress; so, that sufficient provision is made for the convenient arrangement of their domestic and internal trade, whenever it is not injurious to the general interests.

§ 498. Inspection laws are not, strictly speaking, regulations of commerce, though they may have a remote and considerable influence on commerce. The object of inspection laws is to improve the quality of articles produced by the labour of a country; to fit them for exportation, or for domestic use. These laws act upon the subject, before it becomes an article of commerce, foreign or domestic, and prepare it for the purpose. They form a portion of that immense mass of legislation, which embraces every thing in the territory of a state not surrendered to the general government. Inspection laws, quarantine laws, and health laws, as well as laws for regulating the internal commerce of a state, and others, which respect roads, fences, &c. are component parts of state legislation, resulting from the residuary powers of state sovereignty. No direct power over these is given to congress, and consequently they remain subject to state legislation, though they may be controlled by congress, when they interfere with their acknowledged powers. The power to lay duties and imposts on imports and exports, and to lay a tonnage duty, are doubtless properly considered a part of the taxing power; but they may also be applied, as a regulation of commerce.

§ 499. Until a recent period, no difficulty occurred in regard to the prohibitions of this clause. Congress, with a just liberality, gave full effect to the inspection laws of the states, and required them to be observed by the revenue officers of the United States. In the year 1821, the state of Maryland passed an act requiring, {356} that all importers of foreign articles or commodities, &c. by bale or package, or of wine, rum, &c. &c., and other persons selling the same by wholesale, bale, or package, hogshead, barrel, or tierce, should, before they were authorized to sell, take out a license, for which they were to pay *fifty* dollars, under certain penalties. Upon this act a question arose, whether it was, or not a violation of the constitution of the United States, and especially of the prohibitory clause now under consideration. Upon solemn argument, the Supreme Court decided, that it was.

§ 500. As the power of taxation exists in the states concurrently with the United States, subject only to the restrictions imposed by the constitution, several questions have from time to time arisen in regard to the nature and extent, of the state power of taxation.

§ 501. In the year 1818, the state of Maryland passed an act, laying a tax on all banks, and branches thereof, not chartered by the legislature of that state; and a question was made, whether the state had a right under that act to lay a tax on the Branch Bank of the United States in that state. This gave rise to a most animated discussion in the Supreme Court of the United States; where it was finally decided, that the tax was, as to the Bank of the United States, unconstitutional.

§ 502. In another case the question was raised, whether a state had a constitutional authority to tax stock issued for loans to the United States; and it was held by the Supreme Court, that a state had not.

§ 503. It is observable, that these decisions turn upon the point, that no state can have authority to tax an instrument of the United States, or thereby to diminish the means of the United States, used in the {357} exercise a powers confided to it. But there is no prohibition upon any state to tax any bank or other corporation created by its own authority, unless it has restrained itself, by the charter of incorporation, from the power of taxation. It may be added, that congress may, without doubt, tax state banks; for it is clearly within the taxing power confided to the general government. When congress tax the chartered institutions of the states, they tax their own constituents; and such taxes must be uniform. But when a state taxes an institution created by congress, it taxes an instrument of a superior and independent sovereignty, not represented in the state legislature.

CHAPTER XV.

POWER TO BORROW MONEY AND REGULATE COMMERCE.

§ 504. HAVING finished this examination of the power of taxation, and of the accompanying restrictions and prohibitions, the other powers of congress will be now examined in the order, in which they stand in the eighth section.

§ 505. The next, is the power of congress, "to borrow money on the credit of the United States." This power seems indispensable to the sovereignty and existence of a national government. Even under the confederation this power was expressly delegated. The remark is unquestionably just, that it is a power inseparably connected with that of raising a revenue, and with the duty of protection, which that power imposes upon the general government. Though in times of profound peace it may not be ordinarily necessary to anticipate the revenues of a state; yet the experience of all nations must convince us, that the burthen and expenses of one year in time of war may more than equal the ordinary revenue of ten years. Hence, a debt is almost unavoidable, when a nation is plunged into a state of war. The least burthensome mode of contracting a debt is by a loan. Indeed, this recourse becomes the more necessary, because the ordinary duties upon importations are subject to great diminution and fluctuations in times of war; and a resort to direct taxes for the whole supply would, under such circumstances, become oppressive and ruinous to the agricultural interests of the country. Even in times of peace {359} exigencies may occur, which render a loan the most facile, economical, and ready means of supply, either to meet expenses, or to avert calamities, or to save the country from an undue depression of its staple productions. The government of the United States has, on several occasions in times of profound peace, obtained large loans, among which a striking illustration of the economy and convenience of such arrangements will be found in the creation of stock on the purchase of Louisiana. The power to borrow money by the United States cannot (as has been already seen) in any way be controlled, or interfered with by the states. The grant of the power is incompatible with any restraining or controlling power; and the declaration of supremacy in the constitution is a declaration that no such restraining or controlling power shall be exercised.

§ 506. The next power of congress is,

> "to regulate commerce with foreign nations, and among the several states, and with the Indian tribes."

§ 507. The want of this power (as has been already seen) was one of the leading defects of the confederation, and probably, as much as any one cause, conduced to the establishment of the constitution. It is a power vital to the prosperity of the Union; and without it the government would scarcely deserve the name of a national government; and would soon sink into discredit and imbecility. It would stand, as a mere shadow of sovereignty, to mock our hopes, and involve us in a common ruin.

§ 508. The oppressed and degraded state of commerce, previous to the adoption of the constitution, can scarcely be forgotten. It was regulated by foreign nations with a single view to their own interests; and {360} our disunited efforts to counteract their restrictions were rendered impotent by a want of combination. Congress, indeed, possessed the power of making treaties; but the inability of the federal government to enforce them had become so apparent, as to render that power in a great degree useless. Those, who felt the injury arising from this state of things, and those, who were capable of estimating the influence of commerce on the prosperity of nations, perceived the necessity of giving the control over this important subject to a single government. It is not, therefore, matter of surprise, that the grant should be as extensive, as the mischief, and should comprehend all foreign commerce, and all commerce among the states.

§ 509. In considering this clause of the constitution several important inquiries are presented. In the first place, what is the natural import of the terms; in the next place, how far the power is exclusive of that of the states; in the third place, to what purposes and for what objects the power may be constitutionally applied; and in the fourth place, what are the true nature and extent of the power to regulate commerce with the Indian tribes.

§ 510. In the first place, then, what is the constitutional meaning of the words, "to regulate commerce;" for the constitution being (as has been aptly said) one of enumeration, and not of definition, it becomes necessary, in order to ascertain the extent of the power, to ascertain the meaning of the words. The power is to regulate; that is, to prescribe the rule, by which commerce is to be governed. The subject to be regulated is commerce. Is that limited to traffic, to buying and selling, or the interchange of commodities? Or does it comprehend navigation and intercourse? If the former construction is adopted, then a general term applicable {361} to many objects is restricted to one of its significations. If the latter, then a general term is retained in its general sense. To adopt the former, without some guiding grounds furnished by the context, or the nature of the power, would be improper. The words being general, the sense must be general also, and embrace all subjects comprehended under them, unless there be some obvious mischief, or repugnance to other clauses to limit them. In the present case there is nothing to justify such a limitation. Commerce undoubtedly is traffic; but it is something more. It is intercourse. It describes the commercial intercourse between nations, and parts of nations, in all its branches; and is regulated by prescribing rules for carrying on that intercourse. The mind can scarcely conceive a system for regulating commerce between nations, which shall exclude all laws concerning navigation; which shall be silent on the admission of the vessels of one nation into the ports of another; and be confined to prescribing rules for the conduct of individuals in the actual employment of buying and selling, or barter.

§ 511. If commerce does not include navigation, the government of the Union has no direct power over that subject, and can make no law prescribing, what shall constitute American vessels, or requiring, that they shall be navigated by American seamen. Yet this power has been exercised from the commencement of the government; it has been exercised with the consent of all America; and it has been always understood to be a commercial regulation. The power over navigation, and over commercial intercourse, was one of the primary objects, for which the people of America adopted their government; and it is impossible, that the convention should not have understood {362} the word "commerce," as embracing it. Indeed, to construe the power, so as to impair its efficacy, would defeat the very object, for which it was introduced into the constitution; for there cannot be a doubt, that to exclude navigation and intercourse from its scope would be to entail upon us all the prominent defects of the confederation, and subject the Union to the ill-adjusted systems of rival states, and the oppressive preferences of foreign nations in favour of their own navigation.

§ 512. The very exceptions found in the constitution demonstrate this; for it would be absurd, as well as useless, to except from a granted power that, which was not granted, or that, which the words did not comprehend. There are plain exceptions in the constitution from the power over navigation, and plain inhibitions to the exercise of that power in a particular way. Why should these be made, if the power itself was not understood to be granted? The clause already cited, that no preference shall be given by any regulation of commerce or revenue to the ports of one state over those of another, is of this nature. This clause cannot be understood, as applicable to those laws only, which are passed for purposes of revenue, because it is expressly applied to commercial regulations; and the most obvious preference, which can be given to one port over another, relates to navigation. But the remaining part of the sentence directly points to navigation. "Nor shall vessels, bound to or from one state, be obliged to enter, clear, or pay duties in another." In short, our whole system for the encouragement of navigation in the coasting trade and fisheries is exclusively founded upon this supposition. Yet no one has ever been bold enough to question the constitutionality of the laws, creating this system. {363}

§ 513. Foreign and domestic intercourse has been universally understood to be within the reach of the power. How, otherwise, could our systems of prohibition and non-intercourse be defended? From what other source has been derived the power of laying embargoes in a time of peace, and without any reference to war, or its operations? Yet this power has been universally admitted to be constitutional, even in times of the highest political excitement. And although the laying of an embargo in the form of a perpetual law was contested, as unconstitutional, at one period of our political history, it was so, not because an embargo was not a *regulation* of commerce, but because a perpetual embargo was an annihilation, and not a regulation, of commerce. It may, therefore, be safely affirmed, that the terms of the constitution have at all times been understood to include a power over navigation, as well as trade, over intercourse, as well as traffic; and, that, in the practice of other countries, and especially in our own, there has been no diversity of judgment or opinion. During our whole colonial history, this was acted upon by the British parliament, as an uncontested doctrine. That government regulated not merely our traffic with foreign nations, but our navigation, and intercourse, as unquestioned functions of the power to regulate commerce.

§ 514. This power the constitution extends to commerce with foreign nations, and among the several states, and with the Indian tribes. In regard to foreign nations, it is universally admitted, that the words comprehend every species of commercial intercourse. No sort of trade or intercourse can be carried on between this country and another, to which it does not extend. Commerce, as used in the constitution, is a {364} unit, every part of which is indicated by the term. If this be its admitted meaning in its application to foreign nations, it must carry the same meaning throughout the sentence. The next words are "among the several states." The word "among" means intermingled with. A thing, which is among others, is intermingled with them. Commerce among the states cannot stop at the external boundary line of each state, but may be introduced into the interior. It does not, indeed, comprehend any commerce, which is purely internal, between man and man in a single state, or between different parts of the same state, and not extending to, or affecting other states. Commerce among the states means, commerce, which concerns more states than one. It is not an apt phrase to indicate the mere interior traffic of a single state. The completely internal commerce of a state may be properly considered, as reserved to the state itself.

§ 515. The importance of the power of regulating commerce among the states, for the purposes of the Union, is scarcely less, than that of regulating it with foreign states. A very material object of this power is the relief of the states, which import and export through other states, from the levy of improper contributions on them by the latter. If each state were at liberty to regulate the trade between state and state, it is easy to foresee, that ways would be found out to load the articles of import and export, during their passage through the jurisdiction, with duties, which should fall on the makers of the latter, and the consumers of the former. The experience of the American states during the confederation abundantly establishes, that such arrangements could be, and would be made under the stimulating influence of local interests, and the desire of undue gain. {365} Instead of acting as a nation in regard to foreign powers, the states individually commenced a system of restraint upon each other, whereby the interests of foreign powers were promoted at their expense. When one state imposed high duties on the goods or vessels of a foreign power to countervail the regulations of such powers, the next adjoining states imposed lighter duties to invite those articles into their ports, that they might be transferred thence into the other states, securing the duties to themselves. This contracted policy in some of the states was soon counteracted by others. Restraints were immediately laid on such commerce by the suffering states; and thus a state of affairs disorderly and unnatural grew up, the necessary tendency of which was to destroy the Union itself. The history of other nations, also, furnishes the same admonition. In Switzerland, where the Union is very slight, it has been found necessary to provide, that each canton shall be obliged to allow a passage to merchandise through its jurisdiction into other cantons without any augmentation of tolls. In Germany, it is a law of the empire, that the princes shall not lay tolls on customs or bridges, rivers, or passages, without the consent of the emperor and diet. But these regulations are but imperfectly obeyed; and great public mischiefs have consequently followed. Indeed, without this power to regulate commerce among the states, the power of regulating foreign commerce would be incomplete and ineffectual. The very laws of the Union in regard to the latter, whether for revenue, for restriction, for retaliation, or for encouragement of domestic products or pursuits, might be evaded at pleasure, or rendered impotent. In short, in a practical view, it is impossible to separate the regulation of foreign commerce and domestic commerce {366} among the states from each other. The same public policy applies to each; and not a reason can be assigned for confiding the power over the one, which does not conduce to establish the propriety of conceding the power over the other.

§ 516. The next inquiry is, whether this power to regulate commerce is exclusive of the same power in the states, or is concurrent with it. It has been settled upon the most solemn deliberation, that the power is exclusive in the government of the United States. The reasoning, upon which this doctrine is founded, is to the following effect. The power to regulate commerce is general and unlimited in its terms. The full power to regulate a particular subject implies the whole power, and leaves no *residuum*. A grant of the whole is incompatible with the existence of a right in another to any part of it. A grant of a power to regulate necessarily excludes the action of all others, who would perform the same operation on the same thing. Regulation is designed to indicate the entire result, applying to those parts, which remain as they were, as well as to those, which are altered. It produces a uniform whole, which is as much disturbed and deranged by changing, what the regulating power designs to hate unbounded, as that, on which it has operated.

§ 517. The power to regulate commerce is not at all like that to lay taxes. The latter may well be concurrent, while the former is exclusive, resulting from the different nature of the two powers. The power of congress in laying taxes is not necessarily, or naturally inconsistent with that of the states. Each may lay a tax on the same property, without interfering with the action of the other; for taxation is but taking small portions {367} from the mass of property, which is susceptible of almost infinite division. In imposing taxes for state purposes, a state is not doing, what congress is empowered to do. Congress is not empowered to tax for those purposes, which are within the exclusive province of the states. When, then, each government exercises the power of taxation, neither is exercising the power of the other. But when a state proceeds to regulate commerce with foreign nations, or among the several states, it is exercising the very power, which is granted to congress; and is doing the very thing, which congress is authorized to do. There is no analogy, then, between the power of taxation, and the power of regulating commerce.

§ 518. Nor can any power be inferred in the states to regulate commerce from other clauses in the constitution, or the acknowledged rights exercised by the states. The constitution has prohibited the states from laying any impost or duty on imports or exports; but this does not admit, that the state might otherwise have exercised the power, as a regulation of commerce. The laying of such imposts and duties may be, and indeed often is used, as a mere regulation of commerce, by governments possessing that power. But the laying of such imposts and duties is as certainly, and more, usually, a right exercised as a part of the power to lay taxes; and with this latter power the states are clearly entrusted. So, that the prohibition is an exception from the acknowledged power of the state to lay taxes, and not from the questionable power to regulate commerce. Indeed, the constitution treats these as distinct and independent powers. The same remarks apply to a duty on tonnage.

§ 519. Nor do the acknowledged powers of the {368} states over certain subjects, having a connexion with commerce, in any degree impugn this reasoning. These powers are entirely distinct in their nature from that to regulate commerce; and though the same means may be resorted to, for the purpose of carrying each of these powers into effect, this by no just reasoning furnishes any ground to assert, that they are identical. Among these, are inspection laws, health laws, laws regulating turnpikes, roads, and ferries, all of which, when exercised by a state, are legitimate, arising from the general powers belonging to it, unless so far as they conflict with the powers delegated to congress. They are not so much regulations of commerce, as of police; and may truly be said to belong, if at all to commerce, to that which is purely internal. The pilotage laws of the states may fall under the same description. But they have been adopted by congress; and without question are controllable by it.

§ 520. The power in congress, then, being exclusive, no state is at liberty to pass any laws imposing a tax upon importers, importing goods from foreign countries, or from other states. It is wholly immaterial whether the tax be laid on the goods imported, or on the person of the importer. In each case, it is a restriction of the right of commerce, not conceded to the states. As the power of congress to regulate commerce reaches the interior of a state, it might be capable of authorizing the sale of the articles, which it introduces. Commerce is intercourse; and one of its most ordinary ingredients is traffic. It is inconceivable, that the power to authorize traffic, when given in the most comprehensive terms, with the intent, that its efficacy should be complete, should cease at the point, when its continuance is indispensable to its value. To what {369} purpose should the power to allow importation be given, unaccompanied with the power to authorize the sale of the thing imported? Sale is the object of importation; and it is an essential ingredient of that intercourse, of which importation constitutes a part. As congress have the right to authorize importation, they must have a right to authorize the importer to sell. What would be the language of a foreign government, which should be informed, that its merchants after importation were forbidden to sell the merchandize imported? What answer could the United States give to the complaints and just reproaches, to which such extraordinary conduct would expose them? No apology could be received, or offered. Such a state of things would annihilate commerce. It is no answer, that the tax may be moderate; for, if the power exists in the states, it may be carried to any extent they may choose. If it does not exist, every exercise of it is, *pro tanto*, a violation of the power of congress to regulate commerce.

§ 521. In the next place, to what extent, and for what objects and purposes the power to regulate commerce may be constitutionally applied.

§ 522. And first, among the states. It is not doubted, that it extends to the regulation of navigation, and to the coasting trade and fisheries, within, as well as without any state, wherever it is connected with the commerce or intercourse with any other state, or with foreign nations. It extends to the regulation and government of seamen on board of American ships; and to conferring privileges upon ships built and owned in the United States in domestic, as well as in foreign trade. It extends to quarantine laws, and pilotage laws, and wrecks of the sea. It extends, to the navigation of vessels engaged in carrying passengers, (whether {370} steam vessels, or of any other description,) as well as to the navigation of vessels engaged in traffic and general coasting business. It extends to the laying of embargoes, as well on domestic, as on foreign voyages. It extends to the construction of light-houses, the placing of buoys and beacons, the removal of obstructions to navigation in creeks, rivers, sounds, and bays, and the establishment of securities to navigation against the inroads of the ocean. It extends also to the designation of particular ports of entry and delivery for the purposes of commerce. The power has been actually exerted for these purposes by the national government under systems of laws, some of which are almost coeval with the establishment of the constitution; and these laws have continued unquestioned unto our day, if not to the utmost range of their reach, at least to that of their ordinary application.

§ 523. Secondly. Many like applications of the power may be traced in the regulations of the commerce of the United States with foreign nations. It has also been employed sometimes for the purpose of revenue; sometimes for the purpose of prohibition; sometimes for the purpose of retaliation and commercial reciprocity; sometimes to lay embargoes; sometimes to encourage domestic navigation, and the shipping and mercantile interest by bounties, by discriminating duties, and by special preferences and privileges; and sometimes to regulate intercourse with a view to mere political objects, such as to repel aggressions, increase the pressure of war, or vindicate the rights of neutral sovereignty. In all these cases, the right and duty have been conceded to the national government by the unequivocal voice of the people. {371}

§ 524. A question has been recently made, whether congress have a constitutional authority to apply the power to regulate commerce for the purpose of encouraging and protecting domestic manufactures. It is not denied, that congress may, incidentally, in its arrangements for revenue, or to countervail foreign restrictions, encourage the growth of domestic manufactures. But it is earnestly and strenuously insisted, that, under the colour of regulating commerce, congress have no right permanently to prohibit any importations, or to tax them unreasonably for the purpose of securing the home market to the domestic manufacturer, as they thereby destroy the commerce entrusted to them to regulate, and foster an interest, with which they have no constitutional power to interfere. This opinion constitutes the leading doctrine of several states in the Union at the present moment; and is asserted by them to be vital to the existence of the Union.

§ 525. The reasoning, by which the doctrine is maintained, that the power to regulate commerce cannot be constitutionally applied, as a means, directly to encourage domestic manufactures, has been already in part adverted to in considering the extent of the power to lay taxes. It is proper, however, to present it entire in its present connexion. It is to the following effect. — The constitution is one of limited and enumerated powers; and none of them can be rightfully exercised beyond the scope of the objects, specified in those powers. It is not disputed, that, when the power is given, all the appropriate means to carry it into effect are included. Neither is it disputed, that the laying of duties is, or may be an appropriate means of regulating commerce. But the question is a very different one, whether, under pretence of an exercise of the power to {372} regulate commerce, congress may in fact impose duties for objects wholly distinct from commerce. The question comes to this, whether a power, exclusively for the regulation of commerce, is a power for the regulation of manufactures? The statement of such a question would seem to involve its own answer. Can a power, granted for one purpose, be transferred to another? If it can, where is the limitation in the constitution? Are not commerce and manufactures as distinct, as commerce and agriculture If they are, how can a power to regulate one arise from a power to regulate the other? It is true, that commerce and manufactures are, or may be, intimately connected with each other. A regulation of one may injuriously or beneficially affect the other. But this is not the point in controversy. It is, whether congress have a right to regulate that, which is not committed to them, under a power, which is committed to them, simply because there is, or may be an intimate connexion between the powers. If this were admitted, the enumeration of the powers of congress would be wholly unnecessary and nugatory. Agriculture, colonies, capital, machinery, the wages of labour, the profits of stock, the rents of land, the punctual performance of contracts, and the diffusion of knowledge would all be within the scope of the power; for all of them bear an intimate relation to commerce. The result would be, that the powers of congress would embrace the widest extent of legislative functions, to the utter demolition of all constitutional boundaries between the state and national governments. When duties are laid, not for purposes of revenue, but of retaliation and restriction, to countervail foreign restrictions, they are strictly within the scope of the power, as a regulation of commerce. But when laid to encourage {373} manufactures, they have nothing to do with it. The power to regulate manufactures is no more confided to congress, than the power to interfere with the systems of education, the poor laws, or the road laws of the states. It is notorious, that, in the convention, an attempt was made to introduce into the constitution a power to encourage manufactures; but it was withheld. Instead of granting the power to congress, permission was given to the states to impose duties, with the consent of that body, to encourage their own manufactures; thus, in the true spirit of justice, imposing the burthen on those, who were to be benefited. It is true, that congress may, incidentally, when laying duties for revenue, consult the other interests of the country. They may so arrange the details, as indirectly to aid manufactures. And this is the whole extent, to which congress have ever gone until the tariffs, which have given rise to the present controversy. The former precedents of congress are not, even if admitted to be authoritative, applicable to the question now presented.

§ 526. The reasoning of those, who maintain the doctrine, that congress has authority to apply the power to regulate commerce to the purpose of protecting and encouraging domestic manufactures, is to the following effect. The power to regulate commerce, being in its terms unlimited, includes all means appropriate to the end, and all means, which have been usually exerted under the power. No one can doubt or deny, that a power to regulate trade involves a power to tax it. It is a familiar mode, recognised in the practice of all nations, and was known and admitted by the United States, while they were colonies, and has ever since been acted upon without opposition or question. The American colonies wholly denied the authority of the {374} British parliament to tax them, except as a regulation of commerce; but they admitted this exercise of power, as legitimate and unquestionable. The distinction was with difficulty maintained in practice between laws for the regulation of commerce by way of taxation, and laws, which were made for mere monopoly, or restriction, when they incidentally produced revenue. And it is certain, that the main and admitted object of parliamentary regulations of trade with the colonies was the encouragement of manufactures in Great-Britain. Other nations have, in like manner, for like purposes, exercised the like power. So, that there is no novelty in the use of the power, and no stretch in the range of the power.

§ 527. Indeed, the advocates of the opposite doctrine admit, that the power may be applied, so as incidentally to give protection to manufactures, when revenue is the principal design; and that it may also be applied to countervail the injurious regulations of foreign powers, when there is no design of revenue. These concessions admit, then, that the regulations of commerce are not wholly for purposes of revenue, or wholly confined to the purposes of commerce, considered *per se*. If this be true, then other objects may enter into commercial regulations; and if so, what restraint is there, as to the nature or extent of the objects, to which they may reach, which does not resolve itself into a question of expediency and policy? It may be admitted, that a power, given for one purpose, cannot be perverted to purposes wholly opposite, or beside its legitimate scope. But what perversion is there in applying a power to the very purposes, to which it has been usually applied? Under such circumstances, does not the grant of the power without restriction concede, {375} that it may be legitimately applied to such purposes? If a different intent had existed, would not that intent be manifested by some corresponding limitation?

§ 528. The terms, then, of the constitution are sufficiently large to embrace the power; the practice of other nations, and especially of Great-Britain and of the American states, has been to use it in this manner; and this exercise of it was one of the very grounds, upon which the establishment of the constitution was urged and vindicated. The argument, then, in its favour would seem to be absolutely irresistible under this aspect. But there are other very weighty considerations, which enforce it.

§ 529. In the first place, if congress does not possess the power to encourage domestic manufactures by regulations of commerce, the power is annihilated for the whole nation. The states are deprived of it. They have made a voluntary surrender of it; and yet it exists not in the national government. It is then a mere nonentity. Such a policy, voluntarily adopted by a free people, in subversion of some of their dearest rights and interests, would be most extraordinary in itself, without any assignable motive or reason for so great a sacrifice, and utterly without example in the history of the world. No man can doubt, that domestic agriculture and manufactures may be most essentially promoted and protected by regulations of commerce. No man can doubt, that it is the most usual, and generally the most efficient means of producing those results. No man can question, that in these great objects the different states of America have as deep a stake, and as vital interests, as any other nation. Why, then, should the power be surrendered and annihilated? It would produce the most serious mischiefs at home; and would {376} secure the most complete triumph over us by foreign nations. It would introduce and perpetuate national debility, if not national ruin. A foreign nation might, as a conqueror, impose upon us this restraint, as a badge of dependence, and a sacrifice of sovereignty, to sub-serve its own interests; but that we should impose it upon ourselves, is inconceivable. The achievement of our independence was almost worthless, if such a system was to be pursued. It would be in effect a perpetuation of that very system of monopoly, of encouragement of foreign manufactures, and depression of domestic industry, which was so much complained of during our colonial dependence; and which kept all America in a state of poverty, and slavish devotion to British interests. Under such circumstances, the constitution would be established, not for the purposes avowed in the preamble, but for the exclusive benefit and advancement of foreign nations, to aid their manufactures, and sustain their agriculture. Suppose cotton, rice, tobacco, wheat, corn, sugar, and other raw materials could be, or should hereafter be, abundantly produced in foreign countries, under the fostering hands of their governments, by bounties and commercial regulations, so as to become cheaper with such aids than our own; are all our markets to be opened to such products without any restraint, simply because we may not want revenue, to the ruin of our products and industry? Is America ready to give every thing to Europe, without any equivalent; and take in return whatever Europe may choose to give, upon its own terms? The most servile provincial dependence could not do more evils. Of what consequence would it be, that the national government could not tax our exports, if foreign governments might tax them to an unlimited extent, so as {377} to favour their own, and thus to supply us with the same articles by the overwhelming depression of our own by foreign taxation? When it is recollected, with what extreme discontent and reluctant obedience the British colonial restrictions were enforced in the manufacturing and navigating states, while they were colonies, it is incredible, that they should be willing to adopt a government, which should, or might entail upon them equal evils in perpetuity. Commerce itself would ultimately be as great a sufferer by such a system, as the other domestic interests. It would languish, if it did not perish. Let any man ask himself, if New-England, or the Middle states, would ever have consented to ratify a constitution, which would afford no protection to their manufactures or home industry. If the constitution was ratified under the belief, sedulously propagated on all sides, that such protection was afforded, would it not now be a fraud upon the whole people to give a different construction to its powers

§ 530. Passing by these considerations, let the practice of the government and the doctrines maintained by those. who have administered it, be deliberately examined; and they will be found to be in entire consistency with this reasoning. The very first congress, that ever sat under the constitution, composed in a considerable degree of those, who had framed, or assisted in the discussion of its provisions in the state conventions, deliberately adopted this view of the power. And what is most remarkable, upon a subject of deep interest and excitement, which at the time occasioned long and vehement debates, not a single syllable of doubt was breathed from any quarter against the constitutionality of protecting agriculture and manufactures by laying duties, although the intention to protect, and {378} encourage them was constantly avowed. Nay, it was contended to be a paramount duty, upon the faithful fulfilment of which the constitution had been adopted, and the omission of which would be a political fraud, without a whisper of dissent from any side. It was demanded by the people from various parts of the Union; and was resisted by none. Yet, state jealousy was never more alive than at this period, and state interests never more actively mingled in the debates of congress. The two great parties, which afterwards so much divided the country upon the question of a liberal and strict construction of the constitution, were then distinctly formed, and proclaimed their opinions with firmness and freedom. If, therefore, there had been a point of doubt, on which to hang an argument, it cannot be questioned, but that it would have been brought into the array of opposition. Such a silence, under such circumstances, is most persuasive and convincing.

§ 531. If ever, therefore, contemporaneous exposition, and the uniform and progressive operations of the government itself in all its departments, can be of any weight to settle the construction of the constitution, there never has been, and there never can be more decided evidence in favour of the power, than is furnished by the history of our national laws for the encouragement of domestic agriculture and manufactures. To resign an exposition so sanctioned, would be to deliver over the country to interminable doubts; and to make the constitution, not a written system of government, but a false and delusive text, upon which every successive age of speculatists and statesmen might build any system, suited to their own views and opinions. But if it be added to this, that the constitution {379} gives the power in the most unlimited terms, and neither assigns motives, nor objects for its exercise; but leaves these wholly to the discretion of the legislature, acting for the common good, and the general interests; the argument in its favour becomes as absolutely irresistible, as any demonstration of a moral or political nature ever can be. Without such a power, the government would be absolutely worthless, and made merely subservient to the policy of foreign nations, incapable of self-protection or self-support; with it, the country will have a right to assert its equality, and dignity, and sovereignty among the other nations of the earth.

§ 532. The power of congress also extends to regulate commerce with the Indian tribes. This power was not contained in the first draft of the constitution. It was afterwards referred to the committee on the constitution (among other propositions) to consider the propriety of giving to congress the power "to regulate affairs with the Indians, as well within, as without the limits of the United States." And, in the revised draft, the committee reported the clause, "and with the Indian Tribes," as it now stands.

§ 533. Antecedently to the American Revolution the authority to regulate trade and intercourse with the Indian tribes, whether they were within, or without the boundaries of the colonies, was understood to belong to the prerogative of the British crown. And after the American Revolution, the like power would naturally fall to the federal government, with a view to the general peace and interest of all the states. Two restrictions, however, upon the power were incorporated with it into the confederation, which occasioned endless embarrassments and doubts.

The {380} power of congress was restrained to Indians, not members of any of the states; and was not to be exercised, so as to violate or infringe the legislative right of any state within its own limits. What descriptions of Indians were to be deemed members of a state was never settled under the confederation; and the question was one of frequent perplexity and contention in the federal councils. And how the trade with Indians, though not members of a state, yet residing within its legislative jurisdiction; was to be regulated by an external authority, without so far intruding on the internal rights of legislation, was absolutely incomprehensible. In this case, as in some other cases, the articles of confederation inconsiderately endeavoured to accomplish impossibilities; to reconcile a partial sovereignty in the Union, with complete sovereignty in the states; to subvert a mathematical axiom, by taking away a part, and letting the whole remain. The constitution has wisely disembarrassed the power of these two limitations; and has thus given to congress, as the only safe and proper depositary, the exclusive power, which belonged to the crown in the ante-revolutionary times; a power indispensable to the peace of the states, and to the just preservation of the rights and territory of the Indians. In the former illustrations of this subject, it was stated, that the Indians, from the first settlement of the country, were always treated, as distinct, though in some sort, as dependent nations. Their territorial rights and sovereignty were respected. They were deemed incapable of carrying on trade or intercourse with any foreign nations, or of ceding their territories to them. But their right of self-government was admitted; and they were allowed a national existence, under the protection of the parent country, which exempted them {381} from the ordinary operations of the legislative power of the colonies. During the revolution and afterwards they were secured in the like enjoyment of their rights and property, as separate communities. The government of the United States, since the constitution, has always recognised the same attributes of dependent sovereignty, as belonging to them, and claimed the same right of exclusive regulation of trade and intercourse with them, and the same authority to protect and guarantee their territorial possessions, immunities, and jurisdiction.

§ 534. The power, then, given to congress to regulate commerce with the Indian tribes, extends equally to tribes living within or without the boundaries of particular states, and within or without the territorial limits of the United States. It is (says a learned commentator) wholly immaterial, whether such tribes continue seated within the boundaries of a state, inhabit part of a territory, or roam at large over lands, to which the United States have no claim. The trade with them is, in all its forms, subject exclusively to the regulation of congress. And in this particular, also, we trace the wisdom of the constitution. The Indians, not distracted by the discordant regulations of different states, are taught to trust one great body, whose justice they respect, and whose power they fear.

§ 535. It has lately been made a question, whether an Indian tribe, situated within the territorial boundaries of a state, but exercising the powers of government, and national sovereignty, under the guarantee of the general government, is a foreign state in the sense of the constitution, and as such entitled to sue in the courts of the United States. Upon solemn argument, it has been held, that such a tribe is to be deemed politically {382} a state; that is, a distinct political society, capable of self-government; but it is not to be deemed a *foreign state*, in the sense of the constitution. It is rather a domestic dependent nation. Such a tribe may properly be deemed to be in a state of pupilage; and its relation to the United States resembles that of a ward to a guardian.

CHAPTER XVI.

POWER OVER NATURALIZATION AND BANKRUPTCY.

§ 536. THE next clause is, that congress

> "shall have power to establish an uniform rule of naturalization, and uniform laws on the subject of bankruptcies throughout the United States."

§ 537. The propriety of confiding the power to establish an uniform rule of naturalization to the national government seems not to have occasioned any doubt or controversy in the convention. For aught that appears on the journals, it was conceded without objection. Under the confederation, the states possessed the sole authority to exercise the power; and the dissimilarity of the system in different states was generally admitted, as a prominent defect, and laid the foundation of many delicate and intricate questions. As the free inhabitants of each state were entitled to all the privileges and immunities of citizens in all the other states, it followed, that a single state possessed the power of forcing upon other states, with the enjoyment of every immunity and privilege, any alien, whom it might choose to incorporate into its own society, however repugnant such admission might be to their polity, convenience, and even prejudices. In effect every state possessed the power of naturalizing aliens in every other state; a power as mischievous in its nature, as it was indiscreet in its actual exercise. In some states, residence for a short time might, and did confer the rights of citizenship. In others, qualifications of greater importance were required. An alien, {384} therefore, incapacitated for the possession of certain rights by the laws of the latter, might, by a previous residence and naturalization in the former, elude at pleasure all their salutary regulations for self-protection. Thus, the laws of a single state were preposterously rendered paramount to the laws of all the others, even within their own jurisdiction. And it has been remarked with equal truth and justice, that it was owing to mere casualty, that the exercise of this power during the confederation did not involve the Union in the most serious embarrassments. There is great wisdom, therefore, in confiding to the national government the power to establish a uniform rule of naturalization throughout the United States. It is of the deepest interest to the whole Union to know, who are entitled to enjoy the rights of citizens in each state, since they thereby, in effect, become entitled to the rights of citizens in all the states. If aliens might be admitted indiscriminately to enjoy all the rights of citizens at the will of a single state, the Union might itself be endangered by an influx of foreigners, hostile to its institutions, ignorant of its powers, and incapable of a due estimate of its privileges.

§ 538. It follows, from the very nature of the power, that to be useful, it must be exclusive; for a concurrent power in the states would bring back all the evils and embarrassments, which the uniform rule of the constitution was designed to remedy. And accordingly, though there was a momentary hesitation, when the constitution first went into operation, whether the power might not still be exercised by the states, subject only to the control of congress, so far as the legislation of the latter extended, as the supreme law; yet the power is now firmly established to be exclusive in congress. {385}

§ 539. Before the adoption of the constitution the states severally possessed the exclusive right, as matter belonging to their general sovereignty, to pass laws upon the subject of bankruptcy and insolvency. Without stopping at present to consider, what is the precise meaning of each of these terms, as contradistinguished from the other; it may be stated, that the general object of all bankrupt and insolvent laws is, on the one hand, to secure to creditors an appropriation of the property of their debtors, *pro tanto*, to the discharge of their debts, whenever the latter are unable to discharge the whole amount; and, on the other hand, to relieve unfortunate and honest debtors from perpetual bondage to their creditors, either in the shape of unlimited imprisonment to coerce payment of their debts, or of an absolute right to appropriate and monopolize all their future earnings. The latter course obviously destroys all encouragement to industry and enterprize on the part of the unfortunate debtor, by taking from him all the just rewards of his labour, and leaving him a miserable pittance, dependent upon the bounty or forbearance of his creditors. The former is, if possible, more harsh, severe, and indefensible. It makes poverty and misfortune, in themselves sufficiently heavy burthens, the subject or the occasion of penalties and punishments. Imprisonment, as a civil remedy, admits of no defence, except so far as it is used to coerce fraudulent debtors to yield up their present property to their creditors, in discharge of their engagements. But when the debtors have no property, or have yielded up the whole to their creditors, to allow the latter at their mere pleasure to imprison them, is a refinement in cruelty, and an indulgence of private passions, which could hardly find apology in an enlightened despotism; and is utterly {386} at war with all the rights and duties of free governments. Such a system of legislation is as unjust, as it is unfeeling. It is incompatible with the first precepts of Christianity; and is a living reproach to the nations of christendom, carrying them back to the worst ages of paganism. One of the first duties of legislation, while it provides amply for the sacred obligation of contracts, and the remedies to enforce them, certainly is, *pari passu*, to relieve the unfortunate and meritorious debtor from a slavery of mind and body, which cuts him off from a fair enjoyment of the common benefits of society, and robs his family of the fruits of his labour, and the benefits of his paternal superintendence. A national government, which did not possess this power of legislation, would be little worthy of the exalted functions of guarding the happiness, and supporting the rights of a free people. It might guard them against political oppressions, only to render private oppressions more intolerable, and more glaring.

§ 540. But there are peculiar reasons, independent of these general considerations, why the government of the United States should be entrusted with this power. They result from the importance of preserving harmony, promoting justice, and securing equality of rights and remedies among the citizens of all the states. It is obvious, that if the power is exclusively vested in the states, each one will be at liberty to frame such a system of legislation upon the subject of bankruptcy and insolvency, as best suits its own local interests, and pursuits. Under such circumstances no uniformity of system or operations can be expected. One state may adopt a system of general insolvency; another, a limited or temporary system; one may relieve from the obligation of contracts; another only from {387} imprisonment; one may adopt a still more restrictive course of occasional relief; and another may refuse to act in any manner upon the subject. The laws of one state may give undue preferences to one class of creditors, as for instance, to creditors by bond, or judgment; another may provide for an equality of debts, and a distribution *pro rata* without distinction among all. One may prefer creditors living within the state to all living without; securing to the former an entire priority of payment out of the assets. Another may, with a more liberal justice, provide for the equal payment of all, at home and abroad, without favour or preference. In short, diversities of almost infinite variety and objects may be introduced into the local system, which may work gross injustice and inequality, and nourish feuds and discontents in neighbouring states. What is here stated, is not purely speculative. It has occurred among the American states in the most offensive forms, without any apparent reluctance or compunction on the part of the offending state. There will always be found in every state a large mass of politicians, who will deem it more safe to consult their own temporary interests and popularity, by a narrow system of preferences, than to enlarge the boundaries, so as to give to distant creditors a fair share of the fortune of a ruined debtor. There can be no other adequate remedy, than giving a power to the general government, to introduce and perpetuate a uniform system.

§ 541. In the next place it is clear, that no state can introduce any system, which shall extend beyond its own territorial limits, and the persons, who are subject to its jurisdiction. Creditors residing in other states cannot be bound by its laws; and debts contracted in other states are beyond the reach of its {388} legislation. It can neither discharge the obligation of such contracts, nor touch the remedies, which relate to them in any other jurisdiction. So that the most meritorious insolvent debtor will be harassed by new suits, and new litigations, as often as he moves out of the state boundaries. His whole property may be absorbed by his creditors residing in a single state, and he may be left to the severe retributions of judicial process in every other state in the Union. Among a people, whose general and commercial intercourse must be so great, and so constantly increasing, as in the United States, this alone would be a most enormous evil, and bear with peculiar severity upon all the commercial states. Very few persons engaged in active business will be without debtors or creditors in many states in the Union. The evil is incapable of being redressed by the states. It can be adequately redressed only by the power of the Union. One of the most pressing grievances, bearing upon commercial, manufacturing, and agricultural interests at the present moment, is the total want of a general system of bankruptcy. It is well known, that the power has lain dormant, except for a short period, ever since the constitution was adopted; and the excellent system, then put into operation, was repealed, before it had any fair trial, upon grounds generally believed to be wholly beside its merits, and from causes more easily understood, than deliberately vindicated.

§ 542. In the next place, the power is important in regard to foreign countries, and to our commercial credit and intercourse with them. Unless the general government were invested with authority to pass suitable laws, which should give reciprocity and equality in cases of bankruptcies here, there would be danger, {389} that the state legislation might, by undue domestic preferences and favours, compel foreign countries to retaliate; and instead of allowing creditors in the United States to partake an equality of benefits in cases of bankruptcies, to postpone them to all others. The existence of the power is, therefore, eminently useful; first, as a check upon undue state legislation; and secondly, as a means of redressing any grievances sustained by foreigners in commercial transactions.

§ 543. What laws are to be deemed bankrupt laws within the meaning of the constitution has been a matter of much forensic discussion and argument. Attempts have been made to distinguish between bankrupt laws and insolvent laws. For example, it has been said, that laws, which merely liberate the person of the debtor, are insolvent laws, and those, which discharge the contract, are bankrupt laws. But it would be very difficult to sustain this distinction by any uniformity of laws at home or abroad. In some of the states, laws, known as insolvent laws, discharge the person only; in others, they discharge the contract. And if congress were to pass a bankrupt act, which should discharge the person only of the bankrupt, and leave his future acquisitions liable to his creditors, there would be great difficulty in saying, that such an act was not in the sense of the constitution a bankrupt act, and so within the power of congress. Again; it has been said, that insolvent laws act on imprisoned debtors only at their own instance; and bankrupt laws only at the instance of creditors. But, however true this may have been in past times, as the actual course of English legislation, it is not true, and never was true, as a distinction in colonial legislation. In England it was an accident in the system, and not a material ground to {390} discriminate, who were to be deemed, in a legal sense, insolvents, or bankrupts. And if an act of congress should be passed, which should authorize a commission of bankruptcy to issue at the instance of the debtor, no court would on this account be warranted in saying, that the act was unconstitutional, and the commission a nullity. It is believed, that no laws ever were passed in America by the colonies or states, which had the technical denomination of "bankrupt laws." But insolvent laws, quite co-extensive with the English bankrupt system in their operations and objects, have not been unfrequent in colonial and state legislation. No distinction was ever practically, or even theoretically, attempted to be made between bankruptcies and insolvencies. And an historical review of the colonial and state legislation will abundantly show, that a bankrupt law may contain those regulations, which are generally found in insolvent laws; and that an insolvent law may contain those, which are common to bankrupt laws.

§ 544. How far the power of congress to pass uniform laws on the subject of bankruptcies supersedes the authority of state legislation on the same subject, has been a matter of much elaborate forensic discussion. It has been strenuously maintained by some learned minds, that the power in congress is exclusive of that of the states; and whether exerted or not, it supersedes state legislation. On the other hand, it has been maintained, that the power in congress is not exclusive;

that when congress has acted upon the subject, to the extent of the national legislation the power of the states is controlled and limited; but when unexerted, the states are at liberty to exercise the power in its full extent, unless so far as they are controlled by other constitutional provisions. And this latter opinion is now {391} firmly established by judicial decisions. As this doctrine seems now to have obtained a general acquiescence, it is not necessary to review the reasoning, on which the different opinions are founded; although, as a new question, it is probably as much open to controversy, as any one, which has ever given rise to judicial argumentation. But upon all such subjects it seems desirable to adopt the sound practical maxim, *Interest reipublicæ, ut finis sit litium.*

§ 545. It is, however, to be understood, that although the states still retain the power to pass insolvent and bankrupt laws, that power is not unlimited, as it was before the constitution. It does not, as will be presently seen, extend to the passing of insolvent or bankrupt acts, which shall discharge the obligation of antecedent contracts. It can discharge such contracts only, as are shade subsequently to the passing of such acts, and such, as are made within the state between citizens of the same state. It does not extend to contracts made with a citizen of another state within the state, nor to any contracts made in other states.

CHAPTER XVII.

POWER TO COIN MONEY AND FIX THE STANDARD OF WEIGHTS AND MEASURES.

{392}

§ 546. THE next power of congress is

> "to coin money, regulate the value thereof, and of foreign coin, and fix the standard of weights and measures."

§ 547. Under the confederation, the continental congress had delegated to them, "the sole and exclusive right and power of regulating the alloy and value of coin struck by their own authority, or by that of the states," and of "fixing the standard of weights and measures throughout the United States." It is observable, that, under the confederation, there was no power given to regulate the value of foreign coin, an omission, which in a great measure would destroy any uniformity in the value of the current coin, since the respective states might, by different regulations, create a different value in each. The constitution has, with great propriety, cured this defect; and, indeed, the whole clause, as it now stands, does not seem to have attracted any discussion in the convention. It has been justly remarked, that the power "to coin money" would, doubtless, include that of regulating its value, had the latter power not been expressly inserted. But the constitution abounds with pleonasms and repetitions of this nature.

§ 548. The grounds, upon which the general power to coin money, and regulate the value of foreign and domestic coin, is granted to the national government, cannot require much illustration in order to vindicate it. The object of the power is to produce uniformity of {393} value throughout the Union, and thus to preclude us from the embarrassments of a perpetually fluctuating and variable currency. Money is the universal medium or common standard, by a comparison with which the value of all merchandise may be ascertained, or, it is a sign, which represents the respective values of all commodities. It is, therefore, indispensable for the wants and conveniences of commerce, domestic as well as foreign. The power to coin money is one of the ordinary prerogatives of sovereignty, and is almost universally exercised in order to preserve a proper circulation of good coin of a known value in the home market. In order to secure it from debasement it is necessary, that it should be exclusively under the control and regulation of the government; for if every individual were permitted to make and circulate, what coin he should please, there would be an opening to the grossest frauds and impositions upon the public, by the use of base and false coin. And the same remark applies with equal force to foreign coin, if allowed to circulate freely in a country without any control by the government. Every civilized government, therefore, with a view to prevent such abuses, to facilitate exchanges, and thereby to encourage all sorts of industry and commerce, as well as to guard itself against the embarrassments of an undue scarcity of currency, injurious to its own interests and credits, has found it necessary to coin money, and affix to it a public stamp and value, and to regulate the introduction and use of foreign coins. In England, this prerogative belongs to the crown; and, in former ages, it was greatly abused; for base coin was often coined and circulated by its authority, at a value far above its intrinsic worth; and thus taxes of a burthensome nature {394} were indirectly laid upon the people. There is great propriety, therefore, in confiding it to the legislature, not only as the more immediate representatives of the public interests, but as the more safe depositaries of the power.

§ 549. The other, power, "to fix the standard of weights and measures," is, doubtless, given from like motives of public policy, for the sake of uniformity, and the convenience of commerce. Hitherto, however, it has remained a dormant power, from the many difficulties attendant upon the subject, although it has been repeatedly brought to the attention of congress in most elaborate reports. Until congress shall fix a standard, the understanding seems to be, that the states possess the power to fix their own weights and measures; or, at least, the existing standards at the adoption of the constitution remain in full force. Under the confederation, congress possessed the like exclusive power. In England the power to regulate weights and measures is said by Mr. Justice Blackstone to belong to the royal prerogative. But it has been remarked by a learned commentator on his work, that the power cannot, with propriety, be referred to the king's prerogative; for, from Magna Charta to the present time, there are above twenty acts of parliament to fix and establish the standard and uniformity of weights and measures.

§ 550. The next power of congress is,

"to provide for the punishment of counterfeiting the securities and current coin of the United States."

This power would naturally flow, as an incident, from the antecedent powers to borrow money, and regulate the coinage; and, indeed, without it the latter would be deficient in {395} any adequate sanction. This power would seem to be exclusive in congress, since it grows out of the constitution, as an appropriate means to carry into effect other delegated powers, not antecedently existing in the states.

CHAPTER XVIII.

POWER TO ESTABLISH POST-OFFICES AND POST-ROADS.

{396}

§ 551. THE next power of congress is, "to establish post-offices and post-roads." The nature and extent of this power, both theoretically and practically, are of great importance, and have given rise to much ardent controversy. It deserves, therefore, a deliberate examination. It was passed over by the Federalist with a single remark, as a power not likely to be disputed in its exercise, or to be deemed dangerous by its scope. The "power," says the Federalist, "of establishing post-roads must, in every view, be a harmless power; and may, perhaps, by judicious management, become productive of great public conveniency. Nothing, which tends to facilitate the intercourse between the states, can be deemed unworthy of the public care." One cannot but feel, at the present time, an inclination to smile at the guarded caution of these expressions, and the hesitating avowal of the importance of the power. It affords, perhaps, one of the most striking proofs, how much the growth and prosperity of the country have outstripped the most sanguine anticipations of our most enlightened patriots.

§ 552. The post-office establishment has already become one of the most beneficent, and useful establishments under the national government. It circulates intelligence of a commercial, political, intellectual, and private nature, with incredible speed and regularity. It thus administers, in a very high degree, to the comfort, {397} the interests, and the necessities of persons, in every rank and station of life. It brings the most distant places and persons, as it were, in contact with each other; and thus softens the anxieties, increases the enjoyments, and cheers the solitude of millions of hearts. It imparts a new influence and impulse to private intercourse; and, by a wider diffusion of knowledge, enables political rights and duties to be performed with more uniformity and sound judgment. It is not less effective, as an instrument of the government in its own operations. In peace, it enables it without ostentation or expense to send its orders, and direct its measures for the public good, and transfer its funds, and apply its powers, with a facility and promptitude, which, compared with the tardy operations, and imbecile expedients of former times, seem like the wonders of magic. In war it is, if possible, still more important and useful, communicating intelligence vital to the movements of armies and navies, and the operations and duties of warfare, with a rapidity, which, if it does not always ensure victory, at least, in many instances, guards against defeat and ruin. Thus, its influences have become, in a public, as well as private view, of incalculable value to the permanent interests of the Union. It is obvious at a moment's glance at the subject, that the establishment in the hands of the states would have been wholly inadequate to these objects; and the impracticability of any uniformity of system would have introduced infinite delays and inconveniences; and burthened the mails with an endless variety of vexatious taxations, and regulations. No one, accustomed to the retardations of the post in passing through independent states on the continent of Europe, can fail to appreciate the benefits of a power, which pervades the {398} Union. The national government is that alone, which can safely or effectually execute it, with equal promptitude and cheapness, certainty and uniformity. Already the post-office establishment realizes a revenue exceeding two millions of dollars, from which it defrays all its own expenses, and transmits mails in various directions over more than one hundred and twenty thousand miles. It transmits intelligence in one day to distant places, which, when the constitution was first put into operation, was scarcely transmitted through the same distance in the course of a week. The rapidity of its movements has been in a general view doubled within the last twenty years. There are now more than eight thousand five hundred post-offices in the United States; and at every session of the legislature new routes are constantly provided for, and new post-offices established. It may, therefore, well be deemed a most beneficent power, whose operations can scarcely be applied, except for good; accomplishing in an eminent degree some of the high purposes set forth in the preamble of the constitution; forming a more perfect union; providing for the common defence; and promoting the general welfare.

§ 553. Upon the construction of this clause of the constitution, two opposite opinions have been expressed. One maintains, that the power to establish post-offices and post-roads can intend no more, than the power to direct, where post-offices shall be kept, and on what roads the mails shall be carried. Or, as it has been on other occasions expressed, the power to establish post-roads is a power to designate, or point out, what roads shall be mail-roads, and the right of passage or way along them, when so designated. The other maintains, that although these modes of exercising the {399} power are perfectly constitutional; yet they are not the whole of the power, and do not exhaust it. On the contrary, the power comprehends the right to make, or construct any roads, which congress may deem proper for the conveyance of the mail, and to keep them in due repair for such purpose.

§ 554. The whole practical course of the government upon this subject, from its first organization down to the present time, under every administration, has repudiated the strict and narrow construction of the words above mentioned. The power to establish post-offices and post-roads has never been understood to be limited to the power to point out and designate post-offices and post-roads. Resort has been constantly had to the more expanded sense of the word "establish;" and no other sense can include the objects, which the post-office laws have constantly included. Nay, it is not only not true, that these laws have stopped short of an exposition of the words sufficiently broad to justify the making of roads; but they have included exercises of power far more remote from the immediate objects. If the practice of the government is, therefore, of any weight in giving a constitutional interpretation, it is in favour of the liberal interpretation of the clause.

§ 555. But passing by considerations of this nature, why does not the power to establish post-offices and post-roads include the power to make and construct them, when wanted, as well as the power to establish a navy-hospital, or a custom-house, a power to make and construct them? The latter is not doubted by any persons; why then is the former? In each case, the sense of the ruling term "establish" would seem to be the same; in each, the power may be carried into effect {400} by means short of constructing, or purchasing the things authorized. A temporary use of a suitable site or building may possibly be obtained with, or without hire. Besides; why may not congress purchase, or erect a post-office building, and buy the necessary land, if it be in their judgment advisable? Can there be a just doubt, that a power to establish post-offices includes this power, just as much, as a power to establish custom-houses would to build the latter? Would it not be a strange construction to say, that the abstract office might be created, but not the officina, or place, where it should be exercised? There are many places peculiarly fit for local post-offices, where no suitable building could be found. And, if a power to construct post-office buildings exists, where is the restraint upon constructing roads?

§ 556. But whatever be the extent of the power, narrow or large, there will still remain another inquiry, whether it is an exclusive power, or concurrent in the states. This is not, perhaps, a very important inquiry, because it is admitted on all sides, that it can be exercised only in subordination to the power of congress, if it be concurrent in the states. A learned commentator deems it concurrent, inasmuch as there seems nothing in the constitution, or in the nature of the thing itself, which may not be exercised by both governments at the same time, without prejudice or interference; but subordinate, because, whenever any power is expressly granted to congress, it is to be taken for granted, that it is not to be contravened by the authority of any particular state. A state might, therefore, establish a post-road, or post-office, on any route, where congress had not established any. On the other hand, another learned commentator is of opinion, that the power is exclusive {401} in congress, so far as relates to the conveyance of letters. Hitherto the question has been purely speculative; and it cannot now be important to discuss it. It is highly improbable, that any state will attempt any exercise of the power, considering the difficulty of carrying it into effect, without the co-operation of congress.

CHAPTER XIX.

POWER TO PROMOTE SCIENCE AND USEFUL ARTS.

§ 557. THE next power of congress is,

> "to promote the progress of science and the useful arts, by securing, for limited times, to authors and inventors the exclusive right to their respective writings and discoveries."

§ 558. This power did not exist under the confederation; and its utility does not seem to have been questioned. The copyright of authors in their works had, before the revolution, been decided in Great Britain to be a common law right; and it was regulated and limited under statutes passed by parliament upon that subject. The right to useful inventions seems, with equal reason, to belong to the inventors; and, accordingly, it was saved out of the statute of monopolies in the reign of King James the First, and has ever since been allowed for a limited period, not exceeding fourteen years. It is doubtless to this knowledge of the common law and statuteable rights of authors and inventors, that we are to attribute this constitutional provision. It is beneficial to all parties, that the national government should possess this power; to authors and inventors, because, otherwise, they would be subjected to the varying laws and systems of the different states on this subject, which would impair, and might even destroy the value of their rights; to the public, as it will promote the progress of science and the useful arts, and admit the people at large, after a short interval, to the full possession and {403} enjoyment of all writings and invention without restraint. In short, the only boon that could be offered to inventors to disclose the secrets of their discoveries, would be the exclusive right and profit of them, as a monopoly, for a limited period. And authors would have little inducement to prepare elaborate works for the public, if the publication of them would be at a large expense, and, as soon as they were published, there would be an unlimited right of depredation and piracy of their copyright. The states could not separately make effectual provision for either of the cases; and most of them, at the time of the adoption of the constitution, had anticipated the propriety of such a grant of power, by passing laws on the subject, at the instance of the continental congress.

§ 559. The power, in its terms, is confined to authors and inventors; and cannot be extended to the introducers of any new works or inventions. This has been thought by some persons of high distinction to be a defect in the constitution. But perhaps the policy of further extending the right is questionable; and, at all events, the restriction has not hitherto operated as any discouragement of science or the arts. It has been doubted, whether congress has authority to decide the fact, that a person is an author or inventor in the sense of the constitution, so as to preclude that question from judicial inquiry. But, at all events, such a construction ought never to be put upon the general terms of any act in favour of a particular inventor, unless it be inevitable.

§ 560. The next power of congress is, "to constitute tribunals inferior to the Supreme Court." This clause properly belongs to the third article of the constitution; {404} and will come in review, when we survey the structure and powers of the judicial department. It will, therefore, be, for the present, passed over.

CHAPTER XX.

POWER TO PUNISH PIRACIES AND FELONIES.

§ 561. THE next power of congress is,

> "to define and punish piracies and felonies committed on the high seas, and offences against the law of nations."

§ 562. If the clause of the constitution had been confined to piracies, there would not have been any necessity of conferring the power to define the crime, since the power to punish would necessarily be held to include the power of ascertaining and fixing the definition of the crime. Indeed, there would not seem to be the slightest reason to define the crime at all; for piracy is perfectly well known, and understood in the law of nations, though it is often found defined in mere municipal codes. By the law of nations, robbery, or forcible depredation upon the sea, *animo furandi*, is piracy. The common law, too, recognises, and punishes piracy as an offence, not against its own municipal code, but as an offence against the universal law of nations; a pirate being deemed an enemy of the human race. The common law, therefore, deems piracy to be robbery on the sea; that is, the same crime, which it denominates robbery, when committed on land. And if congress had simply declared, that piracy should be punished with death, the crime would have been sufficiently defined. Congress may as well define by using a term of a known and determinate meaning, as by an express enumeration of all the particulars included in that term; for that is certain, which, by reference, is made certain. If congress should declare murder a {406} felony, no body would doubt, what was intended by murder. And, indeed, if congress should proceed to declare, that homicide, "with malice aforethought," should be deemed murder, and a felony; there would still be the same necessity of ascertaining, from the common law, what constitutes malice aforethought. So, that there would be no end to difficulties or definitions; for each successive definition might involve some terms, which would still require some new explanation. The true intent of the constitution in this clause, is not merely to define piracy, as known to the law of nations, but to enumerate what crimes in the national code shall be deemed piracies. And so the power has been practically expounded by congress.

§ 563. But the power is not merely to define and punish piracies, but *felonies*, and *offences* against *the law of nations*; and on this account, the power to define, as well as to punish, is peculiarly appropriate. It has been remarked, that felony is a term of loose signification, even in the common law; and of various import in the statute law of England. Mr. Justice Blackstone says, that felony, in the general acceptation of the English law, comprises every species of crime, which occasioned at common law the forfeiture of lands and goods. This most frequently happens in those crimes, for which a capital punishment either is, or was liable to be inflicted. All offences now capital by the English law are felonies; but there are still some offences, not capital, which are yet felonies, (such as suicide, petty larceny, and homicide by chance medley;) that is, they subject the committers of them to some forfeiture, either of lands or goods. But the idea of capital punishment has now become so associated, in the English law, with the idea of felony, that if {407} an act of parliament makes a new offence felony, the law implies, that it shall be punished with death, as well as with forfeiture.

§ 564. But whatever may be the true import of the word felony at the common law, in regard to municipal offences, its meaning, in regard to offences on the high seas, is necessarily somewhat indeterminate; since the term is not used in the criminal jurisprudence of the Admiralty in the technical sense of the common law. Lord Coke long ago stated, that a pardon of felonies would not pardon piracy; for "piracy or robbery on the high seas was no felony, whereof the common law took any knowledge, &c.; but was only punishable by the civil law, &c.; the attainder by which law wrought no forfeiture of lands or corruption of blood." And he added, that the statute of 28 Henry 8, ch. 15, which created the High Commission Court for the trial of "all treasons, felonies, robberies, murders, and confederacies, committed in or upon the high sea, &c.," did not alter the offence, or make the offence felony, but left the offence as it was before the act, viz. felony only by the civil law.

§ 565. Offences against the law of nations are quite as important, and cannot with any accuracy be said to be completely ascertained, and defined in any public code, recognised by the common consent of nations. In respect, therefore, as well to felonies on the high seas, as to offences against the law of nations, there is a peculiar fitness in giving to congress the power to define, as well as to punish. And there is not the slightest reason to doubt, that this consideration had very great weight with the convention, in producing the phraseology of the clause. On both subjects it would have been inconvenient, if not impracticable, to have referred {408} to the codes of the states, as well from their imperfection, as their different enumeration of the offences. Certainty, as well as uniformity, required, that the power to define and punish should reach over the whole of these classes of offences.

§ 566. What is the meaning of "high seas," within the intent of this clause, does not seem to admit of any serious doubt. The phrase embraces not only the waters of the ocean, which are out of sight of land, but the waters on the sea coast below low water mark, whether within the territorial boundaries of a foreign nation, or of a domestic state. Mr. Justice Blackstone has remarked, that the *main sea* or high sea begins at the low water mark. But between the high water mark and low water mark, where the tide ebbs and flows, the common law and the admiralty have *divisum imperium*, an alternate jurisdiction, one upon the water, when it is full sea; the other upon the land, when it is an ebb. He doubtless here refers to the waters of the ocean on the sea-coast, and not in creeks and inlets. Lord Hale says, that the sea is either that, which lies within the body of the county, or without. That, which lies without the body of a county, is called the main sea, or ocean. So far, then, as regards the states of the Union, "high seas" may be taken to mean that part of the ocean, which washes the sea-coast, and is without the body of any county, according to the common law; and, so far as regards foreign nations, any waters on their sea-coast, below low water mark.

CHAPTER XXI.

THE POWER TO DECLARE WAR AND MAKE CAPTURES.

{409}

§ 567. THE next power of congress is to

> "declare war, grant letters of marque and reprisal, and make rules concerning captures on land and water."

§ 568. A similar exclusive power was given to congress by the confederation. That such a power ought to exist in the national government, no one will deny, who believes, that it ought to have any powers whatsoever, either for offence or defence, for the common good, or for the common protection. It is, therefore, wholly superfluous to reason out the propriety of granting the power. It is self-evident, unless the national government is to be a mere mockery and shadow. The power could not be left without extreme mischief, if not absolute ruin, to the separate authority of the several states; for then it would be at the option of any one to involve the whole in the calamities and burthens of warfare. In the general government it is safe, because war can be declared only by the majority of the states, in congress.

§ 569. The only practical question upon this subject would seem to be, to what department of the national government it would be most wise and safe to confide this high prerogative, emphatically called the last resort of sovereigns, *ultima ratio regum.* In Great Britain it is the exclusive prerogative of the crown; and in other countries, it is usually, if not universally, confided to the executive department. It might by the constitution {410} have been confided to the executive, or to the senate, or to both conjointly.

§ 570. In the plan offered by an eminent statesman in the convention, it was proposed, that the senate should have the sole power of declaring war. The reasons, which may be urged in favour of such an arrangement, are, that the senate would be composed of representatives of the states, of great weight, sagacity, and experience, and that being a small and select body, promptitude of action, as well as wisdom, and firmness, would, as they ought, accompany the possession of the power. Large bodies necessarily move slowly; and where the co-operation of different bodies is required, the retardation of any measure must be proportionally increased. In the ordinary course of legislation this may be no inconvenience. But in the exercise of such a prerogative, as declaring war, despatch, secrecy, and vigour are often indispensable, and always useful towards success. On the other hand it may be urged in reply, that the power of declaring war is not only the highest sovereign prerogative, but that it is in its own nature and effects so critical and calamitous, that it requires the utmost deliberation, and the successive review of all the councils of the nation. War, in its best estate, never fails to impose upon the people the most burthensome taxes, and personal sufferings. It is always injurious to, and sometimes subversive of the great commercial, manufacturing, and agricultural interests. Nay, it always involves the prosperity, and not unfrequently the existence, of a nation. It is sometimes fatal to public liberty itself, by introducing a spirit of military glory, which is ready to follow, wherever a successful commander will lead; and in a republic, whose institutions are essentially {411} founded on the basis of peace, there is infinite danger, that war will find it both imbecile in defence, and eager for contest. Indeed, the history of republics has but too fatally proved, that they are too ambitious of military fame and conquest, and too easily devoted to the views of demagogues, who flatter their pride, and betray their interests. It should therefore be difficult in a republic to declare war; but not to make peace. The representatives of the people are to lay the taxes to support a war, and therefore have a right to be consulted, as to its propriety and necessity. The executive is to carry it on, and therefore should be consulted, as to its time, and the ways and means of making it effective. The co-operation of all the branches of the legislative power ought, upon principle, to be required in this the highest act of legislation, as it is in all others. Indeed, there might be a propriety even in enforcing still greater restrictions, as by requiring a concurrence of two thirds of both houses.

§ 571. This reasoning appears to have had great weight with the convention, and to have decided its choice. Its judgment has hitherto obtained the unqualified approbation of the country.

§ 572. The power to declare war would of itself carry the incidental power to grant letters of marque and reprisal, and make rules concerning captures. It is most probable, that an extreme solicitude to follow out the powers, enumerated in the confederation, occasioned the introduction of these clauses into the constitution. In the former instrument, where all powers, not *expressly* delegated, were prohibited, this enumeration was peculiarly appropriate. But in the latter, where incidental powers were expressly contemplated, and provided, for, the same necessity did not exist. As has been already {412} remarked in another place, and will abundantly appear from the remaining clauses auxiliary to the power to declare war, the constitution abounds with pleonasms and repetitions, sometimes introduced from caution, sometimes from inattention, and sometimes from the imperfections of language.

§ 573. But the express power "to grant letters of marque and reprisal" may not have been thought wholly unnecessary, because it is often a measure of peace, to prevent the necessity of a resort to war. Thus, individuals of a nation sometimes suffer from the depredations of foreign potentates; and yet it may not be deemed either expedient or necessary to redress such grievances by a general declaration of war. Under such circumstances the law of nations authorizes the sovereign of the injured individual to grant him this mode of redress, whenever justice is denied to him by the state, to which the party, who has done the injury, belongs. In this case the letters of marque and reprisal (words used as synonymous, the latter (reprisal) signifying, a taking in return, the former (letters of marque) the license to pass the frontiers in order to such taking,) contain an authority to seize the bodies or goods of the subjects of the offending state, wherever they may be found, until satisfaction is made for the injury. This power of reprisal seems indeed to be a dictate almost of nature itself, and is nearly related to, and plainly derived from that of making war. It is but an incomplete state of hostilities; and often ultimately leads to a formal denunciation of war, if the injury is undressed, or extensive in its operations.

§ 574. The next power of congress is

"to raise and support armies; but no appropriation of money to that use shall be for a longer term than two years." {413}

§ 575. The power to raise armies is an indispensable incident to the power to declare war; and the latter would literally be *brutum fulmen* without the former, a means of mischief without a power of defence. Under the confederation congress possessed no power whatsoever to raise armies; but only "to agree upon the number of land forces, and to make requisitions from each state for its quota, in proportion to the number of white inhabitants in such state;" which requisitions were to be binding; and thereupon the legislature of each state were to appoint the regimental officers, raise the men, and clothe, arm, and equip them in a soldier-like manner, at the expense of the United States. The experience of the whole country, during the revolutionary war, established, to the satisfaction of every statesman, the utter inadequacy and impropriety of this system of requisition. It was equally at war with economy, efficiency, and safety. It gave birth to a competition between the states, which created a kind of auction of men. In order to furnish the quotas required of them, they outbid each other, till bounties grew to an enormous and insupportable size. On this account many persons procrastinated their enlistment, or enlisted only for short periods. Hence, there were but slow and scanty levies of men in the most critical emergencies of our affairs; short enlistments at an unparalleled expense; and continual fluctuations in the troops, ruinous to their discipline, and subjecting the public safety frequently to the perilous crisis of a disbanded army. Hence also arose those oppressive expedients for raising men, which were occasionally practised, and which nothing, but the enthusiasm of liberty, could have induced the people to endure. The burthen was also very unequally distributed. The states near the seat of {414} war, influenced by motives of self-preservation, made efforts to furnish their quotas, which even exceeded their abilities; while those at a distance were exceedingly remiss in their exertions. In short, the army was frequently composed of three bodies of men; first, raw recruits; secondly, persons, who were just about completing their term of service; and thirdly, of persons, who had served out half their term, and were quietly waiting for its determination. Under such circumstances, the wonder is not, that its military operations were tardy, irregular, and often unsuccessful; but, that it was ever able to make head-way at all against an enemy, possessing a fine establishment, well appointed, well armed, well clothed, and well paid. The appointment, too, by the states, of all regimental officers, had a tendency to destroy all harmony and subordination, so necessary to the success of military life.

§ 576. There is great wisdom and propriety in relieving the government from the ponderous and unwieldly machinery of the requisitions and appointments under the confederation. The present system of the Union is general and direct, and capable of a uniform organization and action. It is essential to the common defence, that the national government should possess the power to raise armies; build and equip fleets; prescribe rules for the government of both; direct their operations; and provide for their support. The power, however, was assailed in the state conventions, and before the people, with incredible zeal and pertinacity, as dangerous to liberty, and subversive of the state governments. Objections were made against the general and indefinite power to raise armies, not limiting the number of troops; and to the maintenance of them in peace, as well as in war. {415}

§ 577. To these suggestions it was replied with equal force and truth, that to be of any value, the power must be unlimited. It is impossible to foresee, or define the extent and variety of national exigencies, and the correspondent extent and variety of the national means necessary to satisfy them. The power must be co-extensive with all possible combinations of circumstances, and under the direction of the councils entrusted with the common defence. To deny this would be to deny the means, and yet require the end. These must therefore, be unlimited in every matter essential to its efficacy, that is, in the formation, direction, and support of the national forces. This was not doubted under the confederation; though the mode adopted to carry it into effect was utterly inadequate and illusory.

§ 578. It is important also to consider, that the surest means of avoiding war is to be prepared for it in peace. If a prohibition should be imposed upon the United States against raising armies in time of peace, it would present the extraordinary spectacle to the world of a nation incapacitated by a constitution of its own choice from preparing for defence before an actual invasion. As formal denunciations of war are in modern times often neglected, and are never necessary, the presence of an enemy within our territories would be required, before the government would be warranted to begin levies of men for the protection of the state. The blow must be received, before any attempts could be made to ward it off, or to return it. Such a course of conduct would at all times invite aggression and insult; and enable a formidable rival or secret enemy to seize upon the country, as a defenceless prey; or to drain its resources by a levy of contributions, at once irresistible and ruinous. It would be in vain to look to the militia {416} for an adequate defence under such circumstances. This reliance came very near losing us our independence, and was the occasion of the useless expenditure of many millions.

§ 579. The next power of congress is

"to provide and maintain a navy."

§ 580. Under the confederation congress possessed the power "to build and equip a navy." The same language was adopted in the original draft of the constitution, and it was amended by substituting the present words, apparently without objection, as more broad and appropriate. In the convention, the propriety of granting the power seems not to have been questioned. But it was assailed in the state conventions as dangerous. It was said, that commerce and navigation are the principal sources of the wealth of the maritime powers of Europe; and if we engaged in commerce, we should soon become their rivals. A navy would soon be thought indispensable to protect it. But the attempt on our part to provide a navy would provoke these powers, who would not suffer us to become a naval power.

Thus, we should be immediately involved in wars with them. The expenses, too, of maintaining a suitable navy would be enormous; and wholly disproportionate to our resources. If a navy should be provided at all, it ought to be limited to the mere protection of our trade. It was further urged, that the Southern states would share a large portion of the burthens of maintaining a navy, without any corresponding advantages.

§ 581. With the nation at large these objections were not deemed of any va-lidity. The necessity of a navy for the protection of commerce and navigation was not only admitted, but made a strong ground for {417} the grant of the power. One of the great objects of the constitution was the encouragement and protection of navigation and trade. Without a navy, it would be utterly impossible to maintain our right to the fisheries, and our trade and navigation on the lakes, and the Mis-sissippi, as well as our foreign commerce. It was one of the blessings of the Union, that it would be able to provide an adequate support and protection for all these important objects. Besides; a navy would be absolutely indispensable to protect our whole Atlantic frontier, in case of a war with a foreign maritime power. We should otherwise be liable, not only to the invasion of strong regular forces of the enemy; but to the attacks and incursions of every predatory adventurer. Our mari-time towns might all be put under contribution; and even the entrance and depar-ture from our own ports be interdicted at the caprice, or the hostility of a foreign power. It would also be our cheapest, as well as our best defence; as it would save us the expense of numerous forts and garrisons upon the sea-coast, which, though not effectual for all, would still be required for some purposes. In short, in a mari-time warfare, without this means of defence, our commerce would be driven from the ocean, our ports would be blockaded, our sea-coast infested with plunderers, and our vital interests put at hazard.

§ 582. Although these considerations were decisive with the people at large in favour of the power, from its palpable necessity and importance to all the great interests of the country, it is within the memory of all of us, that the same ob-jections for a long time prevailed with a leading party in the country. It was not until during the late war with Great Britain, when our little navy, by a gallantry and brilliancy of achievement almost {418} without parallel, had literally fought itself into favour, that the nation at large began to awake from its lethargy on this subject, and to insist upon a policy, which should at once make us respected and formidable abroad, and secure protection and honor at home. It has been proudly said by a learned commentator on the laws of England, that the royal navy of Eng-land hath ever been its greatest defence and ornament. It is its ancient and natural strength; the floating bulwark of the island; an army, from which, however strong and powerful, no danger can be apprehended to liberty. Every American citizen ought to cherish the same sentiment, as applicable to the navy of his own country.

§ 583. The next power of congress is

"to make rules for the government and regulation of the land and naval forces."

This is a natural incident to the preceding powers to make war, to raise armies, and to provide and maintain a navy. Its propriety, therefore, scarcely could be, and never has been denied, and need not now be insisted on. The clause was not in the original draft of the constitution; but was added without objection by way of amendment. It was without question borrowed from a corresponding clause in the articles of confederation, where it was with more propriety given, because there was a prohibition of all implied powers. In Great Britain, the king, in his capacity of generalissimo of the whole kingdom, has the sole power of regulating fleets and armies. But parliament has repeatedly interposed; and the regulation of both is now in a considerable measure provided for by acts of parliament. The whole power is far more safe in the hands of congress, than of the executive; since otherwise the most summary and severe punishments might be inflicted at the mere will of the executive. {419}

§ 584. It is a natural result of the sovereignty over the navy of the United States, that it should be exclusive. Whatever crimes, therefore, are committed on board of public ships of war of the United States, whether they are in port or at sea, they are exclusively cognizable and punishable by the government of the United States. The public ships of sovereigns, wherever they may be, are deemed to be extraterritorial, and enjoy the immunities from the local jurisdiction, which belong to their sovereign.

CHAPTER XXII.

POWER OVER THE MILITIA.

§ 585. THE next power of congress is

"to provide for calling forth the militia to execute the laws of the Union, suppress insurrections, and repel invasions."

§ 586. This clause seems, after a slight amendment, to have passed the convention without opposition. It cured a defect severely felt under the confederation, which contained no provision on the subject.

§ 587. The power of regulating the militia, and of commanding its services to enforce the laws, and to suppress insurrections, and repel invasions, is a natural incident to the duty of superintending the common defence, and preserving the internal peace of the nation. In short, every argument, which is urged, or can be urged against standing armies in time of peace, applies forcibly to the propriety of vesting this power in the national government. There is but one of two alternatives, which can be resorted to in cases of insurrection, invasion, or violent opposition to the laws; either to employ regular troops, or to employ the militia to suppress them. In ordinary cases, indeed, the resistance to the laws may be put down by the *posse comitatus*, or the assistance of the common magistracy. But cases may occur, in which such a resort would be utterly vain, and even mischievous; since it might encourage the factious to more rash measures, and prevent the application of a force, which would at once destroy the hopes and crush the efforts of the disaffected. The general power of the government to pass all laws necessary {421} and proper to execute its declared powers, would doubtless authorize laws to call forth the *posse comitatus*, and employ the common magistracy, in cases, where such measures would suit the emergency. But if the militia could not be called in aid, it would be absolutely indispensable to the common safety to keep up a strong regular force in time of peace. The latter would certainly not be desirable, or economical; and therefore this power over the militia is highly salutary to the public repose, and at the same time an additional security to the public liberty. In times of insurrection or invasion, it would be natural and proper, that the militia of a neighbouring state should be marched into another to resist a common enemy, or guard the republic against the violences of a domestic faction or sedition. But it is scarcely possible, that in the exercise of the power the militia should ever be called to march great distances, since it would be at once the most expensive and the most inconvenient force, which the government could employ for distant expeditions. The regulation of the whole subject is always to be in the power of congress; and it may from time to time be moulded so, as to escape from all dangerous abuses.

§ 588. The next power of congress is,

"to provide for organizing, arming, and disciplining the militia, and for governing such part of them, as may be employed in the service of the United States; reserving to the states respectively the appointment of the officers, and the authority of training the militia according to the discipline prescribed by congress."

§ 589. This power has a natural connexion with the preceding, and, if not indispensable to its exercise, furnishes the only adequate means of giving it promptitude and efficiency in its operations. It requires no {422} skill in the science of war to discern, that uniformity in the organization and discipline of the militia will be attended with the most beneficial effects, whenever they are called into active service. It will enable them to discharge the duties of the camp and field with mutual intelligence and concert, an advantage of peculiar moment in the operations of an army; and it will enable them to acquire, in a much shorter period, that degree of proficiency in military functions, which is essential to their usefulness. Such an uniformity, it is evident, can be attained only through the superintending power of the national government.

§ 590. Several questions of great practical importance have arisen under the clauses of the constitution respecting the militia, which deserve mention in this place. It is observable, that power is given to congress

"to *provide* for calling forth the militia to execute the laws of the Union, suppress insurrections, and repel invasions."

Accordingly, congress in 1795, in pursuance of this authority, and to give it a practical operation, provided by law, "that whenever the United States shall be invaded, or be in imminent danger of invasion from any foreign nation or Indian tribe, it shall be lawful for the president to call forth such number of the militia of the state, or states most convenient to the place of danger, or scene of action, as he may judge necessary, to repel such invasion, and to issue his order for that purpose to such officer or officers of the militia, as he shall think proper." Like provisions are made for the other cases stated in the constitution. The constitutionality of this act has not been questioned, although it provides for calling forth the militia, not only in cases of invasion, but of imminent danger of invasion; for the power to repel invasions {423} must include the power to provide against any attempt and danger of invasion, as the necessary and proper means to effectuate the object. One of the best means to repel invasion is, to provide the requisite force for action, before the invader has reached the territory of the nation. Nor can there be a doubt, that the president, who is (as will be presently seen) by the constitution the commander-in-chief of the army and navy of the United States, and of the militia, when called into the actual service of the United States, is the proper functionary, to whom this high and delicate trust ought to be confided. A free people will naturally be jealous of the exercise of military power; and that of calling forth the militia is certainly one of no ordinary magnitude. It is, however, a power limited in its nature to certain exigencies; and by whomsoever it is to be executed, it carries with it a corresponding responsibility. Who is so fit to exercise the power, and to incur the responsibility, as the president?

§ 591. But a most material question arises: By whom is the exigency to be decided? Is the president the sole and exclusive judge, whether the exigency has arisen? Or is it to be considered, as an open question, which every officer, to whom the orders of the president are addressed, may decide for himself, and equally open to be contested, by every militia-man, who shall refuse to obey the orders of the president?

§ 592. At a very recent period, the question came before the Supreme Court of the United States for a judicial decision; and it was then unanimously determined, that the authority to decide, whether the exigency has arisen, belongs exclusively to the president; and that his decision is conclusive upon all other persons. The court said, that this construction necessarily {424} resulted from the nature of the power itself, and from the manifest objects contemplated by the act of congress. The power itself is to be exercised upon sudden emergencies, upon great occasions of state, and under circumstances, which may be vital to the existence of the Union. A prompt and unhesitating obedience to orders is indispensable to the complete attainment of the object. The service is a military service, and the command of a miltary nature; and in such cases, every delay and every obstacle to an efficient and immediate compliance would necessarily tend to jeopard the public interests. While subordinate officers or soldiers are pausing to consider, whether they ought to obey, or are scrupulously weighing the facts, upon which the commander-in-chief exercises the right to demand their services, the hostile enterprize may be accomplished, without the means of resistance. If the power of regulating the militia, and of commanding its services in times of insurrection and invasion, are, as it has been emphatically said, they are, natural incidents to the duties of superintending the common defence, and of watching over the internal peace of the confederacy, these powers must be so construed, as to the modes of their exercise, as not to defeat the great end in view. If a superior officer has a right to contest the orders of the president, upon his own doubts, as to the exigency having arisen, it must be equally the right of every inferior officer and soldier. And any act done by any person in furtherance of such orders would subject him to responsibility in a civil suit, in which his defence must finally rest upon his ability to establish the facts by competent proofs. Besides; in many instances the evidence, upon which the president might decide, that there was imminent danger of invasion, {425} might be of a nature not constituting strict technical proof; or the disclosure of the evidence might reveal important state secrets, which the public interest, and even safety, might imperiously demand to be kept in concealment.

§ 593. The power to govern the militia, when in the actual service of the United States, is denied by no one to be an exclusive one. Indeed, from its very nature, it must be so construed; for the notion of distinct and independent orders from authorities wholly unconnected, would be utterly inconsistent with that unity of command and action, on which the success of all military operations must essentially depend. But there is nothing in the constitution, which prohibits a state from calling forth its own militia, not detached into the service of the Union, to aid the United States in executing the laws, in suppressing insurrections, and in repelling invasions. Such a concurrent exercise of power in no degree interferes with, or obstructs the exercise of the powers of the Union. Congress may, by suitable laws, provide for the calling forth of the militia, and annex suitable penalties to disobedience of their orders, and direct the manner, in which the delinquents may be tried. But the authority to call forth, and the authority exclusively to govern, are quite distinct in their nature. The question, when the authority of congress over the militia becomes exclusive, must essentially depend upon the fact, when they are to be deemed in the actual service of the United States. There is a clear distinction between calling forth the militia, and their being in actual service. These are not contemporaneous acts, nor necessarily identical in their constitutional bearings. The president is commander-in-chief of the militia, when in actual service; and not, when they are merely {426} ordered into service. They are subjected to martial law only, when in actual service, and not merely when called forth, before they have obeyed the call.

CHAPTER XXIII.

POWER OVER SEAT OF GOVERNMENT AND OTHER CEDED PLACES.

§ 594. THE next power of congress is,

> "to exercise exclusive legislation in all cases whatsoever over such district, not exceeding ten miles square, as may, by cession of particular states and the acceptance of congress, become the SEAT OF THE GOVERNMENT of the United States; and to exercise like authority over all places purchased by the consent of the legislature of the state, in which the same shall be, for the erection of FORTS, MAGAZINES, ARSENALS, and other needful buildings."

§ 595. The indispensable necessity of complete and exclusive power, on the part of the congress, at the seat of government, carries its own evidence with it. It is a power exercised by every legislature of the Union, and one might say of the world, by virtue of its general supremacy. Without it, not only the public authorities might be insulted, and their proceedings be interrupted with impunity; but the public archives might be in danger of violation, and destruction, and a dependence of the members of the national government on the state authorities for protection in the discharge of their functions be created, which would bring upon the national councils the imputation of being subjected to undue awe and influence, and might, in times of high excitement, expose their lives to jeopardy. It never could be safe to leave in possession of any state the exclusive power to decide, whether the functionaries of the national government {428} should have the moral or physical power to perform their duties. It might subject the favoured state to the most unrelenting jealousy of the other states, and introduce earnest controversies from time to time respecting the removal of the seat of government.

§ 596. Nor can the cession be justly an object of jealousy to any state; or in the slightest degree impair its sovereignty. The ceded district is of a very narrow extent; and it rests in the option of the state, whether it shall be made or not. There can be little doubt, that the inhabitants composing it would receive with thankfulness such a blessing, since their own importance would be thereby increased, their interests be subserved, and their rights be under the immediate protection of the representatives of the whole Union. It is not improbable, that an occurrence, at the very close of the revolutionary war, had a great effect in introducing this provision into the constitution. At the period alluded to, the congress, then sitting at Philadelphia, was surrounded, and insulted by a small, but insolent body of mutineers of the continental army. Congress applied to the executive authority of Pennsylvania for defence; but, under the ill-conceived constitution of the state at that time, the executive power was vested in a council consisting of thirteen members; and they possessed, or exhibited so little energy, and such apparent intimidation, that

238

congress indignantly removed to New-Jersey, whose inhabitants welcomed them with promises of defending them. Congress remained for some time at Princeton without being again insulted, till, for the sake of greater convenience, they adjourned to Annapolis. The general dissatisfaction with the proceedings of Pennsylvania, and the degrading spectacle of a fugitive congress, were sufficiently striking to produce this {429} remedy. Indeed, if such a lesson could have been lost upon the people, it would have been as humiliating to their intelligence, as it would have been offensive to their honour.

§ 597. The other part of the power, giving exclusive legislation over places ceded for the erection of forts, magazines, &c., seems still more necessary for the public convenience and safety. The public money expended on such places, and the public property deposited in them, and the nature of the military duties, which may be required there, all demand, that they should be exempted from state authority. In truth, it would be wholly improper, that places, on which the security of the entire Union may depend, should be subjected to the control of any member of it. The power, indeed, is wholly unexceptionable; since it can only be exercised at the will of the state; and it is therefore placed beyond all reasonable scruple.

§ 598. A great variety of cessions have been made by the states under this power. And generally there has been a reservation of the right to serve all state process, civil and criminal, upon persons found therein. This reservation has not been thought at all inconsistent with the provisions of the constitution; for the state process, *quoad hoc*, becomes the process of the United States, and the general power of exclusive legislation remains with congress. Thus, these places are not capable of being made a sanctuary for fugitives, to exempt them from acts done within, and cognizable by, the states, to which the territory belonged; and at the same time congress is enabled to accomplish the great objects of the power.

§ 599. The power of congress to exercise exclusive jurisdiction over these ceded places is conferred on {430} that body, as the legislature of the Union; and cannot be exercised in any other character. A law passed in pursuance of it is the supreme law of the land, and binding on all the states, and cannot be defeated by them. The power to pass such a law carries with it all the incidental powers to give it complete and effectual execution; and such a law may be extended in its operation incidentally throughout the United States, if congress think it necessary so to do. But if intended to have efficiency beyond the district, language must be used in the act expressive of such an intention; otherwise it will be deemed purely local.

CHAPTER XXIV.

POWERS OF CONGRESS — INCIDENTAL.

§ 600. THE next power of congress is,

> "to make all laws, which shall be *necessary* and *proper* for carrying into execution the foregoing powers, and all other powers vested by this constitution in the government of the United States, or in any department, or officer thereof."

§ 601. Few powers of the government were at the time of the adoption of the constitution assailed with more severe invective, and more declamatory intemperance, than this. And it has ever since been made a theme of constant attack, and extravagant jealousy. Yet it is difficult to perceive the grounds, upon which any objection can be maintained, or the logic, by which it can be reasoned out. The clause is only declaratory of a truth, which would have resulted by necessary and unavoidable implication from the very act of establishing the national government, and investing it with certain powers. What is a power, but the ability or faculty of doing a thing? What is the ability to do a thing, but the power of employing the *means* necessary to its execution? What is a legislative power, but a power of making laws? What are the means to execute a legislative power, but laws? What is the power for instance, of laying and collecting taxes, but a legislative power, or a power to make laws to lay and collect taxes? What are the proper means of executing such a power, but necessary and proper laws? In truth, the constitutional operation of the government would be precisely the {432} same, if the clause were obliterated, as if it were repeated in every article. It would otherwise result, that the power could never be exercised; that is, the end would be required, and yet no means allowed. This would be a perfect absurdity. It would be to create powers, and compel them to remain for ever in a torpid, dormant, and paralytic state. It cannot, therefore, be denied, that the powers, given by the constitution, imply, the ordinary means of execution; for without the substance of the power the constitution would be a dead letter.

§ 602. If, then, the clause imports no more, than would result from necessary implication, it may be asked, why it was inserted at all. The true answer is, that such a clause was peculiarly useful, in order to avoid any doubt, which ingenuity or jealousy might raise upon the subject. Much plausible reasoning, might be employed by those, who were hostile to the Union, and in favour of state power, to prejudice the people on such a subject, and to embarrass the government in all its reasonable operations. Besides; as, the confederation contained a positive clause, restraining the authority of congress to powers expressly granted, there was a fitness in declaring, that that rule of interpretation should no longer prevail. The very zeal, indeed, with which the present clause has been always assailed, is the

240

highest proof of its importance and propriety. It has narrowed down the grounds of hostility to the mere interpretation of the terms.

§ 603. The plain import of the clause is, that congress shall have all the incidental and instrumental powers, necessary and proper to carry into execution all the express powers. It neither enlarges any power specifically granted; nor is it a grant of any new power to congress. But it is merely a declaration for the removal of all uncertainty, that the means of carrying into execution those, otherwise granted, are included in the grant. Whenever, therefore, a question arises concerning the constitutionality of a particular power, the first question is, whether the power be *expressed* in the constitution. If it be, the question is decided. If it be not *expressed*, the next inquiry must be, whether it is properly an incident to an express power, and necessary and proper to its execution. If it be, then it may be exercised by congress. If not, congress cannot exercise it.

§ 604. But still a ground of controversy remains open, as to the true interpretation of the terms of the clause; and it has been contested with no small share of earnestness and vigour. What, then, is the true constitutional sense of the words "necessary and proper" in this clause? It has been insisted by the advocates of a rigid interpretation, that the word "necessary" is here used in its close and most intense meaning; so that it is equivalent to *absolutely and indispensably necessary*. It has been said, that the constitution allows only the means, which are *necessary*; not those, which are merely *convenient* for effecting the enumerated powers. If such a latitude of construction be given to this phrase, as to include any non-enumerated power, it will go far to include every one; for there is no one, which ingenuity might not torture into a convenience in some way ox other to some one of so long a list of enumerated powers. It would swallow up all the delegated powers, and reduce the whole to one phrase. Therefore it is, that the constitution has restrained congress to the *necessary* means; that is to say, to those means, *without which the grant of* {434} *the power would be nugatory*. A little difference in the degree of convenience cannot constitute the necessity, which the constitution refers to.

§ 605. The effect of this mode of interpretation is to exclude all choice of means; or, at most, to leave to congress in each case those only, which are most direct and simple. If, indeed, such implied powers, and such only, as can be shown to be indispensably necessary, are within the purview of the clause, there will be no end to difficulties, and the express powers must practically become a mere nullity. It will be found, that the operations of the government, upon any of its powers, will rarely admit of a rigid demonstration of the necessity (in this strict sense) of any particular means. In most cases, various systems or means may be resorted to, to attain the same end; and yet, with respect to each, it may be argued, that it is not constitutional, because it is not indispensable; and the end may be obtained by other means. The consequence of such reasoning would be, that, as no means could be shown to be constitutional, none could be adopted. For instance, congress possess the power to make war, and to raise armies, and incidentally to erect fortifications, and purchase cannon and ammunition and other munitions of war. But war may be carried on without fortifications, cannon, and ammunition. No particular kind of arms can be shown to be absolutely necessary; because various sorts of arms of different convenience, power, and utility are, or may be resorted to by different nations. What then becomes of the power? Congress has power to borrow money, and to provide for the payment of the public debt; yet no particular method is indispensable to these ends. They may be attained by various means. Congress has power to provide a navy; {435} but no particular size, or form, or equipment of ships is indispensable. The means of providing a naval establishment are very various; and the applications of them admit of infinite shades of opinion, as to their convenience, utility, and necessity. What then is to be done? Are the powers to remain dormant? Would it not be absurd to say, that congress did not possess the choice of means under such circumstances, and were not empowered to select, and use any means, which are in fact conducive to the exercise of the powers granted by the constitution? Take another example; congress has, doubtless, the authority, under the power to regulate commerce, to erect lighthouses, beacons, buoys, and public piers, and authorize the employment of pilots. But it cannot be affirmed, that the exercise of these powers is in a strict sense necessary; or that the power to regulate commerce would be nugatory without establishments of this nature. In truth, no particular regulation of commerce can ever be shown to be exclusively and indispensably necessary; and thus we should be driven to admit, that all regulations are within the scope of the power, or that none are. If there be any general principle, which is inherent in the very definition of government, and essential to every step of the progress to be made by that of the United States, it is, that every power, vested in the government, is in its nature sovereign, and includes, by force of the term, a right to employ all the means requisite, and fairly applicable to the attainment of the end of such power; unless they are excepted in the constitution, or are immoral, or are contrary to the essential objects of political society.

§ 606. There is another difficulty in the strict construction above alluded to, that it makes the constitutional {436} authority depend upon casual and temporary circumstances, which may produce a necessity to-day, and change it to-morrow. This alone shows the fallacy of the reasoning. The expediency of exercising a particular power at a particular time must, indeed, depend on circumstances; but the constitutional right of exercising it must be uniform and invariable; the same to-day, as to-morrow.

§ 607. Neither can the degree, in which a measure is necessary, ever be a test of the legal right to adopt it. That must be a matter of opinion, (upon which different men, and different bodies may form opposite judgments,) and can only be a test of expediency. The relation between the measure and the end, between the nature of the means employed towards the execution of a power, and the object of that power, must be the criterion of constitutionality; and not the greater or less necessity or expediency. If the legislature possess a right of choice as to the means, who can limit that choice? Who is appointed an umpire, or arbiter in cases, where a discretion is confided to a government? The very idea of such a controlling authority in the exercise of its powers is a virtual denial of the supremacy of the government in regard to its powers. It repeals the supremacy of the national government, proclaimed in the constitution.

§ 608. It is equally certain, that neither the grammatical, nor the popular sense of the word, "necessary," requires any such construction. According to both, "necessary" often means no more than *needful, requisite, incidental, useful,* or *conducive to.* It is a common mode of expression to say, that it is necessary for a government, or a person, to do this or that thing, when nothing more is intended or understood, than that the {437} interest of the government or person requires, or will be promoted by, the doing of this or that thing. Every one's mind will at once suggest to him many illustrations of the use of the word in this sense. To employ the means, necessary to an end, is generally understood, as employing any means calculated to produce the end, and not as being confined to those means alone, without which the end would be entirely unattainable.

§ 609. Such is the character of human language, that no word conveys to the mind, in all situations, one single definite idea; and nothing is more common, than to use words in a figurative sense. Almost all compositions contain words, which, taken in their rigorous sense, would convey a meaning, different from that, which is obviously intended. It is essential to just interpretation, that many words, which import something excessive, should be understood in a more mitigated sense; in a sense, which common usage justifies. The word "necessary" is of this description. It has not a fixed character peculiar to itself. It admits of all degrees of comparison; and is often connected with other words, which increase or diminish the impression, which the mind receives of the urgency it imports. A thing may be necessary, very necessary, absolutely or indispensably necessary. It may be little necessary, less necessary, or least necessary. To no mind would the same idea be conveyed by any two of these several phrases. The tenth section of the first article of the constitution furnishes a strong illustration of this very use of the word. It contains a prohibition upon any state to "lay any imposts or duties, &c. except what may be *absolutely necessary* for executing its inspection laws." No one can compare this clause with the {438} other, on which we are commenting, without being struck with the conviction, that the word "*absolutely*," here prefixed to "necessary," is intended to distinguish it from the sense, in which, standing alone, it is used in the other.

§ 610. That the restrictive interpretation must be abandoned, in regard to certain powers of the government, cannot be reasonably doubted. It is universally conceded, that the power of punishment appertains to sovereignty, and may be exercised, whenever the sovereign has a right to act, as incidental to his constitutional powers. It is a means for carrying into execution all sovereign powers, and may be used, although not indispensably necessary. If, then, the restrictive interpretation must be abandoned, in order to justify the constitutional exercise of the power to punish; whence is the rule derived, which would reinstate it, when the government would carry its powers into operation, by means not vindictive in their nature? If the word, "necessary" means *needful, requisite, essential, conducive to,* to let in the power of punishment, why is it not equally comprehensive, when applied to other means used to facilitate the execution of the powers of the government?

§ 611. The restrictive interpretation is also contrary to a sound maxim of construction, generally admitted, namely, that the powers contained in a constitution of government, especially those, which concern the general administration of the affairs of the country, such as its finances, its trade, and its defence, ought to be liberally expounded in advancement of the public good. This rule does not depend on the particular form of a government, or on the particular demarcations of the boundaries of its powers; but on the {439} nature and objects of government itself. The means, by which national exigencies are provided for, national inconveniences obviated, and national prosperity promoted, are of such infinite variety, extent, and complexity, that there must of necessity be great latitude of discretion in the selection, and application of those means. Hence, consequently, result the necessity and propriety of exercising the authorities, entrusted to a government, upon principles of a liberal construction.

§ 612. It is no valid objection to this doctrine to say, that it is calculated to extend the powers of the government throughout the entire sphere of state legislation. The same thing may be said, and has been said, in regard to every exercise of power by implication and construction. There is always some chance of error, or abuse of every power; but this furnishes no ground of objection against the power; and certainly no reason for an adherence to the most rigid construction of its terms, which would at once arrest the whole movements of the government. The remedy for any abuse, or misconstruction of the power, is the same, as in similar abuses and misconstructions of the state governments. It is by an appeal to the other departments of the government; and finally to the people, in the exercise of their elective franchises.

§ 613. There are yet other grounds against the restrictive interpretation derived from the language, and the character of the provision. The language is, that congress shall have power "to make all laws, which shall be *necessary* and *proper.*" If the word "necessary" were used in the strict and rigorous sense contended for, it would be an extraordinary departure from the usual course of the human mind, as exhibited in solemn instruments, to add another word "proper;" {440} the only possible effect of which is to qualify that strict and rigorous meaning, and to present clearly the idea of a choice of means in the course of legislation. If no means can be resorted to, but such as are indispensably necessary, there can be neither sense, nor utility in adding the other word; for the necessity shuts out from view all consideration of the propriety of the means, as contradistinguished from the former. But if the intention was to use the word "necessary" in its more liberal sense, then there is a peculiar fitness in the other word. It has a sense at once admonitory, and directory. It requires, that the means should be, *bonâ fide*, appropriate to the end.

§ 614. The character of the clause equally forbids, any presumption of an intention to use the restrictive interpretation. In the first place the clause is placed among the powers of congress, and not among the limitations upon those powers. In the next place, its terms purport to enlarge, and not to diminish, the powers vested in the government. It purports, on its face, to be an additional power, not a restriction on those already granted. If it does not, in fact, (as seems the true construction,) give any new powers, it affirms the right to use all necessary and proper means to carry into execution the other powers; and thus makes an *express* power, what would otherwise be merely an *implied* power. In either aspect, it is impossible to construe it to be a restriction. If it have any effect, it is to remove the implication of any restriction. If a restriction had been intended, it is impossible, that the framers of the constitution should have concealed it under phraseology, which purports to enlarge, or at least give the most ample scope to the other powers. There was every motive on their {441} part to give point and clearness to every restriction of national power; for they well knew, that the national government would be more endangered in its adoption by its supposed strength, than by its weakness. It is inconceivable, that they should have disguised a restriction upon its powers under the form of a grant of power. They would have sought other terms, and have imposed the restraint by negatives. And what is equally strong, no one, in or out of the state conventions, at the time when the constitution was put upon its deliverance before the people, ever dreamed of, or suggested, that this clause contained a restriction of power. The whole argument on each side, of attack and of deference, gave it the positive form of an express power, and not of an express restriction.

§ 615. Upon the whole, the result of the most careful examination of this clause is, that, if it does not enlarge, it cannot be construed to restrain, the powers of congress, or to impair the right of the legislature to exercise its best judgment in the selection of, measures to carry into execution the constitutional powers of the national government. The motive for its, insertion doubtless was, the desire to remove all possible doubt respecting the right to legislate on that vast mass of incidental powers, which must be involved in the constitution, if that instrument be not a splendid pageant, or a delusive phantom of sovereignty. Let the end be legitimate; let it be within the scope of the constitution; and all means, which are appropriate, which are plainly adapted to the end, and which are not prohibited, but are consistent with the letter and spirit of the instrument, are constitutional.

§ 616. It may be well, in this connexion, to mention another sort of implied power, which has been {442} called with great propriety a resulting power, arising from the aggregate powers of the national government. It will not be doubted, for instance, that, if the United States should make a conquest of any of the territories of its neighbours, the national government would possess sovereign jurisdiction over the conquered territory. This would, perhaps, rather be a result from the whole mass of the powers of the national government, and from the nature of political society, than a consequence or incident of the powers specially enumerated. It may, however, be deemed, if an incident to any, an incident to the power to make war. Other instances of resulting powers will easily suggest themselves. The United States are no where declared in the constitution to be a sovereignty entitled to sue, though jurisdiction is given to the national courts over controversies, "to which the United States shall be a party." It is a natural incident, resulting from the sovereignty and character of the national government. So the United States, in their political capacity, have a right to enter into a contract, (although it is not expressly provided for by the constitution;) for it is an incident to their general right of sovereignty, so far as it is appropriate to any of the ends of the government, and within the constitutional range of its powers. So congress possess power to punish offences committed on board of the public ships of war of the government by persons not in the military or naval service of the United States, whether they are in port, or at sea; for the jurisdiction on board of public ships is every where deemed exclusively to belong to the sovereign.

§ 617. And not only may implied powers, but implied exemptions from state authority, exist, although not expressly provided for by law. The collectors of {443} the revenue, the carriers of the mail, the mint establishment, and all those institutions, which are public in their nature, are examples in point. It has never been doubted, that all, who are employed in them, are protected, while in the line of their duty, from state control; and yet this protection is not expressed in any act of congress. It is incidental to, and is implied in, the several acts, by which those institutions are created; and is preserved to them by the judicial department, as a part of its functions. A contractor for supplying a military post with provisions cannot be restrained from making purchases within a state, or from transporting provisions to the place, at which troops are stationed. He cannot be taxed, or fined or lawfully obstructed, in so doing. These incidents necessarily flow from the supremacy of the powers of the Union, within their legitimate sphere of action.

§ 618. It would be almost impracticable, if it were not useless, to enumerate the various instances, in which congress, in the progress of the government, have made use of incidental and implied means to execute its powers. They are almost infinitely varied in their ramifications and details. It is proposed, however, to take notice of the principal measures, which have been contested, as not within the scope of the powers of congress, and which may be distinctly traced in the operations of the government, and in leading party divisions.

CHAPTER XXV.

INCIDENTAL POWERS — NATIONAL BANK.

{444}

§ 619. ONE of the earliest and most important measures, which gave rise to a question of constitutional power, was the act chartering the bank of the United States in 1791. That question has often since been discussed; and though the measure has been repeatedly sanctioned by congress, by the executive, and by the judiciary, and has obtained the like favour in a great majority of the states, yet it is, up to this very hour, still debated upon constitutional grounds, as if it were still new, and untried. It is impossible, at this time, to treat it, as an open question, unless the constitution is for ever to remain an unsettled text, possessing no permanent attributes, and incapable of having any ascertained sense; varying with every change of doctrine, and of party; and delivered over to interminable doubts. If the constitution is to be only, what the administration of the day may wish it to be; and is to assume any, and all shapes, which may suit the opinions and theories of public men, as they successively direct the public councils, it will be difficult, indeed, to ascertain, what its real value is. It cannot possess either certainty, or uniformity, or safety. It will be one thing to-day, and another thing to-morrow, and again another thing on each succeeding day. The past will furnish no guide, and the future no security. It will be the reverse of a law; and entail upon the country the curse of that miserable servitude, so much abhorred and denounced, where all is vague and uncertain in the fundamentals of government. {445}

§ 620. The reasoning, upon which the constitutionality of a national bank is denied, has been already in some degree stated in the preceding remarks. It turns upon the strict interpretation of the clause, giving the auxiliary powers, necessary and proper to execute the other enumerated powers. It is to the following effect. The power to incorporate a bank is not among those enumerated in the constitution. In the next place, all the enumerated powers can be carried into execution without a bank. A bank, therefore, is not *necessary*, and consequently not authorized by this clause of the constitution. It is urged, that a bank will give great facility, or convenience to the collection of taxes. If this were true, yet the constitution allows only the means, which are *necessary*, and not merely those, which are *convenient*, for effecting the enumerated powers. If such a latitude of construction were allowed, as to consider convenience, as justifying the use of such means, it would swallow up all the enumerated powers. Therefore, the constitution restrains congress to those means, without which the power would be nugatory.

§ 621. Nor can the convenience be satisfactorily established. Bank-bills may be a more convenient vehicle, than treasury orders, for the purposes of that department. But a little difference in the degree of convenience cannot constitute the necessity contemplated by the constitution. Besides; the local and state banks now in existence are competent, and would be willing to undertake all the agency required for those very purposes by the government. And if they are able and willing, this establishes clearly, that there can be no necessity for establishing a national bank. If there shall ever be a superior conveniency {446} in a national bank, it does not follow, that there exists a power to establish it, or that the business of the country cannot go on very well without it. Can it be thought, that the constitution intended, that for a shade or two of convenience, more or less, congress should be authorized to break down the most ancient and fundamental laws of the states, such as those against mortmain, the laws of alienage, the rules of descent, the acts of distribution, the laws of escheat and forfeiture, and the laws of monopoly? Nothing but a necessity, invincible by any other means, can justify such a prostration of laws, which constitute the pillars of our whole system of jurisprudence. If congress have the power to create one corporation, they may create all sorts; for the power is no where limited; and they may even establish monopolies. Indeed this very charter is a monopoly.

§ 622. The reasoning, by which the constitutionality of the national bank has been sustained, is contained in the following summary. The powers confided to the national government are unquestionably, so far as they exist, sovereign and supreme. It is not, and cannot be disputed, that the power of creating a corporation is one belonging to sovereignty. But so are all other legislative powers; for the original power of giving the law on any subject whatever is a sovereign power. If the national government cannot create a corporation, because it is an exercise of sovereign power, neither can it, for the same reason, exercise any other legislative power. This consideration alone ought to put an end to the abstract inquiry, whether the national government has power to erect a corporation, that is, to give a legal or artificial capacity to one or more persons, distinct from the natural {447} capacity. For, if it be an incident to sovereignty, and it is not prohibited, it must belong to the national government in relation to the objects entrusted to it. The true difference is this; where the authority of a government is general, it can create corporations in all cases; where it is confined to certain branches of legislation, it can create corporations only as to those cases. It cannot be denied, that implied powers may be delegated, as well as express. It follows, that a power to erect corporations may as well be implied, as any other thing, if it be an instrument or means of carrying into execution any specified power. The only question in any case must be, whether it be such an instrument or means, and have a natural relation to any of the acknowledged objects of government. Thus, congress may not erect a corporation for superintending the police of the city of Philadelphia, because they have no authority to regulate the police of that city. But if they possessed the authority to regulate the police of that city, they might, unquestionably, create a corporation for that purpose; because it is incident to the sovereign legislative power to regulate a thing, to employ all the means, which relate to its regulation, to the best and greatest advantage.

§ 623. A strange fallacy has crept into the reasoning on this subject. It has been supposed, that a corporation is some great, independent thing; and that the power to erect it is a great, substantive, independent power; whereas, in truth, a corporation is but a legal capacity, quality, or means, to an end; and the power to erect it is, or may be, an implied and incidental power. A corporation is never the end, for which other powers are exercised; but a means, by {448} which other objects are accomplished. No contributions are made to charity for the sake of an incorporation; but a corporation is created to administer the charity. No seminary of learning is instituted in order to be incorporated; but the corporate character is conferred to subserve the purposes of education. No city was ever built with the sole object of being incorporated; but it is incorporated, as affording the best means of being well governed. So a mercantile company is formed with a certain capital for carrying on a particular branch of business. Here, the business to be prosecuted is the end. The association, in order to form the requisite capital, is the primary means. If an incorporation is added to the association; it only gives it a new quality, an artificial capacity, by which it is enabled to prosecute the business with more convenience and safety. In truth, the power of creating a corporation is never used for its own sake; but for the purpose of effecting something else. So that there is not a shadow of reason to say, that it may not pass, as an incident to powers expressly given, and as a mode of executing them.

§ 624. It is true, that among the enumerated powers we do not find that of establishing a bank, or creating a corporation. But we do find there the great powers to lay and collect taxes; to borrow money; to regulate commerce; to declare and conduct war; and to raise and support armies and navies. Now, if a bank be a fit means to execute any or all of these powers, it is just as much implied, as any other means. If it be "necessary and proper" for any of them, how is it possible to deny the authority to create it for such purposes? There is no more propriety in giving this power in *express* terms, than in giving any other incidental {449} powers or means in express terms. If it had been intended to grant this power generally, and to make it a distinct and independent power, having no relation to, but reaching beyond the other enumerated powers, there would then have been a propriety in giving it in express terms, for otherwise it would not exist. Thus, it was proposed in the convention, to give a general power "to grant charters of incorporation;" — to "grant charters of incorporation in cases, where the public good may require them, and the authority of a single state may be incompetent;" — and "to grant letters of incorporation for canals, &c." If either of these propositions had been adopted, there would have been an obvious propriety in giving the power in express terms; because, as to the two farmer, the power was general and unlimited, and reaching far beyond any of the other enumerated powers; and as to the latter, it might be far more extensive than any incident to the other enumerated powers. But the rejection of these propositions does not prove, that congress in no case, as an incident to the enumerated powers, could erect a corporation; but only, that they should not have a substantive, independent power to erect corporations beyond those powers.

§ 625. Indeed, it is most manifest, that it never could have been contemplated by the convention, that congress should, in no case, possess the power to erect a corporation. What otherwise would become of the territorial governments, all of which are corporations, created by congress? There is no where an express power given to congress to erect them. But under the confederation, congress did provide for their erection, as a resulting and implied right of sovereignty, by the celebrated ordinance of 1787; and congress, {450} under the constitution, have ever since, without question, and with the universal approbation of the nation, from time to time created territorial governments. Yet congress derive this power by implication, as necessary and proper to carry into effect the express power to regulate the territories of the United States. In the convention, two propositions were made, and referred to a committee at the same time with the propositions already stated respecting granting of charters, "to dispose of the unappropriated lands of the United States," and "to institute temporary governments for new states arising therein." Both of these propositions shared the same fate, as those respecting charters of incorporation. But what would be thought of the argument, built upon this foundation, that congress did not possess the power to erect territorial governments, because these propositions were silently abandoned, or annulled in the convention.

§ 626. This is not the only case, in which congress may erect corporations. Under the power to accept a cession of territory for the seat of government, and to exercise exclusive legislation therein, no one can doubt, that congress may erect corporations therein; not only public, but private corporations. They have constantly exercised the power; and it has never yet been breathed, that it was unconstitutional. Yet it can be exercised only as an incident to the power of general legislation. And if so, why may it not be exercised, as an incident to any specific power of legislation, if it be a means to attain the objects of such power?

§ 627. That a national bank is an appropriate means to carry into effect some of the enumerated powers of the government, and that this can be best done by {451} erecting it into a corporation, may be established by the most satisfactory reasoning. It has a relation, more or less direct, to the power of collecting taxes, to that of borrowing money, to that of regulating trade between the states, and to those of raising and maintaining fleets and armies. And it may be added, that it has a most important bearing upon the regulation of currency between the states. It is an instrument, which has been usually applied by governments in the administration of their fiscal and financial operations. And in the present times it can hardly require argument to prove, that it is a convenient, a useful, and an essential instrument in the fiscal operations of the government of the United States. This is so generally admitted by sound and intelligent statesmen, that it would be a waste of time to endeavour to establish the truth by an elaborate survey of the mode, in which it touches the administration of all the various branches of the powers of the government.

§ 628. In regard to the faculties of the bank, if congress could constitutionally create it, they might confer on it such faculties and powers, as were fit to make it an appropriate means for fiscal operations. They had a right to adapt it in the best manner to its end. No one can pretend, that its having the faculty of holding a capital; of lending and dealing in money; of issuing bank notes; of receiving deposits; and of appointing suitable officers to manage its affairs; are not highly useful and expedient, and appropriate to the purposes of a bank. They are just such as are usually granted to state banks; and just such, as give increased facilities to all its operations. To say, that the bank might have gone on without this or that faculty, is nothing. Who, but congress, shall say, how {452} few, or how many faculties it shall have, if all are still appropriate to it, as an instrument of government, and may make it more convenient, and more useful in its operations? No man can say, that a single faculty in any national charter is useless, or irrelevant, or strictly improper, that is conducive to its end, as a national instrument. Deprive a bank of its trade and business, and its vital principles are destroyed. Its form may remain, but its substance is gone. All the powers given to the bank are to give efficacy to its functions of trade and business.

§ 629. As to another suggestion, that the same objects might have been accomplished through the state banks, it is sufficient to say, that no trace can be found in the constitution of any intention to create a dependence on the states, or state institutions, for the execution of its great powers. Its own means are adequate to its end; and on those means it was expected to rely for their accomplishment. It would be utterly absurd to make the powers of the constitution wholly dependent on state institutions. But, if state banks might be employed, as congress have a choice of means, they have a right to choose a national bank, in preference to state banks, for the financial operations of the government. Proof, that they might use one means, is no proof, that they cannot constitutionally use another means.

§ 630. After all, the subject has been settled repeatedly by every department of the government, legislative, executive, and judicial. The states have acquiesced; and a majority have constantly sustained the power. If it is not now settled, it never can be. If it is settled, it would be too much to expect a re-argument, whenever any person may choose to question it.

CHAPTER XXVI.

POWERS OF CONGRESS — INTERNAL IMPROVEMENTS.

§ 631. ANOTHER question, which has for a long time agitated the public councils of the nation, is, as to the authority of congress to make roads, canals, and other internal improvements.

§ 632. So far, as regards the right to appropriate money to internal improvements generally, the subject has already passed under review in considering the power to lay and collect taxes. The doctrine there contended for, which has been in a great measure borne out by the actual practice of the government, is, that congress may appropriate money, not only to clear obstructions to navigable rivers; to improve harbours; to build breakwaters; to assist navigation; to erect forts, light-houses, and piers; and to other purposes allied to some of the enumerated powers; but may also appropriate it in aid of canals, roads, and other institutions of a similar nature, existing under state authority. The only limitations upon the power are those prescribed by the terms of the constitution, that the objects shall be for the common defence, or the general welfare of the Union. The true test is, whether the object be of a local character, and local use; or, whether it be of general benefit to the states. If it be purely local, congress cannot constitutionally appropriate money for the object. But, if the benefit be general, it matters not, whether in point of locality it be in one state, or several; whether it be of large, or of small extent. Its nature and character determine the right, and congress may {454} appropriate money in aid of it; for it is then in a just sense for the general welfare.

§ 633. But it has been contended, that the constitution is not confined to mere appropriations of money; but authorizes congress directly to undertake, and carry on a system of internal improvements for the general welfare, wherever such improvements fall within the scope of any of the enumerated powers. Congress may not, indeed, engage in such undertakings merely, because they are internal improvements for the general welfare, unless they fall within the scope of the enumerated powers. The distinction between this power, and the power of appropriation is, that in the latter, congress may appropriate to any purpose, which is for the common defence or general welfare; but in the former, they can engage in such undertakings only, as are means, or incidents to its enumerated powers. Congress may, therefore, authorize the making of a canal, as incident to the power to regulate commerce, where such canal may facilitate the intercourse between state and state. They may authorize light-houses, piers, buoys, and beacons to be built for the purposes of navigation. They may authorize the purchase and building of custom-houses, and revenue cutters, and public ware-houses, as incidents to the power to lay and collect taxes. They may purchase places for public uses; and erect forts, arsenals, dock-yards, navy-yards, and magazines, as incidents to

252

the power to make war.

§ 634. For the same reason congress may authorize the laying out and making of a military road, and acquire a right over the soil for such purposes; and as incident thereto they will have a power to keep the road in repair, and prevent all obstructions thereto. But {455} in these, and the like cases, the general jurisdiction of the state over the soil, subject only to the rights of the United States, is not excluded. As, for example, in case of a military road; although a state cannot prevent repairs on the part of the United States, or authorize any obstructions of the road, its general jurisdiction remains untouched. It may punish all crimes committed on the road; and it retains in other respects its territorial sovereignty over it. The right of soil may still remain in the state, or in individuals, and the right to the easement only in the national government. There is a great distinction between the exercise of a power, excluding altogether state jurisdiction, and the exercise of a power, which leaves the state jurisdiction generally in force, and yet includes, on the part of the national government, a power to preserve, what it has created.

§ 635. In all these, and other cases, in which the power of congress is asserted, it is so upon the general ground of its being an incidental power; and the course of reasoning, by which it is supported, is precisely the same, as that adopted in relation to other cases already considered. It is, for instance, admitted, that congress cannot authorize the making of a canal, except for some purpose of commerce among the states, or for some other purpose belonging to the Union; and it cannot make a military road, unless it be necessary and proper for purposes of war. To go over the reasoning at large would, therefore, be little more, than a repetition of what has been already fully expounded. The Journal of the Convention is not supposed to furnish any additional lights on the subject, beyond what have been already stated.

§ 636. The resistance to this extended reach of {456} the national powers turns also upon the same general reasoning, by which a strict construction of the constitution has been constantly maintained. It is said, that such a power is not among those enumerated in the constitution; nor is it implied, as a means of executing any of them. The power to regulate commerce cannot include a power to construct roads and canals, and improve the navigation of water-courses in order to facilitate, promote, and secure such commerce, without a latitude of construction departing from the ordinary import of the terms, and incompatible with the nature of the constitution. The liberal interpretation has been very uniformly asserted by congress; the strict interpretation has not uniformly, but has upon several important occasions been insisted upon by the executive. In the present state of the controversy, the duty of forbearance seems inculcated upon the commentator; and the reader must decide for himself upon his own views of the subject.

§ 637. Another question has been made, how far congress could make a law giving to the United States a preference and priority of payment of their debts, in case of the death, or insolvency, or bankruptcy of their debtors, out of their estates. It has been settled, upon deliberate argument, that congress possess such a constitutional power. It is a necessary and proper power to carry into effect the other powers of the government. The government is to pay the debts of the Union;

and must be authorized to use the means, which appear to itself most eligible to effect that object. It may purchase, and remit bills for this object; and it may take all those precautions, and make all those regulations, which will render the transmission safe. It may, in like manner, pass all laws to render effectual {457} the collection of its debts. It is no objection to this right of priority, that it will interfere with the rights of the state sovereignties respecting the dignity of debts, and will defeat the measures, which they have a right to adopt to secure themselves against delinquencies on the. part of their own revenue or other officers. This objection, if of any avail, is an objection to the powers given by the constitution. The mischief suggested, so far as it can really happen, is the necessary consequence of the supremacy of the laws of the United States on all subjects, to which the legislative power of congress extends.

§ 638. It is under the same implied authority, that the United States have any right even to sue in their own courts; for an express power is no where given in the constitution, though it is clearly implied in that part respecting the judicial power. And congress may not only authorize suits to be brought in the name of the United States, but in the name of any artificial person, (such as the Postmaster-General,) or natural person, for their benefit. Indeed, all the usual incidents appertaining to a *personal* sovereign, in relation to contracts, and suing, and enforcing rights, so far as they are within the scope of the powers of the government, belong to the United States, as they do to other sovereigns. The right of making contracts and instituting suits is an incident to the general right of sovereignty; and the United States, being a body politic, may, within the sphere of the constitutional powers confided to it, and through the instrumentality of the proper department, to which those powers are confided, enter into contracts not prohibited by law, and appropriate to the just exercise of those powers; {458} and enforce the observance of them by suits and judicial process.

§ 639. There are almost innumerable cases, in which the auxiliary and implied powers belonging to congress have been put into operation. But the object of these Commentaries is, rather to take notice of those, which have been the subject of animadversion, than of those, which have hitherto escaped reproof, or have been silently approved.

CHAPTER XXVII.

POWERS OF CONGRESS — PURCHASE OF FOREIGN TERRITORY — EMBARGOES.

§ 640. BUT the most remarkable powers, which have been exercised by the government, as auxiliary and implied powers, and which, if any, go to the utmost verge of liberal construction, are the laying of an unlimited embargo in 1807, and the purchase of Louisiana in 1803, and its subsequent admission into the Union, as a state. These measures were brought forward, and supported, and carried, by the known and avowed friends of a strict construction of the constitution; and they were justified at the time, and can be now justified, only upon the doctrines of those, who support a liberal construction of the constitution. The subject has been already hinted at; but it deserves a more deliberate review.

§ 641. In regard to the acquisition of Louisiana: — The treaty of 1803 contains a cession of the whole of that vast territory by France to the United States, for a sum exceeding eleven millions of dollars. There is a stipulation in the treaty on the part of the United States, that the inhabitants of the ceded territory shall be incorporated into the Union, and admitted, as soon as possible, according to the principles of the federal constitution, to the enjoyment of all the rights, advantages, and immunities of citizens of the United States.

§ 642. It is obvious, that the treaty embraced several very important questions, each of them upon the grounds of a strict construction full of difficulty and delicacy. In the first place, had the United States a {460} constitutional authority to accept the cession and pay for it? In the next place, if they had, was the stipulation for the admission of the inhabitants into the Union, as a state, constitutional, or within the power of congress to give it effect?

§ 643. There is no pretence, that the purchase, or cession of any foreign territory is within any of the powers expressly enumerated in the constitution. It is no where in that instrument said, that congress, or any other department of the national government, shall have a right to purchase, or accept of any cession of foreign territory. The power itself (it has been said) could scarcely have been in the contemplation of the framers of it. It is, in its own nature, as dangerous to liberty, as susceptible of abuse in its actual application, and as likely as any, which could be imagined, to lead to a dissolution of the Union. If congress have the power, it may unite any foreign territory whatsoever to our own, however distant, however populous, and however powerful. Under the form of a cession, we may become united to a more powerful neighbour or rival; and be involved in European, or other foreign interests, and contests, to an interminable extent. And if there may be a stipulation for the admission of foreign states into the Union, the whole balance of the constitution may be destroyed, and the old states sunk into utter insignificance. It is incredible, that it should have been contemplated, that any such overwhelming authority should be confided to the national government with the consent of the people of the old states. If it exists at all, it is unforeseen, and the result of a sovereignty, intended to be limited, and yet not sufficiently guarded. The very case of the cession of Louisiana is a striking illustration of the {461} doctrine. It admits, by consequence, into the Union an immense territory, equal to, if not greater, than that of all the United States under the peace of 1783. In the natural progress of events, it must, within a short period, change the whole balance of power in the Union, and transfer to the West all the important attributes of the sovereignty of the whole. If, as is, well known, one of the strong objections urged against the constitution was, that the original territory of the United States was too large for a national government; it is inconceivable, that it could have, been within the intention of the people, that any additions of foreign territory should be made, which should thus double every danger from this source. The treaty-making power must be construed, as confined to objects within the scope of the constitution. And, although congress have authority to admit new states into the firm, yet it is demonstrable, that this clause had sole reference to the territory then belonging to the United States; and was designed for the admission of the states, which, under the ordinance of 1787, were contemplated to be formed within its old boundaries. In regard to the appropriation of money for the purposes of the cession the case is still stronger. If no appropriation of money can be made, except for cases within the enumerated powers, (and this clearly is not one,) how can the enormous sum of eleven millions be justified for this object? If it be said, that it will be "for the common defence, and general welfare" to purchase the territory, how is this reconcilable with the strict construction of the constitution? If congress can appropriate money for one object, because it is deemed for the common defence and general welfare, why may they not appropriate it for all objects of the same sort? {462} If the territory can be purchased, it must be governed; and a territorial government must be created. But where can congress find authority in the constitution to erect a territorial government, since it does not possess the power to erect corporations?

§ 644. Such were the objections, which were urged against the cession, and the appropriations made to carry the treaty into effect. The friends of the measure were driven to the adoption of the doctrine, that the right to acquire territory was incident to national sovereignty; that it was a resulting power, growing necessarily out of the aggregate powers confided by the federal constitution; that the appropriation might justly be vindicated upon this ground, and also upon the ground, that it was for the common defence and general welfare. In short, there is no possibility of defending the constitutionality of this measure, but upon the principles of the liberal construction, which has been, upon other occasions, so earnestly resisted.

§ 645. The other instance of an extraordinary application of the implied powers of the government, above alluded to, is the embargo laid in the year 1807, by the special recommendation of President Jefferson. It was avowedly recommended, as a measure of safety for our vessels, our seamen, and our merchandise, from the then threatening dangers from the belligerents of Europe; and it was explicitly stated "to be a measure of precaution called for by the occasion;" and "neither hostile in its character, nor as justifying, or inciting, or leading to hostility with any nation whatever." It was in no sense, then, a war measure. If it could be classed at all, as flowing from, or as an incident to, any of the enumerated powers, it was to that of regulating commerce. In its terms, the act provided, that an embargo {463} be, and hereby is, laid on all ships and vessels in the ports, or within the limits or jurisdiction, of the United States, &c. bound to any foreign port or place. It was in its terms unlimited in duration; and could be removed only by a subsequent act of congress, having the assent of all the constitutional branches of the legislature.

§ 646. No one can reasonably doubt, that the laying of an embargo, suspending commerce for a limited period, is within the scope of the constitution. But the question of difficulty was, whether congress, under the power to regulate commerce with foreign nations, could constitutionally suspend and interdict it wholly for an unlimited period, that is, by a permanent act, having no limitation as to duration, either of the act, or of the embargo. It was most seriously controverted, and its constitutionality denied in the Eastern states of the Union, during its existence. An appeal was made to the judiciary upon the question; and it having been settled to be constitutional by that department of the government, the decision was acquiesced in, though the measure bore with almost unexampled severity upon the Eastern states; and its ruinous effects can still be traced along their extensive sea-board. The argument was, that the power to regulate did not include the power to annihilate commerce, by interdicting it permanently and entirely with foreign nations. The decision was, that the power of congress was sovereign, in relation to commercial intercourse, qualified by the limitations and restrictions contained in the constitution itself. Non-intercourse and Embargo laws are within the range of legislative discretion; and if congress have the power, for purposes of safety, of preparation, or of counteraction, to suspend commercial intercourse with foreign {464} nations, they are not limited, as to the duration, any more, than as to the manner and extent of the measure.

§ 647. That this measure went to the utmost verge of constitutional power, and especially of implied power, has never been denied. That it could not be justified by any, but the most liberal construction of the constitution, is equally undeniable. It was the favourite measure of those, who were generally the advocates of the strictest construction. It was sustained by the people from a belief, that it was promotive of the interests, and important to the safety of the Union.

§ 648. There remain one or two other measures of a political nature, whose constitutionality has been denied; but which, being of a transient character, have left no permanent traces in the constitutional jurisprudence of the country. Reference is here made to the Alien and Sedition laws, passed in 1798, both of which were limited to a short duration, and expired by their own limitation.

§ 649. The constitutionality of both the acts was assailed with great earnestness and ability at the time; and was defended with equal masculine vigour. The ground of the advocates, in favour of these laws, was, that they resulted from the right and duty in the government of self-preservation, and the like duty and protection of its functionaries in the proper discharge of their official duties. They were impugned, as not conformable to the letter, or spirit of the constitution; and as inconsistent in their principles with the rights of citizens, and the liberty of the press. The Alien act was denounced, as exercising a power not delegated by the constitution; as uniting legislative and judicial functions, with that of the executive; and by this Union {465} as subverting the general principles of free government, and the particular organization and positive provisions of the constitution. It was added, that the Sedition act was open to the same objection, and was expressly forbidden by one of the amendments of the constitution, on which there will be occasion hereafter to comment. At present it does not seem necessary to present more than this general outline, as the measures are not likely to be renewed; and as the doctrines, on which they are maintained, and denounced, are not materially different from those, which have been already considered.

CHAPTER XXVIII.

POWER OF CONGRESS TO PUNISH TREASON.

§ 650. AND here, in the order of the constitution, terminates the section, which enumerates the powers of Congress. There are, however, other clauses detached from their proper connexion, which embrace other powers delegated to congress; and which for no apparent reason have been so detached. As it will be more convenient to bring the whole in review at once, it is proposed (though it is a deviation from the general method of this work) to submit them in this place to the consideration of the reader.

§ 651. The third section of the fourth article gives a constitutional definition of the crime of treason, (which will be reserved for a separate examination,) and then provides:

> "The congress shall have power to declare the punishment of treason; but no attainder of treason shall work corruption of blood, or forfeiture, except during the life of the person attainted."

§ 652. The propriety of investing the national government with authority to punish the crime of treason against the United States could never become a question with any persons, who deemed the national government worthy of creation, or preservation. If the power had not been expressly granted, it must have been implied, unless all the powers of the national government might be put at defiance, and prostrated with impunity. Two motives, probably, concurred in introducing it, as an express power. One was, not to leave it open to implication, whether treason was to be exclusively punishable {467} with death according to the known rule of the common law, and with the barbarous accompaniments pointed out by it; but to confide the punishment to the discretion of congress. The other was, to impose some limitation upon the nature and extent of the punishment, so that it should not work corruption of blood or forfeiture beyond the life of the offender.

§ 653. The punishment of high treason by the common law, as stated by Mr. Justice Blackstone, is as follows: 1. That the offender be drawn to the gallows, and not be carried or walk, though usually (by connivance at length ripened into law) a sledge or hurdle is allowed, to preserve the offender from the extreme torment of being dragged on the ground or pavement. 2. That he be hanged by the neck, and cut down alive. 3. That his entrails be taken out and burned, while he is yet alive. 4. That his head be cut off. 5. That his body be divided into four parts. 6. That his head and quarters be at the king's disposal. These refinements in cruelty (which if now practised would be disgraceful to the character of the age) were, in former times, literally and studiously executed; and indicate at once a savage and ferocious spirit, and a degrading subserviency to royal resentments, real or supposed.

It was wise to place the punishment solely in the discretion of congress; and the punishment has been since declared to be simply death by hanging; thus inflicting death in a manner becoming the humanity of a civilized society.

§ 654. It is well known, that corruption of blood, and forfeiture of the estate of the offender followed, as a necessary consequence at the common law, upon every attainder of treason. By corruption of blood all inheritable qualities are destroyed; so, that an attainted {468} person can neither inherit lands, nor other hereditamerits from his ancestors, nor retain those, he is already in possession of, nor transmit them to any heir. And this destruction of all inheritable qualities is so complete; that it obstructs all descents to his posterity, whenever they are obliged to derive a title through him to any estate of a remoter ancestor. So, that if a father commits treason, and is attainted, and suffers death, and then the grandfather dies, his grandson cannot inherit any estate from his grandfather; for he must claim through his father, who can convey to him no inheritable blood. Thus the innocent are made the victims of a guilt, in which they did not, and perhaps could not, participate; and the sin is visited upon remote generations. In addition to this most grievous disability; the person attainted forfeits, by the common law, all his lands, and tenements, and rights of entry, and rights of profits in lands or tenements, which he possesses. And this forfeiture relates back to the time of the treason committed, so as to avoid all intermediate sales and incumbrances; and he also forfeits all his goods and chattels from the time of his conviction.

§ 655. The reason commonly assigned for these severe punishments, beyond the mere forfeiture of the life of the party attainted, are these: By committing treason the party has broken his original bond of allegiance, and forfeited his social rights. Among these social rights, that of transmitting property to others is deemed one of the chief and most valuable. Moreover, such forfeitures, whereby the posterity of the offender must suffer, as well as himself, will help to restrain a man, not only by the sense of his duty, and dread of personal punishment, but also by his passions and natural affections; and will interest every dependent {469} and relation, he has, to keep him from offending. But this view of the subject is wholly unsatisfactory. It looks only to the offender himself, and is regardless of his innocent posterity. It really operates, as a posthumous punishment upon them; and compels them to bear, not only the disgrace naturally attendant upon such flagitious crimes; but takes from them the common rights and privileges enjoyed by all other citizens, where they are wholly innocent, and however remote they may be in the lineage from the first offender. It surely is enough for society to take the life of the offender, as a just punishment of his crime, without taking from his offspring and relatives that property, which may be the only means of saving them from poverty and ruin. It is bad policy too; for it cuts off all the attachments, which these unfortunate victims might otherwise feel for their own government, and prepares them to engage in any other service, by which their supposed injuries may be redressed, or their hereditary hatred gratified. Upon these and similar grounds, it may be presumed, that the clause was first introduced into the original draft of the constitution; and, after some amendments, it was adopted without any apparent resistance.

CHAPTER XXIX.

POWER OF CONGRESS AS TO PROOF OF STATE RECORDS AND PROCEEDINGS.

{470}

§ 656. THE first section of the fourth article declares:

> "Full faith and credit shall be given in each state to the public acts, records, and judicial proceedings of every other state. And the congress may by general laws prescribe the manner, in which such acts, records, and proceedings shall be proved, and *the effect thereof.*"

§ 657. It is well known, that the laws and acts of foreign nations are not judicially taken notice of in any other nation; and that they must be proved, like any other facts, whenever they come into operation or examination in any forensic controversy. The nature and mode of the proof depend upon the municipal law of the country, where the suit is depending; and there are known to be great diversities in the practice of different nations on this subject. Even in England and America the subject, notwithstanding the numerous judicial decisions, which have from time to time been made, is not without its difficulties and embarrassments.

§ 658. Independent of the question as to *proof*, there is another question, as to the *effect*, which is to be given to foreign judgments, when duly authenticated, in the tribunals of other nations, either as matter to maintain a suit, or to found a defence to a suit. Upon this subject, also, different nations are not entirely agreed in opinion or practice. Most, if not all of them, profess {471} to give some effect to such judgments; but many exceptions are allowed, which either demolish the whole efficiency of the judgment, as such, or leave it open to collateral proofs, which in a great measure impair its validity. To treat suitably of this subject would require a large dissertation, and appropriately belongs to another branch of public law.

§ 659. The general rule of the common law, recognised both in England and America, is, that foreign judgments are *primâ facie* evidence of the right and matter, which they purport to decide. At least, this may be asserted to be in England the preponderating weight of opinion; and in America it has been held, upon many occasions, though its correctness has been recently questioned, upon principle and authority, with much acuteness.

§ 660. Before the revolution, the colonies were deemed foreign to each other, as the British colonies are still deemed foreign to the mother country; and, of course, their judgments were deemed foreign judgments within the scope of the foregoing rule. It followed, that the judgments of one colony were deemed re-examinable in another, not only as to the jurisdiction of the court, which pronounced them; but also as to the merits of the controversy, to the extent, in which they were then understood to be re-examinable in England. In some of the colonies, however, laws had been passed, which put judgments in the neighbouring colonies upon a like footing with domestic judgments, as to their conclusiveness, when the court possessed jurisdiction. The reasonable construction of the article of the confederation on this subject is, that it was intended to give the same conclusive effect to judgments of all the states, so as to promote uniformity, as well as {472} certainty, in the rule among them. It is probable, that it did not invariably, and perhaps not generally, receive such a construction; and the amendment in the constitution was, without question, designed to cure the defects in the existing provision.

§ 661. The clause of the constitution propounds three distinct objects; first, to declare, that full faith and credit shall be given to the records, &c. of every other state; secondly, to prescribe the manner of authenticating them; and thirdly, to prescribe their effect, when so authenticated. The first is declared, and established by the constitution itself, and is to receive no aid from, nor is it susceptible of any qualification by, congress. The other two are expressly subjected to the legislative power.

CHAPTER XXX

POWERS OF CONGRESS — ADMISSION OF NEW STATES, AND ACQUISITION OF TERRITORY.

{473}

§ 662. THE third section of the fourth article contains two distinct clauses. The first is —

> "New states may be admitted by the congress into this Union. But no new state shall be formed or erected within the jurisdiction of any other state, nor any state be formed by the junction of two or more states, or parts of states, without the consent of the legislature of the states concerned, as well as of the congress."

§ 663. In the articles of confederation no provision is to be found on this important subject. Canada was to be admitted of right, upon her acceding to the measures of the United States. But no other colony (by which was evidently meant no other British colony) was to be admitted, unless by the consent of nine states. The eventual establishment of new states within the limits of the Union seems to have been wholly overlooked by the framers of that instrument. In the progress of the revolution it was not only perceived, that from the acknowledged extent of the territory of several of the states, and its geographical position, it might be expedient to divide it into two states; but a much more interesting question arose, to whom of right belonged the vacant territory appertaining to the crown at the time of the revolution, whether to the states, within whose chartered limits it was situated, or to the Union in its federative capacity. This was a subject of long and ardent controversy, and (as has been already suggested) threatened to disturb the peace, if not to {474} overthrow the government of the Union. It was upon this ground, that several of the states refused to ratify the articles of confederation, insisting upon the right of the confederacy to a portion of the vacant and unpatented territory included within their chartered limits. Some of the states most interested in the vacant and unpatented western territory, at length yielded to the earnest solicitations of congress on this subject. To induce them to make liberal cessions, congress declared, that the ceded territory should be disposed of for the common benefit of the Union, and formed into republican states, with the same rights of sovereignty, freedom, and independence, as the other states; to be of a suitable extent of territory, not less than one hundred, nor more than one hundred and fifty miles square; and that the reasonable expenses incurred by the state, since the commencement of the war, in subduing British posts, or in maintaining and acquiring the territory, should be reimbursed.

§ 664. It was doubtless with reference principally to this territory, that the article of the constitution, now under consideration, was adopted. The general precaution, that no new states shall be formed without the concurrence of the

263

national government, and of the states concerned, is consonant to the principles, which ought to govern all such transactions. The particular precaution against the erection of new states by the partition of a state without its own consent, will quiet the jealousy of the larger states; as that of the smaller will also be quieted by a like precaution against a junction of states without their consent. Under this provision no less than eleven states have, in the space of little more than forty years, been admitted into the Union upon an equality with the original states. And it {475} scarcely requires the spirit of prophecy to foretell, that in a few years the predominance of numbers, of population, and of power, will be unequivocally transferred from the old to the new states. May the patriotic wish be for ever true to the fact, *felix prole parens.*

CHAPTER XXXI.

POWERS OF CONGRESS — TERRITORIAL GOVERNMENTS.

{476}

§ 665. THE next clause of the same article is,

> "The congress shall have power to dispose of, and make all needful rules and regulations respecting the territory and other property belonging to the United States; and nothing in this constitution shall be so construed, as to prejudice any claims of the United States, or of any particular state."

The proviso thus annexed to the power is certainly proper in itself, and was probably rendered necessary by the jealousies and questions concerning the Western territory, which have been already alluded to under the preceding head. It was perhaps suggested by the clause in the ninth article of the confederation, which contained a proviso, "that no state shall be deprived of territory for the benefit of the United States."

§ 666. As the general government possesses the right to acquire territory, either by conquest, or by treaty, it would seem to follow, as an inevitable consequence, that it possesses the power to govern, what it has so acquired. The territory does not, when so acquired, become entitled to self-government, and it is not subject to the jurisdiction of any state. It must, consequently, be under the dominion and jurisdiction of the Union, or it would be without any government at all. In cases of conquest, the usage, of the world is, if a nation is not wholly subdued, to consider the conquered territory, as merely held by military occupation, until {477} its fate shall be determined by a treaty of peace. But during this intermediate period it is exclusively subject to the government of the conqueror. In cases of confirmation or cession by treaty, the acquisition becomes firm and stable; and the ceded territory becomes a part of the nation, to which it is annexed, either on terms stipulated in the treaty, or on such, as its new master shall impose. The relations of the inhabitants with each other do not change; but their relations with their former sovereign are dissolved; and new relations are created between them and their new sovereign. The act transferring the country transfers the allegiance of its inhabitants. But the general laws, not strictly political, remain, as they were, until altered by the new sovereign. If the treaty stipulates, that they shall enjoy the privileges, rights, and immunities of citizens of the United States, the treaty, as a part of the law of, the land, becomes obligatory in these respects. Whether the same effects would result from the mere fact of their becoming inhabitants and citizens by the cession, without any express stipulation, may deserve inquiry, if the question should ever occur. But they do not participate in political power; nor can they share in the powers of the general government, until they become a state, and are admitted into the Union, as such. Until that period, the territory remains subject to be governed in such manner, as congress shall direct, under the clause of the constitution now under consideration.

§ 667. No one has ever doubted the authority of congress to errect territorial governments within the territory of the United States, under the general language of the clause, "to make all needful rules and regulations." Indeed, with the ordinance of 1787 in {478} the very view of the framers, as well as of the people of the states, it is impossible to doubt, that such a power was deemed indispensable to the purposes of the cessions made by the states. So that, notwithstanding the generality of the objection, (already examined,) that congress have no power to erect corporations, and that in the convention the power was refused, we see, that the very power is an incident to that of regulating the territory of the United States; that is, it is an appropriate means of carrying the power into effect. What shall be the form of government established in the territories depends exclusively upon the discretion of congress. Having a right to erect a territorial government, they may confer on it such powers, legislative, judicial, and executive, as they may deem best. They may confer upon it general legislative powers, subject only to the laws and constitution of the United States. If the power to create courts is given to the territorial legislature, those courts are to be deemed strictly territorial; and in no just sense constitutional courts, in which the judicial power conferred by the constitution can be deposited. They are incapable of receiving it. They are legislative courts, created in virtue of the general right of sovereignty in the government, or in virtue of that clause, which enables congress to make all needful rules and regulations respecting the territory of the United States. The power is not confined to the territory of the United States; but extends to "other property belonging to the United States;" so that it may be applied to the due regulation of all other personal and real property rightfully belonging to the United States. And so it has been constantly understood, and acted upon. {479}

§ 668. The power of congress over the public territory is clearly exclusive and universal; and their legislation is subject to no control; but is absolute, and unlimited, unless so far as is affected by stipulations in the cessions, or by the ordinance of 1787, under which any part of it has been settled. But the power of congress to regulate the other national property (unless they have acquired, by cession of the states, exclusive jurisdiction) is not necessarily exclusive in all cases. If the national government own a fort, arsenal, hospital, or lighthouse establishment, not so ceded, the general jurisdiction of the state is not excluded in regard to the site; but, subject to the rightful exercise of the powers of the national government, it remains in full force.

§ 669. There are some other incidental powers given to congress, to carry into effect certain other provisions of the constitution. But they will most properly come under consideration in a future part of these Commentaries. At present, it may suffice to say, that with reference to due energy in the government, due protection of the national interests, and due security to the Union, fewer powers could scarcely have been granted, without jeoparding the whole system. Without the power of the purse, the power to declare war, or to promote the common defence, or general welfare, would have been wholly vain and illusory. Without the power exclusively to regulate commerce, the intercourse between the states would have been constantly liable to domestic dissentions, jealousies, and rivalries, and to foreign hostilities, and retaliatory restrictions. The other powers are principally auxiliary to these; and are dictated at once by an enlightened policy, a devotion to justice, and a regard to the permanence {480} (may it ripen into a perpetuity!) of the Union.

§ 670. As there are incidental powers belonging to the United States in their sovereign capacity, so there are incidental rights, obligations, and duties. It may be asked, how these are to be ascertained. In the first place, as to duties and obligations of a public nature, they are to be ascertained by the law of nations, to which, on asserting our independence, we necessarily became subject. In regard to municipal rights and obligations, whatever differences of opinion may arise in regard to the extent, to which the common law attaches to the national government, no one can doubt, that it must, and ought to be resorted to, in order to ascertain many of its rights and obligations. Thus, when a contract is entered into by the United States, we naturally and necessarily resort to the common law, to interpret its terms, and ascertain its obligations. The same general rights, duties, and limitations, which the common law attaches to contracts of a similar character between private individuals, are applied to the contracts of the government. Thus, if the United States become the holder of a bill of exchange, they are bound to the same diligence, as to giving notice, in order to charge an indorser, upon the dishonour of the bill, as a private holder would be. In like manner, when a bond is entered into by a surety for the faithful discharge of the duties of an office by his principal, the nature and extent of the obligation, created by the instrument, are constantly ascertained by reference to the common law; though the bond is given to the government in its sovereign capacity.

CHAPTER XXXII.

PROHIBITIONS ON THE UNITED STATES.

{481}

§ 671. HAVING finished this review of the powers of congress, the order of the subject next conducts us to the prohibitions and limitations upon these powers, which are contained in the ninth section of the first article. Some of these have already been under discussion, and therefore will be pretermitted.

§ 672. The first clause is as follows:

> "The migration, or importation of such persons, as any of the states now existing shall think proper to admit, shall not be prohibited by the congress, prior to the year one thousand eight hundred and eight; but a tax, or duty, may be imposed on such importation, not exceeding ten dollars for each person."

§ 673. It is to the honour of America, that she should have set the first example of interdicting and abolishing the slave-trade, in modern times. It is well known, that it constituted a grievance, of which some of the colonies complained before the revolution, that the introduction of slaves was encouraged by the crown, and that prohibitory laws were negatived. It was doubtless to have been wished, that the power of prohibiting the importation of slaves had been allowed to be put into immediate operation, and had not been postponed for twenty years. But it is not difficult to account, either for this restriction, or for the manner, in which it is expressed. It ought to be considered, as a great point gained in favour of humanity, that a period of twenty years might forever terminate, within the {482} United States, a traffic, which had so long, and so loudly upbraided the barbarism of modern policy. Even within this period, it might receive a very considerable discouragement, by curtailing the traffic between foreign countries; and it might even be totally abolished by the concurrence of a few states. "Happy," (it was then added by the Federalist,) "would it be for the unfortunate Africans, if an equal prospect lay before them of being redeemed from the oppressions of their European brethren." Let it be remembered, that at this period this horrible traffic was carried on with the encouragement and support of every civilized nation of Europe; and by none with more eagerness and enterprize, than by the parent country. America stood forth alone, uncheered and unaided, in stamping ignominy upon this traffic on the very face of her constitution of government, although there were strong temptations of interest to draw her aside from the performance of this great moral duty.

§ 674. The next clause is,

> "The privilege of the writ of habeas corpus shall not be suspended, unless when, in cases of rebellion or invasion, the public safety may require it."

§ 675. In order to understand the meaning of the terms here used, it will be necessary to have recourse to the common law; for in no other way can we arrive at the true definition of the writ of habeas corpus. At the common law there are various writs, called writs of habeas corpus. But the particular one here spoken of is that great and celebrated writ, used in all cases of illegal confinement, known by the name of the writ of *habeas corpus ad subjiciendum*, directed to the person detaining another, and commanding him to produce the body of the prisoner, with the day and cause of his caption and {483} detention, *ad faciendum, subjiciendum, et recipiendum*, to do, submit to, and receive, whatsoever the judge or court, awarding such writ, shall consider in that behalf. It is, therefore, justly esteemed the great bulwark of personal liberty; since it is the appropriate remedy to ascertain, whether any person is rightfully in confinement or not, and the cause of his confinement; and if no sufficient ground of detention appears, the party is entitled to his immediate discharge. This writ is most beneficially construed; and is applied to every case of illegal restraint, whatever it may be; for every restraint upon a man's liberty is, in the eye of the law, an imprisonment, wherever may be the place, or whatever may be the manner, in which the restraint is effected.

§ 676. It is obvious, that cases of a peculiar emergency may arise, which may justify, nay even require, the temporary suspension of the right to this writ. But as it has frequently happened in foreign countries, and even in England, that the writ has, upon various pretexts and occasions, been suspended, whereby persons, apprehended upon suspicion, have suffered a long imprisonment, sometimes from design, and sometimes, because they were forgotten, the right to suspend it is expressly confined to cases of rebellion or invasion, where the public safety may require it; a very just and wholesome restraint, which cuts down at a blow a fruitful means of oppression, capable of being abused in bad times to the worst of purposes. Hitherto no suspension of the writ has ever been authorized by congress since the establishment of the constitution. It would seem, as the power is given to congress to suspend the writ of habeas corpus in cases of rebellion or invasion, that the right to judge, whether exigency had arisen, must exclusively belong to that body. {484}

§ 677. The next clause is,

"No bill of attainder or *ex post facto* law shall be passed."

§ 678. Bills of attainder, as they are technically called, are such special acts of the legislature, as inflict capital punishments upon persons supposed to be guilty of high offences, such as treason and felony, without any conviction in the ordinary course of judicial proceedings. If an act inflicts a milder degree of punishment than death, it is called a bill of pains and penalties. But in the sense of the constitution, it seems, that bills of attainder include bills of pains and penalties; for the Supreme Court have said, "A bill of attainder may affect the life of an individual, or may confiscate his property, or both." In such cases, the legislature assumes judicial magistracy, pronouncing upon the guilt of the party without any of the common forms and guards of trial, and satisfying itself with proofs, when such proofs are within its reach, whether they are conformable to the rules of evidence, or not. In short, in all such cases, the legislature exercises the highest power of sovereignty, and what may properly be deemed an irresponsible despotic discretion, being governed solely by what it deems political necessity or expediency, and too often under the influence of unreasonable fears, or unfounded suspicions. Such acts have been often resorted to in foreign governments, as a common engine of state; and even in England they have been pushed to the most extravagant extent in bad times, reaching, as well to the absent and the dead, as to the living. Sir Edward Coke has mentioned it to be among the transcendent powers of parliament, that an act may be passed to attaint a man, after he is dead. And the reigning monarch, who was slain at Bosworth, is said to have been attainted by an act of parliament {485} a few months after his death, notwithstanding the absurdity of deeming him at once in possession of the throne and a traitor. The punishment has often been inflicted without calling upon the party accused to answer, or without even the formality of proof; and sometimes, because the law, in its ordinary course of proceedings, would acquit the offender. The injustice and iniquity of such acts, in general, constitute an irresistible argument against the existence of the power. In a free government it would be intolerable; and in the hands of a reigning faction, it might be, and probably would be, abused to the ruin and death of the most virtuous citizens. Bills of this sort have been most usually passed in England in times of rebellion, or of gross subserviency to the crown, or of violent political excitements; periods, in which all nations are most liable (as well the free, as the enslaved) to forget their duties, and to trample upon the rights and liberties of others.

§ 679. Of the same class are *ex post facto* laws, that is to say, (in a literal sense,) laws passed after the act done. The terms, *ex post facto* laws, in a comprehensive sense, embrace all retrospective laws, or laws governing, or controlling past transactions, whether they are of a civil, or a criminal nature. And there have not been wanting learned minds, that have contended with no small force of authority and reasoning, that such ought to be the interpretation of the terms in the constitution of the United States. As an original question, the argument would be entitled to grave consideration; but the current of opinion and authority has been so generally one way, as to the meaning of this phrase in the state constitutions, as well as in that of the United States, ever since their adoption, that it is {486} difficult to feel, that it is now an open question. The general interpretation has been, and is, that the phrase applies to acts of a criminal nature only; and, that the prohibition reaches every law, whereby an act is declared a crime, and made punishable as such, when it was not a crime, when done; or whereby the act, if a crime, is aggravated in enormity, or punishment; or whereby different, or less evidence, is required to convict an offender, than was required, when the act was committed.

§ 680. The next clause (passing by such, as have been already considered) is,

"No money shall be drawn from the treasury, but in consequence of appropriations made by law. And a regular statement and account of the receipts and expenditures of all public money shall be published from time to time."

§ 681. The object is apparent upon the slightest examination. It is to secure regularity, punctuality, and fidelity, in the disbursement of the public money. As all the taxes raised from the people, as well as the revenues arising from other sources, are to be applied to the discharge of the expenses, and debts, and other engagements of the government, it is highly proper, that congress should possess the power to decide, how and when any money should be applied for these purposes. If it were otherwise, the executive would possess an unbounded power over the public purse of the nation; and might apply all its monied resources at his pleasure. The power to control, and direct the appropriations, constitutes a most useful and salutary check upon profusion and extravagance, as well as upon corrupt influence and public peculation. In arbitrary governments the prince levies what money he pleases from his subjects, disposes of it, as he thinks proper, {487} and is beyond responsibility or reproof. It is wise to interpose, in a republic, every restraint, by which the public treasure, the common fund of all, should be applied with unshrinking honesty to such objects, as legitimately belong to the common defence, and the general welfare. Congress is made the guardian of this treasure; and to make their responsibility complete and perfect, a regular account of the receipts and expenditures is required to be published, that the people may know, what money is expended, for what purposes, and by what authority.

§ 682. The next clause is,

> "No title of nobility shall be granted by the United States; and no person holding any office of profit or trust under them shall, without the consent of the congress, accept of any present, emolument, office, or title of any kind whatever, from any king, prince, or foreign state."

§ 683. This clause seems scarcely to require even a passing notice. As a perfect equality is the basis of all our institutions, state and national, the prohibition against the creation of any titles of nobility seems proper, if not indispensable, to keep perpetually alive a just sense of this important truth. Distinctions between citizens, in regard to rank, would soon lay the foundation of odious claims and privileges, and silently subvert the spirit of independence and personal dignity, which are so often proclaimed to be the best security of a republican government.

§ 684. The other clause, as to the acceptance of any emoluments, title, or office, from foreign governments, is founded in a just jealousy of foreign influence of every sort. Whether, in a practical sense, it can produce much effect, has been thought doubtful. A patriot will not be likely to be seduced from his duties {488} to his country by the acceptance of any title, or present, from a foreign power. An intriguing, or corrupt agent, will not be restrained from guilty machinations in the service of a foreign state by such constitutional restrictions. Still, however, the provision is highly important, as it puts it out of the power of any officer of the government to wear borrowed honours, which shall enhance his supposed importance abroad by a titular dignity at home.

CHAPTER XXXIII.

PROHIBITIONS ON THE STATES.

§ 685. THE tenth section of the first article (to which we are now to proceed) contains the prohibitions and restrictions upon the authority of the states. Some of these, and especially those, which regard the power of taxation, and the regulation of commerce, have already passed under consideration; and will, therefore, be here omitted. The others will be examined in the order of the text of the constitution.

§ 686. The first clause is,

> "No state shall enter into any treaty, alliance, or confederation; grant letters of marque or reprisal; coin money; emit bills of credit; make any thing but gold and silver coin a tender in payment of debts; pass any bill of attainder, *ex post facto* law, or law impairing the obligation of contracts; or grant any title of nobility."

The prohibition against treaties, alliances, and confederations, constituted a part of the articles of Confederation, and was from thence transferred in substance into the constitution. The sound policy, nay, the necessity of it, for the preservation of any national government, is so obvious, as to strike the most careless mind. If every state were at liberty to enter into any treaties, alliances, or confederacies, with any foreign state, it would become utterly subversive of the power confided to the national government on the same subject. Engagements might be entered into by different states, utterly hostile to the interests of neighbouring or distant states; and thus the internal peace and harmony {490} of the Union might be destroyed, or put in jeopardy. A foundation might thus be laid for preferences, and retaliatory systems, which would render the power of taxation, and the regulation of commerce, by the national government, utterly futile. Besides; the intimate dangers to the Union ought not to be overlooked, by thus nourishing within its own bosom a perpetual source of foreign corrupt influence, which, in times of political excitement and war, might be wielded to the destruction of the independence of the country. This, indeed, was deemed, by the authors of the Federalist, too clear to require any illustration. The corresponding clauses in the confederation were still more strong, direct, and exact, in their language and import.

§ 688. The prohibition to grant letters of marque and reprisal stands upon the same general ground; for otherwise it would be in the power of a single state to involve the whole Union in war at its pleasure. It is true, that the granting of letters of marque and reprisal is not always a preliminary to war, or necessarily designed to provoke it. But in its essence, it is a hostile measure for unredressed grievances, real or supposed; and therefore it is most generally the precursor of an appeal to arms by general hostilities. The security (as has been justly observed) of the whole Union ought not to be suffered to depend upon the petulance or precipitation of a single state. The constitution has wisely both in peace and war, confided the whole subject to the general government. Uniformity is thus secured in all operations, which relate to foreign powers; and an immediate responsibility to the nation on the part of those, for whose conduct the nation is itself responsible. {490}

§ 689. The next prohibition is to coin money. We have already seen, that the power to coin money, and regulate the value thereof, is confided to the general government. Under the confederation a concurrent power was left in the states, with a restriction, that congress should have the exclusive power to regulate the alloy and value of the coin struck by the states. In this, as in many other cases, the constitution has made a great improvement, upon the existing system. Whilst the alloy and value depended on the general government, a right of coinage in the several states could have no other effect, than to multiply expensive mints, and diversify the forms and weights of the circulating coins. The latter inconvenience would defeat one main purpose, for which the power is given to the general government, viz. uniformity of the currency; and the former might be as well accomplished by local mints established by the national government, if it should ever be found inconvenient to send bullion, or old coin for recoinage to the central mint. The truth is, that the prohibition had a higher motive, the danger of the circulation of base and spurious coin connived at for local purposes, or easily accomplished by the ingenuity of artificers, where the coins are very various in value and denomination, and issued from so many independent and unaccountable authorities. This subject has, however, been already enlarged on in another place.

§ 690. The prohibition to "emit bills of credit" cannot, perhaps, be more forcibly vindicated, than by quoting the glowing language of the Federalist, a language justified by that of almost every contemporary writer, and attested in its truth by facts, from which the mind involuntarily turns away at once with disgust and {492} indignation. "This prohibition," says the Federalist, "must give pleasure to every citizen in proportion to his love of justice, and his knowledge of the true springs of public prosperity. The loss, which America has sustained since the peace from the pestilent effects of paper money on the necessary confidence between man and man; on the necessary confidence in the public councils; on the industry and morals of the people; and on the character of republican government, constitutes an enormous debt against the states, chargeable with this unadvised measure, which must long remain unsatisfied; or rather an accumulation of guilt, which can be expiated no otherwise, than by a voluntary sacrifice on the altar of justice of the power, which has been the instrument of it. In addition to these persuasive considerations, it may be observed, that the same reasons, which show the necessity of denying to the states the power of regulating coin, prove with equal force, that they ought not to be at liberty *to substitute a paper medium, instead of coin.* Had every state a right to regulate the value of its coin, there might be as many different currencies, as states; and thus the intercourse among them would be impeded. Retrospective alterations in its value might be made; and thus the citizens of other states be injured, and animosities be kindled among the states themselves. The subjects of foreign powers might suffer from the same cause; and hence the Union be discredited, and embroiled by the indiscretion of a single member. No one of these mischiefs is less incident to a . power in the states to emit paper money, than to coin gold or silver."

§ 691. Without doubt the melancholy shades of this picture were deepened by the urgent distresses of the {493} revolutionary war, and the reluctance of the states to perform their proper duty. And some apology, if not some justification of the proceedings, may be found in the eventful transactions and sufferings of those times. But the history of paper money, without any adequate funds pledged to redeem it, and resting merely upon the pledge of the public faith, has been in all ages and in all nations the same. It has constantly become more and more depreciated; and in some instances has ceased from this cause to have any circulation whatsoever, whether issued by the irresistible edict of a despot, or by the more alluring order of a republican congress. There is an abundance of illustrative facts scattered over the history of those of the American colonies, which ventured upon this pernicious scheme of raising money to supply the public wants, during their subjection to the British crown; and in the several states, from the declaration of independence down to the present times. Even the United States, with almost inexhaustible resources, and with a population of 9,000,000 of inhabitants, exhibited during the late war with Great-Britain the humiliating spectacle of treasury notes, issued and payable in a year, remaining unredeemed, and sunk by depreciation to about half of their nominal value!

§ 692. It would seem to be obvious, that as the states are expressly prohibited from coining money, the prohibition would be wholly ineffectual, if they might create a paper currency, and circulate it as money. But, as it might become necessary for the states to borrow money, the prohibition could not be intended to prevent such an exercise of power, on giving to the lender a certificate of the amount borrowed, and a promise to repay it. {494}

§ 693. What, then, is the true meaning of the phrase "bills of credit" in the constitution? In its enlarged, and perhaps in its literal sense, it may comprehend any instrument, by which a state engages to pay money at a future day (and of course, for which it obtains a present credit;) and thus it would include a certificate given for money borrowed. But the language of the constitution itself, and the mischief to be prevented, which we know from the history of our country, equally limit the interpretation of the terms. The word "emit" is never employed in describing those contracts, by which a state binds itself to pay money at a future day for services actually received, or for money borrowed for present use. Nor are instruments, executed for such purposes, in common language denominated "bills of credit." To emit bills of credit conveys to the mind the idea of issuing paper, intended to circulate through the community for its ordinary purposes, as money, which paper is redeemable at a future day. This is the sense, in which the terms of the constitution have been generally understood. The phrase (as we have seen) was well known, and generally used to indicate the paper currency, issued by the states during their colonial dependence. During the war of our revolution the paper currency issued by congress was constantly denominated, in the acts of that body, bills of credit; and the like appellation was applied to similar currency issued by the states. The phrase had thus acquired a determinate and appropriate meaning. At the time of the adoption of the constitution, bills of credit were universally understood to signify a paper medium intended to circulate between individuals, and between government and individuals, for the ordinary purposes of society. Such a medium has always been liable to {495} considerable fluctuation. Its value is continually changing; and these changes, often great and sudden, expose individuals to immense losses, are the sources of ruinous speculations, and destroy all proper confidence between man and man. In no country, more than our own, had these truths been felt in all their force. In none had more intense suffering, or more wide-spreading ruin accompanied the system. It was, therefore, the object of the prohibition to cut up the whole mischief by the roots, because it had been deeply felt throughout all the states, and had deeply affected the prosperity of all. The object of the prohibition was not to prohibit the thing, when it bore a particular name; but to prohibit the thing, whatever form or name it might assume. If the words are not merely empty sounds, the prohibition must comprehend the emission of any paper medium by a state government for the purposes of common circulation. It would be preposterous to suppose, that the constitution meant solemnly to prohibit an issue under one denomination, leaving the power complete to issue the same thing under another. It can never be seriously contended, that the constitution means to prohibit names, and not things; to deal with shadows, and to leave substances. What would be the consequence of such a construction? That a very important act, big with great and ruinous mischief, and on that account forbidden by words the most appropriate for its description, might yet be performed by the substitution of a name. That the constitution, even in one of its vital provisions, might be openly evaded by giving a new name to an old thing. Call the thing a bill of credit, and it is prohibited. Call the same thing a certificate, and it is constitutional. {496}

§ 694. The next prohibition is, that no state shall "make any thing but gold and silver coin, a tender in payment of debts." This clause was manifestly founded in the same general policy, which procured the adoption of the preceding clause. The history, indeed, of the various laws, which were passed by the states in their colonial and independent character upon this subject, is startling at once to our morals, to our patriotism, and to our sense of justice. Not only was paper money issued, and declared to be a tender in payment of debts; but laws of another character, well known under the appellation of tender laws, appraisement laws, instalment laws, and suspension laws, were from time to time enacted, which prostrated all private credit, and all private morals. By some of these laws, the due payment of debts was suspended; debts were, in violation of the very terms of the contract, authorized to be paid by instalments at different periods; property of any sort, however worthless, either real or personal, might be tendered by the debtor in payment of his debts; and the creditor was compelled to take the property of the debtor, which he might seize on execution, at an appraisement wholly disproportionate to its known value. Such grievances, and oppressions, and others of a like nature, were the ordinary results of legislation during the revolutionary war, and the intermediate period down to the formation of the constitution. They entailed the most enormous evils on the country; and introduced a system of fraud, chicanery, and profligacy, which destroyed all private confidence, industry, and enterprise.

§ 695. The next prohibition is, that no state shall

"pass any bill of attainder, *ex post facto* law, or law impairing the obligation of contracts."

The two former {497} require no commentary, beyond what has been already offered, under a similar prohibitory clause applied to the government of the United States. The same policy and principles apply to each. It would have been utterly useless, if not absurd, to deny a power to the Union, which might at the same time be applied by the states to purposes equally mischievous, and tyrannical; and which might, when applied by the states, be for the very purpose of subverting the Union. Before the constitution of the United States was adopted, every state, unless prohibited by its own constitution, might pass a bill of attainder, or *ex post facto* law, as a general result of its sovereign legislative power. And such a prohibition would not be implied from a constitutional provision, that the legislative, executive, and judiciary departments shall be separate, and distinct; that crimes shall be tried in the county, where they are committed; or that the trial by jury shall remain inviolate. The power to pass such laws would still remain, at least so far as respects crimes committed without the state. During the revolutionary war, bills of attainder, and *ex post facto* acts of confiscation were passed to a wide extent; and the evils resulting therefrom were supposed, in times of more cool reflection, to have far outweighed any imagined good. (Abr. 63}

CHAPTER XXXIV.

PROHIBITIONS ON THE STATES — IMPAIRING CONTRACTS.

{498}

§ 696. THE remaining clause, as to impairing the obligation of contracts, will require a more full and deliberate examination.

§ 697. In the first place, what is to be deemed a contract, in the constitutional sense of this clause g A contract is an agreement to do, or not to do, a particular thing; or (as was said on another occasion) a contract is a compact between two or more persons. A contract is either executory, or executed. An executory contract is one, in which a party binds himself to do, or not to do, a particular thing. An executed contract is one, in which the object of the contract is performed. This differs in nothing from a grant; for a contract executed conveys a chose in possession; a contract executory conveys only a chose in action. Since, then, a grant is in fact a contract executed, the obligation of which continues; and since the constitution uses the general term, *contract*, without distinguishing between those, which are executory, and those, which are executed; it must be construed to comprehend the former, as well as the latter. A state law, therefore, annulling conveyances between individuals, and declaring, that the grantors shall stand seized of their former estates notwithstanding those grants, would be as repugnant to the constitution, as a state law discharging the vendors from the obligation of executing their contracts of sale {499} by conveyances. It would be strange, indeed, if a contract to convey were secured by the constitution, while an absolute conveyance remained unprotected. That the contract, while executory, was obligatory; but when executed, might be avoided.

§ 698. Contracts, too, are express, or implied. Express contracts are, where the terms of the agreement are openly avowed, and uttered at the time of the making of it. Implied contracts are such, as reason and justice dictate from the nature of the transaction, and which therefore the law presumes, that every man undertakes to perform. The constitution makes no distinction between the one class of contracts and the other. It then equally embraces, and applies to both. Indeed, as by far the largest class of contracts in civil society, in the ordinary transactions of life, are implied, there would be very little object in securing the inviolability of express contracts, if those, which are implied, might be impaired by state legislation. The constitution is not chargeable with such folly, or inconsistency. Every grant in its own nature amounts to an extinguishment of the right of the grantor, and implies a contract not to re-assert it. A party is, therefore, always estopped by his own grant. How absurd would it be to provide, that an express covenant by him, as a muniment attendant upon the estate, should bind him for ever, because executory, and resting in action; and yet, that he might re-assert his title to the estate, and dispossess his grantee, because there was only an implied covenant not to re-assert it.

§ 699. In the next place, what is the obligation of a contract? It would seem difficult to substitute words more intelligible, or less liable to misconstruction, than these. And yet they have given rise to much acute {500} disquisition, as to their real meaning in the constitution. It has been said, that right and obligation are correlative terms. Whatever I, by my contract, give another a right to require of me, I, by that act lay myself under an obligation to yield or bestow. The obligation of every contract, then, will consist of that right, or power over my will or actions, which I, by my contract, confer on another. And that right and power will be found to be measured, neither by moral law alone, nor by universal law alone, nor by the laws of society alone; but by a combination of the three; an operation, in which the moral law is explained, and applied by the law of nature, and both modified, and adapted to the exigencies of society by positive law. In an advanced state of society, all contracts of men receive a relative, and not a positive interpretation. The state construes them, the state applies them, the state controls them, and the state decides, how far the social exercise of the rights, which they give over each party, can be justly asserted. Again, it has been said, that the constitution distinguishes between a contract, and the obligation of a contract. The latter is the law, which binds the parties to perform their agreement. The law, then, which has this binding obligation, must govern and control the contract in every shape, in which it is intended to bear upon it. Again, it has been said, that the obligation of a contract consists in the power and efficacy of the law, which applies to, and enforces performance of it, or an equivalent for non-performance. The obligation does not inhere, and subsist in the contract itself, *proprio vigore*, but in the law applicable to the contract. And again, it has been said, that a contract is an agreement of the parties; and, if it be not illegal, it binds them to the extent of their stipulations. Thus, if a {501} party contracts to pay a certain sum on a certain day, the contract binds him to perform it on that day, and this is its obligation.

§ 700. It seems agreed, that, when the obligation of contracts is spoken of in the constitution, we are to understand, not the mere moral, but the legal obligation of contracts. The moral obligation of contracts is, so far as human society is concerned, of an imperfect kind, which the parties are left free to obey or not, as they please. It is addressed to the conscience of the parties, under the solemn admonitions of accountability to the Supreme Being. No human lawgiver can either impair or reach it. The constitution has not in contemplation any such obligation, but such only, as might be impaired by a state, if not prohibited. It is the civil obligation of contracts, which it is designed to reach, that is, the obligation, which is recognised by, and results from the law of the state, in which it is made. If, therefore, a contract, when made, is by the law of the place declared to be illegal, or deemed to be a nullity, or a *nude pact*, it has no civil obligation, because the law in such cases forbids its having any binding efficacy, or force. It confers no legal right on the one party, and no correspondent legal duty on the other. There is no means allowed, or recognised, to enforce it; for the maxim is, *ex nudo pacto non oritur actio*. But when it does not fall within the predicament of being either illegal, or void, its obligatory force is coextensive with its stipulations.

§ 701. Nor is this obligatory force so much the result of the, positive declarations of the municipal law, as of the general principles of natural, or, (as it is sometimes called) universal law. In a state of nature, independent of the obligations of positive law, contracts {502} may be formed, and their obligatory force be complete. Between independent nations, treaties and compacts are formed, which are deemed universally obligatory; and yet in no just sense can they be deemed dependent on municipal law. Nay, there may exist (abstractly speaking) a perfect obligation in contracts, where there are no known and adequate means to enforce them; as, for instance, between independent nations, where their relative strength and power preclude the possibility, on the side of the weaker party, of enforcing them. So in the same government, where a contract is made by a state with one of its own citizens, which yet its laws do not permit to be enforced by any action or suit. In this predicament are the United States, who are not suable on any contracts made by themselves; but no one doubts, that these are still obligatory on the United States. Yet their obligation is not recognised by any positive municipal law in a great variety of cases. It depends altogether upon principles of public or universal law. Still, in these cases there is a right in the one party to have the contract performed, and the duty on the other side to perform it. But, generally speaking, when we speak of the obligation of a contract, we include in the idea some known means acknowledged by the municipal law to enforce it. Where all such means are absolutely denied, the obligation of the contract is understood to be impaired, though it may not be completely annihilated. Rights may, indeed, exist without any present adequate correspondent remedies between private persons. Thus, a state may refuse to allow imprisonment for debt; and the debtor may have no property. But still the right of the creditor remains; and he may enforce it against the future property of the debtor. So {503} a debtor may die without leaving any known estate, or without any known representative. In such cases we should not say, that the right of the creditor was gone; but only, that there was nothing, on which it could presently operate. But suppose an administrator should be appointed, and property in contingency should fall in, the right might then be enforced to the extent of the existing means.

§ 702. The civil obligation of a contract, then, though it can never arise, or exist contrary to positive law, may arise or exist independently of it; and it may exist, notwithstanding there may be no present adequate remedy to enforce it. Wherever the municipal law recognises an absolute duty to perform a contract, there the obligation to perform it is complete, although there may not be a perfect remedy.

§ 703. In the next place, what may properly be deemed impairing the obligation of contracts in the sense of the constitution? It is perfectly clear, that any law, which enlarges, abridges, or in any manner changes the intention of the parties, resulting from the stipulations in the contract, necessarily impairs it. The manner or degree, in which this change is effected, can in no respect influence the conclusion; for whether the law affect the validity, the construction, the duration, the discharge, or the evidence of the contract, it impairs its obligation, though it may not do so to the same extent in all the supposed cases. Any deviation from its terms by postponing, or accelerating the period of performance, which it prescribes; imposing conditions not expressed in the contract; or dispensing with the performance of those, which are a part of the contract; however minute, or apparently immaterial in their effect upon it, impair its obligation. *A fortiori*, {504} a law, which makes the contract wholly invalid, or extinguishes, or releases it, is a law impairing it. Nor is this all. Although there is a distinction between the obligation of a contract, and a remedy upon it; yet if there are certain remedies existing at the time, when it is made, all of which are afterwards wholly extinguished by new laws, so that there remain no means of enforcing its obligation, and no redress; such an abolition of all remedies, operating *in presenti*, is also an impairing of the obligation of such contract. But every change and modification of the remedy does not involve such a consequence. No one will doubt, that the legislature may vary the nature and extent of remedies, so always, that some substantive remedy be in fact left. Nor can it be doubted, that the legislature may prescribe the times and modes, in which remedies may be pursued; and bar suits not brought within such periods, and not pursued in such modes. Statutes of limitations are of this nature; and have never been supposed to destroy the obligation of contracts; but to prescribe the times, within which that obligation shall be enforced by a suit; and in default, to deem it either satisfied, or abandoned. The obligation to perform a contract is coeval with the undertaking to perform it. It originates with the contract itself, and operates anterior to the time of performance. The remedy acts upon the broken contract, and enforces a pre-existing obligation. And a state legislature may discharge a party from imprisonment upon a judgment in a civil case of contract, without infringing the constitution; for this is but a modification of the remedy, and does not impair the obligation of the contract. So, if a party should be in gaol, and give a bond for the prison liberties, and to remain a true prisoner, until lawfully discharged, {505} a subsequent discharge by an act of the legislature would not impair the contract; for it would be a lawful discharge in the sense of the bond.

§ 704. These general considerations naturally conduct us to some more difficult inquiries growing out of them; and upon which there has been a very great diversity of judicial opinion. The great object of the framers of the constitution undoubtedly was, to secure the inviolability of contracts. This principle was to be protected, in whatever form it might be assailed. No enumeration was attempted to be made of the modes, by which contracts might be impaired. It would have been unwise to have made such an enumeration, since it might have been defective; and the intention was to prohibit every mode or device for such purpose. The prohibition was universal.

§ 705. The question has arisen, and has been most elaborately discussed, how far the states may constitutionally pass an insolvent law, which shall discharge the obligation of contracts. It is not doubted, that the states may pass insolvent laws, which shall discharge the person, or operate in the nature of a *cessio bonorum*, provided such laws do not discharge, or intermeddle with the obligation of contracts. Nor is it denied, that insolvent laws, which discharge the obligation of contracts, made antecedently to their passage, are unconstitutional. But the question is, how far the states may constitutionally pass insolvent laws, which shall operate upon, and discharge contracts, which are made subsequently to their passage. After the most ample argument it has at length been settled by a majority of the Supreme Court, that the states may constitutionally pass such laws operating upon future contracts. {506}

§ 706. It has been already stated, that a grant is a contract within the meaning of the constitution, as much as an unexecuted agreement. The prohibition, therefore, equally reaches all interferences with private grants and private conveyances, of whatever nature they may be. But it has been made a question, whether it applies, in the same extent, to contracts and grants of a state created directly by a law, or made by some authorized agent in pursuance of a law. It has been suggested, that, in such cases, it is to be deemed an act of the legislative power; and that all laws are repealable by the same authority, which enacted them. But it has been decided upon solemn argument, that contracts and grants made by a state are not less within the reach of the prohibition, than contracts and grants of private persons; that the question is not, whether such contracts or grants are made directly by law in the form of legislation, or in any other form; but whether they exist at all. The legislature may, by a law, directly make a grant; and such grant, when once made, becomes irrevocable, and cannot be constitutionally impaired. So the legislature may make a contract with individuals directly by a law, pledging the state to a performance of it; and then, when it is accepted, it is equally under the protection of the constitution. And it may be laid down, as a general principle, that, whenever a law is in its own nature a contract, and absolute rights have vested under it, a repeal of that law cannot divest those rights, or annihilate, or impair the title so acquired. A grant amounts to an extinguishment of the right of the grantor, and implies a contract not to reassert it.

§ 707. The cases above spoken of are cases, in which rights of property are concerned, and are {507} manifestly within the scope of the prohibition. But a question of a more nice and delicate nature has been also litigated; and that is, how far charters, granted by a state, are contracts within the meaning of the constitution. That the framers of the constitution did not intend to restrain the states in the regulation of their civil institutions, adopted for internal government, is admitted; and it has never been so construed. It has always been understood, that the contracts spoken of in the constitution were those, which respect property, or some other object of value, and which confer rights capable of being asserted in a court of justice. A charter is certainly in form and substance a contract; it is a grant of powers, rights, and privileges; and it usually gives a capacity to take, and to hold property. Where a charter creates a corporation, it emphatically confers this capacity; for it is an incident to a corporation, (unless prohibited,) to take, and to hold property. A charter granted to private persons for private purposes is within the terms, and the reason of the prohibition. It confers rights and privileges, upon the faith of which it is accepted. It imparts obligations and duties on their part, which they are not at liberty to disregard; and it implies a contract on the part of the legislature, that the rights and privileges, so granted, shall be enjoyed. It is wholly immaterial in such cases, whether the corporation take for their own private benefit, or for the benefit of other persons.

§ 708. A charter, then, being a contract within the scope of the constitution, the next consideration, which has arisen upon this important subject is, whether the principle applies to all charters, public, as well as private. Corporations are divisible into two sorts, such as are {508} strictly public, and such as are private.

Within the former denomination are included all corporations, created for public purposes only, such as cities, towns, parishes, and other public bodies. Within the latter denomination all corporations are included, which do not strictly belong to the former. There is no doubt, as to public corporations, which exist only for public purposes, that the legislature may change, modify, enlarge, and restrain them; with this limitation, however, that property, held by such corporations, shall still be secured for the use of those, for whom, and at whose expense it has been acquired. The principle may be stated in a more general form. If a charter be a mere grant of political power, if it create a civil institution, to be employed in the administration of the government, or, if the funds be public property alone, and the government alone be interested in the management of them, the legislative power over such charter is not restrained by the constitution, but remains unlimited. The reason is, that it is only a mode of exercising public rights and public powers, for the promotion of the general interest; and, therefore, it must, from its very nature, remain subject to the legislative will, so always that private rights are not infringed, or trenched upon.

§ 709. But an attempt has been made to press this principle much farther, and to exempt from the constitutional prohibition all charters, which, though granted to private persons, are in reality trusts for purposes and objects, which may, in a certain sense, be deemed public and general. The first great case, in which this doctrine became the subject of judicial examination and decision, was the case of Dartmouth College. The legislature of New-Hampshire had, without the {509} consent of the corporation, passed an act changing the organization of the original provincial charter of the college, and transferring all the rights, privileges, and franchises from the old charter trustees to new trustees, appointed under the act. The constitutionality of the act was contested, and after solemn argument, it was deliberately held by the Supreme Court, that the provincial charter was a contract within the meaning of the constitution, and that the amendatory act was utterly void, as impairing the obligation of that charter. The college was deemed, like other colleges of private foundation, to be a private eleemosynary institution, endowed, by its charter, with a capacity to take property, unconnected with the government. Its funds were bestowed upon the faith of the charter, and those funds consisted entirely of private donations. It is true, that the uses were in some sense public; that is, for the general benefit, and not for the mere benefit of the corporators; but this did not make the corporation a public corporation. It was a private institution for general charity. It was not distinguishable in principle from a private donation, vested in private trustees, for a public charity, or for a particular purpose of beneficence. And the state itself, if it had bestowed funds upon a charity of the same nature, could not resume those funds. In short, the charter was deemed a contract, to which the government, and the donors, and the trustees of the corporation, were all parties. It was for a valuable consideration; for the security and disposition of property, which, was entrusted to the corporation upon the faith of its terms; and the trustees acquired rights under it, which could not be taken away; for they came to them clothed with trusts, which they were obliged to perform, and could not constitutionally disregard. {510}

§ 710. It has also been made a question, whether a compact between two states is within the scope of the prohibition. And this also has been decided in the affirmative. The terms, compact and contract, are synonymous; and, when propositions are offered by one state, and agreed to, and accepted by another, they necessarily, constitute a contract between them. There is no difference, in reason or in law, to distinguish between contracts made by a state with individuals, and contracts made between states. Each ought to be equally inviolable.

§ 711. Before quitting this subject it may be proper to remark, that as the prohibition, respecting *ex post facto* laws, applies only to criminal cases; and the other is confined to impairing the obligation of contracts; there are many laws of a retrospective character, which may yet be constitutionally passed by the state legislatures, however unjust, oppressive, or impolitic they may be. Retrospective laws are, indeed, generally unjust; and, as has been forcibly said, neither accord with sound legislation, nor with the fundamental principles of the social compact. Still they are, with the exceptions above stated, left open to the states, according to their own constitutions of government; and become obligatory, if not prohibited by the latter.

§ 712. Whether, indeed, independently of the constitution of the United States, the nature of republican and free governments does not necessarily impose some restraints upon the legislative power, has been much discussed. It seems to be the general opinion, fortified by a strong current of judicial opinion, that since the American revolution no state government can be presumed to possess the transcendental sovereignty to take away vested rights of property; {511} to take the property of A. and transfer it to B. by a mere legislative act. A government can scarcely be deemed to be free, where the rights of property are left solely depen-dent upon a legislative body, without any restraint. The fundamental maxims of a free government seem to require, that the rights of personal liberty, and private property should be held sacred. At least, no court of justice, in this country, would be warranted in assuming, that any state legislature possessed a power to violate and disregard them; or that such a power, so repugnant to the common principles of justice and civil liberty, lurked under any general grant of legislative authority, or ought to be implied from any general expression of the will of the people, in the usual forms of the constitutional delegation of power. The people ought not to be presumed to part with rights, so vital to their security and well-being, without very strong, and positive declarations to that effect.

§ 713. The remaining prohibition in this clause is, that no state shall "grant any title of nobility." The reason of this prohibition is the same, as that, upon which the like prohibition to the government of the nation is founded. Indeed, it would be almost absurd to provide sedulously against such a power in the latter, if the states were still left free to exercise it. It has been emphatically said, that this is the corner-stone of a republican government; for there can be little danger, while a nobility is excluded, that the government will ever cease to be that of the people.

CHAPTER XXXV.

PROHIBITIONS ON THE STATES.

§ 714. THE next clause of the constitution is,

> "No state shall, without the consent of congress, lay any duty on tonnage; keep troops, or ships of war in time of peace; enter into any agreement or compact with another state, or with a foreign power; or engage in war, unless actually invaded, or in such imminent danger, as will not admit of delay."

§ 715. The first part of this clause, respecting laying a duty on tonnage, has been already considered. The remaining clauses have their origin in the same general policy and reasoning, which forbid any state from entering into any treaty, alliance, or confederation; and from granting letters of marque and reprisal. In regard to treaties, alliances, and confederations, they are wholly prohibited. But a state may, *with the consent of congress*, enter into an agreement, or compact with another state, or with a foreign power. What precise distinction is here intended to be taken between *treaties*, and *agreements*, and *compacts* is nowhere explained; and has never as yet been the subject of any exact judicial, or other examination.

§ 716. The other prohibitions in the clause respect the power of making war, which is appropriately confided to the national government. The setting on foot of an army, or navy by a state, in times of peace, might be a cause of jealousy between neighbouring states, and provoke the hostilities of foreign bordering nations. In other cases, as the protection of the whole {513} Union is confided to the national arm, and the national power, it is not fit, that any state should possess military means to overawe the Union, or to endanger the general safety. Still, a state may be so situated, that it may become indispensable to possess military forces, to resist an expected invasion, or insurrection. The danger may be too imminent for delay; and under such circumstances, a state will have a right to raise troops for its own safety, even without the consent of congress. After war is once begun, there is no doubt, that a state may, and indeed it ought to possess the power, to raise forces for its own defence; and its co-operation with the national forces may often be of great importance, to secure success and vigour in the operations of war. The prohibition is, therefore, wisely guarded by exceptions sufficient for the safety of the states, and not justly open to the objection of being dangerous to the Union.

§ 717. It has been already seen, and it will hereafter more fully appear, that there are implied, as well as express, prohibitions in the constitution upon the power of the states. Among the former, one clearly is, that no state can control, or abridge, or interfere with the exercise of any authority under the national government. And it may be added, that state laws, as, for instance, states statutes of limitations, and state insolvent laws, have no operation upon the rights or contracts of the United States.

§ 718. And here end our commentaries upon the first article of the constitution, embracing the organization and powers of the legislative department of the government, and the prohibitions upon the state and national governments. If we here pause, but for a {514} moment, we cannot but be struck with the reflection, how admirably this division and distribution of legislative powers between the state and national governments is adapted to preserve the liberty, and promote the happiness of the people of the United States. To the general government are assigned all those powers, which relate to the common interests of all the states, as comprising one confederated nation. While to each state is reserved all those powers, which may affect, or promote its own domestic interests, its peace, its prosperity, its policy, and its local institutions. At the same time, such limitations and restraints are imposed upon each government, as experience has demonstrated to be wise in order to control the public functionaries, or indispensable to secure the harmonious operations of the Union.

CHAPTER XXXVI.

EXECUTIVE DEPARTMENT — ORGANIZATION OF.

§ 719. IN the progress of our examination of the constitution, we are now arrived at the second article, which contains an enumeration of the organization and powers of the executive department. What is the best constitution for the executive department, and what are the powers, with which it should be entrusted, are problems among the most important, and probably the most difficult to be satisfactorily solved, of all, which are involved in the theory of free governments. No man, who has ever studied the subject with profound attention, has risen from the labour without an increased and almost overwhelming sense of its intricate relations, and perplexing doubts. No man, who has thoroughly read the human history, and especially the history of republics, but has been struck with the consciousness, how little has been hitherto done to establish a safe depositary of power in any hands; and how often in the hands of one, or a few, or many, of an hereditary monarch, or of an elective chief, the executive power has brought ruin upon the state, or sunk under the oppressive burthen of its own imbecility. Perhaps our own history, hitherto, does not establish, that we have wholly escaped all the dangers; and that here is not to be found, as has been the case in other nations, the vulnerable part of the republic.

§ 720. The first clause of the first section of the second article is as follows:

"The executive power shall be vested in a President of the United States {516} of America. He shall hold his office during the term of four years; and together with the Vice-President, chosen for the same term, be chosen as follows."

§ 721. In considering this clause, three practical questions are naturally suggested: First, whether there should be a distinct executive department; secondly, whether it should be composed of more than one person; and, thirdly, what should be the duration of office.

§ 722. Upon the first question, little need be said. All America have at length concurred in the propriety of establishing a distinct executive department. The principle is embraced in every state constitution; and it seems now to be assumed among us, as a fundamental maxim of government, that the legislative, executive, and judicial departments ought to be separate, and the powers of one ought not to be exercised by either of the others. The same maxim is found recognised in express terms in many of our state constitutions. It is hardly necessary to repeat, that where all these powers are united in the same hands, there is a real despotism, to the extent of their coercive exercise. Where, on the other hand, they exist together, and yet depend for their exercise upon the mere authority of recommendation, (as they did under the confederation,) they become at once imbecile and arbitrary, subservient to popular clamour, and incapable of steady action.

§ 723. Taking it, then, for granted, that there ought to be an executive department, the next consideration is, how it ought to be organized. It may be stated in general terms, that that organization is best, which will at once secure energy in the executive, and safety to the people. The notion, however, is not uncommon, and {517} occasionally finds ingenious advocates, that a vigorous executive is inconsistent with the genius of a republican government. It is difficult to find any sufficient grounds, on which to rest this notion; and those, which are usually stated, belong principally to that class of minds, which readily indulge in the belief of the general perfection, as well as perfectibility, of human nature, and deem the least possible quantity of power, with which government can subsist, to be the best. To those, who look abroad into the world, and attentively read the history of other nations, ancient and modern, far different lessons are taught with a severe truth and force. Those lessons instruct them, that energy in the executive is a leading character in the definition of a good government. It is essential to the protection of the community against foreign attacks. It is not less essential to the steady administration of the laws, to the protection of property against those irregular and high-handed combinations, which sometimes interrupt the ordinary course of justice, and to the security of liberty against the enterprises and assaults of ambition, of faction, and of anarchy. Every man the least conversant with Roman history knows, how often that republic was obliged to take refuge in the absolute power of a single man, under the formidable name of a dictator, as well against the intrigues of ambitious individuals, aspiring to tyranny, and the seditions of whole classes of the community, threatening the existence of the government, as against foreign enemies, menacing the destruction and conquest of the state. A feeble executive implies a feeble execution of the government. A feeble execution is but another phrase for a bad execution; and a government ill executed, whatever may be its theory, must, in practice, be a bad government. {518}

§ 724. The ingredients, which constitute energy in the executive, are unity, duration, an adequate provision for its support, and competent powers. The ingredients, which constitute safety in a republican form of government, are a due dependence on the people, and a due responsibility to the people.

§ 725. That unity is conducive to energy will scarcely be disputed. Decision, activity, secrecy, and despatch will generally characterise the proceedings of one man in a much more eminent degree, than the proceedings of a greater number; and in proportion, as the number is increased, these qualities will be diminished.

§ 726. This unity may be destroyed in two ways; first, by vesting the power in two or more magistrates of equal dignity; secondly, by vesting it ostensibly in one man, subject, however, in whole or in part, to the control and advice of a council. Of the first, the two consuls of Rome may serve, as an example in ancient times; and in modern times, the brief and hasty history of the three consuls of France, during its shortlived republic. Of the latter, several states in the Union furnish examples, as some of the colonies did before the revolution. Both these methods of destroying the unity of the executive have had their advocates. They are both liable to similar, if not to equal objections.

§ 727. But independent of any of the lights derived from history, it is obvious, that a division of the executive power between two or more persons must always tend to produce dissensions, and fluctuating councils. Whenever two or more persons are engaged in any common enterprise, or pursuit, there is always danger of difference of opinion. If it be a public trust, or office, {519} in which they are clothed with equal dignity and authority, there are peculiar dangers arising from personal emulation, or personal animosity; from superior talents on one side, encountering strong jealousies on the other; from pride of opinion on one side, and weak devotion to popular prejudices on the other; from the vanity of being the author of a plan, or resentment from some imagined slight by the approval of that of another. From these, and other causes of the like nature, the most bitter rivalries and dissensions often spring. Whenever these happen, they lessen the respectability, weaken the authority, and distract the plans and operations of those whom they divide. The wisest measures are thus often defeated, or delayed, even in the most critical moments. And what constitutes even a greater evil, the community often becomes split up into rival factions, adhering to the different persons, who compose the magistracy; and temporary animosities become thus the foundation of permanent calamities to the state. Indeed, the ruinous effects of rival factions in free states, struggling for power, have been the constant theme of reproach by the admirers of monarchy, and of regret by the lovers of republics. The Guelphs and the Ghibelins, the white and the black factions, have been immortalized in the history of the Italian states; and they are but an epitome of the same unvarying scenes in all other republics.

§ 728. Objections of a like nature apply, though in some respects with diminished force, to the scheme of an executive council, whose constitutional concurrence is rendered indispensable. An artful cabal in that council would be able to distract and enervate the whole public councils. And even without such a cabal, the mere diversity of views and opinions would almost {520} always mark the exercise of the executive authority with a spirit of habitual feebleness and dilatoriness, or a degrading inconsistency. But an objection, in a republican government quite as weighty, is, that such a participation in the executive power has a direct tendency to conceal faults, and destroy responsibility. Responsibility is of two kinds, to censure, and to punishment. The first is the more important of the two, especially in an elective government. Men in public trust will more often act in such a manner, as to render themselves unworthy of public favour, than to render themselves liable to legal punishment. But the multiplication of voices in the business of the executive renders it difficult to fix responsibility of either kind; for it is perpetually shifted from one to another. It often becomes impossible amidst mutual accusations to determine, upon whom the blame ought to rest. A sense of mutual impropriety sometimes induces the parties to resort to plausible pretexts to disguise their misconduct; or a dread of public responsibility to cover up, under the lead of some popular demagogue, their own faults and vacillations. Thus, a council often becomes the means, either of shifting off all effective responsibility from the chief magistrate, or of intrigues and oppositions, which destroy his power, and supplant his influence.

§ 729. The proper conclusion to be drawn from these considerations is, that plurality in the executive deprives the people of the two greatest securities for the faithful exercise of delegated power. First, it removes the just restraints of public opinion; and, secondly, it diminishes the means, as well as the power, of fixing responsibility for bad measures upon the real authors.

§ 730. The question as to the unity of the executive being disposed of, the next consideration is, as to {521} the proper duration of his term of office. It has been already mentioned, that duration in office constitutes an essential requisite to the energy of the executive department. This has relation to two objects; first, the personal firmness of the chief magistrate in the employment of his constitutional powers; and, secondly, the stability of the system of administration, which may have been adopted under his auspices. With regard to the first, it is evident, that the longer the duration in office, the greater will be the probability of obtaining so important an advantage. A man will naturally be interested in whatever he possesses, in proportion to the firmness or precariousness of the tenure, by which he holds it. He will be less attached to what he holds by a momentary, or uncertain title, than to what he enjoys by a title durable, or certain; and of course he will be willing to risk more for the one, than for the other. This remark is not less applicable to political privilege, or honour, or trust, than to any article of ordinary property. A chief magistrate, acting under the consciousness, that in a very short time he must lay down office, will be apt to feel himself too little interested in it to hazard any material censure or perplexity from an independent exercise of his powers, or from those ill humours, which are apt at times to prevail in all governments. If the case should be, that he might, notwithstanding, be re-eligible, his wishes, if he should have any for office, would combine with his fears to debase his fortitude, or weaken his integrity, or enhance his irresolution.

§ 731. The other ground, that of stability in the system of administration, is still more strikingly connected with duration in office. Few men will be found willing to commit themselves to a course of policy, whose wisdom {522} may be perfectly clear to themselves, if they cannot be permitted to complete, what they have begun. Of what consequence will it be to form the best plans of executive administration, if they are perpetually passing into new hands, before they are matured, or may be defeated at the moment, when their reasonableness and their value cannot be understood, or realized by the public? One of the truest rewards to patriots and statesmen is the consciousness, that the objections raised against their measures will disappear upon a fair trial; and that the gratitude and affection of the people will follow their labours, long after they have ceased to be actors upon the public scenes. But who will plant, when he can never reap? Who will sacrifice his present ease, and reputation, and popularity, and encounter obloquy and persecution, for systems, which he can neither mould so, as to ensure success, nor direct so, as to justify the experiment?

§ 732. The natural result of a change of the head of the government will be a change in the course of administration, as well as a change in the subordinate persons, who are to act as ministers to the executive. A successor in office will feel little sympathy with the plans of his predecessor. To undo, what has been done by the latter, will be supposed to give proofs of his own capacity; and will recommend him to all those, who were adversaries of the past administration; and perhaps will constitute the main grounds of elevating him to office. Personal pride, party principles, and an ambition for public distinction will thus naturally prompt him to an abandonment of old schemes, and combine with that love of novelty so congenial to all free states, to make every new administration the founders of new systems of government. {523}

§ 733. It is observable, that the period actually fixed is intermediate between the term of office of the senate, and that of the house of representatives. In the course of one presidential term, the house is, or may be, twice re-composed; and two-thirds of the senate changed, or re-elected. So far, as executive influence can be presumed to operate upon either branch of the legislature unfavourably to the rights of the people, the latter possess, in their elective franchise, ample means of redress. On the other hand, so far, as uniformity and stability in the administration of executive duties are desirable, they are in some measure secured by the more permanent tenure of office of the senate, which will check too hasty a departure from the old system, by a change of the executive, or representative branch of the government.

§ 734. Hitherto our experience has demonstrated, that the period is not found practically so long, as to create danger to the people, or so short, as to take away a reasonable independence and energy from the executive. Still it cannot be disguised, that sufficient time has scarcely yet elapsed to enable us to pronounce a decisive opinion upon the subject; since the executive has generally acted with a majority of the nation; and in critical times he has been sustained by the force of that majority in strong measures, and in times of more tranquillity, by the general moderation of the policy of his administration.

§ 735. Another question, connected with the duration of office of the president, was much agitated in the convention, and has often since been a topic of serious discussion; and that is, whether he should be re-eligible to office. In support of the opinion, that the president ought to be ineligible after one period of office, it {524} was urged, that the return of public officers into the mass of the common people, where they would feel the tone, which they had given to the administration of the laws, was the best security the public could have for their good behaviour. It would operate as a check upon the restlessness of ambition, and at the same time promote the independence of the executive. It would prevent him from a cringing subserviency to procure a re-election; or from a resort to corrupt intrigues for the maintenance of his power. And it was even added by some, whose imaginations were continually haunted by terrors of all sorts from the existence of any powers in the national government, that the re-eligibility of the executive would furnish an inducement to foreign governments to interfere in our elections, and would thus inflict upon us all the evils, which had desolated, and betrayed Poland.

§ 736. In opposition to these suggestions it was stated, that one ill effect of the exclusion would be a diminution of the inducements to good behaviour. There are few men, who would not feel much less zeal in the discharge of a duty, when they were conscious, that the advantage of the station, with which it is connected, must be relinquished at a determinate period, than, when they were permitted to entertain a hope of obtaining by their merit a continuance of it. A desire of reward is one of the strongest incentives of human conduct; and the best security for the fidelity of mankind is to make interest coincide with duty. Another ill effect of the exclusion would be the temptation to sordid views, to peculation, to the corrupt gratification of favourites, and in some instances to usurpation. A selfish or avaricious executive might, under such circumstances, be disposed to make the most he could for {525} himself, and his friends, and partisans, during his brief continuance in office, and to introduce a system of official patronage and emoluments, at war with the public interests, but well adapted to his own. If he were vain and ambitious, as well as avaricious and selfish, the transient possession of his honors would depress the former passions, and give new impulses to the latter. He would dread the loss of gain more, than the loss of fame; since the power must drop from his hands too soon to ensure any substantial addition to his reputation. On the other hand, his very ambition, as well as his avarice, might tempt him to usurpation; since the chance of impeachment would scarcely be worthy of thought; and the present power of serving friends might easily surround him with advocates for every stretch of authority, which would flatter his vanity, or administer to their necessities.

§ 737. Another ill effect of the exclusion would be, depriving the community of the advantage of the experience, gained by an able chief magistrate in the exercise of office. Experience is the parent of wisdom. And it would seem almost absurd to say, that it ought systematically to be excluded from the executive office. It would be equivalent to banishing merit from the public councils, because it had been tried. What could be more strange, than to declare, at the moment, when wisdom was acquired, that the possessor of it should no longer be enabled to use it for the very purposes, for which it was acquired?

§ 738. Another ill effect of the exclusion would be, that it might banish men from the station in certain emergencies, in which their services might be eminently useful, and indeed almost indispensable for the safety of their country. There is no nation, which has not, at {526} some period or other in its history, felt an absolute necessity of the services of particular men in particular stations; and, perhaps it is not too much to say, as vital to the preservation of its political existence. In a time of war, or other pressing calamity, the very confidence of a nation in the tried integrity and ability of a single man may of itself ensure a triumph. Is it wise to substitute in such cases inexperience for experience, and to set afloat public opinion, and change the settled course of administration? One should suppose, that it would be sufficient to possess the right to change a bad magistrate, without making the singular merit of a good one the very ground of excluding him from office.

§ 739. It was added, that the advantages proposed by the exclusion, (1.) greater independence in the executive, (2.) greater security to the people, were not well founded. The former could not be attained in any moderate degree, unless the exclusion was made perpetual. And, if it were, there might be many motives to induce the executive to sacrifice his independence to friends, to partisans, to selfish objects, and private gain, to the fear of enemies, and the desire to stand well with majorities. As to the latter supposed advantage, the exclusion would operate no check upon a man of irregular ambition, or corrupt principles, and against such men alone could the exclusion be important. In truth, such men would easily find means to cover up their usurpations and dishonesty under fair pretensions, and mean subserviency to popular prejudices. They would easily delude the people into a belief, that their acts were constitutional, because they were in harmony with the public wishes, or held out some specious, but false projects for the public good. {527}

§ 740. Still it must be confessed, that where the duration is for a considerable length of time, the right of re-election becomes less important, and perhaps less safe to the public. A president chosen for ten years might be made ineligible with far less impropriety, than one chosen for four years. And a president chosen for twenty years ought not to be again eligible, upon the plain ground, that by such a term of office his responsibility would be greatly diminished, and his means of influence and patronage immensely increased, so as to check in a great measure the just expression of public opinion, and the free exercise of the elective franchise.

§ 741. The remaining part of the clause respects the Vice-President. If such an officer was to be created, it is plain, that the duration of his office should be co-extensive with that of the president. Indeed, as we shall immediately see, the scheme of the government necessarily embraced it; for when it was decided, that two persons were to be voted for, as president, it was decided, that he, who had the greatest number of votes of the electors, after the person chosen as president, should be vice-president. The principal question, therefore, was, whether such an officer ought to be created.

§ 742. The reasons in favour of the appointment were as follows. It was seen, that a presiding officer must be chosen for the senate, where all the states were equally represented, and where an extreme jealousy might naturally be presumed to exist of the preponderating influence, of any one state. If a member of the senate were appointed, either the state would be deprived of one vote, or would enjoy a double vote in case of an equality of votes, or there would be a tie, {528} and no decision. Each of these alternatives was equally undesirable, and might lay the foundation of great practical inconveniences. An officer, therefore, chosen by the whole Union, would be a more suitable person to preside, and give a casting vote, since he would be more free, than any member of the senate, from local attachments, and local interests; and being the representative of the Union, would naturally be induced to consult the interests of all the states. Having only a casting vote, his influence could only operate exactly, when most beneficial; that is, to procure a decision. A still more important consideration is the necessity of providing some suitable person to perform the executive functions, when the president is unable to perform them, or is removed from office. Every reason, which recommends the mode of election of the president, prescribed by the constitution, with a view either to dignity, independence, or personal qualifications for office, applies with equal force to the appointment of his substitute. He is to perform the same duties, and to possess the same rights; and it seems, if not indispensable, at least peculiarly proper, that the choice of the person, who should succeed to the executive functions, should belong to the people at large, rather than to a select body chosen for another purpose. If (as was suggested) the president of the senate, chosen by that body, might have been designated, as the constitutional substitute; it is by no means certain, that he would either possess so high qualifications, or enjoy so much public confidence, or feel so much responsibility for his conduct, as a vice-president selected directly by and from the people. The president of the senate would generally be selected from other motives, and with reference to other {529} qualifications, than what ordinarily belonged to the executive department. His political opinions might be in marked contrast with those of a majority of the nation; and while he might possess a just influence in the senate, as a presiding officer, he might be deemed wholly unfit for the various duties of the chief executive magistrate. In addition to these considerations, there was no novelty in the appointment of such an officer for similar purposes in some of the state governments; and it therefore came recommended by experience, as a safe and useful arrangement, to guard the people against the inconveniences of an interregnum in the government, or a devolution of power upon an officer, who was not their choice, and might not possess their confidence.

§ 743. The next clause embraces the mode of election of the President and Vice-President; and although it has been repealed by an amendment of the constitution, (as will be hereafter shown,) yet it still deserves consideration, as a part of the original scheme, and more especially, as very grave doubts have been entertained, whether the substitute is not inferior to it in wisdom and convenience.

§ 744. The clause is as follows:

"Each state shalt appoint in such manner, as the legislature thereof may direct, a number of electors, equal to the whole number of senators and representatives, to which the state may be entitled in the congress. But no senator, or representative, or person holding an office of trust or profit under the United States, shall be appointed an elector.

The electors shall meet in their respective states, and vote by ballot for two persons, of whom one at least shall not be an inhabitant of the same state with {530} themselves. And they shall make a list of all the persons voted for, and of the number of votes for each; which list they shall sign and certify, and transmit, sealed, to the seat of the government of the United States, directed to the president of the senate. The president of the senate shall, in the presence of the senate and house of representatives, open all the certificates, and the votes shall then be counted. The person having the greatest number of votes shall be the president, if such number be a majority of the whole number of electors appointed; and if there be more than one, who have such majority, and have an equal number of votes, then the house of representatives shall immediately choose by ballot one of them for president; and if no person have a majority, then from the five highest on the list the said house shall in like manner choose the president. But in choosing the president, the votes shall be taken by states, the representation from each state having one vote; a quorum for this purpose shall consist of a member or members from two-thirds of the states, and a majority of all the states shall be necessary to a choice. In every case, after the choice of the president, the person having the greatest number of votes of the electors shall be the vice-president. But if there should remain two or more, who have equal votes, the senate shall choose from them by ballot the vice president."

§ 745. Assuming that the choice ought not to be confided to the national legislature, (which was at one time proposed, and after deliberation rejected,) there remained various other modes, by which it might be effected; by the people directly; by the state legislatures; or by electors, chosen by the one, or the other. The latter {531} mode was deemed most advisable; and the reasoning, by which it was supported, was to the following effect. The immediate election should be made by men, the most capable of analyzing the qualities adapted. to the station, and acting under circumstances favorable, to deliberation, and to a judicious combination of all the inducements, which ought to govern their choice. A small number of persons, selected by their fellow citizens from the general mass for this special object, would be most likely to possess the information, and discernment, and independence, essential for the proper discharge of the duty. It is also highly important to afford as little opportunity, as possible, to tumult and disorder. These evils are not unlikely to occur in the election of a chief magistrate directly by the people, considering the strong excitements and interests, which such an occasion may naturally be presumed to produce. The choice of a number of persons, to form an intermediate body of electors, would be far less apt to convulse the community with any extraordinary or violent movements, than the choice of one, who was himself the final object of the public wishes. And as the electors chosen in each state are to assemble, and vote in the state, in which they are chosen, this detached and divided situation would expose them much less to heats and ferments, which might be communicated from them to the people, than if they were all convened at one time in one place. The same circumstances would naturally lessen the dangers of cabal, intrigue, and corruption, especially, if congress should, as they undoubtedly would, prescribe the same day for the choice of the electors, and for giving their votes, throughout the United States. The scheme, indeed, presents every reasonable guard against these fatal evils to republican governments. {532} The appointment of the president is not made to depend upon any pre-existing body of men, who might be tampered with beforehand to prostitute their votes; but is delegated to persons chosen by the immediate act of the people, for that sole and temporary purpose. All those persons, who, from their situation, might be suspected of too great a devotion to the president in office, such as senators, and representatives, and other persons holding offices of trust or profit under the United States, are excluded from eligibility to the trust. Thus, without corrupting the body of the people, the immediate agents in the election may fairly be presumed to enter upon their duty free from any sinister bias. Their transitory existence and dispersed situation would present formidable obstacles to any corrupt combinations; and time, as well as means, would be wanting to accomplish, by bribery or intrigue of any considerable number, a betrayal of their duty. The president, too, who should be thus appointed, would be far more independent, than if chosen by a legislative body, to whom he might be expected to make correspondent sacrifices, to gratify their wishes, or reward their services. And on the other hand, being chosen by the voice of the people, his gratitude would take the natural direction, and sedulously guard their rights.

§ 746. The other parts of the scheme are no less entitled to commendation. The number of electors is equal to the number of senators and representatives of each state; thus giving to each state as virtual a representation in the electoral colleges, as that, which it enjoys in congress. The votes, when given, are to be transmitted to the seat of the national government, and there opened and counted in the presence of both houses. The person, having a majority of the whole {533} number of votes, is to be president. But, if no one of the candidates has such a majority, then the house of representatives, the popular branch of the government, is to elect, from the five highest on the list, the person, whom they may deem best qualified for the office, each state having one vote in the choice. The person, who has the next highest number of votes after the choice of president, is to be vice-president. But, if two or more shall have equal votes, the senate are to choose the vice-president. Thus, the ultimate functions are to be shared alternately by the senate and representatives in the organization of the executive department.

§ 747. The principal difficulty, which has been felt in the mode of election, is the constant tendency, from the number of candidates, to bring the choice into the house of representatives. This has already occurred twice in the progress of the government; and in the future there is every probability of a far more frequent occurrence. This was early foreseen; and, even in one of the state conventions, a most distinguished statesman, and one of the framers of the constitution, admitted, that it would probably be found impracticable to elect a president by the immediate suffrages of the people; and that in so large a country many persons would probably be voted for, and that the lowest of the five highest on the list might not have an inconsiderable number of votes. It cannot escape the discernment of any attentive observer, that if the house of representatives is often to choose a president, the choice will, or at least may, be influenced by many motives, independent of his merits and qualifications. There is danger, that intrigue and cabal may mix in the rivalries and strife. And the discords, if not the corruptions, generated by the occasion, will probably {534} long outlive the immediate choice, and scatter their pestilential influences over all the great interests of the country. One fearful crisis was passed in the choice of Mr. Jefferson over his competitor, Mr. Burr, in 1801; which threatened a dissolution of the government, and put the issue upon the tried patriotism of one or two individuals, who yielded from a sense of duty their preference of the candidate, generally supported by their friends.

§ 748. The issue of the contest of 1801 gave rise to an amendment of the constitution materially changing in several respects, the mode of election of president. In the first place it provides, that the ballots of the electors shall be separately given for president and vice-president, instead of one ballot for two persons, as president; that the vice-president (like the president) shall be chosen by a majority of the whole number of electors appointed; that the number of candidates, out of whom the selection of president is to be made by the house of representatives, shall be three, instead of five; that the senate shall choose the vice-president from the two highest numbers on the list; and that, if no choice is made of president before the fourth of March following, the vice-president shall act as president.

§ 749. The amendment was proposed in October, 1803, and was ratified before September, 1804, and is in the following terms.

"The electors shall meet in their respective states, and vote by ballot for president and vice-president, one of whom, at least, shall not be an inhabitant of the same state with themselves; they shall name in their ballots the person voted for as president, and in distinct ballots the, person voted for as vice-president; and they shall make distinct lists of all persons voted {535} for as president, and of all persons voted for as vice-president, and of the number of votes for each; which lists they shall sign and certify, and transmit sealed to the seat of government of the United States; directed to the president of the senate. The president of the senate shall, in the presence of the senate and house of representatives, open all the certificates, and the votes shall then be counted. The person having the greatest number of votes for president shall be the president, if such number be a majority of the whole number of electors appointed; and if no person have such majority, then from the persons having the highest numbers, not exceeding three, on the list of those voted for as president, the house of representatives shall choose immediately, by ballot, the president. But in choosing the president, the votes shall be taken by states, the representation from each state having one vote; a quorum for this purpose shall consist of a member, or members, from two-thirds of the states; and a majority of all the states shall be necessary to a choice. And if the house of representatives shall not choose a president, whenever the right of choice shall devolve upon them, before the fourth day of March next following, then the vice president shall act as president, as in the case of the death or other constitutional disability of the president.

"The person, having the greatest number of votes as vice-president, shall be the vice-president, if such number be a majority of the whole number of electors appointed; and if no person have a majority, then from the two highest numbers on the list, the senate shall choose the vice-president; a quorum for the purpose shall consist of two-thirds of the whole {536} number of senators, and a majority of the whole number shall be necessary to a choice.

"But no person, constitutionally ineligible to the office of president, shall be eligible to that of vice-president of the United States."

§ 750. This amendment has alternately been the subject of praise and blame, and experience alone can decide, whether the changes proposed by it are in all respects for the better, or the worse. In some respects it is a substantial improvement. In the first place, under the original mode, the senate was restrained from acting, until the house of representatives had made their selection, which, if parties ran high, might be considerably delayed. By the amendment the senate may proceed to a choice of the vice-president, immediately on ascertaining the returns of the votes. In the next place, under the original mode, if no choice should be made of a president by the house of representatives until after the expiration of the term of the preceding officer, there would be no person to perform the functions of the office, and an *interregnum* would ensue, and a total suspension of the powers of government. By the amendment, the new vice-president would in such case act as president. By the original mode, the senate are to elect the vice-president by ballot; by the amendment, the mode of choice is left open, so that it may be *vivâ voce*. Whether this be an improvement, or not, may be doubted.

§ 751. On the other hand, the amendment has certainly greatly diminished the dignity and importance of the office of vice-president. Though the duties remain the same, he is no longer a competitor for the presidency, and selected, as possessing equal merit, talents, and qualifications, with the other candidate. {537} As every state was originally compelled to vote for two candidates (one of whom did not belong to the state) for the same office, a choice was fairly given to all other states to select between them; thus excluding the absolute predominance of any local interest, or local partiality.

§ 752. It is obversable, that the language of the constitution is, that "each state shall appoint in such manner, as the legislature thereof may direct," the number of electors, to which the state is entitled. Under this authority the appointment of electors has been variously provided for by the state legislatures. In some states the legislature have directly chosen the electors by themselves; in others they have been chosen by the people by a general ticket throughout the whole state; and in others by the people in electoral districts, fixed by the legislature, a certain number of electors being apportioned to each district. No question has ever arisen, as to the constitutionality of either mode, except that of a direct choice by the legislature. But this, though often doubted by able and ingenious minds, has been firmly established in practice, ever since the adoption of the constitution, and does not now seem to admit of controversy, even if a suitable tribunal existed to adjudicate upon it. At present, in nearly all the states, the electors are chosen either by the people by a general ticket, or by the state legislature. The choice in districts has been gradually abandoned; and is now persevered in, but by two states. The inequality of this mode of choice, unless it should become general throughout the Union, is so obvious, that it is rather matter of surprise, that it should not long since have been wholly abandoned. In case of any party divisions in a state, it may neutralize {538} its whole vote, while all the other states give an unbroken electoral vote. On this account, and for the sake of uniformity, it has been thought desirable by many statesmen to have the constitution amended so, as to provide for an uniform mode of choice by the people.

§ 753. The remaining part of the clause, which precludes any senator, representative, or person holding an office of trust or profit under the United States, from being an elector, has been already alluded to, and requires little comment. The object is, to prevent persons, holding public stations under the government of the United States, from any direct influence in the choice of a president. In respect to persons holding office, it is reasonable to suppose, that their partialities would all be in favour of the re-election of the actual incumbent, and they might have strong inducements to exert their official influence in the electoral college. In respect to senators and representatives, there is this additional reason for excluding them, that they would be already committed by their vote in the electoral college; and thus, if there should be no election by the people, they could not bring to the final vote either the impartiality, or the independence, which the theory of the constitution contemplates.

§ 754. The next clause is,

"The congress may determine the time of choosing the electors, and the day, on which they shall give their votes, which day shall be the same throughout the United States."

§ 755. The propriety of this power would seem to be almost self-evident. Every reason of public policy and convenience seems in favour of a fixed time of giving the electoral votes, and that it should be the same throughout the Union. Such a measure is calculated to repress political intrigues and speculations, {539} by rendering a combination among the electoral colleges, as to their votes, if not utterly impracticable, at least very difficult; and thus secures the people against those ready expedients, which corruption never fails to employ to accomplish its designs. The arts of ambition are thus in some degree checked, and the independence of the electors against external influence in some degree secured. This power, however, did not escape objection in the general, or the state conventions, though the objection was not extensively insisted on.

§ 756. In pursuance of the authority given by this clause, congress, in 1792, passed an act declaring, that the electors shall be appointed in each state within thirty-four days, preceding the first Wednesday in December in every fourth year, succeeding the last election of president, according to the apportionment of representatives and senators then existing. The electors chosen are required to meet and give their votes on the said first Wednesday of December, at such place in each state, as shall be directed by the legislature thereof. They are then to make and sign three certificates of all the votes by them given, and to seal up the same, certifying on each, that a list of the votes of such state for president and vice-president is contained therein, and are to appoint a person to take charge of, and deliver, one of the same certificates to the president of the senate at the seat of government, before the first Wednesday of January then next ensuing; another of the certificates is to be forwarded forthwith by the post-office to the president of the senate at the seat of government; and the third is to be delivered to the judge of the district, in which the electors assembled. Other auxiliary provisions are made by the same act for the due transmission and preservation of the electoral votes, and {540} authenticating the appointment of the electors. The president's term of office is also declared to commence on the fourth day of March next succeeding the day, on which the votes of the electors shall be given.

§ 757. The next clause respects the qualifications of the president of the United States.

"No person, except a natural born citizen, or a citizen of the United States at the time of the adoption of this constitution, shall be eligible to the office of president. Neither shall any person be eligible to that office, who shall not have attained to the age of thirty-five years, and been fourteen years a resident within the United States."

§ 758. Considering the nature of the duties, the extent of the information, and the solid wisdom and experience required in the executive department, no one can reasonably doubt the propriety of some qualification of age. That, which has been selected, is the middle age of life, by which period the character and talents of individuals are generally known, and fully developed; and opportunities have usually been afforded for public service, and for experience in the public councils. The faculties of the mind, if they have not then attained to their highest maturity, are in full vigour, and hastening towards their ripest state. The judgment, acting upon large materials, has, by that time, attained a solid cast; and the principles, which form the character, and the integrity, which gives lustre to the virtues of life, must then, if ever, have acquired public confidence and approbation.

§ 759. It is indispensable, too, that the president should be a natural born citizen of the United States, or a citizen at the adoption of the constitution, and for fourteen years before his election. This permission of a {541} naturalized citizen to become president is an exception from the great fundamental policy of all governments, to exclude foreign influence from their executive councils and duties. It was doubtless introduced (for it has now become by lapse of time merely nominal, and will soon become wholly extinct) out of respect to those distinguished revolutionary patriots, who were born in a foreign land, and yet had entitled themselves to high honours in their adopted country. A positive exclusion of them from the office would have been unjust to their merits, and painful to their sensibilities.

But the general propriety of the exclusion of foreigners, in common cases, will scarcely be doubted by any sound statesman. It cuts off all chances for ambitious foreigners, who might otherwise be intriguing for the office; and interposes a barrier against those corrupt interferences of foreign governments in executive elections, which have inflicted the most serious evils upon the elective monarchies of Europe, Germany, Poland, and even the pontificate of Rome, are sad, but instructive examples of the enduring mischiefs arising from this source. A residence of fourteen years in the United States is also made an indispensable requisite for every candidate; so, that the people may have a full opportunity to know his character and merits, and that he may have mingled in the duties, and felt the interests, and understood the principles, and nourished the attachments, belonging to every citizen in a republican government. By "residence," in the constitution, is to be understood, not an absolute inhabitancy within the United States during the whole period; but such an inhabitancy, as includes a permanent domicil in the United States. No one has supposed, that a temporary absence abroad on public business, and especially {542} on an embassy to a foreign nation, would interrupt the residence of a citizen, so as to disqualify him for office. If the word were to be construed with such strictness, then a mere journey through any foreign adjacent territory for health, or for pleasure, or a commorancy there for a single day, would amount to a disqualification. Under such a construction a military or civil officer, who should have been in Canada during the late war on public business, would have lost his eligibility. The true sense of residence in the constitution is fixed domicil, or being out of the United States, and settled abroad for the purpose of general inhabitancy, *animo manendi*, and not for a mere temporary and fugitive purpose, *in transitu*.

§ 760. The next clause is,

> "In case of the removal of the president from office, or his death, resignation, or inability to discharge the duties of the said office, the same shall devolve on the vice-president. And the congress may by law provide for the case of removal, death, resignation, or inability of the president and vice-president, declaring what officer shall then act as president; and such officer shall act accordingly, until the disability be removed, or a president shall be elected."

§ 761. The original scheme of the constitution did not embrace (as has been already stated) the appointment of any vice-president; and in case of the death, resignation, or disability of the president, the president of the senate was to perform the duties of his office. The appointment of a vice-president was carried by a vote of ten states to one. Congress, in pursuance of the power here given, have provided, that in case of the removal, death, resignation, or inability of the president and vice-president, the president of the senate {543} *pro tempore*, and in case there shall be no president, then the speaker of the house of representatives for the time being shall act as president, until the disability be removed, or a president shall be elected.

§ 762. What shall be the proper proof of the resignation of the president, or vice-president, or of their refusal to accept the office, is left open by the constitution. But congress, with great wisdom and forecast, have provided, that it shall be by some instrument in writing, declaring the same, subscribed by the party, and delivered into the office of the secretary of state.

§ 763. The next clause is,

> "The president shall, at stated times, receive for his services a compensation, which shall neither be increased, nor diminished during the period, for which he shall have been elected, and he shall not receive within that period any other emolument from the United States, or any of them."

§ 764. It is obvious, that without due attention to the proper support of the president, the separation of the executive from the legislative department would be merely nominal and nugatory. The legislature, with a discretionary power over his salary and emolument, would soon render him obsequious to their will. A control over a man's living is in most cases a control over his actions. To act upon any other view of the subject would be to disregard the voice of experience, and the operation of the invariable principles, which regulate human conduct. There are, indeed, men, who could neither be distressed, nor won into a sacrifice of their duty. But this stern virtue is the growth of few soils; and it will be found, that the general lesson of human life is, that men obey their interests; {544} that they may be driven by poverty into base compliances, or tempted by largesses to a desertion of duty. Nor have there been wanting examples in our own country of the intimidation, or seduction of the executive, by the terrors, or allurements of the pecuniary arrangements of the legislative body. The wisdom of this clause can scarcely be too highly commended. The legislature, on the appointment of a president, is once for all to declare, what shall be the compensation for his services during the time, for which he shall have been elected. This done, they will have no power to alter it, either by increase or diminution, until a new period of service by a new election commences. They can neither weaken his fortitude by operating upon his necessities, nor corrupt his integrity by appealing to his avarice. Neither the Union, nor any of its members, will be at liberty to give, nor will he be at liberty to receive, any other emolument. He can, of course, have no pecuniary inducement to renounce, or desert, the independence intended for him by the constitution. The salary of the first president was fixed by congress at the sum of twenty-five thousand dollars per annum, and of the vice-president, at five thousand dollars. And to prevent any difficulty, as to future presidents, congress, by a permanent act, a few years afterwards established the same compensation for all future presidents and vice-presidents. So that, unless some great changes should intervene, the independence of the executive is permanently secured by an adequate maintenance; and it can scarcely be diminished, unless some future executive shall basely betray his duty to his successor.

§ 765. The next clause is,

> "Before he enters on the execution of his office, he shall take the following oath or affirmation: I do solemnly swear, (or affirm,) {545} that I will faithfully execute the office of President of the United States, and will, to the best of my ability, preserve, protect, and defend the constitution of the United States."

§ 765. There is little need of commentary upon this clause. No man can well doubt the propriety of placing a president of the United States under the most solemn obligations to preserve, protect, and defend the constitution. It is a suitable pledge of his fidelity and responsibility to his country; and creates upon his conscience a deep sense of duty, by an appeal, at once in the presence of God and man, to the most sacred and solemn sanctions, which can operate upon the human mind.

CHAPTER XXXVII.

EXECUTIVE — POWERS AND DUTIES.

§ 766. HAVING thus considered the manner, in which the executive department is organized, the next inquiry is, as to the powers, with which it is entrusted. These, and the corresponding duties, are enumerated in the second and third sections of the second article of the constitution.

§ 767. The first clause of the second section is,

> "The President shall be commander-in-chief of the army and navy of the United States, and of the militia of the several states, when called into the actual service of the United States. He may require the opinion in writing of the principal officer in each of the executive departments, upon any subject relating to the duties of their respective offices. And he shall have power to grant reprieves and pardons for offences against the United States, except in cases of impeachment."

§ 768. The command and application of the public force, to execute the laws, to maintain peace, and to resist foreign invasion, are powers so obviously of an executive nature, and require the exercise of qualities so peculiarly adapted to this department, that a well-organized government can scarcely exist, when they are taken away from it. Of all the cases and concerns of government, the direction of war most peculiarly demands those qualities, which distinguish the exercise of power by a single hand. Unity of plan, promptitude, activity, and decision, are indispensable to success; and these can scarcely exist, except {547} when a single magistrate is entrusted exclusively with the power. Even the coupling of the authority of an executive council with him, in the exercise of such powers, enfeebles the system, divides the responsibility, and not unfrequently defeats every energetic measure. Timidity, indecision, obstinacy, and pride of opinion, must mingle in all such councils, and infuse a torpor and sluggishness, destructive of all military operations. Indeed, there would seem to be little reason to enforce the propriety of giving this power to the executive department, (whatever may be its actual organization,) since it is in exact coincidence with the provisions of our state constitutions; and therefore seems to be universally deemed safe, if not vital to the system.

§ 769. The next provision is, as to the power of the president, to require the opinions in writing of the heads of the executive departments. It has been remarked, that this is a mere redundancy, and the right would result from the very nature of the office. Still, it is not without use, as it imposes a more strict responsibility, and recognises a public duty of high importance and value in critical times. It has, in the progress of the government, been repeatedly acted upon; but by no president with more wisdom and propriety, than by President Washington.

§ 770. The next power is, "to grant reprieves and pardons." It has been said by the marquis Beccaria, that the power of pardon does not exist under a perfect administration of the laws; and that the admission of the power is a tacit acknowledgment of the infirmity of the course of justice. But if this be a defect at all, it arises from the infirmity of human nature generally; and in this view, is up more objectionable, than any {548} other power of government; for every such power, in some sort, arises from human infirmity. But if it be meant, that it is an imperfection in human legislation to admit the power of pardon in any case, the proposition may well be denied, and some proof, at least, be required of its sober reality. The common argument is, that where punishments are mild, they ought to be certain; and that the clemency of the chief magistrate is a tacit disapprobation of the laws. But surely no man in his senses will contend, that any system of laws can provide for every possible shade of guilt a proportionate degree of punishment. The most, that ever has been, and ever can be done, is to provide for the punishment of crimes by some general rules, and within some general limitations. The total exclusion of all power of pardon would necessarily introduce a very dangerous power in judges and juries, of following the spirit, rather than the letter of the laws; or, out of humanity, of suffering real offenders wholly to escape punishment; or else, it must be holden, (what no man will seriously avow,) that the situation and circumstances of the offender, though they alter not the essence of the offence, ought to make no distinction in the punishment. There are not only various gradations of guilt in the commission of the same crime, which are not susceptible of any previous enumeration and definition; but the proofs must, in many cases, be imperfect in their own nature, not only as to the actual commission of the offence, but also as to the aggravating or mitigating circumstances. In many cases, convictions must be founded upon presumptions and probabilities. Would it not be at once unjust and unreasonable to exclude all means of mitigating punishment, when subsequent inquiries should demonstrate, {549} that the accusation was wholly unfounded, or the crime greatly diminished in point of atrocity and aggravation, from what the evidence at the trial seemed to establish? A power to pardon seems, indeed, indispensable under the most common administration of the law by human tribunals; since, otherwise, men would sometimes fall a prey to the vindictiveness of accusers, the inaccuracy of testimony, and the fallibility of jurors and courts. Besides; the law may be broken, and yet the offender be placed in such circumstances, that he will stand, in a great measure, and perhaps wholly, excused in moral and general justice, though not in the strictness of the law. What then is to be done? Is he to be acquitted against the law; or convicted, and to suffer punishment infinitely beyond his deserts? If an arbitrary power is to be given to meet such cases, where can it be so properly lodged, as in the executive department?

§ 771. So far from the power of pardon being incompatible with the fundamental principles of a republic, (as has sometimes been stated) it may be boldly asserted to be peculiarly appropriate, and safe in all free states; because the power can there be guarded by a just responsibility for its exercise. Little room will be left for favouritism, personal caprice, or personal resentment. If the power should ever be abused, it would be far less likely to occur in opposition, than in obedience to the will of the people. The danger is not, that in republics the victims of the law will too often escape punishment by a pardon; but that the power will not be sufficiently exerted in cases, where public feeling accompanies the prosecution, and assigns the ultimate doom to persons, who have been convicted upon slender testimony, or popular suspicions.

§ 772. The power to pardon, then, being a fit one to be entrusted to all governments, humanity and sound policy dictate, that this benign prerogative should be, as little as possible, fettered, or embarrassed. The criminal code of every country partakes so much of necessary severity, that, without an easy access to exceptions in favour of unfortunate guilt, justice would assume an aspect too sanguinary and cruel. The only question is, in what department of the government it can be most safely lodged; and that must principally refer to the executive, or legislative department. The reasoning in favour of vesting it in the executive department may be thus stated. A sense of responsibility is always strongest in proportion, as it is undivided. A single person would, therefore, be most ready to attend to the force of those motives, which might plead for a mitigation of the rigour of the law; and the least apt to yield to considerations, which were calculated to shelter a fit object of its vengeance. The consciousness, that the life, or happiness of an offender was exclusively within his discretion, would inspire scrupulousness and caution; and the dread of being accused of weakness, or connivance, would beget circumspection of a different sort. On the other hand, as men generally derive confidence from numbers, a large assembly might naturally encourage each other in acts of obduracy, as no one would feel much apprehension of public censure. A public body, too, ordinarily engaged in other duties, would be little apt to sift cases of this sort thoroughly to the bottom, and would be disposed to yield to the solicitations, or be guided by the prejudices of a few; and thus shelter their own acts of yielding too much, or too little, under the common apology of ignorance {551} or confidence. A single magistrate would be compelled to search, and act upon his own responsibility; and therefore would be at once a more enlightened dispenser of mercy, and a more firm administrator of public justice.

§ 773. There is an exception to the power of pardon, that it shall not extend to cases of impeachment, which takes from the president every temptation to abuse it in cases of political and official offences by persons in the public service. The power of impeachment will generally be applied to persons holding high offices under the government; and it is of great consequence, that the president should not have the power of preventing a thorough investigation of their conduct, or of securing them against the disgrace of a public conviction by impeachment, if they should deserve it. The constitution has, therefore, wisely interposed this check upon his power, so that he cannot, by any corrupt coalition with favourites, or dependents in high offices, screen them from punishment.

§ 774. It would seem to result from the principle, on which the power of each branch of the legislature to punish for contempts is founded, that the executive authority cannot interpose between them and the offender. The main object is to secure a purity, independence, and ability of the legislature, adequate to the discharge of all their duties. If they can be overawed by force, or corrupted by largesses, or interrupted in their proceedings by violence, without the means of self-protection, it is obvious, that they will soon be found incapable of legislating with wisdom or independence. If the executive should possess the power of pardoning any such offender, they would be wholly dependent upon his good will and pleasure for the exexcise {552} of their own powers. Thus, in effect, the rights of the people entrusted to them would be placed in perpetual jeopardy. The constitution is silent in respect to the right of granting pardons in such cases, as it is in respect to the jurisdiction to punish for contempts. The latter arises by implication; and to make it effectual the former is excluded by implication.

§ 775. Subject to these exceptions, (and perhaps there may be others of a like nature standing upon special grounds,) the power of pardon is general and unqualified, reaching from the highest to the lowest offences. The power of remission of fines, penalties, and forfeitures is also included in it; and may in the last resort be exercised by the executive, although it is in many cases by our laws confided to the treasury department. No law can abridge the constitutional powers of the executive department, or interrupt its right to interpose by pardon in such cases.

§ 776. The next clause is:

"He (the president) shall have power, by and with the advice and consent of the senate, to make treaties, provided two thirds of the senators present concur. And he shall nominate, and, by and with the advice and consent of the senate, shall appoint, ambassadors, other public ministers, and consuls, judges of the Supreme Court, and all other officers of the United States, whose appointments are not herein otherwise provided for, and which shall be established by law. But the congress may by law vest the appointment of such inferior officers, as they think proper, in the president alone, in the courts of law, or in the heads of departments."

§ 777. The power "to make treaties" is by the constitution general; and of course it embraces all {553} sorts of treaties, for peace or war; for commerce or territory; for alliance or succours; for indemnity for injuries or payment of debts; for the recognition or enforcement of principles of public law; and for any other purposes, which the policy or interests of independent sovereigns may dictate in their intercourse with each other. But, though the power is thus general and unrestricted, it is not to be so construed, as to destroy the fundamental laws of the state. A power given by the constitution cannot be construed to authorize a destruction of other powers given in the same instrument. It must be construed, therefore, in subordination to it; and cannot supersede, or interfere with any other of its fundamental provisions. Each is equally obligatory, and of paramount authority within its scope; and no one embraces a right to annihilate any other. A treaty to change the organization of the government, to annihilate its sovereignty, to overturn its republican form, or to deprive it of its constitutional powers, would be void; because it would destroy, what it was designed merely to fulfil, the will of the people. Whether there are any other restrictions, necessarily growing out of the structure of the government, will remain to be considered, whenever the exigency shall arise.

§ 778. The power of making treaties is indispensable to the due exercise of national sovereignty, and very important, especially as it relates to war, peace, and commerce. That it should belong to the national government would seem to be irresistibly established by every argument deduced from experience, from public policy, and a close survey of the objects of government. It is difficult to circumscribe the power within any definite limits, applicable to all times and {554} exigencies, without impairing its efficacy, or defeating its purposes. The constitution has, therefore, made it general and unqualified. This very circumstance, however, renders it highly important, that it should be delegated in such a mode, and with such precautions, as will afford the highest security, that it will be exercised by men the best qualified for the purpose, and in the manner most conducive to the public good. With such views, the question was naturally presented in the convention, to what body shall it be delegated? It might be delegated to congress generally, as it was under the confederation, exclusive of the president, or in conjunction with him. It might be delegated to either branch of the legislature, exclusive of, or in conjunction with him. Or it might be exclusively delegated to the president.

§ 779. In the formation of treaties, secrecy and immediate despatch are generally requisite, and sometimes absolutely indispensable. Intelligence may often be obtained, and measures matured in secrecy, which could never be done, unless in the faith and confidence of profound secrecy. No man at all acquainted with diplomacy, but must have felt, that the success of negotiations as often depends upon their being unknown by the public, as upon their justice or their policy. Men will assume responsibility in private, and communicate information, and express opinions, which they would feel the greatest repugnance publicly to avow; and measures may be defeated by the intrigues and management of foreign powers, if they suspect them to be in progress, and understand their precise nature and extent. In this view the executive department is a far better depositary of the power, than congress would be. The delays incident to a large {555} assembly; the differences of opinion; the time consumed in debate; and the utter impossibility of secrecy, all combine to render them unfitted for the purposes of diplomacy. And our own experience during the confederation abundantly demonstrated all the evils, which the theory would lead us to expect. Besides; there are tides in national affairs, as well as in the affairs of private life. To discern and profit by them is the part of true political wisdom; and the loss of a week, or even of a day, may sometimes change the whole aspect of affairs, and render negotiations wholly nugatory, or indecisive. The loss of a battle, the death of a prince, the removal of a minister, the pressure or removal of fiscal embarrassments at the moment, and other circumstances, may change the whole posture of affairs, and ensure success, or defeat the best concerted project. The executive, having a constant eye upon foreign affairs, can promptly meet, and even anticipate such emergencies, and avail himself of all the advantages accruing from them; while a large assembly would be coldly deliberating on the chances of success, and the policy of opening negotiations. It is manifest, then, that congress would not be a suitable depositary of the power.

§ 780. The same difficulties would occur from confiding it exclusively to either branch of congress. Each is too numerous for prompt and immediate action, and secrecy. The matters in negotiations, which usually require these qualities in the highest degree, are the preparatory and auxiliary measures; and which are to be seized upon, as it were, in an instant. The president could easily arrange them. But the house, or the senate, if in session, could not act, until after great delays; and in the recess could not act at all. To {556} have entrusted the power to either would have been to relinquish the benefits of the constitutional agency of the president in the conduct of foreign negotiations. It is true, that the branch so entrusted might have the option to employ the president in that capacity; but they would also have the option of refraining from it; and it cannot be disguised, that pique, or cabal, or personal or political hostility, might induce them to keep their pursuits at a distance from his inspection and participation. Nor could it be expected, that the president, as a mere ministerial agent of such branch, would enjoy the confidence and respect of foreign powers to the same extent, as he would, as the constitutional representative of the nation itself; and his interposition would of course have less efficacy and weight.

§ 781. On the other hand, considering the delicacy and extent of the power, it is too much to expect, that a free people would confide to a single magistrate, however respectable, the sole authority to act conclusively, as well as exclusively upon the subject of treaties. In England, the power to make treaties is exclusively vested in the crown. But however proper it may be in a monarchy, there is no American statesman, but must feel, that such a prerogative in an American president would be inexpedient and dangerous. It would be inconsistent with that wholesome jealousy, which all republics ought to cherish of all depositaries of power; and which, experience teaches us, is the best security against the abuse of it. The check, which acts upon the mind from the consideration, that what is done is but preliminary, and requires the assent of other independent minds to give it a legal conclusiveness, is a restraint, which awakens caution, and compels to deliberation. {557}

§ 782. The plan of the constitution is happily adapted to attain all just objects in relation to foreign negotiations. While it confides the power to the executive department, it guards it from serious abuse by placing it under the ultimate superintendence of a select body of high character and high responsibility. It is indeed clear to a demonstration, that this joint possession of the power affords a greater security for its just exercise, than the separate possession of it by either. The president is the immediate author and finisher of all treaties; and all the advantages, which can be derived from talents, information, integrity, and deliberate investigation on the one hand, and from secrecy and despatch on the other, are thus combined in the system. But no treaty, so formed, becomes binding upon the country, unless it receives the deliberate assent of two thirds of the senate. In that body all the states are equally represented; and, from the nature of the appointment and duration of the office, it may fairly be presumed at all times to contain a very large portion of talents, experience, political wisdom, and sincere patriotism, a spirit of liberality, and a deep devotion to all the substantial interests of the country. The constitutional check of requiring two thirds to confirm a treaty is, of itself, a sufficient guaranty against any wanton sacrifice of private rights, or any betrayal of public privileges. To suppose otherwise would be to suppose, that a representative republican government was a mere phantom; that the state legislatures were incapable, or unwilling to choose senators possessing due qualifications; and that the people would voluntarily confide power to those, who were ready to promote their ruin, and endanger, or destroy their liberties. Without supposing a case of utter indifference, or utter {558} corruption in the people, it would be impossible, that the senate should be so constituted at any time, as that the honour and interests of the country would not be safe in their hands. When such an indifference, or corruption shall have arrived, it will be in vain to prescribe any remedy; for the constitution will have crumbled into ruins, or have become a mere shadow, about which it would be absurd to disquiet ourselves.

§ 783. Some doubts appear to have been entertained in the early stages of the government, as to the correct exposition of the constitution in regard to the agency of the senate in the formation of treaties. The question was, whether the agency of the senate was admissible previous to the negotiation, so as to advise on the instructions to be given to the ministers; or was limited to the exercise of the power of advice and consent, after the treaty was formed; or whether the president possessed an option to adopt one mode, or the other, as his judgment might direct. The practical exposition assumed on the first occasion, which seems to have oc- curred in President Washington's administration, was, that the option belonged to the executive to adopt either mode, and the senate might advise before, as well as after, the formation of a treaty. Since that period, the senate have been rarely, if ever, consulted, until after a treaty has been completed, and laid before them for ratification. When so laid before the senate, that body is in the habit of deliberat- ing upon it, as, indeed, it does on all *executive* business, in secret, and with closed doors. The senate may wholly reject the treaty, or advise and consent to a ratifica- tion of part of the articles, rejecting others, or recommend additional or explana- tory articles. In the event of a partial ratification, the treaty does not {559} become the law of the land, until the president and the foreign sovereign have each as- sented to the modifications proposed by the senate. But, although the president may ask the advice and consent of the senate to a treaty, he is not absolutely bound by it; for he may, after it is given, still constitutionally refuse to ratify it. Such an occurrence will probably be rare, because the president will scarcely incline to lay a treaty before the senate, which he is not disposed to ratify.

§ 784. The next part of the clause respects appointments to office. The presi- dent is to nominate, and by and with the advice and consent of the senate, to ap- point ambassadors, other public ministers, and consuls, judges of the Supreme Court, and other officers, whose appointments are not otherwise provided for.

§ 785. Under the confederation, an exclusive power was given to congress of "sending and receiving ambassadors." The term "ambassador," strictly construed, (as would seem to be required by the second article of that instrument,) compre- hends the highest grade only of public ministers; and excludes those grades, which the United States would be most likely to prefer, whenever foreign embassies may be necessary. But under no latitude of construction could the term, "ambassa- dors," comprehend consuls. Yet it was found necessary by congress to employ the inferior grades of ministers, and to send and receive consuls. It is true, that the mutual appointment of consuls might have been provided for by treaty; and where no treaty existed, congress might perhaps have had the authority under the ninth article of the confederation, which conferred a general authority to ap- point officers, for managing the general affairs of the United {560} States. But the admission of foreign consuls into the United States, when not stipulated for by treaty, was no where provided for. The whole subject was full of embarrassment and constitutional doubts; and the provision in the constitution, extending the appointment to other public ministers and consuls, as well as to ambassadors, is a decided improvement upon the confederation.

§ 786. The mode of appointment to office, pointed out by the constitution, seems entitled to peculiar commendation. There are several ways, in which in ordinary cases the power may be vested. It may be confided to congress; or to one branch of the legislature or to the executive alone; or to the executive in concurrence with any selected branch. The exercise of it by the people at large will readily be admitted by all considerate statesmen to be impracticable; and therefore need not be examined. The suggestions, already made upon the treaty-making power, and the inconveniences of vesting it in congress, apply with great force to that of vesting the power of appointment to office in the same body. It would enable candidates for office to introduce all sorts of intrigues, and coalitions into congress; and not only distract their attention from their proper legislative duties; but probably in a very high degree influence all legislative measures. A new source of division and corruption would thus be infused into the public councils, stimulated by private interests, and pressed by personal solicitations. What would be to be done, in case the senate and house should disagree in an appointment? Are they to vote in convention, or at distinct bodies? There would be practical difficulties attending both courses; and experience has not justified {561} the belief, that either would conduce to good appointments, or to due responsibility.

§ 787. The same reasoning would apply to vesting the power exclusively in either branch of the legislature. It would make the patronage of the government subservient to private interests, and bring into suspicion the motives and conduct of members of the appointing body. There would be great danger, that the elections at the polls might be materially influenced by this power, to confer, or to withhold favours of this sort.

§ 788. Those, who are accustomed to profound reflection upon the human character and human experience, will readily adopt the opinion, that one man of discernment is better fitted to analyze and estimate the peculiar qualities, adapted to particular offices, than any body of men of equal, or even of superior discernment. His sole and undivided responsibility will naturally beget a livelier sense of duty, and a more exact regard to reputation. He will inquire with more earnestness, and decide with more impartiality. He will have fewer personal attachments to gratify, than a body of men; and will be less liable to be misled by his private friendships and affections; or, at all events, his conduct will be more open to scrutiny, and less liable to be misunderstood. If he ventures upon a system of favoritism, he will not escape censure, and can scarcely avoid public detection and disgrace. But in a public body appointments will be materially influenced by party attachments and dislikes; by private animosities, and antipathies, and partialities; and will be generally founded in compromises, having little to do with the merit of candidates, and much to do with the selfish interests of individuals and cabals. They will be too much governed by local, {562} or sectional, or party arrangements. A president, chosen from the nation at large, may well be presumed to possess high intelligence, integrity, and sense of character. He will be compelled to consult public opinion in the most important appointments; and must be interested to vindicate the propriety of his appointments by selections from those, whose qualifications are unquestioned, and unquestionable. If he should act otherwise, and surrender the public patronage into the hands of profligate men, or low adventurers, it will be impossible for him long to retain public favour. Nothing, no, not even the whole influence of party, could long screen him from the just indignation of the people. Though slow, the ultimate award of popular opinion would stamp upon his conduct its merited infamy. No president, however weak, or credulous, (if such a person could ever under any conjuncture of circumstances obtain the office,) would fail to perceive, or to act upon admonitions of this sort. At all events, he would be less likely to disregard them, than a large body of men, who would share the responsibility, and encourage each other in the division of the patronage of the government.

§ 789. But, though these general considerations might easily reconcile us to the choice of vesting the power of appointment exclusively in the president, in preference to the senate, or house of representatives alone; yet the patronage of the government, and the appointments to office are too important to the public welfare, not to induce great hesitation in vesting them exclusively in the president. The power may be abused; and, assuredly, it will be abused, except in the hands of an executive of great firmness, independence, integrity, and public spirit. It should never {563} be forgotten, that in a republican government offices are established, and are to be filled, not to gratify private interests and private attachments; not as a means of corrupt influence, or individual profit; not for cringing favourites, or court sycophants; but for purposes of the highest public good; to give dignity, strength, purity, and energy to the administration of the laws. It would not, therefore, be a wise course to omit any precaution, which, at the same time, that it should give to the president a power over the appointments of those, who are in conjunction with himself to execute the laws, should also interpose a salutary check upon its abuse, acting by way of preventive, as well as of remedy.

§ 790. Happily, this difficult task has been achieved by the constitution. The president is to nominate, and thereby has the sole power to select for office; but his nomination cannot confer office, unless approved by a majority of the senate. His responsibility and theirs is thus complete, and distinct. He can never be compelled to yield to their appointment of a man unfit for office; and, on the other hand, they may withhold their advice and consent from any candidate, who in their judgment does not possess due qualifications for office. Thus, no serious abuse of the power can take place without the co-operation of two co-ordinate branches, of the government, acting in distinct spheres; and, if there Should be any improper concession on either side, it is obvious, that from the structure and changes, incident to each department, the evil cannot long endure, and will be remedied, as it should be, by the elective franchise. The consciousness of this check will make the president more circumspect, and deliberate in his nominations {564} for office. He will feel, that, in case of a disagreement of opinion with the senate, his principal vindication must depend upon the unexceptionable character of his nomination. And in case of a rejection, the most, that can be said, is, that he had not his first choice. He will still have a wide range of selection; and his responsibility to present another candidate, entirely qualified for the office, will be complete and unquestionable.

§ 791. Nor is it to be expected, that the senate will ordinarily fail of ratifying the appointment of a suitable person for the office. Independent of the desire, which such a body may naturally be presumed to feel, of having offices suitably filled, (when they cannot make the appointment themselves,) there will be a responsibility to public opinion for a rejection, which will overcome all common private wishes. Cases, indeed, may be imagined, in which the senate from party motives, from a spirit of opposition, and eves from motives of a more private nature, may reject at nomination absolutely unexceptionable. But such occurrences will be rare. The more common error, (if there shall be any) will be too great a facility to yield to the executive wishes, as a means of personal, or popular favour. A president will rarely want means, if he shall choose to use them, to induce some members of such a body to aid his nominations; since a correspondent influence may be fairly presumed to exist, to gratify such persons in other recommendations for office, and thus to make them indirectly the dispensers of local patronage. It will be, principally, with regard to high officers, such as ambassadors, judges, heads of departments, and other appointments of great public importance, that the senate will interpose {565} to prevent an unsuitable choice. Their own dignity, and sense of character, their duty to their country, and their very title to office, will be materially dependent upon a firm discharge of their duty on such occasions.

§ 792. Perhaps the duties of the president, in the discharge of this most delicate and important duty of his office, were never better summed up, than in the following language of a distinguished commentator. "A proper selection or appointment of subordinate officers is one of the strongest marks of a powerful mind. It is a duty of the president to acquire, as far as possible, an intimate knowledge of the capacities and characters of his fellow citizens; to disregard the importunities of friends; the hints or menaces of enemies; the bias of party; and the hope of popularity. The latter is sometimes the refuge of feeble-minded men; but its gleam is transient, if it is obtained by a dereliction of honest duty and sound discretion. Popular favour is best secured by carefully ascertaining, and strictly pursuing the true interests of the people. The president himself is elected on the supposition, that he is the most capable citizen to understand, and promote those interests; and in every appointment he ought to consider himself as executing a public trust of the same nature. Neither should the fear of giving offence to the public, or pain to the individual, deter him from the immediate exercise of his power of removal, on proof of incapacity, or infidelity in the subordinate officer. The public, uninformed of the necessity, may be surprised, and at first dissatisfied; but public approbation ultimately accompanies the fearless and upright discharge of duty."

§ 793. The other part of the clause, while it leaves {566} to the president the appointment to all offices, not otherwise provided for, enables congress to vest the appointment of such inferior officers, as they may think proper, in the president, in the courts of law, or in the heads of departments. The propriety of this discretionary power in congress, to some extent, cannot well be questioned. If any discretion should be allowed, its limits could hardly admit of being exactly defined; and it might fairly be left to congress to act according to the lights of experience. It is difficult to foresee, or to provide for all the combinations of circumstances, which might vary the right to appoint in such cases. In one age the appointment might be most proper in the president; and in another age, in a department.

§ 794. In the practical course of the government, there does not seem to have been any exact line drawn, who are, and who are not, to be deemed *inferior* officers in the sense of the constitution, whose appointment does not necessarily require the concurrence of the senate. In many cases of appointments, congress have required the concurrence of the senate, where, perhaps, it might not be easy to say, that it was required by the constitution. The power of congress has been exerted to a great extent, under this clause, in favour of the executive department. The president is by law invested, either solely, or with the senate, with the appointment of all military and naval officers, and of the most important civil officers, and especially of those connected with the administration of justice, the collection of the revenue, and the supplies and expenditures of the nation. The courts of the Union possess the narrow prerogative of appointing their own clerk, and reporter, without any farther patronage. The heads of department are, in like manner, generally entitled {567} to the appointment of the clerks in their respective offices. But the great anomaly in the system is the enormous patronage of the postmaster general, who is invested with the sole and exclusive authority to appoint, and remove all deputy post-masters; and whose power and influence have thus, by slow degrees, accumulated, until it is, perhaps, not too much to say, that it rivals, if it does not exceed, in value and extent, that of the president himself. How long a power so vast, and so accumulating, shall remain without any check on the part of any other branch of the government, is a question for statesmen, and not for jurists. But it cannot be disguised, that it will be idle to impose constitutional restraints upon high executive appointments, if this power, which pervades every village of the republic, and exerts an irresistible, though silent, influence in the direct shape of office, or in the no less inviting form of lucrative contracts, is suffered to remain without scrutiny or rebuke. It furnishes no argument against the interposition of a check, which shall require the advice and consent of the senate to appointments, that the power has not hitherto been abused. In its own nature, the post-office establishment is susceptible of abuse to such an alarming degree; the whole correspondence of the country is so completely submitted to the fidelity and integrity of the agents, who conduct it; and the means of making it subservient to mere state policy are so abundant, that the only surprise is, that it has not already awakened the public jealousy, and been placed under more effectual control. It may be said, without the slightest disparagement of any officer, who has presided over it, that if ever the people are to be corrupted, or their liberties are to be prostrated, this establishment will furnish the most facile {568} means, arid be the easiest employed, to accomplish such a purpose.

§ 795. It is observable, that the constitution makes no mention of any power of removal by the executive of any officers whatever. As, however, the tenure of office of no officers, except those in the judicial department, is, by the constitution, provided to be during good behaviour, it follows by irresistible inference that all others must hold their offices, during pleasure, unless congress shall have given some other duration to their office. As far as congress constitutionally possess the power to regulate, and delegate the appointment of "inferior officers" so far they may prescribe the term of office, the manner in which, and the persons by whom, the removal, as well as the appointment to office, shall be made. But two questions naturally occur upon this subject. The first is, to whom, in the absence of all such legislation, does the power of removal belong to the appointing power, or to the executive? to the president and senate, who have concurred in the appointment, or to the president, alone? The next is, if the power of removal belongs to the executive, in regard to any appointments confided by the constitution to him; whether congress can give any duration of office in such cases, not subject to exercise of this power of removal? Hitherto the latter has remained a merely speculative question, as all our legislation, giving a limited duration to office, recognises the executive power of removal, as in full force.

§ 796. The other is a vastly important practical question; and, in an early stage of the government, underwent a most elaborate discussion. The language of the constitution is, that the president "shall nominate, and, by and with the advice and consent of the {569} senate, appoint," &c. The power to nominate does not naturally, or necessarily include the power to remove; and if the power to appoint does include it, then the latter belongs conjointly to the executive and the senate. In short, under such circumstances, the removal takes place in virtue of the new appointment, by mere operation of law. It results, and is not separable from the appointment itself.

§ 797. This was the doctrine maintained with great earnestness by the Federalist; and it had a most material tendency to quiet the just alarms of the overwhelming influence, and arbitrary exercise of this prerogative of the executive, which might prove fatal to the personal independence, and freedom of opinion of officers, as well as to the public liberties of the country. Indeed, it is utterly impossible not to feel, that, if this unlimited power of removal does exist, it may be made, in the hands of a bold and designing man, of high ambition, and feeble principles, an instrument of the worst oppression, and most vindictive vengeance. Even in monarchies, while the councils of state are subject to perpetual fluctuations and changes, the ordinary officers of the government are permitted to remain in the silent possession of their offices, undisturbed by the policy, or the passions of the favourites of the court. But in a republic, where freedom of opinion and action are guaranteed by the very first principles of the government, if a successful party may first elevate their candidate to office, and then make him the instrument of their resentments, or their mercenary bargains; if men may be made spies upon the actions of their neighbours, to displace them from office; or if fawning sycophants upon the popular leader of the day may gain his patronage, to the exclusion {570} worthier and abler men, it is most manifest, that elections will be corrupted at the very source; and those, who seek office, will have every motive to delude, and deceive the people. It was not, therefore, without reason, that, in the animated discussion already alluded to, it was urged, that the power of removal was incident to the power of appointment. That it would be a most unjustifiable construction of the constitution, and of its implied powers, to hold otherwise. That such a prerogative in the executive was in its own nature monarchical and arbitrary; and eminently dangerous to the best interests, as well as to the liberties, of the country. It would convert all the officers of the country into the mere tools and creatures of the president. A dependence so servile, on one individual, would deter men of high and honorable minds from engaging in the public service. And if, contrary to expectation, such men should be brought into office, they would be reduced to the necessity of sacrificing every principle of independence to the will of the chief magistrate, or of exposing themselves to the disgrace of being removed from office, and that too at a time, when it might no longer be in their power to engage in other pursuits.

§ 798. On the other hand, those, who after the adoption of the constitution held the doctrine, (for before that period it never appears to have been avowed by any of its friends, although it was urged by its opponents, as a reason for rejecting it,) that the power of removal belonged to the president, argued, that it resulted from the nature of the power, and the convenience, and even necessity of its exercise. It was clearly in its nature a part of the executive power, and was indispensable for a due execution of the laws, and {571} a regular administration of the public affairs. What would become of the public interests, if during the recess of the senate the president could not remove an unfaithful public officer? If he could not displace a corrupt ambassador, or head of department, or other officer engaged in the finances, or expenditures of the government? If the executive, to prevent a non-execution of the laws, or a non-performance of his own proper functions, had a right to suspend an unworthy officer from office, this power was in no respect distinguishable from a power of removal. In fact, it is an exercise, though in a more moderated form, of the same power. Besides; it was argued, that the danger, that a president would remove good men from office was wholly imaginary. It was not by the splendour attached to the character of a particular president, like Washington, that such an opinion was to be maintained. It was founded on the structure of the office. The man, in whose favour a majority of the people of the United States would unite, to elect him to such an office, had every probability at least in favour of his principles. He must be presumed to possess integrity, independence, and high talents. It would be impossible, that he should abuse the patronage of the government, or his power of removal, to the base purposes of gratifying a party, or of ministering to his own resentments, or of displacing upright and excellent officers for a mere difference of opinion. The public odium, which would inevitably attach to such conduct, would be a perfect security against it. And, in truth, removals made from such motives, or with a view to bestow the offices upon dependents, or favourites, would be an impeachable offence.

§ 799. That the final decision of this question in {572} favour of the executive power of removal, was greatly influenced by the exalted character of the president, then in office, was asserted at the time, and has always been believed. Yet the doctrine was opposed, as well as supported, by the highest talents and patriotism of the country. The public, however, acquiesced in this decision; and it constitutes, perhaps, the most extraordinary case in the history of the government of a power, conferred by implication on the executive, by the assent of a bare majority of congress, which has not been questioned on many other occasions. Even the most jealous advocates of state rights seem to have slumbered over this vast reach of authority; and have left it untouched, as the neutral ground of controversy, in which they desired to reap no harvest, and from which they retired without leaving any protestations of title or contest.

§ 800. Whether the predictions of the original advocates of the executive power, or those of the opposers of it, are likely, in the future progress of the government, to be realized, must be left to the sober judgment of the community, and to the impartial award of time. If there has been any aberration from the true constitutional exposition of the power of removal, which the reader must decide for himself, it will be difficult, and perhaps impracticable, after forty years' experience, to recall the practice to the correct theory. But at all events, it will be a consolation to those, who love the Union, and honour a devotion to the patriotic discharge of duty, that in regard to "inferior officers," which appellation probably includes ninety-nine out of a hundred of the lucrative offices in the government, the remedy for any permanent abuse is still within the power of congress, by the simple expedient of requiring {573} the consent of the senate to removals in such cases.

§ 801. Another point of great practical importance is, when the appointment of any officer is to be deemed complete. It will be seen in a succeeding clause, that the president is to "commission all the officers of the United States." In regard to officers, who are removable at the will of the executive, the point is unimportant, since they may be displaced, and their commission arrested at any moment. But if the officer is not so removable, the time, when the appointment is complete, becomes of very deep interest.

§ 802. This subject was very elaborately discussed in the celebrated case of *Marbury v. Madison.* Upon the fullest deliberation, the court were of opinion, that, when a commission has been signed by the president, the appointment is final and complete. The officer appointed has then conferred on him legal rights, which cannot be resumed. Until that period, the discretion of the president may be exercised by him, as to the appointment; but, from that moment, it is irrevocable. His power over the office is then terminated in all cases, where by law the officer is not removable by him. The right to the office is then in the person appointed, and he has the absolute, unconditional power of accepting, or rejecting it. Neither a delivery of the commission, nor an actual acceptance of the office, is indispensable to make the appointment perfect.

§ 803. The next clause of the constitution is,

"The president shall have power to fill up all vacancies, that may happen during the recess of the senate, by granting commissions, which shall expire at the end of their next session."

§ 804. The propriety of this grant is so obvious, {574} that it can require no elucidation. There was but one of two courses to be adopted; either, that the senate should be perpetually in session, in order to provide for the appointment of officers; or, that the president should be authorized to make temporary appointments during the recess, which should expire, when the senate should have had an opportunity to act on the subject. The former course would have been at once burthensome to the senate, and expensive to the public. The latter combines convenience, promptitude of action, and general security.

§ 805. The appointments so made, by the very language of the constitution, expire at the next session of the senate; and the commissions given by the President have the same duration. When the senate is assembled, if the president nominates the same officer to the office, this is to all intents and purposes a new nomination to office; and, if approved by the senate, the appointment is a new appointment, and not a mere continuation of the old appointment. So that, if a bond for fidelity in office has been given under the first appointment and commission, it does not apply to any acts done under the new appointment and commission.

§ 806. The next section of the second article is,

> "He (the president) shall from time to time give to the congress information of the state of the Union, and recommend to their consideration such measures, as he shall judge necessary and expedient. He may, on extraordinary occasions, convene both houses, or either of them, and, in case of a disagreement between them, with respect to the time of adjournment, he may adjourn them to such time, as he shall think proper. He shall receive ambassadors, and other public ministers. He shall take care, that the {575} laws be faithfully executed; and shall commission all the officers of the United States."

§ 807. The first part, relative to the president's giving information and recommending measures to congress, is so consonant with the structure of the executive department of the colonial and state governments, with the usages and practice of other free governments, with the general convenience of congress, and with a due share of responsibility on the part of the executive, that it may well be presumed to be above all real objection. From the nature and duties of the executive department, he must possess more extensive sources of information, as well in regard to domestic as foreign affairs, than can belong to congress. The true workings of the laws; the defects in the nature or arrangements of the general systems of trade, finance, and justice; and the military, naval, and civil establishments of the Union, are more readily seen, and more constantly under the view of the executive, than they can possibly be of any other department. There is great wisdom, therefore, in not merely allowing, but in requiring, the president to lay before congress all facts and information, which may assist their deliberations; and in enabling him at once to point out the evil, and to suggest the remedy. He is thus justly made responsible, not merely for a due administration of the existing systems, but for due diligence and examination into the means of improving them.

§ 808. The power to convene congress on extraordinary occasions is indispensable to the proper operations, and even safety of the government. Occasions may occur in the recess of congress, requiring the government to take vigorous measures to repel foreign aggression, depredations, and direct hostilities; to {576} provide adequate means to mitigate, or overcome unexpected calamities; to suppress insurrections; and to provide for innumerable other important exigencies, arising out of the intercourse and revolutions among nations.

§ 809. The power to adjourn congress in cases of disagreement is equally indispensable; since it is the only peaceable way of terminating a controversy, which can lead to nothing but distraction in the public councils.

§ 810. On the other hand, the duty imposed upon him to take care, that the laws be faithfully executed, follows out the strong injunctions of his oath of office, that he will "preserve, protect, and defend the constitution." The great object of the executive department is to accomplish this purpose; and without it, be the form of government whatever it may, it will be utterly worthless for offence, or defence; for the redress of grievances, or the protection of rights; for the happiness, or good order, or safety of the people.

§ 811. The next power is to receive ambassadors and other public ministers. This subject has been already incidentally touched. A similar power existed under the confederation; but it was confined to receiving "ambassadors," which word, in a strict sense, (as has been already stated,) comprehends the highest grade only of ministers, and not those of an inferior character. The policy of the United States would ordinarily prefer the employment of the inferior grades; and therefore the description is properly enlarged, so as to include all classes of ministers. Why the receiving of consuls was not also expressly mentioned, as the appointment of them is in the preceding clause, is not easily to be accounted for, especially as the defect of {577} the confederation on this head was fully understood. The power, however, may be fairly inferred from other parts of the constitution; and indeed seems a general incident to the executive authority. It has constantly been exercised without objection; and foreign consuls have never been allowed to discharge any functions of office until they have received the exequatur of the president. Consuls, indeed, are no diplomatic functionaries, or political representatives of a foreign nation; but are treated in the character of mere commercial agents.

§ 812. The power to receive ambassadors and ministers is always an important, and sometimes a very delicate function; since it constitutes the only accredited medium, through which negotiations and friendly relations are ordinarily carried on with foreign powers. A government may in its discretion lawfully refuse to receive an ambassador, or other minister, without its affording any just cause of war. But it would generally be deemed an unfriendly act, and might provoke hostilities, unless accompanied by conciliatory explanations. A refusal is sometimes made upon the ground of the bad character of the minister, or his former offensive conduct, or of the special subject of the embassy not being proper, or convenient for discussion. This, however, is rarely done. But a much more delicate occasion is, when a civil war breaks out in a nation, and two nations are formed, or two parties in the same nation, each claiming the sovereignty of the whole, and the contest remains as yet undecided, *flagrante bello.* In such a case a neutral nation may very properly withhold its recognition of the supremacy of either party, or of the existence of two independent nations; and on that account refuse to receive an ambassador {578} from either. It is obvious, that in such cases the simple acknowledgment of the minister of either party, or nation, might be deemed taking part against the other; and thus as affording a strong countenance, or opposition, to rebellion and civil dismemberment. On this account, nations, placed in such a predicament, have not hesitated sometimes to declare war against neutrals, as interposing in the war; and have made them the victims of their vengeance, when they have been anxious to assume a neutral position. The exercise of this prerogative of acknowledging new nations, or ministers, is, therefore, under such circumstances, an executive function of great delicacy, which requires the utmost caution and deliberation. If the executive receives an ambassador, or other minister, as the representative of a new nation, or of a party in a civil war in an old nation, it is an acknowledgment of the sovereign authority *de facto* of such new nation, or party. If such recognition is made, it is conclusive upon the nation, unless, indeed, it can be reversed by an act of congress repudiating it. If, on the other hand, such recognition has been refused by the executive, it is said, that congress may, notwithstanding, solemnly acknowledge the sovereignty of the nation, or party. These, however, are propositions, which have hitherto remained, as abstract statements under the constitution; and, therefore, can be propounded, not as absolutely true, but as still open to discussion, if they should ever arise in the course of our foreign diplomacy. The constitution has expressly invested the executive with power to receive ambassadors, and other ministers. It has not expressly invested congress with the power, either to repudiate, or acknowledge them. At all events, in the case of a revolution, {579} or dismemberment of a nation, the judiciary cannot take notice of any new government, or sovereignty, until it has been duly recognised by some other department of the government, to whom the power is constitutionally confided.

§ 813. As incidents to the power to receive ambassadors and foreign ministers, the president is understood to possess the power to refuse them, and to dismiss those, who, having been received, become obnoxious to censure, or unfit to be allowed the privilege, by their improper conduct, or by political events. While, however, they are permitted to remain, as public functionaries, they are entitled to all the immunities and rights, which the law of nations has provided at once for their dignity, their independence, and their inviolability.

§ 814. There are other incidental powers, belonging to the executive department, which are necessarily implied from the nature of the functions, which are confided to it. Among these must necessarily be included the power to perform them, without any obstruction or impediment whatsoever. The president cannot, therefore, be liable to arrest, imprisonment, or detention, while he is in the discharge of the duties of his office; and for this purpose his person must be deemed, in civil cases at least, to possess an official inviolability. In the exercise of his political powers he is to use his own discretion, and is accountable only to his country, and to his own conscience. His decision, in relation to these powers, is subject to no control; and his discretion, when exercised, is conclusive. But he has no authority to control other officers of the government, in relation to the duties imposed upon them by law, in cases not touching his political powers. {580}

§ 815. We have seen, that by law the president possesses the right to require the written advice and opinions of his cabinet ministers, upon all questions connected with their respective departments. But, he does not possess a like authority, in regard to the judicial department. That branch of the government can be called upon only to decide controversies, brought before them in a legal form; and therefore is bound to abstain from any extra-judicial opinions upon points of law, even though solemnly requested by the executive.

§ 816. The remaining section of the fourth article, declaring that the President, Vice-President, and all civil officers of the United States shall be liable to impeachment, has been already fully considered in another place. And thus is closed the examination of the rights, powers, and duties of the executive department. Unless my judgment has been unduly biassed, I think it will be found impossible to hold from this part of the constitution a tribute of profound respect, if not of the liveliest admiration. All, that seems desirable, in order to gratify the hopes, secure the reverence, and sustain the dignity of the nation, is, that the office should always be occupied by a man of elevated talents, of ripe virtues, of incorruptible integrity, and of tried patriotism; one, who shall forget his own interests, and remember, that he represents not a party, but the whole nation; one, whose fame may be rested with posterity, not upon the false eulogies of favourites, but upon the solid merit of having preserved the glory, and enhanced the prosperity of the country.

CHAPTER XXXVIII.

JUDICIARY — ORGANIZATION AND POWERS.

§ 817. THE order of the subject next conducts us to the consideration of the third article of the constitution, which embraces the organization and powers of the judicial department.

§ 818. The importance of the establishment of a judicial department in the national government has been already incidentally discussed under other heads. The want of it constituted one of the vital defects of the confederation. And every government must, in its essence, be unsafe and unfit for a free people, where such a department does not exist, with powers co-extensive with those of the legislative department. Where there is no judicial department to interpret, pronounce, and execute the law, to decide controversies, and to enforce rights, the government must either perish by its own imbecility, or the other departments of government must usurp powers, for the purpose of commanding obedience, to the destruction of liberty. The will of those, who govern, will, under such circumstances, become absolute and despotic; and it is wholly immaterial, whether power is vested in a single tyrant, or in an assembly of tyrants. No remark is better founded in human experience, than that of Montesquieu, that "there is no liberty, if the judiciary power be not separated from the legislative and executive powers." And it is no less true, that personal security and private property rest entirely upon the wisdom, the stability, and the integrity of the courts of justice. If that government {582} can be truly said to be despotic and intolerable, in which the law is vague and uncertain, it cannot but be rendered still more oppressive and more mischievous, when the actual administration of justice is dependent upon caprice, or favour, upon the will of rulers, or the influence of popularity. When power becomes right, it is of little consequence, whether decisions rest upon corruption, or weakness, upon the accidents of chance, or upon deliberate wrong. In every well organized government, therefore, with reference to the security both of public rights and private rights, it is indispensable, that there should be a judicial department to ascertain, and decide rights, to punish crimes, to administer justice, and to protect the innocent from injury and usurpation.

§ 819. In the national government the power is equally as important, as in the state governments. The laws and treaties, and even the constitution, of the United States, would become a dead letter without it. Indeed, in a complicated government, like ours, where there is an assemblage of republics, combined under a common head, the necessity of some controlling judicial power, to ascertain and enforce the powers of the Union, is, if possible, still more striking. The laws of the whole would otherwise be in continual danger of being contravened by the laws of the parts. The national government would be reduced to a servile dependence upon the states; and the same scenes would be again acted over in solemn mockery, which began in the neglect, and ended in the ruin, of the confederation. Power, without adequate means to enforce it, is like a body in a state of suspended animation. For all practical purposes it is, as if its faculties were extinguished. Even if there were no danger of collision between {583} the laws and powers of the Union, and those of the states, it is utterly impossible, without some superintending judiciary establishment, that there should be any uniform administration, or interpretation of them. The idea of uniformity of decision by thirteen independent and co-ordinate tribunals (and the number is now advanced to twenty-four) is absolutely visionary, if not absurd. The consequence would necessarily be, that neither the constitution, nor the laws, neither the rights and powers of the Union, nor those of the states, would be the same in any two states. And there would be perpetual fluctuations and changes, growing out of the diversities of judgment, as well as of local institutions, interests, and habits of thought.

§ 820. Two ends, then, of paramount importance, and fundamental to a free government, are proposed to be attained by the establishment of a national judiciary. The first is a due execution of the powers of the government; and the second is a uniformity in the interpretation and operation of those powers, and of the laws enacted in pursuance of them. The power of interpreting the laws involves necessarily the function to ascertain, whether they are conformable to the constitution, or not; and if not so conformable, to declare them void and inoperative. As the constitution is the supreme law of the land, in a conflict between that and the laws, either of congress, or of the states, it becomes the duty of the judiciary to follow that only, which is of paramount obligation. This results from the very theory of a republican constitution of government; for otherwise the acts of the legislature and executive would in effect become supreme and uncontrollable, notwithstanding any prohibitions or limitations contained in the constitution; and usurpations of the most unequivocal {584} and dangerous character might be assumed, without any remedy being within the reach of the citizens. The people would thus be at the mercy of their rulers in the state and national governments; and an omnipotence would practically exist, like that claimed for the British Parliament. The universal sense of America has decided, that in the last resort the judiciary must decide upon the constitutionality of the acts and laws of the general and state governments, as far as they are capable of being made the subject of judicial controversy. It follows, that, when they are subjected to the cognizance of the judiciary, its judgments must be conclusive; for otherwise they may be disregarded, and the acts of the legislature and executive enjoy a secure and irresistible triumph.

§ 821. The framers of the constitution, having these great principles in view, adopted two fundamental rules with entire unanimity; first, that a national judiciary ought to be established; secondly, that the national judiciary ought to possess powers co-extensive with those of the legislative department. Indeed, the latter necessarily flowed from the former, and was treated, and must always be treated, as an axiom of political government. But these provisions alone would not be sufficient to ensure a complete administration of public justice, or to give permanency to the republic. The judiciary must be so organized, as to carry into complete effect all the purposes of its establishment. It must possess wisdom, learning, integrity, independence, and firmness. It must at once possess the power and the means to check usurpation, and enforce execution of its judgments. Mr. Burke has, with singular sagacity and pregnant brevity, stated the doctrine, which every republic should steadily sustain, and conscientiously {585} inculcate. "Whatever," says he, "is supreme in a state ought to have, as much as possible, its judicial authority so constituted, as not only not to depend upon it, but in some sort to balance it. It ought to give security to its justice against its power. It ought to make its judicature, as it were, something exterior to the state." The best manner, in which this is to be accomplished, must mainly depend upon the mode of appointment, the tenure of office, the compensation of the judges, and the jurisdiction confided to the department in its various branches.

§ 822. Let us proceed, then, to the consideration of the judicial department, as it is established by the constitution, and see, how far adequate means are provided for all these important purposes.

§ 823. The first section of the third article is as follows:

"The judicial power of the United States shall be vested in one Supreme Court, and in such inferior courts, as the congress may from time to time ordain and establish. The judges, both of the supreme and inferior courts, shall hold their offices during good behaviour; and shall at stated times receive for their services a compensation, which shall not be diminished during their continuance in office."

To this may be added the clause in the enumeration of the powers of congress in the first article, (which is but a mere repetition,) that congress shall have power

"to constitute tribunals inferior to the Supreme Court."

§ 824. To the establishment of one court of supreme and final jurisdiction, there do not seem to have been any strenuous objections generally insisted on in the state conventions, though many were urged against certain portions of the jurisdiction, proposed by the constitution to be vested in the courts of the United {586} States. The principal question seems to have been of a different nature, whether it ought to be a distinct coordinate department, or a branch of the legislature.

§ 825. In regard to the power of constituting inferior courts of the Union, it is evidently calculated to obviate the necessity of having recourse to the Supreme Court in every case of federal cognizance. It enables the national government to institute, or authorize in each state and district of the United States, a tribunal competent to the determination of all matters of national jurisdiction within its limits. One of two courses only could be open for adoption; either to create inferior courts under the national authority, to reach all cases fit for the national jurisdiction, which either constitutionally, or conveniently, could not be of original cognizance in the Supreme Court; or to confide jurisdiction of the same cases to the state courts, with a right of appeal to the Supreme Court. To the latter course solid objections were thought to apply, which rendered it ineligible and unsatisfactory. In the first place, the judges of the state courts would be wholly irresponsible to the national government for their conduct in the administration of national justice; so, that the national government would, or might be, wholly dependent upon the good will, or sound discretion of the states, in regard to the efficiency, promptitude, and ability, with which the judicial authority of the nation should be administered. In the next place, the prevalency of a local, or sectional spirit might be found to disqualify the state tribunals for a suitable discharge of national judicial functions; and the very modes of appointment of someof the state judges might render them improper channels of the judicial authority of the Union. State judges, holding their offices during pleasure, or {587} from year to year, or for other short periods, would, or at least might, be too little independent to be relied upon for an inflexible execution of the national laws. What could be done, where the state itself should happen to be in hostility to the national government, (as might well be presumed occasionally to be, the case, from local interests, party spirit, or peculiar prejudices,) if the state tribunals were to be the sole depositaries of the judicial powers of the Union, in the ordinary administration of criminal, as well as of civil justice? Besides; if the state tribunals were thus entrusted with the ordinary administration of the criminal and civil justice of the Union, there would be a necessity for leaving the door of appeal as widely open, as possible. In proportion to the grounds of confidence in, or distrust of, the subordinate tribunals, ought to be the facility or difficulty of appeals. An unrestrained course of appeals would be a source of much private, as well as public inconvenience. It would encourage litigation, and lead to the most oppressive expenses. Nor should it be omitted, that this very course of appeals would naturally lead to great jealousies, irritations, and collisions between the state courts and the Supreme Court, not only from differences of opinions, but from that pride of character, and consciousness of independence, which would be felt by state judges, possessing the confidence of their own state, and irresponsible to the Union.

§ 826. In considering the first clause of the third section, declaring, that

> "the judicial power of the United States shall be vested in one Supreme Court, and in such inferior courts, as the congress may, from time to time, ordain and establish,"

we are naturally led to the inquiry, whether congress possess any discretion, {588} as to the creation of a Supreme Court and inferior courts, in which the constitutional jurisdiction is to be vested. This was at one time matter of much discussion; and is vital to the existence of the judicial department. If congress possess any discretion on this subject, it is obvious, that the judiciary, as a co-ordinate department of the government, may, at the will of congress, be annihilated, or stripped of all its important jurisdiction; for, if the discretion exists, no one can say in what manner, or at what time, or under what circumstances, it may, or ought to be exercised. The whole argument, upon which such an interpretation has been attempted to be maintained, is, that the language of the constitution, "shall be vested," is not imperative, but simply indicates the future tense. This interpretation has been overruled by the Supreme Court, upon solemn deliberation. "The language of the third article," say the court, "throughout is manifestly designed to be mandatory upon the legislature. Its obligatory force is so imperative, that congress could not, without a violation of its duty, have refused to carry it into operation. The judicial power of the United States *shall be vested* (not may be vested) in one Supreme Court, and in such inferior courts, as congress may, from time to time, ordain and establish. Could congress have lawfully refused to create a Supreme Court, or to vest in it the constitutional jurisdiction? 'The judges, both of the supreme and inferior courts, *shall hold* their offices during good behaviour, and *shall*, at stated times, receive, for their services, a compensation, which shall not be diminished during their continuance in office.' Could congress create, or limit any other tenure of the judicial office? Could they refuse to pay, at stated times, the stipulated salary, or diminish {589} it during the continuance in office? But one answer can be given to these questions. It must be in the negative. The object of the constitution was to establish three great departments of government; the legislative, the executive, and the judicial department. The first was to pass laws, the second to approve and execute them, and the third to expound and enforce them. Without the latter, it would be impossible to carry into effect some of the express provisions of the constitution. How, otherwise, could crimes against the United States be tried and punished? How could causes between two states be heard and determined? The judicial power must, therefore, be vested in some court by congress; and to suppose, that it was not an obligation binding on them, but might, at their pleasure, be omitted, or declined, is to suppose, that, under the sanction of the constitution, they might defeat the constitution itself. A construction, which would lead to such a result, cannot be sound."

§ 827. The constitution has wisely established, that there shall be one Supreme Court, with a view to uniformity of decision in all cases whatsoever, belonging to the judicial department, whether they arise at the common law, or in equity, or within the admiralty and prize jurisdiction; whether they respect the doctrines of mere municipal law, or constitutional law, or the law of nations. It is obvious, that, if there were independent supreme courts of common law, of equity, and of admiralty, a diversity of judgment might, and almost necessarily would spring up, not only, as to the limits of the jurisdiction of each tribunal; but as to the fundamental doctrines of municipal, constitutional, and public law. The effect of this diversity would be, that a different rule would, or might be promulgated on the {590} most interesting subjects by the several tribunals; and thus the citizens be involved in endless doubts, not only as to their private rights, but as to their public duties. The constitution itself would, or might speak a different language according to the tribunal, which was called upon to interpret it; and thus interminable disputes might embarrass the administration of justice throughout the whole country. But the same reason did not apply to the inferior tribunals. These were, therefore, left entirely to the discretion of congress, as to their number, their jurisdiction, and their powers. Experience might, and probably would, show good grounds for varying and modifying them from time to time. It would not only have been unwise, but exceedingly inconvenient, to have fixed the arrangement of these courts in the constitution itself; since congress would have been disabled thereby from adapting them from time to time to the exigencies of the country. But, whatever may be the extent, to which the power of congress reaches, as to the establishment of inferior tribunals, it is clear from what has been already stated, that all the jurisdiction contemplated by the constitution must be vested in some of its courts, either in an original or an appellate form.

§ 828. We next come to the consideration of those securities, which the constitution has provided for the due independence and efficiency of the judicial department.

§ 829. The mode of appointment of the judges has necessarily come under review, in the examination of the structure and powers of the executive department. The president is expressly authorized, by and with the consent of the senate, to appoint the judges of the Supreme Court. The appointment of the {591} judges of the inferior courts is not expressly provided for; but has either been left to the discretion of congress, or silently belongs to the president, under the clause of the constitution authorizing him to appoint "all other officers of the United States, whose appointments are not herein otherwise provided for."

§ 830. The next consideration is the tenure, by which the judges hold their offices. It is declared that

> "the judges, both of the Supreme and Inferior Courts shall hold their offices during good behaviour."

§ 831. It has sometimes been suggested, that, though in monarchical governments the independence of the judiciary is essential to guard the rights of the subjects from the injustice and oppression of the crown; yet that the same reasons do not apply to a republic, where the popular will is sufficiently known, and ought always to be obeyed. A little consideration of the subject will satisfy us, that, so far from this being true, the reasons in favour of the independence of the judiciary apply with augmented force to republics; and especially to such as possess a written constitution with defined powers, and limited rights.

§ 832. In the first place, factions and parties are quite as common, and quite as violent in republics, as in monarchies; and the same safeguards are as indispensable in the one, as in the other, against the encroachments of party spirit, and the tyranny of factions. Laws, however wholesome or necessary, are frequently the objects of temporary aversion, and popular odium, and sometimes of popular resistance. Nothing is more facile in republics, than for demagogues, under artful pretences, to stir up combinations against the regular exercise of authority. Their selfish {592} purposes are too often interrupted by the firmness and independence of upright magistrates, not to make them at all times hostile to a power, which rebukes, and an impartiality, which condemns them. The judiciary, as the weakest point in the constitution, on which to make an attack, is therefore, constantly that, to which they direct their assaults; and a triumph here, aided by any momentary popular encouragement, achieves a lasting victory over the constitution itself. Hence, in republics, those, who are to profit by public commotions, or the prevalence of faction, are always the enemies of a regular and independent administration of justice. They spread all sorts of delusion, in order to mislead the public mind, and excite the public prejudices. They know full well, that, without the aid of the people, their schemes must prove abortive; and they, therefore, employ every art to undermine the public confidence, and to make the people the instruments of subverting their own rights and liberties.

§ 833. It is obvious, that, under such circumstances, if the tenure of office of the judges is not permanent, they will soon be rendered odious, not because they do wrong, but because they refuse to do wrong; and they will be made to give way to others, who shall become more pliant tools of the leading demagogues of the day. There can be no security for the minority in a free government, except through the judicial department. In a monarchy, the sympathies of the people are naturally enlisted against the meditated oppressions of their ruler; and they screen his victims from his vengeance. His is the cause of one against the community. But, in free governments, where the majority, who obtain power for the moment, are supposed to represent the will of the people, persecution, especially {593} of a political nature, becomes the cause of the community against one. It is the more violent and unrelenting, because it is deemed indispensable to attain power, or to enjoy the fruits of victory. In free governments, therefore, the independence of the judiciary becomes far more important to the security of the rights of the citizens, than in a monarchy; since it is the only barrier against the oppressions of a dominant faction, armed for the moment with power, and abusing the influence, acquired under accidental excitements, to overthrow the institutions and liberties, which have been the deliberate choice of the people.

§ 834. In the next place, the independence of the judiciary is indispensable to secure the people against the intentional, as well as unintentional, usurpations of the executive and legislative departments. It has been observed with great sagacity, that power is perpetually stealing from the many to the few; and the tendency of the legislative department to absorb all the other powers of the government has always been dwelt upon by statesmen and patriots, as a general truth, confirmed by all human experience. If the judges are appointed at short intervals, either by the legislative, or the executive department, they will naturally, and, indeed, almost necessarily, become mere dependents upon the appointing power. If they have any desire to obtain, or to hold office, they will at all times evince a desire to follow, and obey the will of the predominant power in the state. Public justice will be administered with a faultering and feeble hand. It will secure nothing, but its own place, and the approbation of those, who value, because they control it. It will decree, what best suits the opinions of the day; and it will forget, that the precepts of the law rest on eternal foundations. The {594} rulers and the citizens will not stand upon an equal ground in litigations. The favourites of the day will overawe by their power, or seduce by their influence; and thus, the fundamental maxim of a republic, that it is a government of laws, and not of men, will be silently disproved, or openly abandoned.

§ 835. In the next place, these considerations acquire (as has been already seen) still more cogency and force, when applied to questions of constitutional law. In monarchies, the only practical resistance, which the judiciary can present, is to the usurpations of a single department of the government, unaided, and acting for itself. But, if the executive and legislative departments are combined in any course of measures, obedience to their will becomes a duty, as well as a necessity. Thus, even in the free government of Great Britain, an act of parliament, combining, as it does, the will of the crown, and the legislature, is absolute and omnipotent. It cannot be lawfully resisted, or disobeyed. The judiciary is bound to carry it into effect at every hazard, even though it should subvert private rights and public liberty. But it is far otherwise in a republic, like our own, with a limited constitution, prescribing at once the powers of the rulers, and the rights of the citizens. This very circumstance would seem conclusively to show, that the independence of the judiciary is absolutely indispensable to preserve the balance of such a constitution. In no other way can there be any practical restraint upon the acts of the government, or any practical enforcement of the rights of the citizens. This subject has been already examined very much at large, and needs only to be touched in this place. No man can deny the necessity of a judiciary to interpret the constitution {595} and laws, and to preserve the citizens against oppression and usurpation in civil and criminal prosecutions. Does it not follow, that, to enable the judiciary to fulfil its functions, it is indispensable, that the judges should not hold their offices at the mere pleasure of those, whose acts they are to check, and, if need be, to declare void? Can it be supposed for a moment, that men holding their offices for the short period of two, or four, or even six years, will be generally found firm enough to resist the will of those, who appoint them, and may remove them?

§ 836. The argument of those, who contend for a short period of office of the judges, is founded upon the necessity of a conformity to the will of the people. But the argument proceeds upon a fallacy, in supposing, that the will of the rulers, and the will of the people are the same. Now, they not only may be, but often actually are, in direct variance to each other. No man in a republican government can doubt, that the will of the people is, and ought to be, supreme. But it is the deliberate will of the people, evinced by their solemn acts, and not the momentary ebullitions of those, who act for the majority, for a day, or a month, or a year. The constitution is the will, the deliberate will, of the people. They have declared under what circumstances, and in what manner it shall be amended, and altered; and until a change is effected in the manner prescribed, it is declared, that it shall be the supreme law of the land, to which all persons, rulers, as well as citizens, must bow in obedience. When it is constitutionally altered, then and not until then, are the judges at liberty to disregard its original injunctions. When, therefore, the argument is pressed, that the judges ought to be subject to the will of the people, {596} no one doubts the propriety of the doctrine in its true and legitimate sense.

§ 837. But those, who press the argument, use it in a far broader sense. In their view, the will of the people, as exhibited in the choice of the rulers, is to be followed. If the rulers interpret the constitution differently from the judges, the former are to be obeyed, because they represent the opinions of the people; and therefore, the judges ought to be removable, or appointed for a short period, so as to become subject to the will of the people, as expressed by and through their rulers. But, is it not at once seen, that this is in fact subverting the constitutions? Would it not make the constitution an instrument of flexible and changeable interpretation, and not a settled form of government with fixed limitations? Would it not become, instead of a supreme law for ourselves and our posterity, a mere oracle of the powers of the rulers of the day; to which implicit homage is to be paid, and speaking at different times the most opposite commands, and in the most ambiguous voices? In short, is not this an attempt to erect, behind the constitution, a power unknown, and unprovided for by the constitution, and greater than itself? What become of the limitations of the constitution, if the will of the people, thus inofficially promulgated, forms, for the time being, the supreme law, and the supreme exposition of the law? If the constitution defines the powers of the government, and points out the mode of changing them; and yet the instrument is to expand in the hands of one set of rulers, and to contract in those of another, where is the standard? If the will of the people is to govern in the construction of the powers of the constitution, and that will is to be gathered at every {597} successive election at the polls, and not from their deliberate judgment, and solemn acts in ratifying the constitution, or in amending it, what certainty can there be in those powers If the constitution is to be expounded, not by its written text, but by the opinions of the rulers for the time being, whose opinions are to prevail, the first, or the last? When, therefore, it is said, that the judges ought to be subjected to the will of the people, and to conform to their interpretation of the constitution, the practical meaning must be, that they should be subjected to the control of the representatives of the people in the executive and legislative departments, and should interpret the constitution, as the latter may, from time to time, deem correct.

§ 838. But it is obvious, that elections can rarely, if ever, furnish any sufficient proofs, what is deliberately the will of the people, as to any constitutional or legal doctrines. Representatives and rulers must be ordinarily chosen for very different purposes; and, in many instances, their opinions upon constitutional questions must be unknown to their constituents. The only means known to the constitution, by which to ascertain the will of the people upon a constitutional question, is in the shape of an affirmative or negative proposition by way of amendment, offered for their adoption in the mode prescribed by the constitution. The elections in one year may bring one party into power; and in the next year their opponents, embracing opposite doctrines, may succeed; and so alternate success and defeat may perpetually recur in the same districts, and in the same, or in different states.

§ 839. Surely it will not be pretended, that any constitution, adapted to the American people, could ever contemplate the executive and legislative departments {598} of the government, as the ultimate depositaries of the power to interpret the constitution; or as the ultimate representatives of the will of the people, to change it at pleasure. If, then, the judges were appointed for two, or four, or six years, instead of during good behaviour, the only security, which the people would have for a due administration of public justice, and a firm support of the constitution, would be, that being dependent upon the executive for their appointment during their brief period of office, they might, and would represent more fully, for the time being, the constitutional opinion of each successive executive; and thus carry into effect his system of government. Would this be more wise, or more safe, more for the permanence of the constitution, or for the preservation of the liberties of the people, than the present system? Would the judiciary, then, be, in fact, an independent co-ordinate department? Would it protect the people against an ambitious or corrupt executive; or restrain the legislature from acts of unconstitutional authority?

§ 840. The truth is, that, even with the most secure tenure of office, during good behaviour, the danger is not, that the judges will be too firm in resisting public opinion, and in defence of private rights or public liberties; but, that they will be too ready to yield themselves to the passions, and politics, and prejudices of the day. In a monarchy, the judges, in the performance of their duties with uprightness and impartiality, will always have the support of some of the departments of the government, or at least of the people. In republics, they may sometimes find the other departments combined in hostility against the judiciary; and even the people, for a while, under the influence of party spirit {599} and turbulent factions, ready to abandon them to their fate. Few men possess the firmness to resist the torrent of popular opinion. Still fewer are content to sacrifice present ease and public favour, in order to earn the slow rewards of a conscientious discharge of duty; the sure, but distant, gratitude of the people; and the severe, but enlightened, award of posterity.

§ 841. If passing from general reasoning, an appeal is made to the lessons of experience, there is every thing to convince us, that the judicial department is safe in a republic with the tenure of office during good behaviour; and that justice will ordinarily be best administered, where there is most independence. Of the state constitutions, five only out of twenty-four have provided for any other tenure of office, than during good behaviour; and those adopted by the new states admitted into the Union, since the formation of the national government, have, with two or three exceptions only, embraced the same permanent tenure of office. No one can hesitate to declare that in the states, where the judges hold their offices during good behaviour, justice is administered with wisdom, moderation, and firmness; and that the public confidence has reposed upon the judicial department, in the most critical times, with unabated respect. If the same can be said in regard to other states, where the judges enjoy a less permanent tenure of office, it will not answer the reasoning, unless it can also be shown, that the latter have never been removed for political causes, wholly distinct from their own merit; and yet have often deliberately placed themselves in opposition to the popular opinion.

§ 842. The considerations above stated lead us to the conclusion, that in republics there are, in reality, stronger {600} reasons for an independent tenure of office by the judges, a tenure during good behaviour, than in a monarchy. Indeed, a republic with a limited constitution, and yet without a judiciary sufficiently independent to check usurpation, to protect public liberty, and to, enforce private rights, would be as visionary and absurd, as a society organized without any restraints of law. It would become s democracy with unlimited powers, exercising through its rulers a universal despotic sovereignty. The very theory of a balanced republic of restricted powers presupposes some organized means to control, and resist, any excesses of authority. The people may, if they please, submit all power to their rulers for the time being; but, then, the government should receive its true appellation and character. It would be a government of tyrants, elective, it is true, but still tyrants; and it would become the more fierce, vindictive, and sanguinary, because it would perpetually generate factions in its own bosom, which could succeed only by the ruin of their enemies. It would be alternately characterized, as a reign of terror, and a reign of imbecility. It would be as corrupt, as it would be dangerous. It would form another model a that profligate and bloody democracy, which, at one time, in the French revolution, darkened by its deeds the fortunes of France, and left, to mankind the appalling lesson, that virtue and religion, genius and learning, the authority of wisdom and the appeals of innocence, are unheard and unfelt in the frenzy of popular excitement; and, that the worst crimes may be sanctioned, and the most desolating principles inculcated, under the banners, and in the name of liberty. In human governments, there are but two controlling powers; the power of arms, and the power of laws. If the latter are {601} not enforced by a judiciary above all fear, and above all reproach, the former must prevail; and thus lead to the triumph of military over civil institutions. The framers of the constitution, with profound wisdom, laid the corner stone of our national republic in the permanent independence of the judicial establishment. Upon this point their vote was unanimous. They adopted the results of an enlightened experience. They were not seduced by the dreams of human perfection into the belief; that all power might be safely left to the unchecked operation of the private ambition, or personal virtue of rulers. Nor, on the other hand, were they so lost to a just estimate of human concerns, as not to feel, that confidence must be reposed somewhere; if either efficiency, or safety are to be consulted in the plan of government. Having provided amply for the legislative and executive authorities, they established a balance-wheel, which, by its independent structure, should adjust the irregularities, and check the occasional excesses of the movements of the system.

§ 843. It is observable, that the constitution, has declared, that the judges of the inferior courts, as well as of the Supreme Court, of the United States, shall hold their offices during good behaviour. In this respect there is a marked contrast between the English government and our own. In England the tenure is exclusively confined to the judges of the superior courts, and does not even embrace all of these. In fact, a great portion of all the civil and criminal business of the whole kingdom is performed by persons delegated, *pro hac vice*, for this purpose, under commissions issued periodically for a single circuit. It is true, that it is, and for a long period has been, ordinarily administered by the judges of the courts of {602} King's Bench, Common Pleas, and Exchequer; but it is not so merely *virtute officii*, but under special commissions investing them from time to time with this authority in conjunction with other persons named in the commissions. Such are the commissions of oyer and terminer, of assize, of gaol delivery, and of *nisi prius*, under which all civil and criminal trials of matters of fact are had at the circuits, and in the metropolis. By the constitution of the United States all criminal and civil jurisdiction must be exclusively confided to judges holding their office during good behaviour; and though congress may from time to time distribute the jurisdiction among such inferior courts, as it may create from time to time, and withdraw it at their pleasure, it is not competent for them to confer it upon temporary judges, or to confide it by special commission. Even if the English system be well adapted to the wants of that nation, and if it secure a wise and beneficent administration of justice in the realm, as it doubtless does; still it is obvious, that, in our popular government, it would be quite too great a power, to trust the whole administration of civil and criminal justice to commissioners, appointed at the pleasure of the president. To the constitution of the United States, and to those, who enjoy its advantages, no judges are known, but such, as hold their offices during good behaviour.

§ 844. The next clause of the constitution declares, that the judges of the supreme and inferiour courts "shall, at stated times, receive for their services a compensation, which shall not be diminished during their continuance in office."

Without this provision the other, as to the tenure of office, would have been utterly nugatory, and indeed a mere mockery. The Federalist has here spoken in language so direct and convincing, that it supercedes all other argument. {603}

§ 845. "Next to permanency in office, nothing can contribute more to the independence of the judges, than a fixed provision for their support. The remark made in relation to the president is equally applicable here. In the general course of human nature, *a power over a man's subsistence amounts to a power over his will.* And we can never hope to see realized in practice the complete separation of the judicial from the legislative power in any system, which leaves the former dependent for pecuniary resource on the occasional grants of the latter. The enlightened friends to good government in every state have seen cause to lament the want of precise and explicit precautions in the state constitutions on this head. Some of these indeed have declared, that *permanent* salaries should be established for the judges; but the experiment has in some instances shown, that such expressions are not sufficiently definite to preclude legislative evasions. Something still more positive and unequivocal has been evinced to be requisite. The plan of the convention accordingly has provided, that the judges of the United States 'shall at *stated times* receive for their services a compensation, which shall not be *diminished* during their continuance in office.'

§ 846. "This, all circumstances considered, is the most eligible provision, that could have been devised. It will readily be understood, that the fluctuations in the value of money, and in the state of society, rendered a fixed rate of compensation in the constitution inadmissible. What might be extravagant to-day, might in half a century become penurious and inadequate. It was therefore necessary to leave it to the discretion of the legislature to vary its provisions in conformity to the variations in circumstances; yet under such restrictions {604} as to put it out of the power of that body to change the condition of the individual for the worse. A man may then be sure of the ground, upon which he stands; and can never be deterred from his duty by the apprehension of being placed in a less eligible situation. The clause, which has been quoted, combines both advantages. The salaries of judicial offices may, from time to time, be altered, as occasion shall require; yet so as never to lessen the allowance, with which any particular judge comes into office, in respect to him. It will be observed, that a difference has been made by the convention between the compensation of the president and that of the judges. That of the former can neither be increased, nor diminished. That of the latter can only not be diminished. This probably arose from the difference in the duration of the respective offices. As the president is to be elected for no more than four years, it can rarely happen, that an adequate salary, fixed at the commencement of that period, will not continue to be such to its end. But with regard to the judges, who, if they behave properly, will be secured in their places for life, it may well happen, especially in the early stages of the government, that a stipend, which would be very sufficient at their first appointment, would become too small in the progress of their service.

§ 847. "This provision for the support of the judges bears every mark of prudence and efficacy; and it may be safely affirmed, that, together with the permanent tenure of their offices, it affords a better prospect of their independence, than is discoverable in the constitutions of any of the states, in regard to their own judges. The precautions for their responsibility are comprised in the article respecting impeachments. They {605} are liable to be impeached for maleconduct by the house of representatives, and tried by the senate; and, if convicted, may be dismissed from office, and disqualified for holding any other. This is the only provision on the point, which is consistent with the necessary independence of the judicial character; and is the only one, which we find in our own constitution, in respect to our own judges."

§ 848. It is almost unnecessary to add, that, although the constitution has, with so sedulous a care, endeavoured to guard the judicial department from the overwhelming influence or power of the other coordinate departments of the government, it has not conferred upon them any inviolability, or irresponsibility for an abuse of their authority. On the contrary for any corrupt violation or omission of the high trusts confided to the judges, they are liable to be impeached, (as we have already seen,) and upon conviction to be removed from office. Thus, on the one hand, a pure and independent administration of public justice is amply provided for; and, on the other hand, an urgent responsibility secured for fidelity to the people.

§ 849. The judges of the inferior courts, spoken of in the constitution, do not include the judges of courts appointed in the territories of the United States under the authority, given to congress, to regulate the territories of the United States. The courts of the territories are not constitutional courts, in which the judicial power conferred by the constitution on the general government, can be deposited. They are legislative courts, created in virtue of the general sovereignty, which exists in the national government over its territories. The jurisdiction, with which they are invested, is not a part {606} of the judicial power, which is defined in the third article of the constitution; but arises from general sovereignty. In legislating for them, congress exercise the combined powers of the general, and of a state government. Congress may, therefore, rightfully limit the tenure of office of the judges of the territorial courts, as well as their jurisdiction; and it has been accordingly limited to a short period of years.

§ 850. The second section of the third article contains an exposition of the jurisdiction appertaining to the judicial power of the national government. The first clause is as follows:

"The judicial power shall extend to all cases in law and equity arising under this constitution, the laws of the United States, and treaties made, or which shall be made, under their authority; to all cases affecting ambassadors, other public ministers, and consuls; to all cases of admiralty and maritime jurisdiction; to controversies, to which the United States shall be a party; to controversies between two or more states; between a state and citizens of another state; between citizens of different states; between citizens of the same state, claiming lands under grants of different states; and between a state, or the citizens thereof, and foreign states, citizens, or subjects."

§ 851. And first, the judicial power extends to all cases in law and equity, arising under the constitution, the laws, and the treaties of the United States. And by cases in this clause we are to understand criminal, as well as civil cases.

§ 852. The propriety of the delegation of jurisdiction, "in cases arising under the constitution," rests on the obvious consideration, that there ought always to be some constitutional method of giving effect to {607} constitutional provisions. What, for instance, would avail restrictions on the authority of the state legislatures, Without some constitutional mode of enforcing the observance of them? The states are by the constitution prohibited from doing a variety of things; some of which are incompatible with the interests of the Union; others with its peace and safety; others with the principles of good government. The imposition of duties on imported articles, the declaration of war, and the emission of paper money, are examples of each kind. No man of sense will believe, that such prohibitions would be scrupulously regarded, without some effectual power in the government to restrains or correct the infractions of them. The power must be either a direct negative on the state laws, or an authority in the national courts to overrule such, as shall manifestly be in contravention to the constitution. The latter course was thought by the convention to be preferable to the former; and it is, without question, by far the most acceptable to the states.

§ 853. The same reasoning applies with equal force to "cases arising under the laws of the United States." In fact, the necessity of uniformity in the interpretation of these laws would of itself settle every doubt, that could be raised on the subject. "Thirteen independent courts of final jurisdiction (says the Federalist) over the same causes is a Hydra in government, from which nothing but contradiction and confusion can proceed."

§ 854. There is still more cogency, if it be possible, in the reasoning, as applied to "cases arising under treaties made, or which shall be made, under the authority of the United States." Without this power, there would be perpetual danger of collision, and even {608} of war, with foreign powers, and an utter incapacity to fulfil the ordinary obligations of treaties. The want of this power was (as we have seen) a most mischievous defect in the confederation; and subjected the country, not only to violations of its plighted faith, but to the gross, and almost proverbial imputation of punic insincerity.

§ 855. It is observable, that the language is, that "the judicial power shall extend to all cases *in law* and *equity*," arising under the constitution, laws, and treaties of the United States. What is to be understood by "cases in law and equity," in this clause? Plainly, cases at the common law, as contradistinguished from cases in equity, according to the known distinction in the jurisprudence of England, which our ancestors brought with them upon their emigration, and with which all the American states were familiarly acquainted. Here, then, at least, the constitution of the United States appeals to, and adopts, the common law to the extent of making it a rule in the pursuit of remedial justice in the courts of the Union. If the remedy must be in law, or in equity, according to the course of proceedings at the common law, in cases arising under the constitution, laws, and treaties, of the United States, it would seem irresistibly to follow, that the principles of decision, by which these remedies must be administered, must be derived from the same

source. Hitherto, such has been the uniform interpretation and mode of administering justice in the courts of the United States in this class of civil cases.

§ 856. Another inquiry may be, what constitutes a *case*, within the meaning
of this clause. It is clear, that the judicial department is authorized to exercise
jurisdiction to the full extent of the constitution, laws, and {609} treaties of the
United States, whenever any question respecting them shall assume such a form,
that the judicial power is capable of acting upon it. When it has assumed such a
form, it then becomes a case; and then, and not till then, the judicial power attaches to it. A case, then, in the sense of this clause of the constitution, arises, when
some subject, touching the constitution, laws, or treaties of the United States, is
submitted to the courts by a party, who asserts his rights in the form prescribed
by law. In other words, a case is a suit in law or equity, instituted according to the
regular course of judicial proceedings; and, when it involves any question arising
under the constitution, laws, or treaties of the United States, it is within the judicial power confided to the Union.

§ 857. Cases arising under the constitution, as contradistinguished from
those, arising under the laws of the United States, are such as arise from the powers conferred, or privileges granted, or rights claimed, or protection secured, or
prohibitions contained in the constitution itself, independent of any particular
statute enactment. Many cases of this sort may easily be enumerated. Thus, if a
citizen of one state should be denied the privileges of a citizen in another state; if
a state should coin money, or make paper money a tender; if a person, tried for a
crime against the United States, should be denied a trial by jury, or a trial in the
state, where the crime is charged to be committed; if a person, held to labour or
service in one state, under the laws thereof, should escape into another, and there
should be a refusal to deliver him up to the party, to whom such service or labour
may be due; in these, and many other cases, the question, to be judicially decided,
would be a case arising under the constitution. {610} On the other hand, cases
arising under the laws of the United States are such, as grow out of the legislation of congress, within the scope of their constitutional authority, whether they
constitute the right, or privilege, or claim, or protection, or defence, in whole or in
part, of the party, by whom they are asserted. The same reasoning applies to cases
arising under treaties. Indeed, wherever, in a judicial proceeding, any question
arises, touching the validity of a treaty, or statute, or authority, exercised under
the United States, or touching the construction of any clause of the constitution, or
any statute, or treaty of the United States; or touching the validity of any statute,
or authority exercised under any state, on the ground of repugnancy to the constitution, laws, or treaties, of the United States, it has been invariably held to be a
case, to which the judicial power of the United States extends.

§ 858. It has sometimes been suggested, that a case, to be within the purview
of this clause, must be one, in which a party comes into court to demand something conferred on him by the constitution, or a law, or a treaty, of the United
States. But this construction is clearly too narrow. A case in law or equity consists of the right of the one party, as well as of the other, and may truly be said to
arise under the constitution, or a law, or a treaty, of the United States, whenever
its correct decision depends on the construction of either. This is manifestly the

construction given to the clause by congress, by the 25th section of the Judiciary Act, (which was almost contemporaneous with the constitution,) and there is no reason to doubt its solidity or correctness. Indeed, the main object of this clause would be defeated by any narrower construction; since the power was conferred for the purpose, in an especial {611} manner, of producing a uniformity of construction of the constitution, laws, and treaties of the United States.

§ 859. Cases may also arise under laws of the United States by implication, as well as by express enactment; so, that due redress may be administered by the judicial power of the United States. It is not unusual for a legislative act to involve consequences, which are not expressed. An officer, for example, is ordered to arrest an individual. It is not necessary, nor is it usual, to say, that he shall not be punished for obeying this order. His security is implied in the order itself. It is no unusual thing for an act of congress to imply, without expressing, this very exemption from state control. The collectors of the revenue, the carriers of the mail, the mint establishment, and all those institutions, which are public in their nature, are examples in point. It has never been doubted, that all persons, who are employed in them, are protected, while in the line of their duty; and yet this protection is not expressed in any act of congress. It is incidental to, and is implied in, the several acts, by which those institutions are created; and is secured to the individuals, employed in them, by the judicial power alone; that is, the judicial power is the instrument employed by the government in administering this security.

§ 860. It has also been asked, and may again be asked, why the words, "cases in equity," are found in this clause? What equitable causes can grow out of the constitution, laws, and treaties of the United States? To this the general answer of the Federalist seems at once clear and satisfactory. "There is hardly a subject of litigation between individuals, which may not involve those ingredients of *fraud, accident, trust,* or *hardship*, which would render the {612} matter an object of equitable, rather than of legal jurisdiction, as the distinction is known and established in several of the states. It is the peculiar province, for instance, of a court of equity, to relieve against what are called hard bargains. These are contracts, in which, though there may have been no direct fraud or deceit, sufficient to invalidate them in a court of law; yet there may have been some undue, and unconscionable advantage taken of the necessities, or misfortunes of one of the parties, which a court of equity would not tolerate. In such cases, where foreigners are concerned on either side, it would be impossible for the federal judicatories to do justice, without an equitable, as well as a legal jurisdiction. Agreements to convey lands, claimed under the grants of different states, may afford another example of the necessity of an equitable jurisdiction in the federal courts. This reasoning may not be so palpable in those states, where the formal and technical distinction between LAW and EQUITY is not maintained, as in this state, where it is exemplified by every day's practice."

§ 861. The next clause, extends the judicial power "to all cases affecting ambassadors, other public ministers, and consuls." The propriety of this delegation of power to the national judiciary will scarcely be questioned by any persons, who have duly reflected upon the subject. There are various grades of public ministers, from ambassadors (which is the highest grade,) down to common resident ministers, whose rank, and diplomatic precedence, and authority, are well known, and well ascertained in the law and usages of nations. But whatever may be their relative rank and grade, public ministers of every class are the immediate representatives of their sovereigns. As such representatives, {613} they owe no subjection to any laws, but those of their own country, any more than their sovereign; and their actions are not generally deemed subject to the control, of the private law of that state, wherein they are appointed to reside. He, that is subject to the coercion of laws, is necessarily dependent on that power, by which those laws were made. But public ministers ought, in order to perform their duties to their own sovereign, to be independent of every power, except that by which they are sent; and, of consequence, ought not to be subject to the mere municipal law of that nation, wherein they are to exercise their functions. The rights, the powers, the duties, and the privileges of public ministers are, therefore, to be determined, not by any municipal constitutions, but by the law of nature and nations, which is equally obligatory upon all sovereigns, and all states. What these rights, powers, duties, and privileges are, are inquiries properly belonging to a treatise on the law of nations, and need not be discussed here. But it is obvious, that every question, in which these rights, powers, duties, and privileges are involved, is so intimately connected with the public peace, and policy, and diplomacy of the nation, and touches the dignity and interest of the sovereigns of the ministers concerned so deeply, that it would be unsafe, that they should be submitted to any other, than the highest judicature of the nation.

§ 862. Consuls, indeed, have not in strictness a diplomatic character. They are deemed mere commercial agents; and therefore partake of the ordinary character of such agents; and are subject to the municipal laws of the countries, where they reside. Yet, as they are the public agents of the nation, to which {614} they belong, and are often entrusted with the performance of very delicate functions of state, and as they might be greatly embarrassed by being subject to the ordinary jurisdiction of inferior tribunals, state and national, it was thought highly expedient to extend the original jurisdiction of the Supreme Court to them also. The propriety of vesting jurisdiction, in such cases, in some of the national courts seems hardly to have been questioned by the most zealous opponents of the constitution. And in cases *against* ambassadors, and other foreign ministers, and consuls, the jurisdiction has been deemed exclusive.

§ 863. The next clause extends the judicial power "to all cases of admiralty and maritime jurisdiction."

§ 864. The admiralty and maritime jurisdiction, (and the word, "maritime," was doubtless added to guard against any narrow interpretation of the preceding word, "admiralty,") conferred by the constitution, embraces two great classes of cases, one dependent upon locality, and the other upon the nature of the contract. The first respects acts or injuries done upon the high sea, where all nations claim a common right and common jurisdiction; or acts, or injuries done upon the coast of the sea; or, at farthest, acts and injuries done within the ebb and flow of the tide. The second respects contracts, claims, and services purely maritime, and touching rights and duties appertaining to commerce and navigation. The former is again divisible into two great branches, one embracing captures, and questions of prize, arising *jure belli*; the other embracing acts, torts, and injuries strictly of civil cognizance, independent of belligerent operations.

§ 865. By the law of nations the cognizance of all captures, *jure belli*, or, as it is more familiarly phrased, {615} of all questions of prize, and their incidents, belongs exclusively to the courts of the country, to which the captors belong, and from whom they derive their authority to make the capture. No neutral nation has any right to inquire into, or to decide upon, the validity of such capture, even though it should concern property belonging to its own citizens or subjects, unless its own sovereign or territorial rights are violated; but the sole and exclusive jurisdiction belongs to the courts of the capturing belligerent. And this jurisdiction, by the common consent of nations, is vested exclusively in courts of admiralty, possessing an original, or an appellate jurisdiction. The courts of common law are bound to abstain from any decision of questions of this sort, whether they arise directly or indirectly in judgment. The remedy for illegal acts of capture is by the institution of proper prize proceedings in the prize courts of the captors. If justice be there denied, the nation itself becomes responsible to the parties aggrieved; and if every remedy is refused, it then becomes a. subject for the consideration of the nation, to which the parties aggrieved belong, which may vindicate their rights, either by a peaceful appeal to negotiation, or by a resort to arms.

§ 866. It is obvious upon the slightest consideration, that cognizance of all questions of prize, made under the authority of the United States, ought to belong exclusively to the national courts. How, otherwise, can the legality of the captures be satisfactorily ascertained, or deliberately vindicated? It seems not only a natural, but a necessary appendage to the power of war, and negotiation with foreign nations. It would otherwise follow, that the peace of the whole nation might be put at hazard at any time by the misconduct of one {616} of its members. It could neither restore property upon an illegal capture; nor in many cases afford any adequate redress for the wrong; nor punish the aggressor. It would be powerless and palsied. It could not perform, or compel the performance of the duties required by the law of nations. It would be a sovereign without any solid attribute of sovereignty; and move *in vinculis* only to betray its imbecility. Even under the confederation, the power to decide upon questions of capture and prize was exclusively conferred in the last resort upon the national court of appeals. But like all other powers conferred by that instrument, it was totally disregarded, wherever it interfered with state policy, or with extensive popular interests. We have seen, that the sentences of the national prize court of appeals were treated, as mere nullities; and were incapable of being enforced, until after the establishment of the present constitution. The same reasoning, which conducts us to the conclusion, that the national courts ought to have jurisdiction of this class of admiralty cases, conducts us equally to the conclusion, that, to be effectual for the administration of international justice, it ought to be exclusive. And accordingly it has been constantly held, that this jurisdiction is exclusive in the courts of the United States.

§ 867. The other branch of admiralty jurisdiction, dependent upon locality, respects civil acts, torts, and injuries done on the sea, or (in certain cases) on waters of the sea, where the tide ebbs and flows, without any claim of exercising the rights of war. Such are cases of assaults, and other personal injuries; cases of collision, or running of ships against each other; cases of spoliation and damage, (as they are technically called,) such as illegal seizures, or depredations upon property; {617} cases of illegal dispossession, or withholding possession from the owners of ships, commonly called possessory suits; cases of seizures under municipal authority for supposed breaches of revenue, or other prohibitory laws; and cases of salvage for meritorious services performed in saving property, whether derelict, or wrecked, or captured, or otherwise in imminent hazard from extraordinary perils.

§ 868. It is obvious, that this class of cases has, or may have, an intimate relation to the rights and duties of foreigners in navigation and maritime commerce. It may materially affect our intercourse with foreign states; and raise many questions of international law, not merely touching private claims, but national sovereignty, and national reciprocity. Thus, for instance, if a collision should take place at sea between an American and a foreign ship, many important questions of public law might be connected with its just decision; for it is obvious, that it could not be governed by the mere municipal law of either country. So, if a case of recapture, or other salvage service performed to a foreign ship, should occur, it must be decided by the general principles of maritime law, and the doctrines of national reciprocity. Where a recapture is made of a friendly ship from the hands of its enemy, the general doctrine now established is, to restore it upon salvage, if the foreign country, to which it belongs, adopts a reciprocal rule; or to condemn it to the recaptors, if the like rule is adopted in the foreign country. And in other cases of salvage the doctrines of international and maritime law come into full activity, rather than those of any mere municipal code. There is, therefore, a peculiar fitness in appropriating this class of cases to the national tribunals; since they will be more likely to be {618} there decided upon large and comprehensive principles, and to receive a more uniform adjudication; and thus to become more satisfactory to foreigners.

§ 869. The remaining class respects contracts, claims, and services purely maritime. Among these are the claims of material-men and others for repairs and outfits of ships, belonging to foreign nations, or to other states; bottomry bonds for monies lent to ships in foreign ports to relieve their distresses, and enable them to complete their voyages; surveys of vessels damaged by perils of the seas; pilotage on the high seas; and suits for mariners' wages. These, indeed, often arise in the course of the commerce and navigation of the United States; and seem emphatically to belong, as incidents, to the power to regulate commerce. But they may also affect the commerce and navigation of foreign nations. Repairs may be done, and supplies furnished to foreign ships; money may be lent on foreign bottoms; pilotage and mariners' wages may become due in voyages in foreign employment; and in such cases the general maritime law enables the courts of admiralty to administer a wholesome and prompt justice. Indeed, in many of these cases, as the courts of admiralty entertain suits *in rem*, as well as *in personam*, they are often the only courts, in which an effectual redress can be afforded, especially when it is desirable to enforce a specific maritime lien.

§ 870. So that we see, that the admiralty jurisdiction naturally connects itself, on the one hand, with our diplomatic relations and duties to foreign nations, and their subjects; and, on the other hand, with the great interests of navigation and commerce, foreign and domestic. There is, then, a peculiar wisdom in giving to the national government a jurisdiction of this sort, which {619} cannot, be wielded, except for the general good; and which multiplies the securities for the public peace abroad, and gives to commerce and navigation the most encouraging support at home. It may be added, that, in many of the cases included in these latter classes, the same reasons do not exist, as in cases of prize, for an exclusive jurisdiction; and, therefore, whenever the common law is competent to give a remedy in the state courts, they may retain their accustomed concurrent jurisdiction in the administration of it.

§ 871. We have been thus far considering the admiralty and maritime jurisdiction in civil cases only. But it also embraces all public offences, committed on the high seas, and in creeks, havens, basins, and bays within the ebb and flow of the tide, at least in such as are out of the body of any county of a state. In these places the jurisdiction of the courts of admiralty over offences is exclusive; for that of the courts of common law is limited to such offences, as are committed within the body of some county. And on the sea coast, there is an alternate, or divided jurisdiction of the courts of common law, and admiralty, in places between high and low water mark; the former having jurisdiction when, and as far as the tide is out, and the latter when, and as far as the tide is in, *usque ad filum aguæ*; or to high water mark. This criminal jurisdiction of the admiralty is therefore exclusively vested in the national government; and may be exercised over such crimes and offences, as congress may, from time to time, delegate to the cognizance of the national courts. The propriety of vesting this criminal jurisdiction in the national government depends upon the same reasoning, and is established by the same general considerations, as have been already suggested in regard to civil cases {620} it is essentially connected with the due regulation, and protection of our commerce and navigation on the high seas, and with our rights and duties in regard to foreign nations, and their subjects, in the exercise of common sovereignty on the ocean. The states, as such, are not known in our intercourse with foreign nations, and not recognised as common sovereigns on the ocean. And if they were permitted to exercise criminal or civil jurisdiction thereon, there would be endless embarrassments, arising from the conflict of their laws, and the most serious dangers of perpetual controversies with foreign nations. In short, the peace of the Union would be constantly put at hazard by acts, over which it had no control; and by assertions of right, which it might wholly disclaim.

§ 872. The next clause extends the judicial power "to controversies, to which the United States shall be a party." It seems scarcely possible to raise a reasonable doubt, as to the propriety of giving to the national courts jurisdiction of cases, in which the United States are a party. It would be a perfect novelty in the history of national jurisprudence, as well as of public law, that a sovereign had no authority to sue in his own courts. Unless this power were given to the United States, the enforcement of all their rights, powers, contracts, and privileges in their sovereign capacity would be at the mercy of the states. They must be enforced, if at all, in the state tribunals. And there would not only not be any compulsory power over those courts to perform such functions; but there would not be any means of producing uniformity in their decisions. A sovereign, without the means of enforcing civil rights, or compelling the performance, either civilly or criminally, of public duties on the part of the citizens, {621} would be a most extraordinary anomaly. Such a defect would prostrate the Union at the feet of the states. It would compel the national government to become a supplicant for justice before the judicature of those, who were by other parts of the constitution placed in subordination to it.

§ 873. The next clause extends the judicial power

"to controversies between two or more states; be tween a state and the citizens of another state; between citizens of different states, claiming lands under grants of different states; and between a state or the citizens thereof, and foreign states, citizens, or subjects."

Of these, we will speak in their order. And, first; "controversies between two or more states." This power seems to be essential to the preservation of the peace of the Union. "History" (says the Federalist,) "gives us a horrid picture of the dissensions and private wars, which distracted and desolated Germany, prior to the institution of the imperial chamber by Maximilian, towards the close of the fifteenth century; and informs us at the same time of the vast influence of that institution, in appeasing the disorders, and establishing the tranquillity of the empire. This was a court invested with authority to decide finally all differences among the members of the Germanic body." But we need not go for illustrations to the history of other countries. Our own has presented, in past times, abundant proofs of the irritating effects resulting from territorial disputes, and interfering claims, of boundary between the states. And there are yet controversies of this sort, which have brought on a border warfare, at once dangerous to public repose, and incompatible with the public interests.

§ 874. Under the confederation, authority was given {622} to the national government, to hear and determine, (in the manner pointed out in the article,) in the last resort, on appeal, all disputes and differences between two or more states concerning boundary, jurisdiction, or any other cause whatsoever. Before the adoption of this instrument, as well as afterwards, very irritating and vexatious controversies existed between several of the states, in respect to soil, jurisdiction, and boundary; and threatened the most serious public mischiefs. Some of these controversies were heard and determined by the court of commissioners, appointed by congress. But, notwithstanding these adjudications, the conflict was maintained in some cases, until after the establishment of the present constitution.

§ 875. Before the revolution, controversies between the colonies, concerning the extent of their rights of soil, territory, jurisdiction, and boundary, under their respective charters, were heard and determined before the king in council, who exercised original jurisdiction therein, upon the principles of feudal sovereignty. This jurisdiction was often practically asserted, as in the case of the dispute between Massachusetts and New-Hampshire, decided by the privy council, in 1679; and in the case of the dispute between New-Hampshire and New-York, in 1764. Lord Hardwicke recognised this appellate jurisdiction in the most deliberate manner, in the great case of *Penn v. Lord Baltimore*. The same necessity, which gave rise to it in our colonial state, must continue to operate through all future time. Some tribunal, exercising such authority, is essential to prevent an appeal to the sword, and a dissolution of the government. That it ought to be established under the national, rather than under the state, government; or, to speak {623} more properly, that it can be safely established under the former only, would seem to be a position self-evident, and requiring no reasoning to support it. It may justly be presumed, that under the national government in all controversies of this sort, the decision will be impartially made according to the principles of justice; and all the usual and most effectual precautions are taken to secure this impartiality, by confiding it to the highest judicial tribunal.

§ 876. Next; "controversies between a state and the citizens of another state." "There are other sources," says the Federalist, "besides interfering claims of boundary, from which bickerings and animosities may spring up among the members of the Union. To some of these we have been witnesses in the course of our past experience. It will be readily conjectured, that I allude to the fraudulent laws, which have been passed in too many of the states. And though the proposed constitution establishes particular guards against the repetition of those instances, which have hitherto made their appearance; yet it is warrantable to apprehend, that the spirit, which produced them, will assume new shapes, that could not be foreseen, nor specifically provided against. Whatever practices may have a tendency to distract the harmony of the states are proper objects of federal superintendence and control. It may be esteemed the basis of the Union, that 'the citizens of each state shall be entitled to all the privileges and immunities of citizens of the several states.' And if it be a just principle, that every government ought to possess the means of executing its own provisions by its own authority, it will follow, that, in order to the inviolable maintenance of that equality of privileges and {624} immunities, to which the citizens of the Union will be entitled, the national judiciary ought to preside in all cases, in which one state, or its citizens, are opposed to another state, or its citizens. To secure the full effect of so fundamental a provision against all evasion and subterfuge, it is necessary, that its construction should be committed to that tribunal, which, having no local attachments, will be likely to be impartial between the different states and their citizens, and which, owing its official existence to the Union, will never be likely to feel any bias inauspicious to the principles, on which it is founded." It is added, "The reasonableness of the agency of the national courts in cases, in which the state tribunals cannot be supposed to be impartial, speaks for it. No man ought certainly to be a judge in his own cause, or in any cause, in respect to which he has the least interest or bias. This principle has no inconsiderable weight in designating the federal courts, as the proper tribunals for the determination of controversies between different states and their citizens."

§ 877. And here a most important question of a constitutional nature was formerly litigated; and that is, whether the jurisdiction given by the constitution in cases, in which a state is a party, extended to suits brought *against* a state, as well as *by* it, or was exclusively confined to the latter. It is obvious, that, if a suit could be brought by any citizen of one state against another state upon any contract, or matter of property, the state would be constantly subjected to judicial action, to enforce private rights against it in its sovereign capacity. Accordingly at a very early period numerous suits were brought against states by their creditors to enforce the payment of debts, {625} or other claims. The question was made, and most elaborately considered in the celebrated case of *Chisholm v. Georgia*; and the majority of the Supreme Court held, that the judicial power under the constitution applied equally to suits brought *by*, and *against* a state. The learned judges, on that occasion, delivered *seriatim* opinions, containing the grounds of their respective opinions. It is not thy intention to go over these grounds, though they are stated with great ability and legal learning, and exhibit a very thorough mastery of the whole subject. The decision created general alarm among the states; and an amendment was proposed, and ratified by the states, by which the power was entirely taken away, so far as it regards suits brought *against* a state. It is in the following words:

> "The judicial power of the United States shall not be construed to extend to any suit in law, or equity, commenced or prosecuted *against* one of the United States *by* citizens of another state, or by citizens, or subjects of any foreign state."

This amendment was construed to include suits then pending, as well as suits to be commenced thereafter; and accordingly all the suits then pending were dismissed, without any further adjudication.

§ 878. Since this amendment has been made, a question of equal importance has arisen; and that is, whether the amendment applies to original suits only brought against a state, leaving the appellate jurisdiction of the Supreme Court in its full vigour over all constitutional questions, arising in the progress of any suit brought by a state in any state court against any private citizen or alien. But this question will more properly come under review, when we are considering {626} the nature and extent of the appellate jurisdiction of the Supreme Court. At present, it is only necessary to state, that it has been solemnly adjudged, that the amendment applies only to original suits against a state; and does not touch the appellate jurisdiction of the Supreme Court to re-examine, on an appeal or writ of error, a judgment or decree rendered in any state court, in a suit brought originally by a state against any private person.

§ 879. Another inquiry suggested by the original clause, as well as by the amendment, is, when a state is properly to be deemed a party to a suit, so as to avail itself of, or to exempt itself from, the operation of the jurisdiction conferred by the constitution. To such an inquiry, the proper answer is, that a state, in the sense of the constitution, is a party only, when it is on the record as such; and it sues, or is sued in its political capacity. It is not sufficient that it may have an interest in a suit between other persons, or that its rights, powers, privileges, or duties, may come therein incidentally in question. It must be in terms a plaintiff or defendant, so that the judgment, or decree may be binding upon it, as it is in common suits binding upon parties and privies. The point arose in an early stage of the government, in a suit between private persons, where one party asserted the land in controversy to be in Connecticut and the other in New-York; and the court held, that neither state could be considered as a party. It has been again discussed in some late cases; and the doctrine now firmly established is, that a state is not a party in the sense of the constitution, unless it appears on the record, as such, either as plaintiff or defendant. It is not sufficient, that it may have an interest in the cause, or that the parties {627} before the court are sued for acts done, as agents of the state. In short, the very immunity of a state from being made a party, constitutes, or may constitute, a solid ground, why the suit should be maintained against other parties, who act as its agents, or claim under its title; though otherwise, as the principal, it might be fit, that the state should be made a party upon the common principles of a court of equity.

§ 880. The same principle applies to cases, where a state has an interest in a corporation; as when it is a stockholder in an incorporated bank, the corporation is still suable, although the state, as such, is exempted from any action. The state does not, by becoming a corporator, identify itself with the corporation. The bank, in such a case, is not the state, although the state holds an interest in it. Nor will it make any difference in the case, that the state has the sole interest in the corporation, if in fact it creates other persons corporators. An analogous case will be found in the authority, given by an act of congress to the postmaster-general, to bring suits in his official capacity. In such suits the United States are not understood to be a party, although the suits solely regard their interests. The postmaster-general does not, in such cases, sue under the clause giving jurisdiction, "in controversies, to which the United States shall be a party;" but under the clause extending the jurisdiction to cases arising under the laws of the United States.

§ 881. It may, then, be laid down, as a rule, which admits of no exception, that in all cases under the constitution of the United States, where jurisdiction depends upon the party, it is the party named on the record. Consequently the amendment above referred {628} to, which restrains the jurisdiction granted by the constitution over suits against states, is of necessity limited to those suits, in which a state is a party on the record. The amendment has its full effect, if the constitution is construed, as it would have been construed, had the jurisdiction never been extended to suits brought against a state by the citizens of another state, or by aliens.

§ 882. Next. "Controversies between citizens of different states." Although the necessity of this power may not stand upon grounds quite as strong, as some of the preceding, there are high motives of state policy and public justice, by which it can be clearly vindicated. There are many cases, in which such a power may be indispensable, or in the highest degree expedient, to carry into effect some of the privileges and immunities conferred, and some of the prohibitions upon states expressly declared, in the constitution. For example; it is declared, that the citizens of each state shall be entitled to all the privileges and immunities of citizens of the several states. Suppose an attempt is made to evade, or withhold these privileges and immunities, would it not be right to allow the party aggrieved an opportunity of claiming them, in a contest with a citizen of the state, before a tribunal, at once national and impartial? Suppose a state should pass a tender law, or law impairing the obligation of private contracts, or should in the course of its legislation grant unconstitutional preferences to its own citizens, is it not dear, that the jurisdiction, to enforce the obligations of the constitution in such cases, ought to be confided to the national tribunals? These cases are not purely imaginary. They have actually occurred; and may again occur, under peculiar circumstances, in the course of {629} state legislation. What was the fact under the confederation? Each state was obliged to acquiesce in the degree of justice, which another state might choose to yield to its citizens. There was not only danger of animosities growing up from this source; but, in point of fact, there did grow up retaliatory legislation, to meet such real or imagined grievances.

§ 883. Nothing can conduce more to general harmony and confidence among all the states, than a consciousness, that controversies are not exclusively to be decided by the state tribunals; but may, at the election of the party, be brought before the national tribunals. Besides; it cannot escape observation, that the judges in different states hold their offices by a very different tenure. Some hold during good behaviour; some for a term of years; some for a single year; some are irremovable, except upon impeachment; and others may be removed upon address of the legislature. Under such circumstances it cannot but be presumed, that there may arise a course of state policy, or state legislation, exceedingly injurious to the interests of the citizens of other states, both as to real and to personal property. It would require an uncommon exercise of candour or credulity to affirm, that in cases of this sort all the state tribunals would be wholly without state prejudice, or state feelings; or, that they would be as earnest in resisting the encroachments of state authority upon the just rights, and interests of the citizens of other states, as a tribunal differently constituted, and wholly independent of state authority. And if justice should be as fairly, and as firmly administered in the former, as in the latter, still the mischiefs would be most serious, if the public opinion did not indulge such a belief. Justice, in cases of this sort, should not only {630} be above all reproach, but above all suspicion. The sources of state irritations and state jealousies are sufficiently numerous, without leaving open one so copious and constant, as the belief, or the dread of wrong in the administration of state justice. Besides; if the public confidence should continue to follow the state tribunals, (as in many cases it doubtless will,) the provision will become inert and harmless; for, as the party will have his election of the forum, he will not be inclined to desert the state courts, unless for some sound reason, founded either in the nature of his cause, or in the influence of state prejudices. On the other hand, there can be no real danger of injustice to the other side in the decisions of the national tribunals; because the cause must still be decided upon the true principles of the local law, and not by any foreign jurisprudence. There is another circumstance of no small importance, as a matter of policy; and that is, the tendency of such a power to increase the confidence and credit between the commercial and agricultural states. No man can be insensible to the value, in promoting credit, of the belief of there being a prompt, efficient, and impartial administration of justice in enforcing contracts.

§ 884. The next inquiry growing out of this part of the clause is, who are to be deemed citizens of different states within the meaning of it. Are all persons born within a state to be always deemed citizens of that state, notwithstanding any change of domicil; or does their citizenship change with their change of domicil? The answer to this inquiry is equally plain and satisfactory. The constitution having declared, that the citizens of each state shall be entitled to all privileges and immunities of citizens in the several states, every person, who is a citizen of one state, and removes {631} into another, with the intention of taking up his residence and inhabitancy there, becomes, *ipso facto, a* citizen of the state, where he resides; and he then ceases to be a citizen of the state, from which he has removed his residence. Of course, when he gives up his new residence or domicil, and returns to his native, or other state residence or domicil, he re-acquires the character of the latter. What circumstances shall constitute such a change of residence or domi- cil, is an inquiry, more properly belonging to a treatise upon public or municipal law, than to commentaries upon constitutional law. In general, however, it may be said, that a removal from one state into another, *animo manendi*, or with a design of becoming an inhabitant, constitutes a change of domicil, and of course a change of citizenship. But a person, who is a native citizen of one state, never ceases to be a citizen thereof, until he has acquired a new citizenship elsewhere. Residence in a foreign country has no operation upon his character, as a citizen, although it may, for purposes of trade and commerce, impress him with the character of the country. To change allegiance is one thing; to change inhabitancy is quite another thing. The right and the power are not co-extensive in each case. Every citizen of a state is, *ipso, facto*, a citizen of the United States.

§ 885. And a person, who is a naturalized citizen of the United States, by a like residence in any state in the Union, becomes, *ipso facto, a* citizen of that state. So a citizen of a territory of the Union by a like residence acquires the character of the state, where he resides. But a naturalized citizen of the United States, or a citizen, of a territory, is not a citizen of a state, entitled to sue in the courts of the United States in {632} virtue of that character, while he resides in any such terri- tory, nor until he has acquired a residence or domicil in the particular state.

§ 886. A corporation, as such, is not a citizen of a state in the sense of the constitution. But, if all the members of the corporation are citizens, their character will confer jurisdiction; for then it is substantially a suit by citizens suing in their corporate name. And a citizen of a state is entitled to sue, as such, notwithstanding he is a trustee for others, or sues in *autre droit*, as it is technically called, that is, as representative of another. Thus, a citizen may sue, who is a trustee at law, for the benefit of the person entitled to the trust. And an administrator, and an execu- tor may sue for the benefit of the estate, which they represent; for in each of these cases it is their personal suit. But if citizens, who are parties to a suit, are merely nominally, so, as, for instance, if magistrates are officially required to allow suits to be brought in their names for the use or benefit of a citizen or alien, the latter are deemed the substantial parties entitled to sue.

§ 887. Next. "Controversies between citizens of the same state, claiming lands under grants of different states." This clause was not in the first draft of the constitution, but was added without any known objection to its propriety. It is the only instance, in which the constitution directly contemplates the cognizance of disputes between citizens of the same state; but certainly not the only one, in which they may indirectly upon constitutional questions have the benefit of the judicial power of the Union. The Federalist has remarked, that the reasonableness of the agency of the national courts in cases, in which the state tribunals cannot be supposed to be impartial, speaks for itself. {633} No man ought certainly to be a judge in his own cause; or in any cause, in respect to which he has the least inter- est or bias. This principle has no inconsiderable weight in designating the federal courts, as the proper tribunals for the determination of controversies between dif- ferent states and their citizens. And it ought to have the same operation in regard to some cases between citizens of the same state. Claims to land under grants of different states, founded upon adverse pretensions of boundary, are of this description. The courts of neither of the granting states could be expected to be un-biassed. The laws may have even prejudged the question; and tied the courts down to decisions in favour of the grants of the state, to which they belonged. Where this has not been done, it would be natural, that the judges, as men, should feel a strong predilection for the claims of their own government. And, at all events, the providing of a tribunal, having no possible interest on the one side, more than the other, would have a most salutary tendency in quieting the jealousies, and disarming the resentments of the state, whose grants should be held invalid. This jurisdiction attaches not only to grants made, by different states, which were never united; but also to grants made by different states, which were originally united under one jurisdiction, if made since the separation, although the origin of the title may be traced back to an antecedent period.

§ 888. Next. "Controversies between a state, or the citizens thereof; and for-eign states, citizens, or subjects." The Federalist has vindicated this provision in the following brief, but powerful manner: "The peace of the whole ought not to be left at the disposal of a part. The Union will undoubtedly be answerable {634} to foreign powers for the conduct of its members. And the responsibility for an injury ought ever to be accompanied with the faculty of preventing it. As the denial or perversion of justice by the sentences of courts is with reason classed among the just causes of war, it will follow, that the federal judiciary ought to have cognizance of all causes, in which the citizens of other countries are concerned. This is not less essential to the preservation of the public faith, than to the security of the public tranquillity. A distinction may perhaps be imagined between cases arising upon treaties and the laws of nations, and those, which may stand merely on the foot-ing of the municipal law. The former kind may be supposed proper for the federal jurisdiction; the latter for that of the states. But it is at least problematical, wheth-er an unjust sentence against a foreigner, where the subject of controversy was wholly relative to the *lex loci*, would not, if unredressed, be an aggression upon his sovereign, as well as one, which violated the stipulations of a treaty, or the general law of nations. And a still greater objection to the distinction would result from the immense difficulty, if not impossibility, of a practical discrimination between the cases of one complexion, and those of the other. So great a proportion of the controversies, in which foreigners are parties, involve national questions, that it is by far the most safe, and most expedient, to refer all those, in which they are concerned, to the national tribunals."

§ 889. In addition to these suggestions, it may be remarked, that it is of great national importance to advance public, as well as private credit, in our intercourse with foreign nations and their subjects. Nothing can be more beneficial in this respect, than to {635} create an impartial tribunal, to which they may have resort upon all occasions, when it may be necessary to ascertain, or enforce their rights. Besides; it is not wholly immaterial, that the law to be administered in cases of foreigners is often very distinct from the mere municipal code of a state, and de-pendent upon the, law merchant, or the more enlarged consideration of interna-tional rights and duties, in a case of conflict of the foreign and domestic laws. And it may fairly be presumed, that the national tribunals will, from the nature of their ordinary functions, become better acquainted with the general principles, which regulate subjects of this nature, than other courts, however enlightened, which are rarely required to discuss them.

§ 890. In regard to controversies between an American and a foreign state, it is obvious, that the suit must, on one side at least, be wholly voluntary. No foreign state can be compelled to become a party, plaintiff or defendant, in any of our tribunals. If, therefore, it chooses to consent to the institution of any suit, it is its consent alone, which can give effect to the jurisdiction of the court. It is certainly desirable to furnish some peaceable mode of appeal in cases, where any controversy may exist between an American and a foreign state, sufficiently important to require the grievance to be redressed by any other mode, than through the instrumentality of negotiations.

§ 891. The inquiry may here be made, who are to be deemed aliens entitled to sue in the courts of the United States. The general answer is, any person, who is not a citizen of the United States. A foreigner, who is naturalized, is no longer entitled to the character of an alien. And when an alien is the substantial party, it matters not, whether he is a {636} suitor in his oven right; or whether he acts, as a trustee, or personal representative; or whether he is compellable by the local law to sue through some official organ. A foreign corporation, established in a foreign country, all of whose members are aliens, is entitled to sue in the same manner, that an alien may personally sue in the courts of the Union. It is not sufficient to vest the jurisdiction, that an alien is a party to the suit, unless the other party be a citizen. British subjects, born before the American revolution, are to be deemed aliens; and may sue American citizens, born before the revolution, as well as those born since that period. The revolution severed the ties of allegiance; and made the inhabitants of each country aliens to each other. In relation to aliens, however, it should be stated, that they have a right to sue only, while peace exists between their country and our own. For if a war break out, and they thereby become alien enemies, their right to sue is suspended, until the return of peace.

§ 892. We have now finished our review of the classes of cases, to which the judicial power of the United States extends. The next inquiry naturally presented is, in what mode it is to be exercised, and in what courts it is to be vested. The succeeding clause of the constitution answers this inquiry. It is in the following words.

> "In all cases affecting ambassadors, other public ministers, and consuls, and those, in which a state shall be a party, the Supreme Court shall have *original* jurisdiction. In all the other cases before mentioned, the Supreme Court shall have *appellate* jurisdiction, both as to law and fact, with such exceptions and under such regulations, as the congress shall make." {637}

§ 893. The first remark arising out of this clause is, that, as the judicial power of the United States extends to all the cases enumerated in the constitution, it may extend to all such cases in any form, in which judicial power may be exercised. It may, therefore extend to them in the shape of original, or appellate jurisdiction, or both; for there is nothing in the nature of the cases, which binds to the exercise of the one in preference to the other. But it is clear, from the language of the constitution, that, in one form or the other, it is absolutely obligatory upon congress, to vest all the jurisdiction in the national courts, in that class of cases at least, where it has declared, that it shall extend to "*all cases.*"

§ 894. In the next place, the jurisdiction, which is by the constitution to be exercised by the Supreme Court in an *original* form, is very limited, and extends only to cases affecting ambassadors, and other public ministers, and consuls, and cases, where a state is a party. And congress cannot constitutionally confer on it any other, or further original jurisdiction. This is one of the appropriate illustrations of the rule, that the affirmation of a power in particular cases, excludes it in all others. The clause itself would otherwise be wholly inoperative and nugatory. If it had been intended to leave it to the discretion of congress, to apportion the judicial power between the supreme and inferior courts, according to the will of that body, it would have been useless to have proceeded further, than to define the judicial power, and the tribunals, in which it should be vested. Affirmative words often, in their operation, imply a negative of other objects, than those affirmed; and in this case a negative, or exclusive sense, must be given to the words, {638} or they have no operation at all. If the solicitude of the convention, respecting our peace with foreign powers, might induce a provision to be made, that the Supreme Court should have original jurisdiction in cases, which might be supposed to affect them; yet the clause would have proceeded no further, than to provide for such cases, unless some further restriction upon the powers of congress had been intended. The direction, that the Supreme Court shall have appellate jurisdiction in all cases, with such exceptions, as congress shall make, will be no restriction, unless the words are to be deemed exclusive of original jurisdiction. And accordingly, the doctrine is firmly established, that the Supreme Court cannot constitutionally exercise any original jurisdiction, except in the enumerated cases. If congress should confer it, it would be a mere nullity.

§ 895. But although the Supreme Court cannot exercise original jurisdiction in any cases, except those specially enumerated, it is certainly competent for congress to vest in any inferior courts of the United States original jurisdiction of all other cases, not thus specially assigned to the Supreme Court; for there is nothing in the constitution, which excludes such inferior courts from the exercise of such original jurisdiction. Original jurisdiction, so far as the constitution gives a rule, is co-extensive with the judicial power; and except, so far as the constitution has made any distribution of it among the courts of the United States, it remains to be exercised in an original, or appellate form, or both, as congress may in their wisdom deem fit. Now, the constitution has made no distribution, except of the original and appellate jurisdiction of the Supreme Court. It has no where {639} insinuated, that the inferior tribunals shall have no original jurisdiction. It has no where affirmed, that they shall have appellate jurisdiction. Both are left unrestricted and undefined. Of course, as the judicial power is to be vested in the supreme and inferior courts of the Union, both are under the entire control and regulation of congress.

§ 896. Another question of a very different nature is, whether the Supreme Court can exercise appellate jurisdiction in the class of cases, of which original jurisdiction is delegated to it by the constitution; in other words, whether the original jurisdiction excludes the appellate; and so, *e converso*, the latter implies a negative of the former. It has been said, that the very distinction taken in the constitution, between original and appellate jurisdiction, presupposes, that where the one can be exercised, the other cannot. For example, since the original jurisdiction extends to cases, where a state is a party, this is the proper form, in which such cases are to be brought before the Supreme Court; and, therefore, a case, where a state is a party, cannot be brought before the court, in the exercise of its appellate jurisdiction; for the affirmative here, as well as in the cases of original jurisdiction, includes a negative of the cases not enumerated.

§ 897. If the correctness of this reasoning were admitted, it would establish no more, than that the Supreme Court could not exercise appellate jurisdiction in cases, where a state is a party. But it would by no means establish the doctrine, that the judicial power of the United States did not extend, in an appellate form, to such cases. The exercise of appellate jurisdiction is far from being limited, by the terms of {640} the constitution, to the Supreme Court. There can be no doubt, that congress may create a succession of inferior tribunals, in each of which it may vest appellate, as well as original jurisdiction. This results from the very nature of the delegation of the judicial power in the constitution. It is delegated in the most general terms; and may, therefore, be exercised under the authority of congress, under every variety of form of original and appellate jurisdiction. There is nothing in the instrument, which restrains, or limits the power; and it must, consequently, subsist in the utmost latitude, of which it is in its nature susceptible. The result then would be, that, if the appellate jurisdiction over cases, to which a state is a party, could not, according to the terms of the constitution, be exercised by the Supreme Court, it might be exercised exclusively by an inferior tribunal. The soundness of any reasoning, which would lead us to such a conclusion, may well be questioned.

§ 898. But the reasoning itself is not well founded. It proceeds upon the ground, that, because the character of the *party* alone, in some instances, entitles the Supreme Court to maintain original jurisdiction, without any reference to the nature of the case, therefore, the character of the *case*, which in other instances is made the very foundation of appellate jurisdiction, can not attach. Now, that is the very point of controversy. It is not only not admitted, but it is solemnly denied. The argument might just as well, and with quite as much force, be pressed in the opposite direction. It might be said, that the appellate jurisdiction is expressly extended by the constitution to all cases in law and equity, arising under the constitution, laws, and treaties of the United States, and, therefore, in {641} no such cases could the Supreme Court exercise original jurisdiction, even though a state were a party.

§ 899. The next inquiry is, whether the eleventh amendment to the constitution has effected any change of the jurisdiction, thus confided to the judicial power of the United States. The words of the amendment are, "the judicial power of the United States shall not be construed to extend to any suit in law or equity, commenced or prosecuted against one of the states by citizens of another state, or by citizens or subjects of any foreign state." It is a part of our history, that, at the adoption of the constitution, all the states were greatly indebted; and the apprehension, that these debts might be prosecuted in the federal courts, formed a very serious objection to that instrument. Suits were instituted; and the Supreme

Court maintained its jurisdiction. The alarm was general; and, to quiet the apprehensions, that were so extensively entertained, this amendment was proposed in Congress, and adopted by the state legislatures. That its motive was not to maintain the sovereignty of a state from the degradation, supposed to attend a compulsory appearance before the tribunal of the nation, may be inferred from the terms of the amendment. It does not comprehend controversies between two or more states, or between a state and a foreign state. The jurisdiction of the court still extends to these cases; and in these a state may still be sued. We must ascribe the amendment, then, to some other cause, than the dignity of a state. There is no difficulty in finding this cause. Those, who were inhibited from commencing a suit against a state, or from prosecuting one, which might be commenced before the adoption of the amendment, were {642} persons, who might probably be its creditors. There was not much reason to fear, that foreign or sister states would be creditors to any considerable amount; and there was reason to retain the jurisdiction of the court in those cases, because it might be essential to the preservation of peace. The amendment, therefore, extended to suits commenced, or prosecuted by individuals, but not to those brought by states.

§ 900. The first impression made on the mind by this amendment is, that it was intended for those cases, and for those only, in which some demand against a state is made by an individual in the courts of the Union. If we consider the cause, to which it is to be traced, we are conducted to the same conclusion. A general interest might well be felt in leaving to a state the full power of consulting its convenience in the adjustment of its debts, or of other claims upon it. But no interest could be felt in so changing the relations between the whole and its parts, as to strip the government of the means of protecting, by the instrumentality of its courts, the constitution and laws from active violation.

§ 901. This amendment, then, was designed to prevent any suit being originally commenced *by* any private person *against* a state; but it was not designed to control or interfere with the appellate jurisdiction of the Supreme Court in cases, to which that appellate jurisdiction extended before the amendment. A case, therefore, originally commenced *by* a state *against* a private person in any other court, which involved any question arising under the constitution, laws or treaties of the United States, might still be revised by the Supreme Court upon an appeal or writ of Error, as the case might require. {643}

§ 902. Another inquiry, touching the appellate jurisdiction of the Supreme Court, of a still more general character, is, whether it extends only to the inferior courts of the Union, constituted by congress, or reaches to cases decided in the state courts. This question has been made on several occasions; and has been most deliberately and solemnly decided by the Supreme Court that it reaches the latter cases.

§ 903. We have already seen, that appellate jurisdiction is given by the constitution to the Supreme Court in all cases, where it has not original jurisdiction; subject, however, to such exceptions and regulations, as congress may prescribe. It is, therefore, capable of embracing every case enumerated in the constitution, which is not exclusively to be decided by way of original jurisdiction. But the exercise of appellate jurisdiction is far from being limited by the terms of the constitution to the Supreme Court. There can be no doubt, that congress may create a succession of inferior tribunals, in each of which it may vest appellate, as well as original jurisdiction. The judicial power is delegated by the constitution in the most general terms, and may, therefore, be exercised by congress, under every variety of form of appellate, or original jurisdiction. And as there is nothing in the constitution, which restrains, or limits this power, it must, therefore, in all these cases, subsist in the utmost latitude, of which, in its own nature, it is susceptible.

§ 904. If the constitution meant to limit the appellate jurisdiction to cases pending in the courts of the United States, it would necessarily follow, that the jurisdiction of these courts would, in all the cases enumerated in the constitution, be exclusive of state {644} tribunals. How, otherwise, could the jurisdiction extend to *all cases*, arising under the constitution, laws, and treaties of the United States, or, to *all cases* of admiralty and maritime jurisdiction? If some of these cases might be entertained by state tribunals, and no appellate jurisdiction, as to them, should exist, then the appellate power would not extend to *all*, but, to *some*, cases. If state tribunals might exercise concurrent jurisdiction over all, or some of the other classes of cases in the constitution, without control, then the appellate jurisdiction of the United States might, as to such cases, have no real existence, contrary to the manifest intent of the constitution. Under such circumstances, to give effect to the judicial power, it must be construed to be exclusive; and this, not only when the *casus fœderis* should arise directly; but when it should arise incidentally in cases pending in state courts. This construction would abridge the jurisdiction of such courts far more, than has been ever contemplated in any act of congress.

§ 905. But it is plain, that the framers of the constitution did contemplate, that cases within the judicial cognizance of the United States, not only might, but would arise in the state courts in the exercise of their ordinary jurisdiction. With this view, the sixth article declares, that 'this constitution, and the laws of the United States, which shall be made in pursuance thereof, and all treaties made, or which shall be made, under the authority of the United States, shall be the supreme law of the land, and the judges, in every state, shall be bound thereby, any thing, in the constitution or laws of any state, to the contrary notwithstanding.' It is obvious, that this obligation is imperative upon the state judges in their official, and {645} not merely in their private capacities. From the very nature of their judicial duties, they would be called upon to pronounce the law, applicable to the case in judgment. They were not to decide, merely according to the laws, or constitution of the state, but according to the constitution, laws, and treaties of the United States, — 'the supreme law of the land.'

§ 906. A moment's consideration will show us the necessity and propriety of this provision in cases, where the jurisdiction of the state courts is unquestionable. Suppose a contract, for the payment of money, is made between citizens of the same state, and performance thereof is sought in the courts of that state; no person can doubt, that the jurisdiction completely and exclusively attaches, in the first instance, to such courts. Suppose at the trial, the defendant sets up, in his defence, a tender under a state law, making paper money a good tender, or a state law, impairing the obligation of such contract, which law, if binding, would defeat the suit. The constitution of the United States has declared, that no state shall make any thing but gold or silver coin a tender in payment of debts, or pass a law impairing the obligation of contracts. If congress shall not have passed a law, providing for the removal of such a suit to the courts of the United States, must not the state court proceed to hear, and determine it? Can a mere plea in defence be, of itself, a bar to further proceedings, so as to prohibit an inquiry into its truth, or legal propriety, when no other tribunal exists, to whom judicial cognizance of such cases is confided? Suppose an indictment for a crime in a state court and the defendant should allege in his defence, that the crime was created by an *ex post facto* act of the state, {646} must not the state court, in the exercise of a jurisdiction, which has already rightfully attached, have a right to pronounce on the validity, and sufficiency of the defence? It would be extremely difficult, upon any legal principles, to give a negative answer to these inquiries. Innumerable instances of the same sort might be stated, in illustration of the position; and unless the state courts could sustain jurisdiction in such cases, this clause of the sixth article would be without meaning or effect; and public, mischiefs, of a most enormous magnitude, would inevitably ensue.

§ 907. It must, therefore, be conceded, that the constitution, not only contemplated, but meant to provide for cases within the scope of the judicial power of the United States, which might yet depend before state tribunals. It was foreseen, that, in the exercise of their ordinary jurisdiction, state courts would, incidentally, take cognizance of cases arising under the constitution, the laws, and treaties of the United States. Yet to all these cases the judicial power, by the very terms of the constitution, is to extend. It cannot extend by original jurisdiction, if that has already rightfully and exclusively attached in the state courts, which (as has been already shown) may occur; it must, therefore, extend by appellate jurisdiction, or not at all. It would seem to follow, that the appellate power of the United States must, in such cases, extend to state tribunals; and, if in such cases, there is no reason, why it should not equally attach upon all others within the purview of the constitution.

§ 908. It is manifest, that the constitution has proceeded upon a theory of its own, and given, and withheld, powers according to the judgment of the American {647} people, by whom it was adopted. We can only construe its powers, and cannot inquire into the policy, or principles, which induced the grant of them. The constitution has presumed (whether rightly or wrongly, we do not inquire) that state attachments, state prejudices, state jealousies, and state interests, might sometimes obstruct, or control, or be supposed to obstruct, or control, the regular administration of justice. Hence, in controversies between states; between citizens of different states; between citizens, claiming grants under different states; between a state and its citizens, or foreigners; and between citizens and foreigners; it enables the parties, under the authority of congress, to have the controversies heard, tried, and determined before the national tribunals. No other reason, than that, which has been stated, can be assigned, why some, at least, of these cases should not have been left to the cognizance of the state courts. In respect to the other enumerated cases; cases arising under the constitution, laws, and treaties of the United States; cases affecting ambassadors and other public ministers; and cases of admiralty and maritime jurisdiction; reasons of a higher and more extensive nature, touching the safety, peace, and sovereignty of the nation, might well justify a grant of exclusive jurisdiction.

§ 909. This is not all. A motive of another kind, perfectly compatible with the most sincere respect for state tribunals, might induce the grant of appellate power over their decisions. That motive is the importance, and even necessity, of *uniformity* of decisions throughout the whole United States upon all subjects within the purview of the constitution. Judges of equal learning and integrity, in different states, {648} might differently interpret a statute, or a treaty of the United States, or even the constitution itself. If there were no revising authority to control these jarring and discordant judgments, and harmonise them into uniformity, the laws, the treaties, and the constitution of the United States, would be different in different states; and might, perhaps, never have precisely the same construction, obligation, or efficacy, in any two states. The public mischiefs, which would attend such a state of things, would be truly deplorable; and it cannot be believed, that they could have escaped the enlightened convention, which formed the constitution. What, indeed, might then have been only prophecy, has now become fact; and the appellate jurisdiction must continue to be the only adequate remedy for such evils.

§ 910. There is an additional consideration, which is entitled to great weight. The constitution of the United States was designed for the common and equal benefit of all the people of the United States. The judicial power was granted for the same benign and salutary purposes. It was not to be exercised exclusively for the benefit of parties, who might be plaintiffs, and would elect the national forum; but also for the protection of defendants, who might be entitled to try their rights, or assert their privileges, before the same forum. Yet, if the appellate jurisdiction does not extend to such cases, it, will follow, that, as the plaintiff may always elect the state courts, the defendant may be deprived of all the security, which the constitution intended in aid of his rights. Such a state of things can, in no respect, be considered, as giving equal rights.

§ 911. Strong as this conclusion stands upon the {649} general language of the constitution, it may still derive support from other sources. It is an historical fact, that this exposition of the constitution, extending its appellate power to state courts, was, previous to its adoption, uniformly and publicly avowed by its friends, and admitted by its enemies, as the basis of their respective reasonings, both in and out of the state conventions. It is an historical fact, that, at the time, when the judiciary act was submitted to the deliberations of the first congress, composed, as it was, not only of men of great learning and ability, but of men, who had acted a principal part in framing, supporting, or opposing that constitution, the same exposition was explicitly declared, and admitted by the friends, and by the opponents of that system. It is an historical fact, that the Supreme Court of the United States have, from time to time, sustained this appellate jurisdiction in a great variety of cases, brought from the tribunals of many of the most important states in the Union; and that no state tribunal has ever breathed a judicial doubt on the subject, or declined to obey the mandate of the Supreme Court, until a late occasion. This weight of contemporaneous exposition by all parties, this acquiescence of enlightened state courts, and these judicial decisions of the Supreme

Court, through so long a period, places the doctrine upon a foundation of authority, which cannot be shaken, without delivering over the subject to perpetual, and irremediable doubts.

§ 912. It would be difficult, and perhaps not desirable, to lay down any general rules in relation to the cases, in which the judicial power of the courts of the United States is exclusive of the state courts, or in which it may be made so by congress, until they {650} shall be settled by some positive adjudication of the Supreme Court. That there are some cases, in which that power is exclusive, cannot well be doubted; that there are others, in which it may be made so by congress, admits of as little doubt; and that in other cases it is concurrent in the state courts, at least until congress shall have passed some act excluding the concurrent jurisdiction, will scarcely be denied. It seems to be admitted, that the jurisdiction of the courts of the United States is, or at least may be, made exclusive in all cases arising under the constitution, laws, and treaties of the United States; in all cases affecting ambassadors, other public ministers and consuls; in all cases (*in their character exclusive*) of admiralty and maritime jurisdiction; in controversies, to which the United States shall be a party; in controversies between two or more states; in controversies between a state and citizens of another state; and in controversies between a state and foreign states, citizens, or subjects. And it is only in those cases, where, previous to the constitution, state tribunals possessed jurisdiction, independent of national authority, that they can now constitutionally exercise a concurrent jurisdiction.

§ 913. In the exercise of the jurisdiction confided respectively to the state courts, and to those courts of the United States, (where the latter have not appellate jurisdiction,) it is plain, that neither can have any right to interfere with, or control, the operations of the other. It has accordingly been settled, that no state court can issue an injunction upon any judgment in a court of the United States; the latter having an exclusive authority over its own judgments and proceedings. Nor can any state court, or any state legislature, {651} annul the judgments of the courts of the United States, or destroy the rights acquired under them; nor in any manner deprive the Supreme Court of its appellate jurisdiction; nor in any manner interfere with, or control the process (whether mesne or final) of the courts of the United States; nor prescribe the rules or forms of proceeding, nor effect of process, in the courts of the United States; nor issue a mandamus to an officer of the United States, to compel him to perform duties, devolved on him by the laws of the United States. And although writs of *habeas corpus* have been issued by state judges, and state courts, in cases, where the party has been in custody under the authority of process of the courts of the United States, there has been considerable diversity of opinion, whether such an exercise of authority is constitutional; and it yet remains to be decided, whether it can be maintained.

§ 914. On the other hand the national courts have no authority (in cases not within the appellate jurisdiction of the United States) to issue injunctions to judgments in the state courts; or in any other manner to interfere with their jurisdiction or proceedings.

§ 915. Having disposed of these points, we may again recur to the language of the constitution for the purpose of some farther illustrations. The language is, that "the Supreme Court shall have appellate jurisdiction, both as to law and fact, with such exceptions, and under such regulations, as the congress shall make."

§ 916. In the first place, it may not be without use to ascertain, what is here meant by appellate jurisdiction; and what is the mode, in which it may be exercised. The essential criterion of appellate {652} jurisdiction is, that it revises and corrects the proceedings in a cause already instituted, and does not create that cause. In reference to judicial tribunals, an appellate jurisdiction, therefore, necessarily implies, that the subject matter has been already instituted in, and acted upon, by some other court, whose judgment or proceedings are to be revised. This appellate jurisdiction may be exercised in a variety of forms, and indeed in any form, which the legislature may choose to prescribe; but, still, the substance must exist, before the form can be applied to it. To operate at all, then, under the constitution of the United States, it is not sufficient, that there has been a decision by some officer, or department of the United States; it must be by one clothed with judicial authority, and acting in a judicial capacity. A power, therefore, conferred by congress on the Supreme. Court, to issue a mandamus to public officers of the United States generally, is not warranted by the constitution; for it is, in effect, under such circumstances, an exercise of original jurisdiction. But where the object is to revise a judicial proceeding, the mode is wholly immaterial; and a writ of *habeas corpus*, or mandamus, a writ of error, or an appeal, may be used, as the legislature may prescribe.

§ 917. The most usual modes of exercising appellate jurisdiction, at least those, which are most known in the United States, are by a writ of error, or by an appeal, or by some process of removal of a suit from an inferior tribunal. An appeal is a process of civil law origin, and removes a cause entirely, subjecting the fact, as well as the law, to a review and a re-trial. A writ of error is a process of common law origin and it removes nothing for re-examination, but the {653} law. The former mode is usually adopted in cases of equity and admiralty jurisdiction; the latter, in suits at common law tried by a jury.

§ 918. It is observable, that the language of the constitution is, that "the Supreme Court shall have appellate jurisdiction, *both as to law and fact.*" This provision was a subject of no small alarm and misconstruction at the time of the adoption of the constitution, as it was supposed to confer on the Supreme Court, in the exercise of its appellate jurisdiction, the power to review the decision of a jury in mere matters of fact; and thus, in effect, to destroy the validity of their verdict, and to reduce to a mere form the right of a trial by jury in civil cases. The objection was at once seized hold of by the enemies of the constitution; and it was pressed with an urgency and zeal, which were well nigh preventing its ratification. There is certainly some foundation, in the ambiguity of the language, to justify an interpretation, that such a review might constitutionally be within the reach of the appellate power, if congress should choose to carry it to that extreme latitude. But, practically speaking, there was not the slightest danger, that congress would ever adopt such a course, even if it were within their constitutional authority; since it would be at variance with all the habits, feelings, and institutions of the whole country. At least it might be affirmed, that congress would scarcely take such a step, until the people were prepared to surrender all the great securities of their civil, as well as of their political, rights and liberties; and in such an event the retaining of the trial by jury would be a mere mockery. The real object of the provision was to retain the power of reviewing the fact, as well as the law, in cases of equity {654} and admiralty and maritime jurisdiction. And the manner, in which it is expressed, was probably occasioned by the desire to avoid the introduction of the subject of trial by jury in civil cases, upon which the convention were greatly divided in opinion.

§ 919. These views, however reasonable they may seem to considerate minds, did not wholly satisfy the popular opinion; and as the objection had a vast influence upon public opinion, and amendments were proposed by various state conventions on this subject, congress at its first session under the guidance of the friends of the constitution, proposed an amendment, which was ratified by the people, and is now incorporated into the constitution. It is in these words. "In suits at common law, where the value in controversy shall exceed twenty dollars, the right of a trial by jury shall be preserved. And no fact tried by a jury shall be otherwise re-examined in any court of the United States, than according to the rules of the common law." This amendment completely struck down the objection; and has secured the right of a trial by jury, in civil cases, in the fullest latitude of the common law. It is a most important and valuable amendment; and places upon the high ground of constitutional right the inestimable privilege of a trial by jury in civil cases, a privilege scarcely inferior to that in criminal cases, which is conceded by all persons to be essential to political and civil liberty.

§ 920. The appellate jurisdiction is to be "with such exceptions, and under such regulations, as the congress shall prescribe." But, here, a question is presented upon the construction of the constitution, whether the appellate jurisdiction attaches to the Supreme Court, subject to be withdrawn and modified {655} by congress; or, whether an act of congress is necessary to confer the jurisdiction upon the court. If the former be the true construction, then the entire appellate jurisdiction, if congress should make no exceptions or regulations, would attach *proprio vigore* in the Supreme Court. If the latter, then, notwithstanding the imperative language of the constitution, the Supreme Court is lifeless, until congress have conferred power on it. And if congress may confer power, they may repeal it. So that the whole efficiency of the judicial power is left by the constitution wholly unprotected and inert, if congress shall refrain to act. There is certainly very strong ground to maintain, that the language of the constitution meant to confer the appellate jurisdiction absolutely on the Supreme Court, independent of any action by congress; and to require this action to divest, or regulate it. The language, as to the original jurisdiction of the Supreme Court, admits of no doubt. It confers it without any action of congress. Why should not the same language, as to the appellate jurisdiction, have the same interpretation? It leaves the power of congress complete to make exceptions and regulations; but it leaves nothing to their inaction. This construction was asserted in argument at an earlier period of the constitution. And it has since been deliberately confirmed by the Supreme Court.

§ 921. The functions of the judges of the courts of the United States are strictly and exclusively judicial. They cannot, therefore, be called upon to advise the president in any executive measures; or to give extrajudicial interpretations of law; or to act, as commissioners in cases of pensions, or other like proceedings.

§ 922. The next clause of the first section of the {656} third article is:

"The trial of all crimes, except in cases of impeachment, shall be by jury; and such trial shall be held in the state, where such crimes shall have been committed. But when not committed within any state, the trial shall be at such place or places, as the congress may by law have directed."

§ 923. It seems hardly necessary in this place to expatiate upon the antiquity, or importance of the trial by jury in criminal cases. It was from very early times insisted on by our ancestors in the parent country, as the great bulwark of their civil and political liberties, and watched with an unceasing jealousy and solicitude. The right constitutes one of the fundamental articles of Magna Charta, in which it is declared, "*nullus homo capiatur, nec imprisonetur, aut exulet, aut aliquo modo destruatur, &c.; nisi per legale judicium parium suorum, vel per legem terræ*"; no man shall be arrested, nor imprisoned, nor banished, nor deprived of life, &c. but by the judgment of his peers, or by the law of the land. The judgment of his peers here alluded to, and commonly called, in the quaint language of former times, a trial *per pais*, or trial by the country, is the trial by a jury, who are called the peers of the party accused, being of the like condition and equality in the state. When our more immediate ancestors removed to America, they brought this great privilege with them, as their birth-right and inheritance, as a part of that admirable common law, which had fenced round, and interposed barriers on every side against the approaches of arbitrary power. It is now incorporated into all our state constitutions, as a fundamental right; and the constitution of the United States would have {657} been justly obnoxious to the most conclusive objection, if it had not recognised, and confirmed it in the most solemn terms.

§ 924. The great object of a trial by jury in criminal cases is, to guard against a spirit of oppression and tyranny on the part of rulers, and against a spirit of violence and vindictiveness on the part of the people. Indeed, it is often more important to guard against the latter, than the former. The sympathies of all mankind are enlisted against the revenge and fury of a single despot; and every attempt will be made to screen his victims. But it is difficult to escape from the vengeance of an indignant people, roused into hatred by unfounded calumnies, or stimulated to cruelty by bitter political enmities, or unmeasured jealousies. The appeal for safety can, under such circumstances, scarcely be made by innocence in any other manner, than by the severe control of courts of justice, and by the firm and impartial verdict of a jury sworn to do right, and guided solely by legal evidence and a sense of duty. In such a course there is a double security, against the prejudices of judges, who may partake of the wishes and opinions of the government, and against the passions of the multitude, who may demand their victim with a clamorous precipitancy. So long, indeed, as this palladium remains sacred and inviolable, the liberties of a free government cannot wholly fall. But to give it real efficiency, it must be preserved in its purity and dignity; and not, with a view to slight inconveniences, or imaginary burthens, be put into the hands of those, who are incapable of estimating its worth, or are too inert, or too ignorant, or too imbecile, to wield its potent armour. Mr. Justice Blackstone, with the warmth and pride, becoming an Englishman living under {658} its blessed protection, has said: "A celebrated French writer, who concludes, that because Rome, Sparta, and

Carthage have lost their liberties, therefore those of England in time must perish, should have recollected, that Rome, Sparta, and Carthage, at the time, when their liberties were lost, were strangers to the trial by jury."

§ 925. It is observable, that the trial of all crimes is not only to be by jury, but to be held in the state, where they are committed. The object of this clause is to secure the party accused from being dragged to a trial in some distant state, away from his friends, and witnesses, and neighbourhood; and thus subjected to the verdict of mere strangers, who may feel no common sympathy, or who may even cherish animosities, or prejudices against him. Besides this; a trial in a distant state or territory might subject the party to the most oppressive expenses, or perhaps even to the inability of procuring the proper witnesses to establish his innocence. There is little danger, indeed, that congress would ever exert their power in so oppressive, and unjustifiable a manner. But upon a subject, so vital to the security of the citizen, it was fit to leave is little as possible to mere discretion. By the common law, the trial of all crimes is required to be in the county, where they are committed. Nay, it originally carried its jealousy still farther, and required, that the jury itself should come from the vicinage of the place, where the crime was alleged to be committed. This was certainly a precaution, which, however justifiable in an early and barbarous state of society, is little commendable in its more advanced stages. It has been justly remarked, that in such cases to summon a jury, labouring under local prejudices, is laying a snare for {659} their consciences; and though they should have virtue and vigour of mind sufficient to keep them upright, the parties will grow suspicious, and indulge many doubts of the impartiality of the trial. It was doubtless by analogy to this rule of the common law, that all criminal trials are required to be in the state, where they were committed. But as crimes may be committed on the high seas, and elsewhere, out of the territorial jurisdiction of a state, it was indispensable, that, in such cases, congress should be enabled to provide the place of trial.

§ 926. But, although this provision of a trial by jury in criminal cases is thus constitutionally preserved to all citizens, the jealousies and alarms of the opponents of the constitution were not quieted. They insisted, that a bill of rights was indispensable upon other subjects, and that upon this, farther auxiliary rights ought to have been secured. These objections found their way into the state conventions, and were urged with great zeal against the constitution. They did not, however, prevent the adoption of that instrument. But they produced such a strong effect upon the public mind, that congress, immediately after their first meeting, proposed certain amendments, embracing all the suggestions, which appeared of most force; and these amendments were ratified by the several states, and are now become a part of the constitution. They are contained in the fifth and six articles of the amendments, and are as follows:

> "No person shall be held to answer for a capital or otherwise infamous crime, unless on a presentment or indictment of a grand jury, except in cases arising in the land or naval forces, or in the militia, when in actual service, in time of war, or public danger: nor shall any person be subject, for the same offence, {660} to be twice put in jeopardy of life or limb; nor shall be compelled, in any criminal case, to be a witness against himself; nor be deprived of life, liberty, or property, without due process of law; nor shall private property be taken for public use,

without just compensation."

"In all criminal prosecutions, the accused shall enjoy the right to a speedy and public trial, by an impartial jury of the state and district, wherein the crime shall have been committed; which district shall have been previously ascertained by law; and to be informed of the nature and cause of the accusation; to be confronted with the witnesses against him; to have compulsory process for obtaining witnesses in his favour; and to have the assistance of counsel for his defence."

§ 927. Upon the main provisions of these articles a few remarks only will be made, since they are almost self-evident, and can require few illustrations to establish their utility and importance.

§ 928. The first clause requires the interposition of a grand jury, by way of presentment or indictment, before the party accused can be required to answer to any capital and infamous crime, charged against him. And this is regularly true at the common law of all offences, above the grade of common misdemeanors. A grand jury, it is well known, are selected in the manner prescribed by law, and duly sworn to make inquiry, and present all offences committed against the authority of the state government, within the body of the county, for which they are impannelled. In the national courts, they are sworn to inquire, and present all offences committed against the authority of the national government within the state or district, for {661} which they are impannelled, or elsewhere within the jurisdiction of the national government. The grand jury may consist of any number, not less than twelve, nor more than twenty-three; and twelve at least must concur in every accusation. They sit in secret, and examine the evidence laid before them by themselves. A presentment, properly speaking, is an accusation made *ex mero motu* by a grand jury of an offence upon their own observation and knowledge, or upon evidence before them, and without any bill of indictment laid before them at the suit of the government. An indictment is a written accusation of an offence preferred to, and presented, upon oath, as true, by a grand jury at the suit of the government. Upon a presentment the proper officer of the court must frame an indictment, before the party accused can be put to answer it. But an indictment is usually in the first instance framed by the officers of the government, and laid before the grand jury. When the grand jury have heard the evidence, if they are of opinion, that the indictment is groundless, or not supported by evidence, they used formerly to endorse on the back of the bill, "ignoramus," or we know nothing of it, whence the bill was said to be *ignored*. But now they assert in plain English, "not a true bill," or which is a better way, "not found;" and then the party is entitled to be discharged, if in custody, without farther answer. But a fresh bill may be preferred against him by another grand jury. If the grand jury are satisfied of the truth of the accusation, then they write on the back of the bill, "a true bill," (or anciently, "*billa vera.*") The bill is then said to be found, and is publicly returned into court; the party stands indicted, and may then be required to answer the matters charged against him. {662}

§ 929. From this summary statement it is obvious, that the grand jury perform most important public functions; and are a great security to the citizens against vindictive prosecutions, either by the government, or by political partisans, or by private enemies. Nor is this all; the indictment must charge the time, and place, and nature, and circumstances, of the offence, with clearness and certainty; so that the party may have full notice of the charge, and be able to make his defence with all reasonable knowledge and ability.

§ 930. Another clause declares, that no person shall be subject, "for the same offence, to be twice put in jeopardy of life and limb." This, again, is another great privilege secured by the common law. The meaning of it is, that a party shall not be tried a second time for the same offence, after he has once been convicted, or acquitted of the offence charged, by the verdict of a jury, and judgment has passed thereon for, or against him. But it does not mean, that he shall not be tried for the offence a second time, if the jury have been discharged without giving any verdict; or, if, having given a verdict, judgment has been arrested upon it, or a new trial has been granted in his favour; for, in such a case, his life or limb cannot judicially be said to have been put in jeopardy.

§ 931. The next clause prohibits any person from being compelled, in any criminal case, to be a witness against himself, or from being deprived of life, liberty, or property, without due process of law. This also is but an affirmance of a common law privilege. But it is of inestimable value. It is well known, that in some countries, not only are criminals compelled to give evidence against themselves, but are subjected to the rack {663} or torture in order to procure a confession of guilt. And what is worse, it has been (as if in mockery or scorn) attempted to excuse, or justify it, upon the score of mercy and humanity to the accused. It has been contrived, (it is pretended,) that innocence should manifest itself by a stout resistance, or guilt by a plain confession; as if a man's innocence were to be tried by the hardness of his constitution, and his guilt by the sensibility of his nerves. Cicero, many ages ago, though he lived in a state, wherein it was usual to put slaves to the torture, in order to furnish evidence, has denounced the absurdity and wickedness of the measure in terms of glowing eloquence, as striking, as they are brief. They are conceived in the spirit of Tacitus, and breathe all his pregnant and indignant sarcasm. Ulpian, also, at a still later period in Roman jurisprudence, stamped the practice with severe reproof.

§ 932. The other part of the clause is but an enlargement of the language of magna charta, "*nec super eum ibimus, nec super eum mittimus, nisi per legale judicium parium suorum, vel per legem terræ,*" neither will we pass upon him, or condemn him, but by the lawful judgment of his peers, or by the law of the land. Lord Coke says, that these latter words, *per legem terræ* (by the law of the land,) mean by due process of law, that is, without due presentment or indictment, and being brought in to answer thereto by due process of the common law. So that this clause in effect affirms the right of trial according to the process and proceedings of the common law.

§ 933. The concluding clause is, that private property shall not be taken for public use without just compensation. This is an affirmance of a great doctrine established by the common law for the protection of {664} private property. It is founded in natural equity, and is laid down by jurists as a principle of universal law. Indeed, in a free government, almost all other rights would become utterly worthless, if the government possessed an uncontrollable power over the private fortune of every citizen. One of the fundamental objects of every good government must be the due administration of justice; and how vain it would be to speak of such an administration, when all property is subject to the will or caprice of the legislature, and the rulers.

§ 934. The other article in declaring, that the accused shall enjoy the right to a speedy and public trial by an impartial jury of the state or district, wherein the crime shall have been committed, (which district shall be previously ascertained by law,) and to be informed of the nature and cause of the accusation, and to be confronted with the witnesses against him, does but follow out the established course of the common law in all trials for crimes. The trial is always public; the witnesses are sworn, and give in their testimony (at least in capital cases) in the presence of the accused; the nature and cause of the accusation is accurately laid down in the indictment; and the trial is at once speedy, impartial, and in the district of the offence. Without in any measure impugning the propriety of these provisions, it may be suggested, that there seems to have been an undue solicitude to introduce into the constitution some of the general guards and proceedings of the common law in criminal trials, (truly admirable in themselves) without sufficiently adverting to the consideration, that unless the whole system is incorporated, and especially the law of evidence, a corrupt legislature, or a debased and servile people, may render {665} the whole little more, than a solemn pageantry. If, on the other hand, the people are enlightened, and honest, and zealous in defence of their rights and liberties, it will be impossible to surprise them into a surrender of a single valuable appendage of the trial by jury.

§ 935. The remaining clauses are of more direct significance, and necessity. The accused is entitled to have compulsory process for obtaining witnesses in his favour, and to have the assistance of counsel. A very short review of the state of the common law, on these points, will put their propriety beyond question. In the first place, it was an anciently and commonly received practice, derived from the civil law, and which Mr. Justice Blackstone says, in his day, still obtained in France, though since the revolution it has been swept away, not to suffer the party accused in capital cases to exculpate himself by the testimony of any witnesses. Of this practice the courts grew so heartily ashamed from its unreasonable and oppressive character, that another practice was gradually introduced, of examining witnesses for the accused, but not upon oath; the consequence of which was, that the jury gave less credit to this latter evidence, than to that produced by the government. Sir Edward Coke denounced the practice as tyrannical and unjust; and contended, that, in criminal cases, the party accused was entitled to have witnesses sworn for him. The house of commons, soon after the accession of the house of Stuart to the throne of England, insisted, in a particular bill, then pending, and, against the efforts both of the crown and the house of lords, carried a clause affirming the right, in cases tried under that act, of witnesses being sworn for, as well as against, the accused. By the statute of {666} 7 Will. 3, ch. 3, the same measure of justice was established throughout the realm, in cases of treason; and afterwards, in the reign of Queen Anne, the like rule was extended to all cases of treason and felony. The right seems never to have been doubted, or denied, in cases of mere misdemeanors. For what causes, and upon what grounds this distinction was maintained, or even excused, it is impossible to assign any satisfactory, or even plausible reasoning. Surely, a man's life must be of infinitely more value, than any subordinate punishment; and if he might protect himself against the latter by proofs of his innocence, there would seem to be irresistible reasons for permitting him to do the same in capital offences. The common suggestion has been, that in capital cases no man could, or rather ought, to be convicted, unless upon evidence so conclusive and satisfactory, as to be above contradiction or doubt. But who can say, whether it be in any case so high, until all the proofs in favour, as well as against, the party have been heard? Witnesses for the government may swear falsely, and directly to the matter in charge; and, until opposing testimony is heard, there may not be the slightest ground to doubt its truth; and yet, when such is heard, it may be incontestible, that it is wholly unworthy of belief. The real fact seems to be, that the practice was early adopted into the criminal law in capital cases, in which the crown was supposed to take a peculiar interest, in base subserviency to the wishes of the latter. It is a reproach to the criminal jurisprudence of England, which the state trials, antecedently to the revolution of 1688, but too strongly sustain. They are crimsoned with the blood of persons, who were condemned to death, not only against law, but against the clearest rules of evidence. {667}

§ 936. Another anomaly in the common law is, that in capital cases the prisoner is not, upon his trial upon the general issue, entitled to have counsel, unless some matter of law shall arise, proper to be debated. That is, in other words, that he shall not have the benefit of the talents and assistance of counsel in examining the witnesses, or making his defence before the jury. Mr. Justice Blackstone, with all his habitual reverence for the institutions of English jurisprudence, as they actually exist, speaks out upon this subject with the free spirit of a patriot and a jurist. This, he says, is "a rule, which, however it may be palliated under cover of that noble declaration of the law, when rightly understood, that the judge shall be counsel for the prisoner, that is, shall see, that the proceedings against him are legal, and strictly regular, seems to be not all of a piece with the rest of the humane treatment of prisoners by the English law. For upon what face of reason can that assistance be denied to save the life of a man, which is yet allowed him in prosecutions for every petty trespass." The defect has indeed been cured in England in cases of treason; but it still remains unprovided for in all other cases, to (what one can hardly help deeming) the discredit of the free genius of the English constitution.

§ 937. The wisdom of both of these provisions is, therefore, manifest, since they make matter of constitutional right, what the common law had left in a most imperfect and questionable state. The right to have witnesses sworn, and counsel employed for the prisoner, are scarcely less important privileges, than the right of a trial by jury. The omission of them in the constitution is a matter of surprise; and their present incorporation is matter of honest congratulation among all the friends of rational liberty. {668}

§ 938. There yet remain one or two subjects connected with the judiciary, which, however, grow out of other amendments made to the constitution; and will naturally find their place in our review of that part of these Commentaries, which embraces a review of the remaining amendments.

CHAPTER XXXIX.

DEFINITION AND EVIDENCE OF TREASON.

§ 939. THE third section of the third article is as follows:

> "Treason against the United States shall consist only in levying war against them, or in adhering to their enemies, giving them aid and comfort. No person shall be convicted of treason, unless on the testimony of two witnesses to the same overt act, or on confession in open court."

§ 940. Treason is generally deemed the highest crime, which can be committed in civil society, since its aim is an overthrow of the government, and a public resistance of its powers by force. Its tendency is to create universal danger and alarm; and on this account it is peculiarly odious, and often visited with the deepest public resentment. Even a charge of this nature, made against an individual, is deemed so opprobrious, that, whether just or unjust, it subjects him to suspicion and hatred; and, in times of high political excitement, acts of a very subordinate nature are often, by popular prejudices, as well as by royal resentment, magnified into this ruinous importance. It is therefore, of very great importance, that its true nature and limits should be exactly ascertained; and Montesquieu was so sensible of it, that he has not scrupled to declare, that if the crime of treason be indeterminate, that alone is sufficient to make any government degenerate into arbitrary power. The history of England itself is full of melancholy instruction on this subject. By the ancient common law it was left very much to discretion to determine, {670} what acts were, and were not, treason; and the judges of those times, holding office at the pleasure of the crown, became but too often instruments in its hands of foul injustice. At the instance of tyrannical princes they had abundant opportunities to create *constructive* treasons; that is, by forced and arbitrary constructions, to raise offences into the guilt and punishment of treason, which were not suspected to be such. The grievance of these constructive treasons was so enormous, and so often weighed down the innocent, and the patriotic, that it was found necessary, as early as the reign of Edward the Third, for parliament to interfere, and arrest it, by declaring and defining all the different branches of treason. This statute has ever since remained the pole star of English jurisprudence upon this subject. And although, upon temporary emergencies, and in arbitrary reigns, since that period, other treasons have been created, the sober sense of the nation has generally abrogated them, or reduced their power within narrow limits.

§ 941. Nor have republics been exempt from violence and tyranny of a similar character. The Federalist has justly remarked, that newfangled and artificial treasons have been the great engines, by which violent factions, the natural offspring of free governments, have usually wreaked their alternate malignity on each other.

§ 942. It was under the influence of these admonitions furnished by history and human experience, that the convention deemed it necessary to interpose an impassable barrier against arbitrary constructions, either by the courts or by congress, upon the crime of treason. It confines it to two species; first, the levying of war against the United States; and secondly, adhering {671} to their enemies, giving them aid and comfort. In so doing, they have adopted the very words of the Statute of Treason of Edward the Third; and thus by implication, in order to cut off at once all chances of arbitrary constructions, they have recognised the well-settled interpretation of these phrases in the administration of criminal law, which has prevailed for ages.

§ 943. The other part of the clause, requiring the testimony of two witnesses to the same overt act, or a confession *in open court*, to justify a conviction is founded upon the same reasoning. A like provision exists in British jurisprudence, founded upon the same great policy of protecting men against false testimony, and unguarded confessions, to their utter ruin. It has been well remarked, that confessions are the weakest and most suspicious of all testimony; ever liable to be obtained by artifice, false hopes, promises of favour, or menaces; seldom remembered accurately, or reported with due precision; and incapable, in their nature, of being disproved by other negative evidence. To which it may be added, that it is easy to be forged, and the most difficult to guard against. An unprincipled demagogue, or a corrupt courtier, might otherwise hold the lives of the purest patriots in his hands, without the means of proving the falsity of the charge, if a secret confession, uncorroborated by other evidence, would furnish a sufficient foundation and proof of guilt. And wisely, also, has the constitution declined to suffer the testimony of a single witness, however high, to be sufficient to establish such a crime, which rouses against the victim at once private honour and public hostility. There must, as there should, be a concurrence of two witnesses to the same overt act, that is, {672} open act of treason, who are above all reasonable exception.

§ 944. The subject of the power of congress to declare the punishment of treason, and the consequent disabilities, have been already commented on in another place.

CHAPTER XL.

PRIVILEGES OF CITIZENS — FUGITIVES — SLAVES.

{673}

§ 945. THE fourth article of the constitution contains several important provisions, some of which have been already considered. Among these are, the faith and credit to be given to state acts, records, and judgments, and the mode of proving them, and the effect thereof; the admission of new states into the Union; and the regulation and disposal of the territory, and other property of the United States. We shall now proceed to those, which still remain for examination.

§ 946. The first is,

> "The citizens of each state shall be entitled to all privileges and immunities of citizens in the several states."

There was an article upon the same subject in the confederation, which declared, "that the free inhabitants of each of these states, paupers, vagabonds, and fugitives from justice excepted, shall be entitled to all privileges and immunities of free citizens in the several states; and the people of each state shall, in every other, enjoy all the privileges of trade and commerce, subject to the same duties, impositions, and restrictions, as the inhabitants thereof respectively," &c. It was remarked by the Federalist, that there is a strange confusion in this language. Why the terms, *free inhabitants*, are used in one part of the article, *free citizens* in another, and *people in* another; or what is meant by superadding to "all privileges and immunities of free citizens," "all the privileges of trade and commerce," cannot easily be determined. It seems to be a construction, however, scarcely {674} avoidable, that those, who come under the denomination of *free inhabitants* of a state, although not citizens of such state, are entitled, in every other state, to all the privileges of *free citizens* of the latter; that is to greater privileges, than they may be entitled to in their own state.

§ 947. The provision in the constitution avoids all this ambiguity. It is plain and simple in its language; and its object is not easily to be mistaken. Connected with the exclusive power of naturalization in the national government, it puts at rest many of the difficulties, which affected the construction of the article of the confederation. It is obvious, that, if the citizens of each state were to be deemed aliens to each other, they could not take, or hold real estate, or other privileges, except as other aliens. The intention of this clause was to confer on them, if one may so say, a general citizenship; and to communicate all the privileges and immunities, which the citizens of the same state would be entitled to under the like circumstances.

§ 948. The next clause is as follows:

> "A person charged in any state with treason, felony, or other crime, who shall

flee from justice, and be found in another state, shall on demand of the executive authority of the state, from which he fled, be delivered up, to be removed to the state having jurisdiction of the crime."

A provision, substantially the same, existed under the confederation.

§ 949. It has been often made a question, how far any nation is, by the law of nations, and independent of any treaty stipulations, bound to surrender upon demand fugitives from justice, who, having committed crimes in another country, have fled thither for shelter. Mr. Chancellor Kent considers it clear upon principle, {975} as well as authority, that every state is bound to deny an asylum to criminals, and, upon application and due examination of the case, to surrender the fugitive to the foreign state, where the crime has been committed. Other distinguished judges and jurists have entertained a different opinion. It is not uncommon for treaties to contain mutual stipulations for the surrender of criminals; and the United States have sometimes been a party to such an arrangement.

§ 950. But, however the point may be, as to foreign nations, it cannot be questioned, that it is of vital importance to the public administration of criminal justice, and the security of the respective states, that criminals, who have committed crimes therein, should not find an asylum in other states; but should be surrendered up for trial and punishment. It is a power most salutary in its general operation, by discouraging crimes, and cutting off the chances of escape from punishment. It will promote harmony and good feelings among the states; and it will increase the general sense of the blessings of the national government. It will, moreover, give strength to a great moral duty, which neighbouring states especially owe to each other, by elevating the policy of the mutual suppression of crimes into a legal obligation. Hitherto it has proved as useful in practice, as it is unexceptionable in its character.

§ 951. The next clause is,

"No person held to service or labor in one state under the laws thereof, escaping into another shall in consequence of any law or regulation therein be discharged from such service or labour; but shall be delivered up on the claim of the party, to whom such service or labour may be due." {676}

§ 952. This clause was introduced into the constitution solely for the benefit of the slave-holding states, to enable them to reclaim their fugitive slaves, who should escape into other states, where slavery is not tolerated. The want of such a provision under the confederation was felt, as a grievous inconvenience, by the slave-holding states, since in many states no aid whatsoever would be allowed to the owners; and sometimes indeed they met with open resistance. In fact, it cannot escape the attention of every intelligent reader, that many sacrifices of opinion and feeling are to be found made by the Eastern and Middle states to the peculiar interests of the south. This forms no just subject of complaint; but it should for ever repress the delusive and mischievous notion, that the south has not at all times had its full share of benefits from the Union.

CHAPTER XLI.

GUARANTY OF REPUBLICAN GOVERNMENT — MODE OF MAKING AMENDMENTS.

{677}

§ 953. THE fourth section of the fourth article is as follows:

"The United States shall guaranty to every state in this Union a republican form of government; and shall protect each of them against invasion; and on application of the legislature, or of the executive, when the legislature cannot be convened, against domestic violence."

§ 954. The want of a provision of this nature was felt, as a capital defect in the plan of the confederation, as it might in its consequences endanger, if not overthrow, the Union. Without a guaranty, the assistance to be derived from the national government in repelling domestic dangers, which might threaten the existence of the state constitutions, could not be demanded, as a right, from the national government. Usurpation might raise its standard, and trample upon the liberties of the people, while the national government could legally do nothing more, than behold the encroachments with indignation and regret. A successful faction might erect a tyranny on the ruins of order and law; while no succour could be constitutionally afforded by the Union to the friends and supporters of the government. But this is not all. The destruction of the national government itself, or of neighbouring states, might result from a successful rebellion in a single state. Who can determine, what would have been the issue, if the insurrection in Massachusetts, in 1787, had been successful, {678} and the malecontents had been headed by a Caesar or a Cromwell? If a despotic or monarchical government were established in one state, it would bring on the ruin of the whole republic. Montesquieu has acutely remarked, that confederated governments should be formed only between states, whose form of government is not only similar, but also republican.

§ 955. The fifth article of the constitution respects the mode of making amendments to it. It is in these words:

"The congress, whenever two thirds of both houses shall deem it necessary, shall propose amendments to this constitution, or, on the application of the legislatures of two thirds of the several states, shall call a convention for proposing amendments, which, in either case, shall be valid to all intents and purposes, as part of this constitution, when ratified by the legislatures of three fourths of the several states, or by conventions in three fourths thereof, as the one or the other mode of ratification may be proposed by the congress; provided, that no amendment, which may be made prior to the year one thousand eight hundred and eight, shall in any manner affect the first and fourth clauses in the ninth section of the first article; and that no state, without its consent, shall be deprived of its equal suffrage in the senate."

§ 956. Upon this subject little need be said to persuade us, at once, of its utility and importance. It is obvious, that no human government can ever be perfect; and that it is impossible to foresee, or guard against all the exigencies, which may, in different ages, require different adaptations and modifications of powers to suit the various necessities of the people. A government, forever changing and changeable, is, indeed, {679} in a state bordering upon anarchy and confusion. A government, which, in its own organization, provides no means of change, but assumes to be fixed and unalterable, must, after a while, become wholly unsuited to the circumstances of the nation; and it will either degenerate into a despotism, or by the pressure of its inequalities bring on a revolution. It is wise, therefore, in every government, and especially in a republic, to provide means for altering, and improving the fabric of government, as time and experience, or the new phases of human affairs, may render proper, in order to promote the happiness and safety of the people. The great principle to be sought is to make the changes practicable, but not too easy; to secure due deliberation, and caution; and to follow experience, rather than to open a way for experiments, suggested by mere speculation or theory.

§ 957. In regard to the constitution of the United States, it is confessedly a new experiment in the history of nations. Its framers were not bold or rash enough to believe, or to pronounce it to be perfect. They made use of the best lights, which they possessed, to form and adjust its parts, and mould its materials. But they knew, that time might develope many defects in its arrangements, and many deficiencies in its powers. They desired, that it might be open to improvement; and under the guidance of the sober judgment and enlightened skill of the country, to be perpetually approaching nearer and nearer to perfection. It was obvious, too, that the means of amendment might avert, or at least have a tendency to avert, the most serious perils, to which confederated republics are liable, and by which all of them have hitherto been shipwrecked. They knew, that the besetting sin of {680} republics is a restlessness of temperament, and a spirit of discontent at slight evils. They knew the pride and jealousy of state power in confederacies; and they wished to disarm them of their potency, by providing a safe means to break the force, if not wholly to ward off the blows, which would, from time to time, under the garb of patriotism, or a love of the people, be aimed at the constitution. They believed, that the power of amendment was, if one may so say, the safety valve to let off all temporary effervescences and excitements; and the real effective instrument to control and adjust the movements of the machinery, when out of order, or in danger of self-destruction.

§ 958. Upon the propriety of the power, in some form, there will probably be little controversy. The only question is, whether it is so arranged, as to accomplish its objects in the safest mode; safest for the stability of the government; and safest for the rights and liberties of the people.

§ 959. Two modes are pointed out, the one at the instance of the government itself, through the instrumentality of congress; the other, at the instance of the states, through the instrumentality of a convention. Congress, whenever two thirds of each house shall concur in the expediency of an amendment, may propose it for adoption. The legislatures of two thirds of the states may require a convention to be called, for the purpose of proposing amendments. In each case, three fourths of the states, either through their legislatures, or conventions, called for the purpose, must concur in every amendment, before it becomes a part of the constitution. That this mode of obtaining amendments is practicable, is abundantly demonstrated by our past experience in the only mode hitherto found {681} necessary, that of amendments proposed by congress. In this mode twelve amendments have already been incorporated into the constitution. The guards, too, against the too hasty exercise of the power, under temporary discontents or excitements, are apparently sufficient. Two thirds of congress, or of the legislatures of the states, must concur in proposing, or requiring amendments to be proposed; and three fourths of the states must ratify them. Time is thus allowed, and ample time, for deliberation, both in proposing and ratifying amendments. They cannot be carried by surprise, or intrigue, or artifice. Indeed, years may elapse before a deliberate judgment may be passed upon them, unless some pressing emergency calls for instant action. An amendment, which has the deliberate judgment of two-thirds of congress, and of three fourths of the states, can scarcely be deemed unsuited to the prosperity, or security of the republic. It must combine as much wisdom and experience in its favour, as ordinarily can belong to the management of any human concerns. In England the supreme power of the nation resides in parliament; and, in a legal sense, it is so omnipotent, that it has authority to change the whole structure of the constitution, without resort to any confirmation of the people. There is, indeed, little danger, that it will so do, as long as the people are fairly represented in it. But still it does, theoretically speaking, possess the power; and it has actually exercised it so far, as to change the succession to the crown, and mould to its will some portions of the internal structure of the constitution.

§ 960. Upon the subject of the national constitution, we may adopt without hesitation the language of a learned commentator. "Nor," says he, "can we {682} too much applaud a constitution, which thus provides a safe and peaceable remedy for its own defects, as they may, from time to time, be discovered. A change of government in other countries is almost always attended with convulsions, which threaten its entire dissolution; and with scenes of horror, which deter mankind from every attempt to correct abuses, or remove oppressions, until they have become altogether intolerable. In America we may reasonably hope, that neither of these evils need be apprehended. Nor is there any reason to fear, that this provision in the constitution will produce any instability in the government. The mode, both of originating and ratifying amendments, (in either mode, which the constitution directs,) must necessarily be attended with such obstacles and delays, as must prove a sufficient bar against light or frequent innovations. And, as a further security against them, the same article further provides, that no amendment, which may be made prior to the year 1808, shall, in any manner affect those clauses of the ninth section of the first article, which relate to the migration or importation of such persons, as the states may think proper to allow; and to the manner, in which direct taxes shall be laid; and that no state shall, without its consent, be deprived of its equal suffrage in the senate."

CHAPTER XLII.

PUBLIC DEBTS — SUPREMACY OF CONSTITUTION AND LAWS.

§ 961. THE next clause of the sixth article of the constitution is:

"All debts contracted and engagements entered into before the adoption of this constitution, shall be as valid against the United States, under this constitution, as under the confederation."

§ 962. This can be considered in no other light, than as a declaratory proposition, resulting from the law of nations, and the moral obligations of society. Nothing is more clear upon reason or general law, than the doctrine, that revolutions in government have, or rather ought to have, no effect whatsoever upon private rights, and contracts, or upon the public obligations of nations. It results from the first principles of moral duty, and responsibility, deducible from the law of nature, and applied to the intercourse and social relations of nations. A change in the political form of a society ought to have no power to produce a dissolution of any of its moral obligations.

§ 963. This declaration was probably inserted in the constitution, not only as a solemn recognition of the obligations of the government resulting from national law; but for the more complete satisfaction and security of the public creditors, foreign as well as domestic. The articles of confederation contained a similar stipulation in respect to the bills of credit emitted, monies borrowed, and debts contracted, by or under the authority of congress, before the ratification of the confederation. {684}

§ 964. The next clause is,

"This constitution, and the laws of the United States, which shall be made in pursuance thereof, and all treaties made, or which shall be made, under the authority of the United States, shall be the supreme law of the land. And the judges in every state shall be bound thereby, any thing in the constitution or laws of any state to the contrary notwithstanding."

§ 965. The propriety of this clause would seem to result from the very nature of the constitution. If it was to establish a national government, that government ought, to the extent of its powers and rights, to be supreme. It would be a perfect solecism to affirm, that, a national government should exist with certain powers; and yet, that in the exercise of those powers it should not be supreme. What other inference could have been drawn, than of their supremacy, if the constitution had been totally silent And surely a positive affirmance of that, which is necessarily implied, cannot in a case of such vital importance be deemed unimportant. The very circumstance, that a question might be made, would irresistibly lead to the conclusion, that it ought not to be left to inference. A law, by the very meaning of the term, includes supremacy. It is a rule, which those, to whom it is prescribed, are bound to observe. This results from every political association. If individuals enter into a state of society, the laws of that society must be the supreme regulator of their conduct. If a number of political societies enter into a larger political society, the laws, which the latter may enact, pursuant to the powers entrusted to it by its constitution, must necessarily be supreme over those societies, and the individuals, of whom they are composed. It would otherwise be a mere treaty, dependent {685} upon the good faith of the parties, and not a government, which is only another name for political power and supremacy. But it will not follow, that acts of the larger society, which are not pursuant to its constitutional powers, but which are invasions of the residuary authorities of the smaller societies, will become the supreme law of the land. They will be merely acts of usurpation, and will deserve to be treated as such. Hence we perceive, that the above clause only declares a truth, which flows immediately and necessarily from the institution of a national government. It will be observed, that the supremacy of the laws is attached to those only, which are made in pursuance of the constitution; a caution very proper in itself, but in fact the limitation would have arisen by irresistible implication, if it had not been expressed.

§ 966. In regard to treaties, there is equal reason, why they should be held, when made, to be the supreme law of the land. It is to be considered, that treaties constitute solemn compacts of binding obligation among nations; and unless they are scrupulously obeyed, and enforced, no foreign nation would consent to negotiate with us; or if it did, any want of strict fidelity on our part in the discharge of the treaty stipulations would be visited by reprisals, or war. It is, therefore, indispensable, that they should have the obligation and force of a law, that they may be executed by the judicial power, and be obeyed like other laws. This will not prevent them from being cancelled or abrogated by the nation upon grave and suitable occasions; for it will not be disputed, that they are subject to the legislative power, and may be repealed, like other laws, at its pleasure; or they may be varied by new treaties. Still, while they do subsist, they ought to {686} have a positive binding efficacy, as laws, upon all the states, and all the citizens of the states. The peace of the nation, and its good faith, and moral dignity, indispensably require, that all state laws should be subjected to their supremacy. The difference between considering them as laws, and considering them as executory, or executed contracts, is exceedingly important in the actual administration of public justice. If they are supreme laws, courts of justice will enforce them directly in all cases, to which they can be judicially applied, in opposition to all state laws, as we all know was done in the case of the British debts secured by the treaty of 1783, after the constitution was adopted. If they are deemed but solemn compacts, promissory in their nature and obligation, courts of justice may be embarrassed in enforcing them, and may be compelled to leave the redress to be administered through other departments of the government. It is notorious, that treaty stipulations (especially those of the treaty of peace of 1783) were grossly disregarded by the states under the confederation. They were deemed by the states, not as laws, but like requisitions, of mere moral obligation, and dependent upon the good will of the states for their execution. Congress, indeed, remonstrated against this construction, as unfounded in principle and justice. But their voice was not heard. Power and right were separated; the argument was all on one side; but the power was on the other. It was probably to obviate this very difficulty, that this clause was inserted in the constitution; and it would redound to the immortal honour of its authors, if it had done no more, than thus to bring treaties within the sanctuary of justice, as laws of supreme obligation. There are, indeed, still cases, in which courts of justice {687} can administer no effectual redress; for when the terms of a stipulation import a contract, as when either of the parties engages to perform a particular act, the treaty addresses itself to the political, and not to the judicial, department; and the legislature must execute the contract, before it can become a rule for the courts.

§ 967. From this supremacy of the constitution and laws and treaties of the United States, within their constitutional scope, arises the duty of courts of justice to declare any unconstitutional law, passed by congress, or by a state legislature, void. So, in like manner, the same duty arises, whenever any other department of the national or state governments exceeds its constitutional functions. But the judiciary of the United States has no general jurisdiction to declare acts of the several states void, unless they are repugnant to the constitution of the United States, notwithstanding they are repugnant to the state constitution. Such a power belongs to it only, when it sits to administer the local law of a state, and acts exactly, as the state tribunal is bound to act. But upon this subject it seems unnecessary to dwell, since the right of all courts, state as well as national, to declare unconstitutional laws void, is now settled beyond the reach of judicial controversy.

CHAPTER XLIII.

OATHS OF OFFICE — RELIGIOUS TEST — RATIFICATION OF CONSTITUTION.

{688}

§ 968. THE next clause is,

> "The senators and representatives before mentioned, and the members of the several state legislatures and all executive and judicial officers, both of the United States and of the several states, shall be bound by oath or affirmation to support the constitution. But no religious test shall ever be required as a qualification to any office or public trust under the United States."

§ 969. That all those, who are entrusted with the execution of the powers of the national government, should be bound by some solemn obligation to the due execution of the trusts reposed in them, and to support the constitution, would seem to be a proposition too clear to render any reasoning necessary in support of it. It results from the plain right of society to require some guaranty from every officer, that he will be conscientious in the discharge of his duty. Oaths have a solemn obligation upon the minds of all reflecting men, and especially upon those, who feel a deep sense of accountability to a Supreme being. If, in the ordinary administration of justice in cases of private rights, or personal claims, oaths are required of those, who try, as well as of those, who give testimony, to guard against malice, falsehood, and evasion, surely like guards ought to be interposed in the administration of high public trusts, and especially in such, as {689} may concern the welfare and safety of the whole community. But there are known denominations of men, who are conscientiously scrupulous of taking oaths (among which is that pure and distinguished sect of Christians, commonly called Friends, or Quakers,) and therefore, to prevent any unjustifiable exclusion from office, the constitution has permitted a solemn affirmation to be made instead of an oath, and as its equivalent.

§ 970. But it may not appear to all persons quite so clear, why the officers of the state governments should be equally bound to take a like oath, or affirmation; and it has been even suggested, that there is no more reason to require that, than to require, that all of the United States officers should take an oath or affirmation to support the state constitutions. A moment's reflection will show sufficient reasons for the requisition of it in the one case, and the omission of it in the other. The members and officers of the national government have no agency in carrying into effect the state constitutions. The members and officers of the state governments have an essential agency in giving effect to the national constitution. The election of the president and the senate will depend, in all cases, upon the legislatures of the several states; and, in many cases, the election of the house of representatives may be affected by their agency. The judges of the state courts will frequently be called upon to decide upon the constitution, and laws, and treaties of the United States; and upon rights and claims growing out of them. Decisions ought to be, as far as possible, uniform; and uniformity of obligation will greatly tend to such a result. The executive authority of the several states may be often called upon to exert {690} powers, or allow rights, given by the constitution, as in filling vacancies in the senate, during the recess of the legislature; in issuing writs of election to fill vacancies in the house of representatives; in officering the militia, and giving effect to laws for calling them; and in the surrender of fugitives from justice. These, and many other functions, devolving on the state authorities, render it highly important, that they should be under a solemn obligation to obey the constitution. In common sense, there can be no well-founded objection to it. There may be serious evils growing out of an opposite course.

§ 971. The remaining part of the clause declares, that "no religious test shall ever be required, as a qualification to any office or public trust, under the United States." This clause is not introduced merely for the purpose of satisfying the scruples of many respectable persons, who feel an invincible repugnance to any religious test, or affirmation. It had a higher object; to cut off for ever every pretence of any alliance between church and state in the national government. The framers of the constitution were fully sensible of the dangers from this source, marked out in the history of other ages and countries; and not wholly unknown to our own. They knew, that bigotry was unceasingly vigilant in its stratagems, to secure to itself an exclusive ascendency over the human mind; and that intolerance was ever ready to arm itself with all the terrors of the civil power to exterminate those, who doubted its dogmas, or resisted its infallibility. The Catholic and the Protestant had alternately waged the most ferocious and unrelenting warfare on each other; and Protestantism itself, at the very moment, when it was proclaiming {691} the right of private judgment, prescribed boundaries to that right, beyond which if any one dared to pass, he must seal his rashness with the blood of martyrdom. The history of the parent country, too, could not fail to instruct them in the uses, and the abuses of religious tests. They there found the pains and penalties of non-conformity written in no equivocal language, and enforced with a stern and vindictive jealousy.

§ 972. Of the English laws respecting papists, Montesquieu observes, that they are so rigorous, though not professedly of the sanguinary kind, that they do all the hurt, that can possibly be done in cold blood. To this just rebuke, (after citing it, and admitting its truth,) Mr. Justice Blackstone has no better reply to make, than that these laws are seldom exerted to their utmost rigour; and, indeed, if they were, it would be very difficult to excuse them. The meanest apologist of the worst enormities of a Roman emperor could not have shadowed out a defence more servile, or more unworthy of the dignity and spirit of a freeman. It was easy to foresee, that without some prohibition of religious tests, a successful sect, in our country, might, by once possessing power, pass test-laws, which would secure to themselves a monopoly of all the offices of trust and profit, under the national government.

§ 973. The seventh and last article of the constitution is:

"The ratification of the conventions of nine states shall be sufficient for the establishment of this constitution between the states so ratifying the same."

§ 974. Upon this article it is now wholly unnecessary to bestow much commentary, since the {692} constitution has been ratified by all the states. If a ratification had been required of all the states, instead of nine, as a condition precedent, to give it life and motion, it is now known, that it would never have been ratified. North Carolina in her first convention rejected it; and Rhode-Island did not accede to it, until more than a year after it had been in operation.

§ 975. And here closes our review of the constitution in the original form, in which it was framed for, and adopted by, the people of the United States. The concluding passage of it is, "Done in convention by the unanimous consent of all the states present, the seventeenth day of September, in the year of our Lord one thousand seven hundred and eighty-seven, and of the Independence of the United States of America, the twelfth." At the head of the illustrious men, who framed, and signed it, (men, who have earned the eternal gratitude of their country,) stands the name of GEORGE WASHINGTON, "President and Deputy from Virginia;" a name, at the utterance of which envy is dumb, and pride bows with involuntary reverence, and piety, with eyes lifted to heaven, breathes forth a prayer of profound gratitude.

CHAPTER XLIV.

AMENDMENTS TO THE CONSTITUTION.

{693}

§ 976. WE have already had occasion to take notice of some of the amendments made to the constitution, subsequent to its adoption, in the progress of our review of the provisions of the original instrument. The present chapter will be devoted to a consideration of those, which have not fallen within the scope of our former commentaries.

§ 977. It has been already stated, that many objections were taken to the constitution, not only on account of its actual provisions, but also on account of its deficiencies and omissions. Among the latter, none were proclaimed with more zeal, and pressed with more effect, than the want of a bill of rights. This, it was said, was a fatal defect; and sufficient of itself to bring on the ruin of the republic. To this objection several answers were given; first, that the constitution did in fact contain many provisions in the nature of a bill of rights, if the whole constitution was not in fact a bill of rights; secondly, that a bill of rights was in its nature more adapted to a monarchy, than to a government, professedly founded upon the will of the people, and executed by their immediate representatives and agents; and, thirdly, that a formal bill of rights, beyond what was contained in it, was wholly unnecessary, and might even be dangerous.

§ 978. It was further added, that in truth the constitution itself was, in every rational sense, and to every useful purpose, a bill of rights for the Union. {694} It specifies, and declares the political privileges of the citizens in the structure and administration of the government. It defines certain immunities and modes of proceeding, which relate to their personal, private, and public rights and concerns. It confers on them the unalienable right of electing their rulers; and prohibits any tyrannical measures, and vindictive prosecutions. So, that, at best, much of the force of the objection rests on mere nominal distinctions, or upon a desire to make a frame of government a code to regulate rights and remedies.

§ 979. Although it must be conceded, that there is much intrinsic force in this reasoning, it cannot in candour be admitted to be wholly satisfactory, or conclusive on the subject. It is rather the argument of an able advocate, than the reasoning of a constitutional statesman. In the first place, a bill of rights (in the very sense of this reasoning) is admitted in some cases to be important; and the constitution itself adopts, and establishes its propriety to the extent of its actual provisions. Every reason, which establishes the propriety of any provision of this sort in the constitution, such as a right of trial by jury in criminal cases, is, *pro tanto*, proof, that it is neither unnecessary nor dangerous. It reduces the question to the consideration, not whether any bill of rights is necessary, but what such a bill of rights should properly contain. This is a point for argument, upon which different minds

376

may arrive at different conclusions. That a bill of rights may contain too many enumerations, and especially such, as more correctly belong to the ordinary legislation of a government, cannot be doubted. Some of our state bills of right contain clauses of this description, being either in {695} their character and phraseology quite too loose, and general, and ambiguous; or covering doctrines quite debatable, both in theory and practice; or even leading to mischievous consequences, by restricting the legislative power under circumstances, which were not foreseen, and if foreseen, the restraint would have been pronounced by all persons inexpedient, and perhaps unjust. Indeed, the rage of theorists to make constitutions a vehicle for the conveyance of their own crude, and visionary aphorisms of government, requires to be guarded against with the most unceasing vigilance.

§ 980. In the next place, a bill of rights is important, and may often be indispensable, whenever it operates, as a qualification upon powers, actually granted by the people to the government. This is the real ground of all the bills of rights in the parent country, in the colonial constitutions and laws, and in the state constitutions. In England, the bills of rights were not demanded merely of the crown, as withdrawing power from the royal prerogative; they were equally important, as withdrawing power from parliament. A large proportion of the most valuable of the provisions in Magna Charta, and the bill of rights of 1688, consists of a solemn recognition of limitations upon the power of parliament; that is, a declaration, that parliament *ought* not to abolish, or restrict those rights. Such are the right of trial by jury; the right to personal liberty and private property according to the law of the land; that the subjects ought to have a right to bear arms; that elections of members of parliament ought to be free; that freedom of speech and debate in parliament ought not to be impeached, or questioned elsewhere; and that excessive bail {696} ought not to be required, nor excessive fines imposed, nor cruel or unusual punishments inflicted. Whenever, then, a general power exists, or is granted to a government, which may in its actual exercise or abuse be dangerous to the people, there seems a peculiar propriety in restricting its operations, and in excepting from it some at least of the most mischievous forms, in which it may be likely to be abused. And the very exception in such cases will operate with a silent, but irresistible influence to control the actual abuse of it in other analogous cases.

§ 981. In the next place, a bill of rights may be important, even when it goes beyond powers supposed to be granted. It is not always possible to foresee the extent of the actual reach of certain powers, which are given in general terms. They may be construed to extend (and perhaps fairly) to certain classes of cases, which did not at first appear to be within them. A bill of rights, then, operates, as a guard upon any extravagant or undue extention of such powers. Besides; (as has been justly remarked,) a bill of rights is of real efficiency in controlling the excesses of party spirit. It serves to guide, and enlighten public opinion, and to render it more quick to detect, and more resolute to resist, attempts to disturb private rights. It requires more than ordinary hardihood and audacity of character, to trample down principles, which our ancestors have consecrated with reverence; which we have imbibed in our early education; which recommend themselves to the judgment of the world by their truth and simplicity; and which are constantly placed before the eyes of the people, accompanied with the imposing force and solemnity of a constitutional sanction. Bills of rights {697} are a part of the muniments of freemen, showing their title to protection; and they become of increased value, when placed under the protection of an independent judiciary instituted, as the appropriate guardian of the public and private rights of the citizens.

§ 982. In the next place, a bill of rights is an important protection against unjust and oppressive conduct on the part of the majority of the people themselves. In a government modified, like that of the United States, (it has been said by a great statesman,) the great danger lies rather in the abuse of the community, than of the legislative body. The prescriptions in favour of liberty ought to be levelled against that quarter, where the greatest danger lies, namely, that which possesses the highest prerogative of power. But this is not found in the executive or legislative departments of government; but in the body of the people, operating by the majority against the minority. It may be thought, that all paper barriers against the power of the community are too weak to be worthy of attention. They are not so strong, as to satisfy all, who have seen, and examined thoroughly the texture of such a defence. Yet, as they have a tendency to impress some degree of respect for them, to establish the public opinion in their favour, and to rouse the attention of the whole community, it may be one means to control the majority from those acts, to which they might be otherwise inclined.

§ 983. The want of a bill of rights, then, is not either an unfounded or illusory objection. The real question is not, whether every sort of right or privilege or claim ought to be affirmed in a constitution; but whether such, as in their own nature are of vital importance, and peculiarly susceptible of abuse, ought {698} not to receive this solemn sanction. Doubtless, the want of a formal bill of rights in the constitution was a matter of very exaggerated declamation, and party zeal, for the mere purpose of defeating the constitution. But, so far as the objection was well founded in fact, it was right to remove it by subsequent amendments; and congress have (as we shall see) accordingly performed the duty with most prompt and laudable diligence.

§ 984. Let us now enter upon the consideration of the amendments, which, (it will be found,) principally regard subjects properly belonging to a bill of rights.

§ 985. The first is

> "Congress shall make no law respecting an establishment of religion, or prohibiting the free exercise thereof; or abridging the freedom of speech, or of the press; or the right of the people peaceably to assemble, and to petition government for a redress of grievances."

§ 986. And first, the prohibition of any establishment of religion, and the freedom of religious opinion and worship.

How far any government has a right to interfere in matters touching religion, has been a subject much discussed by writers upon public and political law. The right and the duty of the interference of government, in matters of religion, have been maintained by many distinguished authors, as well those, who were the warmest advocates of free governments, as those, who were attached to governments of a more arbitrary character. Indeed, the right of a society or government to interfere in matters of religion will hardly be contested by any persons, who believe that piety, religion, and morality are intimately connected with {699} the well being of the state, and indispensable to the administration of civil justice. The promulgation of the great doctrines of religion; the being, and attributes, and providence of one Almighty God; the responsibility to him for all our actions, founded upon moral freedom and accountability; a future state of rewards and punishments; the cultivation of all the personal, social, and benevolent virtues; — these never can be a matter of indifference in any well ordered community. It is, indeed, difficult to conceive, how any civilized society can well exist without them. And at all events, it is impossible for those, who believe in the truth of Christianity, as a divine revelation, to doubt, that it is the especial duty of government to foster, and encourage it among all the citizens and subjects. This is a point wholly distinct from that of the right of private judgment in matters of religion, and of the freedom of public worship according to the dictates of one's own conscience.

§ 987. The real difficulty lies in ascertaining the limits, to which government may rightfully go in fostering and encouraging religion. Three cases may easily be supposed. One, where a government affords aid to a particular religion, leaving all persons free to adopt any other; another, where it creates an ecclesiastical establishment for the propagation of the doctrines of a particular sect of that religion, leaving a like freedom to all others; and a third, where it creates such an establishment, and excludes all persons, not belonging to it, either wholly, or in part, from any participation in the public honours, trusts, emoluments, privileges, and immunities of the state. For instance, a government may simply declare, that the Christian religion shall be the religion of the state, and shall be {700} aided, and encouraged in all the varieties of sects belonging to it; or it may declare, that the Catholic or Protestant religion shall be the religion of the state, leaving every man to the free enjoyment of his own religious opinions; or it may establish the doctrines of a particular sect, as of Episcopalians, as the religion of the state, with a like freedom; or it may establish the doctrines of a particular sect, as exclusively the religion of the state, tolerating others to a limited extent, or excluding all, not belonging to it, from all public honours, trusts, emoluments, privileges, and immunities.

§ 988. Probably at the time of the adoption of the constitution, and of the amendment to it, now under consideration, the general, if not the universal, sentiment in America was, that Christianity ought to receive encouragement from the state, so far as it is not incompatible with the private rights of conscience, and the freedom of religious worship. An attempt to level all religions, and to make it a matter of state policy to hold all in utter indifference, would have created universal disapprobation, if not universal indignation.

§ 989. It yet remains a problem to be solved in human affairs, whether any free government can be permanent, where the public worship of God, and the support of religion, constitute no part of the policy or duty of the state in any assignable shape. The future experience of Christendom, and chiefly of the American states, must settle this problem, as yet new in the history of the world, abundant, as it has been, in experiments in the theory of government.

§ 990. But the duty of supporting religion, and especially the Christian religion, is very different from {701} the right to force the consciences of other men, or to punish them for worshipping God in the manner, which, they believe, their accountability to him requires. It has been truly said, that "religion, or the duty we owe to our Creator, and the manner of discharging it, can be dictated only by reason and conviction, not by force or violence." Mr. Locke himself, who did not doubt the right of government to interfere in matters of religion, and especially to encourage Christianity, has at the same time expressed his opinion of the right of private judgment, and liberty of conscience, in a manner becoming his character, as a sincere friend of civil and religious liberty. "No man, or society of men," says he, "have any authority to impose their opinions or interpretations on any other, the meanest Christian; since, in matters of religion, every man must know, and believe, and give an account for himself." The rights of conscience are, indeed, beyond the just reach of any human power. They are given by God, and cannot be encroached upon by human authority, without a criminal disobedience of the precepts of natural, as well as of revealed religion.

§ 991. The real object of the amendment was, not to countenance, much less to advance Mahometanism, or Judaism, or infidelity, by prostrating Christianity; but to exclude all rivalry among Christian sects, and to prevent any national ecclesiastical establishment, which should give to an hierarchy the exclusive patronage of the national government. It thus sought to cut off the means of religious persecution, (the vice and pest of former ages,) and the power of subverting the rights of conscience in matters of religion, which had been trampled upon almost from the days of the Apostles to the present age. The history of the parent {702} country had afforded the most solemn warnings and melancholy instructions on this head; and even New-England, the land of the persecuted puritans, as well as other colonies, where the Church of England had maintained its superiority, had furnished a chapter, as full of dark bigotry and intolerance, as any, which could be found to disgrace the pages of foreign annals. Apostacy, heresy, and nonconformity have been standard crimes for public appeals, to kindle the flames of persecution, and apologize for the most atrocious triumphs over innocence and virtue.

§ 992. It was under a solemn consciousness of the dangers from ecclesiastical ambition, the bigotry of spiritual pride, and the intolerance of sects, thus exemplified in our domestic, as well as in foreign annals, that it was deemed advisable to exclude from the national government all power to act upon the subject. The situation, too, of the different states equally proclaimed the policy, as well as the necessity, of such an exclusion. In some of the states, episcopalians constituted the predominant sect; in others, presbyterians; in others, congregationalists; in others, quakers; and in others again, there was a close numerical rivalry among contending sects. It was impossible, that there should not arise perpetual strife and perpetual jealousy on the subject of ecclesiastical ascendancy, if the national government were left free to create a religious establishment. The only security was in extirpating the power. But this alone would have been an imperfect security, if it had not been followed up by a declaration of the right of the free exercise of religion, and a prohibition (as we have seen) of all religious tests. Thus, the whole power over the subject of religion is left exclusively to the state governments, to be acted {703} upon according to their own sense of justice, and the state constitutions; and the Catholic and the Protestant, the Calvinist and the Arminian, the Jew and the Infidel, may sit down at the common table of the national councils, without any inquisition into their faith, or mode of worship.

§ 993. The next clause of the amendment respects the liberty of the press. "Congress shall make no law abridging the freedom of speech, or of the press." That this amendment was intended to secure to every citizen an absolute right to speak, or write, or print, whatever he might please, without any responsibility, public or private, therefor, is a supposition too wild to be indulged by any rational man. This would be to allow to every citizen a right to destroy, at his pleasure, the reputation, the peace, the property, and even the personal safety of every other citizen. A man might, out of mere malice and revenge, accuse another of the most infamous crimes; might excite against him the indignation of all his fellow citizens by the most atrocious calumnies; might disturb, nay, overturn all his domestic peace, and embitter his parental affections; might inflict the most distressing punishments upon the weak, the timid, and the innocent; might prejudice all a man's civil, and political, and private rights; and might stir up sedition, rebellion, and treason even against the government itself, in the wantonness of his passions, or the corruption of his heart. Civil society could not go on under such circumstances. Men would then be obliged to resort to private vengeance, to make up for the deficiencies of the law; and assassinations, and savage cruelties would be perpetrated with all the frequency belonging to barbarous and brutal communities. It is {704} plain, then, that the language of this amendment imports no more, than that every man shall have a right to speak, write, and print his opinions upon any subject whatsoever, without any prior restraint, so always, that he does not injure any other person in his rights, person, property, or reputation; and so always, that he does not thereby disturb the public peace, or attempt to subvert the government. It is neither more nor less, than an expansion of the great doctrine, recently brought into operation in the law of libel, that every man shall be at liberty to publish what is true, with good motives and for justifiable ends. And with this reasonable limitation it is not only right in itself, but it is an inestimable privilege in a free government. Without such a limitation, it might become the scourge of the republic, first denouncing the principles of liberty, and then, by rendering the most virtuous patriots odious through the terrors of the press, introducing despotism in its worst form.

§ 994. A little attention to the history of other countries in other ages will teach us the vast importance of this right. It is notorious, that, even to this day, in some foreign countries it is a crime to speak upon any subject, religious, philosophical, or political, what is contrary to, the received opinions of the government, or the institutions of the country, however laudable may be the design, and however virtuous may be the motive. Even to animadvert upon the conduct of public men, of rulers, or representatives, in terms of the strictest truth and courtesy, has been, and is deemed, a scandal upon the supposed sanctity of their stations and characters, subjecting the party to grievous punishment. In some countries no works can be printed at all, whether of science, or literature, or philosophy, {705} without the previous approbation of the government; and the press has been shackled, and compelled to speak only in the timid language, which the cringing courtier, or the capricious inquisitor, would license for publication. The Bible itself, the common inheritance, not merely of Christendom, but of the world, has been put exclusively under the control of government; and not allowed to be seen, or heard, except in, a language unknown to the common inhabitants of the country. To publish a translation in the vernacular tongue, has been in former times a flagrant offence.

§ 995. There is a good deal of loose reasoning on the subject of the liberty of the press, as if its inviolability were constitutionally such, that, like the king of England, it could do no wrong, and was free from every inquiry, and afforded a perfect sanctuary for every abuse; that, in short, it implied a despotic sovereignty to do every sort of wrong, without the slightest accountability to private or public justice. Such a notion is too extravagant to be held by any sound constitutional lawyer, with regard to the rights and duties belonging to governments generally, or to the state governments in particular. If it were admitted to be correct, it might be justly affirmed, that the liberty of the press is incompatible with the permanent existence of any free government. Mr. Justice Blackstone has remarked, that the liberty of the press, properly understood, is essential to the nature of a free state; but that this consists in laying no *previous* restraints upon publications, and not in freedom from censure for criminal matter, when published. Every freeman has an undoubted right to lay what sentiments he pleases before the public; to forbid this is to destroy the freedom of the press. But, if he publishes what is improper, {706} mischievous, or illegal, he must take the consequences of his own temerity. To subject the press to the restrictive power of a licenser, as was formerly done before, and since the revolution (of 1688), is to subject all freedom of sentiment to the prejudices of one man, and make him the arbitrary and infallible judge of all controverted points in learning, religion, and government. But to punish any dangerous or offensive writings, which, when published, shall, on a fair and impartial trial, be adjudged of a pernicious tendency, is necessary for the preservation of peace and good order, of government and religion, the only solid foundations of civil liberty. Thus, the will of individuals is still left free; the abuse only of that free will is the object of legal punishment. Neither is any restraint hereby laid upon freedom of thought or inquiry; liberty of private sentiment is still left; the disseminating, or making public of bad sentiments, destructive of the ends of society, is the crime, which society corrects. A man may be allowed to keep poisons in his closet; but not publicly to vend them as cordials. And after some additional reflections, he concludes with this memorable sentence: "So true will it be found, that to censure the licentiousness, is to maintain the liberty of the press."

§ 996. The doctrine laid down by Mr. Justice Blackstone, respecting the liberty of the press, has not been repudiated (as far as is known) by any solemn decision of any of the state courts, in respect to their own municipal jurisprudence. On the contrary, it has been repeatedly affirmed in several of the states, notwithstanding their constitutions, or laws recognize, that "the liberty of the press ought not to be restrained," or more emphatically, that "the liberty of the press shall be inviolably {707} maintained." Nay; it has farther been held, that the truth of the facts is not alone sufficient to justify the publication, unless it is done from good motives, and for justifiable purposes, or, in other words, upon an occasion, (as upon the canvass of candidates for public office,) when public duty, or private right requires it. And Mr. Chancellor Kent, upon a large survey of the whole subject, has not scrupled to declare, that "it has become a constitutional principle in this country, that every citizen may freely speak, write, and publish his sentiments on all subjects, *being responsible for the abuse of that right*; and, that no law can rightfully be passed, to restrain, or abridge the freedom of the press."

§ 997. The remaining clause secures

"the right of the people peaceably to assemble and to petition the government for a redress of grievances."

§ 998. This would seem unnecessary to be expressly provided for in a republican government, since it results from the very nature of its structure and institutions. It is impossible, that it could be practically denied, until the spirit of liberty had wholly disappeared, and the people had become so servile and debased, as to be unfit to exercise any of the privileges of freemen.

§ 999. The provision was probably borrowed from the declaration of rights in England, on the revolution of 1688, in which the right to petition the king for a redress of grievances was insisted on; and the right to petition parliament in the like manner has been provided for, and guarded by statutes passed before, as well as since that period. Mr. Tucker has indulged himself in a disparaging criticism upon the phraseology of this clause, as savouring too much of that style of {708} condescension, in which favours are supposed to be granted. But this seems to be quite overstrained; since it speaks the voice of the people in the language of prohibition, and not in that of affirmance of a right, supposed to be unquestionable, and inherent.

§ 1000. The next amendment is:

"A well regulated militia being necessary to the security of a free state, the right of the people to keep and bear arms shall not be infringed."

§ 1001. The importance of this article will scarcely be doubted by any persons, who have duly reflected upon the subject. The militia is the natural defence of a free country against sudden foreign invasions, domestic insurrections, and domestic usurpations of power by rulers. It is against sound policy for a free people to keep up large military establishments and standing armies in time of peace, both from the enormous expenses, with which they are attended, and the facile means, which they afford to ambitious and unprincipled rulers, to subvert the government, or trample upon the rights of the people. The right of the citizens to keep, and bear arms has justly been considered, as the palladium of the liberties of a republic; since it offers a strong moral check against the usurpation and arbitrary power of rulers; and will generally, even if these are successful in the first instance, enable the people to resist, and triumph over them. And yet, though this truth would seem so clear, and the importance of a well regulated militia would seem so undeniable, it cannot be disguised, that among the American people there is a growing indifference to any system of militia discipline, and a strong disposition, from a sense of its burthens, to be rid of all regulations. How it is practicable to keep the people duly armed without some organization, it is difficult {709} to see. There is certainly no small danger, that indifference may lead to disgust, and disgust to contempt; and thus gradually undermine all the protection intended by this clause of our national bill of rights.

§ 1002. The next amendment is:

"No soldier shall in time of peace be quartered in any house, without the consent of the owner, nor in time of war, but in a manner to be prescribed by law."

§ 1003. This provision speaks for itself. Its plain object is to secure the perfect enjoyment of that great right of the common law, that a man's house shall be his own castle, privileged against all civil and military intrusion. The billetting of soldiers in time of peace upon the people has been a common resort of arbitrary princes, and is full of inconvenience and peril. In the petition of right (4 Charles I), it was declared by parliament to be a great grievance.

§ 1004. The next amendment is:

"The right of the people to be secure in their persons, houses, papers, and effects against unreasonable searches and seizures shall not be violated; and no warrants shall issue, but upon probable cause, supported by oath or affirmation, and particularly describing the place to be searched, and the person or things to be seized."

§ 1005. This provision seems indispensable to the full enjoyment of the rights of personal security, personal liberty, and private property. It is little more than the affirmance of a great constitutional doctrine of the common law. And its introduction into the amendments was doubtless occasioned by the strong sensibility excited, both in England and America, upon the subject of general warrants almost upon the eve of the American Revolution. Although special warrants upon complaints under oath, stating the crime, and the party by {710} name, against whom the accusation is made, are the only legal warrants, upon which an arrest can be made according to the law of England; yet a practice had obtained in the secretaries' office ever since the restoration, (grounded on some clauses in the acts for regulating the press,) of issuing general warrants to take up, without naming any persons in particular, the authors, printers, and publishers of such obscene, or seditious libels, as were particularly specified in the warrant. When these acts expired, in 1694, the same practice was continued in every reign, and under every administration, except the last four years of Queen Anne's reign, down to the year 1763. The general warrants, so issued, in general terms authorized the officers to apprehend all persons suspected, without naming, or describing any person in special. In the year 1763, the legality of these general warrants was brought before the King's Bench for solemn decision; and they were adjudged to be illegal, and void for uncertainty. A warrant, and the complaint, on which the same is founded, to be legal, must not only state the name of the party, but also the time, and place, and nature of the offence with reasonable certainty.

§ 1006. The next amendment is:

"Excessive bail shall not be required; nor excessive fines imposed; nor cruel and unusual punishments inflicted."

This is an exact transcript of a clause in the bill of rights, framed at the revolution of 1688. The provision would seem to be wholly unnecessary in a free government, since it is scarcely possible, that any department of such a government should authorize, or justify such atrocious conduct. It was, however, adopted, as an admonition to all departments of the national government, to warn them against such violent proceedings, as had taken {711} place in England in the arbitrary reigns of some of the Stuarts. In those times a demand of excessive bail was often made against persons, who were odious to the court, and its favourites; and on failing to procure it, they were committed to prison. Enormous fines and amercements were also sometimes imposed, and cruel and vindictive punishments inflicted. Upon this subject Mr. Justice Blackstone has wisely remarked, that sanguinary laws are a bad symptom of the distemper of any state, or at least of its weak constitution. The laws of the Roman kings, and the twelve tables of the Decemvirs, were full of cruel punishments; the Porcian law, which exempted all citizens from sentence of death, silently abrogated them all. In this period the republic flourished. Under the emperors severe laws were revived, and then the empire fell.

§ 1007. The next amendment is:

> "The enumeration in the constitution of certain rights shall not be construed to deny, or disparage others retained by the people."

This clause was manifestly introduced to prevent any perverse, or ingenious misapplication of the well known maxim, that an affirmation in particular cases implies a negation in all others; and *é converso*, that a negation in particular cases implies an affirmation in all others. The maxim, rightly understood, is perfectly sound and safe; but it has often been strangely forced from its natural meaning into the support of the most dangerous political heresies.

§ 1008. The next and last amendment is:

> "The powers not delegated to the United States by the constitution, nor prohibited by it to the states, are reserved to the states respectively, or to the people."

§ 1009. This amendment is a mere affirmation of what, upon any just reasoning, is a necessary rule of {712} interpreting the constitution. Being an instrument of limited and enumerated powers, it follows irresistibly, that what is not conferred, is withheld, and belongs to the state authorities, if invested by their constitutions of government respectively in them; and if not so invested, it is retained BY THE PEOPLE, as a part of their residuary sovereignty. When this amendment was before congress, a proposition was moved, to insert the word "expressly" before "delegated," so as to read "the powers not *expressly* delegated to the United States by the constitution," &c. On that occasion it was remarked, that it is impossible to confine a government to the exercise of express powers. There must necessarily be powers admitted by implication, unless the constitution should descend to the most minute details. It is a general principle, that all corporate bodies possess all powers incident to a corporate capacity, without being absolutely expressed. The motion was accordingly negatived. Indeed, one of the great defects of the confederation was, (as we have already seen,) that it contained a clause, prohibiting the exercise of any power, jurisdiction, or right, not *expressly delegated*. The consequence was, that congress were crippled at every step of their progress; and were often compelled by the very necessities of the times to usurp powers, which they did not constitutionally possess; and thus, in effect, to break down all the great barriers against tyranny and oppression.

§ 1010. It is plain, therefore, that it could not have been the intention of the framers of this amendment to give it effect, as an abridgment of any of the powers granted under the constitution, whether they are express or implied, direct or incidental. Its sole design is to exclude any interpretation, by which other powers {713} should be assumed beyond those, which are granted. All that are granted in the original instrument, whether express or implied, whether direct or incidental, are left in their original state. All powers not delegated, (not, all powers not *expressly* delegated,) and not prohibited, are reserved. The attempts, then, which have been made from time to time, to force upon this language an abridging, or restrictive influence, are utterly unfounded in any just rules of interpreting the words, or the sense of the instrument. Stripped of the ingenious disguises, in which they are clothed, they are neither more nor less, than attempts to foist into the text the word "expressly;" to qualify, what is general, and obscure, what is clear, and defined. They make the sense of the passage bend to the wishes and prejudices of the interpreter; and employ criticism to support a theory, and not to guide it. One should suppose, if the history of the human mind did not furnish abundant proofs to the contrary, that no reasonable man would contend for an interpretation founded neither in the letter, nor in the spirit of an instrument. Where is controversy to end, if we desert both the letter and the spirit? What is to become of constitutions of government, if they are to rest, not upon the plain import of their words, but upon conjectural enlargements and restrictions, to suit the temporary passions and interests of the day? Let us never forget, that our constitutions of government are solemn instruments, addressed to the common sense of the people and designed to fix, and perpetuate their rights and their liberties. They are not to be frittered away to please the demagogues of the day. They are not to be violated to gratify the ambition of political leaders. They are to speak in the same voice now, and for ever. They are of no man's {714} private interpretation. They are ordained by the will of the people; and can be changed only by the sovereign command of the people.

§ 1011. It has been justly remarked, that the erection of a new government, whatever care or wisdom may distinguish the work, cannot fail to originate questions of intricacy and nicety; and these may, in a particular manner, be expected to flow from the establishment of a constitution, founded upon the total, or partial incorporation of a number of distinct sovereignties. Time alone can mature and perfect so compound a system; liquidate the meaning of all the parts; and adjust them to each other in a harmonious and consistent whole.

CHAPTER XLV.

CONCLUDING REMARKS.

§ 1012. WE have now reviewed all the provisions of the original constitution of the United States, and all the amendments, which have been incorporated into it. And, here, the task originally proposed in these Commentaries is brought to a close. Many reflections naturally crowd upon the mind at such a moment; many grateful recollections of the past; and many anxious thoughts of the future. The past is secure. It is unalterable. The seal of eternity is upon it. The wisdom, which it has displayed, and the blessings, which it has bestowed, cannot be obscured; neither can they be debased by human folly, or human infirmity. The future is that, which may well awaken the most earnest solicitude, both for the virtue and the permanence of our republic. The fate of other republics, their rise, their progress, their decline, and their fall, are written but too legibly on the pages of history, if indeed they were not continually before us in the startling fragments of their ruins. They have perished; and perished by their own hands. Prosperity has enervated them; corruption has debased them; and a venal populace has consummated their destruction. Alternately the prey of military chieftains at home, and of ambitious invaders from abroad, they have been sometimes cheated out of their liberties by servile demagogues; sometimes betrayed into a surrender of them by false patriots; and sometimes they have willingly sold them for a price to the despot, who has bidden highest for his victims. {716} They have disregarded the warning voice of their best statesmen; and have persecuted, and driven from office their truest friends. They have listened to the fawning sycophant, and the base calumniator of the wise and the good. They have reverenced power more in its high abuses and summary movements, than in its calm and constitutional energy, when it dispensed blessings with an unseen, but liberal hand. They have surrendered to faction, what belonged to the country. Patronage and party, the triumph of a leader, and the discontents of a day, have outweighed all solid principles and institutions of government. Such are the melancholy lessons of the past history of republics down to our own.

§ 1013. It is not my design to detain the reader, by any elaborate reflections addressed to his judgment, either by way of admonition or of encouragement. But it may not be wholly without use to glance at one or two considerations, upon which our meditations cannot be too frequently indulged.

§ 1014. In the first place, it cannot escape our notice, how exceedingly difficult it is to settle the foundations of any government upon principles, which do not admit of controversy or question. The very elements, out of which it is to be built, are susceptible of infinite modifications; and theory too often deludes us by the attractive simplicity of its plans, and imagination by the visionary perfection of its

387

speculations. In theory, a government may promise the most perfect harmony of operations in all its various combinations. In practice, the whole machinery may be perpetually retarded, or, thrown out of order by accidental mal-adjustments. In theory, a government may seem deficient in unity of design and symmetry of parts; and yet, in practice, it {717} may work with astonishing accuracy and force for the general welfare. Whatever, then, has been found to work well in experience, should be rarely hazarded upon conjectural improvements. Time, and long and steady operation are indispensable to the perfection of all social institutions. To be of any value they must become cemented with the habits, the feelings, and the pursuits of the people. Every change discomposes for a while the whole arrangements of the system. What is safe is not always expedient; what is new is often pregnant with unforeseen evils, and imaginary good.

§ 1015. In the next place, the slightest attention to the history of the national constitution must satisfy every reflecting mind, how many difficulties attended its formation and adoption, from real or imaginary differences of interests, sectional feelings, and local institutions. It is an attempt to create a national sovereignty, and yet to preserve the state sovereignties; though it is impossible to assign definite boundaries in all cases to the powers of each. The influence of the disturbing causes, which, more than once in the convention, were on the point of breaking up the Union, have since immeasurably increased in concentration and vigour. The very inequalities of a government, confessedly founded in a compromise, were then felt with a strong sensibility; and every new source of discontent, whether accidental or permanent, has since added increased activity to the painful sense of these inequalities. The North cannot but perceive, that it has yielded to the South a superiority of representatives, already amounting to twenty-five, beyond its due proportion; and the South imagines, that, with all this preponderance in representation, the other parts of the Union enjoy a more perfect protection of their interests, than its own. The {718} West feels its growing power and weight in the Union; and the Atlantic states begin to learn, that the sceptre must one day depart from them. If, under these circumstances, the Union should once be broken up, it is impossible, that a new constitution should ever be formed, embracing the whole Territory. We shall be divided into several nations or confederacies, rivals in power and interest, too proud to brook injury, and too close to make retaliation distant or ineffectual. Our very animosities will, like those of all other kindred nations, become more deadly, because our lineage, laws, and language are the same. Let the history of the Grecian and Italian republics warn us of our dangers. The national constitution is our last, and our only security. United we stand; divided we fall.

§ 1016. If these Commentaries shall but inspire the rising generation with a more ardent love of their country, an unquenchable thirst for liberty, and a profound reverence for the constitution and the Union, then they will have accomplished all, that their author ought to desire. Let the American youth never forget, that they possess a noble inheritance, bought by the toils, and sufferings, and blood of their ancestors; and capable, if wisely improved, and faithfully guarded, of transmitting to their latest posterity all the substantial blessings of life, the peaceful enjoyment of liberty, property, religion, and independence. The structure has been erected by architects of consummate skill and fidelity; its foundations are solid; its compartments are beautiful, as well as useful; its arrangements are full of wisdom and order; and its defences are impregnable from without. It has been reared for immortality, if the work of man may justly aspire to such a title. It may, nevertheless, perish in an hour by the folly, or {719} corruption, or negligence of its only keepers, THE PEOPLE. Republics are created by the virtue, public spirit, and intelligence of the citizens. They fall, when the wise are banished from the public councils, because they dare to be honest, and the profligate are rewarded, because they flatter the people, in order to betray them.

———————

INDEX

[The Index below, as in the original printing, references the pagination of the 1833 abridged edition, not the section numbers. These page numbers are inserted into the present print edition by the use of {brackets}. They are retained for purposes of citation and referencing, continuity with the previous edition, functionality of the Index, and standardized pagination within digital formats.]

ACCOUNTS, Public, to be published 486, 487

ACCUSATION, Self, Criminals not bound to 659, 660, 662, 663

ADJOURNMENT of Congress, by whom 295, 412, 574, 576;
of each House 295

ADMIRALTY, Jurisdiction. (*See* JUDICIARY.) 614-620

ADMISSION of new States into the Union 473, 474

ALIENS, who are 631, 633-635;
suits by, and against 635, 636

ALIEN ACT, whether constitutional 464

AMBASSADORS, appointment of 559, 560;
Receiving of 574, 576-579;
Dismission of 579;
Protection, and rights of 612, 613;
Suits by and against 606, 6l2-614

AMENDMENTS OF CONSTITUTION, how made 678-682

APPEAL, Nature and Effect of 651-653

APPEALS from State Courts 643-646, 652

APPELLATE JURISDICTION. (*See* JUDICIA-RY.) 651-655

APPOINTMENTS, to office by president, and senate 552, 559;
By congress, and heads of departments 552, 559;
When discretionary in congress 552;
When complete 573;
When the party is in office 573;
In case of vacancies 573-574

APPORTIONMENT, of Representatives 235-247;
of Direct Taxes 338-341

APPROPRIATIONS, of Money 346, 486;
for Internal Improvements 346-350

ARMS, right to bear 708

ARMY AND NAVY, power to create and regulate 412-419

ARREST of Members of Congress 303, 307, 308

ARTS AND SCIENCE, Promotion of 402-404

ATTAINDER, Prohibition of Bills of, by con-gress 484-485;
by States 489, 496;
Effect of, in Treason 466, 467

AUTHORS, Copyright of 402-404

AYES AND NOES, Call of, in congress 299, 300

BAIL, excessive, Prohibition of 710

BANK OF UNITED STATES, Constitutional-ity of 444-452;
States cannot tax 356, 357

BANKRUPTCY, Power of congress over 383, 384-391

BILL OF RIGHTS, Propriety of 693-698

BILLS OF ATTAINDER, Prohibition of by congress 484, 485;
by States 489, 496

BILLS OF CREDIT, Prohibition of 489, 491-496;
What are 494, 495

BILLS OF EXCHANGE, Purchase of, by U. States 480

BORROW MONEY, Power of congress to 358, 359

CANALS AND ROADS, Power of congress as to 346-350, 443, 458

CAPITATION TAX, Power to lay 340, 341, 350

CAPTURES, Regulation of 409-412

CAROLINAS, Origin and Settlement of 56-60

CASES, What are within the judicial power 608-612

CENSUS, when to be taken 235, 241, 242

CESSIONS, for Seat of Government 427, 428;
    for Forts, Arsenals, &c. 427-430, 473;
    of Foreign Territory 459

CHARTER Governments, what 63, 64

CHARTERS, Whether contracts, protected by constitution 506-510

CITIZENS, who are 630-632;
    Privileges and Immunities of, in each
    State 673, 674;
    Suits by and against 628, 632

COINAGE, Power of congress, over 392, 393;
    Counterfeiting 393;
    Prohibition upon the States 490, 491

COLONIES, AMERICAN, Origin and Settlement of 3-62;
    Title of Territory 3-8;
    General Review of 62-83;
    Common Law in 62-66;
    Governments in 67-70;
    Rights of 70-83

COLONIES, Legislative powers of 71-73

COLUMBIA, District of 427;
    Legislation in 427, 428

COMMERCE, Power of congress to regulate
    (*See* Taxes) 359-378;
    Foreign 359-363;
    Domestic 359, 363-366;
    with Indians 379-382;
    Exclusive power in Congress 366-369;
    Encouragement of Manufactures 369-379

COMMON LAW IN COLONIES, Introduction of 62-66

COMMON DEFENCE, Taxes for 329-331

COMPACTS, by States 489, 490

COMPENSATION (*See* PRESIDENT, JUDGES);
    Representatives 303-307;
    Senators 303-307;
    for Property taken for Public uses 670, 678

CONCURRENT POWERS, when in States 148-154

CONTEMPTS OF CONGRESS, how punishable 301, 302

CONFEDERATION, Origin and Formation of 91, 93;
    Decline and Fall of 94-104

CONGRESS, Adjournment of 300;
    Quorum of 295-297;
    Rules of 298, 299;
    Ayes and Noes 299, 300;
    Compensation of 303-307;
    Disqualifications of members of 310-314;
    Qualifications of Representatives 230-235;
    of Senators 263-267; Organization and
    modes of Proceeding 295, 298,300,309;
    Division into two Branches 199-209;
    House of Representatives 210-251;
    Senate 252-290;
    Elections of 291-294, 295;
    Powers, when exclusive or not 148-154;
    Meetings of 294, 295;
    Privileges of 248, 249, 295-303, 307, 309;
    Journals of, to be kept 299, 300;
    Contempts of 301, 302;
    Mode of passing laws 315-317;
    Impeachments by and before 249-251;
    Power to Lay Taxes 329-346;
    Borrow Money 358-359;
    Regulate Commerce 359-378;
    Naturalization 383, 384;
    Bankrupt Laws 383-391;
    Coin Money 392, 393;
    Weights and Measures 394;
    Counterfeiting Coin 394;
    Post-offices and Post-roads 396-401;
    Promotion of Science and Arts 402-404;
    Piracy and Felonies on the High Seas
    405-406;
    Offences against the Law of Nations 405-
    408;
    War and Captures 409-412;
    Army and Navy 412-419;
    Militia 420-426;
    Seat of Government 427, 428;
    Forts, Arsenals, Dockyards, &c. 427-430;
    Incidental Powers 431-441;
    Resulting Powers 442, 443;
    Bank of United States 444, 452;
    Vacancy in Presidency 542;
    Establishment of Judiciary 587;
    Appellate Jurisdiction 651-655;
    Appropriations of Money . 346, 350, 486;
    Internal Improvements 346-350, 453-458;

Embargoes 462-464;

Alien and Sedition Act 464, 465;

Treason, punishment of 466-469;

State Records, proof and effect of 470-472;

Admission of new States 473, 474;

Government of Territories 476-479;

Purchase of Foreign Territory 459;

of Domestic Territory 473

CONNECTICUT, Origin and Settlement of 34-36

CONQUEST, Laws of, as to Colonies 62-64

CONSCIENCE, Rights of 62-64

CONSTITUTION OF UNITED STATES;

Origin and Adoption of 105-109;

General objections to 110-115;

Whether a Compact or League 116-122;

Formed by the People, and not by States 117-118;

Final Interpreter, who is 123-133;

Rules of Interpretation of 134-162;

Preamble, Exposition of 163-194;

Division of powers, Legislative, Executive, Judicial 195-198;

Legislative power, Division into two Branches 199-208;

The House of Representatives (*See* REPRESENTATIVES.) 210-251;

The Senate. (*See* SENATE.) 252-290;

Mode of passing Laws 315, 316;

President's negative 317-325;

Powers of congress. (*See* CONGRESS.) 329-488;

Executive department (*See* PRESIDENT.) 515-580;

Judicial department (*See* JUDICIARY.) 581-668;

Supremacy of Constitution, Treaties and Laws 684-687;

Ratification of 691, 692;

Amendments, how made, 678-682

CONSTRUCTION, Rules of — of Constitution 134-162

CONSULS, Appointment of 552, 559;

Suits, by and against 606, 612-614

CONTEMPTS OF CONGRESS, how punishable 301, 302;

whether pardonable by President 551

CONTRACTS, Impairing, prohibition of 489, 498-511;

of the United States, how interpreted 480

COPYRIGHT, of Authors 402-404

CORPORATION, composed of citizens, when entitled to sue 632;

Foreign, when it may sue 636

CORRUPTION of Blood, in Treason 466-469

COUNSEL, Right to, in criminal cases 660, 665, 667

COURTS. (*See* JUDICIARY.) 585-590;

State, appellate jurisdiction, over 643-649

CRIMES, how prosecuted and tried 655-658

CRIMINALS, Fugitive 674, 675;

not bound to accuse themselves 659, 660, 662, 663;

Trial of 656-669;

not to be twice tried 662

CROWN, Rights and Prerogatives of, in the Colonies 75-78

DEBTS, Revolutionary, provided for 683;

of United States, priority of payment 456

DEBT, PUBLIC, stock not taxable by a State 356, 357;

Old, declared valid 683

DEFENCE, Common, power to tax for 329-331

DELAWARE, Origin and Settlement of 54-55

DIRECT TAXES, What are 337-341;

How apportioned 338, 339

DISCOVERY, Right of, to America 3-7;

Effect of, on Indian Title 5-7

DISQUALIFICATION, &c., of President 540, 542;

of Members of Congress 310-314, 529, 538;

of Electors 529, 538

DISTRICT of Columbia 427, 428;

Legislation in 427, 428

DIVISION of Legislative, Executive, and Judicial powers, Reasons for 195-198;

of Legislative, Reasons for 199-209

DUTIES, Power to lay 329-357;

Meaning of 329-331;

to be uniform 337-342;

Prohibitions on States 354, 356, 512

ELECTIONS of Representatives 291-294;

of Senators 291-294;

of President and Vice-President 529-540

ELECTORS of President and Vice-President 529-538;

Time of choice of 538-540;

of Representatives and Senators (*See* ELECTIONS.) 291-294;

Disqualifications of 528, 529

EMBARGO, power to lay 462-464;

What constitutional 462-464

ERROR, Writ of, Nature and Effect of 652-655

EXCISES, What are. (*See* DUTIES.) 339, 340

EXCLUSIVE, what powers of congress are, or not 148-154, 366

EXECUTIVE department, Organization of 515-546

EXECUTIVE, Unity of, Reasons for 516-521;

Duration of office 521-523;

Re-eligibility. (*See* PRESIDENT.) 523-527

EXPORTS, Prohibition of Duties on 353, 354

EX POST FACTO LAWS, prohibition of,

by congress 484-486;

by a State 496, 510

FELONIES, What are 405-407;

On High Seas 405-407

FINES and FORFEITURES, Pardon of by President 552;

Prohibition of, excessive 710

FREEDOM of the Press 698, 703-707;

of Speech generally 698-703;

in Congress 303, 309, 310;

of Religion 698-703

FUGITIVE, Criminals 674, 675;

Slaves 675, 676

GENERAL WELFARE, Power to Tax for 329-331

GEORGIA, Origin and Settlement of 61

GOVERNMENT, Republican form of, guarantied 677, 678

GRAND JURY, in Crimes 659-672

GUARANTY of Republican form of Government 677, 678

HABEAS CORPUS WRIT, Privilege of 482-484;

Suspension of 482-489

HIGH SEAS, what is 408;

Crimes on 405-408

HOUSE OF REPRESENTATIVES. (*See* REPRE-SENTATIVES.) 210-252

IMPAIRING CONTRACTS, Prohibition of 498-510

IMPEACHMENT, Power of, in House of Representatives, 249, 251;

Trial of in Senate 271-290;

of President and Vice-President 283, 284;

Judgments on 288-290;

who are liable to 283-286;

for what offences 286-288

IMPLIED POWERS OF CONGRESS 431-441;

Duties of National Government 480

IMPLIED EXEMPTIONS from State Power 356, 357, 442, 443

IMPORTS, a State cannot tax 354-512

IMPOSTS, Meaning of (*See* DUTIES.) 337-340

INCIDENTAL POWERS OF CONGRESS 431-441

INDEPENDENCE, Declaration of 88, 89

INDIANS, Title to Territory, 1-7;

Commerce with 359, 379-382

INDICTMENT, when necessary 659, 661

INFERIOR OFFICERS, who are in sense of Constitution 566, 567

INJUNCTIONS, to or by State Courts 650, 651;

to or by United States Courts 650 651

INSOLVENT LAWS, how far constitutional 390, 391

INSPECTION LAWS, what are 354, 355

INTERNAL IMPROVEMENTS, (*See* APPRO-PRIATION.) Power of Congress 346-350, 453-456

INVENTIONS, Patents for 402-404

JEOPARDY of life or limb, in crimes 659, 660, 662

JOURNALS of each House to be published 299, 300

JUDGES, Appointment of 552, 559, 590;

Tenure of Office 585, 591-602;

Duties of, none but Judicial 655;

Compensation of 585, 602-605;

Impeachment of (*See* JUDICIARY.) 283;

Territorial 605

JUDICIARY, Organization and Powers of 581-606;

Importance of 581-585;

Appointment of Judges 552, 559, 590;

Tenure of Office 585, 591-602;

Compensation of . 585, 602-605;
Establishment of Courts 585-590;
Jurisdiction of Courts 606-636;
When exclusive or not 649, 650;
Power of Congress over 585-590, 639-655;
Original Jurisdiction 636-638;
Appellate Jurisdiction 639-649, 651-655;
from State Courts 643, 653-655;
Cases, what are 608-612;
Parties in suits 606;
when a State a party 626-628;
Suits by and against Ambassadors 612-614;
Admiralty Suits 614-620;
Suits by United States 620, 621;
by or against States 621, 622, 623, 626, 633, 641;
by citizens of different States 621, 628-630;
under grants of different States 621, 632-633;
by or against Foreigners or Foreign States 621, 633-636;
Trial of Crimes 656, 668, 674
JURISDICTION OF COURTS OF UNITED STATES 606-636;
Original 636-638;
Appellate. (*See* JUDICIARY.) 606-649, 651-655;
over Cases from State Courts 643-649;
Regulation of, by Congress 636, 638-640
Removal of Suits from State Courts 643-646, 652;
When exclusive, or concurrent 649, 650;
As to facts 651, 653-655;
By Appeal 651, 652-655;
By Writ of Error 653-655
JURY, TRIAL BY in Criminal Cases 655-659;
in Civil Cases 654;
Grand Jury 659-662
KING, Rights and Prerogatives of, in Colonies 75-78
LANDS PUBLIC, Power of Congress over 428, 429, 459, 473
LAWS OF UNITED STATES, Supremacy of 684-687
LAW OF NATIONS, offences against 405, 407, 408

LAW OF THE LAND, Meaning of 663
LEGISLATION, when exclusive in Congress. (*See* COMMERCE.) 148-154;
in ceded places 427-429;
on high seas 405-407;
when not exclusive. (*See* TAXES.) 148-154
LEGISLATURE. (*See* CONGRESS, SENATE, REPRESENTATIVES.)
LETTERS OF MARQUE AND REPRISAL, Power of Congress 409;
Prohibition on States to issue 489
LIBERTY of the Press 698, 703-707;
of Speech 698-703;
in Congress 303, 309, 310
LOUISIANA, Purchase of 459-462
MAINE, Origin and Settlement of 31-33
MANUFACTURES, Power of Congress to encourage 371-379
MARYLAND, Origin and Settlement of 41-43
MASSACHUSETTS, Origin and Settlement of 19-27
MEASURES AND WEIGHTS, Power of Congress as to 392, 394
MIGRATION AND IMPORTATION OF SLAVES 481, 482
MILITIA, Power of Congress over . 420, 421;
Discipline and Government of 421-423;
Calling forth by Government 421-425;
Command of 421-425;
Right to bear arms 708
MINISTERS, PUBLIC, Appointment of 559, 560;
Receiving of, by Executive 574, 576, 579;
Violations of Rights of 612, 613;
Right to sue 606, 612-614
MONEY, Coinage of 392, 393;
Power to borrow 358, 359;
Bills, or Revenue Bills 358, 359
NATIONAL BANK, Constitutionality of 444-452
NATURALIZATION, Power of 383, 384
NAVIGATION, Regulation of 300 361, 362
NAVY AND ARMY, Power to establish 412-419;
Regulation of 418, 419
"NECESSARY AND PROPER," Meaning of, as to powers of Congress 431-441

NEGATIVE of President on Laws 315, 317-325

NEW-ENGLAND, Origin and Settlement of 13-18

NEW-HAMPSHIRE, Origin and Settlement of 28-30

NEW-HAVEN COLONY, Origin and Settlement of 34-36

NEW-JERSEY, Origin and Settlement of 47-49

NEW-YORK, Origin and Settlement of 44-46

NOBILITY, Prohibition of Titles of, by Congress 487;
 by the States 511

NORTH CAROLINA, Origin and Settlement of 56-60

OATH OF OFFICE, by Officers of United States 688-690;
 of Senators and Representatives 688;
 of President (See IMPEACHMENT.) 544, 545;
 by State Officers 688, 689

OBLIGATION OF A CONTRACT, what it is 499-503

OFFICE, Tenure of, by Judges. (See JUDICIARY.) 585, 591-602;
 by President and Vice-President 521, 522;
 Appointments to. (See APPOINTMENTS.) 552, 559;
 Disqualifications to hold 230, 235, 265, 267, 529, 538, 540, 542;
 Foreign, Prohibition to hold 487;
 When Appointee is in 573

OFFICERS, who are inferior in sense of Constitution 566, 567

ORIGINAL JURISDICTION. (See JUDICIARY.) 638-638

PAPER MONEY, Prohibition of. (See TENDER.) 491, 495

PARDONS AND REPRIEVES, by President 546-552;
 Whether extending to Contempts 551;
 not extending to Impeachments 551, 552

PARLIAMENT, Powers and Rights of, over Colonies 78-80

PARTIES TO A SUIT, who are, and when a State 600, 626-628

PATENTS FOR INVENTIONS 402-404

PENNSYLVANIA, Origin and Settlement

of 50-53

PEOPLE, Constitution framed by 134

PETITION. Right of, 707

PIRACY, Power to define 405-407

PLANTATIONS AND COLONIES, General Law Governing 62-65

PLYMOUTH COLONY, Origin and Settlement of 15-18

POLL TAXES 340, 341, 350

POST-OFFICE AND POST-ROADS, Power respecting 396-401

POST-MASTER GENERAL, Suits by 457;
 his Patronage an anomaly 566-568

POWERS OF CONGRESS, Incidental 431-466;
 Express. (See CONGRESS.);
 Implied 431-466;
 When exclusive, or not 148-154

POWERS, reserved to States or People 711-714

PREAMBLE OF CONSTITUTION, Exposition of 163-194

PRESS, Liberty of the 698, 703-707

PRESENTMENT, what it is 671

PRESIDENT, Negative on Laws 315, 317-325;
 Mode of Choice of 529-538;
 Re-eligibility of 523-529;
 Duration and Tenure of Office 521, 522;
 Non-election of 529, 534;
 Vacancy of Office of 542;
 Powers of 546-580;
 Incidental 579, 580;
 Duties of 574-576;
 Appointments by 552, 559-568;
 when complete 573;
 Vacancies filled by 573, 574;
 Removals by 568-573;
 Power to require Opinions of Departments 546, 547;
 Calling forth Militia 422-425;
 Making Treaties (See Treaties) 552-559;
 Command of Militia 546;
 Resignation of 542, 543;
 Pardon and Reprieves by 546-551;
 Qualifications of 540, 542;
 Compensation of 543, 544;
 Oath of office 544, 545;
 Commander of Army and Navy 546, 547;
 Power to Convene and Adjourn

Congress 574-576;

Receiving Ambassadors 574, 576-579;

Resignation of Office 542, 543;

Impeachment of 283, 284;

Veto of 315, 317-325

PRESIDENT OF THE SENATE (*See* VICE-PRESIDENT.) 268-271

PRESENTS FROM FOREIGN GOVERN-MENTS, Prohibition of 487

PRIORITY OF PAYMENT OF DEBTS DUE TO THE UNITED STATES 456

PROCESS, Due, of Law, what is 670, 673

PROHIBITIONS on the United States 481-489; on the States (*See* STATES.) 489-51

PROPERTY taken for Public Use, Compensation for 670, 673

PROPERTY OF UNITED STATES, Power of Congress over 474, 476-479

PROPRIETARY GOVERNMENTS, what 68, 69

PROTECTIVE DUTIES. (*See* TAXES.) 371-379

PROVINCIAL GOVERNMENTS, what 67, 68

PUBLIC LANDS, 474, 476-479

PUNISHMENTS, CRUEL, not to be inflicted 710

PURCHASE by the United States of Foreign Territory 459; of Bills of Exchange 480

QUALIFICATIONS AND DISQUALIFICA-TIONS OF OFFICE 230, 235, 265, 267, 529, 538, 540, 542; of House of Representatives 230-235, 529; of Senate 265-267, 529; of President 540, 542; of Electors of President 529, 538

QUARTERING TROOPS, 709

QUORUM OF EACH HOUSE 295, 296

RATIFICATION OF CONSTITUTION, how made 691, 692

RECORDS AND LAWS OF STATES, how proved 470-472; Effect of Proof 470-472; of Colonies, effect of 471

RELIGIOUS TEST, Prohibition of 688, 690

RELIGION, Freedom of 698-703

REMITTANCES, how United States may make 480

REMOVALS FROM OFFICE BY PRESIDENT 568-573; Whether the Concurrence of the Senate ought to be required 568-573

REMOVAL of Suits from State Courts 643-646, 652

REPRESENTATIVES, House of, in Colonies 72, 73; first Colonial, in Virginia 9, 10; in Congress 210-251; How chosen 210-219; Term of Service 210, 219-229; Qualifications of 230-235; Apportionment of 235-247; Speaker of House of 248, 249; Impeachment by 248-251; Disqualifications of 310-314, 529, 538

REPRIEVES AND PARDONS, Power of President 346-351

REPRISAL, Letters of Marque and Reprisal (*See* LETTERS OF MARQUE.) 409, 489

RESERVED Powers and Rights of the People 711

RESULTING Powers 441, 442

REVENUE, Bills to raise 315-317

REVENUE BILLS, what 315-316

REVOLUTION, AMERICAN, Origin and History of 75, 84-90; Powers of Government during the 89-90

RHODE-ISLAND, Origin and Settlement of 37-40

RIGHTS RESERVED to the States and People 711

ROADS AND CANALS, Power as to 346-350, 453-458

SEARCH AND SEIZURE OF PERSONS AND PAPERS, Prohibition of 709

SEAT OF GOVERNMENT 427, 428; Power of Legislation over 427, 428

SEDITION ACT, whether Constitutional 464, 465

SENATE, Organization of 252-268 ; How chosen 252-256; Number of 252, 256-264; Term of Service 252, 258-264; Vacancies in, how supplied 264; Qualifications of 265-267;

President of 268-271;
Power to try Impeachments (See IM-
PEACHMENTS.) 271-290;
Disqualifications of 310-314
SLAVES, Representation of 235, 239-241;
Migration and Importation of 481, 482;
Fugitive 675, 676
SLAVE TRADE, Prohibition of 481, 482
SOLDIERS, Quartering of, prohibited 709
SOUTH-CAROLINA, Origin and Settlement
of 56-60
SPEECH, Liberty of, in Congress 303, 309, 310
SPEAKER OF HOUSE OF REPRESENTA-
TIVES 248, 249
STATES, Admission of new 473, 475;
Prohibitions on (See PROHIBITIONS.)
489-514;
Treaties, Alliances, Compacts 489, 490;
Letters of Marque and War 490;
Coining Money 490, 491;
Bills of Credit 491-495;
Tender Laws 496;
Impairing Contracts 489-511;
Bills of Attainder 496;
Ex Post Facto Laws 496, 510;
Titles of Nobility 512;
Keeping Army or Navy 512;
Laying Duties or Imposts 354, 512;
Tax on Bank of United States 356, 357;
on Public Debt 356, 357;
Tax on Importation 354, 356;
Tonnage Duties 354, 512;
Declaring War 512, 514;
Suits by and against (See JUDICIARY.)
521-625;
When a party to a Suit 626, 627;
Courts of, Appeals from 643-646, 652
SUPREMACY of Constitution, Laws, and
Treaties 684, 687
TAXES, Power of Congress to lay 329-357;
Extent of power 329-357;
Whether to regulate Commerce 343, 369;
or encourage Manufactures 369-379;
for Common Defence and General Wel-
fare 329, 330, 343, 369;
for Internal Improvements (See APPRO-
PRIATION.) 343-350;

Direct, what 337-341;
Indirect, what 337-341;
Power not exclusive 148-156, 366, 486;
Restrictions on Power 350, 353, 354;
Prohibitions on the States, as to 354, 355
TENDER LAWS, Prohibition of 496
TERRITORIES OF UNITED STATES, Govern-
ment of 428, 428, 459, 474, 476;
Law of Conquered 62-64;
Law of Plantations (See UNITED
STATES.) 62-65
TEST, Religious, Prohibition of 688, 690
TESTIMONY OF CRIMINALS, not compul-
sive 670, 672, 673
TONNAGE DUTIES, by United States 353;
Prohibitions on States 354-356, 512
TREASON, Definition of 669-672;
Evidence of 669, 691;
Effect of Conviction 466-469;
Punishment of 466-469
TREATIES, Prohibition on States to form 489,
490;
Power of President and Senate to make
552-559
TRIAL OF CRIMES, in what place 660-674;
by Jury, in Criminal Cases 656-668, 674;
in Civil Cases 654
TROOPS, Quartering, Prohibition of 709
UNITED COLONIES, Powers of, during
Revolution 90, 91
UNION, Importance of 163-175
UNITED STATES (See CONSTITUTION.),
Supremacy of Laws of 684, 687;
Priority of Debts to 456;
Right to Sue 442, 620;
Right to Contract and Grant 442;
Right to Purchase Foreign Territory 459;
Right to acquire Domestic Territory 473;
Implied Duties of (See PROHIBITIONS.)
480
UNITY OF EXECUTIVE, Reasons 516-521
VACANCIES, Appointments by State Execu-
tives to Senate 264;
Appointments by President in recess of
Congress 573, 574;
in Office of President and Vice-President
542

VETO, President's 315, 317-325

VICE-PRESIDENT, How chosen 515, 516, 529-538;

Reasons for Creation of 527-529;

President of Senate 268-271;

Powers and Duties 542, 543;

Vacancy of Office of 542;

Impeachment of 283, 284;

Duration of Office of 521, 522;

Resignation of 542, 543

VIRGINIA, Origin and Settlement of 8-18

WARRANTS, General, Prohibition of 709, 710

WAR, Power of Congress to Declare 409-412; Prohibition on the States 512, 513

WEIGHTS AND MEASURES, Power of Congress as to 392, 394

WITNESSES, Criminals not bound to be 659, 660, 662;

in Criminal Cases 660, 666

WRIT OF ERROR, Nature and Effect of 652-655

Visit us at *www.quidprobooks.com.*

Made in the USA
Middletown, DE
14 December 2014